College Accounting

TENTH EDITION

CHAPTERS 1–13

John Ellis Price, Ph.D., C.P.A.
KPMG Professor of Taxation and Chair
Department of Accounting
College of Business Administration
University of North Texas
Denton, Texas

M. David Haddock, Jr., Ed.D., C.P.A.
Professor of Accounting
Chattanooga State Technical Community College
Chattanooga, Tennessee

Horace R. Brock, Ph.D., C.P.A.
Distinguished Professor of Accounting Emeritus
College of Business Administration
University of North Texas
Denton, Texas

Visit the *College Accounting* Web site at:

collegeaccounting.glencoe.com

New York, New York Columbus, Ohio Woodland Hills, California Peoria, Illinois

NOTICE. Information on featured companies, organizations, their products and services is included for educational purposes only, and it does not present or imply endorsement of the Glencoe *College Accounting* program. Permission to use all business logos has been granted by the businesses represented in this text.

Glencoe/McGraw-Hill
A Division of The **McGraw·Hill** *Companies*

College Accounting, Tenth Edition

Send all inquiries to:
Glencoe/McGraw-Hill
21600 Oxnard Street, Suite 500
Woodland Hills, CA 91367

ISBN 0-07-827091-X

Printed in the United States of America.

2 3 4 5 6 7 8 9 027 06 05 04 03 02

Preface

Who do you want to be? Do you hope to become a dynamic leader, one of the inspirational members of a corporate team, an innovative contributor in a new business startup? Do you want to solve tough management challenges while utilizing your business skills to the fullest extent possible? If you answered "yes" to these questions, these desires can become a reality. Career development begins by constructing a framework of necessary knowledge, work experience, and personal skills. Employers today seek candidates who can effectively communicate in a business situation, analyze financial data, work creatively with a team, and proactively find answers to difficult problems.

We wrote this text to help you construct a framework of skills and knowledge necessary for success in the business world today. You will learn the "language of business" used in boardrooms, financial newscasts, and corporate meetings every day. This language will become part of your working vocabulary. Real-world perspectives from companies such as The Home Depot, Southwest Airlines, Guess?, and Wal-Mart give you a deeper understanding of business transactions and how they affect the financial condition and performance of a company.

In the workplace, knowledge of a particular topic is not enough. You will be asked to deliver presentations to your peers, write reports and summaries, lead team meetings, analyze financial options, and solve new business challenges. This textbook offers countless opportunities to enhance these valuable skills as you apply and practice accounting procedures and concepts.

Features and Elements of Your Textbook

Textbook Organization

College Accounting is offered in three versions: Chapters 1–13, Chapters 1–25, or Chapters 1–32. Each chapter is divided into two or three sections. Each section is numbered, titled, and treated as a self-contained learning segment. Sections are again broken down into easy-to-digest portions of information labeled with informative headings.

Content

College Accounting, Chapters 1–13, provides a solid coverage of accounting concepts, procedures, and principles. The textbook first examines the traditional framework of a sole proprietorship accounting cycle, and then builds on these concepts with discussions of asset, liability, and equity accounts.

Learning Objectives. Each chapter opens with a preview of learning objectives for the material. Keep these objectives in mind as you work through the content of the chapter. Note that the running text offers an indicator in the side margin signaling that a new learning objective is being addressed.

Vocabulary. Mastery of the "language of business" is key to success in this course and in the business world. Each chapter provides the following learning aids:

- **New Terms Preview.** All new terms are previewed on chapter-opener pages. Each section within a chapter also previews the terms that will be used in that portion of learning. Before beginning each chapter, read the new terms and recall instances in which you have heard these terms used.
- **Definitions.** As each term is introduced in the running text of a chapter, it appears in boldface type and is highlighted. Take special note of these terms as they appear and make sure you understand the term before you continue reading.
- **Glossaries.** A glossary at the end of each chapter provides definitions and page number references. Use the master glossary located at the end of the textbook for a quick way to find definitions and page number references for terms you need to review.

Chapter Summary. Accounting is a subject that continually builds on learned concepts and procedures. The Chapter Summary offers you the chance to regroup and review the concepts learned with a specific chapter. It is organized by learning objective, providing further reinforcement of your learning milestones.

Exercises and Problems. Once you have studied new accounting concepts and analyzed business transactions, you will be ready to practice what you have learned. At the end of each chapter, exercises and problems challenge you to apply the techniques and procedures you have studied. Track your learning progress by noting the learning objective that each exercise or problem addresses.

Visual Learning Tools

Have you ever heard the saying "A picture is worth a thousand words"? *College Accounting* takes every opportunity to reinforce your learning experience with the effective use of color, eye-catching text treatments, and meaningful visual presentations.

In-Text Worksheet Transparencies. In Chapter 5 you will learn about a helpful tool called the *worksheet.* A special worksheet illustration using multiple overlay transparencies is bound into the chapter and highlights step-by-step procedures for its preparation.

Business Transaction Analysis Models. One of the most important concepts you will learn in this course is how to properly analyze and record business transactions. Step-by-step transaction analysis illustrations show you how to identify the appropriate general ledger accounts affected, determine debit or credit activity for each account, present the transaction in T-account form, and record the entry in the general journal.

Business Transaction

On November 10 Carter Consulting Services purchased office equipment on account for $15,000.

OFFICE *plus*

INVOICE NO. 2223

DATE: Nov. 10, 2004
ORDER NO.: P38
SHIPPED BY: n/a
TERMS: 60 days

TO Carter Consulting Services

QTY.	ITEM	UNIT PRICE	TOTAL
1	Copier	1,000	1,000
1	Fax Machine	600	600
5	Computers	2,200	11,000
3	Printers	500	1,500
2	Scanners	250	500
4	Calculators	100	400
		Total	15,000

Analysis

e. The asset account, **Equipment,** is increased by $15,000.

f. The liability account, **Accounts Payable,** is increased by $15,000.

Debit-Credit Rules

DEBIT Increases to asset accounts are recorded as debits. Debit **Equipment** for $15,000.

CREDIT Increases to liability accounts are recorded as credits. Credit **Accounts Payable** for $15,000.

T-Account Presentation

Equipment	
+	–
(e) 15,000	

Accounts Payable	
–	+
	(f) 15,000

General Journal Entry

GENERAL JOURNAL PAGE 1

	DATE		DESCRIPTION	POST. REF.	DEBIT	CREDIT	
10	Nov.	10	Equipment		15 000 00		10
11			Accounts Payable			15 000 00	11
12			Purchased equipment on				12
13			account from Office Plus,				13
14			Inv. 2223, due in 60 days				14

The Bottom Line. The Bottom Line visuals appear in the margins alongside select transactions and concepts in the textbook. These visuals offer a summary of the effects of these transactions—the end result—on the financial statements of a business.

T Accounts. In this course, you will learn that a T account is a visual tool used by the accountant to help analyze business transactions. T accounts are used extensively throughout the textbook. Note that the account's normal balance is indicated by shading. An increase in the account balance is represented by (+) and a decrease is represented by (−).

Full-Color Illustrations. Tables, flowcharts, diagrams, journals, ledgers, and financial statements are presented in full color to provide you with an understanding of the documents and reports found and used extensively in the real world of business.

Highlighting. Vocabulary terms are highlighted in yellow as they appear in the running text. Pause to absorb the meaning and the context of each term as it appears.

Boldface Text. As you progress through this textbook, you will learn that general ledger accounts are a vital part of the accounting profession. These general ledger account names are presented in boldface text. This helps you distinguish formal general ledger accounts from accounting concepts with similar or identical names.

Reinforcement

Most of us learn most effectively by careful review of materials and by practicing what we have learned. *College Accounting* takes every opportunity to construct concepts in an understandable way and then reinforce them at critical junctures.

Recall and Important! The **Recall** margin feature is a series of brief reinforcements that serve as reminders of material covered in *previous* chapters that are relevant to new information being presented. The **Important!** margin features draw your attention to critical materials introduced in the *current* chapter.

Section Self Reviews. Each section concludes with a Self Review that includes questions, multiple choice exercises, and an analysis assignment. You may check your work with the answers that are provided at the end of each chapter.

End-of-Chapter Review and Applications. Retention and reinforcement of concepts are further enhanced through discussion questions, exercises, problems, challenge problems, and critical thinking problems at the end of each chapter.

Business Connections. New enrichment and alternative assessment activities, collectively known as **Business Connections,** reinforce chapter materials from practical and real-world perspectives.

Real-World Connections

College Accounting transforms academic concepts into real-world applications and associations by integrating materials about well-known companies and organizations.

Part Opener. Each part opener presents a vignette of a real-world company like Avis Group Holdings, Inc., SAS Institute Inc., or Johnson & Johnson, connecting the Part business theme to real-world issues or profiles. An evocative Thinking Critically question stimulates thought on the topics to be explored in the Part.

Chapter Opener. Setting the stage for learning, each chapter opener presents brief features about real-world companies such as Adobe Systems Incorporated, Lands' End, Inc., and The Boeing Company. You will assess a topic presented in the Thinking Critically question that concludes each feature.

Street Wise: Questions from the Real World. Excerpts from The Home Depot, Inc. annual report are presented in Appendix B of the text. In **Street Wise: Questions from the Real World,** you will be asked to research various components of the annual report and answer questions related to content, presentation, and meaning.

Financial Statement Analysis. A brief excerpt of a real-world annual report is also included at the end of each chapter in the **Financial Statement Analysis** activities. Questions presented will lead you through an analysis of the statement and conclude with an Analyze Online activity for which you will research the company's most recent financial reports on the Internet.

Internet Connections. The **Internet Connections** activity provides the opportunity to conduct online research about major companies, accounting trends, organizations, and government agencies.

Real-World Snapshots. As you read through each chapter, you will be presented with relevant news, company profiles, and facts related to real-world businesses or situations.

Career Applications

The Big Picture. Accounting plays a role in every

aspect of our personal and business lives. As you learn key accounting concepts and procedures, it is important to know why these issues are relevant and what role they play in the larger picture of business. **Why It's Important** statements accompany each learning objective, highlighting practical applications for the objective.

Career Paths. Accounting skills are useful, and often critical, to landing and keeping that perfect job. **Accounting on the Job** features, found in each even-numbered chapter, highlight the benefits of accounting in the fields of hospitality and tourism, legal and protective services, information technology services, retail/wholesale sales and service, human services, and business and administration—six "career clusters" defined by the U.S. Department of Education. Optional Internet Application activities and Thinking Critically Questions are included.

The Business Manager. The business environment today requires managers to make strategic business decisions based on a variety of factors. Financial and accounting information, in particular, are elements that managers must be well prepared to consider. Near the end of each chapter, **Managerial Implications** summarizes the chapter's accounting concepts from the point of view of the manager. The feature ends with a Thinking Critically question that requires contemplation of chapter content from management's perspective. End-of-chapter assessment materials include **Managerial Focus** questions where you will apply accounting concepts to business situations.

Business Research and Reporting. In order to be useful, business information must be presented in a meaningful format and must be interpreted for its users. Optional end-of-chapter features such as **Street Wise: Questions from the Real World, Financial Statement Analysis, Teamwork,** and **Internet Connections** provide opportunities for you to review real-world financial data, research current trends, offer interpretations, communicate findings, and work as part of a team. Within the chapters themselves, **Accounting on the Job** and **Computers in Accounting** features provide research opportunities in the realms of careers, business technologies, and software.

The Analyst. Problem Sets A and B, Challenge Problems, and Mini-Practice Sets conclude with an **Analyze** question. You will review your work and extend your learning process with summarizations and conclusions about what you have done.

The Problem Solver. The ability to think critically, solve problems, and create solutions is one of the most sought after attributes in the workplace today. **Thinking Critically** questions are incorporated in **Part Openers, Chapter Openers, Managerial Implications, Accounting on the Job,** and **Computers in Accounting.** Critical thinking skills are flexed in the **Section Self Reviews, Comprehensive Self Reviews,** and the end-of-chapter **Business Connection** activities.

The Team Player. Each chapter contains a collaborative learning activity, **Teamwork,** which will provide learning opportunities to prepare for team-oriented projects and work environments.

The Ethical Worker. Reasoning, societal norms, morals, laws, and personal judgment are factors that play critical roles in decision-making in the business world. An **Ethical Dilemma** activity within each chapter provides the opportunity for you to discuss ethics in the workplace, formulate a course of action for certain scenarios, and support your opinions.

The International Professional. Accounting issues that provide connections to the global world of business are presented in an in-text feature called **International Insights.**

The Effective Communicator. Excellent communication skills are paramount to a successful career. In this course, you will write memos, reports, essays; present oral presentations; create visual presentation aids; communicate via electronic methods; and hone your interpersonal skills via **Business Communications** activities presented in each chapter.

Technology Applications

The world of business today is largely fueled and sustained by process and information technologies. In that spirit, *College Accounting* provides many opportunities to work with and learn about various software applications, communications technologies, and Web-based applications.

***College Accounting* Web Site.** From reinforcement quizzes to case studies, Internet research activities to demonstration problems, the *College Accounting* Web site features a realm of opportunities to review, reinforce, and supplement your learning. You may explore tips for completing end-of-chapter problems or use the online glossary for a quick review of vocabulary and accounting concepts.

Commercial Software. The tenth edition of *College Accounting* offers more than twice as many accounting software problems as the previous edition. Master your skills in the following software products:

Peachtree QuickBooks Spreadsheets

Student Tutorial CD-ROM. Supplement your learning with this interactive CD-ROM utilizing exceptional PowerPoint presentations, chapter quizzes, and ten-key practice exercises.

Computers in Accounting. Highlighting a variety of aspects related to computer technologies in the accounting workplace, **Computers in Accounting** activities bring relevant issues to light with optional Internet Application activities and Thinking Critically questions.

The Tenth Edition at a Glance

We are excited to bring you the Tenth Edition of *College Accounting* complete with new designs, activities, reinforcement opportunities, and real-world connections developed to enhance and strengthen your learning experience.

New design
New high-interest photos and full-color illustrations
New business transaction analysis visuals
New "The Bottom Line" visuals
New part opener business vignettes
New chapter opener business vignettes
New section openers with "Why It's Important" statements for each learning objective
New exercises in Section Self Reviews
New analysis assignments in Section Self Reviews
New Comprehensive Self Review
New Recall margin features
New Important! margin features
New real-world snapshots featured in running text
New International Insights margin features
New Accounting on the Job features
New Thinking Critically questions
New Analyze questions
New Chapter Review organized by learning objectives
New Appendix B, featuring Excerpts from The Home Depot, Inc. *1999 Annual Report*
New Business Connections activities:

- Managerial Focus
- Ethical Dilemma
- Street Wise: Questions from the Real World
- Financial Statement Analysis
- Extending the Thought
- Business Communication
- Teamwork
- Internet Connection

Revised chapter structure, organized into easy-to-grasp learning segments
Revised Computers in Accounting features
Revised Mini-Practice Sets
Revised About Accounting margin features

Content Revisions

Chapter 2: This chapter introduces an important visual tool, the Business Transaction Analysis Model. This tool is expanded on in Chapters 3 and 4, providing a step-by-step process used to analyze transactions from source document through T accounts and general journal entry.

Chapter 5: The term *contra account* is introduced in the discussion of depreciation.

The coverage of depreciation is supplemented with the online Chapter 5 Appendix: Methods of Depreciation on the *College Accounting* Web site.

Chapter 6: The term *interpret* is introduced as a New Term to better explain the last step of the accounting cycle: interpreting the financial information.

The coverage of financial statements is supplemented with the online Chapter 6 Appendix: Statement of Cash Flows on the *College Accounting* Web site.

Chapter 7: The merchandising business chart of accounts separates cost of good sold accounts from the expense accounts. Each category has a different series of account numbers: 500 for cost of goods sold accounts, and 600 for expense accounts.

This chapter introduces The Bottom Line, a visual tool that shows the effect of transactions on the income statement and the balance sheet.

Chapter 8: The term *cost of goods sold* is introduced as a New Term. The concept is explained in the discussion of merchandise purchases.

Chapter 10: The discussion of employees versus independent contractors is supplemented with the online Chapter 10 Appendix: Independent Contractors on the *College Accounting* Web site.

Chapter 11: The Electronic Federal Tax Payment System (EFTPS) is introduced in this chapter.

Focus on Features

Accounting On The Job

Computers in Accounting

TeamWork

Ethical Dilemma

interNET CONNECTION

International INSIGHTS

About Accounting

Exploring the Real World of Business

The Tenth Edition focuses on a **business perspective** by using examples from the business world to illustrate accounting concepts.

Information on featured companies, organizations, their products, and services is included for educational purposes only and does not represent or imply endorsement of the *College Accounting* program. The following companies appear throughout the text:

Openers

Part 1

Avis Group Holdings, Inc.

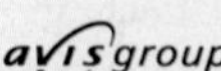

Chapter 1

Yahoo! Inc.

Chapter 2

Southwest Airlines Co.

Chapter 3

Guess? Inc.

Chapter 4

CSX Corporation

Chapter 5

The Boeing Company

Chapter 6

Galileo International Inc.

Part 2

The Home Depot, Inc.

Chapter 7

Wal-Mart Stores, Inc.

Chapter 8

Pier 1 Imports

Chapter 9

H&R Block, Inc.

Part 3

SAS Institute Inc.

Chapter 10

Adobe Systems Incorporated

Chapter 11

Lands' End, Inc.

Part 4

Johnson & Johnson

Chapter 12

American Eagle Outfitters, Inc.

Chapter 13

Safeway Inc.

FINANCIAL STATEMENT ANALYSIS

Chapter 1

American Eagle Outfitters, Inc.

Chapter 2

Southwest Airlines Co.

Chapter 3

Adobe Systems Incorporated

Chapter 4

Wal-Mart Stores, Inc.

Chapter 5

DuPont Company

Chapter 6

CSX Corporation

Chapter 7

Wal-Mart Stores, Inc.

Chapter 8

Lands' End, Inc.

Chapter 9

Armstrong Holdings, Inc.

Chapter 10

Southwest Airlines Co.

Chapter 11

H&R Block, Inc.

Chapter 12

DuPont

Chapter 13

Mattel, Inc.

Acknowledgments

The authors are deeply grateful to the following accounting educators for their ongoing involvement with *College Accounting*. The efforts of these knowledgeable and dedicated instructors provide the authors with valuable assistance in meeting the changing needs of the college accounting classroom.

Ms. Deborah Abercrombie
Wallace Community College,
Sparks Campus
Euflaula, AL

Ms. Terry Aime
Delgado Community College
New Orleans, LA

Mr. Lorenza Balthazar
LTC—Lafayette
Lafayette, LA

Ms. Marilyn Beebe
Kirkwood Community College
Cedar Rapids, IA

Ms. Dianne Bridges
South Plains College
Levelland, TX

Ms. Michele Burleson
McDowell Technical
Community College
Marion, NC

Mr. George Carter
New Hampshire Community
Technical College
Berlin, NH

Mr. Michael Choma
Newport Business Institute
New Kensington, PA

Ms. Juanita Clobes
Gateway Technical College
Racine, WI

Mr. George Converse
Stone Academy
Hamden, CT

Ms. Joan Cook
Milwaukee Area Technical College
Milwaukee, WI

Ms. Karen Cortis
Dorsey Business Schools
Madison Heights, MI

Dr. Michael G. Curran, Jr.
Rider University
Lawrenceville, NJ

Mr. Mike Discello
Pittsburgh Technical Institute
Pittsburgh, PA

Mr. John Dixon
Education America, Dallas Campus
Garland, TX

Dr. Paul Doran
Jefferson State Community College
Birmingham, AL

Ms. Elsie Dubac
The Stuart School of
Business Administration
Wall, NJ

Mr. Richard Dugger
Kilgore College
Kilgore, TX

Mr. Samuel Ehie
Trenholm State Technical College
Montgomery, AL

Ms. Teresa Ferguson
Court Reporting Institute
Seattle, WA

Ms. Tanya Fontenot
LTC—Lamar Salter
Leesville, LA

Mr. Kevin Fura
Allentown Business School
Allentown, PA

Ms. Cheryl Furbee
Cabrillo College
Aptos, CA

Ms. Selena Gardner
International Academy of
Design & Technology
Pittsburgh, PA

Mr. George P. Geran
Florida Metropolitan University,
North Orlando
Orlando, FL

Ms. Deborah Hammons
Shelton State Community College
Tuscaloosa, AL

Mr. Neil Hayes
ECPI College of Technology
Virginia Beach, VA

Dr. Lynn Hogan
Calhoun Community College
Decatur, AL

Mr. Paul Hogan
Northwest Shoals Community College
Muscle Shoals, AL

Mr. Bob Horst
Western Wyoming Community College
Rock Springs, WY

Ms. Verna Mae Johnson
Brown Mackie Business College
Salina, KS

Ms. Janine Jones
Lansdale School of Business
North Wales, PA

Ms. Beverly Kibbie
International Business College
Indianapolis, IN

Ms. Judith Kizzie
Clinton Community College
Clinton, IA

Dr. Tom Land
Bessemer State Technical College
Bessemer, AL

Ms. Lynn LeBlanc
LTC—Lafayette
Lafayette, LA

Mr. Gene Lefort
LTC—Lafourche
Thibodaux, LA

Ms. Sylvia Liverman
Paul D. Camp Community College
Franklin, VA

Ms. Debbie Luna
El Paso Community College,
NW Campus
El Paso, TX

Ms. Linda R. Lyle
Nashville State Tech
Nashville, TN

Ms. Kathy Marino
ESS College of Business
Dallas, TX

Ms. Betty McClain
Mid Florida Tech
Orlando, FL

Mr. Fred McCracken
Indiana Business College
Marion, IN

Ms. Cheryl McQueen
Jones County Junior College
Ellisville, MS

Ms. Catherine Merrikin
Pearl River Junior College
Hattiesburg, MS

Ms. Wanda Metzgar
Boise State University
Boise, ID

Mr. Raymond J. Miller
Lane Community College
Eugene, OR

Ms. Margie Mixon
LTC—Delta Ouachita
West Monroe, LA

Mr. Paul Morgan
Mississippi Gulf Coast
Community College
Gautier, MS

Ms. Judy Parker
North Idaho College
Coeur d'Alene, ID

Mr. David Payne
North Metro Technical College
Acworth, GA

Ms. Linda Petraglia
The Stuart School of Business
Administration
Wall, NJ

Mr. Ellis Plowman
Churchman Business School
Easton, PA

Ms. Betsy Ray
Indiana Business College
Indianapolis, IN

Mr. Phil Reffitt
FMU/Orlando College South
Orlando, FL

Mr. Randy Rogers
Western Business College
Portland, OR

Ms. Peggy Rusek
Mountain Empire Community College
Big Stone Gap, VA

Dr. Francis Sakiey
Mercer County Community College
West Windsor, NJ

Mr. Roman Salazar
Modesto Junior College
Modesto, CA

Mr. Kyle Saunders
Bridgerland ATC
Logan, UT

Mr. Wayne Smith
Indiana Business College
Lafayette, IN

Ms. Linda Stanley
Quapaw Technical Institute
Hot Springs, AR

Ms. Verlindsey Stewart
J. F. Drake State Technical College
Huntsville, AL

Ms. Karla Stroud
Idaho State University
Pocatello, ID

Ms. Lynette Teal
Western Wisconsin Technical College
LaCrosse, WI

Mr. Thomas Tolan
Plaza Business Institute
Jackson Heights, NY

Mr. Gary Tusing
Lord Fairfax Community College
Middletown, VA

Dr. Laverne Ulmer
Jones Junior College
Ellisville, MS

Mr. Jack Verani
New Hampshire Community
Technical College
Berlin, NH

Ms. Patricia Vickers
George Stone Vocational Center
Pensacola, FL

Mr. Philip Waits
Harry M. Ayers State
Technical College
Anniston, AL

Mr. Frank Walker
Lee University
Cleveland, TN

Mr. Douglas Ward
Southwestern Community College
Sylva, NC

Ms. Naomi Ward
Northwest Kansas Technical College
Goodland, KS

Mr. Jeffrey Waybright
Spokane Falls Community College
Spokane, WA

Mr. Jim Weglin
North Seattle Community College
Seattle, WA

Ms. Linda Whitten
Skyline College
San Bruno, CA

Mr. Rick Wilson
Bowling Green Technical College
Bowling Green, KY

Ms. Dawn Wright
Rhodes College
Springfield, MO

Ms. Eileen Yadlowsky
The Cittone Institute
Mt. Laurel, NJ

Brief Contents

Contents

PART 1 The Accounting Cycle 1

PART 4
Summarizing and Reporting Financial Information 427

PART 1

The Accounting Cycle

Chapter 1

Accounting: The Language of Business

Chapter 2

Analyzing Business Transactions

Chapter 3

Analyzing Business Transactions Using T Accounts

Chapter 4

The General Journal and the General Ledger

Chapter 5

Adjustments and the Worksheet

Chapter 6

Closing Entries and the Postclosing Trial Balance

Mini-Practice Set 1

Service Business Accounting Cycle

avis group In 1999 Avis Group Holdings, Inc. expanded its focus by adding new services for corporate customers. Avis now manages leased fleets of autos by tracking fuel usage and maintaining the vehicles. All of these transportation operations amounted to annual revenues of $3.3 billion for the year ended December 31, 1999.

Thinking Critically

Why do you think the leasing services are popular with Avis's corporate clients?

CHAPTER 1

Learning Objectives

1. Define accounting.
2. Identify and discuss career opportunities in accounting.
3. Identify the users of financial information.
4. Compare and contrast the three types of business entities.
5. Describe the process used to develop generally accepted accounting principles.
6. Define the accounting terms new to this chapter.

Accounting: The Language of Business

New Terms

- Accounting
- Accounting system
- Auditing
- Auditor's report
- Certified public accountant (CPA)
- Corporation
- Creditor
- Discussion memorandum
- Economic entity
- Entity
- Exposure draft
- Financial statements
- Generally accepted accounting principles (GAAP)
- Governmental accounting
- International accounting
- Management advisory services
- Managerial accounting
- Partnership
- Public accountants
- Separate entity assumption
- Social entity
- Sole proprietorship
- Statements of Financial Accounting Standards
- Stock
- Stockholders
- Tax accounting

YAHOO!

www.yahoo.com

In the early 1990s Internet users needed an efficient way to organize and find information on the tens of thousands of computers linked to the Internet. In 1994 David Filo and Jerry Yang, the founders of Yahoo! Inc., created software and a customized database to efficiently locate, identify, and categorize material stored on the Internet.

Now a global communications, commerce, and media company, Yahoo! Inc. offers a wide range of services to more than 156 million individuals. As a publicly owned company, Yahoo! Inc. releases its financial information to investors, owners, and managers quarterly.

Thinking Critically

If you were considering becoming a stockholder in Yahoo! Inc., why would it be important for you to have a basic understanding of accounting?

For more information on Yahoo! Inc., go to: collegeaccounting.glencoe.com.

Section 1

Section Objectives

1. **Define accounting.**
   WHY IT'S IMPORTANT
   Business transactions affect many aspects of our lives.
2. **Identify and discuss career opportunities in accounting.**
   WHY IT'S IMPORTANT
   There's something for everyone in the field of accounting. Accounting professionals are found in every workplace from public accounting firms to government agencies, from corporations to nonprofit organizations.
3. **Identify the users of financial information.**
   WHY IT'S IMPORTANT
   A wide variety of individuals and businesses depend on financial information to make decisions.

Terms to Learn

accounting
accounting system
auditing
certified public accountant (CPA)
financial statements
governmental accounting
management advisory services
managerial accounting
public accountants
tax accounting

What Is Accounting?

Accounting provides financial information about a business or a nonprofit organization. Owners, managers, investors, and other interested parties need financial information in order to make decisions. Because accounting is used to communicate financial information, it is often called the "language of business."

The Need for Financial Information

Suppose a relative leaves you a substantial sum of money and you decide to carry out your lifelong dream of opening a small sportswear shop. You rent space in a local shopping center, purchase fixtures and equipment, purchase goods to sell, hire salespeople, and open the store to customers. Before long you realize that, to run your business successfully, you need financial information about the business. You probably need information that provides answers to the following questions:

- How much cash does the business have?
- How much money do customers owe the business?
- What is the cost of the merchandise sold?
- What is the change in sales volume?
- How much money is owed to suppliers?
- What is the profit or loss?

As your business grows, you will need even more financial information to evaluate the firm's performance and make decisions about the future. An efficient accounting system allows owners and managers to quickly obtain a wide range of useful information. The need for timely information is one reason that businesses have an accounting system directed by a professional staff.

Accounting Defined

1 Objective
Define accounting.

Accounting is the process by which financial information about a business is recorded, classified, summarized, interpreted, and communicated to owners, managers, and other interested parties. An **accounting system** is designed to accumulate data about a firm's financial affairs, classify the data in a meaningful way, and summarize it in periodic reports called **financial statements**. Owners and managers obtain a lot of information from financial statements. The accountant

- establishes the records and procedures that make up the accounting system,
- supervises the operations of the system,
- interprets the resulting financial information.

Most owners and managers rely heavily on the accountant's judgment and knowledge when making financial decisions.

Accounting Careers

2 Objective

Identify and discuss career opportunities in accounting.

Many jobs are available in the accounting profession, and they require varying amounts of education and experience. Bookkeepers and accountants are responsible for keeping records and providing financial information about the business. Generally bookkeepers are responsible for recording business transactions. In large firms bookkeepers may also supervise the work of accounting clerks. Accounting clerks are responsible for recordkeeping for a part of the accounting system—perhaps payroll, accounts receivable, or accounts payable. Accountants usually supervise bookkeepers and prepare the financial statements and reports of the business.

Newspapers and Web sites often have job listings for accounting clerks, bookkeepers, and accountants:

- Accounting clerk positions usually require one to two accounting courses and little or no experience.
- Bookkeeper positions usually require one to two years of accounting education plus experience as an accounting clerk.
- Accountant positions usually require a bachelor's degree but are sometimes filled by experienced bookkeepers or individuals with a two-year college degree. Most entry-level accountant positions do not have an experience requirement. Both the education and experience requirements for accountant positions vary according to the size of the firm.

Accountants usually choose to practice in one of three areas:

- public accounting
- managerial accounting
- governmental accounting

Public Accounting

Public accountants work for public accounting firms. Public accounting firms provide accounting services for other companies. Usually they offer three services:

- auditing
- tax accounting
- management advisory services

The largest public accounting firms in the United States are called the "Big Five." The "Big Five" are Andersen, Deloitte & Touche, Ernst & Young, KPMG, and PricewaterhouseCoopers.

Many public accountants are **certified public accountants (CPAs)**. To become a CPA, an individual must have a certain number of college credits in accounting courses, demonstrate good personal character, pass the Uniform CPA Examination, and fulfill the experience requirements of the state of practice. CPAs must follow the professional code of ethics.

Auditing is the review of financial statements to assess their fairness and adherence to generally accepted accounting principles. Accountants who are CPAs perform financial audits.

Tax accounting involves tax compliance and tax planning. *Tax compliance* deals with the preparation of tax returns and the audit of those returns. *Tax planning* involves giving advice to clients on how to structure their financial affairs in order to reduce their tax liability.

About Accounting

Accounting Services

The role of the CPA is expanding. In the past, accounting firms handled audits and taxes. Today accountants provide a wide range of services, including financial planning, investment advice, accounting and tax software advice, and profitability consulting. Accountants provide clients with information and advice on electronic business, health care performance measurement, risk assessment, business performance measurement, and information system reliability.

Management advisory services involve helping clients improve their information systems or their business performance.

Managerial Accounting

Managerial accounting, also referred to as *private accounting*, involves working for a single business in industry. Managerial accountants perform a wide range of activities, including

- establishing accounting policies,
- managing the accounting system,
- preparing financial statements,
- interpreting financial information,
- providing financial advice to management,
- preparing tax forms,
- performing tax planning services,
- preparing internal reports for management.

Governmental Accounting

Governmental accounting involves keeping financial records and preparing financial reports as part of the staff of federal, state, or local governmental units. Governmental units do not earn profits. However, governmental units receive and pay out huge amounts of money and need procedures for recording and managing this money.

Some governmental agencies hire accountants to audit the financial statements and records of the businesses under their jurisdiction and to uncover possible violations of the law. The Securities and Exchange Commission, the Internal Revenue Service, and the Federal Bureau of Investigation employ a large number of accountants.

Users of Financial Information

The results of the accounting process are communicated to many individuals and organizations. Who are these individuals and organizations, and why do they want financial information about a particular firm?

3 Objective

Identify the users of financial information.

Owners and Managers

Assume your sportswear shop is in full operation. One user of financial information about the business is you, the owner. You need information that will help you evaluate the results of your operations and plan and make decisions for the future. Questions such as the following are difficult to answer without financial information:

- Should you drop the long-sleeved pullover that is not selling well from the product line, or should you just reduce the price?
- How much should you charge for the denim jacket that you are adding to the product line?
- How much should you spend on advertising?
- How does this month's profit compare with last month's profit?
- Should you open a new store?

Suppliers

A number of other people are interested in the financial information about your business. For example, businesses that supply you with sportswear need to assess the ability of your firm to pay its bills. They also need to set a credit limit for your firm.

Banks

What if you decide to ask your bank for a loan so that you can open a new store? The bank needs to be sure that your firm will repay the loan on time. The bank will ask for financial information prepared by your accountant. Based on this information, the bank will decide whether to make the loan and the terms of the loan.

Tax Authorities

The Internal Revenue Service (IRS) and other tax authorities are interested in financial information about your firm. This information is used to determine the tax base:

- Income taxes are based on taxable income.
- Sales taxes are based on sales income.
- Property taxes are based on the assessed value of buildings, equipment, and inventory (the goods available for sale).

The accounting process provides all of this information.

Regulatory Agencies and Investors

If an industry is regulated by a governmental agency, businesses in that industry have to supply financial information to the regulating agency. For example, the Federal Communications Commission receives financial information from radio and television stations. The Securities and Exchange Commission (SEC) oversees the financial information provided by publicly owned corporations to their investors and potential investors. Publicly owned corporations trade their shares on stock exchanges and in over-the-counter markets. Congress passed the Securities Act of 1933 and the Securities Exchange Act of 1934 in order to protect those who invest in publicly owned corporations.

The SEC is responsible for reviewing the accounting methods used by publicly owned corporations. The SEC has delegated this review to the accounting profession but still has the final say on any financial accounting issue faced by publicly owned corporations. If the SEC does not agree with the reporting that results from an accounting method, the SEC can suspend trading of a company's shares on the stock exchanges.

> The SEC encourages foreign corporations to file financial data in order to provide U.S. investors protection under U.S. securities laws. More than 1,100 foreign companies from 56 countries file reports with the SEC.

Customers

Customers pay special attention to financial information about the firms with which they do business. For example, before a business spends a lot of money on a mainframe computer, the business wants to know that the computer manufacturer will be around for the next several years in order to service the computer, replace parts, and provide additional components. The business analyzes the financial information about the computer manufacturer in order to determine its economic health and the likelihood that it will remain in business.

Employees and Unions

Often employees are interested in the financial information of the business that employs them. Employees who are members of a profit-sharing plan pay close attention to the financial results because they affect employee income. Employees who are members of a labor union use financial information about the firm to negotiate wages and benefits.

Figure 1-1 illustrates different financial information users. As you learn about the accounting process, you will appreciate why financial information is so important to these individuals and organizations. You will learn how financial information meets users' needs.

FIGURE 1-1 ►
Users of Financial Information

Inside the Business

Owners

Managers

Outside the Business

Tax Authorities

Suppliers

Regulatory Agencies

Unions

Banks

Customers

Investors and Potential Investors

FINANCIAL REPORTS

REPORTS

Section 1 Self Review

Questions

1. Why is accounting called the "language of business"?
2. What are the names of three accounting job positions?
3. What are financial statements?

Exercises

4. One requirement for becoming a CPA is to pass the
   - **a.** State Board Examination
   - **b.** Uniform CPA Examination
   - **c.** SEC Accounting Examination
   - **d.** Final CPA Examination
5. Which organization has the final say on financial accounting issues faced by publicly owned corporations?
   - **a.** Internal Revenue Service
   - **b.** U.S. Treasury Department
   - **c.** Federal Trade Commission
   - **d.** Securities and Exchange Commission

Analysis

6. The owner of the sporting goods store where you work has decided to expand the store. She has decided to apply for a loan. What type of information will she need to give to the bank?

(Answers to Section 1 Self Review are on page 21.)

Section 2

Business and Accounting

The accounting process involves recording, classifying, summarizing, interpreting, and communicating financial information about an economic or social entity. An **entity** is recognized as having its own separate identity. An entity may be an individual, a town, a university, or a business. The term **economic entity** usually refers to a business or organization whose major purpose is to produce a profit for its owners. **Social entities** are nonprofit organizations, such as cities, public schools, and public hospitals. This book focuses on the accounting process for businesses, but keep in mind that nonprofit organizations also need financial information.

Section Objectives

4 Compare and contrast the three types of business entities.

WHY IT'S IMPORTANT
Each type of business entity requires unique legal and accounting considerations.

5 Describe the process used to develop generally accepted accounting principles.

WHY IT'S IMPORTANT
Accounting professionals are required to use common standards and principles in order to produce reliable financial information.

Terms to Learn

auditor's report
corporation
creditor
discussion memorandum
economic entity
entity
exposure draft
generally accepted accounting principles (GAAP)
international accounting
partnership
separate entity assumption
social entity
sole proprietorship
Statements of Financial Accounting Standards
stock
stockholders

Types of Business Entities

The three major legal forms of business entity are the sole proprietorship, the partnership, and the corporation. In general the accounting process is the same for all three forms of business. Later in the book you will study the different ways certain transactions are handled depending on the type of business entity. For now, however, you will learn about the different types of business entities.

Sole Proprietorships

A **sole proprietorship** is a business entity owned by one person. The life of the business ends when the owner is no longer willing or able to keep the business going. Many small businesses are operated as sole proprietorships.

The owner of a sole proprietorship is legally responsible for the debts and taxes of the business. If the business is unable to pay its debts, the **creditors** (those people, companies, or government agencies to whom the business owes money) can turn to the owner for payment. The owner may have to pay the debts of the business from personal resources, including personal savings. When the time comes to pay income taxes, the owner's income and the income of the business are combined to compute the total tax responsibility of the owner.

It is important that the business transactions be kept separate from the owner's personal transactions. If the owner's personal transactions are mixed with those of the business, it will be difficult to measure the performance of the business. The term **separate entity assumption** describes the concept of keeping the firm's financial records separate from the owner's personal financial records.

4 Objective

Compare and contrast the three types of business entities.

Partnerships

A **partnership** is a business entity owned by two or more people. The partnership structure is common in businesses that offer professional services, such as law firms, accounting firms, architectural firms, medical

Computers in Accounting

Computing in the Workplace

Desktop computers, notebooks, handhelds, and networked systems are all distant relatives of the world's first binary digital computer, the Z1, built by Konrad Zuse in 1938. Today, billions of transactions can be quickly stored, analyzed, mined, and communicated using computers.

In the workplace *personal computers*, sometimes called desktop computers, are found in almost every cubicle or office. Companies provide personal computers and software to their employees based on the individual needs of each employee. For example, a company's accounts payable manager may need a computer with high-speed processing capabilities, accounts payable and general ledger software, and connections to the company's computer network and the Internet. Another employee may need a computer equipped only with word processing software, spreadsheet software, and minimal processing speed.

Since their introduction in 1982, *notebook computers* or laptops have exploded into the business computing market. Business travelers often use notebook computers equipped with self-contained battery packs, Internet connectivity, and large memory capacities.

Many business professionals use *handhelds*, or personal digital assistants (PDAs), to organize data, maintain calendars and lists, and communicate using wireless services. A PDA can be used as a portable computing device, holding information that the employee needs while away from the office. Back in the office, PDAs can synchronize with the desktop computer or laptop.

Networked computer systems, *mainframe computers*, and *supercomputers* are large systems that cost from $35,000 to more than $20 million. Large companies often connect personal computers and mainframes to form a network that will support hundreds of users. Supercomputers can work at or near the highest operational rates. A supercomputer is typically used for scientific and engineering applications handling very large databases or lots of computations.

Whether businesses are recording electronic sales or employees are communicating via e-mail, we rely extensively on computer technologies daily.

Thinking Critically

What advantages do you think the global business community enjoys due to the increased use of computer technologies today?

Internet Application

Visit the Web site for a major computing magazine. Find a product review for a notebook or a handheld computer. Write a brief overview of the product. Include the product name, key features, price, and benefits of the product for the professional on the go.

practices, and dental practices. At the beginning of the partnership, two or more individuals enter into a contract that details the rights, obligations, and limitations of each partner, including

- the amount each partner will contribute to the business,
- each partner's percentage of ownership,
- each partner's share of the profits,
- the duties each partner will perform,
- the responsibility each partner has for the amounts owed by the business to creditors and tax authorities.

The partners choose how to share the ownership and profits of the business. They may share equally or in any proportion agreed upon in the contract. When a partner leaves, the partnership is dissolved and a new partnership may be formed with the remaining partners.

> Operating as a partnership since 1911, Woolpert LLP has 17 partners and offers engineering, architecture, and design services internationally. Since 1996 the firm has been ranked as one of the nation's top 100 design firms by *Engineering News-Record.* Woolpert LLP employs approximately 700 in-house professional and technical employees.

Partners are individually, and as a group, responsible for the debts and taxes of the partnership. If the partnership is unable to pay its debts or taxes, the partners' personal property, including personal bank accounts, may be used to provide payment. It is important that partnership transactions be kept separate from the personal financial transactions of the partners.

Corporations

A **corporation** is a business entity that is separate from its owners. A corporation has a legal right to own property and do business in its own name. Corporations are very different from sole proprietorships and partnerships.

Stock, issued in the form of stock certificates, represents the ownership of the corporation. Corporations may be *privately* or *publicly* owned. Privately owned corporations are also called *closely held* corporations. The ownership of privately owned corporations is limited to specific individuals, usually family members. Stock of closely held corporations is not traded on an exchange. In contrast, stock of publicly owned corporations is bought and sold on stock exchanges and in over-the-counter markets. Most large corporations have issued (sold) thousands of shares of stock.

> *Important!*
>
> **Separate Entity Assumption**
> For *accounting* purposes all forms of business are considered separate entities from their owners. However, the corporation is the only form of business that is a separate *legal* entity.

An owner's share of the corporation is determined by the number of shares of stock held by the owner compared to the total number of shares issued by the corporation. Assume that Nancy Ling owns 250 shares of Sample Corporation. If Sample Corporation has issued 1,000 shares of stock, Ling owns 25 percent of the corporation (250 shares ÷ 1,000 shares = 0.25 or 25%). Some corporate decisions require a vote by the owners. For Sample Corporation Ling has 250 votes, one for each share of stock that she owns. The other owners have 750 votes.

> The Boeing Company is the world's largest manufacturer of commercial jetliners and military aircraft. In its 1999 annual report, Boeing reported that 1,001,879,159 shares of common stock have been issued.

One of the advantages of the corporate form of business is the indefinite life of the corporation. A sole proprietorship ends when the owner dies or discontinues the business. A partnership ends on the death or withdrawal of a partner. In contrast, a corporation does not end when ownership changes. Some corporations have new owners daily because their shares are actively traded (sold) on stock exchanges.

Corporate owners, called **stockholders** or *shareholders*, are not personally responsible for the debts or taxes of the corporation. If the corporation is unable to pay its bills, the most stockholders can lose is their investment in the corporation. In other words, the stockholders will not lose more than the cost of the shares of stock.

The accounting process for the corporate entity, like that of the sole proprietorship and the partnership, is separate from the financial affairs of its owners. Usually this separation is easy to maintain. Most stockholders do not participate in the day-to-day operations of the business.

Table 1-1 summarizes the business characteristics for sole proprietorships, partnerships, and corporations.

TABLE 1-1 ▼
Major Characteristics of Business Entities

Characteristic	Type of Business Entity		
	Sole Proprietorship	**Partnership**	**Corporation**
Ownership	One owner	Two or more owners	One or more owners, even thousands
Life of the business	Ends when the owner dies, is unable to carry on operations, or decides to close the firm	Ends when one or more partners withdraw, when a partner dies, or when the partners decide to close the firm	Can continue indefinitely; ends only when the business goes bankrupt or when the stockholders vote to liquidate
Responsibility for debts of the business	Owner is responsible for firm's debts when the firm is unable to pay	Partners are responsible individually and jointly for firm's debts when the firm is unable to pay	Stockholders are not responsible for firm's debts; they can lose only the amount they invested

GAAP
The SEC requires all publicly owned companies to follow generally accepted accounting principles. As new standards are developed or refined, accountants interpret the standards and adapt accounting practices to the new standards.

Generally Accepted Accounting Principles

The Securities and Exchange Commission has the final say on matters of financial reporting by publicly owned corporations. The SEC has delegated the job of determining proper accounting standards to the accounting profession. However, the SEC sometimes overrides decisions the accounting profession makes. To fulfill its responsibility, the accounting profession has developed, and continues to develop, **generally accepted accounting principles (GAAP)**. Generally accepted accounting principles must be followed by publicly owned companies unless they can show that doing so would produce information that is misleading.

5 Objective
Describe the process used to develop generally accepted accounting principles.

The Development of Generally Accepted Accounting Principles

Generally accepted accounting principles are developed by the Financial Accounting Standards Board (FASB), which is composed of seven full-time members. The FASB issues **Statements of Financial Accounting Standards**. The FASB develops these statements and, before issuing them, obtains feedback from interested people and organizations.

First, the FASB writes a **discussion memorandum** to explain the topic being considered. Then public hearings are held where interested parties can express their opinions, either orally or in writing. The groups that consistently express opinions about proposed FASB statements are the

SEC, the American Institute of Certified Public Accountants (AICPA), public accounting firms, the American Accounting Association (AAA), and businesses with a direct interest in a particular statement.

The AICPA is a national association for certified public accountants. The AAA is a group of accounting educators. AAA members research possible effects of a proposed FASB statement and offer their opinions to the FASB.

After public hearings, the FASB releases an **exposure draft**, which describes the proposed statement. Then the FASB receives and evaluates public comment about the exposure draft. Finally, FASB members vote on the statement. If at least four members approve, the statement is issued. The process used to develop GAAP is shown in Figure 1-2 on page 14.

Accounting principles vary from country to country. **International accounting** is the study of the accounting principles used by different countries. In 1973, the International Accounting Standards Committee (IASC) was formed to deal with issues caused by the lack of uniform accounting principles. The IASC was the predecessor of the current standard setter, the International Accounting Standards Board (IASB).

Standards

In 1999 the FASB chairman offered the IASC three guiding principles for its work:

1. Identify a common mission or objective for all parties involved in the process.
2. Develop an accepted and trusted process for creating the standards.
3. Develop standards that achieve high quality.

The Use of Generally Accepted Accounting Principles

Every year publicly traded companies submit financial statements to the SEC. The financial statements are audited by independent certified public accountants (CPAs). The CPAs are called *independent* because they are not employees of the company being audited and they do not have a financial interest in the company. The financial statements include the auditor's report. The **auditor's report** contains the auditor's opinion

Financial Information

- Managers of a business make sure that the firm's accounting system produces financial information that is timely, accurate, and fair.
- Financial statements should be based on generally accepted accounting principles.
- Each year a publicly traded company must submit financial statements, including an independent auditor's report, to the SEC.
- Internal reports for management need not follow generally accepted accounting principles but should provide useful information that will aid in monitoring and controlling operations.
- Financial information can help managers to control present operations, make decisions, and plan for the future.
- The sound use of financial information is essential to good management.

Thinking Critically

If you were a manager, how would you use financial information to make decisions?

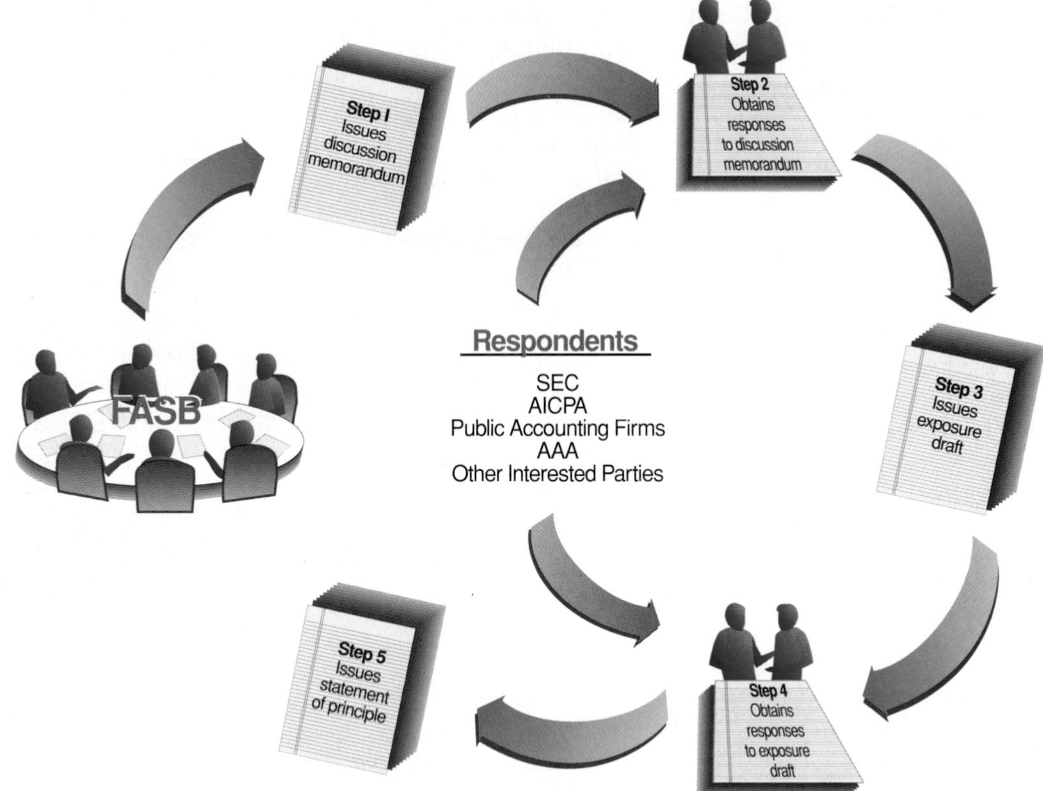

FIGURE 1-2 ▲
The Process Used by FASB to Develop Generally Accepted Accounting Principles

about the fair presentation of the operating results and financial position of the business. The auditor's report also confirms that the financial information is prepared in conformity with generally accepted accounting principles. The financial statements and the auditor's report are made available to the public, including existing and potential stockholders.

Businesses and the environment in which they operate are constantly changing. The economy, technology, and laws change. Generally accepted accounting principles are changed and refined as accountants respond to the changing environment.

Section 2 Self Review

Questions

1. What are generally accepted accounting principles?
2. Why are generally accepted accounting principles needed?
3. How are generally accepted accounting principles developed?

Exercises

4. An organization that has two or more owners who are legally responsible for the debts and taxes of the business is a
   a. corporation
   b. sole proprietorship
   c. partnership
   d. social entity
5. A nonprofit organization such as a public school is a(n)
   a. economic entity
   b. social entity
   c. economic unit
   d. social unit

Analysis

6. You plan to open a business with two of your friends. You would like to form a corporation, but your friends prefer the partnership form of business. What are some of the advantages of the corporate form of business?

(Answers to Section 2 Self Review are on page 21.)

CHAPTER 1 Review and Applications

Review

Chapter Summary

Accounting is often called the "language of business." The financial information about a business is communicated to interested parties in financial statements.

Learning Objectives

1 Define accounting.

Accounting is the process by which financial information about a business is recorded, classified, summarized, interpreted, and communicated to owners, managers, and other interested parties. Accurate accounting information is essential for making business decisions.

2 Identify and discuss career opportunities in accounting.

- There are many job opportunities in accounting.
  - Accounting clerk positions, such as accounts receivable clerk, accounts payable clerk, and payroll clerk, require the least education and experience.
  - Bookkeepers usually have experience as accounting clerks and a minimum of one to two years of accounting education.
  - Most entry-level accounting positions require a college degree or significant experience as a bookkeeper.
- Accountants usually specialize in one of three major areas.
  - Some accountants work for public accounting firms and perform auditing, tax accounting, or management advisory functions.
  - Other accountants work in private industry where they set up and supervise accounting systems, prepare financial reports, prepare internal reports, or assist in determining the prices to charge for the firm's products.
  - Still other accountants work for government agencies. They keep track of public funds and expenditures, or they audit the financial records of businesses and individuals to determine whether the records are in compliance with regulatory laws, tax laws, and other laws. The Securities and Exchange Commission, the Internal Revenue Service, and the Federal Bureau of Investigation employ many accountants.

3 Identify the users of financial information.

All types of businesses need and use financial information. Users of financial information include owners and managers, suppliers, banks, tax authorities, regulatory agencies, and investors. Nonprofit organizations need similar financial information.

4 Compare and contrast the three types of business entities.

- A sole proprietorship is owned by one person. The owner is legally responsible for the debts and taxes of the business.
- A partnership is owned by two or more people. The owners are legally responsible for the debts and taxes of the business.
- A corporation is a separate legal entity from its owners.
- Note that all three types of business entities are considered separate entities for accounting purposes.

5 Describe the process used to develop generally accepted accounting principles.

- The SEC has delegated the authority to develop generally accepted accounting principles to the accounting profession. The Financial Accounting Standards Board handles this task. A series of steps used by the FASB includes issuing a discussion memorandum, an exposure draft, and a statement of principle.
- Each year firms that sell stock on stock exchanges or in over-the-counter markets must publish audited financial reports that follow generally accepted accounting principles. They must submit their reports to the Securities and Exchange Commission. They must also make the reports available to stockholders.

6 Define the accounting terms new to this chapter.

Applications

CHAPTER 1 CRITICAL THINKING PROBLEM

Which Type of Business Entity?

Since graduating from college five years ago, Ned Turner has worked for a national chain of men's clothing stores. Ned has held several positions with the company and is currently manager of a local branch store.

Over the past three years, Ned has observed a pattern in men who purchase suits. He believes that the majority of men's suit purchases are black, brown, blue, gray, and olive. He also notices that French cuff shirts are now fashionable, but few stores carry a wide color selection. Since he has always wanted to be in business for himself, Ned's idea is to open a shop that sells suits that are black, brown, blue, gray, and olive and to carry a wide array of colors of French cuff shirts. The store will also sell fashionable ties and cuff links. Ned already has a name for his store, The Three B's and Go Suit Shop. Ned has discussed his plan with a number of people in the industry and they believe his idea is a viable one.

A new upscale shopping mall is opening nearby and Ned has decided that now is the time to take the plunge and go into business for himself. Ned plans to open The Three B's and Go Suit Shop in the new mall.

One of the things Ned must decide in the process of transforming his idea into reality is the form of ownership for his new business. Should it be organized as a sole proprietorship, a partnership, or corporation?

What advice would you give Ned? What advantages and disadvantages are there to each choice? The following diagram will help you to organize your thoughts.

Business Entity	Advantages	Disadvantages
Sole Proprietorship		
Partnership		
Corporation		

Business Connections

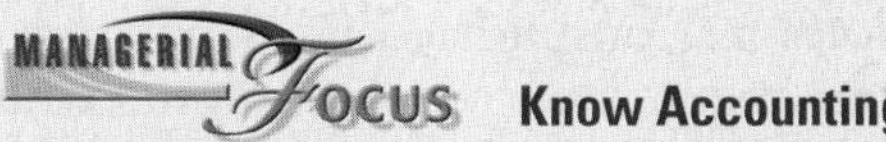

Know Accounting ◄ **Connection 1**

1. Why is it important for managers to have financial information?
2. Do you think a manager will obtain enough financial information to control operations effectively if the manager simply reads a set of financial statements once a year? Why or why not?
3. The owner of a small business commented to a friend that he did not see the need for an accounting system in his firm because he closely supervises day-to-day operations and knows exactly what is happening in the business. Would you agree with his statement? Why or why not?
4. This chapter listed a number of questions that the owner or manager of a firm might ask when trying to evaluate the results of the firm's operations and its financial position. If you were an owner or manager, what other questions would you ask to judge the firm's performance, control operations, make decisions, and plan for the future?
5. The major objective of most businesses is to earn a profit. What other objectives might a business have? How can financial information help management to achieve these objectives?
6. Many business owners and managers are not accountants. Why is it useful for such people to have a basic knowledge of accounting?
7. Are international accounting standards important to management? Why or why not?
8. Why is the separate entity assumption important to a manager?

Ethical DILEMMA ◄ **Connection 2**

Attendance The professor of your *College Accounting* class requires class attendance. Students who miss three or more classes with unexcused absences will have their earned course grade reduced by one letter grade. Because the class is large, the professor's only check on attendance is to have each student sign in upon entering the class. Your roommate is also enrolled in this class and you have observed him sign in and immediately leave class on two occasions. He has indicated that he will continue this practice and intends to get the class notes from you. What would you do if you were in this ethical dilemma?

Street WISE: **Questions from the Real World** ◄ **Connection 3**

Information Refer to The Home Depot, Inc. *1999 Annual Report* in Appendix B.

1. Review the letter written by Arthur M. Blank, President and Chief Executive Officer. To what audiences is the letter directed? Describe the types of financial information presented in the letter. Why would this information be important to readers?
2. Information provided in a company's annual report can also include nonfinancial strategies for merchandising, customer service, or new ventures. Based on the letter presented from The Home Depot, Inc.'s president and CEO, describe three successful strategies that the company implemented in 1999.

Connection 4 ►

AMERICAN EAGLE OUTFITTERS

FINANCIAL STATEMENT ANALYSIS **Notes to Financial Statements** Within a company's annual report, a section called "Notes to Consolidated Financial Statements" offers general information about the company along with detailed notes related to its financial statements. An excerpt from American Eagle Outfitters, Inc.'s, "Notes to Consolidated Financial Statements," *1999 Annual Report*, is presented below.

> American Eagle Outfitters, Inc. ("the Company") is a specialty retailer of all-American casual apparel, accessories, and footwear for men and women between the ages of 16 and 34. The Company designs, markets, and sells its own brand of versatile, relaxed, and timeless classics like AE dungarees, khakis, and T-shirts, providing high-quality merchandise at affordable prices. The Company operates retail stores located primarily in regional enclosed shopping malls principally in the Midwest, Northeast, and Southeast.

Analyze:

1. Would American Eagle Outfitters, Inc., be considered an economic entity or a social entity? Why?
2. What types of merchandise does this company sell?
3. Who are the potential users of the information presented? Why would this information be helpful to these users?

Analyze Online: On the American Eagle Outfitters, Inc., Web site **(www.ae.com),** review the *Company Overview* section, under *Investment Information* within the *Corporate* link.

4. What age consumer does the company target?
5. What types of merchandise does the company offer? Has the merchandise selection changed from the merchandise described in the *1999 Annual Report?*
6. What information is offered to the shareholder on the Web site?

Connection 5 ►

Extending the Thought **Independent Auditor** A certified public accountant (CPA) who audits a company's financial statements must be independent. What is meant by "independent" in this sense? Why is it important? What situations or factors might affect a CPA's independence?

Connection 6 ►

Business Communication **Memo** As the manager of the accounting department, you have been asked by the human resources director to help prepare a job description for a job opening in your department. The company wishes to fill the position of bookkeeper. The heading of your memo should include the following:

Date:
To:
From:
Subject:

The body of your memo should include the job responsibilities, and the training and experience necessary for the position.

TeamWork **Sharing Information** You and your family own a chain of bakeries. Your employees are awarded annual bonuses based on the financial performance of the business. As a group, prepare a list of the types of information that you plan to distribute to your employees that will help them understand the financial condition of the business.

◄ **Connection 7**

interNET CONNECTION **FASB** Visit the Financial Accounting Standards Board Web site **(www.fasb.org)** and select *FASB Facts*.

- What is FASB's mission?
- What is the GASB?

◄ **Connection 8**

Answers to Self Reviews

Answers to Section 1 Self Review

1. The results of the accounting process—financial statements—communicate essential information about a business to concerned individuals and organizations.
2. Clerk, bookkeeper, and accountant.
3. Periodic reports that summarize the financial affairs of a business.
4. **b.** Uniform CPA Examination
5. **d.** Securities and Exchange Commission
6. Current sales and expenses figures, anticipated sales and expenses, and the cost of the expansion.

Answers to Section 2 Self Review

1. Accounting standards that are changed and refined in response to changes in the environment in which businesses operate.
2. GAAP help to ensure that financial information fairly presents a firm's operating results and financial position.
3. FASB develops proposed statements and solicits feedback from interested individuals, groups, and companies. FASB evaluates the opinions received and votes on the statement.
4. **c.** partnership
5. **b.** social entity
6. The shareholders are not responsible for the debts and taxes of the corporation. Corporations can continue in existence indefinitely.

Answers to Comprehensive Self Review

1. To gather and communicate financial information about a business.
2. Recording, classifying, summarizing, interpreting, and communicating financial information about a business.
3. Sole proprietorship, partnership, and corporation.
4. A sole proprietorship is a business entity owned by one person. A corporation is a separate legal entity that has a legal right to own property and do business in its own name.
5. To obtain the objective opinion of a professional accountant from outside the company that the statements fairly present the operating results and financial position of the business and that the information was prepared according to GAAP.

CHAPTER 2

Learning Objectives

1. Record in equation form the financial effects of a business transaction.
2. Define, identify, and understand the relationship between asset, liability, and owner's equity accounts.
3. Analyze the effects of business transactions on a firm's assets, liabilities, and owner's equity and record these effects in accounting equation form.
4. Prepare an income statement.
5. Prepare a statement of owner's equity and a balance sheet.
6. Define the accounting terms new to this chapter.

Analyzing Business Transactions

www.southwest.com

In addition to having low fares, fun flights, and friendly employees, Southwest Airlines Company has been profitable for 27 consecutive years. Chief Executive Officer Herb Kelleher believes an efficient all-Boeing 737 fleet designed for direct short-haul routes, effective cost controls, and a happy, productive workforce are the keys to its success. Voted as CEO of 1999 by his peers, the maverick leader is known for his good humor and creating a company culture brimming with employee chili cook-offs, paper airplane contests, and dance competitions.

Thinking Critically

In what ways do you think a happy workforce contributes to the bottom line, or net profit, of the company?

For more information on Southwest Airlines Company, go to: collegeaccounting.glencoe.com.

New Terms

- **Accounts payable**
- **Accounts receivable**
- **Assets**
- **Balance sheet**
- **Break even**
- **Business transaction**
- **Capital**
- **Equity**
- **Expense**
- **Fair market value**
- **Fundamental accounting equation**
- **Income statement**
- **Liabilities**
- **Net income**
- **Net loss**
- **On account**
- **Owner's equity**
- **Revenue**
- **Statement of owner's equity**
- **Withdrawals**

Section 1

Property and Financial Interest

Section Objectives

1. **Record in equation form the financial effects of a business transaction.**

   WHY IT'S IMPORTANT
   Learning the fundamental accounting equation is a basis for understanding business transactions.

2. **Define, identify, and understand the relationship between asset, liability, and owner's equity accounts.**

   WHY IT'S IMPORTANT
   The relationship between assets, liabilities, and owner's equity is the basis for the entire accounting system.

Terms to Learn

accounts payable
assets
balance sheet
business transaction
capital
equity
liabilities
on account
owner's equity

The accounting process starts with the analysis of business transactions. A **business transaction** is any financial event that changes the resources of a firm. For example, purchases, sales, payments, and receipts of cash are all business transactions. The accountant analyzes each business transaction to decide what information to record and where to record it.

Beginning with Analysis

Let's analyze the transactions of Carter Consulting Services, a firm that provides a wide range of accounting and consulting services. Linda Carter, CPA, has a master's degree in accounting. She is the sole proprietor of Carter Consulting Services. Beatrice Wilson, the office manager, has an associate's degree in business and has taken 12 semester hours of accounting. The firm is located in a large office complex.

Every month Carter Consulting Services bills clients for the accounting and consulting services provided that month. Customers can also pay in cash when the services are rendered.

Starting a Business

Let's start from the beginning. Linda Carter obtained the funds to start the business by withdrawing $80,000 from her personal savings account. The first transaction of the new business was opening a checking account in the name of Carter Consulting Services. The separate bank account helps Carter keep her financial interest in the business separate from her personal funds.

1 Objective
Record in equation form the financial effects of a business transaction.

When a business transaction occurs, it is analyzed to identify how it affects the equation *property equals financial interest.* This equation reflects the fact that in a free enterprise system, all property is owned by someone. In this case Carter owns the business because she supplied the property (cash).

Use these steps to analyze the effect of a business transaction:

1. Describe the financial event.
   - Identify the property.
   - Identify who owns the property.
   - Determine the amount of increase or decrease.
2. Make sure the equation is in balance.

Property	=	Financial Interest
+80,000	=	80,000

Business Transaction

Linda Carter withdrew $80,000 from personal savings and deposited it in a new checking account in the name of Carter Consulting Services.

Analysis

a. The business received $80,000 of *property* in the form of cash.

b. Carter had an $80,000 *financial interest* in the business.

Note that the equation *property equals financial interest* remains in balance.

	Property	=	**Financial Interest**
	Cash	=	Linda Carter, Capital
(a) Invested cash	**+$80,000**		
(b) Increased equity			**+$80,000**
New balances	$80,000	=	$80,000

An owner's financial interest in the business is called **equity**, or **capital**. Linda Carter has $80,000 equity in Carter Consulting Services.

Purchasing Equipment for Cash

The first priority for office manager Beatrice Wilson was to get the business ready for opening day on December 1.

Business Transaction

Carter Consulting Services issued a $20,000 check to purchase a computer and other equipment.

Analysis

c. The firm purchased new property (equipment) for $20,000.

d. The firm paid out $20,000 in cash.

The equation remains in balance.

		Property		=	**Financial Interest**
	Cash	+	Equipment	=	Linda Carter, Capital
Previous balances	$80,000			=	$80,000
(c) Purchased equipment		+	**$20,000**		
(d) Paid cash	**−20,000**				
New balances	$60,000	+	$20,000	=	$80,000

Notice that there is a change in the composition of the firm's property. Now the firm has cash and equipment. The equation shows that the total value of the property remains the same, $80,000. Linda Carter's financial interest, or equity, is also unchanged. Note that property (Cash and Equipment) is equal to financial interest (Linda Carter, Capital).

These activities are recorded for the business entity Carter Consulting Services. Linda Carter's personal assets, such as her personal bank account, house, furniture, and automobile, are kept separate from the property of the firm. Nonbusiness property is not included in the accounting records of the business entity.

Purchasing Equipment on Credit

Wilson purchased additional office equipment. Office Plus, the store selling the equipment, allows Carter Consulting Services 60 days to pay the bill. This arrangement is called buying **on account**. The business has a *charge account*, or *open-account credit*, with its suppliers. Amounts that a business must pay in the future are known as **accounts payable**. The companies or individuals to whom the amounts are owed are called *creditors*.

Business Transaction

Carter Consulting Services purchased office equipment on account from Office Plus for $15,000.

Analysis

e. The firm purchased new property (equipment) that cost $15,000.

f. The firm owes $15,000 to Office Plus.

The equation remains in balance.

	Property			=	Financial Interest		
	Cash	+	Equipment	=	Accounts Payable	+	Linda Carter, Capital
Previous balances	$60,000	+	$20,000	=			$80,000
(e) Purchased equip.			**+15,000**				
(f) Incurred debt					**+$15,000**		
New balances	$60,000	+	$35,000	=	$15,000	+	$80,000

Office Plus is willing to accept a claim against Carter Consulting Services until the bill is paid. Now there are two different financial interests or claims against the firm's property—the creditor's claim (Accounts Payable) and the owner's claim (Linda Carter, Capital). Notice that the total property increases to $95,000. Cash is $60,000 and equipment is $35,000. Linda Carter, Capital stays the same; but the creditor's claim increases to $15,000. After this transaction is recorded, the left side of the equation still equals the right side.

History

For as long as people have been involved in business, there has been a need for accounting. The system of accounting we use is based upon the works of Luca Pacioli, a Franciscan monk in Italy. In 1494, Pacioli wrote about the bookkeeping techniques in practice during his time.

When Ben Cohen and Jerry Greenfield founded Ben & Jerry's Homemade Ice Cream, Inc., in 1978, they invested $8,000 of their own funds and borrowed funds of $4,000. The equation *property equals financial interest* is expressed as

Property	=	**Financial Interest**
cash	=	*creditors' claims*
		+ owners' claims
$12,000	=	$ 4,000
		+ 8,000
		$12,000

Purchasing Supplies

Wilson purchased supplies so that Carter Consulting Services could start operations. The company that sold the items requires cash payments from companies that have been in business less than six months.

Business Transaction

Carter Consulting Services issued a check for $2,000 to Resource Supplies, Inc. to purchase office supplies.

Analysis

g. The firm purchased office supplies that cost $2,000.

h. The firm paid $2,000 in cash.

The equation remains in balance.

	Property					=	Financial Interest		
	Cash	+	Supplies	+	Equipment	=	Accounts Payable	+	Linda Carter, Capital
Previous balances	$60,000			+	$35,000	=	$15,000	+	$80,000
(g) Purchased supplies		+	**$2,000**						
(h) Paid cash	**− 2,000**								
New balances	$58,000	+	$2,000	+	$35,000	=	$15,000	+	$80,000

Notice that total property remains the same, even though the form of the property has changed. Also note that all of the property (left side) equals all of the financial interests (right side).

Paying a Creditor

Wilson decided to reduce the firm's debt to Office Plus by $3,000.

Business Transaction

Carter Consulting Services issued a check for $3,000 to Office Plus.

Analysis

i. The firm paid $3,000 in cash.

j. The claim of Office Plus against the firm decreased by $3,000.

The equation remains in balance.

	Property					=	Financial Interest		
	Cash	+	Supplies	+	Equipment	=	Accounts Payable	+	Linda Carter, Capital
Previous balances	$58,000	+	$2,000	+	$35,000	=	$15,000	+	$80,000
(i) Paid cash	**− 3,000**								
(j) Decreased debt							**− 3,000**		
New balances	$55,000	+	$2,000	+	$35,000	=	$12,000	+	$80,000

Renting Facilities

In November Carter arranged to rent facilities for $3,000 per month, beginning in December. The landlord required that rent for the first two months—December and January—be paid in advance. The firm prepaid (paid in advance) the rent for two months. As a result, the firm obtained the right to occupy facilities for a two-month period. In accounting this right is considered a form of property.

Business Transaction

Carter Consulting Services issued a check for $6,000 to pay for rent for the months of December and January.

Analysis

k. The firm prepaid the rent for the next two months in the amount of $6,000.

l. The firm decreased its cash balance by $6,000.

The equation remains in balance.

	Property							=	Financial Interest		
	Cash	+	Supplies	+	Prepaid Rent	+	Equipment	=	Accounts Payable	+	Linda Carter, Capital
Previous balances	$55,000	+	$2,000			+	$35,000	=	$12,000	+	$80,000
(k) Paid cash	**−6,000**										
(l) Prepaid rent					**+$6,000**						
New balances	$49,000	+	$2,000	+	$6,000	+	$35,000	=	$12,000	+	$80,000

Notice that when property values and financial interests increase or decrease, the total of the items on one side of the equation still equals the total on the other side.

Property		=	**Financial Interest**	
Cash	$49,000		Accounts Payable	$12,000
Supplies	2,000		Linda Carter, Capital	80,000
Prepaid Rent	6,000			
Equipment	35,000			
Total	$92,000	=	Total	$92,000

The balance sheet is also called the *statement of financial position.* Caterpillar Inc., reported assets of $26.6 billion, liabilities of $21.2 billion, and owners' equity of $5.4 billion on its statement of financial position at December 31, 1999.

2 Objective

Define, identify, and understand the relationship between asset, liability, and owner's equity accounts.

Assets, Liabilities, and Owner's Equity

Accountants use special accounting terms when they refer to property and financial interests. For example, they refer to the property that a business owns as **assets** and to the debts or obligations of the business as **liabilities**. The owner's financial interest is called **owner's equity**. (Sometimes owner's equity is called *proprietorship* or *net worth.* Owner's equity is

Carter Consulting Services			
Balance Sheet			
November 30, 2004			
Assets		*Liabilities*	
Cash	49 000 00	*Accounts Payable*	12 000 00
Supplies	2 000 00		
Prepaid Rent	6 000 00	*Owner's Equity*	
Equipment	35 000 00	*Linda Carter, Capital*	80 000 00
Total Assets	92 000 00	*Total Liabilities and Owner's Equity*	92 000 00

▲ **FIGURE 2-1**
Balance Sheet for Carter Consulting Services

the preferred term and is used throughout this book.) At regular intervals Carter reviews the status of the firm's assets, liabilities, and owner's equity in a financial statement called a **balance sheet**. The balance sheet shows the firm's financial position on a given date. Figure 2-1 shows the firm's balance sheet on November 30, the day before the company opened for business.

The assets are listed on the left side of the balance sheet and the liabilities and owner's equity are on the right side. This arrangement is similar to the equation *property equals financial interest.* Property is shown on the left side of the equation, and financial interest appears on the right side.

The balance sheet in Figure 2-1 shows

- the amount and types of property the business owns,
- the amount owed to creditors,
- the owner's interest.

This statement gives Linda Carter a complete picture of the financial position of her business on November 30.

Section 1 Self Review

Questions

1. What is a business transaction?
2. Describe a transaction that increases an asset and the owner's equity.
3. What does the term "accounts payable" mean?

Exercises

4. Maria Sanders purchased a computer for $2,000 on account for her business. What is the effect of this transaction?
   a. Cash decrease of $2,000 and owner's equity increase of $2,000.
   b. Equipment increase of $2,000 and cash increase of $2,000.
   c. Equipment decrease of $2,000 and accounts payable increase of $2,000.
   d. Equipment increase of $2,000 and accounts payable increase of $2,000.
5. Tara Swift began a new business by depositing $40,000 in the business bank account. She wrote two checks from the business account: $5,000 for office furniture and $1,000 for office supplies. What is her financial interest in the company?
   a. $34,000
   b. $35,000
   c. $39,000
   d. $40,000

Analysis

6. T. D. Whatley Co. has no liabilities. The asset and owner's equity balances are as follows. What is the balance of "Supplies"?

Cash	$12,000
Office Equipment	$8,000
Supplies	????
T. D. Whatley, Capital	$22,500

(Answers to Section 1 Self Review are on page 55.)

Section 2

Section Objectives

3 **Analyze the effects of business transactions on a firm's assets, liabilities, and owner's equity and record these effects in accounting equation form.**

WHY IT'S IMPORTANT
Property will always equal financial interest.

4 **Prepare an income statement.**

WHY IT'S IMPORTANT
The income statement shows the results of operations.

5 **Prepare a statement of owner's equity and a balance sheet.**

WHY IT'S IMPORTANT
These financial statements show the financial condition of a business.

Terms to Learn

accounts receivable
break even
expense
fair market value
fundamental accounting equation
income statement
net income
net loss
revenue
statement of owner's equity
withdrawals

The Accounting Equation and Financial Statements

The word *balance* in the title "balance sheet" has a special meaning. It emphasizes that the total on the left side of the report must equal, or balance, the total on the right side.

The Fundamental Accounting Equation

In accounting terms the firm's assets must equal the total of its liabilities and owner's equity. This equality can be expressed in equation form, as illustrated here. The amounts are for Carter Consulting Services on November 30.

Assets	=	Liabilities	+	Owner's Equity
$92,000	=	$12,000	+	$80,000

The relationship between assets and liabilities plus owner's equity is called the **fundamental accounting equation**. The entire accounting process of analyzing, recording, and reporting business transactions is based on the fundamental accounting equation.

If any two parts of the equation are known, the third part can be determined. For example, consider the basic accounting equation for Carter Consulting Services on November 30, with some information missing.

	Assets	=	Liabilities	+	Owner's Equity
1.	?	=	$12,000	+	$80,000
2.	$92,000	=	?	+	$80,000
3.	$92,000	=	$12,000	+	?

In the first case, we can solve for assets by adding liabilities to owner's equity ($12,000 + $80,000) to determine that assets are $92,000. In the second case, we can solve for liabilities by subtracting owner's equity from assets ($92,000 − $80,000) to determine that liabilities are $12,000. In the third case, we can solve for owner's equity by subtracting liabilities from assets ($92,000 − $12,000) to determine that owner's equity is $80,000.

3 **Objective**

Analyze the effects of business transactions on a firm's assets, liabilities, and owner's equity and record these effects in accounting equation form.

Earning Revenue and Incurring Expenses

Carter Consulting Services opened for business on December 1. Some of the other businesses in the office complex became the firm's first clients. Carter also used her contacts in the community to identify other clients. Providing services to clients started a stream of revenue for the business. **Revenue**, or *income*, is the inflow of money or other assets that results from the sales of goods or services or from the use of money or property. A sale on account does not increase money, but it does create a claim to money. When a sale occurs, the revenue increases assets and also increases owner's equity.

An **expense**, on the other hand, involves the outflow of money, the use of other assets, or the incurring of a liability. Expenses include the costs of any materials, labor, supplies, and services used to produce revenue. Expenses cause a decrease in owner's equity.

A firm's accounting records show increases and decreases in assets, liabilities, and owner's equity as well as details of all transactions involving revenue and expenses. Let's use the fundamental accounting equation to show how revenue and expenses affect the business.

Important!

Revenues increase owner's equity. Expenses decrease owner's equity.

Selling Services for Cash

During the month of December, Carter Consulting Services earned a total of $21,000 in revenue from clients who paid cash for accounting and bookkeeping services. This involved several transactions throughout the month. The total effect of these transactions is analyzed below.

Analysis

m. The firm received $21,000 in cash for services provided to clients.

n. Revenues increased by $21,000, which results in a $21,000 increase in owner's equity.

The fundamental accounting equation remains in balance.

	Assets							=	Liabilities +		Owner's Equity		
	Cash	+	Supplies	+	Prepaid Rent	+	Equipment	=	Accounts Payable	+	Linda Carter, Capital	+	Revenue
Previous balances	$49,000	+	$2,000	+	$6,000	+	$35,000	=	$12,000	+	$80,000		
(m) Received cash	+**21,000**												
(n) Increased owner's equity by earning revenue												+	**$21,000**
New balances	$70,000	+	$2,000	+	$6,000	+	$35,000	=	$12,000	+	$80,000	+	$21,000
	$113,000								$113,000				

Notice that revenue amounts are recorded in a separate column under owner's equity. Keeping revenue separate from the owner's equity will help the firm compute total revenue more easily when the financial statements are prepared.

Selling Services on Credit

Carter Consulting Services has some charge account clients. These clients are allowed 30 days to pay. Amounts owed by these clients are known as **accounts receivable**. This is a new form of asset for the firm—claims for future collection from customers. During December Carter Consulting Services earned $7,000 of revenue from charge account clients. The effect of these transactions is analyzed on page 32.

Analysis

o. The firm acquired a new asset, accounts receivable, of $7,000.

p. Revenues increased by $7,000, which results in a $7,000 increase in owner's equity.

The fundamental accounting equation remains in balance.

	Assets					=	Liab.	+	Owner's Equity	
	Cash	+ Accts. Rec.	+ Supp.	+ Prepaid Rent	+ Equip.	=	Accts. Pay.	+	Linda Carter, Capital	+ Rev.
Previous balances	$70,000		+ $2,000	+ $6,000	+ $35,000	=	$12,000	+	$80,000	+ $21,000
(o) Received new asset—accts. rec.		+ **$7,000**								
(p) Increased owner's equity by earning revenue										+ **7,000**
New balances	$70,000	+ $7,000	+ $2,000	+ $6,000	+ $35,000	=	$12,000	+	$80,000	+ $28,000
			$120,000						$120,000	

Collecting Receivables

During December Carter Consulting Services received $3,000 on account from clients who owed money for services previously billed. The effect of these transactions is analyzed below.

Analysis

q. The firm received $3,000 in cash.

r. Accounts receivable decreased by $3,000.

The fundamental accounting equation remains in balance.

	Assets					=	Liab.	+	Owner's Equity	
	Cash	+ Accts. Rec.	+ Supp.	+ Prepaid Rent	+ Equip.	=	Accts. Pay.	+	Linda Carter, Capital	+ Rev.
Previous balances	$70,000	+ $7,000	+ $2,000	+ $6,000	+ $35,000	=	$12,000	+	$80,000	+ $28,000
(q) Received cash	+ **3,000**									
(r) Decreased accounts receivable		− **3,000**								
New balances	$73,000	+ $4,000	+ $2,000	+ $6,000	+ $35,000	=	$12,000	+	$80,000	+ $28,000
			$120,000						$120,000	

In this type of transaction one asset is changed for another asset (accounts receivable for cash). Notice that revenue is not increased when cash is collected from charge account clients. The revenue was recorded when the sale on account took place (see entry (p)). Notice that the fundamental accounting equation, *assets equal liabilities plus owner's equity,* stays in balance regardless of the changes arising from individual transactions.

Paying Employees' Salaries

So far Carter has done very well. Her equity has increased by the revenues earned. However, running a business costs money, and these expenses reduce owner's equity.

During the first month of operations, Carter Consulting Services hired an accounting clerk. The salaries for the new accounting clerk and the office manager are considered an expense to the firm.

Business Transaction

In December Carter Consulting Services paid $5,000 in salaries for the accounting clerk and Beatrice Wilson.

Analysis

s. The firm decreased its cash balance by $5,000.

t. The firm paid salaries expense in the amount of $5,000, which decreased owner's equity.

The fundamental accounting equation remains in balance.

	Assets									=	Liab.	+	Owner's Equity				
	Cash	+	Accts. Rec.	+	Supp.	+	Prepaid Rent	+	Equip.	=	Accts. Pay.	+	L. Carter, Capital	+	Rev.	−	Exp.
Previous balances	$73,000	+	$4,000	+	$2,000	+	$6,000	+	$35,000	=	$12,000	+	$80,000	+	$28,000		
(s) Paid cash	**−5,000**																
(t) Decreased owner's equity by incurring salaries exp.																−	**$5,000**
New balances	$68,000	+	$4,000	+	$2,000	+	$6,000	+	$35,000	=	$12,000	+	$80,000	+	$28,000	−	$5,000
	$115,000										$115,000						

Notice that expenses are recorded in a separate column under owner's equity. The separate record of expenses is kept for the same reason that the separate record of revenue is kept—to analyze operations for the period.

Paying Utilities Expense

At the end of December, the firm received a $600 utilities bill.

Business Transaction

Carter Consulting Services issued a check for $600 to pay the utilities bill.

Analysis

u. The firm decreased its cash balance by $600.

v. The firm paid utilities expense of $600, which decreased owner's equity.

The fundamental accounting equation remains in balance.

	Assets									=	Liab.	+	Owner's Equity				
	Cash	+	Accts. Rec.	+	Supp.	+	Prepaid Rent	+	Equip.	=	Accts. Pay.	+	L. Carter, Capital	+	Rev.	−	Exp.
Previous balances	$68,000	+	$4,000	+	$2,000	+	$6,000	+	$35,000	=	$12,000	+	$80,000	+	$28,000	−	$5,000
(u) Paid cash	**−600**																
(v) Decreased owner's equity by utilities exp.																	**−600**
New balances	$67,400	+	$4,000	+	$2,000	+	$6,000	+	$35,000	=	$12,000	+	$80,000	+	$28,000	−	$5,600
	$114,400										$114,400						

Effect of Owner's Withdrawals

On December 30, Carter withdrew $3,000 in cash for personal expenses. **Withdrawals** are funds taken from the business by the owner for personal use. Withdrawals are not a business expense but a decrease in the owner's equity.

Business Transaction

Linda Carter wrote a check to withdraw $3,000 cash for personal use.

Analysis

w. The firm decreased its cash balance by $3,000.

x. Owner's equity decreased by $3,000.

The fundamental accounting equation remains in balance.

	Assets									=	Liab.	+	Owner's Equity				
	Cash	+	Accts. Rec.	+	Supp.	+	Prepaid Rent	+	Equip.	=	Accts. Pay.	+	L. Carter, Capital	+	Rev.	−	Exp.
Previous bal.	$67,400	+	$4,000	+	$2,000	+	$6,000	+	$35,000	=	$12,000	+	$80,000	+	$28,000	−	$5,600
(w) Withdrew cash	**−3,000**																
(x) Decreased owner's equity													**−3,000**				
New bal.	$64,400	+	$4,000	+	$2,000	+	$6,000	+	$35,000	=	$12,000	+	$77,000	+	$28,000	−	$5,600
	$111,400										$111,400						

Summary of Transactions

Figure 2-2 on page 35 summarizes the transactions of Carter Consulting Services through December 31. Notice that after each transaction, the fundamental accounting equation is in balance. Test your understanding by describing the nature of each transaction. Then check your results by referring to the discussion of each transaction.

4 Objective

Prepare an income statement.

The Income Statement

To be meaningful to owners, managers, and other interested parties, financial statements should provide information about revenue and expenses, assets and claims on the assets, and owner's equity.

	Assets					=	Liab. +	Owner's Equity		
	Cash +	Accts. Rec. +	Supp. +	Prepaid Rent +	Equip.	=	Accts. Pay. +	L. Carter, Cap. +	Rev. −	Exp.
(a) & (b)	+80,000							80,000		
Balances	80,000					=		80,000		
(c) & (d)	−20,000				20,000					
Balances	60,000				20,000	=		80,000		
(e) & (f)					15,000	=	+15,000			
Balances	60,000				35,000	=	15,000	80,000		
(g) & (h)	−2,000		2,000							
Balances	58,000		2,000		35,000	=	15,000	80,000		
(i) & (j)	−3,000						−3,000			
Balances	55,000		2,000		35,000	=	12,000	80,000		
(k) & (l)	−6,000			6,000						
Balances	49,000		2,000	6,000	35,000	=	12,000	80,000		
(m) & (n)	+21,000								21,000	
Balances	70,000		2,000	6,000	35,000	=	12,000	80,000	21,000	
(o) & (p)		7,000							+7,000	
Balances	70,000	7,000	2,000	6,000	35,000	=	12,000	80,000	28,000	
(q) & (r)	+3,000	−3,000								
Balances	73,000	4,000	2,000	6,000	35,000	=	12,000	80,000	28,000	
(s) & (t)	−5,000									5,000
Balances	68,000	4,000	2,000	6,000	35,000	=	12,000	80,000	28,000	5,000
(u) & (v)	−600									−600
Balances	67,400	4,000	2,000	6,000	35,000	=	12,000	80,000	28,000	5,600
(w) & (x)	−3,000							−3,000		
Balances	$64,400	$4,000	$2,000	$6,000	$35,000	=	$12,000	$77,000	$28,000	$5,600
	$111,400						$111,400			

▲ **FIGURE 2-2**
Transactions of Carter Consulting Services Through December 31, 2004

The **income statement** shows the results of business operations for a specific period of time such as a month, a quarter, or a year. The income statement shows the revenue earned and the expenses of doing business. (The income statement is sometimes called a *profit and loss statement* or a *statement of income and expenses.* The most common term, income statement, is used throughout this text.) Figure 2-3 shows the income statement for Carter Consulting Services for its first month of operation.

◀ **FIGURE 2-3**
Income Statement for Carter Consulting Services

Carter Consulting Services Income Statement Month Ended December 31, 2004		
Revenue		
Fees Income		28 000 00
Expenses		
Salaries Expense	5 000 00	
Utilities Expense	600 00	
Total Expenses		5 600 00
Net Income		22 400 00

Financial Statements
Financial statements are reports that summarize a firm's financial affairs.

The income statement shows the difference between income from services provided or goods sold and the amount spent to operate the business. **Net income** results when revenue is greater than the expenses for the period. When expenses are greater than revenue, the result is a **net loss**. In the rare case when revenue and expenses are equal, the firm is said to **break even**. The income statement in Figure 2-3 shows a net income; revenue is greater than expenses.

The three-line heading of the income statement shows *who, what,* and *when.*

- Who—the business name appears on the first line.
- What—the report title appears on the second line.
- When—the period covered appears on the third line.

The third line of the income statement heading in Figure 2-3 indicates that the report covers operations for the "Month Ended December 31, 2004." Review how other time periods are reported on the third line of the income statement heading.

Period Covered	Third Line of Heading
Jan., Feb., Mar.	Three-Month Period Ended March 31, 20--
Jan. to Dec.	Year Ended December 31, 20--
July 1 to June 30	Fiscal Year Ended June 30, 20--

Business Etiquette

In Japan, business cards are always offered with two hands. The receiver should accept the card with two hands, study it, and bow slightly before placing it into a shirt or jacket pocket. Placing the card near the heart shows respect for both the person and the company.

Note the use of single and double rules in amount columns. A single line is used to show that the amounts above it are being added or subtracted. Double lines are used under the final amount in a column or section of a report to show that the amount is complete. Nothing is added to or subtracted from an amount with a double line.

Some companies refer to the income statement as the *statement of operations.* American Eagle Outfitters, Inc. reported $832 million in sales on consolidated statements of operations for the fiscal year ended January 29, 2000. American Eagle Outfitters, Inc. was ranked as the sixteenth fastest-growing company in the United States by *Fortune* magazine in September 2000.

The income statement for Carter Consulting Services does not have dollar signs because it was prepared on accounting paper with ruled columns. However, dollar signs are used on income statements that are prepared on plain paper, that is, not on a ruled form.

The Statement of Owner's Equity and the Balance Sheet

5 Objective
Prepare a statement of owner's equity and a balance sheet.

The **statement of owner's equity** reports the changes that occurred in the owner's financial interest during the reporting period. This statement is prepared before the balance sheet so that the amount of the ending capital balance is available for presentation on the balance sheet. Figure 2-4 on page 38 shows the statement of owner's equity for Carter Consulting Services. Note that the statement of owner's equity has a three-line heading: *who, what,* and *when.*

Accounting On The Job

Hospitality and Tourism

Industry Overview

Hospitality is the world's largest industry, accounting for more jobs, sales, and tax revenue than any other industry. The hospitality industry, also known as the travel or tourism industry, is composed of hotels, restaurants, institutional food service, cruise lines, arenas, travel agencies, meeting and convention centers, sport complexes, resorts, parks, clubs, spas, and tourism-related transportation. In the United States, the hospitality industry's employment growth is twice that of any other industry. Hospitality is forecasted to become the nation's largest industry by the year 2010.

Career Opportunities

- State Tourism Bureau Director
- Director of Resort Contracts and Purchasing
- Executive Chef
- Travel Technology Specialist
- Tour Promotions Manager
- Vice President of Hotel Operations
- Airport Passenger Services Supervisor
- Catering Director

Preparing for a Hospitality and Tourism Career

- Gain expertise in database administration or programming. Hotels, spas, golf courses, and airlines use sophisticated computerized systems to track reservations and memberships.
- Obtain an associate's or bachelor's degree in hotel, restaurant, and institutional management or a degree in hospitality and tourism management. Core course requirements include database management, electronic spreadsheets, and accounting.
- Enroll in an advanced internship program. The Disney College Program offers specialties in marketing, hotel management, finance, and communications. Marriott International offers paid internships from 8 to 16 weeks in duration. Opportunities exist in accounting and finance, catering, front office, human resources, sales, and culinary arts.
- Receive training on the latest Worldspan computer reservation system developed by Delta, TWA, and Northwest Airlines.

Thinking Critically

What skills and education might be required for the position of hotel general manager with a major hotel chain such as Marriott International?

Internet Application

Visit the Web site of a trade organization such as the Travel Industry Association of America to learn about potential career paths within the industry. Describe the purpose of the association. What resources are offered on the site?

- The first line of the statement of owner's equity is the capital balance at the beginning of the period.
- Net income is an increase to owner's equity; net loss is a decrease to owner's equity.
- Withdrawals by the owner are a decrease to owner's equity.
- Additional investments by the owners are an increase to owner's equity.
- The total of changes in equity is reported on the line "Increase in Capital" (or "Decrease in Capital").
- The last line of the statement of owner's equity is the capital balance at the end of the period.

FIGURE 2-4 ►
Statement of Owner's Equity for Carter Consulting Services

Carter Consulting Services		
Statement of Owner's Equity		
Month Ended December 31, 2004		
Linda Carter, Capital, December 1, 2004		80,000 00
Net Income for December	22,400 00	
Less Withdrawals for December	3,000 00	
Increase in Capital		19,400 00
Linda Carter, Capital, December 31, 2004		99,400 00

If Linda Carter had made any additional investments during December, this would appear as a separate line on Figure 2-4. Additional investments can be cash or other assets such as equipment. If an investment is made in a form other than cash, the investment is recorded at its fair market value. **Fair market value** is the current worth of an asset or the price the asset would bring if sold on the open market.

The ending balances in the asset and liability accounts are used to prepare the balance sheet.

	Assets					=	Liab. +	Owner's Equity		
	Cash +	Accts. Rec. +	Supp. +	Prepaid Rent +	Equip.	=	Accts. Pay. +	L. Carter, Capital +	Rev. –	Exp.
New balances	$64,400 +	$4,000 +	$2,000 +	$6,000 +	$35,000	=	$12,000 +	$77,000 +	$28,000 –	$5,600
			$111,400					$111,400		

The ending capital balance from the statement of owner's equity is also used to prepare the balance sheet. Figure 2-5 on page 39 shows the balance sheet for Carter Consulting Services on December 31, 2004.

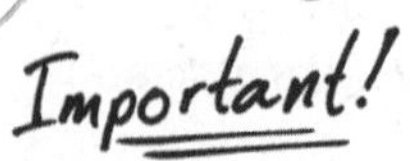

Financial Statements
The balance sheet is a snapshot of the firm's financial position on a specific date. The income statement, like a movie or video, shows the results of business operations over a period of time.

The balance sheet shows

- Assets—the types and amounts of property that the business owns,
- Liabilities—the amounts owed to creditors,
- Owner's Equity—the owner's equity on the reporting date.

In preparing a balance sheet, remember the following.

- The three-line heading gives the firm's name (who), the title of the report (what), and the date of the report (when).
- Balance sheets prepared using the account form (as in Figure 2-5) show total assets on the same horizontal line as the total liabilities and owner's equity.
- Dollar signs are omitted when financial statements are prepared on paper with ruled columns. Statements that are prepared on plain paper, not ruled forms, show dollar signs with the first amount in each column and with each total.
- A single line shows that the amounts above it are being added or subtracted. Double lines indicate that the amount is the final amount in a column or section of a report.

Figure 2-6 on page 40 shows the connections among the financial statements. Financial statements are prepared in a specific order:

- income statement
- statement of owner's equity
- balance sheet

Carter Consulting Services
Balance Sheet
December 31, 2004

Assets		*Liabilities*	
Cash	64,400.00	*Accounts Payable*	12,000.00
Accounts Receivable	4,000.00		
Supplies	2,000.00		
Prepaid Rent	6,000.00	*Owner's Equity*	
Equipment	35,000.00	*Linda Carter, Capital*	99,400.00
Total Assets	111,400.00	*Total Liabilities and Owner's Equity*	111,400.00

▲ **FIGURE 2-5**
Balance Sheet for Carter Consulting Services

Net income from the income statement is used to prepare the statement of owner's equity. The ending capital balance from the statement of owner's equity is used to prepare the balance sheet.

The Importance of Financial Statements

Preparing financial statements is one of the accountant's most important jobs. Each day millions of business decisions are made based on the information in financial statements.

Business managers and owners use the balance sheet and the income statement to control current operations and plan for the future. Creditors, prospective investors, governmental agencies, and others are interested in the profits of the business and in the asset and equity structure.

Accounting Systems

- Sound financial records and statements are necessary so that businesspeople can make good decisions.
- Financial statements show
  - the amount of profit or loss,
  - the assets on hand,
  - the amount owed to creditors,
  - the amount of owner's equity.
- Well-run and efficiently managed businesses have good accounting systems that provide timely and useful information.
- Transactions involving revenue and expenses are recorded separately from owner's equity in order to analyze operations for the period.

Thinking Critically

If you were buying a business, what would you look for in the company's financial statements?

Step 1: Prepare the Income Statement

FIGURE 2-6
Process for Preparing Financial Statements

Carter Consulting Services		
Income Statement		
Month Ended December 31, 2004		
Revenue		
Fees Income		28 000 00
Expenses		
Salaries Expense	5 000 00	
Utilities Expense	600 00	
Total Expenses		5 600 00
Net Income		22 400 00

Net income (or loss) is transferred to the statement of owner's equity.

Step 2: Prepare the Statement of Owner's Equity

Carter Consulting Services		
Statement of Owner's Equity		
Month Ended December 31, 2004		
Linda Carter, Capital, December 1, 2004		80 000 00
Net Income for December	22 400 00	
Less Withdrawals for December	3 000 00	
Increase in Capital		19 400 00
Linda Carter, Capital, December 31, 2004		99 400 00

The ending capital balance is transferred to the balance sheet.

Step 3: Prepare the Balance Sheet

Carter Consulting Services			
Balance Sheet			
December 31, 2004			
Assets		*Liabilities*	
Cash	64 400 00	*Accounts Payable*	12 000 00
Accounts Receivable	4 000 00		
Supplies	2 000 00		
Prepaid Rent	6 000 00	*Owner's Equity*	
Equipment	35 000 00	*Linda Carter, Capital*	99 400 00
Total Assets	111 400 00	*Total Liabilities and Owner's Equity*	111 400 00

Section 2 Self Review

Questions

1. What are withdrawals and how do they affect the basic accounting equation?
2. If an owner gives personal tools to the business, how is the transaction recorded?
3. What information is included in the financial statement headings?

Exercises

4. Hartwell Sporting Goods has assets of $50,000 and liabilities of $35,000. What is the owner's equity?
   - **a.** $85,000
   - **b.** $20,000
   - **c.** $35,000
   - **d.** $15,000
5. What information is contained on the income statement?
   - **a.** revenues and expenses for a period of time
   - **b.** revenue and expenses on a specific date
   - **c.** assets, liabilities, and owner's equity for a period of time
   - **d.** assets, liabilities, and owner's equity on a specific date

Analysis

6. Jensen Computers had revenues of $35,000 and expenses of $28,000. How does this affect owner's equity?

(Answers to Section 2 Self Review are on page 55.)

CHAPTER 2

Review and Applications

Review

Chapter Summary

Accounting begins with the analysis of business transactions. Each transaction changes the financial position of a business. In this chapter, you have learned how to analyze business transactions and how they affect assets, liabilities, and owner's equity. After transactions are analyzed and recorded, financial statements reflect the summarized changes to and results of business operations.

Learning Objectives

1 Record in equation form the financial effects of a business transaction.

The equation *property equals financial interest* reflects the fact that in a free enterprise system all property is owned by someone. This equation remains in balance after each business transaction.

2 Define, identify, and understand the relationship between asset, liability, and owner's equity accounts.

The term *assets* refers to property. The terms *liabilities* and *owner's equity* refer to financial interest. The relationship between assets, liabilities, and owner's equity is shown in equation form.

Assets = Liabilities + Owner's Equity
Owner's Equity = Assets − Liabilities
Liabilities = Assets − Owner's Equity

3 Analyze the effects of business transactions on a firm's assets, liabilities, and owner's equity and record these effects in accounting equation form.

1. Describe the financial event.
   - Identify the property.
   - Identify who owns the property.
   - Determine the amount of the increase or decrease.
2. Make sure the equation is in balance.

4 Prepare an income statement.

The income statement summarizes changes in owner's equity that result from revenue and expenses. The difference between revenue and expenses is the net income or net loss of the business for the period.

An income statement has a three-line heading:

- who
- what
- when

For the income statement, "when" refers to a period of time.

5 Prepare a statement of owner's equity and a balance sheet.

Changes in owner's equity for the period are summarized on the statement of owner's equity.

- Net income increases owner's equity.
- Added investments increase owner's equity.
- A net loss for the period decreases owner's equity.
- Withdrawals by the owner decrease owner's equity.

A statement of owner's equity has a three-line heading:

- who
- what
- when

For the statement of owner's equity, "when" refers to a period of time.

The balance sheet shows the assets, liabilities, and owner's equity on a given date.

A balance sheet has a three-line heading:

- who
- what
- when

For the balance sheet, "when" refers to a single date.

The financial statements are prepared in the following order.

1. Income Statement
2. Statement of Owner's Equity
3. Balance Sheet

6 Define the accounting terms new to this chapter.

CHAPTER 2 GLOSSARY

Accounts payable (p. 26) Amounts a business must pay in the future

Accounts receivable (p. 31) Claims for future collection from customers

Assets (p. 28) Property owned by a business

Balance sheet (p. 29) A formal report of a business's financial condition on a certain date; reports the assets, liabilities, and owner's equity of the business

Break even (p. 36) A point at which revenue equals expenses

Business transaction (p. 24) A financial event that changes the resources of a firm

Capital (p. 25) Financial investment in a business; equity

Equity (p. 25) An owner's financial interest in a business

Expense (p. 31) An outflow of cash, use of other assets, or incurring of a liability

Fair market value (p. 38) The current worth of an asset or the price the asset would bring if sold on the open market

Fundamental accounting equation (p. 30) The relationship between assets and liabilities plus owner's equity

Income statement (p. 35) A formal report of business operations covering a specific period of time; also called a profit and loss statement or a statement of income and expenses

Liabilities (p. 28) Debts or obligations of a business

Net income (p. 36) The result of an excess of revenue over expenses

Net loss (p. 36) The result of an excess of expenses over revenue

On account (p. 26) An arrangement to allow payment at a later date; also called a charge account or open-account credit

Owner's equity (p. 28) The financial interest of the owner of a business; also called proprietorship or net worth

Revenue (p. 30) An inflow of money or other assets that results from the sales of goods or services or from the use of money or property; also called income

Statement of owner's equity (p. 36) A formal report of changes that occurred in the owner's financial interest during a reporting period

Withdrawals (p. 34) Funds taken from the business by the owner for personal use

Comprehensive Self Review

1. What is the difference between buying for cash and buying on account?
2. Describe a transaction that will cause Accounts Payable and Cash to decrease by $500.
3. In what order are the financial statements prepared? Why?
4. If one side of the fundamental accounting equation is decreased, what will happen to the other side? Why?
5. What effect do revenue and expenses have on owner's equity?

(Answers to Comprehensive Self Review are on page 55.)

Discussion Questions

1. What are assets, liabilities, and owner's equity?
2. What information does the balance sheet contain?
3. What is the fundamental accounting equation?
4. What is revenue?
5. What are expenses?
6. Describe the effects of each of the following business transactions on assets, liabilities, and owner's equity.
   a. Bought equipment on credit.
   b. Paid salaries to employees.
   c. Sold services for cash.
   d. Paid cash to a creditor.
   e. Bought furniture for cash.
   f. Sold services on credit.
7. What information does the income statement contain?
8. How is net income determined?
9. What information is shown in the heading of a financial statement?
10. Why does the third line of the headings differ on the balance sheet and the income statement?
11. What information does the statement of owner's equity contain?
12. How does net income affect owner's equity?

Applications

EXERCISES

Exercise 2-1 ► Objectives 1, 2

Completing the accounting equation.

The fundamental accounting equation for several businesses follows. Supply the missing amounts.

Assets	=	Liabilities	+	Owner's Equity
1. $43,500	=	$7,500	+	$?
2. $34,600	=	$6,750	+	$?
3. $26,000	=	$?	+	$22,950
4. $?	=	$1,750	+	$14,250
5. $12,900	=	$?	+	$ 9,350

Exercise 2-2 ► Objectives 1, 2

Determining accounting equation amounts.

Just before Medical Supply Laboratories opened for business, Wes Rowland, the owner, had the following assets and liabilities. Determine the totals that would appear in the firm's fundamental accounting equation (Assets = Liabilities + Owner's Equity).

Cash	$17,900
Laboratory Equipment	42,500
Laboratory Supplies	2,400
Loan Payable	6,800
Accounts Payable	4,100

Exercise 2-3 ► Objectives 1, 2, 3

Determining balance sheet amounts.

The following financial data is for the dental practice of Dr. Steve Smith when he began operations in July. Determine the amounts that would appear in Dr. Smith's balance sheet.

1. Owes $7,500 to the Jones Equipment Company.
2. Has cash balance of $2,825.
3. Has dental supplies of $1,170.
4. Owes $1,400 to the Nolen Furniture Company.
5. Has dental equipment of $11,850.
6. Has office furniture of $1,725.

Exercise 2-4 ► Objectives 1, 2, 3

Determining the effects of transactions on the accounting equation.

Indicate the impact of each of the transactions below on the fundamental accounting equation (Assets = Liabilities + Owner's Equity) by placing a "+" to indicate an increase and a "−" to indicate a decrease. The first transaction is entered as an example.

	Assets	=	Liabilities	+	Owner's Equity
Transaction 1	+				+

TRANSACTIONS

1. Owner invested $20,000 in the business.
2. Purchased $2,000 supplies on account.

3. Purchased equipment for $10,000 cash.
4. Paid $1,400 for rent.
5. Performed services for $2,400 cash.
6. Paid $400 for utilities.
7. Performed services for $3,000 on account.
8. Received $1,500 from charge customers.
9. Paid salaries of $2,400 to employees.
10. Paid $1,000 to a creditor on account.

Determining the effects of transactions on the accounting equation.

◄ **Exercise 2-5**
Objectives 1, 2, 3

Delta Copy Shop had the transactions listed below during the month of April. Show how each transaction would be recorded in the accounting equation. Compute the totals at the end of the month. The headings to be used in the equation follow.

Assets					=	Liabilities	+	Owner's Equity				
Cash	+	Accounts Receivable	+	Equipment	=	Accounts Payable	+	Lacie Hodges, Capital	+	Revenue	−	Expenses

TRANSACTIONS

1. Lacie Hodges started the business with a cash investment of $18,000.
2. Purchased equipment for $7,000 on credit.
3. Performed services for $900 in cash.
4. Purchased additional equipment for $1,500 in cash.
5. Performed services for $2,100 on credit.
6. Paid salaries of $1,600 to employees.
7. Received $700 cash from charge account customers.
8. Paid $3,500 to a creditor on account.

Identifying transactions.

◄ **Exercise 2-6**
Objectives 1, 2, 3

The following equation shows the effects of a number of transactions that took place at Auto Mart Repair Company during the month of August. Describe each transaction.

	Assets					=	Liabilities	+	Owner's Equity				
	Cash	+	Accounts Receivable	+	Equipment	=	Accounts Payable	+	Capital	+	Revenue	−	Expenses
Bal.	$30,000	+	$1,000	+	$36,000	=	$17,000	+	$50,000	+	0	−	0
1.	+4,000										+$4,000		
2.	−3,400				+3,400								
3.	−1,000						−1,000						
4.	−3,800												−$3,800
5.	+600		−600										
6.			+4,000								+4,000		
7.	−1,800												−1,800

Exercise 2-7 ► Objective 4

Computing net income or net loss.

Millennium Computer Center had the following revenue and expenses during the month ended June 30. Did the firm earn a net income or incur a net loss for the period? What was the amount?

Fees for computer repairs	$16,400
Advertising expense	1,800
Salaries expense	8,550
Telephone expense	360
Fees for printer repairs	2,520
Utilities expense	750

Exercise 2-8 ► Objective 4

Computing net income or net loss.

On December 1 Emilio Flores opened a speech and hearing clinic. During December his firm had the following transactions involving revenue and expenses. Did the firm earn a net income or incur a net loss for the period? What was the amount?

Paid $400 for advertising.
Provided services for $525 in cash.
Paid $75 for telephone service.
Paid salaries of $950 to employees.
Provided services for $650 on credit.
Paid $50 for office cleaning service.

Exercise 2-9 ► Objective 4

Preparing an income statement.

At the beginning of September, Jody Seed started Seed's Investment Services, a firm that offers advice about investing and managing money. On September 30, the accounting records of the business showed the following information. Prepare an income statement for the month of September 20--.

Cash	$15,200	Fees Income	$33,400
Accounts Receivable	1,200	Advertising Expense	2,100
Office Supplies	800	Salaries Expense	6,800
Office Equipment	17,100	Telephone Expense	400
Accounts Payable	1,400	Withdrawals	2,000
Jody Seed, Capital, September 1, 20--	10,800		

Exercise 2-10 ► Objective 5

Preparing a statement of owner's equity and a balance sheet.

Using the information provided in Exercise 2-9, prepare a statement of owner's equity and a balance sheet for Seed's Investment Services as of September 30, 20--.

Problems

Selected problems can be completed using:
Peachtree QuickBooks Spreadsheets

PROBLEM SET A

Analyzing the effects of transactions on the accounting equation.

◄ **Problem 2-1A**
Objectives 1, 2, 3

On July 1, Perry Aaron established Expert Opinions, a firm that specializes in providing expert witness testimony.

INSTRUCTIONS

Analyze the following transactions. Record in equation form the changes that occur in assets, liabilities, and owner's equity. (Use plus, minus, and equals signs.)

TRANSACTIONS

1. The owner invested $36,000 in cash to begin the business.
2. Paid $9,180 in cash for the purchase of equipment.
3. Purchased additional equipment for $5,600 on credit.
4. Paid $4,500 in cash to creditors.
5. The owner made an additional investment of $11,200 in cash.
6. Performed services for $3,200 in cash.
7. Performed services for $1,900 on account.
8. Paid $1,300 for rent expense.
9. Received $850 in cash from credit clients.
10. Paid $2,500 in cash for office supplies.
11. The owner withdrew $2,000 in cash for personal expenses.

Analyze: What is the ending balance of cash after all transactions have been recorded?

Analyzing the effects of transactions on the accounting equation.

◄ **Problem 2-2A**
Objectives 1, 2, 3

Don Roganne is a painting contractor who specializes in painting commercial buildings. At the beginning of June, his firm's financial records showed the following assets, liabilities, and owner's equity.

Cash	$10,350	Accounts Payable	$ 3,900
Accounts Receivable	7,000	Don Roganne, Capital	45,000
Office Furniture	15,400	Revenue	18,600
Auto	26,000	Expenses	8,750

INSTRUCTIONS

Set up an accounting equation using the balances given above. Record the effects of the following transactions in the equation. (Use plus, minus, and equals signs.) Record new balances after each transaction has been entered. Prove the equality of the two sides of the final equation on a separate sheet of paper.

TRANSACTIONS

1. Performed services for $2,400 on credit.
2. Paid $500 in cash for a new office chair.
3. Received $1,500 in cash from credit clients.
4. Paid $160 in cash for telephone service.
5. Sent a check for $600 in partial payment of the amount due creditors.
6. Paid salaries of $3,700 in cash.
7. Sent a check for $250 to pay electric bill.
8. Performed services for $3,900 in cash.
9. Paid $860 in cash for auto repairs.
10. Performed services for $3,500 on account.

Analyze: What is the amount of total assets after all transactions have been recorded?

Problem 2-3A ► Objective 5

Preparing a balance sheet.

Abalos' Equipment Repair Service is owned by Donald Abalos.

INSTRUCTIONS

Use the following figures to prepare a balance sheet dated February 28, 20--. (You will need to compute the owner's equity.)

Cash	$15,250	Equipment	$35,600
Supplies	2,780	Accounts Payable	10,400
Accounts Receivable	5,000		

Analyze: What is the net worth, or owner's equity, at February 28, 20-- for Abalos' Equipment Repair Service?

Problem 2-4A ► Objectives 4, 5

Preparing an income statement, a statement of owner's equity, and a balance sheet.

The following equation shows the transactions of Perfection Cleaning Service during March. The business is owned by Raymond Abbey.

	Assets							=	Liab.	+	Owner's Equity				
	Cash	+	Accts. Rec.	+	Supp.	+	Equip.	=	Accts. Pay.	+	R. Abbey, Capital	+	Rev.	−	Exp.
Balances, March 1	3,500	+	500	+	1,200	+	8,200	=	1,500	+	11,900	+	0	−	0
Paid for utilities	−220														−220
New balances	3,280	+	500	+	1,200	+	8,200	=	1,500	+	11,900	+	0	−	220
Sold services for cash	+1,220												+1,220		
New balances	4,500	+	500	+	1,200	+	8,200	=	1,500	+	11,900	+	1,220	−	220
Paid a creditor	−400								−400						
New balances	4,100	+	500	+	1,200	+	8,200	=	1,100	+	11,900	+	1,220	−	220
Sold services on credit			+600										+600		
New balances	4,100	+	1,100	+	1,200	+	8,200	=	1,100	+	11,900	+	1,820	−	220
Paid salaries	−2,100														−2,100
New balances	2,000	+	1,100	+	1,200	+	8,200	=	1,100	+	11,900	+	1,820	−	2,320
Paid telephone bill	−76														−76
New balances	1,924	+	1,100	+	1,200	+	8,200	=	1,100	+	11,900	+	1,820	−	2,396
Withdrew cash for personal expenses	−500										−500				
New balances	1,424	+	1,100	+	1,200	+	8,200	=	1,100	+	11,400	+	1,820	−	2,396

INSTRUCTIONS

Analyze each transaction carefully. Prepare an income statement and a statement of owner's equity for the month. Prepare a balance sheet for March 31, 20--. List the expenses in detail on the income statement.

Analyze: In order to complete the balance sheet, which amount was transferred from the statement of owner's equity?

PROBLEM SET B

Analyzing the effects of transactions on the accounting equation.

◄ **Problem 2-1B**
Objectives 1, 2, 3

On September 1, Selena Rodriguez opened Better Grades Tutoring Service.

INSTRUCTIONS

Analyze the following transactions. Use the fundamental accounting equation form to record the changes in property, claims of creditors, and owner's equity. (Use plus, minus, and equals signs.)

TRANSACTIONS

1. The owner invested $6,000 in cash to begin the business.
2. Purchased equipment for $3,500 in cash.
3. Purchased $750 of additional equipment on credit.
4. Paid $375 in cash to creditors.
5. The owner made an additional investment of $1,250 in cash.
6. Performed services for $780 in cash.
7. Performed services for $390 on account.
8. Paid $450 for rent expense.
9. Received $275 in cash from credit clients.
10. Paid $650 in cash for office supplies.
11. The owner withdrew $500 in cash for personal expenses.

Analyze: Which transactions increased the company's debt? By what amount?

Analyzing the effects of transactions on the accounting equation.

◄ **Problem 2-2B**
Objectives 1, 2, 3

SPREADSHEET

Stacy Abrams owns Abrams' Consulting Service. At the beginning of September, her firm's financial records showed the following assets, liabilities, and owner's equity.

Cash	$7,750	Accounts Payable	$ 1,200
Accounts Receivable	1,500	Stacy Abrams, Capital	12,000
Supplies	1,600	Revenue	6,000
Office Furniture	5,000	Expenses	3,350

INSTRUCTIONS

Set up an equation using the balances given above. Record the effects of the following transactions in the equation. (Use plus, minus, and equals signs.) Record new balances after each transaction has been entered. Prove the equality of the two sides of the final equation on a separate sheet of paper.

TRANSACTIONS

1. Performed services for $1,000 on credit.
2. Paid $360 in cash for utilities.
3. Performed services for $1,200 in cash.
4. Paid $200 in cash for office cleaning service.
5. Sent a check for $600 to a creditor.
6. Paid $240 in cash for the telephone bill.
7. Issued checks for $2,060 to pay salaries.
8. Performed services for $1,780 in cash.
9. Purchased additional supplies for $180 on credit.
10. Received $800 in cash from credit clients.

Analyze: What is the ending balance for owner's equity after all transactions have been recorded?

Problem 2-3B ►
Objective 5

Preparing a balance sheet.

Paul Price is opening a tax preparation service on December 1, which will be called Paul's Tax Service. Paul plans to open the business by depositing $6,000 cash into a business checking account. The following assets will also be owned by the business: furniture (fair market value of $2,000), and a computer and printer (fair market value of $4,400). There are no outstanding debts of the business as it is formed.

INSTRUCTIONS

Prepare a balance sheet for December 1, 20--, for Paul's Tax Service by entering the correct balances in the appropriate accounts. (You will need to use the accounting equation to compute owner's equity.)

Analyze: If Paul's Tax Service had an outstanding debt of $2,000 when the business was formed, what amount should be reported on the balance sheet for owner's equity?

Problem 2-4B ►
Objectives 4, 5

Preparing an income statement, a statement of owner's equity, and a balance sheet.

The equation on page 51 shows the transactions of LaToya Hailey, Attorney and Counselor of Law, during August. This law firm is owned by LaToya Hailey.

INSTRUCTIONS

Analyze each transaction carefully. Prepare an income statement and a statement of owner's equity for the month. Prepare a balance sheet for August 31, 20--. List the expenses in detail on the income statement.

Analyze: In order to complete the statement of owner's equity, which amount was transferred from the income statement?

	Assets							=	Liab.	+	Owner's Equity				
			Accts.						Accts.		L. Hailey				
	Cash	+	Rec.	+	Supp.	+	Equip.	=	Pay.	+	Capital	+	Rev.	−	Exp.
Balances, Aug. 1	1,800	+	450	+	1,350	+	2,500	=	300	+	5,800	+	0	−	0
Paid for utilities	−150														−150
New balances	1,650	+	450	+	1,350	+	2,500	=	300	+	5,800	+	0	−	150
Sold services for cash	+1,500												+1,500		
New balances	3,150	+	450	+	1,350	+	2,500	=	300	+	5,800	+	1,500	−	150
Paid a creditor	−150								−150						
New balances	3,000	+	450	+	1,350	+	2,500	=	150	+	5,800	+	1,500	−	150
Sold services on credit			+1,200										+1,200		
New balances	3,000	+	1,650	+	1,350	+	2,500	=	150	+	5,800	+	2,700	−	150
Paid salaries	−1,350														−1,350
New balances	1,650	+	1,650	+	1,350	+	2,500	=	150	+	5,800	+	2,700	−	1,500
Paid telephone bill	−150														−150
New balances	1,500	+	1,650	+	1,350	+	2,500	=	150	+	5,800	+	2,700	−	1,650
Withdrew cash for personal expenses	−300										−300				
New balances	1,200	+	1,650	+	1,350	+	2,500	=	150	+	5,500	+	2,700	−	1,650

CHAPTER 2 CHALLENGE PROBLEM

Financial Statements

The following account balances are for Don Adler, Certified Public Accountant, as of April 30, 20--.

Cash	$3,250
Accounts Receivable	1,410
Maintenance Expense	550
Advertising Expense	450
Fees Earned	4,750
Don Adler, Capital, April 1	?
Salaries Expense	1,500
Machinery	4,250
Accounts Payable	1,600
Don Adler, Drawing	600

INSTRUCTIONS

Using the accounting equation form, determine the balance for Don Adler, Capital, April 1, 20--. Prepare an income statement for the month of April, a statement of owner's equity, and a balance sheet as of April 30, 20--. List the expenses on the income statement in alphabetical order.

Analyze: What net change in owner's equity occurred during the month of April?

CHAPTER 2 CRITICAL THINKING PROBLEM

Accounting for a New Company

Melissa Branson opened a gym and fitness studio called Melissa's Body Builders Studio at the beginning of November of the current year. It is now the end of December, and Melissa is trying to determine whether she made a profit during her first month of operations. You offer to help her and ask to see her accounting records. She shows you a shoe box and tells you that every piece of paper pertaining to the business is in that box.

As you go through the material in the shoe box, you discover the following:

- **a.** A receipt from Kekich Properties for $3,000 for November's rent on the exercise studio.
- **b.** Bank deposit slips totaling $3,140 for money collected from customers who attended exercise classes.
- **c.** An invoice for $24,000 for exercise equipment. The first payment is not due until December 31.
- **d.** A bill for $900 from the maintenance service that cleans the studio. Melissa has not yet paid this bill.
- **e.** A December 20 parking ticket for $50. Melissa says she was in a hurry that morning to get to the studio on time and forgot to put money in the parking meter.
- **f.** A handwritten list of customers and fees for the classes they have taken. As the customers attend the classes, Melissa writes their names and the amount of each customer's fee on the list. As customers pay, Melissa crosses their names off the list. Fees not crossed off the list amount to $720.
- **g.** A credit card receipt for $200 for printing flyers advertising the grand opening of the studio. For convenience, Melissa used her personal credit card.
- **h.** A credit card receipt for $300 for two warm-up suits Melissa bought to wear at the studio. She also put this purchase on her personal credit card.

Use the concepts you have learned in this chapter to help Melissa.

1. Prepare an income statement for the first month of operation of Melissa's Body Builders Studio.
2. How would you evaluate the results of Melissa's first month of operation?
3. What advice would you give Melissa concerning her system of accounting?

Business Connections

MANAGERIAL FOCUS **Interpreting Results** ◄ **Connection 1**

1. How does an accounting system help managers control operations and make sound decisions?
2. Why should managers be concerned with changes in the amount of creditors' claims against the business?
3. Is it reasonable to expect that all new businesses will have a net income from the first month's operations? From the first year's operations?
4. After examining financial data for a monthly period, the owner of a small business expressed surprise that the firm's cash balance had decreased during the month even though there was substantial net income. Do you think that this owner is right to expect cash to increase whenever there is a net income? Why or why not?

Ethical DILEMMA **It's Only a Game!** You just purchased a copy of Xandress II, the hottest computer game on the market. Xandress II is a copyrighted program that is protected under U.S. copyright law. You and some of your friends have just finished playing the game. Chris, your best friend, asks to borrow your computer disk of Xandress II to install the program on a computer at home. ◄ **Connection 2**

1. What are the ethical issues?
2. What are your alternatives?
3. Who are the affected parties?
4. How do the alternatives affect the parties?
5. What is your decision?
6. Would your decision be different if you were the branch manager of a local bank and a friend who works for a competing bank asked to borrow a loan evaluation program developed especially for your bank?

***Street* WISE: Questions from the Real World** **Financial Information** Refer to The Home Depot, Inc. *1999 Annual Report* in Appendix B. ◄ **Connection 3**

1. Locate the consolidated balance sheets. Based on this financial statement, what is the fundamental accounting equation for the year ended January 30, 2000? Note: Because this company is publicly traded, owners' equity is represented as stockholders' equity.
2. Locate the consolidated statements of earnings. The statement presents the results of operations for what periods of time? What result of operation is presented for the most recent operating period?

Connection 4 ►

FINANCIAL STATEMENT ANALYSIS **Income Statement** Review the following excerpt from the 1999 consolidated statement of income for Southwest Airlines Co. Answer the questions that follow.

Southwest Airlines Co.
Consolidated Statement of Income
Years Ended December 31,

	1999	*1998*	*1997*
Operating Revenues: (in thousands)			
Passenger	*$4,499,360*	*$3,963,781*	*$3,639,193*
Freight	*102,990*	*98,500*	*94,758*
Other	*133,237*	*101,699*	*82,870*
Total operating revenues	*4,735,587*	*4,163,980*	*3,816,821*
Net Income	*$474,378*	*$433,431*	*$317,772*

Analyze:

1. Although the format for the heading of an income statement can vary from company to company, the heading should contain the answers to who, what, and when. List the answers to each question for the statement presented above.
2. What three types of revenue are reflected on this statement?
3. The net income of $474,378,000 reflected on Southwest Airlines Co.'s consolidated statement of income for 1999 will be transferred to the next financial statement to be prepared. Net income is needed to complete which statement?

Analyze Online: Find the *Investor Relations* section of the Southwest Airlines Co. Web site **(www.southwest.com)** and answer the following questions.

4. What total operating revenues did Southwest Airlines Co. report for the most recent quarter?
5. Find the most recent press release posted on the Web site. Read the press release, and summarize the topic discussed. What effect, if any, do you think this will have on company earnings? Why?

Connection 5 ►

Extending the Thought **Personal Financial Statements** The balance sheet for an individual is called a "statement of financial condition." What kinds of assets and liabilities would appear on a statement of financial condition?

Connection 6 ►

Business Communication **Creating an Outline** You are a senior accountant for a mid-size apparel corporation. You have been asked to give a presentation on the basics of financial statements to the managers of the marketing, advertising, manufacturing, and sales departments. Each manager needs to understand what each financial statement presents and why each is important. Prepare an outline for your presentation. Be sure to cover the income statement, the statement of owner's equity, and the balance sheet.

TeamWork **Transaction Analysis** As a team, prepare a diagram showing four transactions for a neighborhood ice cream shop. List transactions that affect only the balance sheet. Include dollar amounts for each transaction and show the effect of the transactions on owner's equity.

◄ **Connection 7**

interNET CONNECTION **Careers in Accounting** How much can you expect to earn as an accountant? Visit the student page of the AICPA Web site at **www.aicpa.org** and look for salary information. List three career paths in accounting. How much can you expect to earn working for a small firm as a tax accountant if you have 1–3 years experience? How much can you expect to earn as a senior corporate accountant working for a large company? How much can you expect to earn as an entry-level (less than one year experience) cost accountant for a medium-size company?

◄ **Connection 8**

Answers to Self Reviews

Answers to Section 1 Self Review

1. A financial event that changes the resources of the firm.
2. An example is the initial investment of cash in a business by the owner.
3. Amounts that a company must pay to creditors in the future.
4. **d.** Equipment is increased by $2,000 and accounts payable is increased by $2,000.
5. **d.** $40,000
6. $2,500

Answers to Section 2 Self Review

1. Funds taken from the business to pay for personal expenses. They decrease the owner's equity in the business.
2. As an additional investment by the owner recorded on the basis of fair market value.
3. The firm's name (who), the title of the statement (what), and the time period covered by the report (when).
4. **d.** $15,000
5. **a.** revenue and expenses for a period of time
6. $7,000 increase

Answers to Comprehensive Self Review

1. Buying for cash results in an immediate decrease in cash; buying on account results in a liability recorded as accounts payable.
2. The payment of $500 to a creditor on account.
3. The income statement is prepared first because the net income or loss is needed to complete the statement of owner's equity. The statement of owner's equity is prepared next to update the change in owner's equity. The balance sheet is prepared last.
4. The opposite side of the accounting equation will decrease because a decrease in assets results in a corresponding decrease in either a liability or the owner's equity.
5. Revenue increases owner's equity. Expenses decrease owner's equity.

Section 1

Section Objectives

1. **Set up T accounts for assets, liabilities, and owner's equity.**

   WHY IT'S IMPORTANT
   The T account is an important visual tool used as an alternative to the fundamental accounting equation.

2. **Analyze business transactions and enter them in the accounts.**

   WHY IT'S IMPORTANT
   Accountants often use T accounts to help analyze and classify business transactions.

3. **Determine the balance of an account.**

   WHY IT'S IMPORTANT
   Accurate account balances contribute to a reliable accounting system.

Terms to Learn

account balance
accounts
classification
footing
normal balance
T account

Transactions That Affect Assets, Liabilities, and Owner's Equity

In this chapter you will learn how to record the changes caused by business transactions. This recordkeeping is a basic part of accounting systems.

Asset, Liability, and Owner's Equity Accounts

The accounting equation is one tool for analyzing the effects of business transactions. However, businesses do not record transactions in equation form. Instead, businesses establish separate records, called **accounts**, for assets, liabilities, and owner's equity. Use of accounts helps owners and staff analyze, record, classify, summarize, and report financial information. Accounts are recognized by their **classification** as assets, liabilities, or owner's equity. Asset accounts show the property a business owns. Liability accounts show the debts of the business. Owner's equity accounts show the owner's financial interest in the business. Each account has a name that describes the type of property, the debt, or the financial interest.

Accountants use T accounts to analyze transactions. A **T account** consists of a vertical line and a horizontal line that resemble the letter **T.** The name of the account is written on the horizontal (top) line. Increases and decreases in the account are entered on either side of the vertical line.

The following are T accounts for assets, liabilities, and owner's equity.

ASSETS		=	LIABILITIES		+	OWNER'S EQUITY	
+	−		−	+		−	+
Record increases	Record decreases		Record decreases	Record increases		Record decreases	Record increases

1 Objective

Set up T accounts for assets, liabilities, and owner's equity.

The Accounting Equation
Assets = Liabilities + Owner's Equity

Recording a Cash Investment

Asset accounts show items of value owned by a business. Linda Carter invested $80,000 in the business. Beatrice Wilson, the office manager for Carter Consulting Services, set up a **Cash** account. Cash is an asset. Assets appear on the left side of the accounting equation. Cash increases appear on the left side of the **Cash** T account. Decreases are shown on the right side. Wilson entered the cash investment of $80,000 **(a)** on the left side of the **Cash** account.

T accounts normally do not have plus and minus signs. We show them to help you identify increases (+) and decreases (−) in accounts.

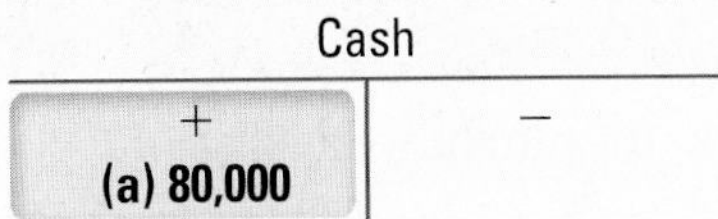

Beatrice Wilson set up an account for owner's equity called **Linda Carter, Capital.** Owner's equity appears on the right side of the accounting equation (Assets = Liabilities + Owner's Equity). Increases in owner's equity appear on the right side of the T account. Decreases in owner's equity appear on the left side. Wilson entered the investment of $80,000 **(b)** on the right side of the **Linda Carter, Capital** account.

2 Objective

Analyze business transactions and enter them in the accounts.

Use these steps to analyze the effects of the business transactions:

1. Analyze the financial event.
   - Identify the accounts affected.
   - Classify the accounts affected.
   - Determine the amount of increase or decrease for each account.
2. Apply the left-right rules for each account affected.
3. Make the entry in T-account form.

Business Transaction

Linda Carter withdrew $80,000 from personal savings and deposited it in the new business checking account for Carter Consulting Services.

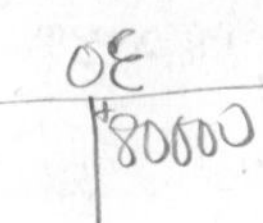

Analysis

a. The asset account, **Cash,** is increased by $80,000.

b. The owner's equity account, **Linda Carter, Capital,** is increased by $80,000.

Left-Right Rules

LEFT Increases to asset accounts are recorded on the left side of the T account. Record $80,000 on the left side of the **Cash** T account.

RIGHT Increases to owner's equity accounts are recorded on the right side of the T account. Record $80,000 on the right side of the **Linda Carter, Capital** T account.

T-Account Presentation

Cash		**Linda Carter, Capital**	
+	−	−	+
(a) 80,000			(b) 80,000

Recording a Cash Purchase of Equipment

Beatrice Wilson set up an asset account, **Equipment,** to record the purchase of a computer and other equipment.

Business Transaction

Carter Consulting Services issued a $20,000 check to purchase a computer and other equipment.

Analysis

c. The asset account, **Equipment,** is increased by $20,000.

d. The asset account, **Cash,** is decreased by $20,000.

Left-Right Rules

LEFT Increases to asset accounts are recorded on the left side of the T account. Record $20,000 on the left side of the **Equipment** T account.

RIGHT Decreases to asset accounts are recorded on the right side of the T account. Record $20,000 on the right side of the **Cash** T account.

T-Account Presentation

Let's look at the T accounts to review the effects of the transactions. Wilson entered $20,000 **(c)** on the left (increase) side of the **Equipment** account. She entered $20,000 **(d)** on the right (decrease) side of the **Cash** account. Notice that the **Cash** account shows the effects of two transactions.

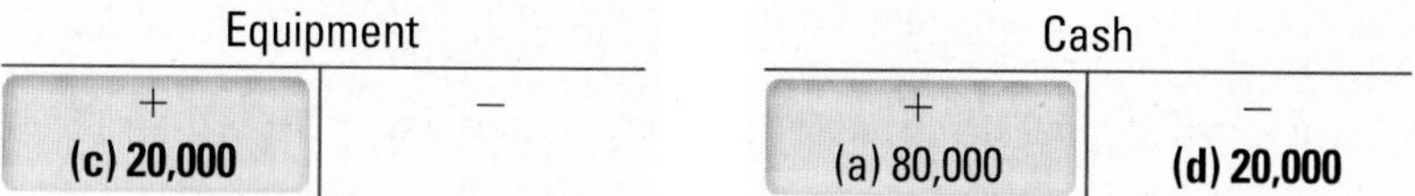

Recording a Credit Purchase of Equipment

Liabilities are amounts a business owes its creditors. Liabilities appear on the right side of the accounting equation (Assets = Liabilities + Owner's Equity). Increases in liabilities are on the right side of liability T accounts. Decreases in liabilities are on the left side of liability T accounts.

Business Transaction

The firm bought office equipment for $15,000 on account from Office Plus.

Analysis

e. The asset account, **Equipment,** is increased by $15,000.

f. The liability account, **Accounts Payable,** is increased by $15,000.

Left-Right Rules

LEFT Increases to asset accounts are recorded on the left side of the T account. Record $15,000 on the left side of the **Equipment** T account.

RIGHT Increases to liability accounts are recorded on the right side of the T account. Record $15,000 on the right side of the **Accounts Payable** T account.

T-Account Presentation

Equipment	
+	−
(e) 15,000	

Accounts Payable	
−	+
	(f) 15,000

Let's look at the T accounts to review the effects of the transactions. Wilson entered $15,000 **(e)** on the left (increase) side of the **Equipment** account. It now shows two transactions. She entered $15,000 **(f)** on the right (increase) side of the **Accounts Payable** account.

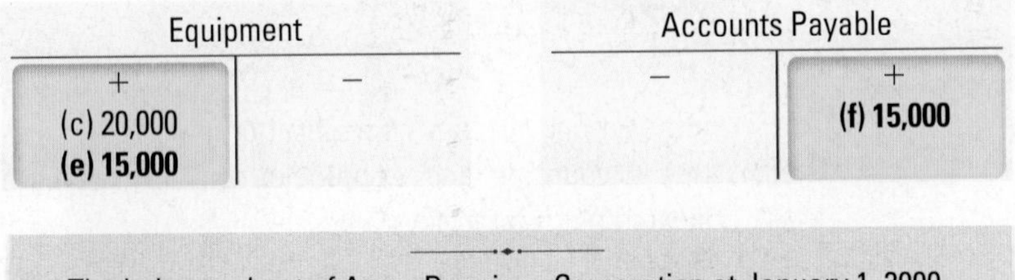

Important!

For liability T accounts
- right side shows increases,
- left side shows decreases.

The balance sheet of Avery Dennison Corporation at January 1, 2000, showed machinery and equipment balances of $1.32 billion.

Recording a Cash Purchase of Supplies

Beatrice Wilson set up an asset account called **Supplies.**

Business Transaction

Carter Consulting Services issued a check for $2,000 to Resource Supplies Inc. to purchase office supplies.

Analysis

g. The asset account, **Supplies,** is increased by $2,000.

h. The asset account, **Cash,** is decreased by $2,000.

Left-Right Rules

LEFT Increases to asset accounts are recorded on the left side of the T account. Record $2,000 on the left side of the **Supplies** T account.

RIGHT Decreases to asset accounts are recorded on the right side of the T account. Record $2,000 on the right side of the **Cash** T account.

Wilson entered $2,000 **(g)** on the left (increase) side of the **Supplies** account and $2,000 **(h)** on the right (decrease) side of the **Cash** account.

Supplies		Cash	
+	−	+	−
(g) 2,000		(a) 80,000	(d) 20,000
			(h) 2,000

Notice that the **Cash** account now shows three transactions: the initial investment by the owner (a), the cash purchase of equipment (d), and the cash purchase of supplies (h).

Computers in Accounting

Hardware and Software: A Working Partnership

When you arrive at work and turn on your computer, many processes happen behind the scenes. Computers are made up of hardware and software. *Hardware* includes a CPU (central processing unit), disk drives, memory, monitor, keyboard, and printer. *Software* makes computer hardware perform tasks. Without software, a computer can do nothing. Software programs come in two basic types: system software and application software.

System software controls the operation of the application software and coordinates the activities of the hardware. Think of your system software as the air-traffic controller of your computer. Popular operating systems include MacOS, Windows, Unix, and Linux.

Application software tells your computer to perform a task. A word processing application such as Microsoft Word has the tools to create, edit, and format text. Spreadsheet applications such as Microsoft Excel or Lotus 1-2-3 organize numbers and words into meaningful columns and rows. Software applications are developed to create efficient and fast ways to convert data into meaningful information. Accounting applications such as Peachtree Accounting and AccuBooks convert data into meaningful information.

Accounting software application programs range from simple and inexpensive to sophisticated and costly. These applications provide tools to enter business transactions and automatically transfer the details to the appropriate accounts. Standardized financial statements and reports can be generated using simple menus. From start to finish, these applications help the accountant maintain accurate records and provide management a wide variety of financial reports.

Thinking Critically

What software applications have you used? What suggestions would you make for improvement to these applications?

Internet Application

Use an Internet search engine to find accounting software applications. Choose two applications suitable for small businesses and write a brief review of each product. Based on your research, which product do you prefer? Why?

Recording a Payment to a Creditor

On November 30 the business paid $3,000 to Office Plus to apply against the debt of $15,000 shown in **Accounts Payable.**

Business Transaction

Carter Consulting Services issued a check in the amount of $3,000 to Office Plus.

Analysis

i. The asset account, **Cash,** is decreased by $3,000.

j. The liability account, **Accounts Payable,** is decreased by $3,000.

Left-Right Rules

LEFT Decreases to liability accounts are recorded on the left side of the T account. Record $3,000 on the left side of the **Accounts Payable** T account.

RIGHT Decreases to asset accounts are recorded on the right side of the T account. Record $3,000 on the right side of the **Cash** T account.

T-Account Presentation

Accounts Payable	
(j) 3,000	

Cash	
+	−
	(i) 3,000

Let's look at the T accounts to review the effects of the transactions. Wilson entered $3,000 **(i)** on the right (decrease) side of the **Cash** account. She entered $3,000 **(j)** on the left (decrease) side of the **Accounts Payable** account. Notice that both accounts show the effects of several transactions.

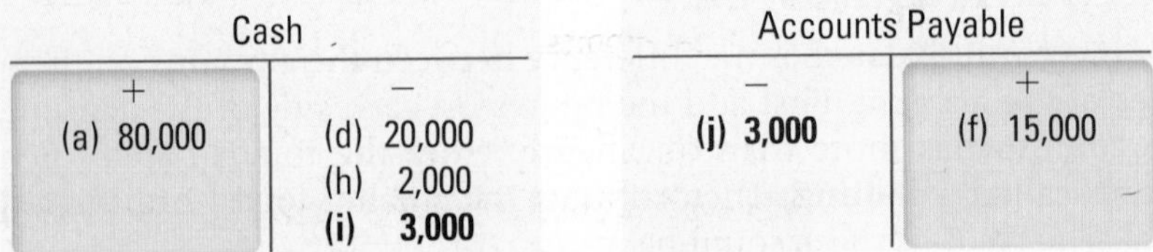

Cash	
+	−
(a) 80,000	(d) 20,000
	(h) 2,000
	(i) 3,000

Accounts Payable	
−	+
(j) 3,000	(f) 15,000

Recording Prepaid Rent

In November Carter Consulting Services was required to pay the December and January rent in advance. Wilson set up an asset account called **Prepaid Rent.**

Business Transaction

Carter Consulting Services issued a check for $6,000 to pay rent for the months of December and January.

k. The asset account, **Prepaid Rent,** is increased by $6,000.
l. The asset account, **Cash,** is decreased by $6,000.

Left-Right Rules

LEFT Increases to asset accounts are recorded on the left side of the T account. Record $6,000 on the left side of the **Prepaid Rent** T account.

RIGHT Decreases to asset accounts are recorded on the right side of the T account. Record $6,000 on the right side of the **Cash** T account.

T-Account Presentation

Prepaid Rent	
+	−
(k) 6,000	

Cash	
+	−
	(l) 6,000

Let's review the T accounts to see the effects of the transactions. Wilson entered $6,000 **(k)** on the left (increase) side of the **Prepaid Rent** account. She entered $6,000 **(l)** on the right (decrease) side of the **Cash** account.

Notice that the **Cash** account shows the effects of numerous transactions. It shows initial investment (a), equipment purchase (d), supplies purchase (h), payment on account (i), and advance rent payment (l).

Prepaid Rent	
+	−
(k) 6,000	

Cash	
+	−
(a) 80,000	(d) 20,000
	(h) 2,000
	(i) 3,000
	(l) 6,000

3 Objective

Determine the balance of an account.

Account Balances

An **account balance** is the difference between the amounts on the two sides of the account. First add the figures on each side of the account. If the column has more than one figure, enter the total in small pencil figures called a **footing**. Then subtract the smaller total from the larger total. The result is the account balance.

- If the total on the right side is larger than the total on the left side, the balance is recorded on the right side.
- If the total on the left side is larger, the balance is recorded on the left side.
- If an account shows only one amount, that amount is the balance.
- If an account contains entries on only one side, the total of those entries is the account balance.

Let's look at the **Cash** account for Carter Consulting Services. The left side shows $80,000. The total of the right side is $31,000. Subtract the footing of $31,000 from $80,000. The result is the account balance of $49,000. The account balance is shown on the left side of the account.

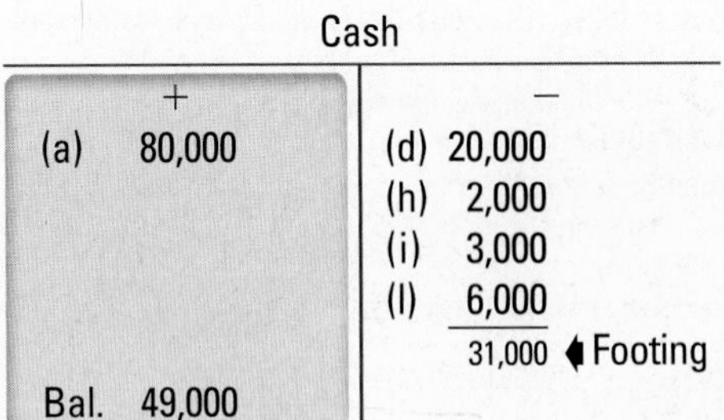

Usually account balances appear on the increase side of the account. The increase side of the account is the **normal balance** of the account.

The following is a summary of the procedures to increase or decrease accounts and shows the normal balance of accounts.

ASSETS		=	LIABILITIES		+	OWNER'S EQUITY	
+	–		–	+		–	+
Increase (Normal Balance)	Decrease		Decrease	Increase (Normal Balance)		Decrease	Increase (Normal Balance)

Figure 3-1 shows a summary of the account balances for Carter Consulting Services.

About Accounting

Law Enforcement
The FBI and other law enforcement agencies recruit accountants to investigate criminal conduct. Perhaps the most famous use of accounting by law enforcers is the conviction of Al Capone for tax evasion after he could not be jailed for his ties to organized crime.

▼ FIGURE 3-1
T-Account Balances for Carter Consulting Services

ASSETS = **LIABILITIES** + **OWNER'S EQUITY**

Cash

+		–	
(a)	80,000	(d)	20,000
		(h)	2,000
		(i)	3,000
		(l)	6,000
			31,000
Bal.	49,000		

Supplies

+		–	
(g)	2,000		

Prepaid Rent

+		–	
(k)	6,000		

Equipment

+		–	
(c)	20,000		
(e)	15,000		
Bal.	35,000		

Accounts Payable

–		+	
(j)	3,000	(f)	15,000
		Bal.	12,000

Linda Carter, Capital

–		+	
		(b)	80,000

Figure 3-2 shows a balance sheet prepared for November 30, 2004.

Carter Consulting Services
Balance Sheet
November 30, 2004

Assets		Liabilities	
Cash	49,000.00	Accounts Payable	12,000.00
Supplies	2,000.00		
Prepaid Rent	6,000.00	Owner's Equity	
Equipment	35,000.00	Linda Carter, Capital	80,000.00
Total Assets	92,000.00	Total Liabilities and Owner's Equity	92,000.00

▲ **FIGURE 3-2**
Balance Sheet for Carter Consulting Services

In equation form the firm's position after these transactions is:

Assets							=	Liabilities	+	Owner's Equity
Cash	+	Supp.	+	Prepaid Rent	+	Equip.	=	Accounts Payable	+	Linda Carter, Capital
$49,000	+	$2,000	+	$6,000	+	$35,000	=	$12,000	+	$80,000

Notice how the balance sheet reflects the fundamental accounting equation.

Section 1 Self Review

Questions

1. Increases are recorded on which side of asset, liability, and owner's equity accounts?
2. What is a footing?
3. What is meant by the "normal balance" of an account? What is the normal balance side for asset, liability, and owner's equity accounts?

Exercises

4. Foot and find the balance of the **Cash** account.

Cash	
+	−
45,000	15,000
10,500	7,500
	3,000
	6,000

a. 55,500
b. 31,500
c. 24,000
d. 14,000

5. The Sullivan Company purchased new computers for $4,500 from Office Supplies, Inc., to be paid in 30 days. Which of the following is correct?
   a. **Equipment** is increased by $4,500. **Cash** is decreased by $4,500.
   b. **Equipment** is decreased by $4,500. **Accounts Payable** is increased by $4,500.
   c. **Equipment** is increased by $4,500. **Accounts Payable** is increased by $4,500.
   d. **Equipment** is increased by $4,500. **Accounts Payable** is decreased by $4,500.

Analysis

6. From the following accounts, show that the fundamental accounting equation is in balance. All accounts have normal balances.

Cash—$15,400
Accounts Payable—$10,000
T. R. Murphy, Capital—$30,000
Equipment—$20,000
Supplies—$4,600

(Answers to Section 1 Self Review are on page 93.)

Transactions That Affect Revenue, Expenses, and Withdrawals

Section Objectives

4 **Set up T accounts for revenue and expenses.**

WHY IT'S IMPORTANT
T accounts help you understand the effects of all business transactions.

5 **Prepare a trial balance from T accounts.**

WHY IT'S IMPORTANT
The trial balance is an important check of accuracy at the end of the accounting period.

6 **Prepare an income statement, a statement of owner's equity, and a balance sheet.**

WHY IT'S IMPORTANT
Financial statements summarize the financial activities and condition of the business.

7 **Develop a chart of accounts.**

WHY IT'S IMPORTANT
Businesses require a system that allows accounts to be easily identified and located.

Terms to Learn

chart of accounts
credit
debit
double-entry system
drawing account
permanent account
slide
temporary account
transposition
trial balance

Let's examine the revenue and expense transactions of Carter Consulting Services for December to see how they are recorded.

Revenue and Expense Accounts

Some owner's equity accounts are classified as revenue or expense accounts. Separate accounts are used to record revenue and expense transactions.

Recording Revenue from Services Sold for Cash

During December the business earned $21,000 in revenue from clients who paid cash for bookkeeping, accounting, and consulting services. This involved several transactions. Beatrice Wilson entered $21,000 **(m)** on the left (increase) side of the asset account **Cash.**

Cash			
+		–	
Bal.	49,000		
(m)	**21,000**		

How is the increase in owner's equity recorded? One way would be to record the $21,000 on the right side of the **Linda Carter, Capital** account. However, the preferred way is to keep revenue separate from the owner's investment until the end of the accounting period. Therefore, Wilson opened a revenue account for **Fees Income.**

Wilson entered $21,000 **(n)** on the right side of the **Fees Income** account. Revenues increase owner's equity. Increases in owner's equity appear on the right side of the T account. Therefore, increases in revenue appear on the right side of revenue T accounts.

Fees Income			
–		+	
		(n)	**21,000**

The right side of the revenue account shows increases and the left side shows decreases. Decreases in revenue accounts are rare but might occur because of corrections or transfers.

Let's review the effects of the transactions. Wilson entered $21,000 **(m)** on the left (increase) side of the **Cash** account and $21,000 **(n)** on the right (increase) side of the **Fees Income** account.

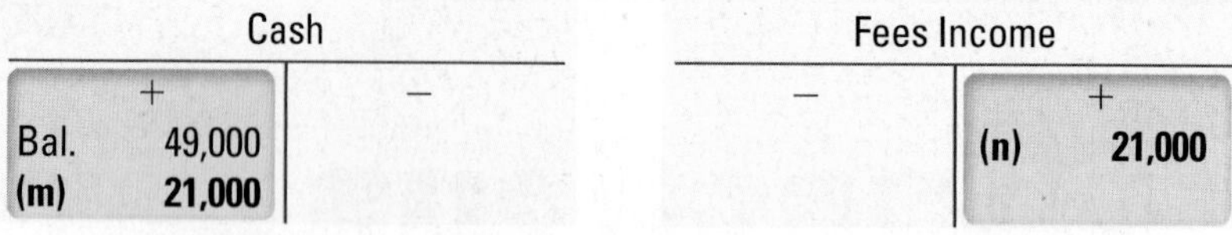

Cash +	Cash −
Bal. 49,000	
(m) 21,000	

Fees Income −	Fees Income +
	(n) 21,000

4 Objective

Set up T accounts for revenue and expenses.

At this point the firm needs just one revenue account. Most businesses have separate accounts for different types of revenue. For example, sales of goods such as clothes are recorded in the revenue account *Sales.*

Recording Revenue from Services Sold on Credit

In December Carter Consulting Services earned $7,000 from various charge account clients. Wilson set up an asset account, **Accounts Receivable.**

Analysis

o. The asset account, **Accounts Receivable,** is increased by $7,000.

p. The revenue account, **Fees Income,** is increased by $7,000.

Left-Right Rules

LEFT Increases to asset accounts are recorded on the left side of the T account. Record $7,000 on the left side of the **Accounts Receivable** T account.

RIGHT Increases in revenue appear on the right side of the T account. Record $7,000 on the right side of the **Fees Income** T account.

T-Account Presentation

Accounts Receivable +	Accounts Receivable −
(o) 7,000	

Fees Income −	Fees Income +
	(p) 7,000

Let's review the effects of the transactions. Wilson entered $7,000 **(o)** on the left (increase) side of the **Accounts Receivable** account and $7,000 **(p)** on the right (increase) side of the **Fees Income** account.

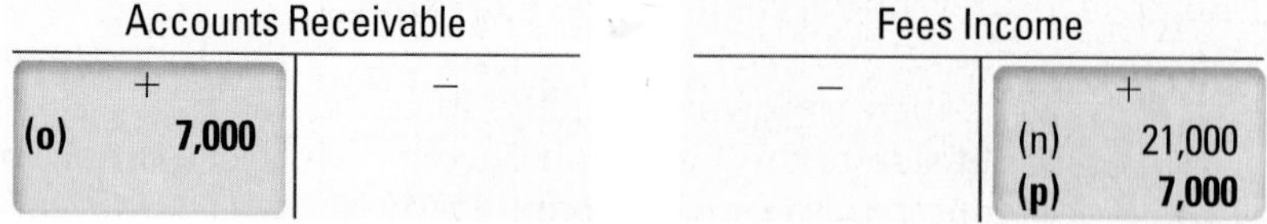

Accounts Receivable +	Accounts Receivable −
(o) 7,000	

Fees Income −	Fees Income +
	(n) 21,000
	(p) 7,000

Recording Collections from Accounts Receivable

Charge account clients paid $3,000, reducing the amount owed to Carter Consulting Services.

Analysis

q. The asset account, **Cash,** is increased by $3,000.

r. The asset account, **Accounts Receivable,** is decreased by $3,000.

Left-Right Rules

LEFT Increases to asset accounts are recorded on the left side of the T account. Record $3,000 on the left side of the **Cash** T account.

RIGHT Decreases to asset accounts are recorded on the right side of the T account. Record $3,000 on the right side of the **Accounts Receivable** T account.

T-Account Presentation

Cash		Accounts Receivable	
+	−	+	−
(q) 3,000			(r) 3,000

Let's review the effects of the transactions. Wilson entered $3,000 **(q)** on the left (increase) side of the **Cash** account and $3,000 **(r)** on the right (decrease) side of the **Accounts Receivable** account. Notice that revenue is not recorded when cash is collected from charge account clients. The revenue was recorded when the sales on credit were recorded (p).

Cash			Accounts Receivable			
+		−	+		−	
Bal.	49,000		(o)	7,000	**(r)**	**3,000**
(m)	21,000					
(q)	**3,000**					

Recording an Expense for Salaries

Expenses decrease owner's equity. Decreases in owner's equity appear on the left side of the T account. Therefore, increases in expenses (which are decreases in owner's equity) are recorded on the left side of expense T accounts. Decreases in expenses are recorded on the right side of the T accounts. Decreases in expenses are rare but may result from corrections or transfers.

Expense
An expense is an outflow of cash, the use of other assets, or the incurring of a liability.

Business Transaction

In December Carter Consulting Services paid $5,000 in salaries.

Analysis

s. The asset account, **Cash,** is decreased by $5,000.

t. The expense account, **Salaries Expense,** is increased by $5,000.

Left-Right Rules

LEFT Increases in expenses appear on the left side of the T account. Record $5,000 on the left side of the **Salaries Expense** T account.

RIGHT Decreases in asset accounts are recorded on the right side of the T account. Record $5,000 on the right side of the **Cash** T account.

T-Account Presentation

Salaries Expense	
+	−
(t) 5,000	

Cash	
+	−
	(s) 5,000

Wilson entered $5,000 **(s)** on the right (decrease) side of the **Cash** T account.

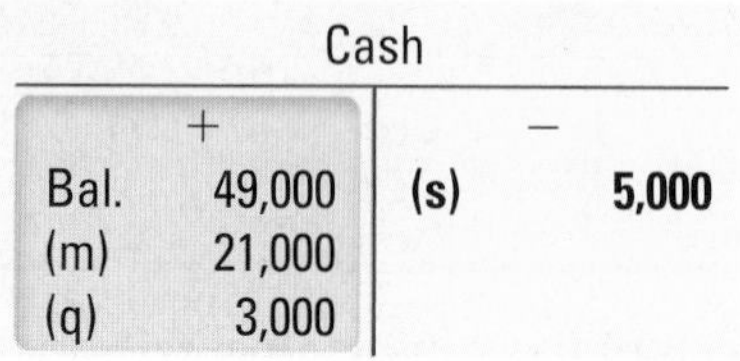

Cash			
+		−	
Bal.	49,000	**(s)**	**5,000**
(m)	21,000		
(q)	3,000		

> ***International* INSIGHTS**
>
> **Electricity**
>
> Accountants who travel with laptop computers should know the voltage used at their destinations. Power in the United States is 110 volts, but in most other countries it is 220 volts.

How is the decrease in owner's equity recorded? One way would be to record the $5,000 on the left side of the **Linda Carter, Capital** account. However, the preferred way is to keep expenses separate from owner's investment. Therefore, Wilson set up a **Salaries Expense** account.

To record the salary expense, Wilson entered $5,000 **(t)** on the left (increase) side of the **Salaries Expense** account. Notice that the plus and minus signs in the **Salaries Expense** account show the effect on the expense account, not on owner's equity.

Salaries Expense	
+	−
(t) 5,000	

Most companies have numerous expense accounts. The various expense accounts appear in the Expenses section of the income statement.

Recording an Expense for Utilities

At the end of December, Carter Consulting Services received a $600 bill for utilities. Wilson set up an account for **Utilities Expense.**

Business Transaction

Carter Consulting Services issued a check for $600 to pay the utilities bill.

Analysis

u. The asset account, **Cash,** is decreased by $600.

v. The expense account, **Utilities Expense,** is increased by $600.

Left-Right Rules

LEFT Increases in expenses appear on the left side of the T account. Record $600 on the left side of the **Utilities Expense** T account.

RIGHT Decreases to asset accounts are recorded on the right side of the T account. Record $600 on the right side of the **Cash** T account.

Let's review the effects of the transactions.

Utilities Expense

+		−	
(v)	**600**		

Cash

+		−	
Bal.	49,000	(s)	5,000
(m)	21,000	**(u)**	**600**
(q)	3,000		

The Drawing Account

In sole proprietorships and partnerships, the owners generally do not pay themselves salaries. To obtain funds for personal living expenses, owners make withdrawals of cash. The withdrawals are against previously earned profits that have become part of capital or against profits that are expected in the future.

Since withdrawals decrease owner's equity, withdrawals could be recorded on the left side of the capital account. However, the preferred way is to keep withdrawals separate from the owner's capital account until the end of the accounting period. An owner's equity account called a **drawing account** is set up to record withdrawals. Increases in the drawing account (which are decreases in owner's equity) are recorded on the left side of the drawing T accounts.

Business Transaction

Linda Carter wrote a check to withdraw $3,000 cash for personal use.

Analysis

w. The asset account, **Cash,** is decreased by $3,000.

x. The owner's equity account, **Linda Carter, Drawing,** is increased by $3,000.

Left-Right Rules

LEFT Increases to drawing accounts are recorded on the left side of the T account. Record $3,000 on the left side of the **Linda Carter, Drawing** T account.

RIGHT Decreases to asset accounts are recorded on the right side of the T account. Record $3,000 on the right side of the **Cash** T account.

Let's review the transactions. Wilson entered $3,000 **(w)** on the right (decrease) side of the asset account, **Cash,** and $3,000 **(x)** on the left (increase) side of **Linda Carter, Drawing.** Note that the plus and minus signs show the effect on the drawing account, not on owner's equity.

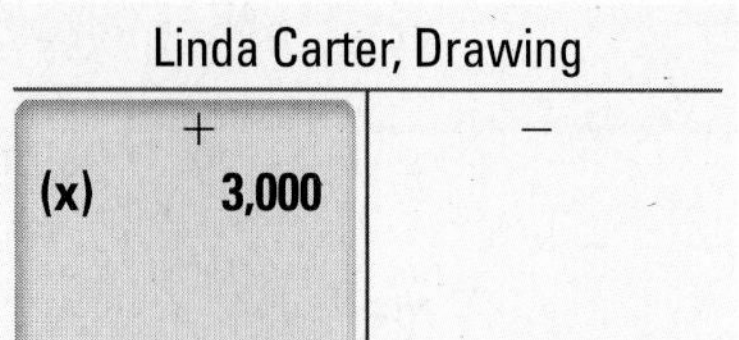

Linda Carter, Drawing		
+		−
(x)	**3,000**	

Cash			
+		−	
Bal.	49,000	(s)	5,000
(m)	21,000	(u)	600
(q)	3,000	**(w)**	**3,000**

Figure 3-3 shows a summary of the relationship between the capital account and the revenue, expense, and drawing accounts.

FIGURE 3-3 ►
The Relationship Between Owner's Equity and Revenue, Expenses, and Withdrawals

Linda Carter, Capital	
− Decrease	+ Increase

Expenses	
+ Increase	− Decrease

Withdrawals	
+ Increase	− Decrease

Revenue	
− Decrease	+ Increase

Important!

Normal Balances

Debit:	*Credit:*
Asset	Liability
Expense	Revenue
Drawing	Capital

The Rules of Debit and Credit

Accountants do not use the terms *left side* and *right side* when they talk about making entries in accounts. Instead, they use the term **debit** for an entry on the left side and **credit** for an entry on the right side. Figure 3-4 summarizes the rules for debits and credits. The accounting system is called the **double-entry system**. This is because each transaction has at least two entries—a debit and a credit.

FIGURE 3-4 ▼
Rules for Debits and Credits

ASSET ACCOUNTS	
Debit + Increase Side (Normal Bal.)	Credit − Decrease Side

LIABILITY ACCOUNTS	
Debit − Decrease Side	Credit + Increase Side (Normal Bal.)

OWNER'S CAPITAL ACCOUNT	
Debit − Decrease Side	Credit + Increase Side (Normal Bal.)

OWNER'S DRAWING ACCOUNT	
Debit + Increase Side (Normal Bal.)	Credit − Decrease Side

REVENUE ACCOUNTS	
Debit − Decrease Side	Credit + Increase Side (Normal Bal.)

EXPENSE ACCOUNTS	
Debit + Increase Side (Normal Bal.)	Credit − Decrease Side

After the December transactions for Carter Consulting Services are recorded, the account balances are calculated. Figure 3-5 on page 73 shows the account balances at the end of December. Notice that the fundamental accounting equation remains in balance (Assets = Liabilities + Owner's Equity).

ASSETS = LIABILITIES + OWNER'S EQUITY

Cash

	Debit		Credit
Bal.	49,000	(s)	5,000
(m)	21,000	(u)	600
(q)	3,000	(w)	3,000
	73,000		8,600
Bal.	64,400		

Accounts Payable

	Debit		Credit
		Bal.	12,000

Linda Carter, Capital

	Debit		Credit
		Bal.	80,000

Accounts Receivable

	Debit		Credit
(o)	7,000	(r)	3,000
Bal.	4,000		

Linda Carter, Drawing

	Debit		Credit
(x)	3,000		

Supplies

	Debit		Credit
Bal.	2,000		

Fees Income

	Debit		Credit
		(n)	21,000
		(p)	7,000
		Bal.	28,000

Prepaid Rent

	Debit		Credit
Bal.	6,000		

Salaries Expense

	Debit		Credit
(t)	5,000		

Equipment

	Debit		Credit
Bal.	35,000		

Utilities Expense

	Debit		Credit
(v)	600		

▲ **FIGURE 3-5** End-of-December 2004 Account Balances

The Trial Balance

5 Objective

Prepare a trial balance from T accounts.

Once the account balances are computed, a trial balance is prepared. The **trial balance** is a statement that tests the accuracy of total debits and credits after transactions have been recorded. If total debits do not equal total credits, there is an error. Figure 3-6 on page 74 shows the trial balance for Carter Consulting Services. To prepare a trial balance, perform the following steps:

1. Enter the trial balance heading showing the company name, report title, and closing date for the accounting period.
2. List the account names in the same order as they appear on the financial statements.
   - Assets
   - Liabilities
   - Owner's Equity
   - Revenue
   - Expenses
3. Enter the ending balance of each account in the appropriate Debit or Credit column.

4. Total the Debit column.
5. Total the Credit column.
6. Compare the total debits with the total credits.

FIGURE 3-6 ►
Trial Balance

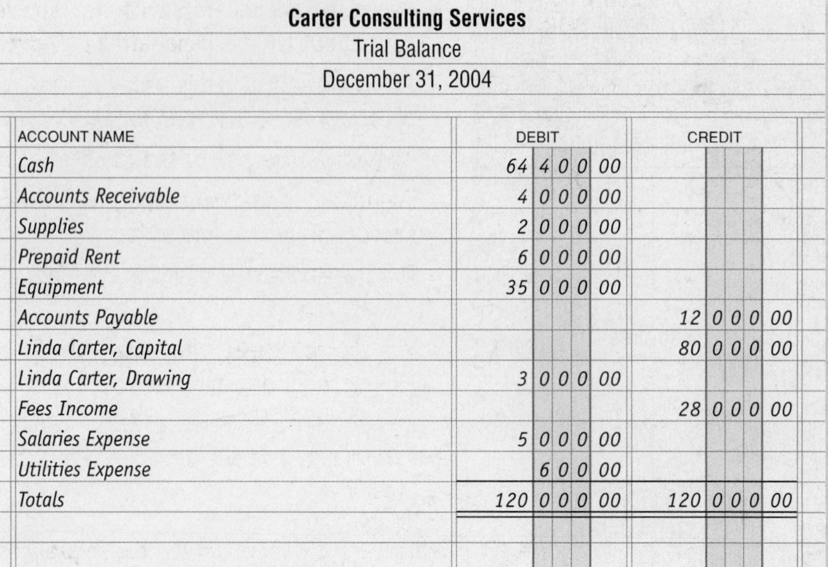

Carter Consulting Services		
Trial Balance		
December 31, 2004		
ACCOUNT NAME	DEBIT	CREDIT
Cash	64 400 00	
Accounts Receivable	4 000 00	
Supplies	2 000 00	
Prepaid Rent	6 000 00	
Equipment	35 000 00	
Accounts Payable		12 000 00
Linda Carter, Capital		80 000 00
Linda Carter, Drawing	3 000 00	
Fees Income		28 000 00
Salaries Expense	5 000 00	
Utilities Expense	600 00	
Totals	120 000 00	120 000 00

Financial Statement Headings
The financial statement headings answer three questions:

Who—the company name

What—the report title

When—the date of, or the period covered by, the report

Understanding Trial Balance Errors

If the totals of the Debit and Credit columns are equal, the financial records are in balance. If the totals of the Debit and Credit columns are not equal, there is an error. The error may be in the trial balance, or it may be in the financial records. Some common errors are

- adding trial balance columns incorrectly;
- recording only half a transaction—for example, recording a debit but not recording a credit, or vice versa;
- recording both halves of a transaction as debits or credits rather than recording one debit and one credit;
- recording an amount incorrectly from a transaction;
- recording a debit for one amount and a credit for a different amount;
- making an error when calculating the account balances.

Finding Trial Balance Errors

If the trial balance does not balance, try the following procedures.

1. Check the arithmetic. If the columns were originally added from top to bottom, verify the total by adding from bottom to top.
2. Check that the correct account balances were transferred to the correct trial balance columns.
3. Check the arithmetic used to compute the account balances.
4. Check that each transaction was recorded correctly in the accounts by tracing the amounts to the analysis of the transaction.

Sometimes you can determine the type of the error by the amount of the difference. Compute the difference between the debit total and the credit total. If the difference is divisible by 2, a debit might be recorded as a credit, or a credit recorded as a debit.

Financial Statements

- Recording entries into accounts provides an efficient method of gathering data about the financial affairs of a business.
- A chart of accounts is usually similar from company to company; balance sheet accounts are first, followed by income statement accounts.
- A trial balance proves the financial records are in balance.
- The income statement reports the revenue and expenses for the period and shows the net income or loss.
- The statement of owner's equity shows the change in owner's equity during the period.
- The balance sheet summarizes the assets, liabilities, and owner's equity of the business on a given date.
- Owners, managers, creditors, banks, and many others use financial statements to make decisions about the business.

Thinking Critically:

What are some possible consequences of not recording financial data correctly?

If the difference is divisible by 9, there might be a transposition. A **transposition** occurs when the digits of a number are switched (357 for 375). The test for a transposition is

$$\begin{array}{r} 375 \\ -357 \\ \hline 18 \end{array} \qquad 18/9 = 2$$

Also check for slides. A **slide** occurs when the decimal point is misplaced (375 for 37.50). We can test for a slide in the following manner.

$$\begin{array}{r} 375.00 \\ -37.50 \\ \hline 337.50 \end{array} \qquad 337.50/9 = 37.50$$

Financial Statements

6 Objective

Prepare an income statement, a statement of owner's equity, and a balance sheet.

After the trial balance is prepared, the financial statements are prepared. Figure 3-7 on page 76 shows the financial statements for Carter Consulting Services. The amounts are taken from the trial balance. As you study the financial statements, note that net income from the income statement is used on the statement of owner's equity. Also note that the ending balance of the **Linda Carter, Capital** account, computed on the statement of owner's equity, is used on the balance sheet.

Chart of Accounts

7 Objective

Develop a chart of accounts.

A **chart of accounts** is a list of all the accounts used by a business. Figure 3-8 on page 77 shows the chart of accounts for Carter Consulting Services. Each account has a number and a name. The balance sheet accounts are listed first, followed by the income statement accounts. The account number is assigned based on the type of account.

FIGURE 3-7 ►
Financial Statements for Carter Consulting Services

Carter Consulting Services Income Statement Month Ended December 31, 2004		
Revenue		
Fees Income		28,000.00
Expenses		
Salaries Expense	5,000.00	
Utilities Expense	600.00	
Total Expenses		5,600.00
Net Income		22,400.00

Carter Consulting Services Statement of Owner's Equity Month Ended December 31, 2004		
Linda Carter, Capital, December 1, 2004		80,000.00
Net Income for December	22,400.00	
Less Withdrawals for December	3,000.00	
Increase in Capital		19,400.00
Linda Carter, Capital, December 31, 2004		99,400.00

Carter Consulting Services Balance Sheet December 31, 2004			
Assets		Liabilities	
Cash	64,400.00	Accounts Payable	12,000.00
Accounts Receivable	4,000.00		
Supplies	2,000.00		
Prepaid Rent	6,000.00	Owner's Equity	
Equipment	35,000.00	Linda Carter, Capital	99,400.00
Total Assets	111,400.00	Total Liabilities and Owner's Equity	111,400.00

Asset Accounts	100–199	Revenue Accounts	400–499
Liability Accounts	200–299	Expense Accounts	500–599
Owner's Equity Accounts	300–399		

Notice that the accounts are not numbered consecutively. For example, asset account numbers jump from 101 to 111 and then to 121, 137, and 141. In each block of numbers, gaps are left so that additional accounts can be added when needed.

Permanent and Temporary Accounts

The asset, liability, and owner's equity accounts appear on the balance sheet at the end of an accounting period. The balances of these accounts are then carried forward to start the new period. Because they continue from one accounting period to the next, these accounts are called **permanent accounts** or *real accounts.*

CARTER CONSULTING SERVICES Chart of Accounts	
Account Number	**Account Name**
Balance Sheet Accounts	
100–199	**ASSETS**
101	Cash
111	Accounts Receivable
121	Supplies
137	Prepaid Rent
141	Equipment
200–299	**LIABILITIES**
202	Accounts Payable
300–399	**OWNER'S EQUITY**
301	Linda Carter, Capital
Statement of Owner's Equity Account	
302	Linda Carter, Drawing
Income Statement Accounts	
400–499	**REVENUE**
401	Fees Income
500–599	**EXPENSES**
511	Salaries Expense
514	Utilities Expense

◄ **FIGURE 3-8**
Chart of Accounts

Important!

Balance Sheet Accounts
The amounts on the balance sheet are carried forward to the next accounting period.

Important!

Income Statement Accounts
The amounts on the income statement are transferred to the capital account at the end of the accounting period.

Revenue and expense accounts appear on the income statement. The drawing account appears on the statement of owner's equity. These accounts classify and summarize changes in owner's equity during the period. They are called **temporary accounts** or *nominal accounts* because the balances in these accounts are transferred to the capital account at the end of the accounting period. In the next period, these accounts start with zero balances.

Section 2 Self Review

Questions

1. What is the increase side for **Cash; Accounts Payable;** and **Linda Carter, Capital?**
2. What is a trial balance and what is its purpose?
3. What is a transposition? A slide?

Exercises

4. Which account has a normal debit balance?
   a. **Fees Income**
   b. **T. C., Drawing**
   c. **T. C., Capital**
   d. **Accounts Payable**
5. The company owner took $1,000 cash for personal use. What is the entry for this transaction?
   a. Debit **Cash** and credit **Vijay Shah, Capital.**
   b. Debit **Vijay Shah, Capital** and credit **Cash.**
   c. Debit **Vijay Shah, Drawing** and credit **Cash.**
   d. Debit **Cash** and credit **Vijay Shah, Drawing.**

Analysis

6. Describe the errors in the Ames Interiors trial balance.

Ames Interiors Trial Balance December 31, 2004		
	DEBIT	CREDIT
Cash	15 000 00	
Accts. Rec.	10 000 00	
Equip.	7 000 00	
Accts. Pay.		15 000 00
A. Ames, Capital		22 000 00
A. Ames, Drawing		10 000 00
Fees Income	14 000 00	
Rent Exp.	2 000 00	
Supplies Exp.	2 000 00	
Telephone Exp.	5 000 00	
Totals	55 000 00	47 000 00

(Answers to Section 2 Self Review are on page 93.)

CHAPTER 3 Review and Applications

Review

Chapter Summary

In this chapter, you have learned how to use T accounts to help analyze and record business transactions. A chart of accounts can be developed to easily identify all the accounts used by a business. After determining the balance for all accounts, the trial balance is prepared to ensure that all transactions have been recorded accurately.

Learning Objectives

1 Set up T accounts for assets, liabilities, and owner's equity.
T accounts consist of two lines, one vertical and one horizontal, that resemble the letter **T**. The account name is written on the top line. Increases and decreases to the account are entered on either the left side or the right side of the vertical line.

2 Analyze business transactions and enter them in the accounts.
Each business transaction is analyzed for its effects on the fundamental accounting equation, Assets = Liabilities + Owner's Equity. Then these effects are recorded in the proper accounts. Accounts are classified as assets, liabilities, or owner's equity.

- Increases in an asset account appear on the debit, or left, side because assets are on the left side of the accounting equation. The credit, or right, side records decreases.
- An increase in a liability account is recorded on the credit, or right, side. The left, or debit, side of a liability account is used for recording decreases.
- Increases in owner's equity are shown on the credit (right) side of an account. Decreases appear on the debit (left) side.
- The drawing account is used to record the withdrawal of cash from the business by the owner. The drawing account decreases owner's equity.

3 Determine the balance of an account.
The difference between the amounts recorded on the two sides of an account is known as the balance of the account.

4 Set up T accounts for revenue and expenses.

- Revenue accounts increase owner's equity; therefore, increases are recorded on the credit side of revenue accounts.
- Expenses are recorded on the debit side of the expense accounts because expenses decrease owner's equity.

5 Prepare a trial balance from T accounts.
The trial balance is a statement to test the accuracy of the financial records. Total debits should equal total credits.

6 Prepare an income statement, a statement of owner's equity, and a balance sheet.
The income statement is prepared to report the revenue and expenses for the period. The statement of owner's equity is prepared to analyze the change in owner's equity during the period. Then the balance sheet is prepared to summarize the assets, liabilities, and owner's equity of the business at a given point in time.

7 Develop a chart of accounts.
A firm's list of accounts is called its chart of accounts. Accounts are arranged in a predetermined order and are numbered for handy reference and quick identification. Typically, accounts are numbered in the order in which they appear on the financial statements. Balance sheet accounts come first, followed by income statement accounts.

8 Define the accounting terms new to this chapter.

CHAPTER 3 GLOSSARY

Account balance (p. 64) The difference between the amounts recorded on the two sides of an account

Accounts (p. 58) Written records of the assets, liabilities, and owner's equity of a business

Chart of accounts (p. 75) A list of the accounts used by a business to record its financial transactions

Classification (p. 58) A means of identifying each account as an asset, liability, or owner's equity

Credit (p. 72) An entry on the right side of an account

Debit (p. 72) An entry on the left side of an account

Double-entry system (p. 72) An accounting system that involves recording the effects of each transaction as debits and credits

Drawing account (p. 71) A special type of owner's equity account set up to record the owner's withdrawal of cash from the business

Footing (p. 64) A small pencil figure written at the base of an amount column showing the sum of the entries in the column

Normal balance (p. 65) The increase side of an account

Permanent account (p. 76) An account that is kept open from one accounting period to the next

Slide (p. 75) An accounting error involving a misplaced decimal point

T account (p. 58) A type of account, resembling a T, used to analyze the effects of a business transaction

Temporary account (p. 77) An account whose balance is transferred to another account at the end of an accounting period

Transposition (p. 75) An accounting error involving misplaced digits in a number

Trial balance (p. 73) A statement to test the accuracy of total debits and credits after transactions have been recorded

Comprehensive Self Review

1. On which side of asset, liability, and owner's equity accounts are decreases recorded?
2. What are withdrawals and how are they recorded?
3. What is a chart of accounts?
4. Your friend has prepared financial statements for her business. She has asked you to review the statements for accuracy. The trial balance debit column totals $81,000 and the credit column totals $94,000. What steps would you take to find the error?
5. What type of accounts are found on the balance sheet?

(Answers to Comprehensive Self Review are on page 93.)

Discussion Questions

1. What are accounts?
2. Why is **Prepaid Rent** considered an asset account?
3. Why is the modern system of accounting usually called the double-entry system?
4. The terms *debit* and *credit* are often used in describing the effects of transactions on different accounts. What do these terms mean?
5. Indicate whether each of the following types of accounts would normally have a debit balance or a credit balance.
   - **a.** An asset account
   - **b.** A liability account
   - **c.** The owner's capital account
   - **d.** A revenue account
   - **e.** An expense account
6. How is the balance of an account determined?
7. What is the purpose of a chart of accounts?
8. In what order do accounts appear in the chart of accounts?
9. When a chart of accounts is created, number gaps are left within groups of accounts. Why are these number gaps necessary?
10. Accounts are classified as permanent or temporary accounts. What do these classifications mean?
11. Are the following accounts permanent or temporary accounts?
    - **a.** Fees Income
    - **b.** Cecil Blakeman, Drawing
    - **c.** Accounts Payable
    - **d.** Accounts Receivable
    - **e.** Cecil Blakeman, Capital
    - **f.** Prepaid Rent
    - **g.** Cash
    - **h.** Advertising Expense
    - **i.** Utilities Expense
    - **j.** Equipment
    - **k.** Salaries Expense
    - **l.** Prepaid Insurance

Applications

EXERCISES

Setting up T accounts.

◄ **Exercise 3-1**
Objective 1

Lake Watch and Jewelry Repair Service has the following account balances on December 31, 20--. Set up a T account for each account and enter the balance on the proper side of the account.

Cash	$4,000	Accounts Payable	$2,000
Equipment	4,000	Richard Lake, Capital	6,000

Using T accounts to analyze transactions.

◄ **Exercise 3-2**
Objective 2

Jessica Mason decided to start a dental practice. The first five transactions for the business follow. For each transaction, (1) determine which two accounts are affected, (2) set up T accounts for the affected accounts, and (3) enter the debit and credit amounts in the T accounts.

1. Jessica invested $10,000 cash in the business.
2. Paid $2,500 in cash for equipment.
3. Performed services for cash amounting to $1,000.
4. Paid $350 in cash for advertising expense.
5. Paid $250 in cash for supplies.

Identifying debits and credits.

◄ **Exercise 3-3**
Objective 3

In each of the following sentences, fill in the blanks with the word *debit* or *credit.*

1. Asset accounts normally have __?__ balances. These accounts increase on the __?__ side and decrease on the __?__ side.
2. Liability accounts normally have __?__ balances. These accounts increase on the __?__ side and decrease on the __?__ side.
3. The owner's capital account normally has a __?__ balance. This account increases on the __?__ side and decreases on the __?__ side.
4. Revenue accounts normally have __?__ balances. These accounts increase on the __?__ side and decrease on the __?__ side.
5. Expense accounts normally have __?__ balances. These accounts increase on the __?__ side and decrease on the __?__ side.

Determining debit and credit balances.

◄ **Exercise 3-4**
Objective 3

Indicate whether each of the following accounts normally has a debit balance or a credit balance.

1. Accounts Payable
2. Fees Income
3. Cash
4. Bob Childers, Capital
5. Equipment
6. Accounts Receivable
7. Salaries Expense
8. Supplies

Exercise 3-5 ►
Objective 3

Determining account balances.

The following T accounts show transactions that were recorded by Baker's Antique Repair, a firm that specializes in restoring antique furniture. The entries for the first transaction are labeled with the letter (a), the entries for the second transaction with the letter (b), and so on. Determine the balance of each account.

Cash

(a)	40,000	(b)	10,000
(d)	5,000	(e)	150
(g)	500	(h)	2,500
		(i)	1,000

Equipment

(c)	15,000		

Accounts Receivable

(f)	2,000	(g)	500

Accounts Payable

		(c)	15,000

Supplies

(b)	10,000		

Aaron Baker, Capital

		(a)	40,000

Fees Income

		(d)	5,000
		(f)	2,000

Telephone Expense

(e)	150		

Aaron Baker, Drawing

(i)	1,000		

Salaries Expense

(h)	2,500		

Exercise 3-6 ►
Objectives 5, 6

Preparing a trial balance and an income statement.

Using the account balances from Exercise 3-5, prepare a trial balance and an income statement for Baker's Antique Repair. The trial balance is for December 31, 20--, and the income statement is for the month ended December 31, 20--.

Exercise 3-7 ►
Objective 6

Preparing a statement of owner's equity and a balance sheet.

From the trial balance and the net income or net loss determined in Exercise 3-6, prepare a statement of owner's equity and a balance sheet for Baker's Antique Repair as of December 31, 20--.

Exercise 3-8 ►
Objective 7

Preparing a chart of accounts.

The accounts that will be used by Chastain Supply Company follow. Prepare a chart of accounts for the firm. Classify the accounts by type, arrange them in an appropriate order, and assign suitable account numbers.

Kelly Chastain, Capital
Office Supplies
Accounts Payable
Cash
Utilities Expense
Office Equipment
Salaries Expense
Prepaid Rent
Fees Income
Accounts Receivable
Telephone Expense
Kelly Chastain, Drawing

Problems

Selected problems can be completed using:
Peachtree **QuickBooks** **Spreadsheets**

PROBLEM SET A

Using T accounts to record transactions involving assets, liabilities, and owner's equity.

◄ **Problem 3-1A**
Objectives 1, 2

The following transactions took place at Mill's Oil Field Equipment Service.

INSTRUCTIONS

For each transaction, set up T accounts from the following list: **Cash; Shop Equipment; Store Equipment; Truck; Accounts Payable; Judd Mill, Capital;** and **Judd Mill, Drawing.** Analyze each transaction. Record the effects of the transactions in the T accounts. Use plus and minus signs before the amounts to show the increases and decreases.

TRANSACTIONS

1. Judd Mill invested $9,000 cash in the business.
2. Purchased shop equipment for $450 in cash.
3. Bought store fixtures for $300; payment is due in 30 days.
4. Purchased a used truck for $1,500 in cash.
5. Mill gave the firm his personal tools that have a fair market value of $500.
6. Bought a used cash register for $250; payment is due in 30 days.
7. Paid $100 in cash to apply to the amount owed for store fixtures.
8. Mill withdrew $400 in cash for personal expenses.

Analyze: Which transactions affect the **Cash** account?

Using T accounts to record transactions involving assets, liabilities, and owner's equity.

◄ **Problem 3-2A**
Objectives 1, 2

The following transactions occurred at several different businesses and are not related.

INSTRUCTIONS

Analyze each of the transactions. For each transaction, set up T accounts. Record the effects of the transaction in the T accounts. Use plus and minus signs to show the increases and decreases.

TRANSACTIONS

1. A firm purchased equipment for $4,000 in cash.
2. The owner John Cain withdrew $1,000 cash.
3. A firm sold a piece of surplus equipment for $500 in cash.
4. A firm purchased a used delivery truck for $4,000 in cash.
5. A firm paid $800 in cash to apply against an account owed.
6. A firm purchased office equipment for $900. The amount is to be paid in 60 days.
7. Holly Call, owner of the company, made an additional investment of $5,000 in cash.

8. A firm paid $300 by check for office equipment that it had previously purchased on credit.

Analyze: Which transactions affect liability accounts?

Problem 3-3A ►
Objectives 2, 4

INSTRUCTIONS

Using T accounts to record transactions involving revenue and expenses.

The following transactions took place at Factory Cleaning Service.

Analyze each of the transactions. For each transaction, decide what accounts are affected and set up T accounts. Record the effects of the transaction in the T accounts. Use plus and minus signs before the amounts to show the increases and decreases.

TRANSACTIONS

1. Paid $800 for the current month's rent.
2. Performed services for $1,000 in cash.
3. Paid salaries of $1,200.
4. Performed additional services for $1,800 on credit.
5. Paid $150 for the monthly telephone bill.
6. Collected $500 from accounts receivable.
7. Received a $30 refund for an overcharge on the telephone bill.
8. Performed services for $1,200 on credit.
9. Paid $100 in cash for the monthly electric bill.
10. Paid $220 in cash for gasoline purchased for the firm's van during the month.
11. Received $900 from charge account customers.
12. Performed services for $1,800 in cash.

Analyze: What total cash was collected for accounts receivable during the month?

Problem 3-4A ►
Objectives 1, 2, 4

INSTRUCTIONS

Using T accounts to record all business transactions.

The accounts and transactions of Justin Malone, Attorney at Law, follow.

Analyze the transactions. Record each in the appropriate T accounts. Use plus and minus signs in front of the amounts to show the increases and decreases. Identify each entry in the T accounts by writing the letter of the transaction next to the entry.

ASSETS

Cash
Accounts Receivable
Office Equipment
Automobile

LIABILITIES

Accounts Payable

OWNER'S EQUITY

Justin Malone, Capital
Justin Malone, Drawing

REVENUE

Fees Income

EXPENSES

Automobile Expense
Rent Expense
Utilities Expense
Salaries Expense
Telephone Expense

TRANSACTIONS

a. Justin Malone invested $54,000 in cash to start the business.
b. Paid $1,600 for the current month's rent.
c. Bought a used automobile for the firm for $16,000 in cash.
d. Performed services for $3,000 in cash.
e. Paid $400 for automobile repairs.
f. Performed services for $3,750 on credit.
g. Purchased office chairs for $2,100 on credit.
h. Received $1,800 from credit clients.
i. Paid $1,000 to reduce the amount owed for the office chairs.
j. Issued a check for $560 to pay the monthly utility bill.
k. Purchased office equipment for $8,400 and paid half of this amount in cash immediately; the balance is due in 30 days.
l. Issued a check for $5,680 to pay salaries.
m. Performed services for $1,850 in cash.
n. Performed services for $2,600 on credit.
o. Paid $192 for the monthly telephone bill.
p. Collected $1,600 on accounts receivable from charge customers.
q. Purchased additional office equipment and received a bill for $1,360 due in 30 days.
r. Paid $300 in cash for gasoline purchased for the automobile during the month.
s. Justin Malone withdrew $2,000 in cash for personal expenses.

Analyze: What outstanding amount is owed to the company from its credit customers?

Preparing financial statements from T accounts.

◄ **Problem 3-5A**
Objectives 3, 5, 6

SPREADSHEET

The accountant for the firm owned by Justin Malone prepares financial statements at the end of each month.

INSTRUCTIONS

Use the figures in the T accounts for Problem 3-4A to prepare a trial balance, an income statement, a statement of owner's equity, and a balance sheet. (The first line of the statement headings should read "Justin Malone, Attorney at Law.") Assume that the transactions took place during the month ended April 30, 20--. Determine the account balances before you start work on the financial statements.

Analyze: What net change in owner's equity occurred during the month of April?

PROBLEM SET B

Problem 3-1B ►
Objectives 1, 2

Using T accounts to record transactions involving assets, liabilities, and owner's equity.

The following transactions took place at the legal services business established by Jill Morris.

INSTRUCTIONS

For each transaction, set up T accounts from this list: **Cash; Office Furniture; Office Equipment; Automobile; Accounts Payable; Jill Morris, Capital;** and **Jill Morris, Drawing.** Analyze each transaction. Record the amounts in the T accounts affected by that transaction. Use plus and minus signs to show increases and decreases in each account.

TRANSACTIONS

1. Jill Morris invested $15,000 cash in the business.
2. Purchased office furniture for $4,000 in cash.
3. Bought a fax machine for $1,300; payment is due in 30 days.
4. Purchased a used car for the firm for $4,000 in cash.
5. Morris invested an additional $4,000 cash in the business.
6. Bought a new computer for $5,000; payment is due in 60 days.
7. Paid $1,300 to settle the amount owed on the fax machine.
8. Morris withdrew $1,000 in cash for personal expenses.

Analyze: Which transactions affected asset accounts?

Problem 3-2B ►
Objectives 1, 2

Using T accounts to record transactions involving assets, liabilities, and owner's equity.

The following transactions occurred at several different businesses and are not related.

INSTRUCTIONS

Analyze each of the transactions. For each, decide what accounts are affected and set up T accounts. Record the effects of the transaction in the T accounts. Use plus and minus signs before the amounts to show the increases and decreases.

TRANSACTIONS

1. Roby Black, an owner, made an additional investment of $3,000 in cash.
2. A firm purchased equipment for $1,750 in cash.
3. A firm sold some surplus office furniture for $150 in cash.
4. A firm purchased a computer for $1,300, to be paid in 60 days.
5. A firm purchased office equipment for $1,750 on credit. The amount is due in 60 days.
6. Debbie Allen, owner of Allen Travel Agency, withdrew $500 of her original cash investment.
7. A firm bought a delivery truck for $4,500 on credit; payment is due in 90 days.
8. A firm issued a check for $125 to a supplier in partial payment of an open account balance.

Analyze: List the transactions that directly affected an owner's equity account.

Using T accounts to record transactions involving revenues and expenses.

◄ **Problem 3-3B**
Objectives 2, 4

The following occurred during April at Loan Accounting Service.

INSTRUCTIONS

Analyze each transaction. Use T accounts to record these transactions and be sure to put the name of the account on the top of each account. Record the effects of the transaction in the T accounts. Use plus and minus signs before the amounts to show the increases and decreases.

TRANSACTIONS

1. Purchased office supplies for $500.
2. Delivered monthly accounting statements, collected fee income of $350.
3. Paid the current month's office rent of $1,150.
4. Completed monthly audit, billed client for $500.
5. Client paid fee of $250 for monthly audit.
6. Paid office salary of $800.
7. Paid telephone bill of $120.
8. Billed client for $500 fee for preparing return.
9. Purchased office supplies of $250 on account.
10. Paid office salary of $800.
11. Collected $500 from client who was billed.
12. Clients paid a total of $5,000 cash in fees.

Analyze: How much cash did the business spend during the month of April?

Using T accounts to record all business transactions.

◄ **Problem 3-4B**
Objectives 1, 2, 4

The following accounts and transactions are for Richard Wall, Consulting Engineer.

INSTRUCTIONS

Analyze the transactions. Record each in the appropriate T accounts. Use plus and minus signs in front of the amounts to show the increases and decreases. Identify each entry in the T accounts by writing the letter of the transaction next to the entry.

ASSETS

Cash
Accounts Receivable
Office Furniture
Office Equipment

LIABILITIES

Accounts Payable

OWNER'S EQUITY

Richard Wall, Capital
Richard Wall, Drawing

REVENUE

Fees Income

EXPENSES

Rent Expense
Utilities Expense
Salaries Expense
Telephone Expense
Miscellaneous Expense

TRANSACTIONS

a. Wall invested $90,000 in cash to start the business.

b. Paid $4,500 for the current month's rent.

c. Bought office furniture for $15,600 in cash.

d. Performed services for $6,300 in cash.

e. Paid $1,350 for the monthly telephone bill.

f. Performed services for $7,650 on credit.

g. Purchased a computer and copier for $23,700 on credit; paid $5,700 in cash immediately with the balance due in 30 days.

h. Received $4,200 from credit clients.

i. Paid $1,800 in cash for office cleaning services for the month.

j. Purchased additional office chairs for $4,800; received credit terms of 30 days.

k. Purchased office equipment for $33,000 and paid half of this amount in cash immediately; the balance is due in 30 days.

l. Issued a check for $19,500 to pay salaries.

m. Performed services for $6,150 in cash.

n. Performed services for $6,900 on credit.

o. Collected $3,600 on accounts receivable from charge customers.

p. Issued a check for $2,400 in partial payment of the amount owed for office chairs.

q. Paid $600 to a duplicating company for photocopy work performed during the month.

r. Paid $1,500 for the monthly electric bill.

s. Wall withdrew $6,000 in cash for personal expenses.

Analyze: What liabilities does the business have after all transactions have been recorded?

Problem 3-5B ► Objectives 3, 5, 6

SPREADSHEET

Preparing financial statements from T accounts.

The accountant for the firm owned by Richard Wall prepares financial statements at the end of each month.

INSTRUCTIONS

Use the figures in the T accounts for Problem 3-4B to prepare a trial balance, an income statement, a statement of owner's equity, and a balance sheet. (The first line of the statement headings should read "Richard Wall, Consulting Engineer.") Assume that the transactions took place during the month ended June 30, 20--. Determine the account balances before you start work on the financial statements.

Analyze: What is the change in owner's equity for the month of June?

CHAPTER 3 CHALLENGE PROBLEM

Sole Proprietorship

Kim Chumley is an architect who operates her own business. The accounts and transactions for the business follow.

INSTRUCTIONS

(1) Analyze the transactions for January 20--. Record each in the appropriate T accounts. Use plus and minus signs in front of the amounts to show the increases and decreases. Identify each entry in the T account by writing the letter of the transaction next to the entry.

(2) Determine the account balances. Prepare a trial balance, an income statement, a statement of owner's equity, and a balance sheet.

ASSETS

Cash
Accounts Receivable
Office Furniture
Office Equipment

LIABILITIES

Accounts Payable

OWNER'S EQUITY

Kim Chumley, Capital
Kim Chumley, Drawing

REVENUE

Fees Income

EXPENSES

Advertising Expense
Utilities Expense
Salaries Expense
Telephone Expense
Miscellaneous Expense

TRANSACTIONS

a. Kim Chumley invested $20,000 in cash to start the business.

b. Paid $1,000 for advertisements in a design magazine.

c. Purchased office furniture for $3,000 in cash.

d. Performed services for $2,400 in cash.

e. Paid $270 for the monthly telephone bill.

f. Performed services for $2,160 on credit.

g. Purchased a fax machine for $1,500; paid $600 in cash with the balance due in 30 days.

h. Paid a bill for $330 from the office cleaning service.

i. Received $1,080 from clients on account.

j. Purchased additional office chairs for $900; received credit terms of 30 days.

k. Paid $2,000 for salaries.

l. Issued a check for $550 in partial payment of the amount owed for office chairs.

m. Received $1,400 in cash for services performed.

n. Issued a check for $480 for utilities expense.

o. Performed services for $2,400 on credit.

p. Collected $400 from clients on account.

q. Kim Chumley withdrew $1,400 in cash for personal expenses.

r. Paid $300 to Kevin's Photocopy Service for photocopy work performed during the month.

Analyze: Using the basic accounting equation, what is the financial condition of Kim Chumley's business at month-end?

CHAPTER 3 CRITICAL THINKING PROBLEM

Financial Condition

At the beginning of the summer, Adam McCoy was looking for a way to earn money to pay for his college tuition in the fall. He decided to start a lawn service business in his neighborhood. To get the business started, Adam used $750 from his savings account to open a checking account for his new business, AM Lawn Care. He purchased two used power mowers and various lawn care tools for $250, and paid $450 for a second-hand truck to transport the mowers.

Several of his neighbors hired him to cut their grass on a weekly basis. He sent these customers monthly bills. By the end of the summer, they had paid him $100 in cash and owed him another $175. Adam also cut grass on an as-needed basis for other neighbors who paid him $50.

During the summer, Adam spent $50 for gasoline for the truck and mowers. He paid $125 to a friend who helped him on several occasions. An advertisement in the local paper cost $15. Now, at the end of the summer, Adam is concerned because he has only $10 left in his checking account. He says, "I worked hard all summer and have only $10 to show for it. It would have been better to leave the money in the bank."

Prepare an income statement, a statement of owner's equity, and a balance sheet for AM Lawn Care. Explain to Adam whether or not he is "better off" than he was at the beginning of the summer. (Hint: T accounts might be helpful in organizing the data.)

Business Connections

MANAGERIAL FOCUS **Informed Decisions** ◄ Connection 1

1. How do the income statement and the balance sheet help management make sound decisions?
2. How can management find out, at any time, whether a firm can pay its bills as they become due?
3. If a firm's expenses equal or exceed its revenue, what actions might management take?
4. In discussing a firm's latest financial statements, a manager says that it is the "results on the bottom line" that really count. What does the manager mean?

Ethical DILEMMA **Reporting Cash Sales** Joe's Quick Stop is a convenience store that sells an array of products. The store is owned by Joseph Lawson, who has offered you a job in the store as a clerk. On your first day on the job, Joseph informs you that when customers pay cash for certain items, the cash should be deposited in a cigar box that is kept under the cash register. At the end of the day, you notice that Joseph empties the cash in the cigar box into his money bag. The cash deposited in the cash register is recorded as the amount of cash received for the day and does not include the cash in the cigar box. You are concerned that Joseph is not properly recording his total amount of cash received. What would you do? ◄ Connection 2

Street WISE: Questions from the Real World **Account Categories** Refer to the *1999 Annual Report* for The Home Depot, Inc. in Appendix B. ◄ Connection 3

THE HOME DEPOT

1. To prepare financial statements, The Home Depot, Inc. summarizes general ledger account balances into summary categories for presentation on statements. List five "permanent" summarized account categories reflected in these statements. List five "temporary" summarized account categories found in the statements.
2. Locate the consolidated balance sheets for The Home Depot, Inc. If The Home Depot, Inc. purchased new store fixtures on account for $25,000, describe the effect on the company's balance sheet categories.

FINANCIAL STATEMENT ANALYSIS **Management Letter** Annual reports released by publicly held companies include a letter to the stockholders written by the chief executive officer, chairman of the board, or president. Excerpts from the Adobe Systems Incorporated *1999 Annual Report* "To Our Stockholders" letter are presented below. The appearance of an ellipsis (. . .) indicates that some of the text of the letter has been deleted to save space. ◄ Connection 4

Adobe

> For everyone at Adobe Systems, 1999 will be remembered as a year of turnaround . . . Adobe stock began a steady ascent, and by the end of fiscal year 1999, its value had increased fourfold . . . our operating profit increased by 107% year over year . . .

. . . net income reached a record level of $238 million, a 126% increase compared with fiscal 1998 . . .

. . . by improving operational efficiency, Adobe was able to enhance operations . . . by outsourcing functions such as order fulfillment and utilizing the Internet to work more efficiently with our customers . . .

Analyze:

1. Based on the excerpts above, what types of information can a company's management deliver using the letter to stockholders?
2. What net income did Adobe Systems Incorporated report for fiscal 1999?
3. What operational efficiencies are discussed for fiscal 1999?

Analyze Online: Locate the Adobe Systems Incorporated Web site **(www.adobe.com).** Within *Investor Relations* in the *About Adobe* link, find the annual report for the current year. Read the letter to the stockholders within the annual report.

4. Are the financial results presented in the current year more or less favorable than those presented for fiscal 1999?
5. What new products were introduced in the current year and mentioned in the stockholders' letter?

Connection 5 ► *Extending the Thought* **Systems** A company's chart of accounts is an organization system. Discuss similar organization systems in subject areas other than accounting.

Connection 6 ► **Business Communication** **Memo** The junior accountant in your department does not agree that a trial balance should be prepared before the financial statements are completed. As the senior accountant, write a memo to your co-worker explaining your position on the topic. Express possible ramifications that you foresee if the trial balance is not prepared.

Connection 7 ► **TeamWork** **Chart of Accounts** As a team, develop a chart of accounts for a retail garden supply store. Brainstorm with your team about the types of revenue and expense accounts that would be required. List asset, liability, and owner's equity accounts. Finally, assign an organized numeric scheme to your chart of accounts. Write instructions for adding new accounts if it becomes necessary.

Connection 8 ► **interNET CONNECTION** **SBA** The Small Business Administration (SBA) offers a wide variety of resources to the entrepreneur. Go to the Web site at **www.sba.gov.** List two counseling or resource services available through the Small Business Administration. Based on the information at the Web site, what goes into a business plan?

Answers to Self Reviews

Answers to Section 1 Self Review

1. Increases in asset accounts are recorded on the left side. Increases in liability and owner's equity accounts are recorded on the right side.
2. The sum of several entries on either side of an account that is entered in small pencil figures.
3. The increase side of an account. The normal balance of an asset account is on the left side. The normal balance of liability and owner's equity accounts is on the right side.
4. c. $24,000
5. c. **Equipment** is increased by $4,500. **Accounts Payable** is increased by $4,500.
6. Cash + Equipment + Supplies = Accounts Payable + T. R. Murphy, Capital

Cash		Equipment		Supplies		Accounts Payable		T. R. Murphy, Capital
15,400	+	20,000	+	4,600	=	10,000	+	30,000
				40,000	=	40,000		

Answers to Section 2 Self Review

1. The increase side of **Cash** is the left, or debit, side. The increase side of **Accounts Payable** is the right, or credit, side. The increase side of **Linda Carter, Capital** is the right, or credit, side.
2. The trial balance is a list of all the accounts and their balances. Its purpose is to prove the equality of the total debits and credits.
3. A transposition is an error in which the digits of a number are switched, for example, when 517 is recorded as 571.

   A slide is an error in which the decimal point is misplaced, for example, when 317 is written as 3.17.
4. b. **T. C., Drawing**
5. c. **Vijay Shah, Drawing** would be debited and **Cash** would be credited.
6. **A. Ames, Drawing**—10,000 should be in the Debit column.

   Fees Income—14,000 should be in the Credit column.

   The new column totals will be 51,000.

Answers to Comprehensive Self Review

1. Decreases in asset accounts are recorded on the credit side. Decreases in liability and owner's equity accounts are recorded on the debit side.
2. Cash taken from the business by the owner to obtain funds for personal living expenses. Withdrawals are recorded in a special type of owner's equity account called a drawing account.
3. A list of the numbers and names of the accounts of a business. It provides a system by which the accounts of the business can be easily identified and located.
4. • Check the math by adding the columns again.
   • Determine whether the account balances are in the correct columns.
   • Check the accounts to see whether the balances in the accounts were computed correctly.
   • Check the accuracy of transactions recorded during the period.
5. The asset, liability, and owner's equity accounts.

CHAPTER 4

Learning Objectives

1. Record transactions in the general journal.
2. Prepare compound journal entries.
3. Post journal entries to general ledger accounts.
4. Correct errors made in the journal or ledger.
5. Define the accounting terms new to this chapter.

The General Journal and the General Ledger

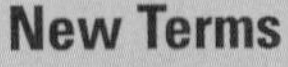

www.csx.com

Economic development in a geographic area often hinges on the transportation infrastructure of the region. No one understands this better than CSX Corporation. Founded originally as the Louisa Railroad Company in 1836, this Fortune 500 company now moves consumer products, automobiles, forest products, coal, and iron from location to location via ocean liners, barges, trucks, and trains. CSX Corporation played a key role from 1994 to 2000 helping approximately 500 companies locate and expand along its rail lines. In addition to rail services, customers contract with CSX Corporation for warehouse management, container shipping, and equipment maintenance services.

Thinking Critically

Why would CSX Corporation expand its services beyond transportation?

For more information on CSX Corporation, go to: collegeaccounting.glencoe.com.

New Terms

Accounting cycle	**General journal**
Audit trail	**General ledger**
Balance ledger form	**Journal**
Chronological order	**Journalizing**
Compound entry	**Ledger**
Correcting entry	**Posting**

Section 1

Section Objectives

1. **Record transactions in the general journal.**

   WHY IT'S IMPORTANT
   Written records for all business transactions are necessary. The general journal acts as the "diary" of the business.

2. **Prepare compound journal entries.**

   WHY IT'S IMPORTANT
   Compound entries contain several debits or credits for a single business transaction, creating efficiencies in journalizing.

Terms to Learn

accounting cycle
audit trail
chronological order
compound entry
general journal
journal
journalizing

The General Journal

The **accounting cycle** is a series of steps performed during each accounting period to classify, record, and summarize data for a business and to produce needed financial information. The first step in the accounting cycle is to analyze business transactions. You learned this skill in Chapter 3. The second step in the accounting cycle is to prepare a record of business transactions.

Journals

Business transactions are recorded in a **journal**, which is a diary of business activities. The journal lists transactions in **chronological order**, that is, in the order in which they occur. The journal is sometimes called the *record of original entry* because it is where transactions are first entered in the accounting records. There are different types of journals. This chapter will examine the general journal. You will become familiar with other journals in later chapters.

> Most corporations use accounting software to record business transactions. Texaco International uses Solomon IV accounting software.

The General Journal

1 Objective
Record transactions in the general journal.

The **general journal** is a financial record for entering all types of business transactions. **Journalizing** is the process of recording transactions in the general journal.

Figure 4-1 shows the general journal for Carter Consulting Services. Notice that the general journal has a page number. To record a transaction, enter the year at the top of the Date column. In the Date column, write the month and day on the first line of the first entry. After the first entry, enter the year and month only when a new page is started or when the year or the month changes. In the Date column, write the day of each transaction on the first line of each transaction.

FIGURE 4-1 ► General Journal Entry

GENERAL JOURNAL PAGE 1

	DATE		DESCRIPTION	POST. REF.	DEBIT	CREDIT	
1	2004						1
2	Nov.	6	Cash		80 000 00		2
3			Linda Carter, Capital			80 000 00	3
4			Investment by owner				4
5							5

Record the year first, then the month and day. →
Record the debit first. →
Indent about one-half inch and record the credit. →
Indent again and write the description.

In the Description column, enter the account to be debited. Write the account name close to the left margin of the Description column, and enter the amount on the same line in the Debit column.

Enter the account to be credited on the line beneath the debit. Indent the account name about one-half inch from the left margin. Enter the amount on the same line in the Credit column.

Then enter a complete but concise description of the transaction in the Description column. Begin the description on the line following the credit. The description is indented about one inch from the left margin.

Write account names exactly as they appear in the chart of accounts. This will minimize errors when amounts are transferred from the general journal to the accounts.

Leave a blank line between general journal entries. Some accountants use this blank line to number each general journal entry.

When possible, the journal entry description should refer to the source of the information. For example, the journal entry to record a payment should include the check number in the description. Document numbers are part of the audit trail. The **audit trail** is a chain of references that makes it possible to trace information, locate errors, and prevent fraud. The audit trail provides a means of checking the journal entry against the original data on the documents.

Important!

The Diary of a Business

The general journal is similar to a diary. The general journal details, in chronological order, the economic events of the business.

Important!

Audit Trail

To maintain the audit trail, descriptions should refer to document numbers whenever possible.

Recording November Transactions in the General Journal

In Chapters 2 and 3, you learned a step-by-step method for analyzing business transactions. In this chapter you will learn how to complete the journal entry for a business transaction in the same manner. Review the following steps before you continue.

1. Analyze the financial event.
   - Identify the accounts affected.
   - Classify the accounts affected.
   - Determine the amount of increase or decrease for each account affected.
2. Apply the rules of debit and credit.
   - **a.** Which account is debited? For what amount?
   - **b.** Which account is credited? For what amount?
3. Make the entry in T-account form.
4. Record the complete entry in general journal form.

Business Transaction

On November 6 Linda Carter withdrew $80,000 from personal savings and deposited it in a new business checking account for Carter Consulting Services.

MEMORANDUM 01

TO: Beatrice Wilson
FROM: Linda Carter
DATE: November 6, 2004
SUBJECT: Contributed personal funds to the business

I contributed $80,000 from my personal savings to Carter Consulting Services.

Analysis

a. The asset account, **Cash,** is increased by $80,000.

b. The owner's equity account, **Linda Carter, Capital,** is increased by $80,000.

Debit-Credit Rules

DEBIT Increases to asset accounts are recorded as debits. Debit **Cash** for $80,000.

CREDIT Increases to the owner's equity account are recorded as credits. Credit **Linda Carter, Capital** for $80,000.

T-Account Presentation

Cash +	Cash −
(a) 80,000	

Linda Carter, Capital −	Linda Carter, Capital +
	(b) 80,000

General Journal Entry

GENERAL JOURNAL PAGE 1

	DATE		DESCRIPTION	POST. REF.	DEBIT	CREDIT	
1	2004						1
2	Nov.	6	Cash		80 000 00		2
3			Linda Carter, Capital			80 000 00	3
4			Investment by owner,				4
5			Memo 01				5

Business Transaction

On November 7 Carter Consulting Services issued Check 1001 for $20,000 to purchase a computer and other equipment.

$ 20,000.00 No. 1001
Date November 7, 20 04
To SBM Tech
For Office Equipment

	Dollars	Cents
Balance brought forward	80,000	00
Add deposits		
Total	80,000	00
Less this check	20,000	00
Balance carried forward	60,000	00

Analysis

c. The asset account, **Equipment,** is increased by $20,000.

d. The asset account, **Cash,** is decreased by $20,000.

Debit-Credit Rules

DEBIT Increases to asset accounts are recorded as debits. Debit **Equipment** for $20,000.

CREDIT Decreases to asset accounts are recorded as credits. Credit **Cash** for $20,000.

T-Account Presentation

Equipment +	Equipment −
(c) 20,000	

Cash +	Cash −
	(d) 20,000

General Journal Entry

GENERAL JOURNAL PAGE 1

	DATE		DESCRIPTION	POST. REF.	DEBIT	CREDIT	
6	Nov.	7	Equipment		20 000 00		6
7			Cash			20 000 00	7
8			Purchased equip., Check 1001				8

The check number appears in the description and forms part of the audit trail for the transaction.

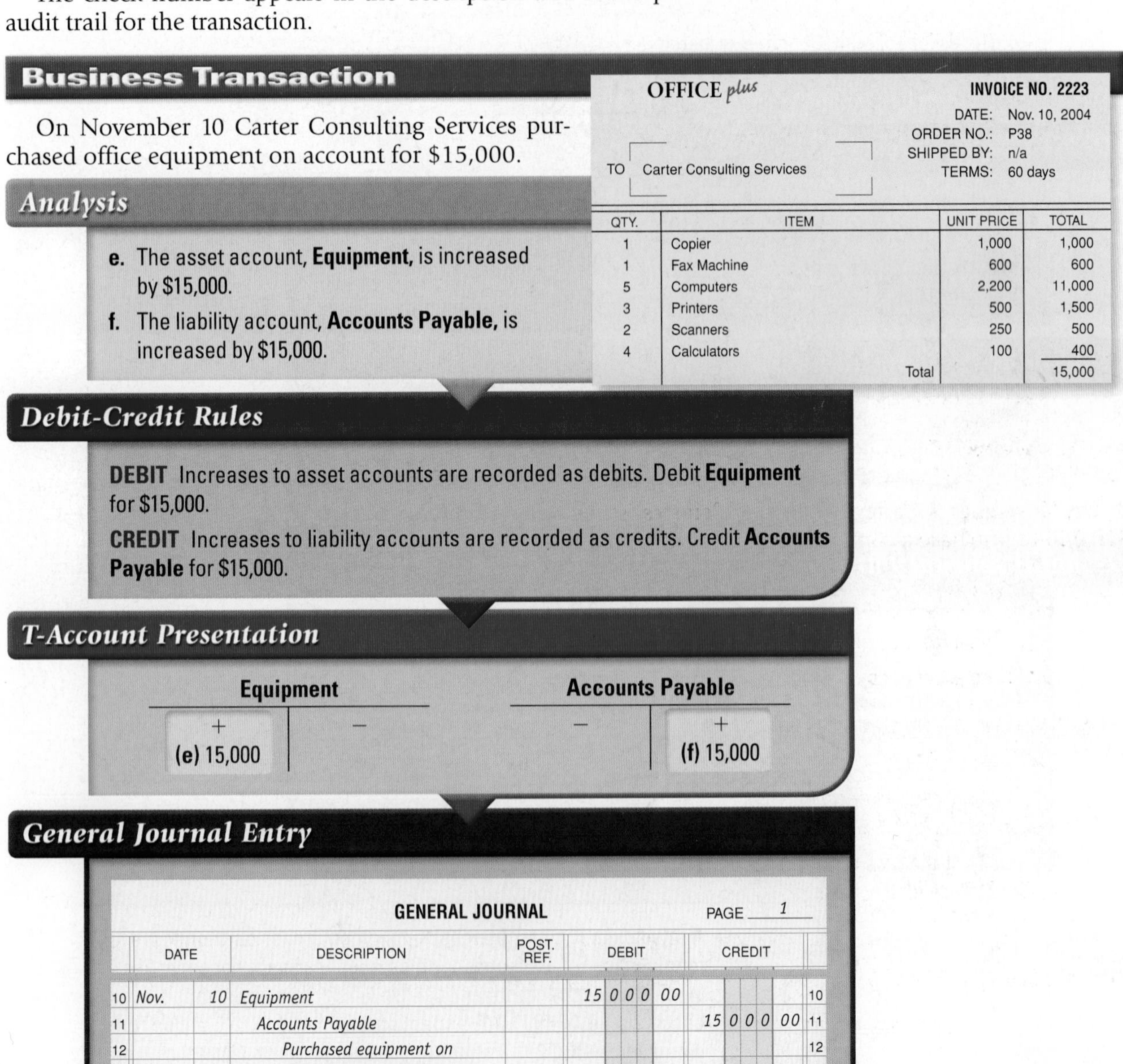

Business Transaction

On November 10 Carter Consulting Services purchased office equipment on account for $15,000.

OFFICE *plus*

INVOICE NO. 2223

DATE: Nov. 10, 2004
ORDER NO.: P38
SHIPPED BY: n/a
TERMS: 60 days

TO Carter Consulting Services

QTY.	ITEM	UNIT PRICE	TOTAL
1	Copier	1,000	1,000
1	Fax Machine	600	600
5	Computers	2,200	11,000
3	Printers	500	1,500
2	Scanners	250	500
4	Calculators	100	400
		Total	15,000

Analysis

e. The asset account, **Equipment,** is increased by $15,000.

f. The liability account, **Accounts Payable,** is increased by $15,000.

Debit-Credit Rules

DEBIT Increases to asset accounts are recorded as debits. Debit **Equipment** for $15,000.

CREDIT Increases to liability accounts are recorded as credits. Credit **Accounts Payable** for $15,000.

T-Account Presentation

Equipment

+	−
(e) 15,000	

Accounts Payable

−	+
	(f) 15,000

General Journal Entry

GENERAL JOURNAL PAGE 1

	DATE		DESCRIPTION	POST. REF.	DEBIT	CREDIT	
10	Nov.	10	Equipment		15 000 00		10
11			Accounts Payable			15 000 00	11
12			Purchased equipment on				12
13			account from Office Plus,				13
14			Inv. 2223, due in 60 days				14

The supplier's name (Office Plus) and invoice number (2223) appear in the journal entry description and form part of the audit trail for the transaction. The journal entry can be checked against the data on the original document, Invoice 2223.

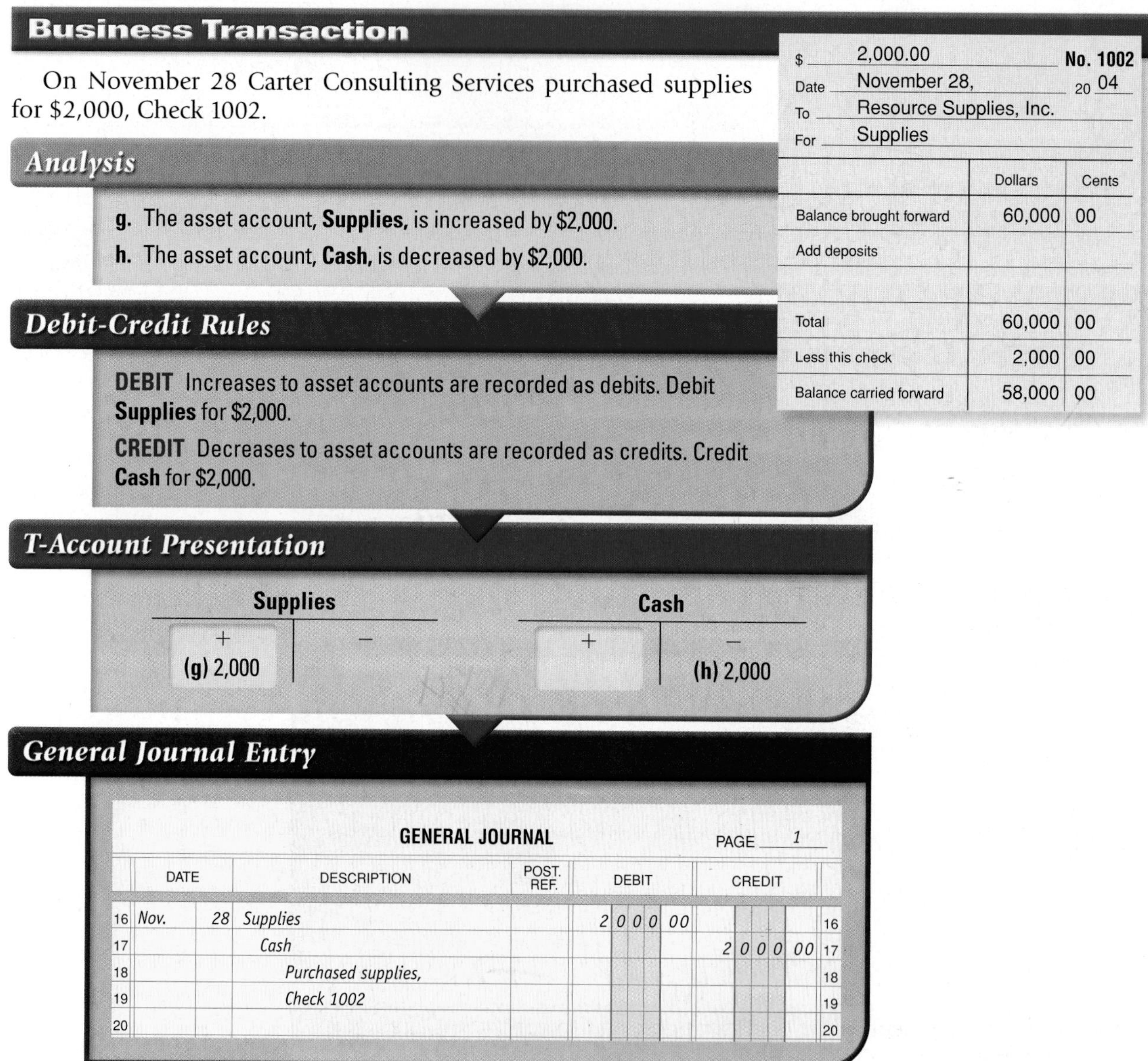

Business Transaction

On November 28 Carter Consulting Services purchased supplies for $2,000, Check 1002.

$ 2,000.00		No. 1002
Date November 28, 20 04		
To Resource Supplies, Inc.		
For Supplies		
	Dollars	Cents
Balance brought forward	60,000	00
Add deposits		
Total	60,000	00
Less this check	2,000	00
Balance carried forward	58,000	00

Analysis

g. The asset account, **Supplies,** is increased by $2,000.

h. The asset account, **Cash,** is decreased by $2,000.

Debit-Credit Rules

DEBIT Increases to asset accounts are recorded as debits. Debit **Supplies** for $2,000.

CREDIT Decreases to asset accounts are recorded as credits. Credit **Cash** for $2,000.

T-Account Presentation

Supplies +	Supplies −
(g) 2,000	

Cash +	Cash −
	(h) 2,000

General Journal Entry

GENERAL JOURNAL PAGE 1

	DATE		DESCRIPTION	POST. REF.	DEBIT	CREDIT	
16	Nov.	28	Supplies		2 000 00		16
17			Cash			2 000 00	17
18			Purchased supplies,				18
19			Check 1002				19
20							20

A few boxes of pens, pencils, highlighters, toner cartridges, several reams of paper—the cost of office supplies might not seem like much. The accountants at Duke University can attest that these costs add up. In 1999 Duke spent approximately $12.5 million for office supplies.

Beatrice Wilson decided to reduce the firm's debt to Office Plus. Recall that the firm had purchased equipment on account in the amount of

$15,000. On November 30 Carter Consulting Services issued a check to Office Plus. Beatrice Wilson analyzed the transaction and recorded the journal entry as follows.

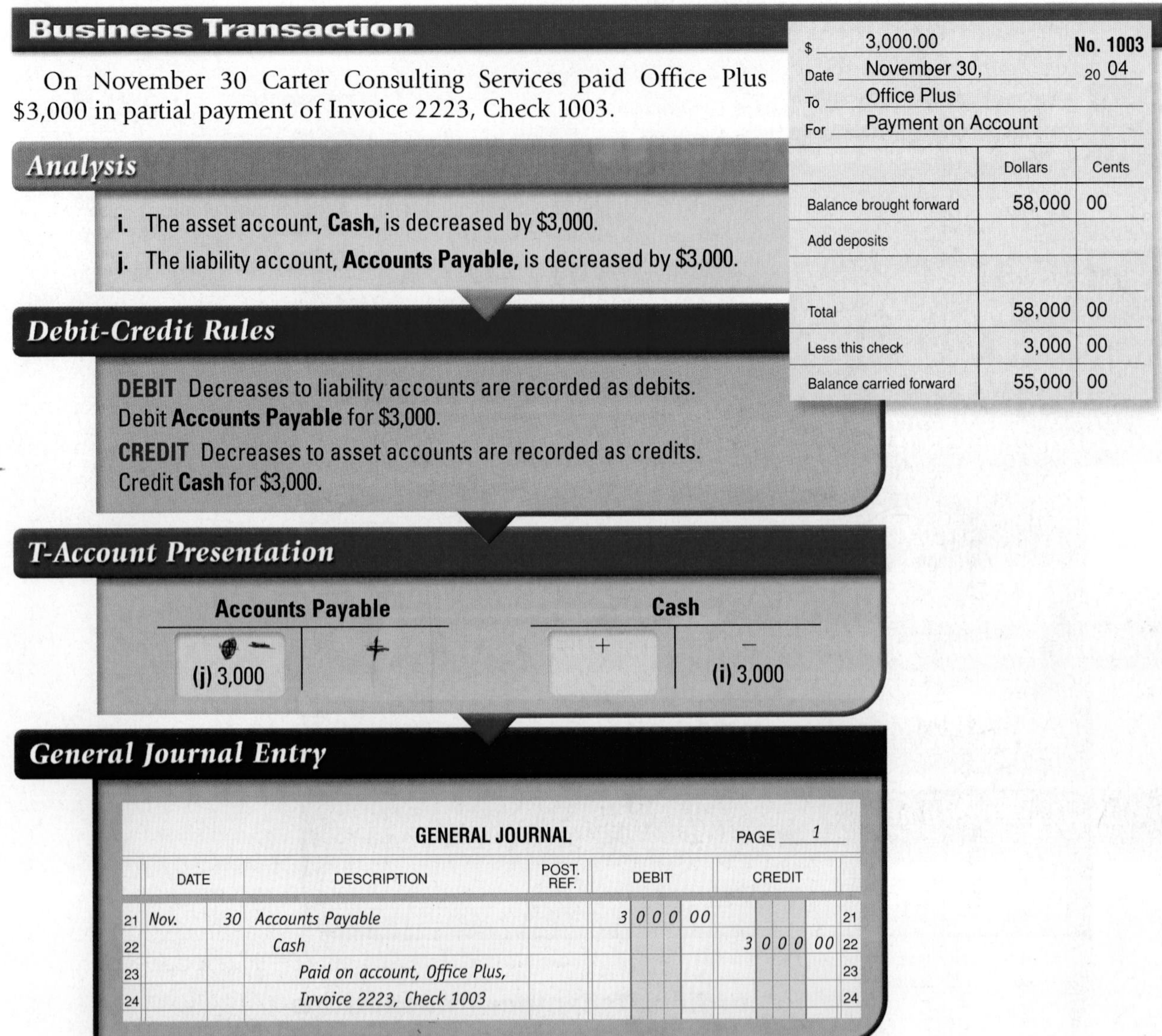

Business Transaction

On November 30 Carter Consulting Services paid Office Plus $3,000 in partial payment of Invoice 2223, Check 1003.

$ 3,000.00		No. 1003
Date November 30, 20 04		
To Office Plus		
For Payment on Account		
	Dollars	Cents
Balance brought forward	58,000	00
Add deposits		
Total	58,000	00
Less this check	3,000	00
Balance carried forward	55,000	00

Analysis

i. The asset account, **Cash,** is decreased by $3,000.

j. The liability account, **Accounts Payable,** is decreased by $3,000.

Debit-Credit Rules

DEBIT Decreases to liability accounts are recorded as debits. Debit **Accounts Payable** for $3,000.

CREDIT Decreases to asset accounts are recorded as credits. Credit **Cash** for $3,000.

T-Account Presentation

Accounts Payable	
−	+
(j) 3,000	

Cash	
+	−
	(i) 3,000

General Journal Entry

GENERAL JOURNAL PAGE 1

	DATE		DESCRIPTION	POST. REF.	DEBIT	CREDIT	
21	Nov.	30	Accounts Payable		3 000 00		21
22			Cash			3 000 00	22
23			Paid on account, Office Plus,				23
24			Invoice 2223, Check 1003				24

Notice that the general journal Description column includes three important items for the audit trail:

- the supplier name,
- the invoice number,
- the check number.

In the general journal, always enter debits before credits. This is the case even if the credit item is considered first when mentally analyzing the transaction.

Carter Consulting Services issued a check in November to pay December and January rent in advance. Recall that the right to occupy facilities is considered a form of property. Beatrice Wilson analyzed the transaction and recorded the journal entry as follows.

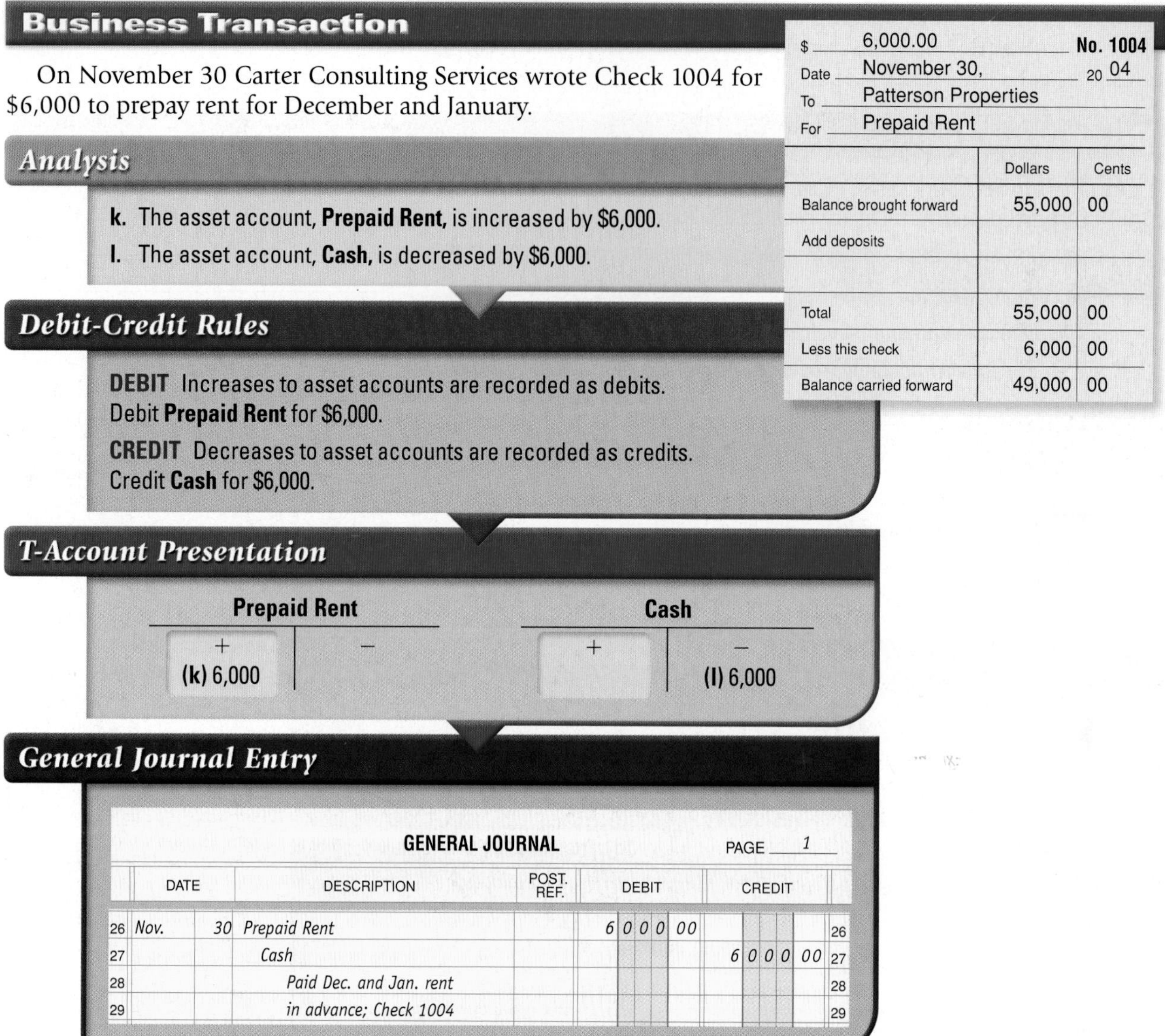

Business Transaction

On November 30 Carter Consulting Services wrote Check 1004 for $6,000 to prepay rent for December and January.

$ 6,000.00	No. 1004
Date November 30,	20 04
To Patterson Properties	
For Prepaid Rent	

	Dollars	Cents
Balance brought forward	55,000	00
Add deposits		
Total	55,000	00
Less this check	6,000	00
Balance carried forward	49,000	00

Analysis

k. The asset account, **Prepaid Rent,** is increased by $6,000.
l. The asset account, **Cash,** is decreased by $6,000.

Debit-Credit Rules

DEBIT Increases to asset accounts are recorded as debits. Debit **Prepaid Rent** for $6,000.

CREDIT Decreases to asset accounts are recorded as credits. Credit **Cash** for $6,000.

T-Account Presentation

Prepaid Rent +	Prepaid Rent −
(k) 6,000	

Cash +	Cash −
	(l) 6,000

General Journal Entry

GENERAL JOURNAL PAGE 1

	DATE		DESCRIPTION	POST. REF.	DEBIT	CREDIT	
26	Nov.	30	Prepaid Rent		6 000 00		26
27			Cash			6 000 00	27
28			Paid Dec. and Jan. rent				28
29			in advance; Check 1004				29

Recording December Transactions in the General Journal

Carter Consulting Services opened for business on December 1. Let's review the transactions that occurred in December. Refer to items **m** through **x** in Chapter 3 for the analysis of each transaction.

1. Performed services for $21,000 in cash.
2. Performed services for $7,000 on credit.
3. Received $3,000 in cash from credit clients on their accounts.
4. Paid $5,000 for salaries.
5. Paid $600 for a utility bill.
6. The owner withdrew $3,000 for personal expenses.

Figure 4-2 shows the entries in the general journal. In an actual business, transactions involving fees income and accounts receivable occur throughout the month and are recorded when they take place. For the sake of simplicity, these transactions are summarized and recorded as of December 31 for Carter Consulting Services.

GENERAL JOURNAL				PAGE 2	
DATE		DESCRIPTION	POST. REF.	DEBIT	CREDIT
2004					
Dec.	31	Cash		21 000 00	
		Fees Income			21 000 00
		Performed services for cash			
	31	Accounts Receivable		7 000 00	
		Fees Income			7 000 00
		Performed services on credit			
	31	Cash		3 000 00	
		Accounts Receivable			3 000 00
		Received cash from credit			
		clients on account			
	31	Salaries Expense		5 000 00	
		Cash			5 000 00
		Paid monthly salaries to			
		employees, Checks			
		1005–1006			
	31	Utilities Expense		600 00	
		Cash			600 00
		Paid monthly bill for utilities,			
		Check 1007			
	31	Linda Carter, Drawing		3 000 00	
		Cash			3 000 00
		Owner withdrew cash for			
		personal expenses,			
		Check 1008			

FIGURE 4-2
General Journal Entries for December

International **INSIGHTS**

Trade Agreements

The General Agreement on Tariffs and Trade (GATT) is both an organization and a set of agreements. The organization began in 1947 with 223 member nations. Its purpose is to end quotas and lower tariffs. GATT has had a beneficial effect on world trade.

Preparing Compound Entries

2 Objective

Prepare compound journal entries.

So far, each journal entry consists of one debit and one credit. Some transactions require a **compound entry**—a journal entry that contains more than one debit or credit. In a compound entry, record all debits first followed by the credits.

In 1999 Allstate purchased an insurance division of CNA Financial Corporation. Allstate paid cash and issued a 10-year note payable (a promise to pay). Detailed accounting records are not available to the public, but a compound journal entry was probably used to record this transaction.

Suppose that on November 7, when Carter Consulting Services purchased the equipment for $20,000, Linda Carter paid $10,000 in cash and agreed to pay the balance in 30 days. This transaction is analyzed on page 104.

Business Transaction

On November 7 the firm purchased equipment for $20,000, issued Check 1001 for $10,000, and agreed to pay the balance in 30 days.

Analysis

The asset account, **Equipment,** is increased by $20,000. The asset account, **Cash,** is decreased by $10,000.

The liability account, **Accounts Payable,** is increased by $10,000.

Debit-Credit Rules

DEBIT Increases to assets are recorded as debits. Debit **Equipment** for $20,000.

CREDIT Decreases to assets are credits. Credit **Cash** for $10,000. Increases to liabilities are credits. Credit **Accounts Payable** for $10,000.

T-Account Presentation

Equipment		Cash		Accounts Payable	
+	−	+	−	−	+
20,000			10,000		10,000

General Journal Entry

GENERAL JOURNAL — PAGE 1

	DATE		DESCRIPTION	POST. REF.	DEBIT	CREDIT	
6	Nov.	7	Equipment		20 000 00		6
7			Cash			10 000 00	7
8			Accounts Payable			10 000 00	8
9			Bought equip. from SBM Tech,				9
10			Inv. 11, issued Ck. 1001 for				10
11			$10,000, bal. due in 30 days				11

Recall

Debits = Credits

No matter how many accounts are affected by a transaction, total debits must equal total credits.

Section 1 Self Review

Questions

1. Why are check and invoice numbers included in the journal entry description?
2. In a compound journal entry, if two accounts are debited, must two accounts be credited?
3. Why is the journal referred to as the "record of original entry"?

Exercises

4. A general journal is like a(n)
   a. address book.
   b. appointment calendar.
   c. diary.
   d. to-do list.
5. The part of the journal entry to be recorded first is the
   a. asset.
   b. credit.
   c. debit.
   d. liability.

Analysis

6. The accountant for Luxury Lawncare never includes descriptions when making journal entries. What effect will this have on the accounting system?

(Answers to Section 1 Self Review are on page 127.)

Section 2

The General Ledger

You learned that a journal contains a chronological (day-by-day) record of a firm's transactions. Each journal entry shows the accounts and the amounts involved. Using the journal as a guide, you can enter transaction data in the accounts.

Section Objectives

3 Post journal entries to general ledger accounts.

WHY IT'S IMPORTANT
The general ledger provides a permanent, classified record for a company's accounts.

4 Correct errors made in the journal or ledger.

WHY IT'S IMPORTANT
Errors must be corrected to ensure a proper audit trail and to provide good information.

Terms to Learn

balance ledger form
correcting entry
general ledger
ledger
posting

Ledgers

T accounts are used to analyze transactions quickly but are not used to maintain financial records. Instead, businesses keep account records on a special form that makes it possible to record all data efficiently. There is a separate form for each account. The account forms are kept in a book or binder called a **ledger**. The ledger is called the *record of final entry* because the ledger is the last place that accounting transactions are recorded.

The process of transferring data from the journal to the ledger is known as **posting**. Posting takes place after transactions are journalized. Posting is the third step of the accounting cycle.

The General Ledger

Every business has a general ledger. The **general ledger** is the master reference file for the accounting system. It provides a permanent, classified record of all accounts used in a firm's operations.

Ledger Account Forms

There are different types of general ledger account forms. Beatrice Wilson decided to use a balance ledger form. A **balance ledger form** shows the balance of the account after each entry is posted. Look at Figure 4-3 on page 106. It shows the first general journal entry, the investment by the owner. It also shows the general ledger forms for **Cash** and **Linda Carter, Capital**. On the ledger form, notice the

- account name and number;
- columns for date, description, and posting reference (post. ref.);
- columns for debit, credit, balance debit, and balance credit.

Important!

General Journal and General Ledger
The general journal is the record of *original* entry. The general ledger is the record of *final* entry.

Posting to the General Ledger

3 Objective
Post journal entries to general ledger accounts.

Examine Figure 4-4 on page 107. On November 7 Beatrice Wilson made a general journal entry to record the purchase of equipment. To post the data from the journal to the general ledger, Wilson entered the debit amount in the Debit column in the **Equipment** account and the credit amount in the Credit column in the **Cash** account.

In the general journal, identify the first account listed. In Figure 4-4, **Equipment** is the first account. In the general ledger, find the ledger form for the first account listed. In Figure 4-4 this is the **Equipment** ledger form.

The steps to post from the general journal to the general ledger follow.

FIGURE 4-3 ►
Posting from the General Journal to the General Ledger

GENERAL JOURNAL — PAGE 1

DATE		DESCRIPTION	POST. REF.	DEBIT	CREDIT
2004					
Nov.	6	Cash	101	80 000 00	
		Linda Carter, Capital	301		80 000 00
		Investment by owner			

ACCOUNT Cash — ACCOUNT NO. 101

DATE		DESCRIPTION	POST. REF.	DEBIT	CREDIT	BALANCE DEBIT	BALANCE CREDIT
2004							
Nov.	6		J1	80 000 00		80 000 00	

ACCOUNT Linda Carter, Capital — ACCOUNT NO. 301

DATE		DESCRIPTION	POST. REF.	DEBIT	CREDIT	BALANCE DEBIT	BALANCE CREDIT
2004							
Nov.	6		J1		80 000 00		80 000 00

1. On the ledger form, enter the date of the transaction. Enter a description of the entry, if necessary. Usually routine entries do not require descriptions.
2. On the ledger form, enter the general journal page in the Posting Reference column. On the **Equipment** ledger form, the **J1** in the Posting Reference column indicates that the journal entry is recorded on page 1 of the general journal. The letter **J** refers to the general journal.
3. On the ledger form, enter the debit amount in the Debit column or the credit amount in the Credit column. In Figure 4-4 on the **Equipment** ledger form, $20,000 is entered in the Debit column.
4. On the ledger form, compute the balance and enter it in the Debit Balance column or the Credit Balance column. In Figure 4-4 the balance in the **Equipment** account is a $20,000 debit.
5. On the general journal, enter the ledger account number in the Posting Reference column. In Figure 4-4 the account number 141 is entered in the Posting Reference column next to "Equipment."

Repeat the process for the next account in the general journal. In Figure 4-4 Wilson posted the credit amount from the general journal to the **Cash** ledger account. Notice on the **Cash** ledger form that she entered the credit of $20,000 and then computed the account balance. After the transaction is posted, the balance of the **Cash** account is $60,000.

Be sure to enter the numbers in the Posting Reference columns. This indicates that the entry was posted and ensures against posting the same entry twice. Posting references are part of the audit trail. They allow a transaction to be traced from the ledger to the journal entry, and then to the source document.

Figure 4-5 on pages 108–109 shows the general ledger after all the entries for November and December are posted.

About Accounting

Careers
How do you get to be the president of a large corporation in the United States? Probably by beginning your career as an accountant. More accountants have advanced to be presidents of large corporations than people with any other background.

Normal Balance
The normal balance of an account is its increase side.

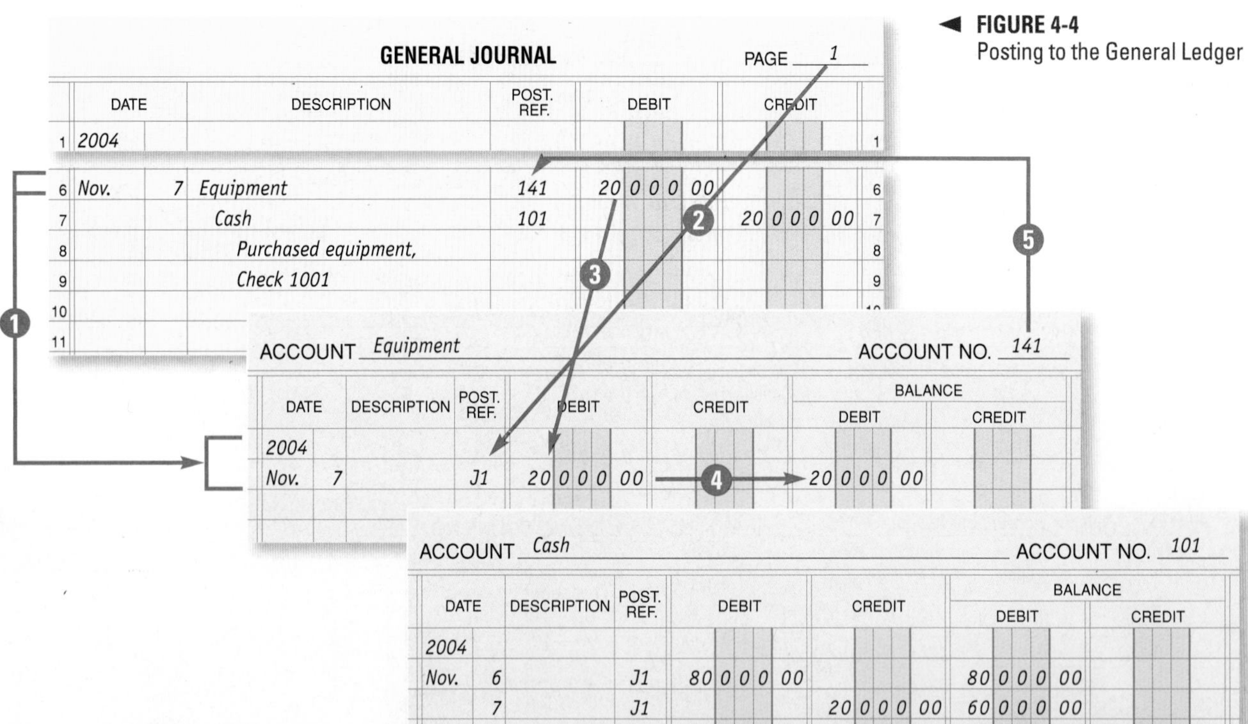

FIGURE 4-4
Posting to the General Ledger

Accounting On The Job

Legal & Protective Services

Industry Overview

U.S. legal and protective services workers include lawyers, judicial workers, and persons trained in specialized community services like fire protection and law enforcement. The U.S. Department of Justice is the largest employer of law enforcement professionals.

Career Opportunities

- Tax Attorney
- Criminal Investigator
- Corrections Administrator
- Director of Emergency Services
- FBI Agent

Preparing for a Legal or Protective Services Career

- For a career in law:
    - Complete a four-year college degree, three years in law school, and the bar exam.
    - Develop skills in writing, speaking, researching, analyzing, and thinking logically.
    - Gain extensive accounting knowledge to specialize in tax law or corporate law.
    - Apply for a court clerkship.
- For a career in protective services:
    - Obtain a four-year degree, professional certification, or master's degree for specialized protective service careers.
    - For an entry level emergency services job, pass the Medical First Responder (MFR) certification test.

Thinking Critically

If you were a corporate attorney for an airline, what issues do you think you might be required to handle? Hint: Review news releases on companies' Web sites.

Internet Application

Use the Internet to research job responsibilities, education requirements, and recommended skills for one of the following: Paralegal, Fire Department Chief, Correctional Officer.

ACCOUNT Cash ACCOUNT NO. 101

DATE		DESCRIPTION	POST. REF.	DEBIT	CREDIT	BALANCE DEBIT	BALANCE CREDIT
2004							
Nov.	6		J1	80 000 00		80 000 00	
	7		J1		20 000 00	60 000 00	
	28		J1		2 000 00	58 000 00	
	30		J1		3 000 00	55 000 00	
	30		J1		6 000 00	49 000 00	
Dec.	31		J2	21 000 00		70 000 00	
	31		J2	3 000 00		73 000 00	
	31		J2		5 000 00	68 000 00	
	31		J2		600 00	67 400 00	
	31		J2		3 000 00	64 400 00	

ACCOUNT Accounts Receivable ACCOUNT NO. 111

DATE		DESCRIPTION	POST. REF.	DEBIT	CREDIT	BALANCE DEBIT	BALANCE CREDIT
2004							
Dec.	31		J2	7 000 00		7 000 00	
	31		J2		3 000 00	4 000 00	

ACCOUNT Supplies ACCOUNT NO. 121

DATE		DESCRIPTION	POST. REF.	DEBIT	CREDIT	BALANCE DEBIT	BALANCE CREDIT
2004							
Nov.	28		J1	2 000 00		2 000 00	

ACCOUNT Prepaid Rent ACCOUNT NO. 137

DATE		DESCRIPTION	POST. REF.	DEBIT	CREDIT	BALANCE DEBIT	BALANCE CREDIT
2004							
Nov.	30		J1	6 000 00		6 000 00	

ACCOUNT Equipment ACCOUNT NO. 141

DATE		DESCRIPTION	POST. REF.	DEBIT	CREDIT	BALANCE DEBIT	BALANCE CREDIT
2004							
Nov.	7		J1	20 000 00		20 000 00	
	10		J1	15 000 00		35 000 00	

ACCOUNT Accounts Payable ACCOUNT NO. 202

DATE		DESCRIPTION	POST. REF.	DEBIT	CREDIT	BALANCE DEBIT	BALANCE CREDIT
2004							
Nov.	10		J1		15 000 00		15 000 00
	30		J1	3 000 00			12 000 00

FIGURE 4-5 ►
Posted General Ledger Accounts

ACCOUNT *Linda Carter, Capital* ACCOUNT NO. *301*

DATE		DESCRIPTION	POST. REF.	DEBIT	CREDIT	BALANCE DEBIT	BALANCE CREDIT
2004							
Nov.	6		J1		80 000 00		80 000 00

ACCOUNT *Linda Carter, Drawing* ACCOUNT NO. *302*

DATE		DESCRIPTION	POST. REF.	DEBIT	CREDIT	BALANCE DEBIT	BALANCE CREDIT
2004							
Dec.	31		J2	3 000 00		3 000 00	

ACCOUNT *Fees Income* ACCOUNT NO. *401*

DATE		DESCRIPTION	POST. REF.	DEBIT	CREDIT	BALANCE DEBIT	BALANCE CREDIT
2004							
Dec.	31		J2		21 000 00		21 000 00
	31		J2		7 000 00		28 000 00

ACCOUNT *Salaries Expense* ACCOUNT NO. *511*

DATE		DESCRIPTION	POST. REF.	DEBIT	CREDIT	BALANCE DEBIT	BALANCE CREDIT
2004							
Dec.	31		J2	5 000 00		5 000 00	

ACCOUNT *Utilities Expense* ACCOUNT NO. *514*

DATE		DESCRIPTION	POST. REF.	DEBIT	CREDIT	BALANCE DEBIT	BALANCE CREDIT
2004							
Dec.	31		J2	600 00		600 00	

Each ledger account provides a complete record of the increases and decreases to that account. The balance ledger form also shows the current balance for the account.

In the general ledger accounts, the balance sheet accounts appear first and are followed by the income statement accounts. The order is:

- assets
- liabilities
- owner's equity
- revenue
- expenses

This arrangement speeds the preparation of the trial balance and the financial statements.

Order of Accounts

The general ledger lists accounts in the same order as they appear on the trial balance: assets, liabilities, owner's equity, revenue, and expenses.

Accounting Systems

- Business managers should be sure that their firms have efficient procedures for recording transactions.
- A well-designed accounting system allows timely and accurate posting of data to the ledger accounts.
- The information that appears in the financial statements is taken from the general ledger.
- Since management uses financial information for decision making, it is essential that the financial statements be prepared quickly at the end of each period and that they contain the correct amounts.
- The promptness and accuracy of the statements depend on the efficiency of the recording process.
- A well-designed accounting system has a strong audit trail.
- Every business should be able to trace amounts through the accounting records and back to the documents where the transactions were first recorded.

Thinking Critically

What are three situations you might encounter in which you need to "follow" the audit trail?

4 Objective

Correct errors made in the journal or ledger.

Correcting Journal and Ledger Errors

Sometimes errors are made when recording transactions in the journal. For example, a journal entry may show the wrong account name or amount. The method used to correct an error depends on whether or not the journal entry has been posted to the ledger:

- If the error is discovered *before* the entry is posted, neatly cross out the incorrect item and write the correct data above it. Do not erase the error. To ensure honesty and provide a clear audit trail, erasures are not made in the journal.
- If the error is discovered *after* posting, a **correcting entry**—a journal entry made to correct the erroneous entry—is journalized and posted. Do not erase or change the journal entry or the postings in the ledger accounts.

Note that erasures are never permitted in the journal or ledger.

Let's look at an example. On September 1 an automobile repair shop purchased some shop equipment for $8,000 in cash. By mistake the journal entry debited the **Office Equipment** account rather than the **Shop Equipment** account, as follows.

GENERAL JOURNAL PAGE 16

DATE		DESCRIPTION	POST. REF.	DEBIT	CREDIT
2004					
Sept.	1	Office Equipment	141	8000 00	
		Cash	101		8000 00
		Purchased equipment,			
		Check 2141			

The error was discovered after the entry was posted to the ledger. To correct the error, a correcting journal entry was prepared and posted. The correcting entry debits **Shop Equipment** and credits **Office Equipment** for $8,000. This entry transfers $8,000 out of the **Office Equipment** account and into the **Shop Equipment** account.

GENERAL JOURNAL PAGE 28

DATE		DESCRIPTION	POST. REF.	DEBIT	CREDIT
2004					
Oct.	1	Shop Equipment	151	8000 00	
		Office Equipment	141		8000 00
		To correct error made on			
		Sept. 1 when a purchase			
		of shop equipment was			
		recorded as office			
		equipment			

Suppose that the error was discovered before the journal entry was posted to the ledger. In that case the accountant would neatly cross out "Office Equipment" and write "Shop Equipment" above it. The correct account **(Shop Equipment)** would be posted to the ledger in the usual manner.

Section 2 Self Review

Questions

1. What is entered in the Posting Reference column of the general journal?
2. Why are posting references made in ledger accounts and in the journal?
3. Are the following statements true or false? Why?
   a. "If a journal entry that contains an error has been posted, erase the entry and change the posting in the ledger accounts."
   b. "Once an incorrect journal entry has been posted, the incorrect amounts remain in the general ledger accounts."

Exercises

4. The general ledger organizes accounting information in
   a. account order.
   b. alphabetical order.
   c. date order.
5. The general journal organizes accounting information in
   a. account order.
   b. alphabetical order.
   c. date order.

Analysis

6. Draw a diagram of the first three steps of the accounting cycle.

(Answers to Section 2 Self Review are on page 127.)

CHAPTER 4 Review and Applications

Review

Chapter Summary

In this chapter, you have studied the method for journalizing business transactions in the records of a company. The details of each transaction are then posted to the general ledger. A well-designed accounting system provides for prompt and accurate journalizing and posting of all transactions.

Learning Objectives

1 Record transactions in the general journal.

- Recording transactions in a journal is called journalizing, the second step in the accounting cycle.
  - A journal is a daily record of transactions.
  - A written analysis of each transaction is contained in a journal.
- The general journal is widely used in business. It can accommodate all kinds of business transactions. Use the following steps to record a transaction in the general journal:
  - Number each page in the general journal. The page number will be used as a posting reference.
  - Enter the year at the top of the Date column. After that, enter the year only when a new page is started or when the year changes.
  - Enter the month and day in the Date column of the first line of the first entry. After that, enter the month only when a new page is started or when the month changes. Always enter the day on the first line of a new entry.
  - Enter the name of the account to be debited in the Description column.
  - Enter the amount to be debited in the Debit column.
  - Enter the name of the account to be credited on the next line. Indent the account name about one-half inch.
  - Enter the amount to be credited in the Credit column.
  - Enter a complete but concise description on the next line. Indent the description about one inch.
- Note that the debit portion is always recorded first.
- If possible, include source document numbers in descriptions in order to create an audit trail.

2 Prepare compound journal entries.

A transaction might require a journal entry that contains several debits or credits. All debits are recorded first, followed by the credits.

3 Post journal entries to general ledger accounts.

- Posting to the general ledger is the third step in the accounting cycle. Posting is the transfer of data from journal entries to ledger accounts.
- The individual accounts together form a ledger. All the accounts needed to prepare financial statements are found in the general ledger.
- Use the following steps to post a transaction.
  - On the ledger form:
    1. Enter the date of the transaction. Enter the description, if necessary.
    2. Enter the posting reference in the Posting Reference column. When posting from the general journal, use the letter **J** followed by the general journal page number.
    3. Enter the amount in either the Debit column or the Credit column.
    4. Compute the new balance and enter it in either the Debit Balance column or the Credit Balance column.
  - On the general journal:
    5. Enter the ledger account number in the Posting Reference column.
- To summarize the steps of the accounting cycle discussed so far:
  1. Analyze transactions.
  2. Journalize transactions.
  3. Post transactions.

4 Correct errors made in the journal or ledger.

To ensure honesty and to provide a clear audit trail, erasures are not permitted in a journal. A correcting entry is journalized and posted to correct a previous mistake. Posting references in the journal and the ledger accounts cross reference the entries and form another part of the audit trail. They make it possible to trace or recheck any transaction.

5 Define the accounting terms new to this chapter.

CHAPTER 4 GLOSSARY

Accounting cycle (p. 96) A series of steps performed during each accounting period to classify, record, and summarize data for a business and to produce needed financial information

Audit trail (p. 97) A chain of references that makes it possible to trace information, locate errors, and prevent fraud

Balance ledger form (p. 105) A ledger account form that shows the balance of the account after each entry is posted

Chronological order (p. 96) Organized in the order in which the events occur

Compound entry (p. 103) A journal entry with more than one debit or credit

Correcting entry (p. 110) A journal entry made to correct an erroneous entry

General journal (p. 96) A financial record for entering all types of business transactions; a record of original entry

General ledger (p. 105) A permanent, classified record of all accounts used in a firm's operation; a record of final entry

Journal (p. 96) The record of original entry

Journalizing (p. 96) Recording transactions in a journal

Ledger (p. 105) The record of final entry

Posting (p. 105) Transferring data from a journal to a ledger

Comprehensive Self Review

1. Give examples of items that might appear in an audit trail.
2. Which of the following shows both the debits and credits of the entire transaction?
   a. An entry in the general journal
   b. A posting to a general ledger account
3. Why is the ledger called the "record of final entry"?
4. What is recorded in the Posting Reference column of a general journal?
5. How do you correct a journal entry that has not been posted?

(Answers to Comprehensive Self Review are on page 127.)

Discussion Questions

1. What is posting?
2. In what order are accounts arranged in the general ledger? Why?
3. What are posting references? Why are they used?
4. What is an audit trail? Why is it desirable to have an audit trail?
5. How should corrections be made in the general journal?
6. What is the accounting cycle?
7. What is the purpose of a journal?
8. What procedure is used to record an entry in the general journal?
9. What is the value of having a description for each general journal entry?
10. What is a compound journal entry?
11. What is a ledger?

Applications

EXERCISES

Exercise 4-1 ► Objective 1

Analyzing transactions.

Selected accounts from the general ledger of the Express Mail Service follow. Analyze the following transactions and indicate by number what accounts should be debited and credited for each transaction.

101 Cash
111 Accounts Receivable
121 Supplies
131 Equipment
202 Accounts Payable
301 Calvin Jefferson, Capital
401 Fees Income
511 Rent Expense
514 Salaries Expense
517 Utilities Expense

TRANSACTIONS

1. Issued a check for $1,700 to pay the monthly rent.
2. Purchased supplies for $1,000 on credit.
3. The owner made an additional investment of $16,000 in cash.
4. Collected $2,800 from credit customers.
5. Performed services for $3,900 in cash.
6. Issued a check for $1,500 to pay a creditor on account.
7. Purchased new equipment for $2,150 and paid for it immediately by check.
8. Provided services for $5,600 on credit.
9. Sent a check for $600 to the utility company to pay the monthly bill.
10. Gave a cash refund of $180 to a customer because of a lost package. (The customer had previously paid in cash.)

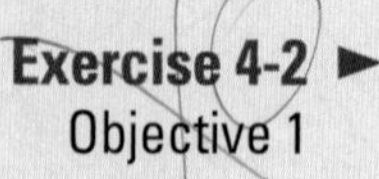

Exercise 4-2 ► Objective 1

Recording transactions in the general journal.

Selected accounts from the general ledger of Custom Decorating Company follow. Record the general journal entries that would be made to record the following transactions. Be sure to include dates and descriptions in these entries.

101 Cash
111 Accounts Receivable
121 Supplies
131 Equipment
141 Automobile
202 Accounts Payable
301 Dan Baxter, Capital
302 Dan Baxter, Drawing
401 Fees Income
511 Rent Expense
514 Salaries Expense
517 Telephone Expense

DATE		TRANSACTIONS
Sept.	1	Dan Baxter invested $26,000 in cash to start the firm.
	4	Purchased office equipment for $5,800 on credit from Zen, Inc.; received Invoice 2398, payable in 30 days.
	16	Purchased an automobile that will be used to visit clients; issued Check 1001 for $10,400 in full payment.
	20	Purchased supplies for $160; paid immediately with Check 1002.
	23	Returned damaged supplies for a cash refund of $50.
	30	Issued Check 1003 for $2,800 to Zen, Inc., as payment on account for Invoice 2398.
	30	Withdrew $1,000 in cash for personal expenses.
	30	Issued Check 1004 for $600 to pay the rent for October.
	30	Performed services for $850 in cash.
	30	Paid $50 for monthly telephone bill, Check 1005.

Posting to the general ledger.

◄ **Exercise 4-3**
Objectives 1, 3

Post the journal entries that you prepared for Exercise 4-2 to the general ledger. Use the account names shown in Exercise 4-2.

Compound journal entries.

◄ **Exercise 4-4**
Objective 2

The following transactions took place at the Talent Search Agency during November 20--. Give the general journal entries that would be made to record these transactions. Use a compound entry for each transaction.

DATE		TRANSACTIONS
Nov.	5	Performed services for Screen Artist, Inc., for $16,000; received $6,000 in cash and the client promised to pay the balance in 60 days.
	18	Purchased a graphing calculator for $150 and some supplies for $200 from Office Supply Center; issued Check 1008 for the total.
	23	Received Invoice 2601 for $900 from Sam's Automotive Services for repairs to the firm's automobile; issued Check 1009 for half the amount and arranged to pay the other half in 30 days.

Recording a correcting entry.

◄ **Exercise 4-5**
Objective 4

On June 5, 20--, an employee of Harris Corporation mistakenly debited **Utilities Expense** rather than **Telephone Expense** when recording a bill of $450 for the May telephone service. The error was discovered on June 30. Prepare a general journal entry to correct the error.

Recording a correcting entry.

◄ **Exercise 4-6**
Objective 4

On August 16, 20--, an employee of Barker Company mistakenly debited the **Truck** account rather than the **Repair Expense** account when recording a bill of $345 for repairs. The error was discovered on September 1. Prepare a general journal entry to correct the error.

Problems

Selected problems can be completed using:
Peachtree QuickBooks Spreadsheets

PROBLEM SET A

Problem 4-1A ►
Objective 1

Recording transactions in the general journal.

The transactions that follow took place at the Fitness Tennis Center during December 20--. This firm has indoor courts where customers can play tennis for a fee. It also rents equipment and offers tennis lessons.

INSTRUCTIONS

Record each transaction in the general journal, using the following chart of accounts. Be sure to number the journal page 1 and to write the year at the top of the Date column. Include a description for each entry.

ASSETS
101 Cash
111 Accounts Receivable
121 Supplies
141 Equipment

LIABILITIES
202 Accounts Payable

OWNER'S EQUITY
301 Martina Garcia, Capital
302 Martina Garcia, Drawing

REVENUE
401 Fees Income

EXPENSES
511 Equipment Repair Expense
512 Rent Expense
513 Salaries Expense
514 Telephone Expense
517 Utilities Expense

DATE		TRANSACTIONS
Dec.	1	Issued Check 2169 for $1,150 to pay the December rent.
	5	Performed services for $2,200 in cash.
	6	Performed services for $1,950 on credit.
	10	Paid $120 for monthly telephone bill; issued Check 2170.
	11	Paid for equipment repairs of $105 with Check 2171.
	12	Received $600 on account from credit clients.
	15	Issued Checks 2172–2177 for $3,200 for salaries.
	18	Issued Check 2178 for $250 to purchase supplies.
	19	Purchased new tennis rackets for $1,850 on credit from The Sports Shop; received Invoice 1133, payable in 30 days.
	20	Issued Check 2179 for $490 to purchase new nets. (Equip.)
	21	Received $650 on account from credit clients.
	21	Returned a damaged net and received a cash refund of $106.
	22	Performed services for $2,980 in cash.
	23	Performed services for $3,520 on credit.
	26	Issued Check 2180 for $280 to purchase supplies.
	28	Paid the monthly electric bill of $475 with Check 2181.
		Continued

DATE	4-1A (cont.) TRANSACTIONS
Dec. 31	Issued Checks 2182–2187 for $3,200 for salaries.
31	Issued Check 2188 for $500 cash to Martina Garcia for personal expenses.

Analyze: If the company paid a bill for supplies on January 1, what check number would be included in the journal entry description?

Journalizing and posting transactions.

◄ **Problem 4-2A**
Objectives 1, 2, 3

QB

On October 1, 20--, Cathy Landers opened an advertising agency. She plans to use the chart of accounts listed below.

INSTRUCTIONS

1. Journalize the transactions. Number the journal page 1, write the year at the top of the Date column, and include a description for each entry.
2. Post to the ledger accounts. Before you start the posting process, open accounts by entering account names and numbers in the headings. Follow the order of the accounts in the chart of accounts.

ASSETS

101 Cash
111 Accounts Receivable
121 Supplies
141 Office Equipment
151 Art Equipment

LIABILITIES

202 Accounts Payable

OWNER'S EQUITY

301 Cathy Landers, Capital
302 Cathy Landers, Drawing

REVENUE

401 Fees Income

EXPENSES

511 Office Cleaning Expense
514 Rent Expense
517 Salaries Expense
520 Telephone Expense
523 Utilities Expense

DATE	TRANSACTIONS
Oct. 1	Cathy Landers invested $60,000 cash in the business.
2	Paid October office rent of $1,900; issued Check 1001.
5	Purchased desks and other office furniture for $12,000 from Discount Mart, Inc.; received Invoice 4767 payable in 60 days.
6	Issued Check 1002 for $3,900 to purchase art equipment.
7	Purchased supplies for $700; paid with Check 1003.
10	Issued Check 1004 for $210 for office cleaning service.
12	Performed services for $1,600 in cash and $4,300 on credit. (Use a compound entry.)
15	Returned damaged supplies for a cash refund of $150.
18	Purchased a computer for $2,100 from Discount Mart, Inc., Invoice 5003; issued Check 1005 for a $1,050 down payment, with the balance payable in 30 days. (Use one compound entry.)
	Continued

DATE	4-2A (cont.) TRANSACTIONS
Oct. 20	Issued Check 1006 for $6,000 to Discount Mart, Inc., as payment on account for Invoice 4767.
26	Performed services for $2,750 on credit.
27	Paid $230 for monthly telephone bill; issued Check 1007.
30	Received $1,600 in cash from credit customers.
30	Mailed Check 1008 to pay the monthly utility bill of $696.
30	Issued Checks 1009–1011 for $5,750 for salaries.

Analyze: What is the balance of account 202 in the general ledger?

Problem 4-3A ► Recording correcting entries.

Objective 4

The following journal entries were prepared by an employee of ABC Company who does not have an adequate knowledge of accounting.

INSTRUCTIONS

Examine the journal entries carefully to locate the errors. Provide a brief written description of each error. Assume that **Office Equipment** and **Office Supplies** were recorded at the correct values.

GENERAL JOURNAL PAGE 3

DATE		DESCRIPTION	POST. REF.	DEBIT	CREDIT
20--					
Mar.	1	Accounts Payable		2 600 00	
		Fees Income			2 600 00
		Performed services on credit			
	2	Cash		2 20 00	
		Telephone Expense			2 20 00
		Paid for February telephone			
		service, Check 1801			
	3	Office Equipment		4 500 00	
		Office Supplies		500 00	
		Cash			5 200 00
		Purchased file cabinet and			
		office supplies, Check 1802			

Analyze: After the correcting journal entries have been posted, what effect do the corrections have on the company's reported assets?

Journalizing and posting transactions.

◄ **Problem 4-4A**
Objectives 1, 2, 3

Four transactions for Traditions Repair Service that took place in November 20-- appear below, along with the general ledger accounts used by the company.

INSTRUCTIONS

Record the transactions in the general journal and post them to the appropriate ledger accounts. Be sure to number the journal page 1 and to write the year at the top of the Date column.

Cash	101	Accounts Payable	202
Accounts Receivable	111	Barbara Doyle, Capital	301
Office Supplies	121	Fees Income	401
Tools	131		
Machinery	141		
Equipment	151		

DATE		TRANSACTIONS
Nov.	1	Barbara Doyle invested $12,500 in cash plus tools with a fair market value of $250 to start the business.
	2	Purchased equipment for $750 and supplies for $250 from Office Ready, Invoice 110; issued Check 100 for $250 as a down payment with the balance due in 30 days.
	10	Performed services for Brian Marshall for $750, who paid $250 in cash with the balance due in 30 days.
	20	Purchased machinery for $1,250 from Zant Machinery, Inc., Invoice 850; issued Check 101 for $250 in cash as a down payment with the balance due in 30 days.

Analyze: What liabilities does the business owe as of November 30?

PROBLEM SET B

Recording transactions in the general journal.

◄ **Problem 4-1B**
Objective 1

The transactions listed on page 120 took place at Chang Commercial Cleaning Service during October 20--. This firm cleans commercial buildings for a fee.

INSTRUCTIONS

Analyze and record each transaction in the general journal. Choose the account names from the chart of accounts shown below. Be sure to number the journal page 1 and to write the year at the top of the Date column.

ASSETS

101 Cash
111 Accounts Receivable
141 Equipment

LIABILITIES

202 Accounts Payable

OWNER'S EQUITY

301 Raymond Chang, Capital
302 Raymond Chang, Drawing

REVENUE

401 Fees Income

EXPENSES

501 Cleaning Supplies Expense
502 Equipment Repair Expense
503 Office Supplies Expense
511 Rent Expense
514 Salaries Expense
521 Telephone Expense
524 Utilities Expense

DATE		TRANSACTIONS
Oct.	1	Raymond Chang invested $36,000 in cash to start the business.
	5	Performed services for $2,400 in cash.
	6	Issued Check 1000 for $1,700 to pay the October rent.
	7	Performed services for $1,800 on credit.
	9	Paid $300 for monthly telephone bill; issued Check 1001.
	10	Issued Check 1002 for $240 for equipment repairs.
	12	Received $850 from credit clients.
	14	Issued Checks 1003–1004 for $7,200 to pay salaries.
	18	Issued Check 1005 for $600 for cleaning supplies.
	19	Issued Check 1006 for $500 for office supplies.
	20	Purchased equipment for $5,000 from Casey's Equipment, Inc., Invoice 2010; issued Check 1007 for $1,000 with the balance due in 30 days.
	22	Performed services for $3,950 in cash.
	24	Issued Check 1008 for $380 for the monthly electric bill.
	26	Performed services for $1,800 on account.
	30	Issued Checks 1009–1010 for $7,200 to pay salaries.
	30	Issued Check 1011 for $2,000 to Raymond Chang to pay for personal expenses.

Analyze: How many transactions affected expense accounts?

Problem 4-2B ►
Objectives 1, 2, 3

Journalizing and posting transactions.

In July 20-- Richard Hailey opened a photography studio that provides services to public and private schools. His firm's financial activities for the first month of operations are listed on page 121. The chart of accounts appears below.

INSTRUCTIONS

1. Journalize the transactions. Number the journal page 1 and write the year at the top of the Date column. Describe each entry.
2. Post to the ledger accounts. Before you start the posting process, open the accounts by entering the names and numbers in the headings. Follow the order of the accounts in the chart of accounts.

ASSETS
101 Cash
111 Accounts Receivable
121 Supplies
141 Office Equipment
151 Photographic Equipment

LIABILITIES
202 Accounts Payable

OWNER'S EQUITY
301 Richard Hailey, Capital
302 Richard Hailey, Drawing

REVENUE
401 Fees Income

EXPENSES
511 Office Cleaning Expense
514 Rent Expense
517 Salaries Expense
520 Telephone Expense
523 Utilities Expense

DATE		TRANSACTIONS
July	1	Richard Hailey invested $28,000 cash in the business.
	2	Issued Check 1001 for $800 to pay the July rent.
	5	Purchased desks and other office furniture for $6,500 from Craft, Inc.; received Invoice 4762, payable in 60 days.
	6	Issued Check 1002 for $1,600 to purchase photographic equipment.
	7	Purchased supplies for $416; paid with Check 1003.
	10	Issued Check 1004 for $110 for office cleaning service.
	12	Performed services for $600 in cash and $1,300 on credit. (Use one compound entry.)
	15	Returned damaged supplies; received a $60 cash refund.
	18	Purchased a computer for $1,050 from Brown Office Supply, Invoice 430; issued Check 1005 for a $250 down payment. The balance is payable in 30 days. (Use one compound entry.)
	20	Issued Check 1006 for $3,250 to Craft, Inc., as payment on account for office furniture, Invoice 4762.
	26	Performed services for $1,400 on credit.
	27	Paid $120 for monthly telephone bill; issued Check 1007.
	30	Received $1,100 in cash from credit clients on account.
	30	Issued Check 1008 to pay the monthly utility bill of $250.
	30	Issued Checks 1009–1011 for $4,800 for salaries.

Analyze: What was the **Cash** account balance after the transaction of July 20 was recorded?

Recording correcting entries.

◄ **Problem 4-3B**
Objective 4

All the journal entries shown on page 122 contain errors. The entries were prepared by an employee of Becknell Corporation who does not have an adequate knowledge of accounting.

INSTRUCTIONS

Examine the journal entries carefully to locate the errors. Provide a brief written description of each error. Assume that **Office Equipment** and **Office Supplies** were recorded at the correct values.

GENERAL JOURNAL					PAGE 1
DATE		DESCRIPTION	POST. REF.	DEBIT	CREDIT
20--					
Jan.	1	*Accounts Payable*		*750 00*	
		Fees Income			*750 00*
		Performed services on credit			
	2	*Cash*		*65 00*	
		Telephone Expense			*65 00*
		Paid for January telephone			
		service, Check 1706			
	3	*Office Equipment*		*675 00*	
		Office Supplies		*85 00*	
		Cash			*700 00*
		Purchased file cabinet and			
		office supplies, Check 1707			

Analyze: After the correcting journal entries have been posted, what effect do the corrections have on the reported assets of the company?

Problem 4-4B ► Objectives 1, 2, 3

Journalizing and posting transactions.

Several transactions that occurred during December 20--, the first month of operation for Louise's Accounting Services, follow. The company uses the general ledger accounts listed below.

INSTRUCTIONS

Record the transactions in the general journal (page 1) and post to the appropriate accounts.

Cash	101	Accounts Payable	202
Accounts Receivable	111	Louise Hodges, Capital	301
Office Supplies	121	Fees Income	401
Computers	131		
Office Equipment	141		
Furniture & Fixtures	151		

DATE		TRANSACTIONS
Dec.	3	Louise Hodges began business by depositing $20,000 cash into a business checking account.
	4	Purchased a computer for $4,400 cash.
	5	Purchased furniture and fixtures on account for $6,000.
	6	Purchased office equipment for $1,190 cash.
	10	Rendered services to client and sent bill for $1,000.
	11	Purchased office supplies for $450.
	15	Received invoice for furniture purchased on December 5 and paid it.

Analyze: Describe the activity for account 202 during the month.

CHAPTER 4 CHALLENGE PROBLEM

Start-Up Business

On June 1, 20--, Darren McDonald opened the Dance and Voice Agency. He plans to use the chart of accounts given below.

INSTRUCTIONS

1. Journalize the transactions. Be sure to number the journal pages and write the year at the top of the Date column. Include a description for each entry.
2. Post to the ledger accounts. Before you start the posting process, open the accounts by entering the account names and numbers in the headings. Using the list of accounts below, assign appropriate account numbers and place them in the correct order in the ledger.
3. Prepare a trial balance.
4. Prepare the income statement.
5. Prepare a statement of owner's equity.
6. Prepare the balance sheet.

ACCOUNTS

Accounts Payable	Darren McDonald, Drawing
Office Furniture	Recording Equipment
Accounts Receivable	Rent Expense
Advertising Expense	Salaries Expense
Cash	Supplies
Fees Income	Telephone Expense
Darren McDonald, Capital	Utilities Expense

DATE		TRANSACTIONS
June	1	Darren McDonald invested $40,000 cash to start the business.
	2	Issued Check 301 for $1,600 to pay the June rent for the office.
	3	Purchased desk and other office furniture for $10,000 from Lawson Office Supply, Invoice 3105; issued Check 302 for a $2,000 down payment with the balance due in 30 days.
	4	Issued Check 303 for $1,800 for supplies.
	6	Performed services for $5,000 in cash.
	7	Issued Check 304 for $1,000 to pay for advertising expense.
	8	Purchased recording equipment for $12,000 from Top Ten Dance and Sounds, Inc., Invoice 3330; issued Check 305 for a down payment of $4,000 with the balance due in 30 days.
	10	Performed services for $3,700 on account.
	11	Issued Check 306 for $2,000 to Lawson Office Supply as payment on account.
	12	Performed services for $6,000 in cash.

Continued

DATE	(cont.) TRANSACTIONS
15	Issued Check 307 for $4,000 to pay an employee's salary.
18	Received payments of $2,000 from credit clients on account.
20	Issued Check 308 for $3,000 to Top Ten Dance and Sounds, Inc. as payment on account.
25	Issued Check 309 in the amount of $750 for the monthly telephone bill.
27	Issued Check 310 in the amount of $900 for the monthly electric bill.
28	Issued Check 311 to Darren McDonald for $3,000 for personal living expenses.
30	Issued Check 312 for $4,000 to pay salary of an employee.

Analyze: How many postings were made to the **Cash** account?

CHAPTER 4 CRITICAL THINKING PROBLEM

Financial Statements

Jim Hall is a new staff accountant for Sutton Cleaning Chemicals. He has asked you to review the financial statements prepared for April to find and correct any errors. Review the income statement and balance sheet that follow and identify the errors Hall made (he did not prepare a statement of owner's equity). Prepare a corrected income statement and balance sheet as well as a statement of owner's equity, for Sutton Cleaning Chemicals.

Sutton Cleaning Chemicals
Income Statement
April 30, 20--

Revenue		
Fees Income		*6 200 00*
Expenses		
Salaries Expense	*2 250 00*	
Rent Expense	*450 00*	
Repair Expense	*75 00*	
Utilities Expense	*650 00*	
Drawing	*1 000 00*	
Total Expenses		*4 425 00*
Net Income		*10 625 00*

Sutton Cleaning Chemicals
Balance Sheet
Month Ended April 30, 20--

Assets		*Liabilities*	
Land	*5 000 00*	*Accounts Receivable*	*2 500 00*
Building	*15 000 00*		
Cash	*6 775 00*	*Owner's Equity*	
Accounts Payable	*2 500 00*	*Scott Jones, Capital, April 1, 20--*	*25 000 00*
Total Assets	*29 275 00*	*Total Liabilities and Owner's Equity*	*27 500 00*

Business Connections

MANAGERIAL FOCUS **Business Records** ◄ **Connection 1**

1. The owner of a new business recently questioned the accountant about the value of having both a journal and a ledger. The owner believes that it is a waste of effort to enter data about transactions in two different records. How would you explain the value of having both records?
2. Why should management insist that a firm's accounting system have a strong audit trail?
3. Why should management be concerned about the efficiency of a firm's procedures for journalizing and posting transactions?
4. How might a poor set of recording procedures affect the flow of information to management?

Ethical DILEMMA **Testing** You and your roommate are taking principles of accounting from the same professor but at different times. After the first exam, you discover that the professor gives the same exam to both sections. Your roommate has not been studying as much since this discovery and is depending on you to furnish him with the answers to questions on the second exam. What will you do? ◄ **Connection 2**

Street **WISE:** Questions from the Real World **General Ledger Accounts** Refer to The Home Depot, Inc. *1999 Annual Report* in Appendix B. ◄ **Connection 3**

1. Review the report called *Selected Consolidated Statements of Earnings Data.* How many sales transactions were reported for 1999? For sales on account transactions, which accounts would be affected when the transactions are recorded?
2. Based on the financial statements, which account categories would be affected by the following transactions?
   a. Paid $5,000 cash for store rent.
   b. Paid $2,000 cash for store utility bill.
   c. Received $1,000 from a customer in payment of their account.

FINANCIAL STATEMENT ANALYSIS **Balance Sheet** Review the following excerpt taken from the Wal-Mart Stores, Inc. consolidated balance sheet as of January 31, 2000. ◄ **Connection 4** WAL★MART

(Amounts in millions) January 31, 2000	
Property, Plant and Equipment at cost:	
Land	$ 8,785
Building and improvements	21,169
Fixtures and equipment	10,362
Transportation equipment	747

Analyze:

1. When the accountant for Wal-Mart Stores, Inc. records a purchase of transportation equipment, what type of account is debited? If Wal-Mart purchases transportation equipment on credit, what account might be credited?
2. What type of source document might be reflected in the journal entry to record the purchase of equipment?
3. If the accounting manager reviewed the **Transportation Equipment** account in the general ledger, what types of information might be listed there? What ending balance would be reflected at January 31, 2000?

Analyze Online: Locate the Web site for the Wal-Mart Stores, Inc. (**www.walmartstores.com**), which provides an online store for consumers as well as corporation information. Within the Web site, locate the consolidated balance sheet for the current year.

4. What kinds of property, plant, and equipment are listed on the balance sheet?
5. What is the balance reported for transportation equipment?

Connection 5 ► *Extending the Thought* **Getting Organized** Business transactions are recorded in a financial record called a journal. List and discuss other organizational records and devices used in everyday life. Why are these records and devices used? What similarities do these records share with the journal used in accounting?

Connection 6 ► **Business Communication** **Training Manual** You have been asked to teach a new accounting clerk how to journalize business transactions. Create a written step-by-step guide to give to the new accounting clerk on his first day at work. Use a sample business transaction of your choice to illustrate the process.

Connection 7 ► **TeamWork** **Interview** Business owners use financial information to prepare for future operations and to make business decisions. As a team, choose a local business in your area and interview the owner or manager to discover how financial data has influenced the operations of the business. First, make a list of questions to ask the business owner. Prepare a summary report of your findings.

Connection 8 ► **interNET CONNECTION** **SEC** The Securities and Exchange Commission is an independent regulatory agency that administers the federal laws related to securities such as stock in corporations. Go to **www.sec.gov** and select *Investor Education.* Search terms for *Annual Report.* What information is usually contained in an annual report? What is a Form 10K? What is an IPO?

Answers to Self Reviews

Answers to Section 1 Self Review

1. To provide an audit trail to trace information through the accounting system.
2. No. The only requirement is that the total debits must equal the total credits.
3. It is the first accounting record where transactions are entered.
4. **c.** diary.
5. **c.** debit.
6. The audit trail will not exist.

Answers to Section 2 Self Review

1. The ledger account number.
2. They indicate that the entry has been posted and ensure against posting the same entry twice.
3. Both statements are false. If an incorrect journal entry was posted, a correcting entry should be journalized and posted. To ensure honesty and provide a clear audit trail, erasures are not permitted in the journal.
4. **a.** account order.
5. **c.** date order.
6. 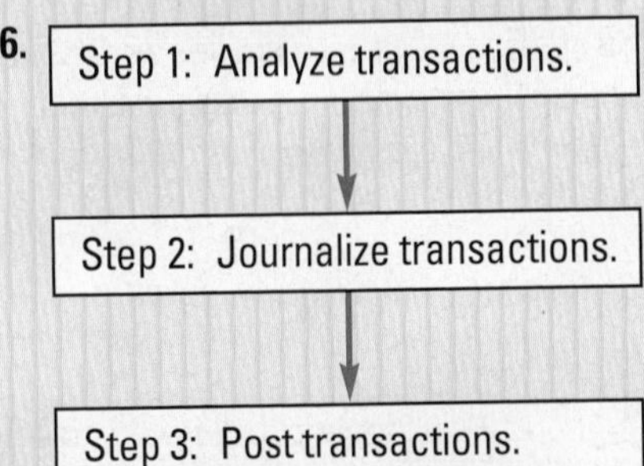

Answers to Comprehensive Self Review

1. Check number
   Invoice number for goods purchased on credit from a vendor
   Invoice number for services billed to a charge account customer
   Memorandum number
2. **a.** An entry in the general journal
3. It is the last accounting record in which a transaction is recorded.
4. The general ledger account number.
5. Neatly cross out the incorrect item and write the correct data above it.

CHAPTER 5

Learning Objectives

1. Complete a trial balance on a worksheet.
2. Prepare adjustments for unrecorded business transactions.
3. Complete the worksheet.
4. Prepare an income statement, statement of owner's equity, and balance sheet from the completed worksheet.
5. Journalize and post the adjusting entries.
6. Define the accounting terms new to this chapter.

Adjustments and the Worksheet

www.boeing.com

The construction and development of the International Space Station (ISS) has been characterized by Boeing Chairman and CEO Phil Condit as "one of the most complex and challenging projects ever undertaken."[1] Boeing is the ISS's prime contractor.

In early 2001 the Boeing-built *Destiny* laboratory was successfully installed on the ISS, providing a shirtsleeve workstation environment where science experiments can be performed in the near zero gravity of space. *Destiny* also provides command and control capabilities as well as maintenance of the proper orientation of the outpost.

Efforts in the space and communications sectors have proven successful for the company. In the first quarter of 2001, the Space and Communications division reported a 35 percent increase in revenue as compared to the first quarter of 2000.

1 Boeing Web site: International Space Station/Boeing's Role

Thinking Critically

How do you think the company accounts for the wear and tear of its own equipment?

For more information on Boeing, go to: collegeaccounting.glencoe.com.

New Terms

- **Account form balance sheet**
- **Adjusting entries**
- **Adjustments**
- **Book value**
- **Contra account**
- **Contra asset account**
- **Depreciation**
- **Prepaid expenses**
- **Report form balance sheet**
- **Salvage value**
- **Straight-line depreciation**
- **Worksheet**

Section 1

Section Objectives

1. **Complete a trial balance on a worksheet.**

   Why It's Important
   Time and effort can be saved when the trial balance is prepared directly on the worksheet. Amounts can be easily transferred to other sections of the worksheet.

2. **Prepare adjustments for unrecorded business transactions.**

   Why It's Important
   Not all business transactions occur between separate business entities. Some financial events occur within a business and need to be recorded.

Terms to Learn

adjusting entries
adjustments
book value
contra account
contra asset account
depreciation
prepaid expenses
salvage value
straight-line depreciation
worksheet

The Worksheet

Financial statements are completed as soon as possible in order to be useful. One way to speed the preparation of financial statements is to use a worksheet. A **worksheet** is a form used to gather all data needed at the end of an accounting period to prepare the financial statements. Preparation of the worksheet is the fourth step in the accounting cycle.

Figure 5-1 shows a common type of worksheet. The heading shows the company name, report title, and period covered. In addition to the Account Name column, this worksheet contains five sections: Trial Balance, Adjustments, Adjusted Trial Balance, Income Statement, and Balance Sheet. Each section includes a Debit column and a Credit column. The worksheet has 10 columns in which to enter dollar amounts.

The Trial Balance Section

Refer to Figure 5-2 on page 132 as you read about how to prepare the Trial Balance section of the worksheet.

1. Enter the general ledger account names.
2. Transfer the general ledger account balances to the Debit and Credit columns of the Trial Balance section.
3. Total the Debit and Credit columns to prove that the trial balance is in balance.
4. Place a double rule under each Trial Balance column to show that the work in that column is complete.

Notice that the trial balance has four new accounts: **Accumulated Depreciation—Equipment, Supplies Expense, Rent Expense,** and **Depreciation Expense—Equipment.** These accounts have zero balances now, but they will be needed later as the worksheet is completed.

The Adjustments Section

Usually account balances change because of transactions with other businesses or individuals. For Carter Consulting Services, the account changes recorded in Chapter 4 were caused by transactions with the

1 Objective
Complete a trial balance on a worksheet.

Trial Balance
If total debits do not equal total credits, there is an error in the financial records. The error must be found and corrected.

Carter Consulting Services
Worksheet
Month Ended December 31, 2004

	ACCOUNT NAME	TRIAL BALANCE		ADJUSTMENTS	
		DEBIT	CREDIT	DEBIT	CREDIT
1					
2					
3					
4					
5					

firm's suppliers, customers, the landlord, and employees. It is easy to recognize, journalize, and post these transactions as they occur.

Some changes are not caused by transactions with other businesses or individuals. They arise from the internal operations of the firm during the accounting period. Journal entries made to update accounts for previously unrecorded items are called **adjustments** or **adjusting entries**. These changes are first entered on the worksheet at the end of each accounting period. The worksheet provides a convenient form for gathering the information and determining the effects of the changes. Let's look at the adjustments made by Carter Consulting Services on December 31, 2004.

❷ Objective

Prepare adjustments for unrecorded business transactions.

Trial Balance

On the trial balance, accounts are listed in this order: assets, liabilities, owner's equity, revenue, and expenses.

Adjusting for Supplies Used

On November 28, 2004, Carter Consulting Services purchased $2,000 of supplies. On December 31 the trial balance shows a $2,000 balance in the **Supplies** account. This amount is too high because some of the supplies were used during December.

An adjustment must be made for the supplies used. Otherwise, the asset account, **Supplies,** is overstated because fewer supplies are actually on hand. The expense account, **Supplies Expense,** is understated. The cost of the supplies used represents an operating expense that has not been recorded.

On December 31 Beatrice Wilson counted the supplies. Remaining supplies totaled $1,500. This meant that supplies amounting to $500 were used during December ($2,000 − $1,500 = $500). At the end of December, an adjustment must be made to reflect the supplies used. The adjustment reduces the **Supplies** account to $1,500, the amount of supplies remaining. It increases the **Supplies Expense** account by $500 for the amount of supplies used. Notice that the adjustment for supplies is based on actual usage.

Refer to Figure 5-2 on page 132 to review the adjustment on the worksheet: a debit of $500 to **Supplies Expense** and a credit of $500 to **Supplies.** Both the debit and credit are labeled **(a)** to identify the two parts of the adjustment.

Supplies is a type of prepaid expense. **Prepaid expenses** are items that are acquired and paid for in advance of their use. Other common prepaid expenses are prepaid rent, prepaid insurance, and prepaid advertising. When cash is paid for these items, amounts are debited to **Prepaid Rent, Prepaid Insurance,** and **Prepaid Advertising;** all are asset accounts. As prepaid expenses are used, an adjustment is made to reduce the asset accounts and to increase the related expense accounts.

About Accounting

E-business

E-commerce and e-business are not the same thing. *E-commerce* is only a small piece of e-business. *E-business* relates to automating an entire company and all its business processes, including electronic transaction workflows, online storefronts, self-service data access, and the reengineering of business processes.

ADJUSTED TRIAL BALANCE		INCOME STATEMENT		BALANCE SHEET		
DEBIT	CREDIT	DEBIT	CREDIT	DEBIT	CREDIT	
						1
						2
						3
						4
						5

◄ **FIGURE 5-1**
Ten-column Worksheet

Carter Consulting Services
Worksheet
Month Ended December 31, 2004

	ACCOUNT NAME	TRIAL BALANCE DEBIT	TRIAL BALANCE CREDIT	ADJUSTMENTS DEBIT	ADJUSTMENTS CREDIT
1	*Cash*	64 400 00			
2	*Accounts Receivable*	4 000 00			
3	*Supplies*	2 000 00			(a) 500 00
4	*Prepaid Rent*	6 000 00			(b) 3 000 00
5	*Equipment*	35 000 00			
6	*Accumulated Depreciation—Equipment*				(c) 583 00
7	*Accounts Payable*		12 000 00		
8	*Linda Carter, Capital*		80 000 00		
9	*Linda Carter, Drawing*	3 000 00			
10	*Fees Income*		28 000 00		
11	*Salaries Expense*	5 000 00			
12	*Utilities Expense*	600 00			
13	*Supplies Expense*			(a) 500 00	
14	*Rent Expense*			(b) 3 000 00	
15	*Depreciation Expense—Equipment*			(c) 583 00	
16	*Totals*	120 000 00	120 000 00	4 083 00	4 083 00
17					

▲ **FIGURE 5-2** A Partial Worksheet

Adjustment

Record the adjustment for supplies.

Analysis

The expense account, **Supplies Expense,** is increased by $500. The asset account, **Supplies,** is decreased by $500.

Debit-Credit Rules

DEBIT Increases to expense accounts are recorded as debits. Debit **Supplies Expense** for $500.

CREDIT Decreases to asset accounts are recorded as credits. Credit **Supplies** for $500.

T-Account Presentation

Supplies Expense +	Supplies Expense −
500	

Supplies +	Supplies −
	500

Let's review the effect of the adjustment on the asset account, **Supplies.** Recall that the **Supplies** account already had a balance of $2,000. If no adjustment is made, the balance would remain at $2,000, even though only $1,500 of supplies are left.

Supplies			
+		−	
Bal.	2,000		
		Adj.	500
Bal.	1,500		

Adjusting for Expired Rent

On November 30, 2004, Carter Consulting Services paid $6,000 rent for December and January. The right to occupy facilities for the specified period is an asset. The $6,000 was debited to **Prepaid Rent,** an asset account. On December 31, 2004, the **Prepaid Rent** balance is $6,000. This is too high because one month of rent has been used. The expired rent is $3,000 ($6,000 ÷ 2 months). At the end of December, an adjustment is made to reflect the expired rent.

Adjustment

Record the adjustment for expired rent.

Analysis

The expense account, **Rent Expense,** is increased by $3,000. The asset account, **Prepaid Rent,** is decreased by $3,000.

Debit-Credit Rules

DEBIT Increases to expense accounts are recorded as debits. Debit **Rent Expense** for $3,000.

CREDIT Decreases to asset accounts are recorded as credits. Credit **Prepaid Rent** for $3,000.

T-Account Presentation

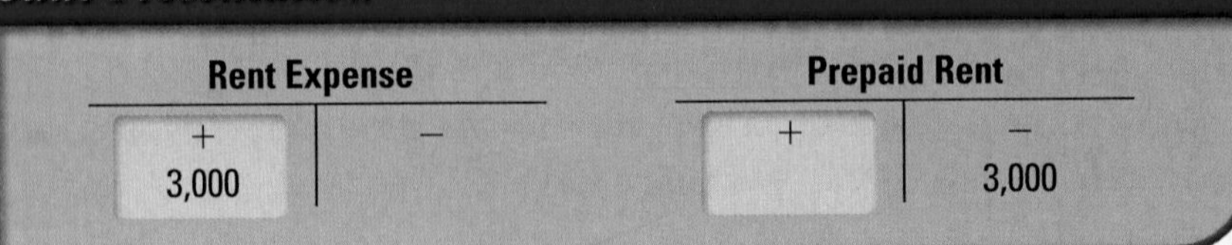

Rent Expense	
+	−
3,000	

Prepaid Rent	
+	−
	3,000

Let's review the effect of the adjustment on the asset account, **Prepaid Rent.** The beginning balance of $6,000 represents prepaid rent for the months of December and January. By December 31, the prepaid rent for the month of December is "used up." The adjustment reducing **Prepaid Rent** recognizes the expense of occupying the facilities in December. The $3,000 ending balance represents prepaid rent for the month of January.

Prepaid Rent			
+		−	
Bal.	6,000		
		Adj.	3,000
Bal.	3,000		

Important!

Prepaid Expense

Prepaid rent is recorded as an asset at the time it is paid. As time elapses, the asset is used up. An adjustment is made to reduce the asset and to recognize rent expense.

Computers in Accounting

Computerized Accounting Systems

Computerized systems are widely used by companies to record, summarize, and analyze large volumes of financial data. From the Disney corporate offices in Burbank, California, to the Southwest Airlines headquarters in Dallas, Texas, accountants prepare paychecks, track bank accounts, and generate financial statements using computerized applications. Accounting systems can be standard commercial packages or customized to fit the unique needs of a company. Six common types of accounting applications are available: general ledger, accounts receivable, accounts payable, sales/order processing, inventory control, and payroll.

General ledger programs are basic to any computerized accounting system and are used to record general journal entries. Posting is completed automatically by the computer. The accountant can easily generate reports such as the trial balance, income statement, balance sheet, or statement of owner's equity. At the end of the accounting period, the general ledger program will complete the closing process, preparing the records for the next accounting period.

Other programs provide tools to the accountant for managing accounts receivable, accounts payable, payroll, and inventory.

Companies may use one or more of these accounting applications, or they may build or purchase a completely integrated package of applications. An "integrated" accounting system means that each module, or application, communicates and transfers data to other modules, keeping the accounting records in balance across all programs.

Thinking Critically

What benefits can you identify to using an integrated computerized accounting system?

Internet Application

Using an Internet search engine, locate information on the general ledger module for AccuBooks accounting software. Create a summary report describing the features of the general ledger module.

Refer to Figure 5-2 to review the adjustment on the worksheet: a debit of $3,000 to **Rent Expense** and a credit of $3,000 to **Prepaid Rent.** Both parts of the adjustment are labeled **(b).**

Adjusting for Depreciation

There is one more adjustment to make at the end of December. It involves the equipment purchased in November. The cost of long-term assets such as equipment is not recorded as an expense when purchased. Instead the cost is recorded as an asset and spread over the time the assets are used for the business. **Depreciation** is the process of allocating the cost of long-term assets over their expected useful lives. There are many ways to calculate depreciation. Carter Consulting Services uses the **straight-line depreciation** method. This method results in an equal amount of depreciation being charged to each accounting period during the asset's useful life. The formula for straight-line depreciation is

$$\text{Depreciation} = \frac{\text{Cost} - \text{Salvage value}}{\text{Estimated useful life}}$$

Salvage value is an estimate of the amount that may be received by selling or disposing of an asset at the end of its useful life.

Carter Consulting Services purchased $35,000 worth of equipment. The equipment has an estimated useful life of five years and no salvage value. The depreciation for December, the first month of operations, is $583 (rounded).

$$\frac{\$35{,}000 - \$0}{60 \text{ months}} = \$583 \text{ (rounded)}$$

1. Convert the asset's useful life from years to months: 5 years × 12 months = 60 months.
2. Divide the total depreciation to be taken by the total number of months: $35,000 ÷ 60 = $583 (rounded).
3. Record depreciation expense of $583 each month for the next 60 months.

Conoco Inc. depreciates property such as refinery equipment, pipelines, and deepwater drill ships on a straight-line basis over the estimated life of each asset, ranging from 15 to 25 years.

As the cost of the equipment is gradually transferred to expense, its recorded value as an asset must be reduced. This procedure cannot be carried out by directly decreasing the balance in the asset account. Generally accepted accounting principles require that the original cost of a long-term asset continue to appear in the asset account until the firm has used up or disposed of the asset.

The adjustment for depreciation is recorded in a contra account named **Accumulated Depreciation—Equipment.** A **contra account** has a normal balance that is opposite that of a related account. For example, the **Equipment** account is an asset and has a normal debit balance. **Accumulated Depreciation—Equipment** is a **contra asset account** with a normal credit balance, which is opposite the normal balance of an asset account. The adjustment to reflect depreciation for December is a $583 debit to **Depreciation Expense—Equipment** and a $583 credit to **Accumulated Depreciation—Equipment.**

The **Accumulated Depreciation—Equipment** account is a record of all depreciation taken on the equipment. The financial records show the original cost of the equipment (**Equipment,** $35,000) and all depreciation taken (**Accumulated Depreciation—Equipment,** $583). The difference between the two accounts is called book value. **Book value** is that portion of an asset's original cost that has not yet been depreciated. Three amounts are reported on the financial statements for equipment:

Important!

Contra Accounts

The normal balance for a contra account is the opposite of the related account. **Accumulated Depreciation** is a contra asset account. The normal balance of an asset account is a *debit.* The normal balance of a contra asset account is a *credit.*

Adjustment

Record the adjustment for depreciation.

Analysis

The expense account, **Depreciation Expense—Equipment,** is increased by $583. The contra asset account, **Accumulated Depreciation—Equipment,** is increased by $583.

Debit-Credit Rules

DEBIT Increases to expense accounts are recorded as debits. Debit **Depreciation Expense—Equipment** for $583.

CREDIT Increases to contra asset accounts are recorded as credits. Credit **Accumulated Depreciation—Equipment** for $583.

T-Account Presentation

Depreciation Expense—Equipment	
+	−
583	

Accumulated Depreciation—Equipment	
−	+
	583

Equipment	$35,000
Less accumulated depreciation	− 583
Equipment at book value	$34,417

Refer to Figure 5-2 on page 132 to review the depreciation adjustment on the worksheet. The two parts of the adjustment are labeled **(c)**.

If Carter Consulting Services had other kinds of long-term assets, an adjustment for depreciation would be made for each one. Long-term assets include land, buildings, equipment, trucks, automobiles, furniture, and fixtures. Depreciation is calculated on all long-term assets except land. Land is not depreciated.

Notice that each adjustment involved a balance sheet account (an asset or a contra asset) and an income statement account (an expense). When all adjustments have been entered, total and rule the Adjustments columns. Be sure that the totals of the Debit and Credit columns are equal. If they are not, locate and correct the error or errors before continuing. Figure 5-2 shows the completed Adjustments section.

Section 1 Self Review

Questions

1. Why is the worksheet prepared?
2. What are adjustments?
3. Why are prepaid expenses adjusted at the end of an accounting period?

Exercises

4. A firm paid $500 for supplies during the accounting period. At the end of the accounting period, the firm had $150 of supplies on hand. What adjustment is entered on the worksheet?
   a. **Supplies Expense** is debited for $350 and **Supplies** is credited for $350.
   b. **Supplies** is debited for $150 and **Supplies Expense** is credited for $150.
   c. **Supplies Expense** is debited for $150 and **Supplies** is credited for $150.
   d. **Supplies** is debited for $350 and **Supplies Expense** is credited for $350.
5. On January 1 a firm paid $9,000 for six months' rent, January through June. What is the adjustment for rent expense at the end of January?
   a. **Rent Expense** is debited for $9,000 and **Prepaid Rent** is credited for $9,000.
   b. **Rent Expense** is debited for $1,500 and **Prepaid Rent** is credited for $1,500.
   c. **Prepaid Rent** is debited for $1,500 and **Rent Expense** is credited for $1,500.
   d. No adjustment is made until the end of June.

Analysis

6. Three years ago T.K. Systems bought a delivery truck for $25,000. The truck has no salvage value and a five-year useful life. What is the book value of the truck at the end of three years?

(Answers to Section 1 Self Review are on page 161.)

Section 2

Financial Statements

The worksheet is used to prepare the financial statements. Preparing financial statements is the fifth step in the accounting cycle.

Section Objectives

3. **Complete the worksheet.**

   Why It's Important
   The worksheet summarizes both internal and external financial events of a period.

4. **Prepare an income statement, statement of owner's equity, and balance sheet from the completed worksheet.**

   Why It's Important
   Using a worksheet saves time in preparing the financial statements.

5. **Journalize and post the adjusting entries.**

   Why It's Important
   Adjusting entries update the financial records of the business.

Terms to Learn

account form balance sheet
report form balance sheet

The Adjusted Trial Balance Section

The next task is to prepare the Adjusted Trial Balance section.

1. Combine the figures from the Trial Balance section and the Adjustments section of the worksheet. Record the computed results in the Adjusted Trial Balance columns.
2. Total the Debit and Credit columns in the Adjusted Trial Balance section. Confirm that debits equal credits.

3 Objective

Complete the worksheet.

Figure 5-3 on pages 138–139 shows the completed Adjusted Trial Balance section of the worksheet. The accounts that do not have adjustments are simply extended from the Trial Balance section to the Adjusted Trial Balance section. For example, the **Cash** account balance of $64,400 is recorded in the Debit column of the Adjusted Trial Balance section without change.

The balances of accounts that are affected by adjustments are recomputed. Look at the **Supplies** account. It has a $2,000 debit balance in the Trial Balance section and shows a $500 credit in the Adjustments section. The new balance is $1,500 ($2,000 − $500). It is recorded in the Debit column of the Adjusted Trial Balance section.

Use the following guidelines to compute the amounts for the Adjusted Trial Balance section.

- If the account has a debit balance in the Trial Balance section and a debit entry in the Adjustments section, add the two amounts.
- If the account has a debit balance in the Trial Balance section and a credit entry in the Adjustments section, subtract the credit amount.
- If the account has a credit balance in the Trial Balance section and a credit entry in the Adjustments section, add the two amounts.
- If the account has a credit balance in the Trial Balance section and a debit entry in the Adjustments section, subtract the debit amount.

If the Trial Balance section has a:	AND if the entry in the Adjustments section is a:	Then:
Debit balance	Debit	Add the amounts.
Debit balance	Credit	Subtract the credit amount.
Credit balance	Credit	Add the amounts.
Credit balance	Debit	Subtract the debit amount.

	Carter Consulting Services Worksheet Month Ended December 31, 2004				
	ACCOUNT NAME	TRIAL BALANCE		ADJUSTMENTS	
		DEBIT	CREDIT	DEBIT	CREDIT
1	*Cash*	64,400.00			
2	*Accounts Receivable*	4,000.00			
3	*Supplies*	2,000.00			(a) 500.00
4	*Prepaid Rent*	6,000.00			(b) 3,000.00
5	*Equipment*	35,000.00			
6	*Accumulated Depreciation—Equipment*				(c) 583.00
7	*Accounts Payable*		12,000.00		
8	*Linda Carter, Capital*		80,000.00		
9	*Linda Carter, Drawing*	3,000.00			
10	*Fees Income*		28,000.00		
11	*Salaries Expense*	5,000.00			
12	*Utilities Expense*	600.00			
13	*Supplies Expense*			(a) 500.00	
14	*Rent Expense*			(b) 3,000.00	
15	*Depreciation Expense—Equipment*			(c) 583.00	
16	*Totals*	120,000.00	120,000.00	4,083.00	4,083.00
17	*Net Income*				

▲ **FIGURE 5-3**
Partial Worksheet

Prepaid Rent has a Trial Balance debit of $6,000 and an Adjustments credit of $3,000. Enter $3,000 ($6,000 − $3,000) in the Adjusted Trial Balance Debit column.

Four accounts that started with zero balances in the Trial Balance section are affected by adjustments. They are **Accumulated Depreciation—Equipment, Supplies Expense, Rent Expense,** and **Depreciation Expense—Equipment.** The figures in the Adjustments section are simply extended to the Adjusted Trial Balance section. For example, **Accumulated Depreciation—Equipment** has a zero balance in the Trial Balance section and a $583 credit in the Adjustments section. Extend the $583 to the Adjusted Trial Balance Credit column.

Once all account balances are recorded in the Adjusted Trial Balance section, total and rule the Debit and Credit columns. Be sure that total debits equal total credits. If they are not equal, find and correct the error or errors.

Locating Errors
If total debits do not equal total credits, find the difference between total debits and total credits. If the difference is divisible by 9, there could be a transposition error. If the difference is divisible by 2, an amount could be entered in the wrong (Debit or Credit) column.

The Income Statement and Balance Sheet Sections

The Income Statement and Balance Sheet sections of the worksheet are used to separate the amounts needed for the balance sheet and the income statement. For example, to prepare an income statement, all revenue and expense account balances must be in one place.

Starting at the top of the Adjusted Trial Balance section, examine each general ledger account. For accounts that appear on the balance sheet, enter the amount in the appropriate column of the Balance Sheet section. For accounts that appear on the income statement, enter the amount in the appropriate column of the Income Statement section. Take care to enter debit amounts in the Debit column and credit amounts in the Credit column.

ADJUSTED TRIAL BALANCE		INCOME STATEMENT		BALANCE SHEET		
DEBIT	CREDIT	DEBIT	CREDIT	DEBIT	CREDIT	
64 400 00						1
4 000 00						2
1 500 00						3
3 000 00						4
35 000 00						5
	583 00					6
	12 000 00					7
	80 000 00					8
3 000 00						9
	28 000 00					10
5 000 00						11
600 00						12
500 00						13
3 000 00						14
583 00						15
120 583 00	120 583 00					16
						17

Preparing the Balance Sheet Section

Refer to Figure 5-4 on pages 140–141 as you learn how to complete the worksheet. Asset, liability, and owner's equity accounts appear on the balance sheet. The first five accounts that appear on the worksheet are assets. Extend the asset accounts to the Debit column of the Balance Sheet section. The next account, **Accumulated Depreciation—Equipment,** is a contra asset account. Extend it to the Credit column of the Balance Sheet section. Extend **Accounts Payable** and **Linda Carter, Capital** to the Credit column of the Balance Sheet section. Extend **Linda Carter, Drawing** to the Debit column of the Balance Sheet section.

Preparing the Income Statement Section

Revenue and expense accounts appear on the income statement. Extend the **Fees Income** account to the Credit column of the Income Statement section. The last five accounts on the worksheet are expense accounts. Extend these accounts to the Debit column of the Income Statement section.

After all account balances are transferred from the Adjusted Trial Balance section of the worksheet to the financial statement sections, total the Debit and Credit columns in the Income Statement section. For Carter Consulting Services, the debits (expenses) total $9,683 and the credits (revenue) total $28,000.

Next total the columns in the Balance Sheet section. For Carter Consulting Services the debits (assets and drawing account) total $110,900 and the credits (contra asset, liabilities, and owner's equity) total $92,583.

Return to the Income Statement section. The totals of these columns are used to determine the net income or net loss. Subtract the smaller

Proper Names

When conducting business in the international marketplace, it is important to address individuals in the proper manner. Some countries do not use the "first name-last name" style as used in the United States. For example, in Spanish-speaking Latin America, the surname is a combination of the mother's and father's last names. The father's name comes first and is the only one used in conversations.

					Carter Consulting Services Worksheet Month Ended December 31, 2004
	ACCOUNT NAME	TRIAL BALANCE		ADJUSTMENTS	
		DEBIT	CREDIT	DEBIT	CREDIT
1	*Cash*	*64 400 00*			
2	*Accounts Receivable*	*4 000 00*			
3	*Supplies*	*2 000 00*			*(a) 500 00*
4	*Prepaid Rent*	*6 000 00*			*(b) 3 000 00*
5	*Equipment*	*35 000 00*			
6	*Accumulated Depreciation—Equipment*				*(c) 583 00*
7	*Accounts Payable*		*12 000 00*		
8	*Linda Carter, Capital*		*80 000 00*		
9	*Linda Carter, Drawing*	*3 000 00*			
10	*Fees Income*		*28 000 00*		
11	*Salaries Expense*	*5 000 00*			
12	*Utilities Expense*	*600 00*			
13	*Supplies Expense*			*(a) 500 00*	
14	*Rent Expense*			*(b) 3 000 00*	
15	*Depreciation Expense—Equipment*			*(c) 583 00*	
16	*Totals*	*120 000 00*	*120 000 00*	*4 083 00*	*4 083 00*
17	*Net Income*				
18					

▲ **FIGURE 5-4**
Completed Worksheet

column total from the larger one. Enter the difference on the line below the smaller total. In the Account Name column, enter "Net Income" or "Net Loss."

In this case the total of the Credit column, $28,000, exceeds the total of the Debit column, $9,683. The Credit column total represents revenue. The Debit column total represents expenses. The difference between the two amounts is a net income of $18,317. Enter $18,317 in the Debit column of the Income Statement section.

Net income causes a net increase in owner's equity. As a check on accuracy, the amount in the Balance Sheet Debit column is subtracted from the amount in the Credit column and compared to net income. In the Balance Sheet section, subtract the smaller column total from the larger one. The difference should equal the net income or net loss computed in the Income Statement section. Enter the difference on the line below the smaller total. For Carter Consulting Services, enter $18,317 in the Credit column of the Balance Sheet section.

Total the Income Statement and Balance Sheet columns. Make sure that total debits equal total credits for each section.

Carter Consulting Services had a net income. If it had a loss, the loss would be entered in the Credit column of the Income Statement section and the Debit column of the Balance Sheet section. "Net Loss" would be entered in the Account Name column on the worksheet.

Important!

Net Income
The difference between the Debit and Credit columns of the Income Statement section represents net income. The difference between the Debit and Credit columns of the Balance Sheet section should equal the net income amount.

4 Objective
Prepare an income statement, statement of owner's equity, and balance sheet from the completed worksheet.

Preparing Financial Statements

When the worksheet is complete, the next step is to prepare the financial statements, starting with the income statement. Preparation of the financial statements is the fifth step in the accounting cycle.

ADJUSTED TRIAL BALANCE		INCOME STATEMENT		BALANCE SHEET		
DEBIT	CREDIT	DEBIT	CREDIT	DEBIT	CREDIT	
64 400 00				64 400 00		1
4 000 00				4 000 00		2
1 500 00				1 500 00		3
3 000 00				3 000 00		4
35 000 00				35 000 00		5
	583 00				583 00	6
	12 000 00				12 000 00	7
	80 000 00				80 000 00	8
3 000 00				3 000 00		9
	28 000 00		28 000 00			10
5 000 00		5 000 00				11
600 00		600 00				12
500 00		500 00				13
3 000 00		3 000 00				14
583 00		583 00				15
120 583 00	120 583 00	9 683 00	28 000 00	110 900 00	92 583 00	16
		18 317 00			18 317 00	17
		28 000 00	28 000 00	110 900 00	110 900 00	18

Preparing the Income Statement

Use the Income Statement section of the worksheet to prepare the income statement. Figure 5-5 shows the income statement for Carter Consulting Services. Compare it to the worksheet in Figure 5-4.

If the firm had incurred a net loss, the final amount on the income statement would be labeled "Net Loss for the Month."

FIGURE 5-5
Income Statement

Carter Consulting Services
Income Statement
Month Ended December 31, 2004

Revenue		
Fees Income		28 000 00
Expenses		
Salaries Expense	5 000 00	
Utilities Expense	600 00	
Supplies Expense	500 00	
Rent Expense	3 000 00	
Depreciation Expense—Equipment	583 00	
Total Expenses		9 683 00
Net Income for the Month		18 317 00

Preparing the Statement of Owner's Equity

The statement of owner's equity reports the changes that have occurred in the owner's financial interest during the reporting period. Use the data in the Balance Sheet section of the worksheet, as well as the net income or net loss figure, to prepare the statement of owner's equity.

- From the Balance Sheet section of the worksheet, use the amounts for owner's capital; owner's withdrawals, if any; and owner's investments, if any.
- From the Income Statement section of the worksheet, use the amount calculated for net income or net loss.

The statement of owner's equity is prepared before the balance sheet because the ending capital balance is needed to prepare the balance sheet. The statement of owner's equity reports the change in owner's capital during the period ($15,317) as well as the ending capital ($95,317). Figure 5-6 shows the statement of owner's equity for Carter Consulting Services.

FIGURE 5-6 ►
Statement of Owner's Equity

Carter Consulting Services Statement of Owner's Equity Month Ended December 31, 2004		
Linda Carter, Capital, December 1, 2004		80 000 00
Net Income for December	18 317 00	
Less Withdrawals for December	3 000 00	
Increase in Capital		15 317 00
Linda Carter, Capital, December 31, 2004		95 317 00

Preparing the Balance Sheet

The accounts listed on the balance sheet are taken directly from the Balance Sheet section of the worksheet. Figure 5-7 shows the balance sheet for Carter Consulting Services.

FIGURE 5-7 ►
Balance Sheet

Carter Consulting Services Balance Sheet December 31, 2004		
Assets		
Cash		64 400 00
Accounts Receivable		4 000 00
Supplies		1 500 00
Prepaid Rent		3 000 00
Equipment	35 000 00	
Less Accumulated Depreciation	583 00	34 417 00
Total Assets		107 317 00
Liabilities and Owner's Equity		
Liabilities		
Accounts Payable		12 000 00
Owner's Equity		
Linda Carter, Capital		95 317 00
Total Liabilities and Owner's Equity		107 317 00

Note that the equipment's book value is reported on the balance sheet ($34,417). Do not confuse book value with market value. Book value is

FIGURE 5-8A
Worksheet Summary

The worksheet is used to gather all the data needed to prepare the financial statements. The worksheet heading contains the name of the company (WHO), the title of the statement (WHAT), and the period covered (WHEN). In addition to the Account Name column, the worksheet contains five sections: Trial Balance, Adjustments, Adjusted Trial Balance, Income Statement, and Balance Sheet. Each section includes a Debit column and a Credit column, resulting in ten money columns.

Below is the worksheet for Carter Consulting Services for the period ended December 31, 2004. The illustrations that follow will highlight the preparation of each part of the worksheet.

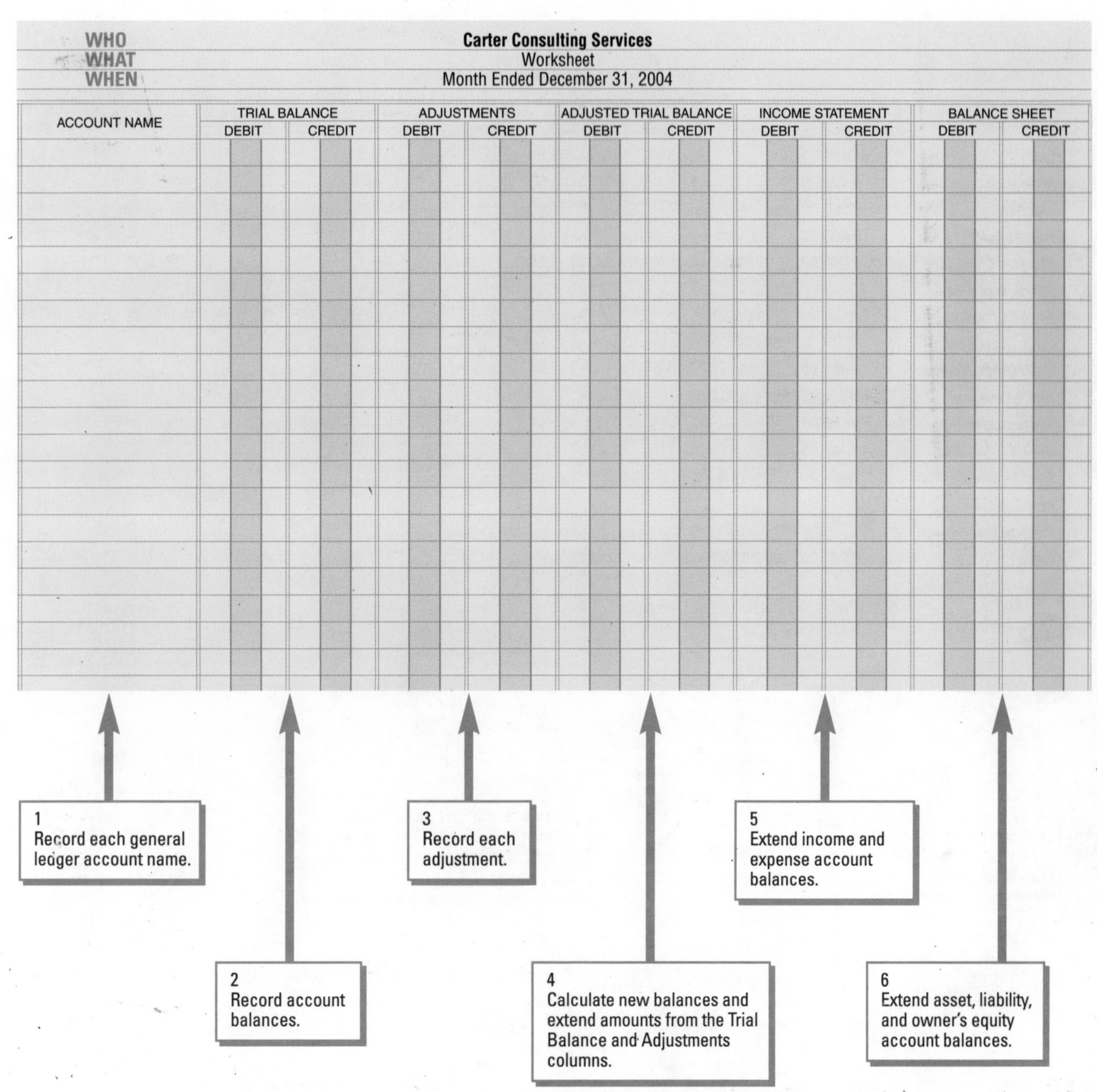

FIGURE 5-8B
Trial Balance Columns

The first step in preparing the worksheet is to list the general ledger account names and their balances in the Account Name and Trial Balance sections of the worksheet. Total the Debit and Credit columns to verify that total debits equal total credits.

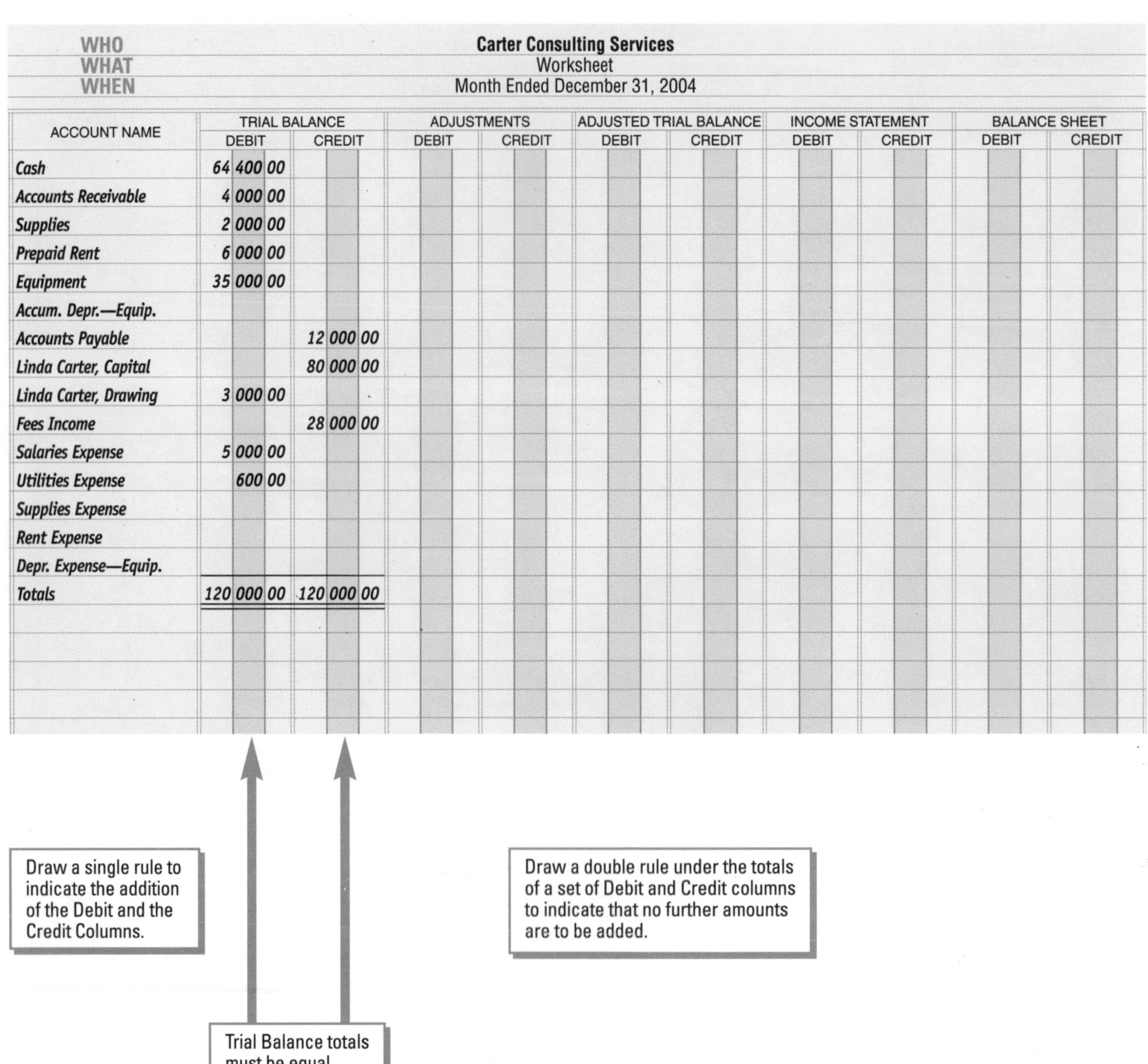

WHO **Carter Consulting Services**
WHAT Worksheet
WHEN Month Ended December 31, 2004

ACCOUNT NAME	TRIAL BALANCE		ADJUSTMENTS		ADJUSTED TRIAL BALANCE		INCOME STATEMENT		BALANCE SHEET	
	DEBIT	CREDIT	DEBIT	CREDIT	DEBIT	CREDIT	DEBIT	CREDIT	DEBIT	CREDIT
Cash	*64 400 00*									
Accounts Receivable	*4 000 00*									
Supplies	*2 000 00*									
Prepaid Rent	*6 000 00*									
Equipment	*35 000 00*									
Accum. Depr.—Equip.										
Accounts Payable		*12 000 00*								
Linda Carter, Capital		*80 000 00*								
Linda Carter, Drawing	*3 000 00*									
Fees Income		*28 000 00*								
Salaries Expense	*5 000 00*									
Utilities Expense	*600 00*									
Supplies Expense										
Rent Expense										
Depr. Expense—Equip.										
Totals	*120 000 00*	*120 000 00*								

FIGURE 5-9G
Preparing the Financial Statements

The information needed to prepare the financial statements is obtained from the worksheet.

Carter Consulting Services Income Statement Month Ended December 31, 2004		
Revenue		
Fees Income		28 000 00
Expenses		
Salaries Expense	5 000 00	
Utilities Expense	600 00	
Supplies Expense	500 00	
Rent Expense	3 000 00	
Depreciation Expense—Equipment	583 00	
Total Expenses		9 683 00
Net Income for the Month		18 317 00

When expenses for the period are less than revenue, a net income results. The net income is transferred to the statement of owner's equity.

Carter Consulting Services Statement of Owner's Equity Month Ended December 31, 2004		
Linda Carter, Capital, December 1, 2004		80 000 00
Net Income for December	18 317 00	
Less Withdrawals for December	3 000 00	
Increase in Capital		15 317 00
Linda Carter, Capital, December 31, 2004		95 317 00

The withdrawals are subtracted from the net income for the period to determine the change in owner's equity.

Carter Consulting Services Balance Sheet December 31, 2004		
Assets		
Cash		64 400 00
Accounts Receivable		4 000 00
Supplies		1 500 00
Prepaid Rent		3 000 00
Equipment	35 000 00	
Less Accumulated Depreciation	583 00	34 417 00
Total Assets		107 317 00
Liabilities and Owner's Equity		
Liabilities		
Accounts Payable		12 000 00
Owner's Equity		
Linda Carter, Capital		95 317 00
Total Liabilities and Owner's Equity		107 317 00

The ending capital balance is transferred from the statement of owner's equity to the balance sheet.

SUMMARY OF FINANCIAL STATEMENTS

THE INCOME STATEMENT

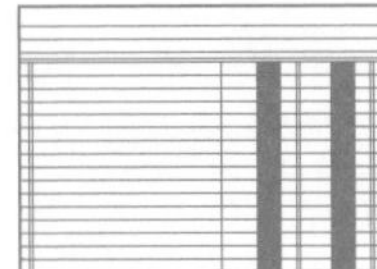

The income statement is prepared from the data in the Income Statement section of the worksheet. The heading of the income statement contains the name of the firm (WHO), the name of the statement (WHAT), and the period covered by the statement (WHEN). The Revenue section of the statement is prepared first. The revenue account name is obtained from the Account Name column of the worksheet. The balance of the revenue account is obtained from the Credit column of the Income Statement section of the worksheet. The Expenses section of the income statement is prepared next. The expense account names are obtained from the Account Name column of the worksheet. The balance of each expense account is obtained from the Debit column of the Income Statement section of the worksheet.

The last step in preparing the income statement is to determine the net income or net loss for the period. If the firm has more revenue than expenses, a net income is reported. If the firm has more expenses than revenue, a net loss is reported. The net income or net loss reported on the income statement must agree with the amount calculated on the worksheet.

THE STATEMENT OF OWNER'S EQUITY

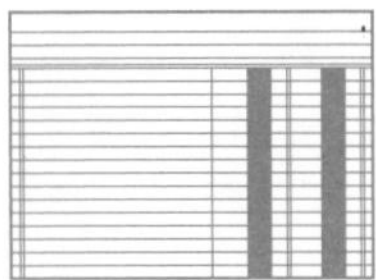

The statement of owner's equity is prepared from the data in the Balance Sheet section of the worksheet as well as the data in the general ledger capital account. The heading of the statement contains the name of the firm (WHO), the name of the statement (WHAT), and the period covered by the statement (WHEN).

The statement begins with the general ledger capital account balance at the beginning of the period. Next the increase or decrease in the owner's capital account is determined: Add the net income or subtract the net loss for the period. Add additional investments made by the owner during the period. Subtract withdrawals for the period. Determine the total increase or total decrease for the period. The increase or decrease is added to the beginning capital balance to obtain the ending capital balance.

THE BALANCE SHEET

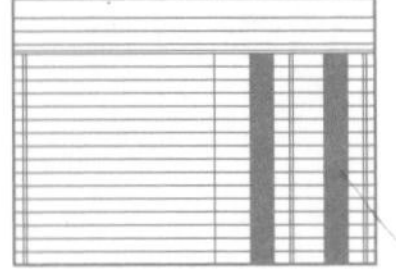

The balance sheet is prepared from the data in the Balance Sheet section of the worksheet and the statement of owner's equity. The balance sheet reflects the assets, liabilities, and owner's equity of the firm on the balance sheet date. The heading of the statement contains the name of the firm (WHO), the name of the statement (WHAT), and the date of the statement (WHEN).

Prepare the Assets section of the statement first. The asset account names are obtained from the Account Name column of the worksheet. The balance of each asset account is obtained from the Debit column of the Balance Sheet section of the worksheet. Contra asset account balances are in the Credit column of the Balance Sheet section. The Liability and Owner's Equity section is prepared next. The liability and owner's equity account names are obtained from the Account Name column of the worksheet. The balance of each liability account is obtained from the Credit column of the Balance Sheet section of the worksheet. The ending balance for the owner's capital account is obtained from the statement of owner's equity. Total liabilities and owner's equity must equal total assets.

the portion of the original cost that has not been depreciated. *Market value* is what a willing buyer will pay a willing seller for the asset. Market value may be higher or lower than book value.

Notice that the amount for **Linda Carter, Capital,** $95,317, comes from the statement of owner's equity.

The balance sheet in Figure 5-7 is prepared using the report form. The **report form balance sheet** lists the asset accounts first, followed by liabilities and owner's equity. Chapters 2 and 3 illustrated the **account form balance sheet,** with assets on the left and liabilities and owner's equity on the right. The report form is widely used because it provides more space for entering account names and its format is easier to prepare.

Some companies show long-term assets at a net amount. "Net" means that accumulated depreciation has been subtracted from the original cost. For example, The Boeing Company's consolidated statement of financial position as of December 31, 1999, states:

Property, plant, and equipment, net: $8,245 million

The accumulated depreciation amount does not appear on the balance sheet.

Figure 5-8 provides a step-by-step demonstration of how to complete the worksheet and financial statements for Carter Consulting Services.

Journalizing and Posting Adjusting Entries

5 Objective

Journalize and post the adjusting entries.

The worksheet is a tool. It is used to determine the effects of adjustments on account balances. It is also used to prepare the financial statements. However, the worksheet is not part of the permanent accounting record.

After the financial statements are prepared, the adjustments shown on the worksheet must become part of the permanent accounting record. Each adjustment is journalized and posted to the general ledger accounts. Journalizing and posting adjusting entries is the sixth step in the accounting cycle.

For Carter Consulting Services, three adjustments are needed to provide a complete picture of the firm's operating results and its financial position. Adjustments are needed for supplies expense, rent expense, and depreciation expense.

Refer to Figure 5-4 on pages 140–141 for data needed to record the adjustments. Enter the words "Adjusting Entries" in the Description column of the general journal. Some accountants prefer to start a new page when they record the adjusting entries. Then journalize the adjustments in the order in which they appear on the worksheet.

After journalizing the adjusting entries, post them to the general ledger accounts. Figure 5-9 on page 144 shows how the adjusting entries for Carter Consulting Services on December 31, 2004 were journalized and posted. Account numbers appear in the general journal Posting Reference column because all entries have been posted. In each general ledger account, the word "Adjusting" appears in the Description column.

◄ FIGURE 5-9
Journalized and Posted Adjusting Entries

GENERAL JOURNAL PAGE 3

	DATE		DESCRIPTION	POST. REF.	DEBIT	CREDIT	
1	2004		Adjusting Entries				1
2	Dec.	31	Supplies Expense	517	500 00		2
3			Supplies	121		500 00	3
4							4
5		31	Rent Expense	520	3000 00		5
6			Prepaid Rent	137		3000 00	6
7							7
8		31	Depr. Expense—Equipment	523	583 00		8
9			Accum. Depr.—Equipment	142		583 00	9
10							10
11							

ACCOUNT Supplies ACCOUNT NO. 121

DATE		DESCRIPTION	POST. REF.	DEBIT	CREDIT	BALANCE DEBIT	BALANCE CREDIT
2004							
Nov.	28		J1	2000 00		2000 00	
Dec.	31	Adjusting	J3		500 00	1500 00	

ACCOUNT Prepaid Rent ACCOUNT NO. 137

DATE		DESCRIPTION	POST. REF.	DEBIT	CREDIT	BALANCE DEBIT	BALANCE CREDIT
2004							
Nov.	30		J1	6000 00		6000 00	
Dec.	31	Adjusting	J3		3000 00	3000 00	

ACCOUNT Accumulated Depreciation—Equipment ACCOUNT NO. 142

DATE		DESCRIPTION	POST. REF.	DEBIT	CREDIT	BALANCE DEBIT	BALANCE CREDIT
2004							
Dec.	31	Adjusting	J3		583 00		583 00

ACCOUNT Supplies Expense ACCOUNT NO. 517

DATE		DESCRIPTION	POST. REF.	DEBIT	CREDIT	BALANCE DEBIT	BALANCE CREDIT
2004							
Dec.	31	Adjusting	J3	500 00		500 00	

ACCOUNT Rent Expense ACCOUNT NO. 520

DATE		DESCRIPTION	POST. REF.	DEBIT	CREDIT	BALANCE DEBIT	BALANCE CREDIT
2004							
Dec.	31	Adjusting	J3	3000 00		3000 00	

ACCOUNT Depreciation Expense—Equipment ACCOUNT NO. 523

DATE		DESCRIPTION	POST. REF.	DEBIT	CREDIT	BALANCE DEBIT	BALANCE CREDIT
2004							
Dec.	31	Adjusting	J3	583 00		583 00	

Worksheets

- The worksheet permits quick preparation of the financial statements. Quick preparation of financial statements allows management to obtain timely information.
- Timely information allows management to
  - evaluate the results of operations,
  - evaluate the financial position of the business,
  - make decisions.
- The worksheet provides a convenient form for gathering information and determining the effects of internal changes such as
  - recording an expense for the use of a long-term asset like equipment,
  - recording the actual use of prepaid items.
- The more accounts that a firm has in its general ledger, the more useful the worksheet is in speeding the preparation of the financial statements.
- It is important to management that the appropriate adjustments are recorded in order to present a complete and accurate picture of the firm's financial affairs.

Thinking Critically

If you skip the adjustment process, how will this affect the financial statements?

Remember that the worksheet is not part of the accounting records. Adjustments that are on the worksheet must be recorded in the general journal and posted to the general ledger in order to become part of the permanent accounting records.

Self Review

Questions

1. What amounts appear on the statement of owner's equity?
2. What is the difference between a report form balance sheet and an account form balance sheet?
3. Why is it necessary to journalize and post adjusting entries even though the data is already recorded on the worksheet?

Exercises

4. On a worksheet, the adjusted balance of the **Supplies** account is extended to the
   a. Income Statement Debit column.
   b. Balance Sheet Debit column.
   c. Income Statement Credit column.
   d. Balance Sheet Credit column.
5. **Accumulated Depreciation—Equipment** is a(n)
   a. asset account.
   b. contra asset account.
   c. liability account.
   d. contra liability account.

Analysis

6. J. Cloves Repair Shop purchased equipment for $12,000. **Depreciation Expense** for the month is $120. What is the balance of the **Equipment** account after posting the depreciation entry? Why?

(Answers to Section 2 Self Review are on page 161.)

CHAPTER 5 Review and Applications

Review

Chapter Summary

At the end of the operating period, adjustments for internal events are recorded to update the accounting records. In this chapter, you have learned how the accountant uses the worksheet and adjusting entries to accomplish this task.

Learning Objectives

1 Complete a trial balance on a worksheet.
A worksheet is normally used to save time in preparing the financial statements. Preparation of the worksheet is the fourth step in the accounting cycle. The trial balance is the first section of the worksheet to be prepared.

2 Prepare adjustments for unrecorded business transactions.
Some changes arise from the internal operations of the firm itself. Adjusting entries are made to record these changes. Any adjustments to account balances should be entered in the Adjustments section of the worksheet.

- Prepaid expenses are expense items that are acquired and paid for in advance of their use. At the time of their acquisition, these items represent assets and are recorded in asset accounts. As they are used, their cost is transferred to expense by means of adjusting entries at the end of each accounting period.

  Examples of general ledger asset accounts and the related expense accounts follow:

Asset Accounts	Expense Accounts
Supplies	Supplies Expense
Prepaid Rent	Rent Expense
Prepaid Insurance	Insurance Expense

- Depreciation is the process of allocating the cost of a long-term asset to operations over its expected useful life. Part of the asset's cost is charged off as an expense at the end of each accounting period during the asset's useful life. The straight-line method of depreciation is widely used. The formula for straight-line depreciation is:

$$\text{Depreciation} = \frac{\text{Cost} - \text{Salvage value}}{\text{Estimated useful life}}$$

3 Complete the worksheet.
An adjusted trial balance is prepared to prove the equality of the debits and credits after adjustments have been entered on the worksheet. Once the Debit and Credit columns have been totaled and ruled, the Income Statement and Balance Sheet columns of the worksheet are completed. The net income or net loss for the period is determined, and the worksheet is completed.

4 Prepare an income statement, statement of owner's equity, and balance sheet from the completed worksheet.
All figures needed to prepare the financial statements are properly reflected on the completed worksheet. The accounts are arranged in the order in which they must appear on the income statement and balance sheet. Preparation of the financial statements is the fifth step of the accounting cycle.

5 Journalize and post the adjusting entries.
After the financial statements have been prepared, the accountant must make permanent entries in the accounting records for the adjustments shown on the worksheet. The adjusting entries are then posted to the general ledger. Journalizing and posting the adjusting entries is the sixth step in the accounting cycle.

To summarize the steps of the accounting cycle discussed so far:

1. Analyze transactions.
2. Journalize transactions.
3. Post the journal entries.
4. Prepare a worksheet.
5. Prepare financial statements.
6. Record adjusting entries.

6 Define the accounting terms new to this chapter.

CHAPTER 5 GLOSSARY

Account form balance sheet (p. 143) A balance sheet that lists assets on the left and liabilities and owner's equity on the right (see Report form balance sheet)

Adjusting entries (p. 131) Journal entries made to update accounts for items that were not recorded during the accounting period

Adjustments (p. 131) See Adjusting entries

Book value (p. 135) That portion of an asset's original cost that has not yet been depreciated

Contra account (p. 135) An account with a normal balance that is opposite that of a related account

Contra asset account (p. 135) An asset account with a credit balance, which is contrary to the normal balance of an asset account

Depreciation (p. 134) Allocation of the cost of a long-term asset to operations during its expected useful life

Prepaid expenses (p. 131) Expense items acquired, recorded, and paid for in advance of their use

Report form balance sheet (p. 143) A balance sheet that lists the asset accounts first, followed by liabilities and owner's equity

Salvage value (p. 134) An estimate of the amount that could be received by selling or disposing of an asset at the end of its useful life

Straight-line depreciation (p. 134) Allocation of an asset's cost in equal amounts to each accounting period of the asset's useful life

Worksheet (p. 130) A form used to gather all data needed at the end of an accounting period to prepare financial statements

Comprehensive Self Review

1. Why are assets depreciated?
2. Why is the net income for a period recorded in the Balance Sheet section of the worksheet as well as the Income Statement section?
3. Is the normal balance for **Accumulated Depreciation** a debit or credit balance?
4. The **Supplies** account has a debit balance of $5,000 in the Trial Balance column. The Credit column in the Adjustments section is $1,750. What is the new balance? The new balance will be extended to which column of the worksheet?
5. The **Drawing** account is extended to which column of the worksheet?

(Answers to Comprehensive Self Review are on page 161.)

Discussion Questions

1. Why is it necessary to journalize and post adjusting entries?
2. What three amounts are reported on the balance sheet for a long-term asset such as equipment?
3. How does a contra asset account differ from a regular asset account?
4. What is book value?
5. Why is an accumulated depreciation account used in making the adjustment for depreciation?
6. How does the straight-line method of depreciation work?
7. Give three examples of assets that are subject to depreciation.
8. A firm purchases machinery, which has an estimated useful life of 10 years and no salvage value, for $15,000 at the beginning of the accounting period. What is the adjusting entry for depreciation at the end of one month if the firm uses the straight-line method of depreciation?
9. What adjustment would be recorded for expired insurance?
10. What are prepaid expenses? Give four examples.
11. Why is it necessary to make an adjustment for supplies used?
12. Are the following assets depreciated? Why or why not?
    - **a.** Prepaid Insurance
    - **b.** Delivery Truck
    - **c.** Land
    - **d.** Manufacturing Equipment
    - **e.** Prepaid Rent
    - **f.** Furniture
    - **g.** Store Equipment
    - **h.** Prepaid Advertising
    - **i.** Computers
13. What effect does each of the following items have on net income?
    - **a.** The owner withdrew cash from the business.
    - **b.** Credit customers paid $1,000 on outstanding balances that were past due.
    - **c.** The business bought equipment on account that cost $10,000.
    - **d.** The business journalized and posted an adjustment for depreciation of equipment.
14. What effect does each item in Question 13 have on owner's equity?

Applications

EXERCISES

Exercise 5-1
Objective 2

Calculating adjustments.

Determine the necessary end-of-June adjustments for Brown Company.

1. On June 1, 20--, Brown Company, a new firm, paid $7,200 rent in advance for a six-month period. The $7,200 was debited to the **Prepaid Rent** account.
2. On June 1, 20--, the firm bought supplies for $1,950. The $1,950 was debited to the **Supplies** account. An inventory of supplies at the end of June showed that items costing $700 were on hand.
3. On June 1, 20--, the firm bought equipment costing $24,000. The equipment has an expected useful life of ten years and no salvage value. The firm will use the straight-line method of depreciation.

Exercise 5-2
Objective 2

Calculating adjustments.

For each of the following situations, determine the necessary adjustments.

1. A firm purchased a two-year insurance policy for $4,800 on July 1, 2004. The $4,800 was debited to the **Prepaid Insurance** account. What adjustment should be made to record expired insurance on the firm's July 31, 2004, worksheet?
2. On December 1, 2004, a firm signed a contract with a local radio station for advertising that will extend over a one-year period. The firm paid $4,080 in advance and debited the amount to **Prepaid Advertising.** What adjustment should be made to record expired advertising on the firm's December 31, 2004, worksheet?

Exercise 5-3
Objectives 1, 2

Worksheet through Adjusted Trial Balance.

On January 31, 20--, the general ledger of Ortiz Company showed the following account balances. Prepare the worksheet through the Adjusted Trial Balance section. Assume that every account has the normal debit or credit balance. The worksheet covers the month of January.

ACCOUNTS			
Cash	$ 57,000	Fees Income	90,000
Accounts Receivable	19,200	Depreciation Exp.—Equip.	0
Supplies	9,000	Insurance Expense	0
Prepaid Insurance	17,100	Rent Expense	7,200
Equipment	95,580	Salaries Expense	8,520
Accum. Depr.—Equip.	0	Supplies Expense	0
Accounts Payable	10,200		
Dennis Ortiz, Capital	113,400		

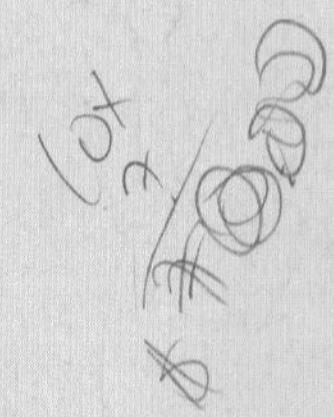

Additional information:

a. Supplies used during January totaled $4,800.
b. Expired insurance totaled $1,500.
c. Depreciation expense for the month was $1,380.

Exercise 5-4 ► Objectives 2, 3

Correcting net income.

Assume that a firm reports net income of $30,000 prior to making adjusting entries for the following items: expired rent, $2,000; depreciation expense, $2,400; and supplies used, $1,000.

Assume that the required adjusting entries have not been made. What effect do these errors have on the reported net income?

Exercise 5-5 ► Objective 5

Journalizing and posting adjustments.

Thomas Company must make three adjusting entries on December 31, 20--.

a. Supplies used, $2,000; (supplies totaling $3,000 were purchased on December 1, 20--, and debited to the **Supplies** account).

b. Expired insurance, $1,600 on December 1, 20--; the firm paid $9,600 for six months' insurance coverage in advance and debited **Prepaid Insurance** for this amount.

c. Depreciation expense for equipment, $800.

Make the journal entries for these adjustments and post the entries to the general ledger accounts. Use page 3 of the general journal for the adjusting entries. Use the following accounts and numbers.

Supplies	121	Depreciation Exp.—Equip.	517
Prepaid Insurance	131	Insurance Expense	521
Accum. Depr.—Equip.	142	Supplies Expense	523

Problems

Selected problems can be completed using:
Peachtree **QuickBooks** **Spreadsheets**

PROBLEM SET A

Problem 5-1A ► Objectives 1, 2, 3

Completing the worksheet.

The trial balance of Dallas Company as of January 31, 20--, after the company completed the first month of operations, is shown in the partial worksheet on page 151.

INSTRUCTIONS

1. Record the trial balance in the Trial Balance section of the worksheet.
2. Complete the worksheet by making the following adjustments: supplies on hand at the end of the month, $1,500; expired insurance, $2,000; depreciation expense for the period, $200.

Analyze: How does the insurance adjustment affect **Prepaid Insurance?**

Problem 5-2A ► Objectives 1, 2, 3

Reconstructing a partial worksheet.

The adjusted trial balance of University Book Store as of September 30, 20--, after the firm's first month of operations, appears on page 151.

Appropriate adjustments have been made for the following items.

a. Supplies used during the month, $1,000.

b. Expired rent for the month, $1,200.

c. Depreciation expense for the month, $600.

	Dallas Company Worksheet (Partial) Month Ended January 31, 20--				
	ACCOUNT NAME	TRIAL BALANCE		ADJUSTMENTS	
		DEBIT	CREDIT	DEBIT	CREDIT
1	*Cash*	*31 000 00*			
2	*Accounts Receivable*	*2 600 00*			
3	*Supplies*	*2 900 00*			
4	*Prepaid Insurance*	*12 000 00*			
5	*Equipment*	*24 000 00*			
6	*Accumulated Depreciation—Equipment*				
7	*Accounts Payable*		*4 000 00*		
8	*J. C. Dallas, Capital*		*60 000 00*		
9	*J. C. Dallas, Drawing*	*2 400 00*			
10	*Fees Income*		*16 300 00*		
11	*Depreciation Expense—Equipment*				
12	*Insurance Expense*				
13	*Salaries Expense*	*4 800 00*			
14	*Supplies Expense*				
15	*Utilities Expense*	*600 00*			
16	*Totals*	*80 300 00*	*80 300 00*		

INSTRUCTIONS

1. Record the Adjusted Trial Balance in the Adjusted Trial Balance columns of the worksheet.
2. Prepare the adjusting entries in the Adjustments columns.
3. Complete the Trial Balance columns of the worksheet prior to making the adjusting entries.

Analyze: What was the balance of **Prepaid Rent** prior to the adjusting entry for expired rent?

University Book Store Adjusted Trial Balance September 30, 20--		
Account Name	Debit	Credit
Cash	19,000	
Accounts Receivable	3,000	
Supplies	2,400	
Prepaid Rent	14,400	
Equipment	24,000	
Accumulated Depreciation—Equipment		600
Accounts Payable		6,000
Chuck Keen, Capital		32,100
Chuck Keen, Drawing	2,000	
Fees Income		36,000
Depreciation Expense—Equipment	600	
Rent Expense	1,200	
Salaries Expense	6,400	
Supplies Expense	1,000	
Utilities Expense	700	
Totals	74,700	74,700

Problem 5-3A ► Objective 4

Preparing financial statements from the worksheet.

The completed worksheet for Penn Corporation as of December 31, 20--, after the company had completed the first month of operation, appears below.

INSTRUCTIONS

1. Prepare an income statement.
2. Prepare a statement of owner's equity. The owner made no additional investments during the month.
3. Prepare a balance sheet (use the report form).

Analyze: If the adjustment to **Prepaid Advertising** had been $700 instead of $1,000, what net income would have resulted?

Problem 5-4A ► Objectives 1, 2, 3, 4, 5

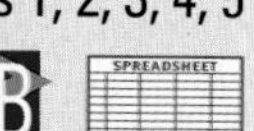

Preparing a worksheet and financial statements, journalizing adjusting entries, and posting to ledger accounts.

David Flores owns Flores Creative Designs. The trial balance of the firm for January 31, 20--, the first month of operations, is shown on page 153.

INSTRUCTIONS

1. Complete the worksheet for the month.
2. Prepare an income statement, statement of owner's equity, and balance sheet. No additional investments were made by the owner during the month.
3. Journalize and post the adjusting entries. Use 3 for the journal page number.

End-of-the-month adjustments must account for the following items:

a. Supplies were purchased on January 1, 20--; inventory of supplies on January 31, 20--, is $200.

Penn Corporation
Worksheet
Month Ended December 31, 20--

	ACCOUNT NAME	TRIAL BALANCE DEBIT	TRIAL BALANCE CREDIT	ADJUSTMENTS DEBIT	ADJUSTMENTS CREDIT
1	*Cash*	36 800 00			
2	*Accounts Receivable*	4 000 00			
3	*Supplies*	4 000 00			(a) 2 000 00
4	*Prepaid Advertising*	6 000 00			(b) 1 000 00
5	*Equipment*	20 000 00			
6	*Accumulated Depreciation—Equipment*				(c) 800 00
7	*Accounts Payable*		4 000 00		
8	*Jeff Penn, Capital*		50 000 00		
9	*Jeff Penn, Drawing*	2 800 00			
10	*Fees Income*		25 000 00		
11	*Advertising Expense*			(b) 1 000 00	
12	*Depreciation Expense—Equipment*			(c) 800 00	
13	*Salaries Expense*	4 800 00			
14	*Supplies Expense*			(a) 2 000 00	
15	*Utilities Expense*	600 00			
16	*Totals*	79 000 00	79 000 00	3 800 00	3 800 00
17	*Net Income*				
18					
19					

Flores Creative Designs
Worksheet (Partial)
Month Ended January 31, 20--

	ACCOUNT NAME	TRIAL BALANCE DEBIT	TRIAL BALANCE CREDIT	ADJUSTMENTS DEBIT	ADJUSTMENTS CREDIT
1	*Cash*	10 200 00			
2	*Accounts Receivable*	3 600 00			
3	*Supplies*	1 150 00			
4	*Prepaid Advertising*	1 200 00			
5	*Prepaid Rent*	8 400 00			
6	*Equipment*	9 600 00			
7	*Accumulated Depreciation—Equipment*				
8	*Accounts Payable*		5 000 00		
9	*David Flores, Capital*		18 100 00		
10	*David Flores, Drawing*	1 500 00			
11	*Fees Income*		16 500 00		
12	*Advertising Expense*				
13	*Depreciation Expense—Equipment*				
14	*Rent Expense*				
15	*Salaries Expense*	3 600 00			
16	*Supplies Expense*				
17	*Utilities Expense*	350 00			
18	*Totals*	39 600 00	39 600 00		
19					

b. The prepaid advertising contract was signed on January 1, 20--, and covers a four-month period.

c. Rent of $700 expired during the month.

ADJUSTED TRIAL BALANCE DEBIT	ADJUSTED TRIAL BALANCE CREDIT	INCOME STATEMENT DEBIT	INCOME STATEMENT CREDIT	BALANCE SHEET DEBIT	BALANCE SHEET CREDIT	
36 800 00				36 800 00		1
4 000 00				4 000 00		2
2 000 00				2 000 00		3
5 000 00				5 000 00		4
20 000 00				20 000 00		5
	800 00				800 00	6
	4 000 00				4 000 00	7
	50 000 00				50 000 00	8
2 800 00				2 800 00		9
	25 000 00		25 000 00			10
1 000 00		1 000 00				11
800 00		800 00				12
4 800 00		4 800 00				13
2 000 00		2 000 00				14
600 00		600 00				15
79 800 00	79 800 00	9 200 00	25 000 00	70 600 00	54 800 00	16
		15 800 00			15 800 00	17
		25 000 00	25 000 00	70 600 00	70 600 00	18
						19

d. … ation is computed using the straight-line method. The equip- … ted useful life of 10 years with no salvage value.

A… … not been made for the month, w…

Problem 5-1B ►
Objectives 1, 2, 3

… ebruary 28, 20--, appears

INSTRUCTIONS

… e section of the worksheet.

… following adjustments: sup- … 1,600; expired rent, $1,800; … 0.

… **Accumulated Depreciation—** … balance shown?

Harding Com…
Worksheet (Partial)
Month Ended February 28, 20--

	ACCOUNT NAME	TRIAL BALANCE		ADJUSTMENTS	
		DEBIT	CREDIT	DEBIT	CREDIT
1	*Cash*	37 000 00			
2	*Accounts Receivable*	4 600 00			
3	*Supplies*	2 400 00			
4	*Prepaid Rent*	21 600 00			
5	*Equipment*	28 000 00			
6	*Accumulated Depreciation—Equipment*				
7	*Accounts Payable*		6 000 00		
8	*Robert Harding, Capital*		67 000 00		
9	*Robert Harding, Drawing*	2 000 00			
10	*Fees Income*		27 000 00		
11	*Depreciation Expense—Equipment*				
12	*Rent Expense*				
13	*Salaries Expense*	3 600 00			
14	*Supplies Expense*				
15	*Utilities Expense*	800 00			
16	*Totals*	100 000 00	100 000 00		
17					

Problem 5-2B ►
Objectives 1, 2, 3

Reconstructing a partial worksheet.

The adjusted trial balance of Cheryl Shore, Attorney-at-Law, as of November 30, 20--, after the company had completed the first month of operations, appears on page 155.

Appropriate adjustments have been made for the following items.

a. Supplies used during the month, $1,600.

b. Expired rent for the month, $1,800.

c. Depreciation expense for the month, $700.

INSTRUCTIONS

1. Record the adjusted trial balance in the Adjusted Trial Balance columns of the worksheet.

2. Prepare the adjusting entries in the Adjustments columns.
3. Complete the Trial Balance columns of the worksheet prior to making the adjusting entries.

Analyze: Which contra asset account is on the adjusted trial balance?

Cheryl Shore, Attorney-at-Law
Adjusted Trial Balance
November 30, 20--

ACCOUNT NAME	DEBIT	CREDIT
Cash	16,480	
Accounts Receivable	3,600	
Supplies	1,400	
Prepaid Rent	19,800	
Equipment	24,000	
Accumulated Depreciation—Equipment		700
Accounts Payable		7,000
Cheryl Shore, Capital		37,530
Cheryl Shore, Drawing	2,000	
Fees Income		31,200
Depreciation Expense—Equipment	700	
Rent Expense	1,800	
Salaries Expense	4,500	
Supplies Expense	1,600	
Utilities Expense	550	
Totals	76,430	76,430

◄ **Problem 5-3B**
Objective 4

Preparing financial statements from the worksheet.

The completed worksheet for Reliable Accounting Services for the month ended December 31, 20--, appears on pages 156–157.

INSTRUCTIONS

1. Prepare an income statement.
2. Prepare a statement of owner's equity. The owner made no additional investments during the month.
3. Prepare a balance sheet.

Analyze: By what total amount did the value of assets reported on the balance sheet decrease due to the adjusting entries?

◄ **Problem 5-4B**
Objectives 1, 2, 3, 4, 5

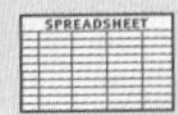

Preparing a worksheet and financial statements, journalizing adjusting entries, and posting to ledger accounts.

Jim Griffith owns Griffith Estate Planning and Investments. The trial balance of the firm for April 30, 20--, the first month of operations, is shown on page 156.

INSTRUCTIONS

1. Complete the worksheet for the month.
2. Prepare an income statement, statement of owner's equity, and balance sheet. No additional investments were made by the owner during the month.
3. Journalize and post the adjusting entries. Use 3 for the journal page number.

Griffith Estate Planning and Investments
Worksheet (Partial)
Month Ended April 30, 20--

	ACCOUNT NAME	TRIAL BALANCE DEBIT	TRIAL BALANCE CREDIT	ADJUSTMENTS DEBIT	ADJUSTMENTS CREDIT
1	Cash	9 400 00			
2	Accounts Receivable	2 600 00			
3	Supplies	1 200 00			
4	Prepaid Advertising	1 600 00			
5	Prepaid Rent	11 400 00			
6	Equipment	12 000 00			
7	Accumulated Depreciation—Equipment				
8	Accounts Payable		2 700 00		
9	Jim Griffith, Capital		25 290 00		
10	Jim Griffith, Drawing	1 000 00			
11	Fees Income		13 450 00		
12	Advertising Expense				
13	Depreciation Expense—Equipment				
14	Rent Expense				
15	Salaries Expense	1 950 00			
16	Supplies Expense				
17	Utilities Expense	290 00			
18	Totals	41 440 00	41 440 00		
19					

End-of-month adjustments must account for the following.

a. The supplies were purchased on April 1, 20--; inventory of supplies on April 30, 20--, showed a value of $400.

Reliable Accounting Services
Worksheet
Month Ended December 31, 20--

	ACCOUNT NAME	TRIAL BALANCE DEBIT	TRIAL BALANCE CREDIT	ADJUSTMENTS DEBIT	ADJUSTMENTS CREDIT
1	Cash	19 500 00			
2	Accounts Receivable	1 100 00			
3	Supplies	600 00			(a) 400 00
4	Prepaid Advertising	2 000 00			(b) 1 000 00
5	Fixtures	11 800 00			
6	Accumulated Depreciation—Fixtures				(c) 1 800 00
7	Accounts Payable		5 000 00		
8	Marsha Lynch, Capital		24 200 00		
9	Marsha Lynch, Drawing	2 000 00			
10	Fees Income		44 000 00		
11	Advertising Expense			(b) 1 000 00	
12	Depreciation Expense—Fixtures			(c) 1 800 00	
13	Rent Expense	7 200 00			
14	Salaries Expense	24 000 00			
15	Supplies Expense			(a) 400 00	
16	Utilities Expense	5 000 00			
17	Totals	73 200 00	73 200 00	3 200 00	3 200 00
18	Net Income				
19					
20					

b. The prepaid advertising contract was signed on April 1, 20--, and covers a four-month period.

c. Rent of $950 expired during the month.

d. Depreciation is computed using the straight-line method. The equipment has an estimated useful life of five years with no salvage value.

Analyze: Why are the costs that reduce the value of equipment not directly posted to the asset account **Equipment?**

CHAPTER 5 CHALLENGE PROBLEM

Worksheet and Financial Statements

The account balances for the Sanchez International Company on January 31, 20--, follow. The balances shown are after the first month of operations.

Account	Balance	Account	Balance
101 Cash	$36,950	401 Fees Income	$14,700
111 Accounts Receivable	1,700	511 Advertising Expense	1,000
121 Supplies	1,800	514 Depr. Expense—Equip.	0
131 Prepaid Insurance	10,000	517 Insurance Expense	0
141 Equipment	12,000	518 Rent Expense	1,600
142 Accum. Depr.—Equip.	0	519 Salaries Expense	8,000
202 Accounts Payable	3,000	520 Supplies Expense	0
301 Jamie Sanchez, Capital	60,000	523 Telephone Expense	750
302 Jamie Sanchez, Drawing	3,000	524 Utilities Expense	900

ADJUSTED TRIAL BALANCE		INCOME STATEMENT		BALANCE SHEET		
DEBIT	CREDIT	DEBIT	CREDIT	DEBIT	CREDIT	
19 500 00				19 500 00		1
1 100 00				1 100 00		2
200 00				200 00		3
1 000 00				1 000 00		4
11 800 00				11 800 00		5
	1 800 00				1 800 00	6
	5 000 00				5 000 00	7
	24 200 00				24 200 00	8
2 000 00				2 000 00		9
	44 000 00		44 000 00			10
1 000 00		1 000 00				11
1 800 00		1 800 00				12
7 200 00		7 200 00				13
24 000 00		24 000 00				14
400 00		400 00				15
5 000 00		5 000 00				16
75 000 00	75 000 00	39 400 00	44 000 00	35 600 00	31 000 00	17
		4 600 00			4 600 00	18
		44 000 00	44 000 00	35 600 00	35 600 00	19
						20

INSTRUCTIONS

1. Prepare the Trial Balance section of the worksheet.
2. Record the following adjustments in the Adjustments section of the worksheet.
   a. Supplies used during the month amounted to $900.
   b. The amount in the **Prepaid Insurance** account represents a payment made on January 1, 20--, for four months of insurance coverage.
   c. The equipment, purchased on January 1, 20--, has an estimated useful life of 10 years with no salvage value. The firm uses the straight-line method of depreciation.
3. Complete the worksheet.
4. Prepare an income statement, statement of owner's equity, and balance sheet (use the report form).
5. Record the balances in the general ledger accounts, then journalize and post the adjusting entries. Use 3 for the journal page number.

Analyze: If the useful life of the equipment had been 12 years instead of 10 years, how would net income have been affected?

CHAPTER 5 CRITICAL THINKING PROBLEM

The Effect of Adjustments

Assume you are the accountant for B&H Enterprises. Charles Brown, the owner of the company, is in a hurry to receive the financial statements for the year and asks you how soon they will be ready. You tell him you have just completed the trial balance and are getting ready to prepare the adjusting entries. Mr. Brown tells you not to waste time preparing adjusting entries but to complete the worksheet without them and prepare the financial statements based on the data in the trial balance. According to him, the adjusting entries will not make that much difference. The trial balance shows the following account balances:

Prepaid Insurance	$ 8,000
Supplies	16,000
Building	360,000
Accumulated Depreciation—Building	54,000

If the income statement were prepared using trial balance amounts, the net income would be $330,000.

A review of the company's records reveals the following information:

1. A two-year insurance policy was purchased three months prior to the end of the year for $8,000.
2. Purchases of supplies during the year totaled $16,000. An inventory of supplies taken at year-end showed supplies on hand of $2,000.
3. The building was purchased three years ago and has an estimated life of 20 years.

Write a memo to Mr. Brown explaining the effect on the financial statements of omitting the adjustments. Indicate the change to net income that results from the adjusting entries.

Business Connections

MANAGERIAL FOCUS **Understanding Adjustments** ◄ Connection 1

1. A building owned by Amos Company was recently valued at $425,000 by a real estate expert. The president of the company is questioning the accuracy of the firm's latest balance sheet because it shows a book value of $275,000 for the building. How would you explain this situation to the president?
2. At the beginning of the year, Wilson Company purchased a new building and some expensive new machinery. An officer of the firm has asked you whether this purchase will affect the firm's year-end income statement. What answer would you give?
3. Suppose the president of a company where you work as an accountant questions whether it is worthwhile for you to spend time making adjustments at the end of each accounting period. How would you explain the value of the adjustments?
4. How does the worksheet help provide vital information to management?

Ethical DILEMMA **Depreciation Expense** One of your clients is preparing for a bank loan and wants to show the highest income possible so that he can obtain the loan. The client uses the straight-line method for depreciating assets. Although you recommend a salvage value of $1,000 for a depreciable asset, the client insists that you use $3,000 in order to show less depreciation on the asset and consequently, a higher net income. What would you do? ◄ Connection 2

Street WISE: Questions from the Real World **Internal Changes** Refer to The Home Depot, Inc. *1999 Annual Report* in Appendix B. ◄ Connection 3

1. Based on the account categories listed on the consolidated statements of earnings and the consolidated balance sheets, what types of adjustments do you think the company makes each fiscal year? List three types of adjustments you believe would be necessary for this company. Describe your reasons for the adjustments you have listed.
2. By what amount has the account category "accumulated depreciation and amortization" increased from fiscal year 1998 to fiscal year 1999? Explain why you think this account has increased from 1998 to 1999.

FINANCIAL STATEMENT ANALYSIS **Depreciation** DuPont reported depreciation expense of $1,444 million on its consolidated income statement for the period ended December 31, 1999. The following excerpt is taken from the company's consolidated balance sheet for the same year. ◄ Connection 4

Consolidated Balance Sheet	
(Dollars in millions, except per share) December 31, 1999	
Property, Plant and Equipment (Note 16)	35,416
Less: Accumulated Depreciation	20,545
Net Property, Plant and Equipment	14,871

Analyze:

1. What percentage of the original cost of property, plant, and equipment was depreciated *during* 1999?
2. What percentage of property, plant, and equipment cost was depreciated *as of* December 31, 1999?
3. If the company continued to record depreciation expense at this level each year, how many years remain until all assets would be fully depreciated? (Assume no salvage values.)

Analyze Online: Connect to the DuPont Web site **(www.dupont.com).** Click on the *For Investor* link to find information on quarterly earnings.

4. What is the most recent quarterly earnings statement presented? What period does the statement cover?
5. For the most recent quarter, what depreciation expense was reported?

Connection 5 ► *Extending the Thought* **Adjusting Entries** Adjusting entries update accounts at the end of an accounting period. Items that belong to the period and were not previously recorded are recorded using an adjusting entry. Suppose that a customer owes money to your business, but you are informed that the customer plans to file bankruptcy. You believe that the customer will never pay the amount owed. Do you think that an entry should be made for this event? Why or why not?

Connection 6 ► Business Communication **Prepare for a Telephone Meeting** The owner of a sparkling water bottling business believes that it is sufficient to record depreciation only at year-end, yet financial statements are prepared at the end of every month. As the accountant for the business, you believe adjusting entries should be made to update equipment depreciation expense on a monthly basis. You plan to call the owner to discuss the issue. How will you begin the conversation? How would you suggest that the situation be handled? Prepare notes on what you plan to say before you make the call to the owner.

Connection 7 ► TeamWork **Research and Apply SFAS** Break into teams of three students. Have two team members research the Statement of Financial Accounting Standards No. 106, "Accounting for Post-Retirement Benefits Other Than Pensions," using library or Internet resources. Prepare notes on your findings. The third team member should prepare a final summary one-page report on the statement and how it relates to adjusting entries. Your report should include answers to these questions:

- When do companies record post-retirement benefits?
- Which adjusting entries are needed to record employee future benefits?

interNET CONNECTION **Big Five** Ernst & Young is one of the "Big Five" accounting firms. Visit their Web site at **www.ey.com.** What services does Ernst & Young provide? What industries does the firm serve?

◄ **Connection 8**

Answers to Self Reviews

Answers to Section 1 Self Review

1. So that the financial statements can be prepared more efficiently.
2. Entries made to update accounts at the end of an accounting period to include previously unrecorded items that belong to the period.
3. To properly reflect the remaining cost to be used by the business (asset) and the amount already used by the business (expense).
4. **a. Supplies Expense** is debited for $350. **Supplies** is credited for $350.
5. **b. Rent Expense** is debited for $1,500. **Prepaid Rent** is credited for $1,500.
6. $10,000

Answers to Section 2 Self Review

1. **(a)** Beginning owner's equity
   (b) Net income or net loss for the period
   (c) Additional investments by the owner for the period
   (d) Withdrawals by the owner for the period
   (e) Ending balance of owner's equity
2. On a report form balance sheet, the liabilities and owner's equity are listed under the assets. On the account form, they are listed to the right of the assets.
3. The worksheet is only a tool that aids in the preparation of financial statements. Any changes in account balances recorded on the worksheet are not shown in the general journal and the general ledger until the adjusting entries have been journalized and posted.
4. **b.** Balance Sheet Debit column.
5. **b.** contra asset account.
6. $12,000. The adjustment for equipment depreciation is a debit to **Depreciation Expense** and a credit to **Accumulated Depreciation—Equipment.** The **Equipment** account is not changed.

Answers to Comprehensive Self Review

1. To allocate the cost of the asset to operations during its expected useful life.
2. Net income causes a net increase in owner's equity.
3. Credit balance.
4. $3,250. Debit column of the Balance Sheet section.
5. Debit column of the Balance Sheet section.

CHAPTER 6

Learning Objectives

1. Journalize and post closing entries.
2. Prepare a postclosing trial balance.
3. Interpret financial statements.
4. Review the steps in the accounting cycle.
5. Define the accounting terms new to this chapter.

Closing Entries and the Postclosing Trial Balance

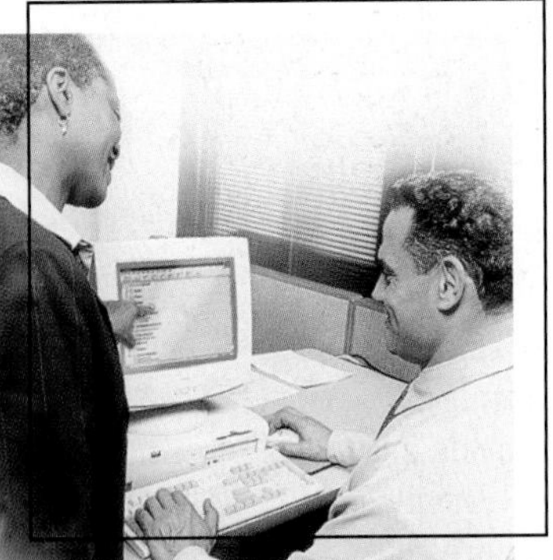

www.galileo.com

If you've ever used a travel agency to plan a vacation, book an airline flight, reserve a hotel room, or rent a car, chances are that your agent used a Galileo International Inc. product or service. The company provides travel agencies with the ability to access schedule and fare information, book reservations, and issue tickets for more than 500 airlines, 37 car rental companies, 47,000 hotel properties, 368 tour operators, and all major cruise lines.

Galileo International Inc. customers select from a wide array of sales, reservations, customer service, and business management products and services. Revenue is generated from electronic global distribution and information services, while expenses are incurred for operating, selling, administrative, and commission costs.

Thinking Critically

How do you think Galileo International Inc. executives and managers use financial statements to evaluate financial performance? How might these evaluations affect business policies or strategies?

For more information on Galileo International Inc., go to: collegeaccounting.glencoe.com.

New Terms

Closing entries
Income Summary account
Interpret
Postclosing trial balance

Section 1

Section Objective

1 Journalize and post closing entries.

Why It's Important
A business ends its accounting cycle at a given point in time. The closing process prepares the accounting records for the beginning of a new accounting cycle.

Terms to Learn

closing entries
Income Summary account

Closing Entries

In Chapter 5 we discussed the worksheet and the adjusting entries. In this chapter you will learn about closing entries.

The Closing Process

The seventh step in the accounting cycle is to journalize and post closing entries. **Closing entries** are journal entries that

- transfer the results of operations (net income or net loss) to owner's equity,
- reduce revenue, expense, and drawing account balances to zero.

The Income Summary Account

The **Income Summary account** is a special owner's equity account that is used only in the closing process to summarize results of operations. **Income Summary** has a zero balance after the closing process, and it remains with a zero balance until after the closing procedure for the next period.

Income Summary is classified as a temporary owner's equity account. Other names for this account are *Revenue and Expense Summary* and *Income and Expense Summary.*

FIGURE 6-1 ▼ Worksheet for Carter Consulting Services

Carter Consulting Services
Worksheet
Month Ended December 31, 2004

	ACCOUNT NAME	TRIAL BALANCE		ADJUSTMENTS	
		DEBIT	CREDIT	DEBIT	CREDIT
1	*Cash*	64 400 00			
2	*Accounts Receivable*	4 000 00			
3	*Supplies*	2 000 00			(a) 500 0
4	*Prepaid Rent*	6 000 00			(b) 3 000 00
5	*Equipment*	35 000 00			
6	*Accumulated Depreciation—Equipment*				(c) 583 00
7	*Accounts Payable*		12 000 00		
8	*Linda Carter, Capital*		80 000 00		
9	*Linda Carter, Drawing*	3 000 00			
10	*Fees Income*		28 000 00		
11	*Salaries Expense*	5 000 00			
12	*Utilities Expense*	600 00			
13	*Supplies Expense*			(a) 500 00	
14	*Rent Expense*			(b) 3 000 00	
15	*Depreciation Expense—Equipment*			(c) 583 00	
16	*Totals*	120 000 00	120 000 00	4 083 00	4 083 00
17	*Net Income*				
18					
19					

Steps in the Closing Process

There are four steps in the closing process:

1. Transfer the balance of the revenue account to the **Income Summary** account.
2. Transfer the expense account balances to the **Income Summary** account.
3. Transfer the balance of the **Income Summary** account to the owner's capital account.
4. Transfer the balance of the drawing account to the owner's capital account.

The worksheet contains the data necessary to make the closing entries. Refer to Figure 6-1 as you study each closing entry.

1 Objective

Journalize and post closing entries.

Step 1: Transfer Revenue Account Balances

On December 31 the worksheet for Carter Consulting Services shows one revenue account, **Fees Income.** It has a credit balance of $28,000. To *close* an account means to reduce its balance to zero. In the general journal, enter a debit of $28,000 to close the **Fees Income** account. To balance the journal entry, enter a credit of $28,000 to the **Income Summary** account. This closing entry transfers the total revenue for the period to the **Income Summary** account and reduces the balance of the revenue account to zero.

The analysis of this closing entry is shown on page 166. In this chapter the visual analyses will show the beginning balances in all T accounts in order to illustrate closing entries.

Important!

Income Summary Account

The **Income Summary** account does not have an increase or decrease side and no normal balance side.

ADJUSTED TRIAL BALANCE		INCOME STATEMENT		BALANCE SHEET		
DEBIT	CREDIT	DEBIT	CREDIT	DEBIT	CREDIT	
64 400 00				64 400 00		1
4 000 00				4 000 00		2
1 500 00				1 500 00		3
3 000 00				3 000 00		4
35 000 00				35 000 00		5
	583 00				583 00	6
	12 000 00				12 000 00	7
	80 000 00				80 000 00	8
3 000 00				3 000 00		9
	28 000 00		28 000 00			10
5 000 00		5 000 00				11
600 00		600 00				12
500 00		500 00				13
3 000 00		3 000 00				14
583 00		583 00				15
120 583 00	120 583 00	9 683 00	28 000 00	110 900 00	92 583 00	16
		18 317 00			18 317 00	17
		28 000 00	28 000 00	110 900 00	110 900 00	18
						19

Closing Entry

First Closing Entry—Close Revenue to Income Summary

Analysis

The revenue account, **Fees Income,** is decreased by $28,000 to zero. The $28,000 is transferred to the temporary owner's equity account, **Income Summary.**

Debit-Credit Rules

DEBIT Decreases in revenue accounts are recorded as debits. Debit **Fees Income** for $28,000.

CREDIT To transfer the revenue to the **Income Summary** account, credit **Income Summary** for $28,000.

T-Account Presentation

Fees Income

−	+
Closing 28,000	Balance 28,000

Income Summary

	Closing 28,000

General Journal Entry

GENERAL JOURNAL PAGE 4

	DATE		DESCRIPTION	POST. REF.	DEBIT	CREDIT	
1	2004		Closing Entries				1
2	Dec.	31	Fees Income		28 000 00		2
3			Income Summary			28 000 00	3
4							4

Write "Closing Entries" in the Description column of the general journal on the line above the first closing entry.

Safeway Inc. reported sales of $28.8 billion for the fiscal year ended January 2, 2000. To close the revenue, the company would debit the **Sales** account and credit the **Income Summary** account.

Recall

Revenue
Revenue increases owner's equity.

Expenses
Expenses decrease owner's equity.

Step 2: Transfer Expense Account Balances

The Income Statement section of the worksheet for Carter Consulting Services lists five expense accounts. Since expense accounts have debit balances, enter a credit in each account to reduce its balance to zero. Debit the total of the expenses, $9,683, to the **Income Summary** account. This closing entry transfers total expenses to the **Income Summary** account and reduces the balances of the expense accounts to zero. This is a compound journal entry; it has more than one credit.

Closing Entry

Second Closing Entry—Close Expenses to Income Summary

Analysis

The five expense account balances are reduced to zero. The total, $9,683, is transferred to the temporary owner's equity account, **Income Summary.**

Debit-Credit Rules

DEBIT To transfer the expenses to the **Income Summary** account, debit **Income Summary** for $9,683.

CREDIT Decreases to expense accounts are recorded as credits. Credit **Salaries Expense** for $5,000, **Utilities Expense** for $600, **Supplies Expense** for $500, **Rent Expense** for $3,000, and **Depreciation Expense—Equipment** for $583.

T-Account Presentation

Income Summary

Closing 9,683	Balance 28,000

Salaries Expense

+	−
Balance 5,000	Closing 5,000

Utilities Expense

+	−
Balance 600	Closing 600

Supplies Expense

+	−
Balance 500	Closing 500

Rent Expense

+	−
Balance 3,000	Closing 3,000

Depreciation Expense—Equip.

+	−
Balance 583	Closing 583

General Journal Entry

GENERAL JOURNAL PAGE 4

	DATE		DESCRIPTION	POST. REF.	DEBIT	CREDIT	
4							4
5	Dec.	31	Income Summary		9 6 8 3 00		5
6			Salaries Expense			5 0 0 0 00	6
7			Utilities Expense			6 0 0 00	7
8			Supplies Expense			5 0 0 00	8
9			Rent Expense			3 0 0 0 00	9
10			Depreciation Expense—Equip.			5 8 3 00	10

After the second closing entry, the **Income Summary** account reflects all of the entries in the Income Statement columns of the worksheet.

Income Summary

Dr.	Cr.
Closing 9,683	Closing 28,000
	Balance 18,317

For the three months ended March 30, 2000, operating expenses for Amazon.com totaled $326 million. At the end of the year, accountants for Amazon.com transferred the balances of all expense accounts to the **Income Summary** account.

Step 3: Transfer Net Income or Net Loss to Owner's Equity

The next step in the closing process is to transfer the balance of **Income Summary** to the owner's capital account. After the revenue and expense accounts are closed, the **Income Summary** account has a credit balance of $18,317, which is net income for the month. The journal entry to transfer net income to owner's equity is a debit to **Income Summary** and a credit to **Linda Carter, Capital** for $18,317. When this entry is posted, the balance of the **Income Summary** account is reduced to zero and the owner's capital account is increased by the amount of net income.

Closing Entry

Third Closing Entry—Close Income Summary to Capital

Analysis

The **Income Summary** account is reduced to zero. The net income amount, $18,317, is transferred to the owner's equity account. **Linda Carter, Capital** is increased by $18,317.

Debit-Credit Rules

DEBIT To reduce **Income Summary** to zero, debit **Income Summary** for $18,317.

CREDIT Net income increases owner's equity. Increases in owner's equity accounts are recorded as credits. Credit **Linda Carter, Capital** for $18,317.

T-Account Presentation

Income Summary

Closing 18,317	Balance 18,317

Linda Carter, Capital

−	+
	Balance 80,000
	Closing 18,317

General Journal Entry

GENERAL JOURNAL PAGE 4

	DATE		DESCRIPTION	POST. REF.	DEBIT	CREDIT	
12	Dec.	31	Income Summary		18 317 00		12
13			Linda Carter, Capital			18 317 00	13

After the third closing entry, the **Income Summary** account has a zero balance. The summarized expenses ($9,683) and revenue ($28,000) have been transferred to the owner's equity account ($18,317 net income).

Income Summary	
Dr.	Cr.
Expenses 9,683	Revenue 28,000
Closing 18,317	
Balance 0	

Linda Carter, Capital	
Dr.	Cr.
−	+
	Balance 80,000
	Net Inc. 18,317
	Balance 98,317

Step 4: Transfer the Drawing Account Balance to Capital

You will recall that withdrawals are funds taken from the business by the owner for personal use. Withdrawals are recorded in the drawing account. Withdrawals are not expenses of the business. They do not affect net income or net loss.

Withdrawals
Withdrawals decrease owner's equity.

Withdrawals appear in the statement of owner's equity as a deduction from capital. Therefore, the drawing account is closed directly to the capital account.

When this entry is posted, the balance of the drawing account is reduced to zero and the owner's capital account is decreased by the amount of the withdrawals.

Closing Entry

Fourth Closing Entry—Close Withdrawals to Capital

Analysis

The drawing account balance is reduced to zero. The balance of the drawing account, $3,000, is transferred to the owner's equity account.

Debit-Credit Rules

DEBIT Decreases in owner's equity accounts are recorded as debits. Debit **Linda Carter, Capital** for $3,000.

CREDIT Decreases in the drawing account are recorded as credits. Credit **Linda Carter, Drawing** for $3,000.

T-Account Presentation

Linda Carter, Capital	
−	+
Closing 3,000	Balance 98,317

Linda Carter, Drawing	
+	−
Balance 3,000	Closing 3,000

General Journal Entry

GENERAL JOURNAL PAGE 4

DATE		DESCRIPTION	POST. REF.	DEBIT	CREDIT
Dec.	31	*Linda Carter, Capital*		*3 000 00*	
		Linda Carter, Drawing			*3 000 00*

The new balance of the **Linda Carter, Capital** account agrees with the amount listed in the Owner's Equity section of the balance sheet.

Linda Carter, Drawing	
Dr.	Cr.
+	−
Balance 3,000	Closing 3,000
Balance 0	

Linda Carter, Capital	
Dr.	Cr.
−	+
	Balance 80,000
Drawing 3,000	Net Inc. 18,317
	Balance 95,317

Figure 6-2 on pages 170–172 shows the general journal and general ledger for Carter Consulting Services after the closing entries are recorded and posted. Note that

- "Closing" is entered in the Description column of the ledger accounts;
- the balance of **Linda Carter, Capital** agrees with the amount shown on the balance sheet for December 31;
- the ending balances of the drawing, revenue, and expense accounts are zero.

This example shows the closing process at the end of one month. Usually businesses make closing entries at the end of the fiscal year only.

FIGURE 6-2 ► Closing Process Completed: General Journal and General Ledger

Step 1 Close revenue.

Step 2 Close expense accounts.

Step 3 Close Income Summary.

Step 4 Close Drawing account.

GENERAL JOURNAL PAGE 4

DATE		DESCRIPTION	POST. REF.	DEBIT	CREDIT
2004		*Closing Entries*			
Dec.	*31*	*Fees Income*	*401*	*28 000 00*	
		Income Summary	*309*		*28 000 00*
	31	*Income Summary*	*309*	*9 683 00*	
		Salaries Expense	*511*		*5 000 00*
		Utilities Expense	*514*		*600 00*
		Supplies Expense	*517*		*500 00*
		Rent Expense	*520*		*3 000 00*
		Depreciation Expense—Equip.	*523*		*583 00*
	31	*Income Summary*	*309*	*18 317 00*	
		Linda Carter, Capital	*301*		*18 317 00*
	31	*Linda Carter, Capital*	*301*	*3 000 00*	
		Linda Carter, Drawing	*302*		*3 000 00*

ACCOUNT *Linda Carter, Capital* ACCOUNT NO. *301*

DATE		DESCRIPTION	POST. REF.	DEBIT	CREDIT	BALANCE DEBIT	BALANCE CREDIT
2004							
Nov.	6		J1		80,000 00		80,000 00
Dec.	31	Closing	J4		18,317 00		98,317 00
	31	Closing	J4	3,000 00			95,317 00

ACCOUNT *Linda Carter, Drawing* ACCOUNT NO. *302*

DATE		DESCRIPTION	POST. REF.	DEBIT	CREDIT	BALANCE DEBIT	BALANCE CREDIT
2004							
Dec.	31		J2	3,000 00		3,000 00	
	31	Closing	J4		3,000 00	—0—	

ACCOUNT *Income Summary* ACCOUNT NO. *309*

DATE		DESCRIPTION	POST. REF.	DEBIT	CREDIT	BALANCE DEBIT	BALANCE CREDIT
2004							
Dec.	31	Closing	J4		28,000 00		28,000 00
	31	Closing	J4	9,683 00			18,317 00
	31	Closing	J4	18,317 00			—0—

ACCOUNT *Fees Income* ACCOUNT NO. *401*

DATE		DESCRIPTION	POST. REF.	DEBIT	CREDIT	BALANCE DEBIT	BALANCE CREDIT
2004							
Dec.	31		J2		21,000 00		21,000 00
	31		J2		7,000 00		28,000 00
	31	Closing	J4	28,000 00			—0—

ACCOUNT *Salaries Expense* ACCOUNT NO. *511*

DATE		DESCRIPTION	POST. REF.	DEBIT	CREDIT	BALANCE DEBIT	BALANCE CREDIT
2004							
Dec.	31		J2	5,000 00		5,000 00	
	31	Closing	J4		5,000 00	—0—	

ACCOUNT *Utilities Expense* ACCOUNT NO. *514*

DATE		DESCRIPTION	POST. REF.	DEBIT	CREDIT	BALANCE DEBIT	BALANCE CREDIT
2004							
Dec.	31		J2	600 00		600 00	
	31	Closing	J4		600 00	—0—	

ACCOUNT *Supplies Expense* ACCOUNT NO. 517

DATE		DESCRIPTION	POST. REF.	DEBIT	CREDIT	BALANCE DEBIT	BALANCE CREDIT
2004							
Dec.	31	Adjusting	J3	500 00		500 00	
	31	Closing	J4		500 00	—0—	

ACCOUNT *Rent Expense* ACCOUNT NO. 520

DATE		DESCRIPTION	POST. REF.	DEBIT	CREDIT	BALANCE DEBIT	BALANCE CREDIT
2004							
Dec.	31	Adjusting	J3	3000 00		3000 00	
	31	Closing	J4		3000 00	—0—	

ACCOUNT *Depreciation Expense—Equipment* ACCOUNT NO. 523

DATE		DESCRIPTION	POST. REF.	DEBIT	CREDIT	BALANCE DEBIT	BALANCE CREDIT
2004							
Dec.	31	Adjusting	J3	583 00		583 00	
	31	Closing	J4		583 00	—0—	

You have now seen seven steps of the accounting cycle. The steps we have discussed are (1) analyze transactions, (2) journalize the transactions, (3) post the transactions, (4) prepare a worksheet, (5) prepare financial statements, (6) record adjusting entries, and (7) record closing entries. Two steps remain. They are (8) prepare a postclosing trial balance, and (9) interpret the financial information.

Section 1 Self Review

Questions

1. How is the **Income Summary** account classified?
2. What are the four steps in the closing process?
3. What is the journal entry to close the drawing account?

Exercises

4. After closing, which accounts have zero balances?
   a. asset and liability accounts
   b. liability and capital accounts
   c. liability, drawing, and expense accounts
   d. revenue, drawing, and expense accounts
5. After the closing entries are posted, which account normally has a balance other than zero?
   a. **Capital**
   b. **Fees Income**
   c. **Income Summary**
   d. **Rent Expense**

Analysis

6. The business owner removes supplies that are worth $600 from the company stockroom. She intends to take them home for personal use. What effect will this have on the company's net income?

(Answers to Section 1 Self Review are on page 195.)

Section 2

Using Accounting Information

In this section we will complete the accounting cycle for Carter Consulting Services.

Preparing the Postclosing Trial Balance

The eighth step in the accounting cycle is to prepare the postclosing trial balance, or *after-closing trial balance.* The **postclosing trial balance** is a statement that is prepared to prove the equality of total debits and credits. It is the last step in the end-of-period routine. The postclosing trial balance verifies that

- total debits equal total credits;
- revenue, expense, and drawing accounts have zero balances.

On the postclosing trial balance, the only accounts with balances are the permanent accounts:

- assets
- liabilities
- owner's equity

Figure 6-3 shows the postclosing trial balance for Carter Consulting Services.

Carter Consulting Services
Postclosing Trial Balance
December 31, 2004

ACCOUNT NAME	DEBIT	CREDIT
Cash	64 400 00	
Accounts Receivable	4 000 00	
Supplies	1 500 00	
Prepaid Rent	3 000 00	
Equipment	35 000 00	
Accumulated Depreciation—Equipment		583 00
Accounts Payable		12 000 00
Linda Carter, Capital		95 317 00
Totals	107 900 00	107 900 00

◄ **FIGURE 6-3**
Postclosing Trial Balance

Section Objectives

2 Prepare a postclosing trial balance.

Why It's Important
The postclosing trial balance helps the accountant identify any errors in the closing process.

3 Interpret financial statements.

Why It's Important
Financial statements contain information that can impact and drive operating decisions and plans for the future of the company.

4 Review the steps in the accounting cycle.

Why It's Important
Proper treatment of data as it flows through the accounting system ensures reliable financial reports.

Terms to Learn

interpret
postclosing trial balance

Finding and Correcting Errors

If the postclosing trial balance does not balance, there are errors in the accounting records. Find and correct the errors before continuing. Refer to Chapter 3 for tips on how to find common errors. Also use the audit trail to trace data through the accounting records to find errors.

2 Objective

Prepare a postclosing trial balance.

Accounting On The Job

Information Technology Services

Industry Overview

The information technology industry is projected to grow 117 percent between 1998 and 2008, making it the fastest growing industry in the United States. Products include software applications, data processing and retrieval systems, network systems, and Internet technologies.

Career Opportunities

- Financial Systems Analyst
- Database Marketing Programmer
- Data Services Manager
- Instructional Design Manager
- Accounting Technologist
- Director of Accounting Applications Development
- E-Commerce Director

Preparing for an Information Technology Services Career

- For a career as an accounting technologist or financial systems analyst, learn installation and implementation procedures for a variety of accounting applications.
- For general programming careers, obtain a bachelor's degree in computer or information science, mathematics, engineering, or the physical sciences.
- Learn current programming languages such as Java, VRML, or Visual C++.
- Gain extensive knowledge of systems and applications software packages.
- Obtain certification in database systems such as DB2, Oracle, or Sybase.
- Develop analytical and communication skills.
- Apply for a summer or co-op internship with a leading technology company like Intel.

Thinking Critically

Peachtree Software, Inc., the developer of Windows-based accounting software, frequently employs senior software engineers. What skills, experience, or education do you think would be desirable for this position?

Internet Application

Use Web sites to research information technology job opportunities in Great Plains, Peachtree, and Microsoft programs. Describe one job opportunity of interest to you. Include job title, position responsibilities, and education and skills requirements.

3 Objective

Interpret financial statements.

Interpreting the Financial Statements

The ninth and last step in the accounting cycle is interpreting the financial statements. Management needs timely and accurate financial information to operate the business successfully. To **interpret** the financial statements means to understand and explain the meaning and importance of information in accounting reports. Information in the financial statements provides answers to many questions:

- What is the cash balance?
- How much do customers owe the business?
- How much does the business owe suppliers?
- What is the profit or loss?

Managers of The Home Depot, Inc. use the corporation's financial statements to answer questions about the business. How much cash does our business have? What net earnings did our company report this year? For the fiscal year ended January 30, 2000, The Home Depot, Inc. reported an ending cash balance of $168 million and net earnings of $2.32 billion.

Figure 6-4 shows the financial statements for Carter Consulting Services at the end of its first accounting period. By interpreting these statements, management learns that

- the cash balance is $64,400,
- customers owe $4,000 to the business,
- the business owes $12,000 to its suppliers,
- the profit was $18,317.

◀ **FIGURE 6-4**
End-of-Month Financial Statements

Carter Consulting Services Income Statement Month Ended December 31, 2004		
Revenue		
Fees Income		28,000.00
Expenses		
Salaries Expense	5,000.00	
Utilities Expense	600.00	
Supplies Expense	500.00	
Rent Expense	3,000.00	
Depreciation Expense—Equipment	583.00	
Total Expenses		9,683.00
Net Income for the Month		18,317.00

Carter Consulting Services Statement of Owner's Equity Month Ended December 31, 2004		
Linda Carter, Capital, December 1, 2004		80,000.00
Net Income for December	18,317.00	
Less Withdrawals for December	3,000.00	
Increase in Capital		15,317.00
Linda Carter, Capital, December 31, 2004		95,317.00

Carter Consulting Services Balance Sheet December 31, 2004		
Assets		
Cash		64,400.00
Accounts Receivable		4,000.00
Supplies		1,500.00
Prepaid Rent		3,000.00
Equipment	35,000.00	
Less Accumulated Depreciation	583.00	34,417.00
Total Assets		107,317.00
Liabilities and Owner's Equity		
Liabilities		
Accounts Payable		12,000.00
Owner's Equity		
Linda Carter, Capital		95,317.00
Total Liabilities and Owner's Equity		107,317.00

About Accounting

Medical Accounting
Professionals in the health field, such as doctors and dentists, need to understand accounting so they can bill for services performed. Because patients have different insurance and payment plans, specialized software is used to manage the paperwork and keep track of the payments.

Review the steps in the accounting cycle.

The Accounting Cycle

You have learned about the entire accounting cycle as you studied the financial affairs of Carter Consulting Services during its first month of operations. Figure 6-5 summarizes the steps in the accounting cycle.

FIGURE 6-5 ►
The Accounting Cycle

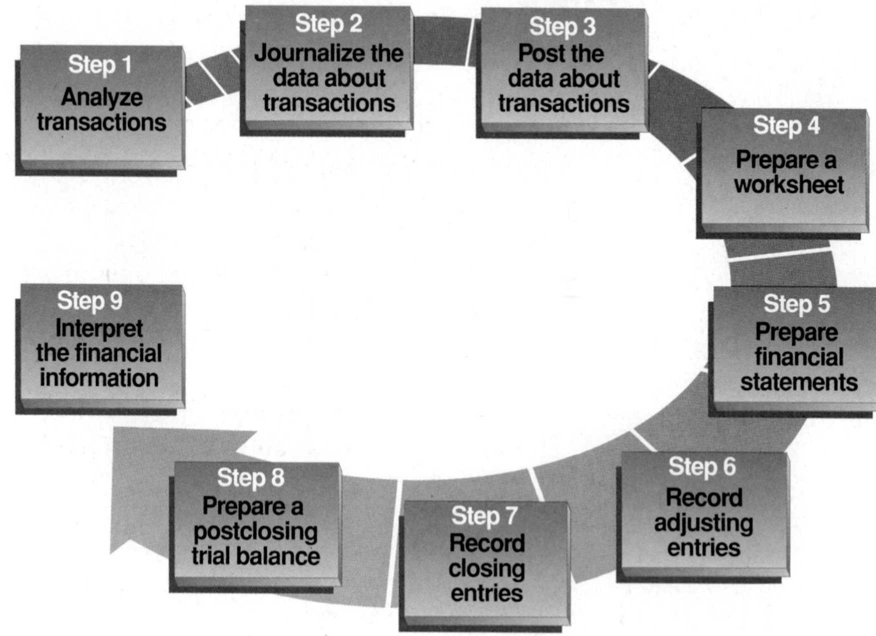

The Accounting Cycle
The accounting cycle is a series of steps performed during each period to classify, record, and summarize data to produce needed financial information.

European Union

The European Economic Community was formed in 1958 to allow goods, services, workers, and money to move freely among its member countries. Now known as the European Union, the organization has developed a single currency, the *euro*. The euro is divided into one hundred cents.

Step 1. **Analyze transactions.** Analyze source documents to determine their effects on the basic accounting equation. The data about transactions appears on a variety of source documents such as:
- sales slips,
- purchase invoices,
- credit memorandums,
- check stubs.

Step 2. **Journalize the transactions.** Record the effects of the transactions in a journal.

Step 3. **Post the journal entries.** Transfer data from the journal to the general ledger accounts.

Step 4. **Prepare a worksheet.** At the end of each period, prepare a worksheet.
- Use the Trial Balance section to prove the equality of debits and credits in the general ledger.
- Use the Adjustments section to enter changes in account balances that are needed to present an accurate and complete picture of the financial affairs of the business.
- Use the Adjusted Trial Balance section to verify the equality of debits and credits after the adjustments. Extend the amounts from the Adjusted Trial Balance section to the Income Statement and Balance Sheet sections.
- Use the Income Statement and Balance Sheet sections to prepare the financial statements.

Financial Information

- Management needs timely and accurate financial information to control operations and make decisions.
- A well-designed and well-run accounting system provides reliable financial statements to management.
- Although management is not involved in day-to-day accounting procedures and end-of-period processes, the efficiency of the procedures affects the quality and promptness of the financial information that management receives.

Thinking Critically

If you owned or managed a business, how often would you want financial statements prepared? Why?

Step 5. Prepare financial statements. Prepare financial statements to report information to owners, managers, and other interested parties.

- The income statement shows the results of operations for the period.
- The statement of owner's equity reports the changes in the owner's financial interest during the period.
- The balance sheet shows the financial position of the business at the end of the period.

Step 6. Record adjusting entries. Use the worksheet to journalize and post adjusting entries. The adjusting entries are a permanent record of the changes in account balances shown on the worksheet.

Step 7. Record closing entries. Journalize and post the closing entries to

- transfer net income or net loss to owner's equity;
- reduce the balances of the revenue, expense, and drawing accounts to zero.

Step 8. Prepare a postclosing trial balance. The postclosing trial balance shows that the general ledger is in balance after the closing entries are posted. It is also used to verify that there are zero balances in revenue, expense, and drawing accounts.

Step 9. Interpret the financial information. Use financial statements to understand and communicate financial information and to make decisions. Accountants, owners, managers, and other interested parties interpret financial statements by comparing such things as profit, revenue, and expenses from one accounting period to the next.

In addition to financial statements, Adobe Systems Incorporated prepares a Financial Highlights report. This report lists total assets, revenue, net income, and number of worldwide employees for the past five years.

After studying the accounting cycle of Carter Consulting Services, you have an understanding of how data flows through a simple accounting system for a small business:

- Source documents are analyzed.
- Transactions are recorded in the general journal.
- Transactions are posted from the general journal to the general ledger.
- Financial information is proved, adjusted, and summarized on the worksheet.
- Financial information is reported on financial statements.

Figure 6-6 illustrates this data flow.

FIGURE 6-6 ▶
Flow of Data through a Simple Accounting System

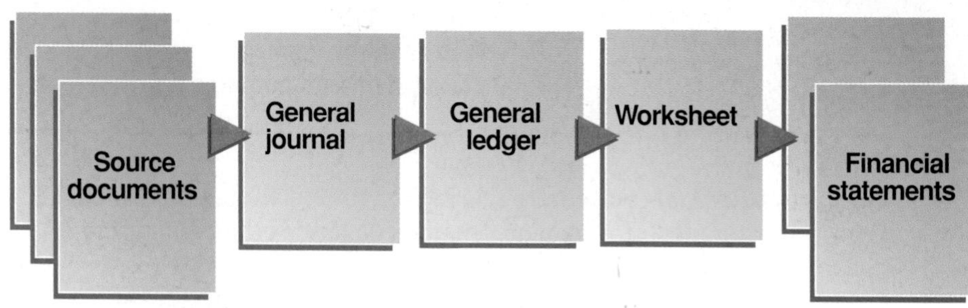

As you will learn in later chapters, some accounting systems have more complex records, procedures, and financial statements. However, the steps of the accounting cycle and the underlying accounting principles remain the same.

Section 2 Self Review

Questions

1. Why is a postclosing trial balance prepared?
2. What accounts appear on the postclosing trial balance?
3. What are the last three steps in the accounting cycle?

Exercises

4. Which of the following accounts will not appear on the postclosing trial balance?
   a. **J. T. Owens, Drawing**
   b. **Cash**
   c. **J. T. Owens, Capital**
   d. **Accounts Payable**
5. After the revenue and expense accounts are closed, **Income Summary** has a debit balance of $15,000. What does this figure represent?
   a. net profit of $15,000
   b. net loss of $15,000
   c. owner's withdrawals of $15,000
   d. increase in owner's equity of $15,000

Analysis

6. On which financial statement would you find the answer to each question?
   - What were the total fees earned this month?
   - How much money is owed to suppliers?
   - Did the business make a profit?
   - Is there enough cash to purchase new equipment?
   - What were the expenses?
   - Do customers owe money to the business?

(Answers to Section 2 Self Review are on page 195.)

CHAPTER 6 Review and Applications

Review

Chapter Summary

After the worksheet and financial statements have been completed and adjusting entries have been journalized and posted, the closing entries are recorded and a postclosing trial balance is prepared.

Learning Objectives

1 Journalize and post closing entries.

Journalizing and posting the closing entries is the seventh step in the accounting cycle. Closing entries transfer the results of operations to owner's equity and reduce the balances of the revenue and expense accounts to zero. The worksheet provides the data necessary for the closing entries. A temporary owner's equity account, **Income Summary,** is used. There are four steps in the closing process:

1. The balance of the revenue account is transferred to the **Income Summary** account.

   Debit **Revenue**
       Credit **Income Summary**

2. The balances of the expense accounts are transferred to the **Income Summary** account.

   Debit **Income Summary**
       Credit **Expenses**

3. The balance of the **Income Summary** account—net income or net loss—is transferred to the owner's capital account.

   If **Income Summary** has a credit balance:

   Debit **Income Summary**
       Credit **Owner's Capital**

   If **Income Summary** has a debit balance:

   Debit **Owner's Capital**
       Credit **Income Summary**

4. The drawing account is closed to the owner's capital account.

   Debit **Owner's Capital**
       Credit **Drawing**

After the closing entries have been posted, the capital account reflects the results of operations for the period. The revenue and expense accounts, with zero balances, are ready to accumulate data for the next period.

2 Prepare a postclosing trial balance.

Preparing the postclosing trial balance is the eighth step in the accounting cycle. A postclosing trial balance is prepared to test the equality of total debit and credit balances in the general ledger after the adjusting and closing entries have been recorded. This report lists only permanent accounts open at the end of the period—asset, liability, and the owner's capital accounts. The temporary accounts—revenue, expenses, drawing, and **Income Summary**—apply only to one accounting period and do not appear on the postclosing trial balance.

3 Interpret financial statements.

The ninth step in the accounting cycle is interpreting the financial statements. Business decisions must be based on accurate and timely financial data.

4 Review the steps in the accounting cycle.

The accounting cycle consists of a series of steps that are repeated in each fiscal period. These steps are designed to classify, record, and summarize the data needed to produce financial information.

The steps of the accounting cycle are:

1. Analyze transactions.
2. Journalize the transactions.
3. Post the journal entries.
4. Prepare a worksheet.
5. Prepare financial statements.
6. Record adjusting entries.
7. Record closing entries.
8. Prepare a postclosing trial balance.
9. Interpret the financial information.

5 Define the accounting terms new to this chapter.

CHAPTER 6 GLOSSARY

Closing entries (p. 164) Journal entries that transfer the results of operations (net income or net loss) to owner's equity and reduce the revenue, expense, and drawing account balances to zero

Income Summary account (p. 164) A special owner's equity account that is used only in the closing process to summarize the results of operations

Interpret (p. 174) To understand and explain the meaning and importance of something (such as financial statements)

Postclosing trial balance (p. 173) A statement that is prepared to prove the equality of total debits and credits after the closing process is completed

Comprehensive Self Review

1. A firm has $25,000 in revenue for the period. Give the entry to close the **Fees Income** account.
2. A firm has the following expenses: **Rent Expense,** $1,600; **Salaries Expense,** $3,360; **Supplies Expense,** $640. Give the entry to close the expense accounts.
3. What three financial statements are prepared during the accounting cycle?
4. What is the last step in the accounting cycle?
5. Is the following statement true or false? Why? "All owner's equity accounts appear on the postclosing trial balance."

(Answers to Comprehensive Self Review are on page 195.)

Discussion Questions

1. Why is a postclosing trial balance prepared?
2. What accounts appear on a postclosing trial balance?
3. What is the accounting cycle?
4. Name the steps of the accounting cycle.
5. Briefly describe the flow of data through a simple accounting system.
6. What three procedures are performed at the end of each accounting period before the financial information is interpreted?
7. Where does the accountant obtain the data needed for the adjusting entries?
8. Why does the accountant record closing entries at the end of a period?
9. How is the **Income Summary** account used in the closing procedure?
10. Where does the accountant obtain the data needed for the closing entries?

Applications

EXERCISES

Journalize closing entries.

◄ **Exercise 6-1**
Objective 1

On December 31 the ledger of McWilliams Company contained the following account balances:

Cash	$18,000	Jerry McWilliams, Drawing	$12,000
Accounts Receivable	1,200	Fees Income	42,500
Supplies	800	Depreciation Expense	1,500
Equipment	15,000	Salaries Expense	14,000
Accumulated Depreciation	1,500	Supplies Expense	2,000
Accounts Payable	2,000	Telephone Expense	1,800
Jerry McWilliams, Capital	23,100	Utilities Expense	3,600

All the accounts have normal balances. Journalize the closing entries. Use 4 as the general journal page number.

Postclosing trial balance.

◄ **Exercise 6-2**
Objective 2

From the following list identify the accounts that will appear on the postclosing trial balance.

ACCOUNTS

1. Cash
2. Accounts Receivable
3. Supplies
4. Equipment
5. Accumulated Depreciation
6. Accounts Payable
7. Theron White, Capital
8. Theron White, Drawing
9. Fees Income
10. Depreciation Expense
11. Salaries Expense
12. Supplies Expense
13. Utilities Expense

Accounting cycle.

◄ **Exercise 6-3**
Objective 4

Following are the steps in the accounting cycle. Arrange the steps in the proper sequence.

1. Journalize the transactions.
2. Prepare a worksheet.
3. Analyze transactions.
4. Record adjusting entries.
5. Post the journal entries.
6. Prepare a postclosing trial balance.
7. Prepare financial statements.
8. Record closing entries.
9. Interpret the financial information.

Exercise 6-4 ► Objective 3

Financial statements.

Managers often consult financial statements for specific types of information. Indicate whether each of the following items would appear on the income statement, statement of owner's equity, or the balance sheet. Use *I* for the income statement, *E* for the statement of owner's equity, and *B* for the balance sheet. If an item appears on more than one statement, use all letters that apply to that item.

1. Cash on hand
2. Revenue earned during the period
3. Total assets of the business
4. Net income for the period
5. Owner's capital at the end of the period
6. Supplies on hand
7. Cost of supplies used during the period
8. Accounts receivable of the business
9. Accumulated depreciation on the firm's equipment
10. Amount of depreciation charged off on the firm's equipment during the period
11. Original cost of the firm's equipment
12. Book value of the firm's equipment
13. Total expenses for the period
14. Accounts payable of the business
15. Owner's withdrawals for the period

Exercise 6-5 ► Objective 1

Closing entries.

The **Income Summary** and **Alexis Wells, Capital** accounts for Alexis Production Company at the end of its accounting period follow.

ACCOUNT *Income Summary* ACCOUNT NO. *399*

DATE		DESCRIPTION	POST. REF.	DEBIT	CREDIT	BALANCE DEBIT	BALANCE CREDIT
20--							
Dec.	*31*	*Closing*	*J4*		*7 750 00*		*7 750 00*
	31	*Closing*	*J4*	*5 050 00*			*2 700 00*
	31	*Closing*	*J4*	*2 700 00*			*—0—*

ACCOUNT *Alexis Wells, Capital* ACCOUNT NO. *301*

DATE		DESCRIPTION	POST. REF.	DEBIT	CREDIT	BALANCE DEBIT	BALANCE CREDIT
20--							
Dec.	*1*		*J1*		*25 000 00*		*25 000 00*
	31	*Closing*	*J4*		*2 700 00*		*27 700 00*
	31	*Closing*	*J4*	*1 400 00*			*26 300 00*

Complete the following statements.

1. Total revenue for the period is ________.
2. Total expenses for the period are ________.
3. Net income for the period is ________.
4. Owner's withdrawals for the period are ________.

◄ **Exercise 6-6**
Objective 1

Closing entries.

The ledger accounts of Cool Streams Internet Company appear as follows on March 31, 20--.

ACCOUNT NO.	ACCOUNT	BALANCE
101	Cash	$11,500
111	Accounts Receivable	2,200
121	Supplies	1,350
131	Prepaid Insurance	3,480
141	Equipment	16,800
142	Accumulated Depreciation—Equipment	3,360
202	Accounts Payable	1,800
301	Alonzo Hernandez, Capital	19,600
302	Alonzo Hernandez, Drawing	1,000
401	Fees Income	46,000
510	Depreciation Expense—Equipment	1,680
511	Insurance Expense	1,600
514	Rent Expense	4,800
517	Salaries Expense	23,600
518	Supplies Expense	650
519	Telephone Expense	900
523	Utilities Expense	1,200

All accounts have normal balances. Journalize and post the closing entries. Use 4 as the page number for the general journal in journalizing the closing entries.

◄ **Exercise 6-7**
Objective 1

Closing entries.

On December 31 the **Income Summary** account of Hensley Company has a debit balance of $9,000 after revenue of $14,000 and expenses of $23,000 were closed to the account. **Ronnie Hensley, Drawing** has a debit balance of $1,000 and **Ronnie Hensley, Capital** has a credit balance of $28,000. Record the journal entries necessary to complete closing the accounts. What is the new balance of **Ronnie Hensley, Capital?**

◄ **Exercise 6-8**
Objective 4

Accounting cycle.

Complete a chart of the accounting cycle by writing the steps of the cycle in their proper sequence.

Problems

Selected problems can be completed using:
Peachtree QuickBooks Spreadsheets

PROBLEM SET A

Problem 6-1A ►
Objective 1

Adjusting and closing entries.

The Longacre Consumer Satisfaction Company, owned by Mary Longacre, is employed by large companies to test consumer reaction to new products. On January 31 the firm's worksheet showed the following adjustments data: (a) supplies used, $280; (b) expired rent, $1,500; and (c) depreciation on office equipment, $560. The balances of the revenue and expense accounts listed in the Income Statement section of the worksheet and the drawing account listed in the Balance Sheet section of the worksheet are given below.

REVENUE AND EXPENSE ACCOUNTS

401	Fees Income	$38,500 Cr.
511	Depr. Expense—Office Equipment	560 Dr.
514	Rent Expense	1,500 Dr.
517	Salaries Expense	20,600 Dr.
520	Supplies Expense	280 Dr.
523	Telephone Expense	470 Dr.
526	Travel Expense	4,460 Dr.
529	Utilities Expense	230 Dr.

DRAWING ACCOUNT

302	Mary Longacre, Drawing	2,400 Dr.

Wilson Talent Agency
Worksheet
Month Ended December 31, 20--

	ACCOUNT NAME	TRIAL BALANCE DEBIT	TRIAL BALANCE CREDIT	ADJUSTMENTS DEBIT		ADJUSTMENTS CREDIT	
1	*Cash*	7,700.00					
2	*Accounts Receivable*	1,000.00					
3	*Supplies*	500.00				(a)	200.00
4	*Prepaid Advertising*	2,000.00				(b)	250.00
5	*Equipment*	5,000.00					
6	*Accumulated Depreciation—Equipment*					(c)	200.00
7	*Accounts Payable*		1,000.00				
8	*Virginia Wilson, Capital*		11,000.00				
9	*Virginia Wilson, Drawing*	700.00					
10	*Fees Income*		6,250.00				
11	*Supplies Expense*			(a)	200.00		
12	*Advertising Expense*			(b)	250.00		
13	*Depreciation Expense—Equipment*			(c)	200.00		
14	*Salaries Expense*	1,200.00					
15	*Utilities Expense*	150.00					
16	*Totals*	18,250.00	18,250.00		650.00		650.00
17	*Net Income*						
18							
19							

INSTRUCTIONS

1. Record the adjusting entries in the general journal, page 3.
2. Record the closing entries in the general journal, page 4.

Analyze: What closing entry is required to close a drawing account?

Journalizing and posting adjusting and closing entries and preparing a postclosing trial balance.

◄ **Problem 6-2A**
Objectives 1, 2

A completed worksheet for Wilson Talent Agency is shown on pages 184–185.

INSTRUCTIONS

1. Record balances as of December 31, 20--, in the ledger accounts.
2. Journalize (use 3 as the page number) and post the adjusting entries.
3. Journalize (use 4 as the page number) and post the closing entries.
4. Prepare a postclosing trial balance.

Analyze: How many accounts are listed in the Adjusted Trial Balance section? How many accounts are listed on the postclosing trial balance?

Journalizing and posting closing entries.

◄ **Problem 6-3A**
Objective 1

On December 31, after adjustments, Preston Company's ledger contains the following account balances.

101	Cash	$ 9,300	Dr.
111	Accounts Receivable	4,200	Dr.
121	Supplies	750	Dr.
131	Prepaid Rent	9,900	Dr.
141	Equipment	13,500	Dr.
142	Accumulated Depreciation—Equip.	375	Cr.

ADJUSTED TRIAL BALANCE		INCOME STATEMENT		BALANCE SHEET		
DEBIT	CREDIT	DEBIT	CREDIT	DEBIT	CREDIT	
7 700 00				7 700 00		1
1 000 00				1 000 00		2
300 00				300 00		3
1 750 00				1 750 00		4
5 000 00				5 000 00		5
	200 00				200 00	6
	1 000 00				1 000 00	7
	11 000 00				11 000 00	8
700 00				700 00		9
	6 250 00		6 250 00			10
200 00		200 00				11
250 00		250 00				12
200 00		200 00				13
1 200 00		1 200 00				14
150 00		150 00				15
18 450 00	18 450 00	2 000 00	6 250 00	16 450 00	12 200 00	16
		4 250 00			4 250 00	17
		6 250 00	6 250 00	16 450 00	16 450 00	18
						19

202	Accounts Payable	1,875 Cr.
301	Sara Preston, Capital (12/1/20--)	13,905 Cr.
302	Sara Preston, Drawing	1,800 Dr.
401	Fees Income	34,500 Cr.
511	Advertising Expense	1,200 Dr.
514	Depreciation Expense—Equip.	225 Dr.
517	Rent Expense	900 Dr.
519	Salaries Expense	7,200 Dr.
523	Utilities Expense	1,680 Dr.

INSTRUCTIONS

1. Record the balances in the ledger accounts as of December 31.
2. Journalize the closing entries in the general journal, page 4.
3. Post the closing entries to the general ledger accounts.

Analyze: What is the balance of the **Salaries Expense** account after closing entries are posted?

Problem 6-4A ► Objectives 1, 2, 4

QB

Worksheet, journalizing and posting adjusting and closing entries, and the postclosing trial balance.

A partially completed worksheet for Bush Auto Detailing Service, a firm that details cars and vans, follows.

Bush Auto Detailing Service
Worksheet
Month Ended December 31, 20--

	ACCOUNT NAME	TRIAL BALANCE DEBIT	TRIAL BALANCE CREDIT	ADJUSTMENTS DEBIT	ADJUSTMENTS CREDIT
1	*Cash*	31 050 00			
2	*Accounts Receivable*	4 950 00			
3	*Supplies*	4 000 00			(a) 1 600 00
4	*Prepaid Advertising*	3 000 00			(b) 1 400 00
5	*Equipment*	20 000 00			
6	*Accumulated Depreciation—Equipment*				(c) 480 00
7	*Accounts Payable*		5 000 00		
8	*Mark Bush, Capital*		35 500 00		
9	*Mark Bush, Drawing*	2 000 00			
10	*Fees Income*		30 000 00		
11	*Supplies Expense*			(a) 1 600 00	
12	*Advertising Expense*			(b) 1 400 00	
13	*Depreciation Expense—Equipment*			(c) 480 00	
14	*Salaries Expense*	4 800 00			
15	*Utilities Expense*	700 00			
16	*Totals*	70 500 00	70 500 00	3 480 00	3 480 00
17					
18					
19					
20					

INSTRUCTIONS

1. Record balances as of December 31 in the ledger accounts.
2. Prepare the worksheet.
3. Journalize (use 3 as the journal page number) and post the adjusting entries.
4. Journalize (use 4 as the journal page number) and post the closing entries.
5. Prepare a postclosing trial balance.

Analyze: What total debits were posted to the general ledger to complete all closing entries for the month of December?

PROBLEM SET B

◄ **Problem 6-1B**
Objective 1

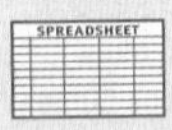

Adjusting and closing entries.

Thrifty Maid Service, owned by Michael Turner, provides cleaning services to hotels, motels, and hospitals. On January 31 the firm's worksheet showed the following adjustment data. The balances of the revenue and expense accounts listed in the Income Statement section of the worksheet and the drawing account listed in the Balance Sheet section of the worksheet are also given.

ADJUSTMENTS

a. Supplies used, $2,860
b. Expired insurance, $370
c. Depreciation on machinery, $1,120

REVENUE AND EXPENSE ACCOUNTS

401 Fees Income	$32,800 Cr.
511 Depreciation Expense—Machinery	1,120 Dr.
514 Insurance Expense	370 Dr.
517 Rent Expense	3,000 Dr.
520 Salaries Expense	16,000 Dr.
523 Supplies Expense	2,860 Dr.
526 Telephone Expense	210 Dr.
529 Utilities Expense	640 Dr.

DRAWING ACCOUNT

302 Michael Turner, Drawing	2,400 Dr.

INSTRUCTIONS

1. Record the adjusting entries in the general journal, page 3.
2. Record the closing entries in the general journal, page 4.

Analyze: What effect did the adjusting entry for expired insurance have on the **Insurance Expense** account?

Dave's Lawn and Garden Service
Worksheet
Month Ended December 31, 20--

	ACCOUNT NAME	TRIAL BALANCE DEBIT	TRIAL BALANCE CREDIT	ADJUSTMENTS DEBIT	ADJUSTMENTS CREDIT
1	*Cash*	2700 00			
2	*Accounts Receivable*	500 00			
3	*Supplies*	500 00			(a) 250 00
4	*Prepaid Advertising*	750 00			(b) 100 00
5	*Equipment*	5000 00			
6	*Accumulated Depreciation—Equipment*				(c) 125 00
7	*Accounts Payable*		750 00		
8	*Dave Andrews, Capital*		6850 00		
9	*Dave Andrews, Drawing*	700 00			
10	*Fees Income*		3900 00		
11	*Supplies Expense*			(a) 250 00	
12	*Advertising Expense*			(b) 100 00	
13	*Depreciation Expense—Equipment*			(c) 125 00	
14	*Salaries Expense*	1200 00			
15	*Utilities Expense*	150 00			
16	*Totals*	11500 00	11500 00	475 00	475 00
17	*Net Income*				
18					
19					
20					
21					

Problem 6-2B ► Objectives 1, 2

Journalizing and posting adjusting and closing entries and preparing a postclosing trial balance.

A completed worksheet for Dave's Lawn and Garden Service is shown above.

INSTRUCTIONS

1. Record the balances as of December 31 in the ledger accounts.
2. Journalize (use 3 as the page number) and post the adjusting entries.
3. Journalize (use 4 as the page number) and post the closing entries.
4. Prepare a postclosing trial balance.

Analyze: What total credits were posted to the general ledger to complete the closing entries?

ADJUSTED TRIAL BALANCE		INCOME STATEMENT		BALANCE SHEET		
DEBIT	CREDIT	DEBIT	CREDIT	DEBIT	CREDIT	
2,700 00				2,700 00		1
500 00				500 00		2
250 00				250 00		3
650 00				650 00		4
5,000 00				5,000 00		5
	125 00				125 00	6
	750 00				750 00	7
	6,850 00				6,850 00	8
700 00				700 00		9
	3,900 00		3,900 00			10
250 00		250 00				11
100 00		100 00				12
125 00		125 00				13
1,200 00		1,200 00				14
150 00		150 00				15
11,625 00	11,625 00	1,825 00	3,900 00	9,800 00	7,725 00	16
		2,075 00			2,075 00	17
		3,900 00	3,900 00	9,800 00	9,800 00	18
						19
						20
						21

◄ **Problem 6-3B**
Objective 1

Journalizing and posting closing entries.

On December 31, after adjustments, The Green House's ledger contains the following account balances.

101	Cash	$ 9,500 Dr.
111	Accounts Receivable	2,400 Dr.
121	Supplies	1,000 Dr.
131	Prepaid Rent	7,700 Dr.
141	Equipment	12,000 Dr.
142	Accumulated Depreciation—Equip.	300 Cr.
202	Accounts Payable	3,250 Cr.
301	Shane McCoy, Capital (12/1/20--)	19,150 Cr.
302	Shane McCoy, Drawing	1,200 Dr.
401	Fees Income	18,000 Cr.
511	Advertising Expense	1,100 Dr.
514	Depreciation Expense—Equip.	300 Dr.
517	Rent Expense	700 Dr.
519	Salaries Expense	3,600 Dr.
523	Utilities Expense	1,200 Dr.

INSTRUCTIONS

1. Record the balances in the ledger accounts as of December 31.
2. Journalize the closing entries in the general journal, page 4.
3. Post the closing entries to the general ledger accounts.

Analyze: List the accounts that required closing entries for the month of December.

Problem 6-4B ► Objectives 1, 2, 4

Worksheet, journalizing and posting adjusting and closing entries, and the postclosing trial balance.

A partially completed worksheet for Lance Wallace, CPA, for the month ending June 30, 20--, is shown below.

INSTRUCTIONS

1. Record the balances as of June 30 in the ledger accounts.
2. Prepare the worksheet.
3. Journalize (use 3 as the journal page number) and post the adjusting entries.
4. Journalize (use 4 as the journal page number) and post the closing entries.
5. Prepare a postclosing trial balance.

Analyze: What is the reported net income for the month of June for Lance Wallace, CPA?

Lance Wallace, CPA
Worksheet
Month Ended June 30, 20--

	ACCOUNT NAME	TRIAL BALANCE DEBIT	TRIAL BALANCE CREDIT	ADJUSTMENTS DEBIT	ADJUSTMENTS CREDIT
1	Cash	3,300.00			
2	Accounts Receivable	2,700.00			
3	Supplies	2,400.00			(a) 450.00
4	Computers	10,800.00			
5	Accumulated Depreciation—Computers		900.00		(b) 180.00
6	Accounts Payable		3,600.00		
7	Lance Wallace, Capital		11,250.00		
8	Lance Wallace, Drawing	3,000.00			
9	Fees Income		17,700.00		
10	Salaries Expense	9,000.00			
11	Supplies Expense			(a) 450.00	
12	Depreciation Expense—Computers			(b) 180.00	
13	Travel Expense	1,500.00			
14	Utilities Expense	750.00			
15	Totals	33,450.00	33,450.00	630.00	630.00
16					
17					
18					
19					

CHAPTER 6 CHALLENGE PROBLEM

The Closing Process

The Trial Balance section of the worksheet for The Car Wash for the period ended December 31, 20--, appears below. Adjustments data is also given.

ADJUSTMENTS

a. Supplies used, $1,200
b. Expired insurance, $800
c. Depreciation expense for machinery, $400

INSTRUCTIONS

1. Complete the worksheet.
2. Prepare an income statement.
3. Prepare a statement of owner's equity.
4. Prepare a balance sheet.
5. Journalize the adjusting entries in the general journal, page 3.
6. Journalize the closing entries in the general journal, page 4.
7. Prepare a postclosing trial balance.

Analyze: If the adjusting entry for expired insurance had been recorded in error as a credit to **Insurance Expense** and a debit to **Prepaid Insurance** for $800, what reported net income would have resulted?

The Car Wash
Worksheet
Month Ended December 31, 20--

	ACCOUNT NAME	TRIAL BALANCE DEBIT	TRIAL BALANCE CREDIT	ADJUSTMENTS DEBIT	ADJUSTMENTS CREDIT
1	*Cash*	13 600 00			
2	*Accounts Receivable*	3 000 00			
3	*Supplies*	2 400 00			(a) 1 200 00
4	*Prepaid Insurance*	3 600 00			(b) 800 00
5	*Machinery*	28 000 00			
6	*Accumulated Depreciation—Machinery*				(c) 400 00
7	*Accounts Payable*		4 500 00		
8	*T. A. Watson, Capital*		24 860 00		
9	*T. A. Watson, Drawing*	2 000 00			
10	*Fees Income*		27 500 00		
11	*Supplies Expense*			(a) 1 200 00	
12	*Insurance Expense*			(b) 800 00	
13	*Salaries Expense*	3 700 00			
14	*Depreciation Expense—Machinery*			(c) 400 00	
15	*Utilities Expense*	560 00			
16	*Totals*	56 860 00	56 860 00	2 400 00	2 400 00
17					
18					

CHAPTER 6 CRITICAL THINKING PROBLEM

Owner's Equity

Brenda Powell, the bookkeeper for Executive Home Designs Company, has just finished posting the closing entries for the year to the ledger. She is concerned about the following balances:

Capital account balance in the general ledger:	$194,200
Ending capital balance on the statement of owner's equity:	111,200

Brenda knows that these amounts should agree and asks for your assistance in reviewing her work.

Your review of the general ledger of Executive Home Designs Company reveals a beginning capital balance of $100,000. You also review the general journal for the accounting period and find the following closing entries.

GENERAL JOURNAL PAGE *15*

	DATE		DESCRIPTION	POST. REF.	DEBIT	CREDIT	
1	*20--*		*Closing Entries*				1
2	*Dec.*	*31*	*Fees Income*		*196 000 00*		2
3			*Accumulated Depreciation*		*17 000 00*		3
4			*Accounts Payable*		*66 000 00*		4
5			*Income Summary*			*279 000 00*	5
6							6
7		*31*	*Income Summary*		*184 800 00*		7
8			*Salaries Expense*			*156 000 00*	8
9			*Supplies Expense*			*10 000 00*	9
10			*Depreciation Expense*			*4 800 00*	10
11			*Brenda Powell, Drawing*			*14 000 00*	11
12							12
13							13
14							14

1. What errors did Ms. Powell make in preparing the closing entries for the period?
2. Prepare a general journal entry to correct the errors made.
3. Explain why the balance of the capital account in the ledger after closing entries have been posted will be the same as the ending capital balance on the statement of owner's equity.

Business Connections

MANAGERIAL FOCUS **Interpreting Financial Statements** ◄ **Connection 1**

1. An officer of Carson Company recently commented that when he receives the firm's financial statements, he looks at just the bottom line of the income statement—the line that shows the net income or net loss for the period. He said that he does not bother with the rest of the income statement because "it's only the bottom line that counts." He also does not read the balance sheet. Do you think this manager is correct in the way he uses the financial statements? Why or why not?
2. The president of Henderson Corporation is concerned about the firm's ability to pay its debts on time. What items on the balance sheet would help her to assess the firm's debt-paying ability?
3. Why is it important that a firm's financial records be kept up to date and that management receive the financial statements promptly after the end of each accounting period?
4. What kinds of operating and general policy decisions might be influenced by data on the financial statements?

Ethical DILEMMA **Overstated Income** You have just taken over as bookkeeper of a company and immediately discover that the firm did not make adjusting entries every year. From your conversations with other employees in the firm, you have determined that the former bookkeeper intentionally did this in order to report a higher net income to impress the owner. What will you do? ◄ **Connection 2**

Street WISE: Questions from the Real World **Closing Process** Refer to The Home Depot, Inc. *1999 Annual Report* in Appendix B. ◄ **Connection 3**

1. Locate the consolidated balance sheets and consolidated statements of earnings. List ten permanent account categories and five temporary account categories found within these statements.
2. Based on the consolidated statements of earnings, what is the closing entry that should be made to zero out all operating expense categories?

FINANCIAL STATEMENT ANALYSIS **Income Statement** In 1999 CSX Corporation reported operating expenses of $10,203 million. A partial list of the company's operating expenses follows. CSX Corporation reported revenues from external customers to be $10,811 million for the year. These revenues are divided among three operations: surface transportation, container shipping, and contract logistics. ◄ **Connection 4**

CSX CORPORATION

Revenues from External Customers *(Dollars in millions)*	
Surface Transportation	$6,566
Container Shipping	3,809
Contract Logistics	436

Operating Expenses (partial list) *(Dollars in millions)*	
Labor and Fringe Benefits	$3,471
Materials, Supplies, and Other	2,662
Conrail Operating Fee, Rent, and Services	280
Building and Equipment Rent	1,211
Inland Transportation	1,044
Depreciation	595
Fuel	484

Analyze:

1. If the given categories represent the related general ledger accounts, what journal entry would be made to close the expense accounts at year-end?
2. What journal entry would be made to close the revenue accounts?

Analyze Online: Locate the Web site for CSX Corporation **(www.csx.com).** Click on *About CSX Corporation.* Within the *Financial Information* link, find the most recent annual report.

3. On the consolidated statement of earnings, what was the amount reported for operating expenses?
4. What percentage increase or decrease does this figure represent from the operating expenses reported in 1999 of $10,203 million?

Connection 5 ► *Extending the Thought* **Worksheets** Suppose that an accountant with many years' experience suggests that you skip preparation of the worksheet. The accountant claims that the financial statements can be prepared using only the general ledger account balances. What risks can you identify if the accountant uses this procedure? Do you agree or disagree with this approach? Why?

Connection 6 ► **Business Communication** **Training** As the general ledger accountant for a music supply store, you have just completed the trial balance, closing entries, and postclosing trial balance for the month. Next month, you will be on vacation during the closing process. Your boss has hired a temporary employee to perform these duties while you are away. Prepare a descriptive report for your replacement explaining the differences between a postclosing trial balance and a trial balance.

Connection 7 ► **TeamWork** **Job Opportunities** Using the Internet or your local newspaper, review job listings to find accounting positions that require knowledge of adjusting and closing entries. Each member of the team should contribute at least two job titles and their related description and required skills. Create a listing for all jobs.

inter NET CONNECTION **GAO** Visit the U.S. General Accounting Office Web site at **www.gao.gov.** When was the GAO founded? What is its purpose? Who is the head of the GAO? When does this person's term expire? What is the purpose of FraudNET?

◄ **Connection 8**

Answers to Self Reviews

Answers to Section 1 Self Review

1. A temporary owner's equity account.
2. Close the revenue account to **Income Summary.**
   Close the expense accounts to **Income Summary.**
   Close the **Income Summary** account to the capital account.
   Close the drawing account to the capital account.
3. Debit **Capital** and credit **Drawing.**
4. **d.** revenue, drawing, and expense accounts
5. **a. Capital**
6. No effect on net income.

Answers to Section 2 Self Review

1. To make sure the general ledger is in balance after the adjusting and closing entries are posted.
2. Asset, liability, and the owner's capital accounts.
3. (7) Record closing entries, (8) prepare a postclosing trial balance, (9) interpret the financial statements.
4. **a. J. T. Owens, Drawing**
5. **b.** net loss of $15,000
6. The income statement will answer questions about fees earned, expenses incurred, and profit. The balance sheet will answer questions about the cash balance, the amount owed by customers, and the amount owed to suppliers.

Answers to Comprehensive Self Review

1. Fees Income	25,000	
Income Summary		25,000
2. Income Summary	5,600	
Rent Expense		1,600
Salaries Expense		3,360
Supplies Expense		640

3. Income statement, statement of owner's equity, and balance sheet.
4. Interpret the financial statements.
5. False. The *temporary* owner's equity accounts do not appear on the postclosing trial balance. The temporary owner's equity accounts are the drawing account and **Income Summary.**

MINI-PRACTICE SET 

Service Business Accounting Cycle

Carter Consulting Services

This project will give you an opportunity to apply your knowledge of accounting principles and procedures by handling all the accounting work of Carter Consulting Services for the month of January 2005.

INTRODUCTION

Assume that you are the chief accountant for Carter Consulting Services. During January the business will use the same types of records and procedures that you learned about in Chapters 1 through 6. The chart of accounts for Carter Consulting Services has been expanded to include a few new accounts. Follow the instructions to complete the accounting records for the month of January.

Carter Consulting Services
Chart of Accounts

Assets	**Revenue**
101 Cash	401 Fees Income
111 Accounts Receivable	**Expenses**
121 Supplies	511 Salaries Expense
134 Prepaid Insurance	514 Utilities Expense
137 Prepaid Rent	517 Supplies Expense
141 Equipment	520 Rent Expense
142 Accumulated Depreciation—Equipment	523 Depreciation Expense—Equipment
Liabilities	526 Advertising Expense
202 Accounts Payable	529 Maintenance Expense
Owner's Equity	532 Telephone Expense
301 Linda Carter, Capital	535 Insurance Expense
302 Linda Carter, Drawing	
309 Income Summary	

INSTRUCTIONS

1. Open the general ledger accounts and enter the balances for January 1, 2005. Obtain the necessary figures from the postclosing trial balance prepared on December 31, 2004, which appears on page 173.
2. Analyze each transaction and record it in the general journal. Use page 3 to begin January's transactions.
3. Post the transactions to the general ledger accounts.
4. Prepare the Trial Balance section of the worksheet.

5. Prepare the Adjustments section of the worksheet.
   a. Compute and record the adjustment for supplies used during the month. An inventory taken on January 31 showed supplies of $1,450 on hand.
   b. Compute and record the adjustment for expired insurance for the month.
   c. Record the adjustment for one month of expired rent of $3,000.
   d. Record the adjustment for depreciation of $583 on the old equipment for the month. The first adjustment for depreciation for the new equipment will be recorded in February.
6. Complete the worksheet.
7. Prepare an income statement for the month.
8. Prepare a statement of owner's equity.
9. Prepare a balance sheet using the report form.
10. Journalize and post the adjusting entries.
11. Journalize and post the closing entries.
12. Prepare a postclosing trial balance.

DATE		TRANSACTIONS
Jan.	2	Purchased supplies for $3,000; issued Check 1015.
	2	Purchased a one-year insurance policy for $2,400; issued Check 1016.
	7	Sold services for $11,600 in cash and $1,490 on credit during the first week of January.
	12	Collected a total of $590 on account from credit customers during the first week of January.
	12	Issued Check 1017 for $790 to pay for special promotional advertising to new businesses on the local radio station during the month.
	13	Collected a total of $1,000 on account from credit customers during the second week of January.
	14	Returned supplies that were damaged for a cash refund of $80.
	15	Sold services for $17,000 in cash and $800 on credit during the second week of January.
	20	Purchased supplies for $1,600 from Partners, Inc.; received Invoice 4823, payable in 30 days.
	20	Sold services for $7,780 in cash and $5,120 on credit during the third week of January.
	20	Collected a total of $1,500 on account from credit customers during the third week of January.

Continued

DATE	(cont.) TRANSACTIONS
Jan. 21	Issued Check 1018 for $2,550 to pay for maintenance work on the office equipment.
22	Issued Check 1019 for $300 to pay for special promotional advertising to new businesses in the local newspaper.
23	Received the monthly telephone bill for $430 and paid it with Check 1020.
26	Collected a total of $3,120 on account from credit customers during the fourth week of January.
27	Issued Check 1021 for $8,000 to Office Plus, as payment on account for Invoice 2223.
28	Sent Check 1022 for $470 in payment of the monthly bill for utilities.
29	Sold services for $11,780 in cash and $1,350 on credit during the fourth week of January.
31	Issued Checks 1023–1027 for $10,800 to pay the monthly salaries of the regular employees and three part-time workers.
31	Issued Check 1028 for $4,000 for personal use.
31	Issued Check 1029 for $830 to pay for maintenance services for the month.
31	Purchased additional equipment for $12,000 from Expert Equipment Company; issued Check 1030 for $2,500 and bought the rest on credit. The equipment has a five-year life and no salvage value.
31	Sold services for $1,090 in cash and $650 on credit on January 31.

Analyze: Compare the January 31 balance sheet you prepared with the December 31 balance sheet shown in Chapter 6 on page 175.

a. What changes occurred in total assets, liabilities, and the owner's ending capital?

b. What changes occurred in the **Cash** and **Accounts Receivable** accounts?

c. Has there been an improvement in the firm's financial position? Why or why not?

PART 2

Recording Financial Data

A large company such as The Home Depot, Inc. must account for millions of transactions each year. The Home Depot, Inc. has been named "America's Most Admired Specialty Retailer" by *Fortune* magazine for seven consecutive years.

Thinking Critically

What do you think it takes to be voted America's Most Admired Specialty Retailer?

CHAPTER 7

Learning Objectives

1. Record credit sales in a sales journal.
2. Post from the sales journal to the general ledger accounts.
3. Post from the sales journal to the customers' accounts in the accounts receivable subsidiary ledger.
4. Record sales returns and allowances in the general journal.
5. Post sales returns and allowances.
6. Prepare a schedule of accounts receivable.
7. Compute trade discounts.
8. Record credit card sales in appropriate journals.
9. Prepare the state sales tax return.
10. Define the accounting terms new to this chapter.

Accounting for Sales and Accounts Receivable

WAL★MART®

www.walmartstores.com

Exploding from a small chain of variety stores that began in Arkansas and Missouri in 1962, Wal-Mart Stores, Inc. has grown into a powerhouse of more than 1,773 Wal-Mart stores, 780 Supercenters, and 466 Sam's Clubs. Founder Sam Walton attributed his company's phenomenal growth to its hometown identity, low prices, and friendly customer service. During store visits, Sam Walton was known to ask his employees to implement the "10-Foot Attitude":

"I want you to promise that whenever you come within 10 feet of a customer, you will look him in the eye, greet him and ask if you can help him."[1]

[1] Wal-Mart Stores, Inc. Web site, Culture Stores

Thinking Critically

What other factors besides customer service have contributed to Wal-Mart's phenomenal success?

For more information on Wal-Mart Stores, Inc., go to: collegeaccounting.glencoe.com.

New Terms

- **Accounts receivable ledger**
- **Charge-account sales**
- **Contra revenue account**
- **Control account**
- **Credit memorandum**
- **Invoice**
- **List price**
- **Manufacturing business**
- **Merchandise inventory**
- **Merchandising business**
- **Net price**
- **Net sales**
- **Open-account credit**
- **Retail business**
- **Sales allowance**
- **Sales journal**
- **Sales return**
- **Schedule of accounts receivable**
- **Service business**
- **Special journal**
- **Subsidiary ledger**
- **Trade discount**
- **Wholesale business**

Section 1

Section Objectives

1. **Record credit sales in a sales journal.**

   WHY IT'S IMPORTANT
   Credit sales are a major source of revenue for many businesses. The sales journal is an efficient option for recording large volumes of credit sales transactions.

2. **Post from the sales journal to the general ledger accounts.**

   WHY IT'S IMPORTANT
   A well-designed accounting system prevents repetitive tasks.

Terms to Learn

manufacturing business
merchandise inventory
merchandising business
retail business
sales journal
service business
special journal
subsidiary ledger

Merchandise Sales

When an accounting system is developed for a firm, one important consideration is the nature of the firm's operations. The three basic types of businesses are a **service business**, which sells services; a **merchandising business**, which sells goods that it purchases for resale; and a **manufacturing business**, which sells goods that it produces.

Carter Consulting Services, the firm that was described in Chapters 2 through 6, is a service business. The firm that we will examine next, The Trend Center, is a merchandising business that sells the latest fashion clothing for men, women, and children. It is a **retail business**, which sells goods and services directly to individual consumers. The Trend Center is a sole proprietorship owned and operated by Stacee Harris, who was formerly a sales manager for a major retail clothing store.

The Trend Center must account for purchases and sales of goods, and for **merchandise inventory**—the stock of goods that is kept on hand. Refer to the chart of accounts for The Trend Center on page 203. You will learn about the accounts in this and following chapters.

To allow for efficient recording of financial data, the accounting systems of most merchandising businesses include special journals and subsidiary ledgers.

Special Journals and Subsidiary Ledgers

A **special journal** is a journal that is used to record only one type of transaction. A **subsidiary ledger** is a ledger that contains accounts of a single type. Table 7-1 lists the journals and ledgers that merchandising businesses generally use in their accounting systems. In this chapter we will discuss the sales journal and the accounts receivable subsidiary ledger.

TABLE 7-1 ► Journals and Ledgers Used by Merchandising Businesses

JOURNALS

Type of Journal	Purpose
Sales	To record sales of merchandise on credit
Purchases	To record purchases of merchandise on credit
Cash receipts	To record cash received from all sources
Cash payments	To record all disbursements of cash
General	To record all transactions that are not recorded in another special journal and all adjusting and closing entries

LEDGERS

Type of Ledger	Content
General	Assets, liabilities, owner's equity, revenue, and expense accounts
Accounts receivable	Accounts for credit customers
Accounts payable	Accounts for creditors

THE T
Char

ASSETS
101 Cash
105 Petty Cash Fund
109 Notes Receivable
111 Accounts Receivable
112 Allowance for Doubtful Accounts
116 Interest Receivable
121 Merchandise Inventory
126 Prepaid Insurance
127 Prepaid Interest
129 Supplies
131 Store Equipment
132 Accumulated Depreciation—Store Equipment
141 Office Equipment
142 Accumulated Depreciation—Office Equipment

LIABILITIES
201 Notes Pa
202 Notes Pa
205 Accounts
216 Interest F
221 Social Se
222 Medicare
223 Employee
225 Federal U Payable
227 State Unemployment Tax Payable
229 Salaries Payable
231 Sales Tax Payable

OWNER'S EQUITY
301 Stacee Harris, Capital
302 Stacee Harris, Drawing
399 Income Summary

REVENUE
401 Sales
451 Sales Returns and Allowances
491 Interest Income
493 Miscellaneous Income

d

es

614 Advertising Expense
617 Cash Short or Over
626 Depreciation Expense—Store Equipment
634 Rent Expense
637 Salaries Expense—Office
639 Insurance Expense
641 Payroll Taxes Expense
643 Utilities Expense
649 Telephone Expense
651 Uncollectible Accounts Expense
657 Bank Fees Expense
658 Delivery Expense
659 Depreciation Expense—Office Equipment
691 Interest Expense
693 Miscellaneous Expense

The Sales Journal

The **sales journal** is used to record only sales of merchandise on credit. To understand the need for a sales journal, consider how credit sales made at The Trend Center would be entered and posted using a general journal and general ledger. Refer to Figure 7-1 on pages 204–205.

Note the word "Balance" in the ledger accounts. To record beginning balances, enter the date in the Date column, the word "Balance" in the Description column, a check mark in the Posting Reference column, and the amount in the Debit or Credit Balance column.

Most state and many local governments impose a sales tax on retail sales of certain goods and services. Businesses are required to collect this tax from their customers and send it to the proper tax agency at regular intervals. When goods or services are sold on credit, the sales tax is usually recorded at the time of the sale even though it will not be collected immediately. A liability account called **Sales Tax Payable** is credited for the sales tax charged.

As you can see, a great amount of repetition is involved in both journalizing and posting these sales. The four credit sales made on January 3, 8, 11, and 15 required four separate entries in the general journal and involved four debits to **Accounts Receivable,** four credits to **Sales Tax Payable,** four

Important!

Business Classifications
The term *merchandising* refers to the type of business operation, not the type of legal entity. The Trend Center could have been a partnership or a corporation instead of a sole proprietorship.

credits to **Sales** (the firm's revenue account), and four descriptions. The posting of twelve items to the three general ledger accounts represents still further duplication of effort. This recording procedure is not efficient for a business that has a substantial number of credit sales each month.

FIGURE 7-1 ►
Journalizing and Posting Credit Sales

GENERAL JOURNAL PAGE 2

DATE		DESCRIPTION	POST. REF.	DEBIT	CREDIT
20--					
Jan.	3	Accounts Receivable	111	214 00	
		Sales Tax Payable	231		14 00
		Sales	401		200 00
		Sold merchandise on			
		credit to John Allen,			
		Sales Slip 1101			
	8	Accounts Receivable	111	535 00	
		Sales Tax Payable	231		35 00
		Sales	401		500 00
		Sold merchandise on			
		credit to Larry Bates,			
		Sales Slip 1102			
	11	Accounts Receivable	111	642 00	
		Sales Tax Payable	231		42 00
		Sales	401		600 00
		Sold merchandise on			
		credit to Blake Howard,			
		Sales Slip 1103			
	15	Accounts Receivable	111	428 00	
		Sales Tax Payable	231		28 00
		Sales	401		400 00
		Sold merchandise on			
		credit to Sarah Gomez,			
		Sales Slip 1104			

ACCOUNT Accounts Receivable ACCOUNT NO. 111

DATE		DESCRIPTION	POST. REF.	DEBIT	CREDIT	BALANCE DEBIT	BALANCE CREDIT
20--							
Jan.	1	Balance	✓			3,210 00	
	3		J2	214 00		3,424 00	
	8		J2	535 00		3,959 00	
	11		J2	642 00		4,601 00	
	15		J2	428 00		5,029 00	

ACCOUNT *Sales Tax Payable* ACCOUNT NO. *231*

DATE		DESCRIPTION	POST. REF.	DEBIT	CREDIT	BALANCE DEBIT	BALANCE CREDIT
20--							
Jan.	*1*	*Balance*	✓				*749 00*
	3		*J2*		*14 00*		*763 00*
	8		*J2*		*35 00*		*798 00*
	11		*J2*		*42 00*		*840 00*
	15		*J2*		*28 00*		*868 00*

ACCOUNT *Sales* ACCOUNT NO. *401*

DATE		DESCRIPTION	POST. REF.	DEBIT	CREDIT	BALANCE DEBIT	BALANCE CREDIT
20--							
Jan.	*3*		*J2*		*200 00*		*200 00*
	8		*J2*		*500 00*		*700 00*
	11		*J2*		*600 00*		*1 300 00*
	15		*J2*		*400 00*		*1 700 00*

Recording Transactions in a Sales Journal

1 Objective

Record credit sales in a sales journal.

A special journal intended only for credit sales provides a more efficient method of recording these transactions. Figure 7-2 shows the January credit sales of The Trend Center recorded in a sales journal. Since The Trend Center is located in a state that has a 7 percent sales tax on retail transactions, its sales journal includes a Sales Tax Payable Credit column. For the sake of simplicity, the sales journal shown here includes a limited number of transactions. The firm actually has many more credit sales each month.

◄ **FIGURE 7-2**
Sales Journal

SALES JOURNAL PAGE *1*

	DATE		SALES SLIP NO.	CUSTOMER'S ACCOUNT DEBITED	POST. REF.	ACCOUNTS RECEIVABLE DEBIT	SALES TAX PAYABLE CREDIT	SALES CREDIT	
1	*20--*								1
2	*Jan.*	*3*	*1101*	*John Allen*		*214 00*	*14 00*	*200 00*	2
3		*8*	*1102*	*Larry Bates*		*535 00*	*35 00*	*500 00*	3
4		*11*	*1103*	*Blake Howard*		*642 00*	*42 00*	*600 00*	4
5		*15*	*1104*	*Sarah Gomez*		*428 00*	*28 00*	*400 00*	5
6		*18*	*1105*	*Ed Ramirez*		*856 00*	*56 00*	*800 00*	6
7		*21*	*1106*	*James Walker*		*321 00*	*21 00*	*300 00*	7
8		*28*	*1107*	*Linda Sanchez*		*107 00*	*7 00*	*100 00*	8
9		*29*	*1108*	*Newton Wu*		*1 070 00*	*70 00*	*1 000 00*	9
10		*31*	*1109*	*Kim Johnson*		*963 00*	*63 00*	*900 00*	10
11		*31*	*1110*	*John Allen*		*267 50*	*17 50*	*250 00*	11
12									12

Notice that the headings and columns in the sales journal speed up the recording process. No general ledger account names are entered. Only one line is needed to record all information for each transaction—date, sales slip number, customer's name, debit to **Accounts Receivable,** credit

Recall

Journals

A journal is a day-to-day record of a firm's transactions.

to **Sales Tax Payable,** and credit to **Sales.** Since the sales journal is used for a single purpose, there is no need to enter any descriptions. Thus a great deal of repetition is avoided.

Entries in the sales journal are usually made daily. In a retail business such as The Trend Center, the data needed for each entry is taken from a copy of the customer's sales slip, as shown in Figure 7-3.

FIGURE 7-3 ►
Customer's Sales Slip

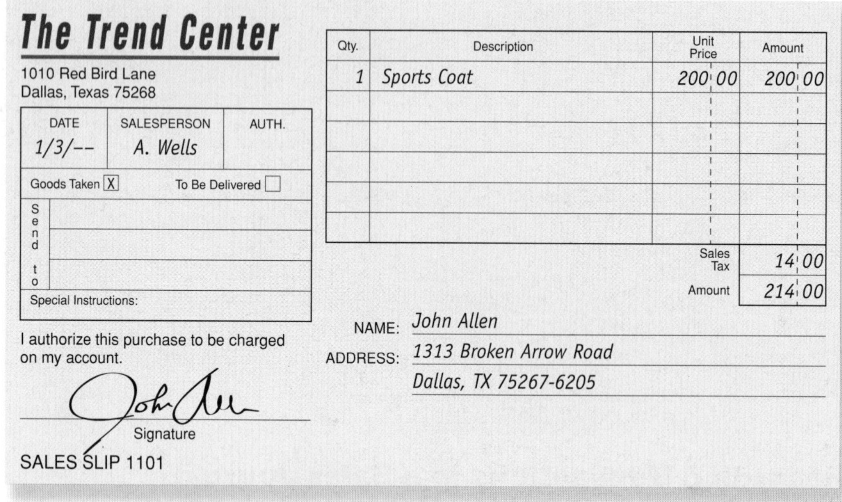

The Trend Center

1010 Red Bird Lane
Dallas, Texas 75268

DATE	SALESPERSON	AUTH.
1/3/--	A. Wells	

Goods Taken [X] To Be Delivered [ ]

Send to

Special Instructions:

I authorize this purchase to be charged on my account.

Signature

SALES SLIP 1101

Qty.	Description	Unit Price	Amount
1	Sports Coat	200 00	200 00
		Sales Tax	14 00
		Amount	214 00

NAME: John Allen
ADDRESS: 1313 Broken Arrow Road
Dallas, TX 75267-6205

Many small retail firms use a sales journal similar to the one shown in Figure 7-2. However, keep in mind that special journals vary in format according to the needs of individual businesses.

2 Objective

Post from the sales journal to the general ledger accounts.

Posting from a Sales Journal

A sales journal not only simplifies the initial recording of credit sales, it also eliminates a great deal of repetition in posting these transactions. With a sales journal, it is not necessary to post each credit sale individually to general ledger accounts. Instead, summary postings are made at the end of the month after the amount columns of the sales journal are totaled. See Figure 7-4 on page 207 for an illustration of posting from the sales journal to the general ledger.

In actual practice, before any posting takes place, the equality of the debits and credits recorded in the sales journal is proved by comparing the column totals. The proof for the sales journal in Figure 7-4 is given below. All multicolumn special journals should be proved in a similar manner before their totals are posted.

PROOF OF SALES JOURNAL

	Debits
Accounts Receivable Debit column	$5,403.50
	Credits
Sales Tax Payable Credit column	$ 353.50
Sales Credit column	5,050.00
	$5,403.50

▼ FIGURE 7-4 End-of-Month Postings

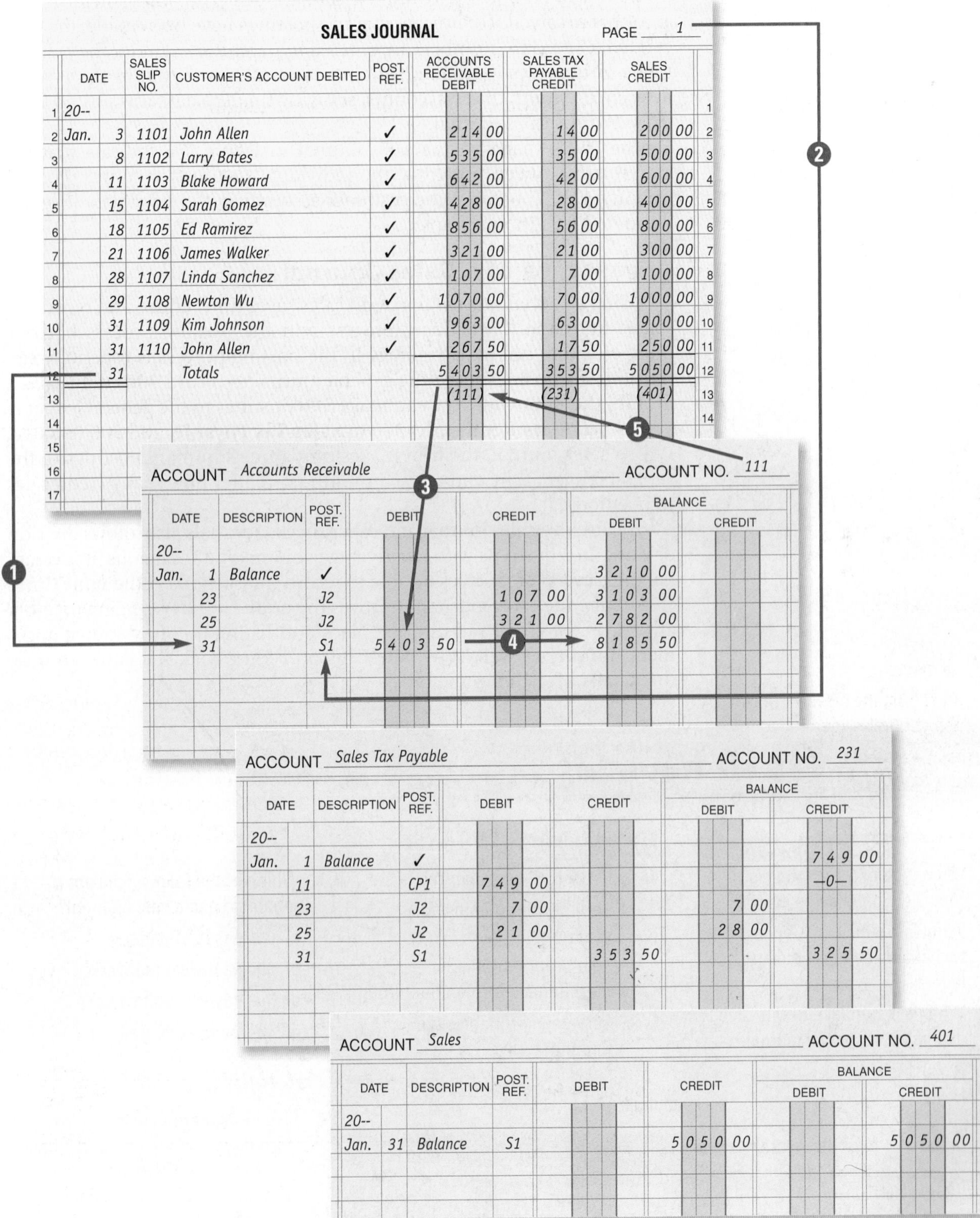

SALES JOURNAL PAGE 1

DATE		SALES SLIP NO.	CUSTOMER'S ACCOUNT DEBITED	POST. REF.	ACCOUNTS RECEIVABLE DEBIT	SALES TAX PAYABLE CREDIT	SALES CREDIT
20--							
Jan.	3	1101	John Allen	✓	214 00	14 00	200 00
	8	1102	Larry Bates	✓	535 00	35 00	500 00
	11	1103	Blake Howard	✓	642 00	42 00	600 00
	15	1104	Sarah Gomez	✓	428 00	28 00	400 00
	18	1105	Ed Ramirez	✓	856 00	56 00	800 00
	21	1106	James Walker	✓	321 00	21 00	300 00
	28	1107	Linda Sanchez	✓	107 00	7 00	100 00
	29	1108	Newton Wu	✓	1 070 00	70 00	1 000 00
	31	1109	Kim Johnson	✓	963 00	63 00	900 00
	31	1110	John Allen	✓	267 50	17 50	250 00
	31		Totals		5 403 50	353 50	5 050 00
					(111)	(231)	(401)

ACCOUNT Accounts Receivable ACCOUNT NO. 111

DATE		DESCRIPTION	POST. REF.	DEBIT	CREDIT	BALANCE DEBIT	BALANCE CREDIT
20--							
Jan.	1	Balance	✓			3 210 00	
	23		J2		107 00	3 103 00	
	25		J2		321 00	2 782 00	
	31		S1	5 403 50		8 185 50	

ACCOUNT Sales Tax Payable ACCOUNT NO. 231

DATE		DESCRIPTION	POST. REF.	DEBIT	CREDIT	BALANCE DEBIT	BALANCE CREDIT
20--							
Jan.	1	Balance	✓				749 00
	11		CP1	749 00			—0—
	23		J2	7 00		7 00	
	25		J2	21 00		28 00	
	31		S1		353 50		325 50

ACCOUNT Sales ACCOUNT NO. 401

DATE		DESCRIPTION	POST. REF.	DEBIT	CREDIT	BALANCE DEBIT	BALANCE CREDIT
20--							
Jan.	31	Balance	S1		5 050 00		5 050 00

Important!

Posting

When posting from the sales journal, post information moving from left to right across the ledger form.

After the equality of the debits and credits has been verified, the sales journal is ruled and the column totals are posted to the general ledger accounts involved. To indicate that the postings have been made, the general ledger account numbers are entered in parentheses under the column totals in the sales journal. The abbreviation S1 is written in the Posting Reference column of the accounts, showing that the data was posted from page 1 of the sales journal.

The check marks in the sales journal in Figure 7-4 indicate that the amounts have been posted to the individual customer accounts. Posting from the sales journal to the customer accounts in the subsidiary ledger is illustrated later in this chapter.

Advantages of a Sales Journal

Using a special journal for credit sales saves time, effort, and recording space. Both the journalizing process and the posting process become more efficient, but the advantage in the posting process is especially significant. If a business used the general journal to record 300 credit sales a month, the firm would have to make 900 postings to the general ledger—300 to **Accounts Receivable,** 300 to **Sales Tax Payable,** and 300 to **Sales.** With a sales journal, the firm makes only three summary postings to the general ledger at the end of each month no matter how many credit sales were entered.

The use of a sales journal and other special journals also allows division of work. In a business with a fairly large volume of transactions, it is essential that several employees be able to record transactions at the same time.

Finally, the sales journal improves the audit trail by bringing together all entries for credit sales in one place and listing them by source document number as well as by date. This procedure makes it easier to trace the details of such transactions.

Section 1 Self Review

Questions

1. What type of transaction is recorded in the sales journal?
2. What is a subsidiary ledger? Give two examples of subsidiary ledgers.
3. What is a special journal? Give four examples of special journals.

Exercises

4. Types of business operations are
   a. service, merchandising, corporation.
   b. sole proprietorship, merchandising, manufacturing.
   c. service, merchandising, manufacturing.
5. Which of the following is not a reason to use a sales journal?
   a. increases efficiency
   b. allows division of work
   c. increases credit sales
   d. improves audit trail

Analysis

6. All sales recorded in this sales journal were made on account and are taxable at a rate of 6 percent. What errors have been made in the entries? Assume the Sales Credit column is correct.

SALES JOURNAL PAGE 1

	DATE		SALES SLIP NO.	CUSTOMER'S ACCOUNT DEBITED	POST. REF.	ACCOUNTS RECEIVABLE DEBIT	SALES TAX PAYABLE CREDIT	SALES CREDIT	
12	Apr.	25	4100	Susan Li		321 00	21 00	300 00	12
13		25	4101	James Hahn		427 00	27 00	450 00	13
14									14

(Answers to Section 1 Self Review are on page 250.)

Section 2

Accounts Receivable

A business that extends credit to customers must manage its accounts receivable carefully. Accounts receivable represents a substantial asset for many businesses, and this asset must be converted into cash in a timely manner. Otherwise, a firm may not be able to pay its bills even though it has a large volume of sales and earns a satisfactory profit.

The Accounts Receivable Ledger

The accountant needs detailed information about the transactions with credit customers and the balances owed by such customers at all times. This information is provided by an **accounts receivable ledger** with individual accounts for all credit customers. The accounts receivable ledger is referred to as a subsidiary ledger because it is separate from and subordinate to the general ledger.

Using an accounts receivable ledger makes it possible to verify that customers are paying their balances on time and that they are within their credit limits. The accounts receivable ledger also provides a convenient way to answer questions from credit customers. Customers may ask about their current balances or about a possible billing error.

The accounts for credit customers are maintained in a balance ledger form with three money columns, as shown in Figure 7-5 on page 210. Notice that this form does not contain a column for indicating the type of account balance. The balances in the customer accounts are presumed to be debit balances since asset accounts normally have debit balances. However, occasionally there is a credit balance because a customer has overpaid an amount owed or has returned goods that were already paid for. One common procedure for dealing with this situation is to circle the balance in order to show that it is a credit amount.

For a small business such as The Trend Center, customer accounts are alphabetized in the accounts receivable ledger. Larger firms and firms that use computers assign an account number to each credit customer and arrange the customer accounts in numeric order. Postings to the accounts receivable ledger are usually made daily so that the customer accounts can be kept up to date at all times.

Posting a Credit Sale

Each credit sale recorded in the sales journal is posted to the appropriate customer's account in the accounts receivable ledger, as shown in Figure 7-5. The date, the sales slip number, and the amount that the customer owes as a result of the sale are transferred from the sales journal to the customer's account. The amount is taken from the Accounts Receivable Debit column of the journal and is entered in the Debit column of the account. Next, the new balance is determined and recorded.

Section Objectives

3 Post from the sales journal to the customers' accounts in the accounts receivable subsidiary ledger.

Why It's Important
This ledger contains individual records that reflect all transactions of each customer.

4 Record sales returns and allowances in the general journal.

Why It's Important
Companies can see how much revenue is lost due to merchandise problems.

5 Post sales returns and allowances.

Why It's Important
Accurate, up-to-date customer records contribute to overall customer satisfaction.

6 Prepare a schedule of accounts receivable.

Why It's Important
This schedule provides a snapshot of amounts due from customers.

Terms to Learn

accounts receivable ledger
contra revenue account
control account
credit memorandum
net sales
sales allowance
sales return
schedule of accounts receivable

❸ Objective

Post from the sales journal to the customers' accounts in the accounts receivable subsidiary ledger.

To show that the posting has been completed, a check mark (✓) is entered in the sales journal and the abbreviation S1 is entered in the Posting Reference column of the customer's account. As noted before, this abbreviation identifies page 1 of the sales journal.

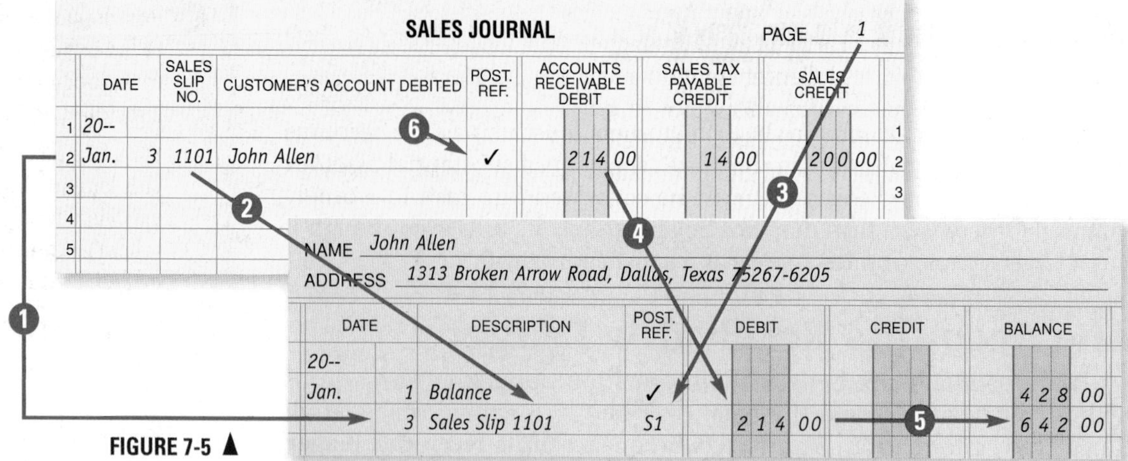

SALES JOURNAL PAGE 1

	DATE		SALES SLIP NO.	CUSTOMER'S ACCOUNT DEBITED	POST. REF.	ACCOUNTS RECEIVABLE DEBIT	SALES TAX PAYABLE CREDIT	SALES CREDIT	
1	20--								1
2	Jan.	3	1101	John Allen	✓	214 00	14 00	200 00	2
3									3
4									
5									

NAME John Allen
ADDRESS 1313 Broken Arrow Road, Dallas, Texas 75267-6205

DATE		DESCRIPTION	POST. REF.	DEBIT	CREDIT	BALANCE
20--						
Jan.	1	Balance	✓			428 00
	3	Sales Slip 1101	S1	214 00		642 00

FIGURE 7-5 ▲
Posting from the Sales Journal to the Accounts Receivable Ledger

Posting Cash Received on Account

When the transaction involves cash received on account from a credit customer, the cash collected is first recorded in a cash receipts journal. (The necessary entry in the cash receipts journal is discussed in Chapter 9.) The cash is then posted to the individual customer account in the accounts receivable ledger. Figure 7-6 shows a posting for cash received on January 7 from John Allen, a credit customer of The Trend Center.

FIGURE 7-6 ►
Posting for Cash Received on Account

NAME John Allen
ADDRESS 1313 Broken Arrow Road, Dallas, Texas 75267-6205

DATE		DESCRIPTION	POST. REF.	DEBIT	CREDIT	BALANCE
20--						
Jan.	1	Balance	✓			428 00
	3	Sales Slip 1101	S1	214 00		642 00
	7		CR1		428 00	214 00

❹ Objective

Record sales returns and allowances in the general journal.

Sales Returns and Allowances

A sale is entered in the accounting records when the goods are sold or the service is provided. If something is wrong with the goods or service, the firm may take back the goods, resulting in a **sales return**, or give the customer a reduction in price, resulting in a **sales allowance**.

When a return or allowance is related to a credit sale, the normal practice is to issue a document called a **credit memorandum** to the customer rather than giving a cash refund. The credit memorandum states that the customer's account is being reduced by the amount of the return or allowance plus any sales tax. A copy of the credit memorandum provides the data needed to enter the transaction in the firm's accounting records.

A debit to the **Sales Returns and Allowances** account is preferred to making a direct debit to **Sales.** This procedure gives a complete record of sales returns and allowances for each accounting period. Business managers use this record as a measure of operating efficiency. The **Sales Returns and Allowances** account is a **contra revenue account** because it has a debit balance, which is contrary, or opposite, to the normal balance for a revenue account.

Business Transaction

On January 23 The Trend Center issued Credit Memorandum 101 for a sales allowance to Ed Ramirez for merchandise purchased on account. The merchandise was damaged but still usable.

The Trend Center
1010 Red Bird Lane, Dallas, TX 75268

DATE: *January 23, 20--*
NAME: *Ed Ramirez*
ADDRESS: *711 Londonderry*
Dallas, TX 75267

Ed Ramirez
CUSTOMER SIGNATURE

CREDIT MEMORANDUM — **NO. 101**

ORIGINAL SALES DATE	ORIGINAL SALES SLIP	APPROVAL	X MDSE RET
Dec. 29, 20--	*No. 1050*	*S.H.*	

QTY	DESCRIPTION	AMOUNT
1	*Athletic Suit*	*$100 00*
REASON FOR RETURN *damaged*	SUB TOTAL	*$100 00*
THE TOTAL SHOWN AT THE RIGHT WILL BE CREDITED TO YOUR ACCOUNT.	SALES TAX	*7 00*
	TOTAL	*$107 00*

Analysis

The contra revenue account, **Sales Returns and Allowances,** is increased by $100. The liability account, **Sales Tax Payable,** is decreased by $7. The asset account, **Accounts Receivable,** is decreased by $107.

Debit-Credit Rules

DEBIT Increases to a contra revenue account are recorded as debits. Debit **Sales Returns and Allowances** for $100. Decreases to liability accounts are recorded as debits. Debit **Sales Tax Payable** for $7.

CREDIT Decreases to an asset account are recorded as credits. Credit **Accounts Receivable** for $107.

T-Account Presentation

Sales Returns and Allowances	
+	−
100	

Sales Tax Payable	
−	+
7	

Accounts Receivable	
+	−
	107

General Journal Entry

GENERAL JOURNAL PAGE *1*

	DATE		DESCRIPTION	POST. REF.	DEBIT	CREDIT	
1	*20--*						1
2	*Jan.*	*23*	*Sales Returns and Allowances*		*100 00*		2
3			*Sales Tax Payable*		*7 00*		3
4			*Accts. Rec.—Ed Ramirez*			*107 00*	4

The Bottom Line

Allowance for Damaged Merchandise

Income Statement

Contra Revenue	↑ 100
Net Income	↓ 100

Balance Sheet

Assets	↓ 107
Liabilities	↓ 7
Equity	↓ 100

What is the ultimate effect of this transaction on the financial statements? An increase in contra revenue causes a decrease in net income. Note that the $100 decrease in net income causes a $100 decrease in owner's equity. The asset **Accounts Receivable** is decreased, and the liability **Sales Tax Payable** is also decreased. The eventual effect of this transaction on the income statement and the balance sheet is summarized in the box titled *The Bottom Line.*

Recording Sales Returns and Allowances

Depending on the volume of sales returns and allowances, a business may use a general journal to record these transactions, or it may use a special sales returns and allowances journal.

Using the General Journal for Sales Returns and Allowances. A small firm that has a limited number of sales returns and allowances each month has no need to establish a special journal for such transactions. Instead, the required entries are made in the general journal.

Using a Sales Returns and Allowances Journal. In a business having many sales returns and allowances, it is efficient to use a special journal for these transactions. An example of a *sales returns and allowances journal* is shown in Figure 7-7.

FIGURE 7-7 ►
Sales Returns and Allowances Journal

SALES RETURNS AND ALLOWANCES JOURNAL PAGE *8*

	DATE		CREDIT MEMO NO.	CUSTOMER'S ACCOUNT CREDITED	POST. REF.	ACCOUNTS RECEIVABLE CREDIT	SALES TAX PAYABLE DEBIT	SALES RET. & ALLOW. DEBIT	
1	*20--*								1
2	*Jan.*	*23*	*101*	*Ed Ramirez*	✓	*107 00*	*7 00*	*100 00*	2
3		*25*	*102*	*James Walker*	✓	*321 00*	*21 00*	*300 00*	3
4									4
17		*31*		*Totals*		*3 210 00*	*210 00*	*3 000 00*	17
18						*(111)*	*(231)*	*(451)*	18
19									19

5 Objective

Post sales returns and allowances.

Posting a Sales Return or Allowance

Whether sales returns and allowances are recorded in the general journal or in a special sales returns and allowances journal, each of these transactions must be posted from the general ledger to the appropriate customer's account in the accounts receivable ledger. Figure 7-8 on page 213 shows how a return of merchandise was posted from the general journal to the account of James Walker.

Because the credit amount in the general journal entry for this transaction requires two postings, the account number 111 and a check mark are entered in the Posting Reference column of the journal. The 111 indicates that the amount was posted to the **Accounts Receivable** account in the general ledger, and the check mark indicates that the amount was posted to the customer's account in the accounts receivable ledger. Notice that a diagonal line was used to separate the two posting references.

Refer to Figure 7-7, which shows a special sales returns and allowances journal instead of a general journal. The account numbers at the bottom of each column are the posting references for the three general ledger accounts: **Accounts Receivable, Sales Tax Payable,** and **Sales Returns and Allowances.** The check marks in the Posting Reference column show that the credits were posted to individual customer accounts in the accounts receivable subsidiary ledger.

Remember that a business can use the general journal or special journals for transactions related to credit sales. A special journal is an efficient option for recording and posting large numbers of transactions.

FIGURE 7-8
Posting a Sales Return to the Customer's Account

GENERAL JOURNAL PAGE 1

	DATE		DESCRIPTION	POST. REF.	DEBIT	CREDIT	
1	20--						1
6	Jan.	25	Sales Returns and Allowances	451	300 00		6
7			Sales Tax Payable	231	21 00		7
8			Accounts Rec./James Walker	111 / ✓		321 00	8
9			Accepted a return of				9
10			defective merchandise,				10
11			Credit Memorandum 102;				11
12			original sale made on Sales				12
13			Slip 1106 of January 21.				13
14							14
15							15
16							16
17							

NAME James Walker
ADDRESS 5415 Stuart Road, Dallas, Texas 75267-6205

DATE		DESCRIPTION	POST. REF.	DEBIT	CREDIT	BALANCE
20--						
Jan.	1	Balance	✓			53 50
	21	Sales Slip 1106	S1	321 00		374 50
	25	CM 102	J1		321 00	53 50

Figure 7-9 on pages 214–215 shows the accounts receivable ledger after posting is completed.

Reporting Net Sales

At the end of each accounting period, the balance of the **Sales Returns and Allowances** account is subtracted from the balance of the **Sales** account in the Revenue section of the income statement. The resulting figure is the **net sales** for the period.

For example, suppose that the **Sales Returns and Allowances** account contains a balance of $400 at the end of January. Also suppose that the **Sales** account has a balance of $20,250 at the end of January. The Revenue section of the firm's income statement will appear as follows.

THE TREND CENTER
Income Statement (Partial)
Month Ended January 31, 20--

Revenue	
Sales	$20,250.00
Less Sales Returns and Allowances	400.00
Net Sales	$19,850.00

About Accounting

Investing in Ethics

Are ethical companies—those with a strong internal enforcement policy—really more profitable? Yes, such companies are listed among the top 100 financial performers twice as often as those without an ethics focus, according to a study by Curtis Verschoor at DePaul University.

FIGURE 7-9 ▼
Accounts Receivable Ledger

NAME *John Allen*
ADDRESS *1313 Broken Arrow Road, Dallas, Texas 75267-6205*

DATE		DESCRIPTION	POST. REF.	DEBIT	CREDIT	BALANCE
20--						
Jan.	1	Balance	✓			428 00
	3	Sales Slip 1101	S1	214 00		642 00
	7		CR1		428 00	214 00
	31	Sales Slip 1110	S1	267 50		481 50

NAME *Larry Bates*
ADDRESS *2712 Broken Arrow Road, Dallas, Texas 75267-6205*

DATE		DESCRIPTION	POST. REF.	DEBIT	CREDIT	BALANCE
20--						
Jan.	8	Sales Slip 1102	S1	535 00		535 00

NAME *Clyde Davis*
ADDRESS *1007 Woodrow Willson Lane, Dallas, Texas 75267-6502*

DATE		DESCRIPTION	POST. REF.	DEBIT	CREDIT	BALANCE
20--						
Jan.	1	Balance	✓			267 50
	11		CR1		267 50	—0—

NAME *Sarah Gomez*
ADDRESS *3111 Berry Lane, Dallas, Texas 75267-6318*

DATE		DESCRIPTION	POST. REF.	DEBIT	CREDIT	BALANCE
20--						
Jan.	1	Balance	✓			642 00
	15	Sales Slip 1104	S1	428 00		1 070 00

NAME *Blake Howard*
ADDRESS *2525 Whetstone Drive, Dallas, Texas 75267-6205*

DATE		DESCRIPTION	POST. REF.	DEBIT	CREDIT	BALANCE
20--						
Jan.	1	Balance	✓			1 070 00
	11	Sales Slip 1103	S1	642 00		1 712 00
	13		CR1		535 00	1 177 00

NAME Kim Johnson
ADDRESS 1501 Ryan Road, Dallas, Texas 75267-6318

DATE		DESCRIPTION	POST. REF.	DEBIT	CREDIT	BALANCE
20--						
Jan.	1	Balance	✓			107 00
	16		CR1		107 00	—0—
	31	Sales Slip 1109	S1	963 00		963 00

NAME Ed Ramirez
ADDRESS 711 Londonderry Lane, Dallas, Texas 75267-6318

DATE		DESCRIPTION	POST. REF.	DEBIT	CREDIT	BALANCE
20--						
Jan.	1	Balance	✓			214 00
	18	Sales Slip 1105	S1	856 00		1070 00
	22		CR1		200 00	870 00
	23	CM 101	J1		107 00	763 00

NAME Linda Sanchez
ADDRESS 1010 Laney Road, Dallas, Texas 75267-6205

DATE		DESCRIPTION	POST. REF.	DEBIT	CREDIT	BALANCE
20--						
Jan.	1	Balance	✓			214 00
	28	Sales Slip 1107	S1	107 00		321 00
	31		CR1		107 00	214 00

NAME James Walker
ADDRESS 5415 Stuart Road, Dallas, Texas 75267-6205

DATE		DESCRIPTION	POST. REF.	DEBIT	CREDIT	BALANCE
20--						
Jan.	1	Balance	✓			53 50
	21	Sales Slip 1106	S1	321 00		374 50
	25	CM 102	J1		321 00	53 50

NAME Newton Wu
ADDRESS 9110 Stella Street, Dallas, Texas 75267-6205

DATE		DESCRIPTION	POST. REF.	DEBIT	CREDIT	BALANCE
20--						
Jan.	1	Balance	✓			214 00
	29	Sales Slip 1108	S1	1070 00		1284 00
	31		CR1		260 00	1024 00

Computers in Accounting

Sales and Fulfillment Systems

One definition of "fulfill" is "to meet the requirements of a business order."[2] Department stores like Macy's and Bloomingdale's have developed sophisticated order processing systems for physical store locations and Web site operations.

When a customer places an order online using a credit card, data such as the customer's account number, the product identification number, product attributes like color and size, and the quantity ordered are transmitted to the company fulfillment and credit processing systems. These computerized systems review the data to verify item availability and to secure credit approval. Seconds later, the customer receives an onscreen confirmation, containing order total, sales tax, and shipping details. Behind the scenes, packing slips are generated at the company's fulfillment centers and the customer's order is packed and shipped per the customer's instructions.

Advanced sales and order systems can also identify sales trends by product and by geographic region, and they can pinpoint the most popular purchasing times of the day.

Thinking Critically

How might management use these reporting features to its benefit?

Internet Application

Visit the Federal Trade Commission Web site to learn more about electronic commerce. Choose an article about e-commerce under *Consumer Protection*. Write a summary of the article.

[2] *Merriam-Webster's Collegiate Dictionary,* Tenth Edition

6 Objective

Prepare a schedule of accounts receivable.

Schedule of Accounts Receivable

The use of an accounts receivable ledger does not eliminate the need for the **Accounts Receivable** account in the general ledger. This account remains in the general ledger and continues to appear on the balance sheet at the end of each fiscal period. However, the **Accounts Receivable** account is now considered a control account. A **control account** serves as a link between a subsidiary ledger and the general ledger. Its balance summarizes the balances of its related accounts in the subsidiary ledger.

At the end of each month, after all the postings have been made from the sales journal, the cash receipts journal, and the general journal to the accounts receivable ledger, the balances in the accounts receivable ledger must be proved against the balance of the **Accounts Receivable** general ledger account. First a **schedule of accounts receivable**, which lists the subsidiary ledger account balances, is prepared. The total of the schedule is compared with the balance of the **Accounts Receivable** account. If the two figures are not equal, errors must be located and corrected.

On January 31 the accounts receivable ledger at The Trend Center contains the accounts shown in Figure 7-9. To prepare a schedule of accounts receivable, the names of all customers with account balances are listed with the amount of their unpaid balances. Next the figures are added to find the total owed to the business by its credit customers.

Federated Department Stores, Inc. reported accounts receivable of $4.31 billion or 24.4 percent of the corporation's total assets at January 30, 2000.

A comparison of the total of the schedule of accounts re pared at The Trend Center on January 31 and the balance of t **Receivable** account in the general ledger shows that the tw the same, as shown in Figure 7-10. The posting reference CR1 cash receipts journal, which is discussed in Chapter 9.

In addition to providing a proof of the subsidiary ledger, of accounts receivable serves another function. It reports about the firm's accounts receivable at the end of the month. can review the schedule to see exactly how much each custom

The Trend Center
Schedule of Accounts Receivable
January 31, 20--

John Allen	481 50
Larry Bates	535 00
Sarah Gomez	1 070 00
Blake Howard	1 177 00
Kim Johnson	963 00
Ed Ramirez	763 00
Linda Sanchez	214 00
James Walker	53 50
Newton Wu	1 024 00
Total	6 281 00

ACCOUNT *Accounts Receivable* ACCOUNT NO. *111*

DATE		DESCRIPTION	POST. REF.	DEBIT	CREDIT	BALANCE DEBIT	BALANCE CREDIT
20--							
Jan.	*1*	*Balance*	✓			3 210 00	
	23		*J1*		107 00	3 103 00	
	25		*J1*		321 00	2 782 00	
	31		*S1*	5 403 50		8 185 50	
	31		*CR1*		1 904 50	6 281 00	

Section 2 Self Review

Questions

1. Which accounts are kept in the accounts receivable ledger?
2. What are net sales?
3. What is a sales return? What is a sales allowance?

Exercises

4. Where would you report net sales?
   a. sales general ledger account
   b. general journal
   c. income statement
   d. sales journal
5. Which of the following general ledger accounts would appear in a sales returns and allowances journal?
   a. **Sales Returns and Allowances, Sales Tax Payable, Accounts Receivable**
   b. **Sales Returns and Allowances, Sales, Accounts Receivable**
   c. **Sales Returns, Sales Allowances, Sales**

Analysis

6. Draw a diagram showing the relationship between the accounts receivable ledger, the schedule of accounts receivable, and the general ledger.

(Answers to Section 2 Self Review are on page 250.)

Section 3

Section Objectives

7 **Compute trade discounts.**

Why It's Important
Trade discounts allow for flexible pricing structures.

8 **Record credit card sales in appropriate journals.**

Why It's Important
Credit cards are widely used in merchandising transactions.

9 **Prepare the state sales tax return.**

Why It's Important
Businesses are legally responsible for accurately reporting and remitting sales taxes.

Terms to Learn

charge-account sales
invoice
list price
net price
open-account credit
trade discount
wholesale business

Special Topics in Merchandising

Merchandisers have many accounting concerns. These include pricing, credit, and sales taxes.

Credit Sales for a Wholesale Business

The operations of The Trend Center are typical of those of many retail businesses—businesses that sell goods and services directly to individual consumers. In contrast, a **wholesale business** is a manufacturer or distributor of goods that sells to retailers or large consumers such as hotels and hospitals. The basic procedures used by wholesalers to handle sales and accounts receivable are the same as those used by retailers. However, many wholesalers offer cash discounts and trade discounts, which are not commonly found in retail operations.

The procedures used in connection with cash discounts are examined in Chapter 9. The handling of trade discounts is described here.

Computing Trade Discounts

7 **Objective**
Compute trade discounts.

A wholesale business offers goods to trade customers at less than retail prices. This price adjustment is based on the volume purchased by trade customers and takes the form of a **trade discount**, which is a reduction from the **list price**—the established retail price. There may be a single trade discount or a series of discounts for each type of goods. The **net price** (list price less all trade discounts) is the amount the wholesaler records in its sales journal.

The same goods may be offered to different customers at different trade discounts, depending on the size of the order and the costs of selling to the various types of customers.

Single Trade Discount. Suppose the list price of goods is $1,000 and the trade discount is 40 percent. The amount of the discount is $400, and the net price to be shown on the invoice and recorded in the sales journal is $600.

List price	$1,000
Less 40% discount ($1,000 × 0.40)	400
Invoice price	$ 600

Important!
Trade Discounts
The amount of sales revenue recorded is the list price *minus* the trade discount.

Series of Trade Discounts. If the list price of goods is $1,000 and the trade discount is quoted in a series such as 25 and 15 percent, a different net price will result.

List price	$1,000.00
Less first discount ($1,000 × 0.25)	250.00
Difference	$ 750.00
Less second discount ($750 × 0.15)	112.50
Invoice price	$ 637.50

same as net price

Using a Sales Journal for a Wholesale Business

Since sales taxes apply only to retail transactions, a wholesale business does not need to account for such taxes. Its sales journal may therefore be as simple as the one illustrated in Figure 7-11. This sales journal has a single amount column. The total of this column is posted to the general ledger at the end of the month as a debit to the **Accounts Receivable** account and a credit to the **Sales** account (Figure 7-12). During the month the individual entries in the sales journal are posted to the customer accounts in the accounts receivable ledger.

Special Journal Format
Special journals such as the sales journal can vary in format from company to company.

◄ **FIGURE 7-11**
Wholesaler's Sales Journal

SALES JOURNAL — PAGE 1

	DATE		INVOICE NO.	CUSTOMER'S ACCOUNT DEBITED	POST. REF.	ACCOUNTS RECEIVABLE DR. SALES CR.	
1	20--						1
2	Jan.	3	9907	Discount Hardware Company		1 600 00	2
25		31	10017	Tyson's Department Store		3 800 00	25
26		31		Total		30 750 00	26
27						(111/401)	27
28							28

◄ **FIGURE 7-12**
General Ledger Accounts

ACCOUNT *Accounts Receivable* — ACCOUNT NO. 111

DATE		DESCRIPTION	POST. REF.	DEBIT	CREDIT	BALANCE DEBIT	BALANCE CREDIT
20--							
Jan.	1	Balance	✓			45 200 00	
	31		S1	30 750 00		75 950 00	

ACCOUNT *Sales* — ACCOUNT NO. 401

DATE		DESCRIPTION	POST. REF.	DEBIT	CREDIT	BALANCE DEBIT	BALANCE CREDIT
20--							
Jan.	31		S1		30 750 00		30 750 00

Wholesale businesses issue invoices. An **invoice** is a customer billing for merchandise bought on credit. Copies of the invoices are used to enter the transactions in the sales journal.

The next merchandising topic, credit policies, applies to both wholesalers and retailers. The discussion in this textbook focuses on credit policies and accounting for retail firms.

Credit Policies

The use of credit is considered to be one of the most important factors in the rapid growth of modern economic systems. Sales on credit are made by large numbers of wholesalers and retailers of goods and by many professional people and service businesses. The assumption is that the volume of both sales and profits will increase if buyers are given a period of a month or more to pay for the goods or services they purchase.

However, the increase in profits a business expects when it grants credit will be realized only if each customer completes the transaction by paying for the goods or services purchased. If payment is not received, the expected profits become actual losses and the purpose for granting the credit is defeated. Business firms try to protect against the possibility of such losses by investigating a customer's credit record and ability to pay for purchases before allowing any credit to the customer.

Professional people, such as doctors, lawyers, and architects, and owners of small businesses like The Trend Center usually make their own decisions about granting credit. Such decisions may be based on personal judgment or on reports available from credit bureaus, information supplied by other creditors, and credit ratings supplied by national firms such as Dun & Bradstreet.

Equifax, a leader in providing consumer and commercial credit information, was founded in Atlanta in 1899. For the fiscal year ended December 1999, 100 years later, the company reported revenues of $1.77 billion dollars.

Larger businesses maintain a credit department to determine the amounts and types of credit that should be granted to customers. In addition to using credit data supplied by institutions, the credit department may obtain financial statements and related reports from customers who have applied for credit. This information is analyzed to help determine the maximum amount of credit that may be granted and suitable credit terms for the customer. Financial statements that have been audited by certified public accountants are used extensively by credit departments.

Even though the credit investigation is thorough, some accounts receivable become uncollectible. Unexpected business developments, errors of judgment, incorrect financial data, and many other causes may lead to defaults in payments by customers. Experienced managers know that some uncollectible accounts are to be expected in normal business operations and that limited losses indicate that a firm's credit policies are sound. Provisions for such limited losses from uncollectible accounts are usually made in budgets and other financial projections.

Each business must develop credit policies that achieve maximum sales with minimum losses from uncollectible accounts:

- A credit policy that is too tight results in a low level of losses at the expense of increases in sales volume.
- A credit policy that is too lenient may result in increased sales volume accompanied by a high level of losses.

Good judgment based on knowledge and experience must be used to achieve a well balanced credit policy.

Different types of credit have evolved with the growing economy and changing technology. The different types of credit require different accounting treatments.

Accounting for Different Types of Credit Sales

The most common types of credit sales are

- open-account credit,
- business credit cards,
- bank credit cards,
- cards issued by credit card companies.

Open-Account Credit. The form of credit most commonly offered by professional people and small businesses permits the sale of services or goods to the customer with the understanding that the amount is to be paid at a later date. This type of arrangement is called **open-account credit**. It is usually granted on the basis of personal acquaintance or knowledge of the customer. However, formal credit checks may also be used. The amount involved in each transaction is usually small, and payment is expected within 30 days or on receipt of a monthly statement. Open-account sales are also referred to as **charge-account sales**.

The Trend Center uses the open-account credit arrangement. Sales transactions are recorded as debits to the **Accounts Receivable** account and credits to the **Sales** account. Collections on account are recorded as debits to the **Cash** account and credits to the **Accounts Receivable** account.

Business Credit Cards. Many retail businesses, especially large ones such as department store chains and gasoline companies, provide their own credit cards (sometimes called charge cards) to customers who have established credit. Whenever a sale is completed using a business credit card, a sales slip is prepared in the usual manner. Then the sales slip and the credit card are placed in a mechanical device that prints the customer's name, account number, and other data on all copies of the sales slip. Some companies use computerized card readers and sales registers that print out a sales slip with the customer information and a line for the customer's signature. Many businesses require that the salesclerk contact the credit department by telephone or computer terminal to verify the customer's credit status before completing the transaction.

Business credit card sales are similar to open-account credit sales. A business credit card sale is recorded as

- a debit to **Accounts Receivable,**
- a credit to a revenue account such as **Sales.**

A customer payment is recorded as

- a debit to **Cash,**
- a credit to **Accounts Receivable.**

Bank Credit Cards

Using a bank credit card is one of the best ways to acquire money when conducting business in another country because you get the bank's exchange rate.

Bank Credit Cards. Retailers can provide credit while minimizing or avoiding the risk of losses from uncollectible accounts by accepting bank credit cards. The most widely accepted bank credit cards are MasterCard and Visa. Many banks participate in one or both of these credit card programs, and other banks have their own credit cards. Bank credit cards are issued to consumers directly by banks.

A business may participate in these credit card programs by meeting the conditions set by the bank. When a sale is made to a cardholder, the business completes a special sales slip such as the one shown in Figure 7-13 on page 222. This form must be imprinted with data from the customer's bank credit card and then signed by the customer. Many businesses continue to complete their regular sales slips for internal control and other purposes.

The Trend Center
06O1X3
851 7007 763
928 6548 421

Shirley Carson
7000 120 362 222
04/X7BWG

DATE	AUTH NO.	IDENTIFICATION	CLERK	REG/DEPT	☐ TAKE ☐ SEND
1/28/--	12				

QTY	CLASS	DESCRIPTION	PRICE	AMOUNT
1		Sweater		80 00
The issuer of the card identified on this itemis authorized to pay the amount shown on TOTAL upon proper authorization. I promis to pay such TOTAL (together with any other charges due) subject to and in accordance with the agreement governing the use of such card.			SUB TOTAL	80 00
CUSTOMER SIGNATURE *Shirley Carson*			TAX	5 60
SALES SLIP			TOTAL	85 60

MERCHANT RETAIN THIS COPY FOR RECORDS

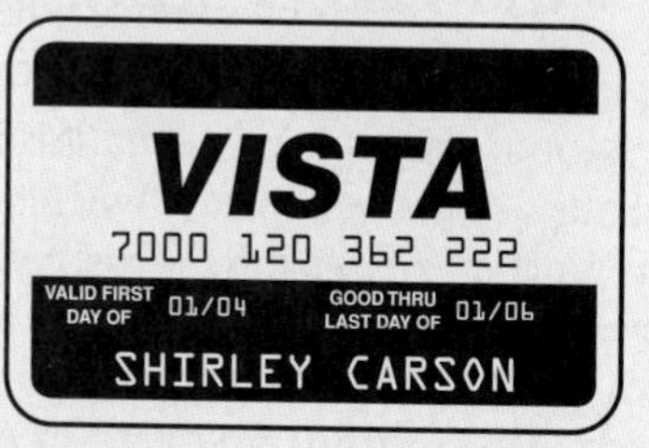

FIGURE 7-13 ▲
Sales Slip for a Bank Credit Card Transaction

When a business makes a sale on a bank credit card, it acquires an asset that can be converted into cash immediately without responsibility for later collection from the customer. Periodically (preferably each day) the completed sales slips from bank credit card sales are totaled. The number of sales slips and the total amount of the sales are recorded on a special deposit form, as shown in Figure 7-14.

FIGURE 7-14 ►
Deposit Form for Bank Credit Card Sales

The Trend Center
851 7007 763
928 6548 421

DATE ______

ITEM	NO. SLIPS	AMOUNT
Total Sales	10	1177 00
LESS: Total Credits		
NET SALES		1177 00
LESS: DISCOUNT 3 %		35 31
NET AMOUNT		1141 69

VISTA MERCHANT SUMMARY SLIP

Attach calculator tape to Bank Copy when more than one sales slip is enclosed.

x *Stacee Harris*
MERCHANT SIGNATURE

The deposit form, along with the completed sales slips, is presented to the firm's bank in much the same manner as a cash deposit. Depending on the arrangements that have been made, either the bank will deduct a fee, called a *discount* (usually between 1 and 8 percent), and immediately credit the depositor's checking account with the net amount of the sales, or it will credit the depositor's checking account for the full amount of the sales and then deduct the discount at the end of the month. If the second procedure is used, the total discount for the month will appear on the bank statement.

The bank is responsible for collecting from the cardholder. If any amounts are uncollectible, the bank sustains the loss. For the retailer, bank credit card sales are like cash sales. The accounting procedures for such sales are therefore quite similar to the accounting procedures for cash sales, which will be discussed in Chapter 9. If the business is billed once each month for the bank's discount, the total amount involved in the daily deposit of the credit card sales slips is debited to **Cash** and credited to **Sales.**

Credit Card Companies. Credit cards such as American Express and Diners Club are issued by business firms or subsidiaries of business firms that are operated for the special purpose of handling credit card transactions. The potential cardholder must submit an application and pay an annual fee to the credit card company. If the credit references are satisfactory, the credit card is issued. It is normally reissued at one-year intervals so long as the company's credit experience with the cardholder remains satisfactory.

Hotels, restaurants, airline companies, many types of retail stores, and a wide variety of other businesses accept these credit cards. When making sales to cardholders, sellers usually prepare their own sales slip or bill and then complete a special sales slip required by the credit card company. As with the sales slips for bank credit cards, the forms must be imprinted with the identifying data on the customer's card and signed by the customer. Such sales slips are sometimes referred to as *sales invoices, sales drafts,* or *sales vouchers.* The term used varies from one credit card company to another.

The seller acquires an account receivable from the credit card company rather than from the customer. At approximately one-month intervals, the credit card company bills the cardholders for all sales slips it has acquired during the period. It is the responsibility of the credit card company to collect from the cardholders.

Accounting for Credit Card Sales

8 Objective

Record credit card sales in appropriate journals.

The procedure used to account for credit card sales is similar to the procedure for recording open-account credit sales. However, the account receivable is with the credit card company, not with the cardholders who buy the goods or services.

There are two basic methods of recording these sales. Businesses that have few transactions with credit card companies normally debit the amounts of such sales to the usual **Accounts Receivable** account in the general ledger and credit them to the same **Sales** account that is used for cash sales and other types of credit sales. An individual account for each credit card company is set up in the accounts receivable subsidiary ledger. This method of recording sales is shown in Figure 7-15.

Payment from a credit card company is recorded in the cash receipts journal, a procedure discussed in Chapter 9. Fees charged by the credit card companies for processing these sales are debited to an account called **Discount Expense on Credit Card Sales.** For example, assume that American Express charges a 7 percent discount fee on the sale charged by Richard Harris on January 3 and remits the balance to the firm.

FIGURE 7-15 Recording Credit Card Company Sales

SALES JOURNAL — PAGE 12

	DATE		SALES SLIP NO.	CUSTOMER'S ACCOUNT DEBITED	POST. REF.	ACCOUNTS RECEIVABLE DEBIT	SALES TAX PAYABLE CREDIT	SALES CREDIT	
1	20--								1
2	Jan.	3	335	American Express		428 00	28 00	400 00	2
3				(Richard Harris)					3
26		11	351	Diners Club		107 00	7 00	100 00	26
27				(Penny Howard)					27
28									28

This transaction would be recorded in the cash receipts journal by debiting **Cash** for $398.04, debiting **Discount Expense on Credit Card Sales** for $29.96, and crediting **Accounts Receivable** for $428.00.

Firms that do a large volume of business with credit card companies may debit all such sales to a special **Accounts Receivable from Credit Card Companies** account in the general ledger, thus separating this type of receivable from the accounts receivable resulting from open-account credit sales. A special account called **Sales—Credit Card Companies** is credited for the revenue from these transactions. Figure 7-16 shows how the necessary entries are made in the sales journal.

FIGURE 7-16 ▼
Recording Sales for Accounts Receivable from Credit Card Companies

SALES JOURNAL PAGE 7

	DATE		SALES SLIP NO.	CUSTOMER'S ACCOUNT DEBITED	POST. REF.	ACCOUNTS RECEIVABLE DEBIT	ACCT. REC.—CREDIT CARD COMPANIES DEBIT	SALES TAX PAYABLE CREDIT	SALES CREDIT	SALES—CREDIT CARD COMPANIES CREDIT	
1	20--										1
2	Jan.	3		*Summary of credit card sales/*							2
3				*American Express*			8560 00	560 00		8000 00	3
16		11		*Summary of credit card sales/*			4280 00	280 00		4000 00	16
17				*Diners Club*							17
29		31		*Totals*			42800 00	2800 00		40000 00	29
30							(114)	(231)		(404)	30
31											31

Sales Taxes

Many cities and states impose a tax on retail sales. Sales taxes imposed by city and state governments vary. However, the procedures used to account for these taxes are similar.

A sales tax may be levied on all retail sales, but often certain items are exempt. In most cases the amount of the sales tax is stated separately and then added to the retail price of the merchandise.

> The California State Board of Equalization collects approximately $22.9 billion dollars annually from sales tax revenues. These revenues foot the bill for state and local programs, including hospitals, social welfare efforts, transportation, schools, and housing.

The retailer is required to collect sales tax from customers, make periodic (usually monthly) reports to the taxing authority, and pay the taxes due when the reports are filed. The government may allow the retailer to retain part of the tax as compensation for collecting it.

9 Objective
Prepare the state sales tax return.

Preparing the State Sales Tax Return

At the end of each month, after the accounts have all been posted, The Trend Center prepares the sales tax return. The information required for the monthly return comes from the accounting data of the current month. Three accounts are involved: **Sales Tax Payable, Sales,** and **Sales**

Returns and Allowances. In some states the sales tax return is filed quarterly rather than monthly.

The procedures to file a sales tax return are similar to those used by The Trend Center on February 7 when it filed the monthly sales tax return for January with the state tax commissioner. The firm's sales are subject to a 7 percent state sales tax. To highlight the data needed, the January postings are shown in the ledger accounts in Figure 7-17.

◀ **FIGURE 7-17**
Ledger Account Postings for Sales Tax

ACCOUNT *Sales Tax Payable* ACCOUNT NO. *231*

DATE		DESCRIPTION	POST. REF.	DEBIT	CREDIT	BALANCE DEBIT	BALANCE CREDIT
20--							
Jan.	*1*	*Balance*	✓				*7 4 9 00*
	11		*CP1*	*7 4 9 00*			*—0—*
	23		*J1*	*7 00*		*7 00*	
	25		*J1*	*2 1 00*		*2 8 00*	
	31		*S1*		*3 5 3 50*		*3 2 5 50*
	31		*CR1*		*1 0 6 4 00*		*1 3 8 9 50*

ACCOUNT *Sales* ACCOUNT NO. *401*

DATE		DESCRIPTION	POST. REF.	DEBIT	CREDIT	BALANCE DEBIT	BALANCE CREDIT
20--							
Jan.	*31*		*S1*		*5 0 5 0 00*		*5 0 5 0 00*
	31		*CR1*		*15 2 0 0 00*		*20 2 5 0 00*

ACCOUNT *Sales Returns and Allowances* ACCOUNT NO. *451*

DATE		DESCRIPTION	POST. REF.	DEBIT	CREDIT	BALANCE DEBIT	BALANCE CREDIT
20--							
Jan.	*23*		*J1*	*1 0 0 00*		*1 0 0 00*	
	25		*J1*	*3 0 0 00*		*4 0 0 00*	

Using these figures as a basis, the amount of the firm's taxable gross sales for January is determined as follows:

Cash Sales	$15,200
Credit Sales	5,050
Total Sales	$20,250
Less Sales Returns and Allowances	400
Taxable Gross Sales for January	$19,850

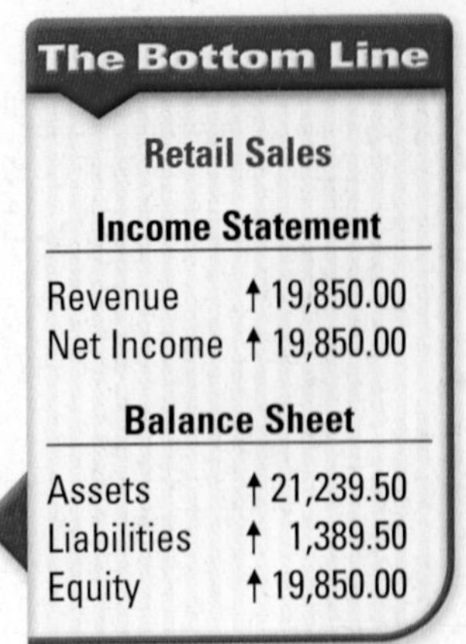

The 7 percent sales tax on the gross sales of $19,850 amounts to $1,389.50. Note that the firm's increase in assets (**Cash** and **Accounts Receivable**) is equal to sales revenue plus the sales tax liability on that revenue.

In the state where The Trend Center is located, a retailer who files the sales tax return (see Figure 7-18 on page 226) on time and who pays the tax when it is due is entitled to a discount. The discount is intended to compensate the retailer, at least in part, for acting as a collection agent for the government. The discount rate depends on the amount of tax to be

SALES TAX RETURN

ALWAYS REFER TO THIS NUMBER WHEN WRITING THE DIVISION →	LICENSE NUMBER 217539
—IMPORTANT— ANY CHANGE IN OWNERSHIP REQUIRES A NEW LICENSE: NOTIFY THIS DIVISION IMMEDIATELY.	
This return DUE on the 1st day of month following period covered by the return, and becomes DELINQUENT on the 21st day.	37-9462315 FED. E.I. NO. OR S.S NO.

STATE TAX COMMISSION
SALES AND USE TAX DIVISION
DRAWER 20
CAPITAL CITY, STATE 78711
RETURN REQUESTED

January 31, 20--
—Sales for period ending—

MAKE ALL REMITTANCES PAYABLE TO STATE TAX COMMISSIOIN
DO NOT SEND CASH
STAMPS NOT ACCEPTED

OWNER'S NAME AND LOCATION

THE TREND CENTER
1010 Red Bird Lane
Dallas, Texas 75268-7783

COMPUTATION OF SALES TAX	For Taxpayer's Use	Do Not Use This Column
1. TOTAL Gross proceeds of sales or Gross Receipts (to include rentals)	19,850.00	
2. Add cost of personal property purchased on a RETAIL LICENSE FOR RESALE but USED BY YOU or YOUR EMPLOYEES, including GIFTS and PREMIUMS	-0-	
3. USE TAX—Add cost of personal property purchased outside of STATE for your use, storage, or consumption	-0-	
4. Total (Lines 1, 2, and 3)	19,850.00	
5. LESS ALLOWABLE DEDUCTIONS (Must be itemized on reverse side)	-0-	
6. Net taxable total (Line 4 minus Line 5)	19,850.00	
7. Sales and Use Tax Due (7% of Line 6)	1,389.50	
8. LESS TAXPAYER'S DISCOUNT—(Deductible only when amount of TAX due is not delinquent at time of payment) →	13.90	
IF LINE 7 IS LESS THAN $100.00 —DEDUCT 3% IF LINE 7 IS $100 BUT LESS THAN $1,000.00 —DEDUCT 2% IF LINE 7 IS $1,000.00 OR MORE —DEDUCT 1%		
9. NET AMOUNT OF TAX PAYABLE (Line 7 minus Line 8)	1,375.60	
Add the following penalty and interest if return or remittance is late. 10. Specific Penalty: 25% of tax $ ______ 11. Interest: 1/2 of 1% per month from due date until paid. $ ______ TOTAL PENALTY AND INTEREST →		
12. TOTAL TAX, PENALTY AND INTEREST	1,375.60	
13. Subtract credit memo No.		
14. TOTAL AMOUNT DUE (IF NO SALES MADE SO STATE)	1,375.60	

I certify that this return, including the accompanying schedules or statements, has been examined by me and to the best of my knowledge and belief, a true and complete return, made in good faith, for the period stated, pursuant to the provisions of the Code of Laws, 20--, and Acts Amendatory Thereto.

URGENT—SEE THAT LICENSE NUMBER IS ON RETURN

Stacee Harris
SIGNATURE

Owner
Owner, partner or title

February 7, 20--
Date

Return must be signed by owner or if corporation, authorized person.

Division Use Only

State Sales Tax Return **FIGURE 7-18** ▲

paid. For amounts over $1,000, the rate is 1 percent of the total tax due. For The Trend Center, the discount for January is determined as follows:

Taxable Gross Sales for January	$19,850.00
7% Sales Tax Rate	× 0.07
Sales Tax Due	$ 1,389.50
1% Discount Rate	× 0.01
Discount	$ 13.90

Sales Tax Due	$ 1,389.50
Discount	(13.90)
Net Sales Tax Due	$ 1,375.60

The firm sends a check for the net sales tax due with the sales tax return. The accounting entry made to record this payment includes a debit to **Sales Tax Payable** and a credit to **Cash** (for $1,375.60 in this case). After the amount of the payment is posted, the balance in the **Sales Tax Payable** account should be equal to the discount, as shown in Figure 7-19. Slight differences can arise because the tax collected at the time of the sale is determined by a tax bracket method that can give results slightly more or less than the final computations on the tax return.

ACCOUNT *Sales Tax Payable* ACCOUNT NO. *231*

DATE		DESCRIPTION	POST. REF.	DEBIT	CREDIT	BALANCE DEBIT	BALANCE CREDIT
20--							
Jan.	1	Balance	✓				749 00
	11		CP1	749 00			—0—
	23		J1	7 00		7 00	
	25		J1	21 00		28 00	
	31		S1		353 50		325 50
	31		CR1		1,064 00		1,389 50
Feb.	6		CP1	1,375 60			13 90

Tax payment — Amount of discount

◄ **FIGURE 7-19**
Effect of Paying Sales Tax

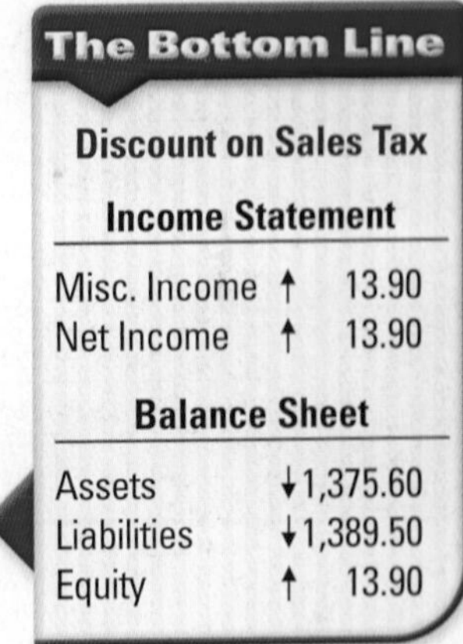

If there is a balance in the **Sales Tax Payable** account after the sales tax liability is satisfied, the balance is transferred to an account called **Miscellaneous Income** by a general journal entry. This entry consists of a debit to **Sales Tax Payable** and a credit to **Miscellaneous Income.**

Recording Sales Tax in the Sales Account

In some states retailers can credit the entire sales price plus tax to the **Sales** account. At the end of each month or quarter, they must remove from the **Sales** account the amount of tax included and transfer that amount to the **Sales Tax Payable** account. Assume that during January a retailer whose sales are all taxable sells merchandise for a total price of $16,050, which includes a 7 percent tax. The entry to record these sales is summarized in general journal form on page 228.

Credit Sales

- Credit sales are a major source of revenue in many businesses, and accounts receivable represent a major asset.
- Management needs up-to-date and correct information about both sales and accounts receivable in order to monitor the financial health of the firm.
- Special journals save time and effort and reduce the cost of accounting work.
- In a retail firm that must handle sales tax, the sales journal and the cash receipts journal provide a convenient method of recording the amounts owed for sales tax.
    - When the data is posted to the Sales Tax Payable account in the general ledger, the firm has a complete and systematic record that speeds the completion of the periodic sales tax return.
    - The firm has detailed proof of its sales tax figures in the case of a tax audit.
- An accounts receivable subsidiary ledger provides management and the credit department with up-to-date information about the balances owed by all customers.
    - This information is useful in controlling credit and collections.
    - Detailed information helps in evaluating the effectiveness of credit policies.
    - Management must keep a close watch on the promptness of customer payments because much of the cash needed for day-to-day operations usually comes from payments on accounts receivable.
- A well-balanced credit policy helps increase sales volume but also keeps losses from uncollectible accounts at an acceptable level.
- Retailers are liable for any undercollection of sales taxes. This situation can be avoided with an efficient control system.

Thinking Critically
What are some possible consequences of out-of-date accounts receivable records?

GENERAL JOURNAL PAGE *4*

	DATE		DESCRIPTION	POST. REF.	DEBIT	CREDIT	
1	*20--*						1
2	*Jan.*	*31*	*Accounts Receivable*	*111*	*16 0 5 0 00*		2
3			*Sales*	*401*		*16 0 5 0 00*	3
4			*To record total sales and*				4
5			*sales tax collected during*				5
6			*the month*				6
7							7

At the end of the month, the retailer must transfer the sales tax from the **Sales** account to the **Sales Tax Payable** account. The first step in the transfer process is to determine the amount of tax involved. The sales tax payable is computed as follows.

Sales + tax	= $16,050
100% of sales + 7% of sales	= $16,050
107% of sales	= $16,050
Sales	= $16,050/1.07
Sales	= $15,000
Tax	= $15,000 × 0.07 = $1,050

The firm then makes the following entry to transfer the liability from the **Sales** account.

GENERAL JOURNAL PAGE 4

	DATE		DESCRIPTION	POST. REF.	DEBIT	CREDIT	
1	20--						1
8	*Jan.*	*31*	*Sales*	*401*	*1 0 5 0 00*		8
9			*Sales Tax Payable*	*231*		*1 0 5 0 00*	9
10			*To transfer sales tax*				10
11			*payable from the Sales*				11
12			*account to the liability*				12
13			*account*				13
14							14
15							15

The retailer in this example originally recorded the entire sales price plus tax in the **Sales** account. The sales tax was transferred to the **Sales Tax Payable** account at the end of the month.

Section 3 Self Review

Questions

1. What are four types of credit sales?
2. What account is used to record sales tax owed by a business to a city or state?
3. What is the difference between list price and net price?

Exercises

4. If a wholesale business offers a trade discount of 35 percent on a sale of $2,400, what is the amount of the discount?
   - **a.** $84
   - **b.** $85
   - **c.** $840
   - **d.** $845
5. A company that buys $3,000 of goods from a wholesaler offering trade discounts of 20 and 10 percent will pay what amount for the goods?
   - **a.** $1,560
   - **b.** $2,100
   - **c.** $2,130
   - **d.** $2,160

Analysis

6. What factors would you consider in deciding whether or not to extend credit to a customer?

(Answers to Section 3 Self Review are on page 251.)

CHAPTER 7 Review and Applications

Review

Chapter Summary

The nature of the operations of a business, the volume of its transactions, and other factors influence the design of an accounting system. In this chapter, you have learned about the use of special journals and subsidiary ledgers suitable for a merchandising business. These additional journals and ledgers increase the efficiency of recording credit transactions and permit the division of labor.

Learning Objectives

1. **Record credit sales in a sales journal.**
   The sales journal is used to record credit sales transactions, usually on a daily basis. For sales transactions that include sales tax, the sales tax liability is recorded at the time of the sale to ensure that company records reflect the appropriate amount of sales tax liability.

2. **Post from the sales journal to the general ledger accounts.**
   At the end of each month, the sales journal is totaled, proved, and ruled. Column totals are then posted to the general ledger. Using a sales journal rather than a general journal to record sales saves the time and effort of posting individual entries to the general ledger during the month.

3. **Post from the sales journal to the customers' accounts in the accounts receivable subsidiary ledger.**
   The accounts of individual credit customers are kept in a subsidiary ledger called the accounts receivable ledger. Daily postings are made to this ledger from the sales journal, the cash receipts journal, and the general journal or the sales returns and allowances journal. The current balance of a customer's account is computed after each posting so that the amount owed is known at all times.

4. **Record sales returns and allowances in the general journal.**
   Sales returns and allowances are usually debited to a contra revenue account. A firm with relatively few sales returns and allowances could use the general journal to record these transactions.

5. **Post sales returns and allowances.**
   Sales returns and allowances transactions must be posted to the general ledger and to the appropriate accounts receivable subsidiary ledgers. The balance of the **Sales Returns and Allowances** account is subtracted from the balance of the **Sales** account to show net sales on the income statement.

6. **Prepare a schedule of accounts receivable.**
   Each month a schedule of accounts receivable is prepared. It is used to prove the subsidiary ledger against the **Accounts Receivable** account. It also reports the amounts due from credit customers.

7. **Compute trade discounts.**
   Wholesale businesses often offer goods to trade customers at less than retail prices. Trade discounts are expressed as a percentage off the list price. Multiply the list price by the percentage trade discount offered to compute the dollar amount.

8. **Record credit card sales in appropriate journals.**
   Credit sales are common, and different credit arrangements are used. Businesses that have few transactions with credit card companies normally record these transactions in the sales journal by debiting the usual **Accounts Receivable** account in the general ledger and crediting the same **Sales** account that is used for cash sales.

9. **Prepare the state sales tax return.**
   In states and cities that have a sales tax, the retailer must prepare a sales tax return and send the total tax collected to the taxing authority.

10. **Define the accounting terms new to this chapter.**

CHAPTER 7 GLOSSARY

Accounts receivable ledger (p. 209) A subsidiary ledger that contains credit customer accounts

Charge-account sales (p. 221) Sales made through the use of open-account credit or one of various types of credit cards

Contra revenue account (p. 211) An account with a debit balance, which is contrary to the normal balance for a revenue account

Control account (p. 216) An account that links a subsidiary ledger and the general ledger since its balance summarizes the balances of the accounts in the subsidiary ledger

Credit memorandum (p. 210) A note verifying that a customer's account is being reduced by the amount of a sales return or sales allowance plus any sales tax that may have been involved

Invoice (p. 219) A customer billing for merchandise bought on credit

List price (p. 218) An established retail price

Manufacturing business (p. 202) A business that sells goods that it has produced

Merchandise inventory (p. 202) The stock of goods a merchandising business keeps on hand

Merchandising business (p. 202) A business that sells goods purchased for resale

Net price (p. 218) The list price less all trade discounts

Net sales (p. 213) The difference between the balance in the **Sales** account and the balance in the **Sales Returns and Allowances** account

Open-account credit (p. 221) A system that allows the sale of services or goods with the understanding that payment will be made at a later date

Retail business (p. 202) A business that sells directly to individual consumers

Sales allowance (p. 210) A reduction in the price originally charged to customers for goods or services

Sales journal (p. 203) A special journal used to record sales of merchandise on credit

Sales return (p. 210) A firm's acceptance of a return of goods from a customer

Schedule of accounts receivable (p. 216) A listing of all balances of the accounts in the accounts receivable subsidiary ledger

Service business (p. 202) A business that sells services

Special journal (p. 202) A journal used to record only one type of transaction

Subsidiary ledger (p. 202) A ledger dedicated to accounts of a single type and showing details to support a general ledger account

Trade discount (p. 218) A reduction from list price

Wholesale business (p. 218) A business that manufactures or distributes goods to retail businesses or large consumers such as hotels and hospitals

Comprehensive Self Review

1. Explain how service, merchandising, and manufacturing businesses differ from each other.
2. Why does a small merchandising business usually need a more complex set of financial records and statements than a small service business?
3. Why is it useful for a firm to have an accounts receivable ledger?
4. What is a control account?
5. Name the two different time periods usually covered in sales tax returns.

(Answers to Comprehensive Self Review are on page 251.)

Discussion Questions

1. What is a trade discount? Why do some firms offer trade discounts to their customers?
2. What is open-account credit?
3. Why are bank credit card sales similar to cash sales for a business?
4. What is the discount on credit card sales? What type of account is used to record this item?
5. When a firm makes a sale involving a credit card issued by a credit card company, does the firm have an account receivable with the cardholder or with the credit card company?
6. What procedure does a business use to collect amounts owed to it for sales on credit cards issued by credit card companies?
7. What two methods are commonly used to record sales involving credit cards issued by credit card companies?
8. In a particular state, the sales tax rate is 5 percent of sales. The retailer is allowed to record both the selling price and the tax in the same account. Explain how to compute the sales tax due when this method is used.
9. The sales tax on a credit sale is not collected from the customer immediately. When is this tax usually entered in a firm's accounting records? What account is used to record this tax?
10. How is a multicolumn special journal proved at the end of each month?
11. What kind of account is **Sales Returns and Allowances**?
12. Why is a sales return or allowance usually recorded in a special **Sales Returns and Allowances** account rather than being debited to the **Sales** account?
13. How are the net sales for an accounting period determined?
14. What purposes does the schedule of accounts receivable serve?
15. How do retail and wholesale businesses differ?

Applications

EXERCISES

Identifying the accounts used to record sales and related transactions.

◄ **Exercise 7-1**
Objective 1

The transactions below took place at Resort Camping Center, a retail business that sells outdoor clothing and camping equipment. Indicate the numbers of the general ledger accounts that would be debited and credited to record each transaction.

GENERAL LEDGER ACCOUNTS

101 Cash
111 Accounts Receivable
231 Sales Tax Payable
401 Sales
451 Sales Returns and Allowances

DATE		TRANSACTIONS
May	1	Sold merchandise on credit; the transaction involved sales tax.
	2	Received checks from credit customers on account.
	3	Accepted a return of merchandise from a credit customer; the original sale involved sales tax.
	4	Sold merchandise for cash; the transaction involved sales tax.
	5	Gave an allowance to a credit customer for damaged merchandise; the original sale involved sales tax.
	6	Provided a cash refund to a customer who returned merchandise; the original sale was made for cash and involved sales tax.

Identifying the journal to record transactions.

◄ **Exercise 7-2**
Objective 1

The accounting system of Resort Camping Center includes the journals listed below. Indicate the specific journal in which each of the transactions listed below would be recorded.

JOURNALS

Cash receipts journal
Cash payments journal
Purchases journal
Sales journal
General journal

DATE		TRANSACTIONS
May	1	Sold merchandise on credit.
	2	Accepted a return of merchandise from a credit customer.
	3	Sold merchandise for cash.
	4	Purchased merchandise on credit.
	5	Gave a $200 allowance for damaged merchandise.
	6	Collected sums on account from credit customers.
	7	Received an additional cash investment from the owner.
	8	Issued a check to pay a creditor on account.

Exercise 7-3 ►
Objective 2

Recording credit sales.

The following transactions took place at Tina's Camp Shop during May. Indicate how these transactions would be entered in a sales journal like the one shown in Figure 7-2.

DATE		TRANSACTIONS
May	1	Sold a tent and other items on credit to Brad Winkler; issued Sales Slip 1101 for $280 plus sales tax of $14.
	2	Sold a backpack, an air mattress, and other items to Mary Fuller; issued Sales Slip 1102 for $120 plus sales tax of $6.
	3	Sold a lantern, cooking utensils, and other items to James Baker; issued Sales Slip 1103 for $100 plus sales tax of $5.

Exercise 7-4 ►
Objective 2

Recording sales returns and allowances.

Record the general journal entries for the following transactions of World of Styles that occurred in May 20--.

DATE		TRANSACTIONS
May	7	Accepted a return of some damaged merchandise from Shanda Perry, a credit customer; issued Credit Memorandum 130 for $636, which includes sales tax of $36; the original sale was made on Sales Slip 1605 of May 5.
	22	Gave an allowance to Jared Lewis, a credit customer, for some merchandise that was slightly damaged but usable; issued Credit Memorandum 131 for $848, which includes sales tax of $48; the original sale was made on Sales Slip 1649 of May 19.

Exercise 7-5 ►
Objective 2

Posting from the sales journal.

The sales journal for Crocker Company is shown below. Describe how the amounts would be posted to the general ledger accounts.

SALES JOURNAL PAGE *1*

	DATE		SALES SLIP NO.	CUSTOMER'S ACCOUNT DEBITED	POST. REF.	ACCOUNTS RECEIVABLE DEBIT	SALES TAX PAYABLE CREDIT	SALES CREDIT	
1	20--								1
2	July	2	1101	Ned Turner		642 00	42 00	600 00	2
3		7	1102	Selena Hines		749 00	49 00	700 00	3
11		31	1110	Julie Sanders		267 50	17 50	250 00	11
12		31		Totals		4,146 25	271 25	3,875 00	12
13						(111)	(231)	(401)	13

Exercise 7-6 ►
Objective 7

Computing a trade discount.

Renquist Wholesale Company made sales using the following list prices and trade discounts. What amount will be recorded for each sale in the sales journal?

1. List price of $350 and trade discount of 40 percent
2. List price of $600 and trade discount of 40 percent

3. List price of $180 and trade discount of 30 percent

Computing a series of trade discounts.

◄ **Exercise 7-7**
Objective 7

Masonville Distributing Company, a wholesale firm, made sales using the following list prices and trade discounts. What amount will be recorded for each sale in the sales journal?

1. List price of $4,000 and trade discounts of 25 and 15 percent
2. List price of $3,600 and trade discounts of 25 and 15 percent
3. List price of $1,880 and trade discounts of 20 and 10 percent

Computing the sales tax due and recording its payment.

◄ **Exercise 7-8**
Objective 9

The balances of certain accounts of Hazelnut Corporation on February 28, 20--, were as follows:

Sales	$212,500
Sales Returns and Allowances	1,750

The firm's net sales are subject to a 6 percent sales tax. Give the general journal entry to record payment of the sales tax payable on February 28, 20--.

Preparing a schedule of accounts receivable.

◄ **Exercise 7-9**
Objective 6

The accounts receivable ledger for Style Corner follows.

1. Prepare a schedule of accounts receivable as of January 31.
2. What should the balance in the **Accounts Receivable** (control) account be?

NAME *Jim Brown*
ADDRESS *2001 5th Avenue, New York, NY 10018*

DATE		DESCRIPTION	POST. REF.	DEBIT	CREDIT	BALANCE
20--						
Jan.	*1*	*Balance*	✓			*1 2 7 2 00*
	2	*Sales Slip 1604*	*S1*	*4 2 4 00*		*1 6 9 6 00*

NAME *Ashley Ellis*
ADDRESS *901 Broadway, New York, NY 10018*

DATE		DESCRIPTION	POST. REF.	DEBIT	CREDIT	BALANCE
20--						
Jan.	*1*	*Balance*	✓			*4 2 4 00*
	27	*Sales Slip 1607*	*S1*	*1 3 0 00*		*5 5 4 00*
	31		*CR1*		*2 1 2 00*	*3 4 2 00*

NAME *Darren Flanagan*
ADDRESS *5021 Park Avenue, New York, NY 10018*

DATE		DESCRIPTION	POST. REF.	DEBIT	CREDIT	BALANCE
20--						
Jan.	*1*	*Balance*	✓			*2 1 2 00*
	15	*Sales Slip 1609*	*CR1*		*2 1 2 00*	*—0—*
	31		*S1*	*7 4 2 00*		*7 4 2 00*

NAME *Maria Gonzalez*

ADDRESS *94 Houston Street, New York, NY 10019*

DATE		DESCRIPTION	POST. REF.	DEBIT	CREDIT	BALANCE
20--						
Jan.	1	Balance	✓			424 00
	20	Sales Slip 1606	S1	212 00		636 00
	21		CR1		400 00	236 00
	22	Sales Slip 1610	S1	848 00		1084 00

NAME *Aaren McCord*

ADDRESS *619 Lexington Avenue, New York, NY 10017*

DATE		DESCRIPTION	POST. REF.	DEBIT	CREDIT	BALANCE
20--						
Jan.	1	Balance	✓			530 00
	31	Sales Slip 1615	S1	2120 00		2650 00

NAME *Ron Thomas*

ADDRESS *2110 West 32nd Street, New York, NY 10027*

DATE		DESCRIPTION	POST. REF.	DEBIT	CREDIT	BALANCE
20--						
Jan.	1	Balance	✓			2120 00
	12		CR1		1060 00	1060 00
	17		S1	848 00		1908 00

Exercise 7-10 ► Objective 5

Posting sales returns and allowances.

Post the journal entries below to the appropriate ledger accounts. Assume the following account balances:

Accounts Receivable (control account)	$901
Accounts Receivable—Marsha Cline	424
Accounts Receivable—Reba Black	477

GENERAL JOURNAL PAGE *42*

	DATE		DESCRIPTION	POST. REF.	DEBIT	CREDIT	
1	20--						1
2	Feb.	14	Sales Returns and Allowances		150 00		2
3			Sales Tax Payable		9 00		3
4			Accounts Rec.—Marsha Cline			159 00	4
5			Accepted return on defective				5
6			merchandise, Credit Memo				6
7			101; original sale of Jan. 12,				7
8			Sales Slip 1101				8
9							9
10		23	Sales Returns and Allowances		50 00		10
11			Sales Tax Payable		3 00		11
12			Accounts Rec.—Reba Black			53 00	12
13			Gave allowance for damaged				13
14			merchandise, Credit Memo				14
15			102; original sale Jan. 20,				15
16			Sales Slip 1150				16

Problems

Selected problems can be completed using:
Peachtree QuickBooks Spreadsheets

PROBLEM SET A

Recording credit sales and posting from the sales journal.

◄ **Problem 7-1A**
Objectives 1, 2

The Metroplex Appliance Center is a retail store that sells household appliances. The firm's credit sales for June are listed below, along with the general ledger accounts used to record these sales. The balance shown for **Accounts Receivable** is for the beginning of the month.

INSTRUCTIONS

1. Open the general ledger accounts and enter the balance of **Accounts Receivable** for June 1, 20--.
2. Record the transactions in a sales journal like the one shown in Figure 7-4. Use 7 as the journal page number.
3. Total, prove, and rule the sales journal as of June 30.
4. Post the column totals from the sales journal to the proper general ledger accounts.

GENERAL LEDGER ACCOUNTS

111 Accounts Receivable, $15,700 Dr.
231 Sales Tax Payable
401 Sales

DATE		TRANSACTIONS
June	1	Sold a dishwasher to Tonya Wonders; issued Sales Slip 105 for $1,700 plus sales tax of $102.
	6	Sold a washer to Denise Permenter; issued Sales Slip 106 for $1,200 plus sales tax of $72.
	11	Sold a high-definition television set to Tucker Allen; issued Sales Slip 107 for $4,100 plus sales tax of $246.
	17	Sold an electric dryer to Arlene Hillman; issued Sales Slip 108 for $800 plus sales tax of $48.
	23	Sold a trash compactor to Mary Alvarez; issued Sales Slip 109 for $600 plus sales tax of $36.
	27	Sold a color television set to Clint Lewis; issued Sales Slip 110 for $600 plus sales tax of $36.
	29	Sold an electric range to Pat Ashley; issued Sales Slip 111 for $1,200 plus sales tax of $72.
	30	Sold a microwave oven to Rusty Ryan; issued Sales Slip 112 for $500 plus sales tax of $30.

Analyze: What percentage of credit sales were for entertainment items?

Problem 7-2A ► Objectives 1, 2, 4

Journalizing, posting, and reporting sales transactions.

Millennium Furniture specializes in modern living room and dining room furniture. Merchandise sales are subject to a 5 percent sales tax. The firm's credit sales and sales returns and allowances for February 20-- are reflected below, along with the general ledger accounts used to record these transactions. The balances shown are for the beginning of the month.

INSTRUCTIONS

1. Open the general ledger accounts and enter the balances for February 1.
2. Record the transactions in a sales journal and in a general journal. Use 8 as the page number for the sales journal and 24 as the page number for the general journal.
3. Post the entries from the general journal to the general ledger.
4. Total, prove, and rule the sales journal as of February 28.
5. Post the column totals from the sales journal.
6. Prepare the heading and the Revenue section of the firm's income statement for the month ended February 28, 20--.

GENERAL LEDGER ACCOUNTS

111 Accounts Receivable, $5,212 Dr.
231 Sales Tax Payable, $2,390 Cr.
401 Sales
451 Sales Returns and Allowances

DATE		TRANSACTIONS
Feb.	1	Sold a living room sofa to Barbara Evans; issued Sales Slip 1516 for $1,750 plus sales tax of $87.50.
	5	Sold three recliners to Richard Clinton; issued Sales Slip 1517 for $1,580 plus sales tax of $79.
	9	Sold a dining room set to Louise Mack; issued Sales Slip 1518 for $5,200 plus sales tax of $260.
	11	Accepted a return of one damaged recliner from Richard Clinton that was originally sold on Sales Slip 1517 of February 5; issued Credit Memorandum 207 for $556.50, which includes sales tax of $26.50.
	17	Sold living room tables and bookcases to Raymond Cheng; issued Sales Slip 1519 for $4,500 plus sales tax of $225.
	23	Sold eight dining room chairs to Anna Wallace; issued Sales Slip 1520 for $3,200 plus sales tax of $160.
	25	Gave Raymond Cheng an allowance for scratches on his bookcases; issued Credit Memorandum 208 for $105, which includes sales taxes of $5; the bookcases were originally sold on Sales Slip 1519 of February 17.
	27	Sold a living room sofa and four chairs to Victor De la Hoya; issued Sales Slip 1521 for $3,680 plus sales tax of $184.
	28	Sold a dining room table to Sue Barker; issued Sales Slip 1522 for $1,300 plus sales tax of $65.
	28	Sold a living room modular wall unit to Mack Slaughter; issued Sales Slip 1523 for $3,140 plus sales tax of $157.

Analyze: Based on the beginning balance of the **Sales Tax Payable** account, what was the amount of net sales for January? (Hint: Sales tax returns are filed and paid to the state quarterly.)

◄ **Problem 7-3A**
Objectives 1, 2, 3, 4, 6

Recording sales transactions, posting to the accounts receivable ledger, and preparing a schedule of accounts receivable.

Bradford China Shop sells china, glassware, and other gift items that are subject to a 6 percent sales tax. The shop uses a general journal and a sales journal similar to those illustrated in this chapter.

INSTRUCTIONS

1. Record the transactions for November in the proper journal. Use 5 as the page number for the sales journal and 15 as the page number for the general journal.
2. Immediately after recording each transaction, post to the accounts receivable ledger.
3. Post the amounts from the general journal daily. Post the sales journal amount as a total at the end of the month.
4. Prepare a schedule of accounts receivable. Compare the balance of the **Accounts Receivable** control account with the total of the schedule.

DATE	TRANSACTIONS
Nov. 1	Sold china to Connie Tolbert; issued Sales Slip 1401 for $1,200 plus $72 sales tax.
5	Sold a brass serving tray to Jill Mason; issued Sales Slip 1402 for $1,800 plus $108 sales tax.
6	Sold a vase to Durwood Cluck; issued Sales Slip 1403 for $600 plus $36 sales tax.
10	Sold a punch bowl and glasses to Amy Sadler; issued Sales Slip 1404 for $1,500 plus $90 sales tax.
14	Sold a set of serving bowls to Troy Dockery; issued Sales Slip 1405 for $450 plus $27 sales tax.
17	Gave Amy Sadler an allowance because of a broken glass discovered when unpacking the punch bowl and glasses sold on November 10, Sales Slip 1404; issued Credit Memorandum 201 for $127.20, which includes sales tax of $7.20.
21	Sold a coffee table to Jeff Marx; issued Sales Slip 1406 for $3,000 plus $180 sales tax.
24	Sold sterling silver teaspoons to Brint Polinksi; issued Sales Slip 1407 for $600 plus $36 sales tax.
25	Gave Jeff Marx an allowance for scratches on his coffee table sold on November 21, Sales Slip 1406; issued Credit Memorandum 202 for $318, which includes $18 in sales tax.
30	Sold a clock to Henry Griffon; issued Sales Slip 1408 for $3,600 plus $216 sales tax

Analyze: How many postings would be made to the general ledger if the business did not use a sales journal?

Problem 7-4A ► Objectives 1, 2, 3, 4, 6

Recording sales transactions, posting to the accounts receivable ledger, and preparing a schedule of accounts receivable.

Flowers & More is a wholesale shop that sells flowers, plants, and plant supplies. The transactions shown below took place during January.

INSTRUCTIONS

1. Record the transactions in the proper journal. Use 6 as the page number for the sales journal and 10 as the page number for the general journal.
2. Immediately after recording each transaction, post to the accounts receivable ledger.
3. Post the amounts from the general journal daily. Post the sales journal amount as a total at the end of the month.
4. Prepare a schedule of accounts receivable. Compare the balance of the **Accounts Receivable** control account with the total of the schedule.

DATE		TRANSACTIONS
Jan.	3	Sold a floral arrangement to Jefferson Florist; issued Invoice 1801 for $300.
	8	Sold potted plants to Goree Garden Supply; issued Invoice 1802 for $751.
	9	Sold floral arrangements to Henderson Flower Shop; issued Invoice 1803 for $361.50.
	10	Sold corsages to Lowe's Flower Shop; issued Invoice 1804 for $530.
	15	Gave Henderson Flower Shop an allowance because of withered blossoms discovered in one of the floral arrangements sold on Invoice 1803 on January 9; issued Credit Memorandum 101 for $20.
	20	Sold table arrangements to Town Floral Shop; issued Invoice 1805 for $424.
	22	Sold plants to Metroplex Nursery; issued Invoice 1806 for $642.50.
	25	Sold roses to Lowe's Flower Shop; issued Invoice 1807 for $383.
	27	Sold several floral arrangements to Jefferson Florist; issued Invoice 1808 for $860.
	31	Gave Jefferson Florist an allowance because of withered blossoms discovered in one of the floral arrangements sold on Invoice 1808 on January 27; issued Credit Memorandum 102 for $106.

Analyze: Damaged goods decreased the net sales by what dollar amount? By what percentage amount?

PROBLEM SET B

Recording credit sales and posting from the sales journal.

◄ **Problem 7-1B**
Objectives 1, 2

The Appliance Mart is a retail store that sells household appliances. The firm's credit sales for July are listed below, along with the general ledger accounts used to record these sales. The balance shown for Accounts Receivable is for the beginning of the month.

INSTRUCTIONS

1. Open the general ledger accounts and enter the balance of **Accounts Receivable** for July 1.
2. Record the transactions in a sales journal like the one shown in Figure 7-4. Use 7 as the journal page number.
3. Total, prove, and rule the sales journal as of July 31.
4. Post the column totals from the sales journal to the proper general ledger accounts.

GENERAL LEDGER ACCOUNTS

111 Accounts Receivable, $36,400 Dr.

231 Sales Tax Payable

401 Sales

DATE		TRANSACTIONS
July	1	Sold a dishwasher to Ted Gates; issued Sales Slip 101 for $1,400 plus sales tax of $84.
	6	Sold a washer to Jay Robinson; issued Sales Slip 102 for $1,000 plus sales tax of $60.
	11	Sold a high-definition television set to Samuel Davis; issued Sales Slip 103 for $3,600 plus sales tax of $216.
	17	Sold an electric dryer to Angela Bush; issued Sales Slip 104 for $800 plus sales tax of $48.
	23	Sold a trash compactor to Selena Lozono; issued Sales Slip 105 for $700 plus sales tax of $42.
	27	Sold a portable color television set to Wes Reeves; issued Sales Slip 106 for $500 plus sales tax of $30.
	29	Sold an electric range to David Turner; issued Sales Slip 107 for $1,300 plus sales tax of $78.
	30	Sold a microwave oven to Lauren Ashford; issued Sales Slip 108 for $400 plus sales tax of $24.

Analyze: What percentage of credit sales were for entertainment items?

Problem 7-2B ► Objectives 1, 2, 4

Journalizing, posting, and reporting sales transactions.

Furniture Future is a retail store that specializes in modern living room and dining room furniture. Merchandise sales are subject to a 6 percent sales tax. The firm's credit sales and sales returns and allowances for May are reflected below, along with the general ledger accounts used to record these transactions. The balances shown are for the beginning of the month.

INSTRUCTIONS

1. Open the general ledger accounts and enter the balances for May 1.
2. Record the transactions in a sales journal and a general journal. Use 8 as the page number for the sales journal and 24 as the page number for the general journal.
3. Post the entries from the general journal to the general ledger.
4. Total, prove, and rule the sales journal as of May 31.
5. Post the column totals from the sales journal.
6. Prepare the heading and the Revenue section of the firm's income statement for the month ended May 31, 20--.

GENERAL LEDGER ACCOUNTS

111 Accounts Receivable, $5,644 Dr.
231 Sales Tax Payable, $960 Cr.
401 Sales
451 Sales Returns and Allowances

DATE		TRANSACTIONS
May	1	Sold a living room sofa to Marion Cherry; issued Sales Slip 1507 for $1,800 plus sales tax of $108.
	5	Sold three recliners to Giffen Cruit; issued Sales Slip 1508 for $1,200 plus sales tax of $72.
	9	Sold a dining room set to Jennifer Ashley; issued Sales Slip 1509 for $6,000 plus sales tax of $360.
	11	Accepted a return of a damaged chair from Giffen Cruit; the chair was originally sold on Sales Slip 1508 of May 5; issued Credit Memorandum 210 for $424, which includes sales tax of $24.
	17	Sold living room tables and bookcases to Victor Salez; issued Sales Slip 1510 for $5,000 plus sales tax of $300.
	23	Sold eight dining room chairs to Nelvia Wilson; issued Sales Slip 1511 for $3,600 plus sales tax of $216.
	25	Gave Victor Salez an allowance for scratches on his bookcases; issued Credit Memorandum 211 for $159, which includes sales taxes of $9; the bookcases were originally sold on Sales Slip 1510 of May 17.
	27	Sold a living room sofa and four chairs to Henry Barker; issued Sales Slip 1512 for $3,200 plus sales tax of $192.
	29	Sold a dining room table to Jenny Lemons; issued Sales Slip 1513 for $1,350 plus sales tax of $81.
	30	Sold a living room modular wall unit to John Morris; issued Sales Slip 1514 for $2,900 plus sales tax of $174.

Analyze: Based on the beginning balance of the **Sales Tax Payable** account, what was the amount of net sales for April? (Hint: Sales tax returns are filed and paid to the state quarterly.)

◄ **Problem 7-3B**
Objectives 1, 2, 3, 4, 6

Recording sales transactions, posting to the accounts receivable ledger, and preparing a schedule of accounts receivable.

Amy's Special Occasions Card Shop sells cards, supplies, and various holiday gift items. All sales are subject to a sales tax of 6 percent. The shop uses a sales journal and general journal.

INSTRUCTIONS

1. Record the credit sale transactions for February in the proper journal. Use 5 as the page number for the sales journal and 15 as the page number for the general journal.
2. Immediately after recording each transaction, post to the accounts receivable ledger.
3. Post the entries to the appropriate accounts.
4. Prepare a schedule of accounts receivable and compare the balance due with the amount shown in the **Accounts Receivable** control account.

DATE	TRANSACTIONS
Feb. 3	Sold Vicki Grey a box of holiday greeting cards for $50 plus sales tax of $3 on Sales Slip 302.
4	Sold to Dave Dorris a Valentine's Day party pack for $100 plus sales tax of $6 on Sales Slip 303.
5	Ken Blackmon bought 10 boxes of Valentine's Day gift packs for his office. Sales Slip 304 was issued for $50 plus sales tax of $3.
8	Sold Misty Woodall a set of crystal glasses for $300 plus sales tax of $18 on Sales Slip 305.
9	Adam Harris purchased two statues for $200 plus $12 sales tax on Sales Slip 306.
9	Gave Ken Blackmon an allowance because of incomplete items in one gift pack; issued Credit Memorandum 1000 for $5.30, which includes sales tax of $0.30.
10	Sold Darryl Wrenn a Valentine Birthday package for $150 plus $9 sales tax on Sales Slip 307.
13	Gave Misty Woodall an allowance of $50 because of two broken glasses in the set she purchased on February 8. Credit Memorandum 1001 was issued for the allowance plus sales tax of $3.
14	Sold Vicki Grey 12 boxes of gift candy for $150 plus sales tax of $9 on Sales Slip 308.
15	Sold a punch serving set with glasses for $100 to Corey Lambert. Sales tax of $6 was included on Sales Slip 309.

Analyze: How many postings were made to the general ledger? How many additional postings would be needed if the business did not use a sales journal?

Problem 7-4B ► Objectives 1, 2, 3, 4, 6

Recording sales transactions, posting to the accounts receivable ledger, and preparing a schedule of accounts receivable.

County Town Nursery is a wholesale shop that sells flowers, plants, and plant supplies. The transactions shown below took place during February.

INSTRUCTIONS

1. Record the transactions in the proper journal. Use 4 as the page number for the sales journal and 9 as the page number for the general journal.
2. Immediately after recording each transaction, post to the accounts receivable ledger.
3. Post the amounts from the general journal daily. Post the sales journal amount as a total at the end of the month.
4. Prepare a schedule of accounts receivable. Compare the balance of the **Accounts Receivable** control account with the total of the schedule.

DATE		TRANSACTIONS
Feb.	3	Sold a floral arrangement to Jamestown Funeral Home; issued Invoice 1101 for $500.
	8	Sold potted plants to The Nursery; issued Invoice 1102 for $900.00.
	9	Sold floral arrangements to Town Flower Shop; issued Invoice 1103 for $1,161.50.
	10	Sold corsages to City Flower Shop; issued Invoice 1104 for $650.
	15	Gave Town Flower Shop an allowance because of withered blossoms discovered in one of the floral arrangements sold on Invoice 1103 on February 9; issued Credit Memorandum 102 for $40.
	20	Sold table arrangements to City Flower Shop; issued Invoice 1105 for $636.
	22	Sold plants to Winter Nursery; issued Invoice 1106 for $750.50.
	25	Sold roses to Lewisville Flower Shop; issued Invoice 1107 for $423.
	27	Sold several floral arrangements to Jamestown Funeral Home; issued Invoice 1108 for $950.
	28	Gave Jamestown Funeral Home an allowance because of withered blossoms discovered in one of the floral arrangements sold on Invoice 1108 on February 27; issued Credit Memorandum 103 for $53.

Analyze: Damaged goods decreased the net sales by what dollar amount? By what percentage amount?

CHAPTER 7 CHALLENGE PROBLEM

Wholesaler Transactions

The Play Therapy Company sells toys and games to retail stores. The firm offers a trade discount of 40 percent on toys and 30 percent on games. Its credit sales and sales returns and allowances transactions for August are shown on page 246. The general ledger accounts used to record these transactions are listed below. The balance shown for **Accounts Receivable** is as of the beginning of August.

INSTRUCTIONS

1. Open the general ledger accounts and enter the balance of **Accounts Receivable** for August 1.
2. Set up an accounts receivable subsidiary ledger. Open an account for each of the credit customers listed below and enter the balances as of August 1.

Zane's Department Store	$14,880
Variety Toy Stores	20,200
Dallas Bookstores	
Pebblebrook Toy Center	
Emporium Game Center	8,420
Hanson's Game Store	

3. Record the transactions in a sales journal and in a general journal. Use 10 as the page number for the sales journal and 30 as the page number for the general journal. Be sure to enter each sale at its net price.
4. Post the individual entries from the sales journal and the general journal.
5. Total and rule the sales journal as of August 31.
6. Post the column total from the sales journal to the proper general ledger accounts.
7. Prepare the heading and the Revenue section of the firm's income statement for the month ended August 31.
8. Prepare a schedule of accounts receivable for August 31.
9. Check the total of the schedule of accounts receivable against the balance of the **Accounts Receivable** account in the general ledger. The two amounts should be equal.

GENERAL LEDGER ACCOUNTS

111 Accounts Receivable, $43,500 Dr.
401 Sales
451 Sales Returns and Allowances

DATE	TRANSACTIONS
August 1	Sold toys to Zane's Department Store; issued Invoice 2501, which shows a list price of $17,600 and a trade discount of 40 percent.
5	Sold games to the Dallas Bookstores; issued Invoice 2502, which shows a list price of $21,300 and a trade discount of 30 percent.
9	Sold games to the Emporium Game Center; issued Invoice 2503, which shows a list price of $7,040 and a trade discount of 30 percent.
14	Sold toys to the Variety Toy Stores; issued Invoice 2504, which shows a list price of $24,400 and a trade discount of 40 percent.
18	Accepted a return of all the games shipped to the Emporium Game Center because they were damaged in transit; issued Credit Memo 162 for the original sale made on Invoice 2503 on August 9.
22	Sold toys to Hanson's Game Store; issued Invoice 2505, which shows a list price of $16,320 and a trade discount of 40 percent.
26	Sold games to the Zane's Department Store; issued Invoice 2506, which shows a list price of $20,300 and a trade discount of 30 percent.
30	Sold toys to the Pebblebrook Toy Center; issued Invoice 2507, which shows a list price of $23,400 and a trade discount of 40 percent.

Analyze: What is the effect on net sales if the company offers a series of trade discounts on toys (25 percent, 15 percent) instead of a single 40 percent discount?

CHAPTER 7 CRITICAL THINKING PROBLEM

Retail Store

Jim Hogan is the owner of The Linen Closet, a housewares store that sells a wide variety of items for the kitchen, bathroom, and home workshop. The Linen Closet offers a company credit card to customers.

The company has experienced an increase in sales since the credit card was introduced. Jim is considering replacing his manual system of recording sales with electronic point-of-sale cash registers that are linked to a computer.

Cash sales are now rung up by the salesclerks on a cash register that generates a tape listing total cash sales at the end of the day. For credit sales, salesclerks prepare handwritten sales slips that are forwarded to the accountant for manual entry into the sales journal and accounts receivable ledger.

The electronic register system Jim is considering would use an optical scanner to read coded labels attached to the merchandise. As the merchandise is passed over the scanner, the code is sent to the computer. The computer is programmed to read the code and identify the item being sold, record the amount of the sale, maintain a record of total sales, update the inventory record, and keep a record of cash received.

If the sale is a credit transaction, the customer's company credit card number is entered into the register. The computer updates the customer's account in the accounts receivable ledger stored in computer memory.

If this system is used, many of the accounting functions are done automatically as sales are entered into the register. At the end of the day, the computer prints a complete sales journal, along with up-to-date balances for the general ledger and the accounts receivable ledger accounts related to sales transactions.

Listed below are four situations that Jim is eager to eliminate. Would use of an electronic point-of-sale system as described above reduce or prevent these problems? Why or why not?

1. The salesclerk was not aware that the item purchased was on sale and did not give the customer the sale price.
2. The customer purchased merchandise using a stolen credit card.
3. The salesclerk did not charge a customer for an item.
4. The accountant did not post a sale to the customer's subsidiary ledger account.

Business Connections

Connection 1 ►  Retail Sales

1. How does the **Sales Returns and Allowances** account provide management with a measure of operating efficiency? What problems might be indicated by a high level of returns and allowances?
2. Suppose you are the accountant for a small chain of clothing stores. Up to now the firm has offered open-account credit to qualified customers but has not allowed the use of bank credit cards. The president of the chain has asked your advice about changing the firm's credit policy. What advantages might there be in eliminating the open-account credit and accepting bank credit cards instead? Do you see any disadvantages?
3. During the past year Cravens Company has had a substantial increase in its losses from uncollectible accounts. Assume that you are the newly hired controller of this firm and that you have been asked to find the reason for the increase. What policies and procedures would you investigate?
4. Suppose a manager in your company has suggested that the firm not hire an accountant to advise it on tax matters and to file tax returns. He states that tax matters are merely procedural in nature and that anyone who can read the tax form instructions can do the necessary work. Comment on this idea.
5. Why is it usually worthwhile for a business to sell on credit even though it will have some losses from uncollectible accounts?
6. How can a firm's credit policy affect its profitability?
7. Why should management insist that all sales on credit and other transactions affecting the firm's accounts receivable be journalized and posted promptly?
8. How can efficient accounting records help management maintain sound credit and collection policies?

Connection 2 ► Ethical DILEMMA **Working in Sales** Assume that you were just hired as a salesclerk at a clothing store. On your first day on the job, you observe the manager making a deal with a customer to sell a designer suit with "no tax." What would you do?

Connection 3 ► Street WISE: Questions from the Real World **Revenue Growth** Refer to the *1999 Annual Report* of The Home Depot, Inc. in Appendix B.

1. Locate Management's Discussion and Analysis of Results of Operations and Financial Condition. By what percentage did net sales increase from fiscal 1998 to fiscal 1999? What factors contributed to this growth?
2. Review the Consolidated Balance Sheets. By what percentage did net accounts receivable change from fiscal 1998 to fiscal 1999? Consider your answer to Question 1 above. Describe the relationship between your answer to Question 1 and the change in net accounts receivable.

FINANCIAL $TATEMENT ANALYSIS **Income Statement** An excerpt from the Consolidated Statements of Income for Wal-Mart Stores, Inc. is presented below. Review the financial data and answer the following analysis questions.

◄ Connection 4
WAL★MART

Amounts in millions **Fiscal years ended January 31**	**2000**	**1999**	**1998**
Revenues:			
Net Sales	$165,013	$137,634	$117,958
Other Income Net	1,796	1,574	1,341
Total Revenues	$166,809	$139,208	$119,299

Analyze:

1. Based on the financial statement presented above, what is Wal-Mart Stores, Inc.'s fiscal year period?
2. Wal-Mart Stores, Inc.'s statement reports one figure for net sales. Name one account whose balance may have been deducted from the **Sales** account balance to determine a net sales amount.
3. The data presented demonstrates a steady increase in net sales over the three-year period. By what percentage have sales of 2000 increased over sales of 1998?

Analyze Online: Find the most recent consolidated statements of income on the Wal-Mart Stores, Inc. Web site **(www.walmartstores.com).** Click on the link *Financial Information,* then select the link for the most recent annual report.

4. What dollar amount is reported for net sales for the most recent year?
5. What is the trend in net sales over the last three years?
6. What are some possible reasons for this trend?

Extending the Thought **e-commerce** Some retailers only operate online and do not have "bricks-and-mortar" physical locations where consumers can shop. What benefits and drawbacks do you see for retailers who operate entirely online?

◄ Connection 5

Business Communication **Memo** You and your partner own three children's bookstores. Your partner comments on the separate general ledger accounts used for **Sales, Sales Tax Payable,** and **Sales Returns and Allowances,** saying this seems like unnecessary "busy work." Write a memo to your partner in response to these concerns.

◄ Connection 6

Connection 7 ► **TeamWork** **Store Policies** As a team, gather information about the sales returns and allowance policies of various stores. Choose stores that sell different types of merchandise, such as

a shoe store,
a hardware store,
a video store,
a supermarket,
a nursery.

Summarize your findings in a one-page report.

Connection 8 ► **interNET CONNECTION** **Privacy and Security** Locate the Web sites for three major online retailers. Research the policy of each retailer regarding privacy and security. Prepare a report that compares the policies.

Answers to Self Reviews

Answers to Section 1 Self Review

1. Sales of merchandise on credit.
2. A ledger that contains accounts of a single type. Examples are the accounts receivable ledger and the accounts payable ledger.
3. A journal that is used to record only one type of transaction. Examples are the sales journal, the purchases journal, the cash receipts journal, and the cash payments journal.
4. **c.** service, merchandising, manufacturing.
5. **c.** increases credit sales
6. The sale to Li was recorded at a taxable rate of 7 percent instead of 6 percent. Therefore, the Sales Tax Payable column should have an entry of $18, not $21. The Accounts Receivable Debit column should have an entry of $318, not $321.

   The sale to Hahn should have an entry in the Accounts Receivable Debit column of $477, not $427.

Answers to Section 2 Self Review

1. Individual accounts for all credit customers.
2. Sales minus sales returns.
3. A sales return results when a customer returns goods and the firm takes them back. A sales allowance results when the firm gives a customer a reduction in the price of the good or service.
4. **c.** income statement
5. **a. Sales Returns and Allowances, Sales Tax Payable, Accounts Receivable**

6.

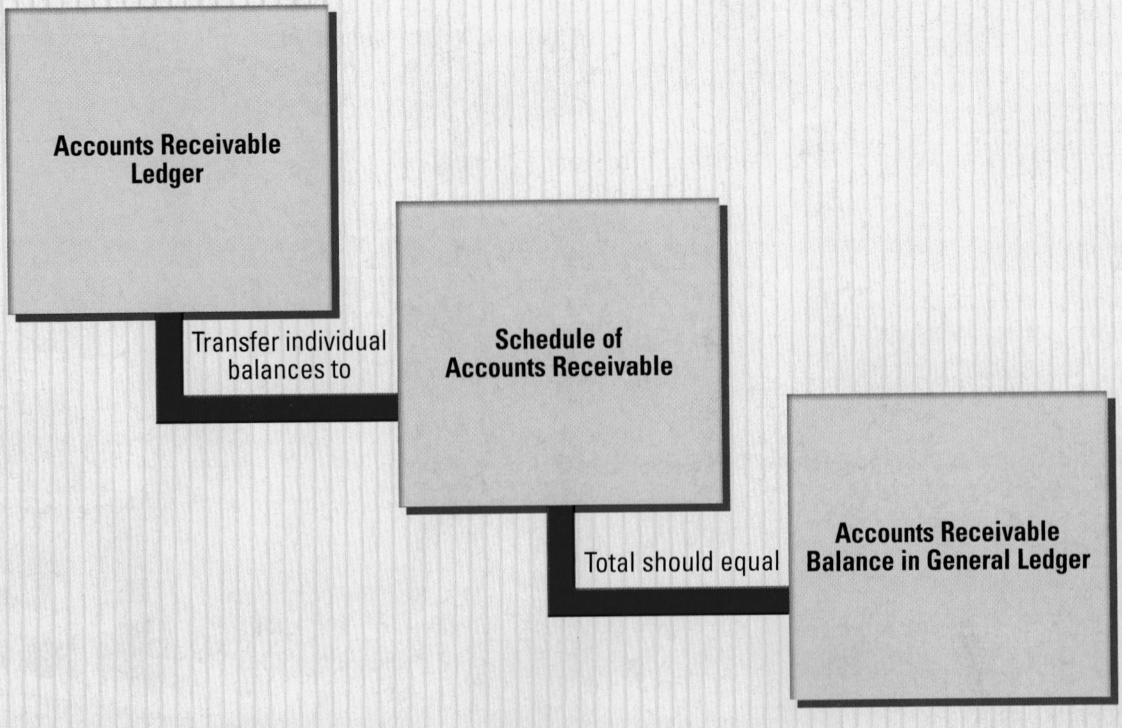

Accounts Receivable Ledger

Transfer individual balances to

Schedule of Accounts Receivable

Total should equal

Accounts Receivable Balance in General Ledger

Answers to Section 3 Self Review

1. Four types of credit sales are open-account credit, business credit card sales, bank credit card sales, and credit card company sales.
2. **Sales Tax Payable** is the account used to record the liability for sales taxes to be paid in the future.
3. List price is the established retail price of an item; net price is the amount left after all trade discounts are subtracted from the list price.
4. **c.** $840
5. **d.** $2,160
6. Possible factors are payment history, amount of current debt, amount of potential debt (available credit cards), employment history, salary, references from other creditors.

Answers to Comprehensive Self Review

1. A service business sells services; a merchandising business sells goods that it has purchased for resale; and a manufacturing business sells goods that it has produced.
2. A merchandising business must account for the purchase and sale of goods and for its merchandise inventory.
3. It contains detailed information about the transactions with credit customers and shows the balances owed by credit customers at all times.
4. A control account is an account that serves as a link between a subsidiary ledger and the general ledger because its balance summarizes the balances of the accounts in the subsidiary ledger.
5. The month and the quarter.

CHAPTER 8

Learning Objectives

1. Record purchases of merchandise on credit in a three-column purchases journal.
2. Post from the three-column purchases journal to the general ledger accounts.
3. Post credit purchases from the purchases journal to the accounts payable subsidiary ledger.
4. Record purchases returns and allowances in the general journal and post them to the accounts payable subsidiary ledger.
5. Prepare a schedule of accounts payable.
6. Compute the net delivered cost of purchases.
7. Demonstrate a knowledge of the procedures for effective internal control of purchases.
8. Define the accounting terms new to this chapter.

Accounting for Purchases and Accounts Payable

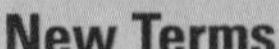

Pier 1 imports®

www.pier1.com

In the 1960s when the first Pier 1 Imports store opened in San Mateo, California, the company offered merchandise such as beanbag chairs, love beads, and incense. Throughout the 1970s and 1980s, the company's merchandise assortment changed along with the demands of its customer base. Pier 1 Imports reshaped its image over the years to sell quality, unique home furnishings and imaginative decorative accessories. By 1989, 500 stores offered items such as occasional tables, Jamaican wicker shelves, and bamboo birdcages. Pier 1 Imports now operates more than 800 stores worldwide, importing products from more than 50 countries.

Thinking Critically

How do you think Pier 1 Imports chooses the products that are offered for sale in its stores?

For more information on Pier 1 Imports, go to: collegeaccounting.glencoe.com.

New Terms

Accounts payable ledger
Cash discount
Cost of goods sold
Freight In account
Purchase allowance
Purchase invoice
Purchase order
Purchase requisition
Purchase return
Purchases account
Purchases discount
Purchases journal
Receiving report
Sales discount
Sales invoice
Schedule of accounts payable
Transportation In account

Section 1

Section Objectives

1. **Record purchases of merchandise on credit in a three-column purchases journal.**

   WHY IT'S IMPORTANT
   Most merchandisers purchase goods on credit, and the use of a special journal improves efficiency when recording these transactions.

2. **Post from the three-column purchases journal to the general ledger accounts.**

   WHY IT'S IMPORTANT
   Summary postings from the purchases journal minimize repetitive tasks.

Terms to Learn

cash discount
cost of goods sold
Freight In account
purchase invoice
purchase order
purchase requisition
Purchases account
purchases discount
purchases journal
receiving report
sales discount
sales invoice
Transportation In account

Merchandise Purchases

In this chapter you will learn how The Trend Center manages its purchases of goods for resale and its accounts payable.

Accounting for Purchases

Most merchandising businesses purchase goods on credit under open-account arrangements. A large firm usually has a centralized purchasing department that is responsible for locating suppliers, obtaining price quotations, negotiating credit terms, and placing orders. In small firms purchasing activities are handled by a single individual, usually the owner or manager.

Purchasing Procedures

When a sales department needs goods, it sends the purchasing department a purchase requisition (Figure 8-1 on page 255). A **purchase requisition** lists the items to be ordered. It is signed by someone with the authority to approve requests for merchandise, usually the manager of the sales department. The purchasing department selects a supplier who can furnish the goods at a competitive price and then issues a purchase order (Figure 8-2 on page 255). The **purchase order** specifies the exact items, quantity, price, and credit terms. It is signed by someone with authority to approve purchases, usually the purchasing agent.

When the goods arrive at the business, they are inspected. A **receiving report** is prepared to show the quantity and condition of the goods received. The purchasing department receives a copy of the receiving report and compares it to the purchase order. If defective goods or the wrong quantity of goods are received, the purchasing department contacts the supplier and settles the problem.

Figure 8-3 on page 255 shows the invoice, or *bill*, for items ordered and shipped. The customer, The Trend Center, calls it a **purchase invoice**. The supplier, Clothes Rack Depot, calls it a **sales invoice**. The customer's accounting department compares the invoice to copies of the purchase order and receiving report. The accounting department checks the quantities, prices, and math on the invoice and then records the purchase. It is important to record purchases in the accounting records as soon as the invoice is verified. Shortly before the due date of the invoice, the accounting department issues a check to the supplier and records the payment.

The purchasing department for The Home Depot, Inc. purchases 40,000 to 50,000 different kinds of home improvement supplies, building materials, and lawn and garden products.

FIGURE 8-1 Purchase Requisition

The Trend Center
1010 Red Bird Lane
Dallas, TX 75268-7783

PURCHASE REQUISITION
No. 325

DEPARTMENT Men's
DATE OF REQUEST January 2, 20--
ADVISE ON DELIVERY Virginia Richey
DATE REQUIRED January 25, 20--

QUANTITY	DESCRIPTION
5	Assorted colors men's suits

APPROVED BY ______
REQUESTED BY ______

FOR PURCHASING DEPARTMENT USE ONLY

PURCHASE ORDER 8001
DATE January 5, 20--
ISSUED TO: Clothes Rack Depot
1677 Mandela Lane
Dallas, TX 75267-6205

FIGURE 8-2 Purchase Order

The Trend Center
1010 Red Bird Lane
Dallas, TX 75268-7783

PURCHASE ORDER

To
Clothes Rack Depot
1677 Mandela Lane
Dallas, TX 75267-6205

Date: January 5, 20--
Order No: 8001
Terms: n/30

QUANTITY	ITEM	UNIT PRICE	TOTAL
5	Assorted colors men's suits	476.00	2,380.00

APPROVED BY ______

FIGURE 8-3 Invoice

Clothes Rack Depot
1677 Mandela Lane
Dallas, TX 75267-6205

INVOICE NO. 7985

SOLD TO: The Trend Center
1010 Red Bird Lane
Dallas, TX 75268-7783

DATE: January 22, 20--
ORDER NO.: 8001
SHIPPED BY: City Express
TERMS: n/30

YOUR ORDER NO.	SALESPERSON	TERMS
8001		n/30
DATE SHIPPED	SHIPPED BY	FOB
January 22, 20--	City Express	Dallas

QUANTITY	DESCRIPTION	UNIT PRICE	TOTAL
5	Assorted colors men's suits	476 00	2,380 00
	Freight		180 00
	Total		2,560 00

National Preferences

When conducting business, the customer's tastes should be considered. Consumers around the world have different preferences in product packaging. For example, in France and Italy, consumers expect stylish looks, while in Germany many consumers look for recyclable materials. Accountants who work with international clients should consider national preferences when designing letterhead, creating portfolios, or choosing paper quality.

The Purchases Account

The purchase of merchandise for resale is a cost of doing business. The purchase of merchandise is debited to the **Purchases account**. **Purchases** is a temporary account classified as a cost of goods sold account. The **cost of goods sold** is the actual cost to the business of the merchandise sold to customers.

Cost of goods sold accounts follow the debit and credit rules of expense accounts. The **Purchases** account is increased by debits and decreased by credits. Its normal balance is a debit. In the chart of accounts, the cost of goods sold accounts appear just before the expense accounts.

Wal-Mart Stores, Inc. purchases private-label products from suppliers and markets these as Wal-Mart brands. Products such as Ol'Roy™ dog food, Spring Valley® vitamins, and EverStart® automotive batteries are purchased at lower costs than nationally known brands. Thus, Wal-Mart Stores, Inc. can sell these items at a lower price to its customers.

Freight Charges for Purchases

Sometimes the buyer pays the freight charge—the cost of shipping the goods from the seller's warehouse to the buyer's location. There are two ways to handle the freight charges paid by the buyer:

- The buyer is billed directly by the transportation company for the freight charge. The buyer issues a check directly to the freight company.
- The seller pays the freight charge and includes it on the invoice. The invoice includes the price of the goods and the freight charge.

The freight charge is debited to the **Freight In** or **Transportation In account**. This is a cost of goods sold account showing transportation charges for merchandise purchased. The buyer enters three elements in the accounting records:

Price of goods	(debit **Purchases**)	$2,380.00
Freight charge	(debit **Freight In**)	180.00
Total invoice	(credit **Accounts Payable**)	$2,560.00

Purchases Dr. +	Purchases Cr. −	Freight In Dr. +	Freight In Cr. −	Accounts Payable Dr. −	Accounts Payable Cr. +
2,380		180			2,560

Important!

Credit Purchases

The purchases journal is used to record *only credit purchases of merchandise for resale.* Credit purchases of other items used in the business are recorded in the general journal.

The Purchases Journal

For most merchandising businesses, it is not efficient to enter purchases of goods in the general journal. Instead, credit purchases of merchandise are recorded in a special journal called the **purchases journal**.

The following illustrates how credit purchases appear in a general journal. Each entry involves a debit to **Purchases** and **Freight In** and a credit to **Accounts Payable** plus a detailed explanation.

GENERAL JOURNAL PAGE 1

DATE		DESCRIPTION	POST. REF.	DEBIT	CREDIT
20--					
Jan.	3	Purchases	501	3 000 00	
		Freight In	502	250 00	
		Accounts Payable	205		3 250 00
		Purchased merchandise from			
		Sebrina's Clothing Store,			
		Invoice 8434, dated December 29,			
		terms 2/10, n/30			
	5	Purchases	501	3 360 00	
		Freight In	502	260 00	
		Accounts Payable	205		3 620 00
		Purchased merchandise from			
		The Style Shop, Invoice 336,			
		dated December 30, terms n/30			
	6	Purchases	501	2 700 00	
		Freight In	502	220 00	
		Accounts Payable	205		2 920 00
		Purchased merchandise from			
		The Women's Shop, Invoice 9080,			
		dated December 31, terms n/30			
	7	Purchases	501	3 850 00	
		Freight In	502	450 00	
		Accounts Payable	205		4 300 00
		Purchased merchandise from			
		Fashion World, Invoice 4321, dated			
		December 31, terms 2/10, n/30			

These four general journal entries require twelve separate postings to general ledger accounts: four to **Purchases,** four to **Freight In,** and four to **Accounts Payable.** As you can see from the ledger accounts that follow, it takes a great deal of time and effort to post these entries.

ACCOUNT *Accounts Payable* ACCOUNT NO. 205

DATE		DESCRIPTION	POST. REF.	DEBIT	CREDIT	BALANCE	
						DEBIT	CREDIT
20--							
Jan.	1	Balance	✓				5 400 00
	3		J1		3 250 00		8 650 00
	5		J1		3 620 00		12 270 00
	6		J1		2 920 00		15 190 00
	7		J1		4 300 00		19 490 00

ACCOUNT *Purchases* ACCOUNT NO. *501*

DATE		DESCRIPTION	POST. REF.	DEBIT	CREDIT	BALANCE DEBIT	BALANCE CREDIT
20--							
Jan.	3		J1	3 000 00		3 000 00	
	5		J1	3 360 00		6 360 00	
	6		J1	2 700 00		9 060 00	
	7		J1	3 850 00		12 910 00	

ACCOUNT *Freight In* ACCOUNT NO. *502*

DATE		DESCRIPTION	POST. REF.	DEBIT	CREDIT	BALANCE DEBIT	BALANCE CREDIT
20--							
Jan.	3		J1	250 00		250 00	
	5		J1	260 00		510 00	
	6		J1	220 00		730 00	
	7		J1	450 00		1 180 00	

Figure 8-4 shows the purchases journal for The Trend Center. Remember that the purchases journal is only for credit purchases of merchandise for resale to customers. Notice how the columns efficiently organize the data about the credit purchases. The purchases journal makes it possible to record each purchase on a single line. In addition, there is no need to enter account names and descriptions.

FIGURE 8-4 ▼
Purchases Journal

PURCHASES JOURNAL PAGE *1*

DATE		CREDITOR'S ACCOUNT CREDITED	INVOICE NUMBER	INVOICE DATE	TERMS	POST. REF.	ACCOUNTS PAYABLE CREDIT	PURCHASES DEBIT	FREIGHT IN DEBIT
20--									
Jan.	3	Sebrina's Clothing Store	8434	12/29/--	2/10, n/30		3 250 00	3 000 00	250 00
	5	The Style Shop	336	12/30/--	n/30		3 620 00	3 360 00	260 00
	6	The Women's Shop	9080	12/31/--	n/30		2 920 00	2 700 00	220 00
	7	Fashion World	4321	01/03/--	2/10, n/30		4 300 00	3 850 00	450 00
	19	Designer's Fashions	9789	01/15/--	2/10, n/30		2 100 00	1 930 00	170 00
	23	Clothes Rack Depot	7985	01/22/--	n/30		2 560 00	2 380 00	180 00
	31						18 750 00	17 220 00	1 530 00

❶ Objective

Record purchases of merchandise on credit in a three-column purchases journal.

Recording Transactions in a Purchases Journal

Use the information on the purchase invoice to make the entry in the purchases journal.

1. Enter the date, supplier name, invoice number, invoice date, and credit terms.
2. In the Accounts Payable Credit column, enter the total owed to the supplier.
3. In the Purchases Debit column, enter the price of the goods purchased.
4. In the Freight In Debit column, enter the freight amount.

Accounting On The Job

Retail/Wholesale Sales & Service

Industry Overview

In the United States today, retailing represents $3 trillion in annual sales. Wholesale markets fuel these sales, supplying products and services for resale in department stores, discount stores, factory outlets, catalogs, and on the Web. The retail industry alone employs more than 20 million workers in the United States.

Career Opportunities

- Store Manager
- Vice President of Acquisitions and Real Estate
- Inventory Specialist
- Manager of Logistics
- Fashion Merchandiser
- Senior Buyer
- Director of E-Commerce Distribution
- Customer Service Manager

Preparing for a Retail/Wholesale Career

- Obtain a business-related degree to open doors to management-level positions.
- Apply to corporate executive training programs for paths to senior buyer, manager of planning and distribution, or regional merchandise manager.
- Complete college courses in marketing, finance, accounting, communications, merchandising, and information systems, as recommended by the National Retail Federation.
- Complete one or two introductory accounting courses, one financial accounting course, and one managerial accounting course for degree programs in fashion merchandising and retail marketing.
- Obtain specialized certifications such as the Buyers Certification or Logistics Certification.

Thinking Critically

Describe why an understanding of credit policies and credit terms might help a retail store manager direct the operations of the store more effectively.

Internet Application

Locate a recruiting Web site for a company such as Federated Department Stores. Review the job description for store manager or buyer. In a half-page report, list the primary responsibilities for this job. What accounting or financial responsibilities does the position entail?

The total of the Purchases Debit and Freight In Debit columns must equal the amount entered in the Accounts Payable Credit column.

The invoice date and credit terms determine when payment is due. The following credit terms often appear on invoices:

- *Net 30 days* or *n/30* means that payment in full is due 30 days after the date of the invoice.
- *Net 10 days EOM*, or *n/10 EOM*, means that payment in full is due 10 days after the end of the month in which the invoice was issued.
- *2% 10 days, net 30 days*, or *2/10, n/30* means that if payment is made within 10 days of the invoice date, the customer can take a 2 percent discount. Otherwise, payment in full is due in 30 days.

The 2 percent discount is a **cash discount**; it is a discount offered by suppliers to encourage quick payment by customers. To the customer it is known as a **purchases discount**. To the supplier it is known as a **sales discount**.

Important!

Cash Discounts

In the purchases journal, record the amount shown on the invoice. The cash discount is recorded when the payment is made.

❷ Objective

Post from the three-column purchases journal to the general ledger accounts.

Posting to the General Ledger

The purchases journal simplifies the posting process. Summary amounts are posted at the end of the month. Refer to Figure 8-5 as you learn how to post from the purchases journal to the general ledger accounts.

Total the Accounts Payable Credit, the Purchases Debit, and the Freight In Debit columns. Before posting, prove the equality of the debits and credits recorded in the purchases journal.

PROOF OF PURCHASES JOURNAL

	Debits
Purchases Debit column	$17,220.00
Freight In Debit column	1,530.00
	$18,750.00
	Credits
Accounts Payable Credit column	$18,750.00

FIGURE 8-5 ▼
Posting to the General Ledger

PURCHASES JOURNAL PAGE 1

DATE		CREDITOR'S ACCOUNT CREDITED	INVOICE NUMBER	INVOICE DATE	TERMS	POST. REF.	ACCOUNTS PAYABLE CREDIT	PURCHASES DEBIT	FREIGHT IN DEBIT
20--									
Jan.	3	Sebrina's Clothing Store	8434	12/29/--	2/10, n/30	✓	3 250 00	3 000 00	250 00
	5	The Style Shop	336	12/30/--	n/30	✓	3 620 00	3 360 00	260 00
	6	The Women's Shop	9080	12/31/--	n/30	✓	2 920 00	2 700 00	220 00
	7	Fashion World	4321	01/03/--	2/10, n/30	✓	4 300 00	3 850 00	450 00
	19	Designer's Fashions	9789	01/15/--	2/10, n/30	✓	2 100 00	1 930 00	170 00
	23	Clothes Rack Depot	7985	01/22/--	n/30	✓	2 560 00	2 380 00	180 00
	31						18 750 00	17 220 00	1 530 00
							(205)	(501)	(502)

ACCOUNT *Accounts Payable* ACCOUNT NO. 205

DATE		DESCRIPTION	POST. REF.	DEBIT	CREDIT	BALANCE DEBIT	BALANCE CREDIT
20--							
Jan.	1	Balance	✓				5 400 00
	31		P1		18 750 00		24 150 00

ACCOUNT *Purchases* ACCOUNT NO. 501

DATE		DESCRIPTION	POST. REF.	DEBIT	CREDIT	BALANCE DEBIT	BALANCE CREDIT
20--							
Jan.	31		P1	17 220 00		17 220 00	

ACCOUNT *Freight In* ACCOUNT NO. 502

DATE		DESCRIPTION	POST. REF.	DEBIT	CREDIT	BALANCE DEBIT	BALANCE CREDIT
20--							
Jan.	31		P1	1 530 00		1 530 00	

After the equality of debits and credits is verified, rule the purchases journal. The steps to post the column totals to the general ledger follow.

1. Locate the **Accounts Payable** ledger account.
2. Enter the date.
3. Enter the posting reference, P1. The **P** is for purchases journal. The **1** is the purchases journal page number.
4. Enter the amount from the Accounts Payable Credit column in the purchases journal in the Credit column of the **Accounts Payable** ledger account.
5. Compute the new balance and enter it in the Balance Credit column.
6. In the purchases journal, enter the **Accounts Payable** ledger account number (205) under the column total.
7. Repeat the steps for the Purchases Debit and Freight In Debit columns.

During the month the individual entries in the purchases journal are posted to the creditor accounts in the accounts payable ledger. The check marks in the purchases journal in Figure 8-5 indicate that these postings have been completed. This procedure is discussed later in this chapter.

Advantages of a Purchases Journal

Every business has certain types of transactions that occur over and over again. A well-designed accounting system includes journals that permit efficient recording of such transactions. In most merchandising firms, purchases of goods on credit take place often enough to make it worthwhile to use a purchases journal.

A special journal for credit purchases of merchandise saves time and effort when recording and posting purchases. The use of a purchases journal and other special journals allows for the division of accounting work among different employees. The purchases journal strengthens the audit trail. All credit purchases are recorded in one place, and each entry refers to the number and date of the invoice.

Section 1 Self Review

Questions

1. What type of transaction is recorded in the purchases journal?
2. What are the advantages of using a purchases journal?
3. What activities does a purchasing department perform?

Exercises

4. When the sales department needs goods, what document is sent to the purchasing department?
   a. Purchase invoice
   b. Purchase order
   c. Purchase requisition
   d. Sales requisition
5. What form is sent to the supplier to order goods?
   a. Purchase invoice
   b. Purchase order
   c. Purchase requisition
   d. Sales invoice

Analysis

6. An invoice dated January 15 for $1,000 shows credit terms 2/10, n/30. What do the credit terms mean?

(Answers to Section 1 Self Review are on page 289.)

Section 2

Section Objectives

3 Post credit purchases from the purchases journal to the accounts payable subsidiary ledger.

WHY IT'S IMPORTANT
Up-to-date records allow prompt payment of invoices.

4 Record purchases returns and allowances in the general journal and post them to the accounts payable subsidiary ledger.

WHY IT'S IMPORTANT
For unsatisfactory goods received, an allowance or return is reflected in the accounting records.

5 Prepare a schedule of accounts payable.

WHY IT'S IMPORTANT
This schedule provides a snapshot of amounts owed to suppliers.

6 Compute the net delivered cost of purchases.

WHY IT'S IMPORTANT
This is an important component in measuring operational results.

7 Demonstrate a knowledge of the procedures for effective internal control of purchases.

WHY IT'S IMPORTANT
Businesses try to prevent fraud, errors, and holding excess inventory.

Terms to Learn

accounts payable ledger
purchase allowance
purchase return
schedule of accounts payable

Accounts Payable

Businesses that buy merchandise on credit can conduct more extensive operations and use financial resources more effectively than if they paid cash for all purchases. It is important to pay invoices on time so that the business maintains a good credit reputation with its suppliers.

The Accounts Payable Ledger

Businesses need detailed records in order to pay invoices promptly. The **accounts payable ledger** provides information about the individual accounts for all creditors. The accounts payable ledger is a subsidiary ledger; it is separate from and subordinate to the general ledger. The accounts payable ledger contains a separate account for each creditor. Each account shows purchases, payments, and returns and allowances. The balance of the account shows the amount owed to the creditor.

Figure 8-6 on page 263 shows the accounts payable ledger for Clothes Rack Depot. Notice that the Balance column does not indicate whether the balance is a debit or a credit. The form assumes that the balance will be a credit because the normal balance of liability accounts is a credit. A debit balance may exist if more than the amount owed was paid to the creditor or if returned goods were already paid for. If the balance is a debit, circle the amount to show that the account does not have the normal balance.

Small businesses like The Trend Center arrange the accounts payable ledger in alphabetical order. Large businesses and businesses that use computerized accounting systems assign an account number to each creditor and arrange the accounts payable ledger in numeric order.

Posting a Credit Purchase

To keep the accounting records up to date, invoices are posted to the accounts payable subsidiary ledger every day. Refer to Figure 8-6 as you learn how to post to the accounts payable ledger.

1. Locate the accounts payable ledger account for the creditor Clothes Rack Depot.
2. Enter the date
3. In the Description column, enter the invoice number and date.
4. In the Posting Reference column, enter the purchases journal page number.
5. Enter the amount from the Accounts Payable Credit column in the purchases journal in the Credit column of the accounts payable subsidiary ledger.
6. Compute and enter the new balance in the Balance column.
7. In the purchases journal (Figure 8-5 on page 260), enter a check mark (✓) in the Posting Reference column. This indicates that the transaction is posted in the accounts payable subsidiary ledger.

NAME Clothes Rack Depot			TERMS n/30		
ADDRESS 1677 Mandela Lane, Dallas, Texas 75267-6205					
DATE	DESCRIPTION	POST. REF.	DEBIT	CREDIT	BALANCE
20--					
Jan. 1	Balance	✓			800 00
23	Invoice 7985, 01/22/--	P1		2560 00	3360 00

◄ **FIGURE 8-6**
Accounts Payable Ledger Account

3 Objective

Post credit purchases from the purchases journal to the accounts payable subsidiary ledger.

Posting Cash Paid on Account

When the transaction involves cash paid on account to a supplier, the payment is first recorded in a cash payments journal. (The cash payments journal is discussed in Chapter 9.) The cash payment is then posted to the individual creditor's account in the accounts payable ledger. Figure 8-7 shows a posting for cash paid to a creditor on January 27.

NAME Clothes Rack Depot			TERMS n/30		
ADDRESS 1677 Mandela Lane, Dallas, Texas 75267-6205					
DATE	DESCRIPTION	POST. REF.	DEBIT	CREDIT	BALANCE
20--					
Jan. 1	Balance	✓			800 00
23	Invoice 7985, 01/22/--	P1		2560 00	3360 00
27		CP1	1200 00		2160 00

◄ **FIGURE 8-7**
Posting a Payment Made on Account

Purchases Returns and Allowances

4 Objective

Record purchases returns and allowances in the general journal and post them to the accounts payable subsidiary ledger.

When merchandise arrives, it is examined to confirm that it is satisfactory. Occasionally, the wrong goods are shipped, or items are damaged or defective. A **purchase return** is when the business returns the goods. A **purchase allowance** is when the purchaser keeps the goods but receives a reduction in the price of the goods. The supplier issues a credit memorandum for the return or allowance. The credit memorandum reduces the amount that the purchaser owes.

Purchases returns and allowances are entered in the **Purchases Returns and Allowances** account, not in the **Purchases** account. The **Purchases Returns and Allowances** account is a complete record of returns and allowances. Business managers analyze this account to identify problem suppliers.

Purchases Returns and Allowances is a contra cost of goods sold account. The normal balance of cost of goods sold accounts is a debit. The normal balance of **Purchases Returns and Allowances,** a contra cost of goods sold account, is a credit.

Recall

Subsidiary Ledger

The total of the accounts in the subsidiary ledger must equal the control account balance.

Recording Purchases Returns and Allowances

The Trend Center received merchandise from Clothes Rack Depot on January 23. Some goods were damaged, and the supplier granted a $500 purchase allowance. The Trend Center recorded the full amount of the invoice, $2,560, in the purchases journal. The purchase allowance was recorded separately in the general journal.

Business Transaction

On January 30 The Trend Center received a credit memorandum for $500 from Clothes Rack Depot as an allowance for damaged merchandise.

Clothes Rack Depot
1677 Mandela Lane
Dallas, TX 75267-6205

CREDIT MEMORANDUM
NUMBER: 73
DATE: January 30, 20--

TO: The Trend Center
1010 Red Bird Lane
Dallas, TX 75268-7783

ORIGINAL INVOICE: 7985
INVOICE DATE: January 22, 20--
DESCRIPTION: Credit for damaged suits: $500.00

Analysis

The liability account, **Accounts Payable,** is decreased by $500. The contra cost of goods sold account, **Purchases Returns and Allowances,** is increased by $500.

Debit-Credit Rules

DEBIT Decreases to liabilities are debits. Debit **Accounts Payable** for $500.

CREDIT Increases to contra cost of goods sold accounts are recorded as credits. Credit **Purchases Returns and Allowances** for $500.

T-Account Presentation

Accounts Payable	
−	+
500	

Purchases Returns and Allowances	
−	+
	500

General Journal Entry

GENERAL JOURNAL PAGE 2

	DATE		DESCRIPTION	POST. REF.	DEBIT	CREDIT	
15	Jan.	30	Accounts Payable/Clothes Rack Depot		500 00		15
16			Purchases Returns and Allowances			500 00	16
17			Received Credit Memo 73 for				17
18			an allowance for damaged				18
19			merchandise; original Invoice				19
20			7985, January 22, 20--				20

The Bottom Line

Purchase Allowance

Income Statement

Contra Cost of Goods Sold	↑ 500
Net Income	↑ 500

Balance Sheet

Liabilities	↓ 500
Equity	↑ 500

Notice that this entry includes a debit to **Accounts Payable** and a credit to **Purchases Returns and Allowances.** In addition, there is a debit to the creditor's account in the accounts payable subsidiary ledger. Businesses that have few returns and allowances use the general journal to record these transactions. Businesses with many returns and allowances use a special journal for purchases returns and allowances.

Posting a Purchases Return or Allowance

Whether recorded in the general journal or in a special journal, it is important to promptly post returns and allowances to the creditor's account in the accounts payable ledger. Refer to Figure 8-8 to learn how to post purchases returns and allowances to the supplier's account.

1. Enter the date.
2. In the Description column, enter the credit memorandum number.
3. In the Posting Reference column, enter the general journal page number.
4. Enter the amount of the return or allowance in the Debit column.
5. Compute the new balance and enter it in the Balance column.
6. In the general journal, enter a check mark (✓) to show that the transaction was posted to the creditor's account in the accounts payable subsidiary ledger.

After the transaction is posted to the general ledger, enter the **Purchases Returns and Allowances** ledger account number in the Posting Reference column.

Recall

Contra Accounts

The **Purchases Returns and Allowances** account is a contra account. Contra accounts have normal balances that are the opposite of related accounts.

◄ **FIGURE 8-8**
Posting to a Creditor's Account

GENERAL JOURNAL PAGE 2

	DATE		DESCRIPTION	POST. REF.	DEBIT	CREDIT	
15	Jan.	30	Accounts Payable/Clothes Rack Depot	205 ✓	500 00		15
16			Purchases Returns and Allowances	503		500 00	16
17			Received Credit Memo 73 for				17
18			an allowance for damaged				18
19			merchandise; original Invoice				19
20			7985, January 22, 20--				20
21							21
22							

NAME *Clothes Rack Depot* TERMS *n/30*
ADDRESS *1677 Mandela Lane, Dallas, Texas 75267-6205*

DATE		DESCRIPTION	POST. REF.	DEBIT	CREDIT	BALANCE
20--						
Jan.	1	Balance	✓			800 00
	23	Invoice 7985, 01/22/--	P1		2 560 00	3 360 00
	27		CP1	1 200 00		2 160 00
	30	CM 73	J2	500 00		1 660 00

Schedule of Accounts Payable

5 Objective

Prepare a schedule of accounts payable.

The total of the individual creditor accounts in the subsidiary ledger must equal the balance of the **Accounts Payable** control account. To prove that the control account and the subsidiary ledger are equal, businesses prepare a **schedule of accounts payable**—a list of all balances owed to creditors. Figure 8-9 on page 266 shows the accounts payable subsidiary ledger for The Trend Center on January 31.

Figure 8-10 on page 267 shows the schedule of accounts payable for The Trend Center. Notice that the accounts payable control account balance is $10,940. This equals the total on the schedule of accounts payable. If the amounts are not equal, it is essential to locate and correct the errors.

◄ **FIGURE 8-9**
The Accounts Payable Ledger

NAME *Clothes Rack Depot* TERMS *n/30*
ADDRESS *1677 Mandela Lane, Dallas, Texas 75267-6205*

DATE		DESCRIPTION	POST. REF.	DEBIT	CREDIT	BALANCE
20--						
Jan.	1	Balance	✓			800 00
	23	Invoice 7985, 01/22/--	P1		2 560 00	3 360 00
	27		CP1	1 200 00		2 160 00
	30	CM 73	J2	500 00		1 660 00

NAME *Designer's Fashions* TERMS *2/10, n/30*
ADDRESS *7701 Holly Hill Drive, Dallas, Texas 75267-6205*

DATE		DESCRIPTION	POST. REF.	DEBIT	CREDIT	BALANCE
20--						
Jan.	19	Invoice 9789, 01/15/--	P1		2 100 00	2 100 00

NAME *Fashion World* TERMS *2/10, n/30*
ADDRESS *2701 George Avenue, Dallas, Texas 75267-6205*

DATE		DESCRIPTION	POST. REF.	DEBIT	CREDIT	BALANCE
20--						
Jan.	1	Balance	✓			1 500 00
	7	Invoice 4321, 01/03/--	P1		4 300 00	5 800 00
	11		CP1	1 000 00		4 800 00
	31		CP1	2 560 00		2 240 00

NAME *Sebrina's Clothing Store* TERMS *2/10, n/30*
ADDRESS *5671 Preston Road, Dallas, Texas 75267-6205*

DATE		DESCRIPTION	POST. REF.	DEBIT	CREDIT	BALANCE
20--						
Jan.	1	Balance	✓			1 100 00
	3	Invoice 8434, 12/29/--	P1		3 250 00	4 350 00
	13		CP1	3 250 00		1 100 00
	30		CP1	400 00		700 00

NAME *The Style Shop* TERMS *n/30*
ADDRESS *3123 Belt Line Road, Dallas, Texas 75267-6205*

DATE		DESCRIPTION	POST. REF.	DEBIT	CREDIT	BALANCE
20--						
Jan.	1	Balance	✓			1 200 00
	5	Invoice 336, 12/30/--	P1		3 620 00	4 820 00
	17		CP1	4 300 00		520 00

NAME *The Women's Shop* TERMS *n/30*
ADDRESS *6028 Audra Lane, Dallas, Texas 75267-6205*

DATE		DESCRIPTION	POST. REF.	DEBIT	CREDIT	BALANCE
20--						
Jan.	1	Balance	✓			800 00
	6	Invoice 9080, 12/31/--	P1		2 920 00	3 720 00

The Trend Center	
Schedule of Accounts Payable	
January 31, 20--	
Clothes Rack Depot	1 660 00
Designer's Fashions	2 100 00
Fashion World	2 240 00
Sebrina's Clothing Store	700 00
The Style Shop	520 00
The Women's Shop	3 720 00
Total	10 940 00

ACCOUNT *Accounts Payable* ACCOUNT NO. 205

DATE		DESCRIPTION	POST. REF.	DEBIT	CREDIT	BALANCE DEBIT	BALANCE CREDIT
20--							
Jan.	*1*	*Balance*	✓				*5 400 00*
	30		*J1*	*500 00*			*4 900 00*
	31		*P1*		*18 750 00*		*23 650 00*
	31		*CP1*	*12 710 00*			*10 940 00*

FIGURE 8-10
Schedule of Accounts Payable and the Accounts Payable Account

Determining the Cost of Purchases

6 Objective

Compute the net delivered cost of purchases.

The **Purchases** account accumulates the cost of merchandise bought for resale. The income statement of a merchandising business contains a section showing the total cost of purchases. This section combines information about the cost of the purchases, freight in, and purchases returns and allowances for the period. Assume that The Trend Center has the following general ledger account balances at January 31:

Purchases	$28,125
Freight In	2,295
Purchases Returns and Allowances	4,250

The net delivered cost of purchases for The Trend Center for January is calculated as follows.

Purchases	$28,125
Freight In	2,295
Delivered Cost of Purchases	$30,420
Less Purchases Returns and Allowances	4,250
Net Delivered Cost of Purchases	$26,170

Lands' End, Inc. reported cost of sales as 55.1 percent of net sales for the period ended January 28, 2000. This means that for every dollar a consumer spent on a product, Lands' End, Inc. paid approximately 55 cents to purchase the item.

Accounting for Purchases

- Management and the accounting staff need to work together to make sure that there are good internal controls over purchasing.
- A carefully designed system of checks and balances protects the business against fraud, errors, and excessive investment in merchandise.
- The accounting staff needs to record transactions efficiently so that up-to-date information about creditors is available.
- Using the purchases journal and the accounts payable subsidiary ledger improves efficiency.
- To maintain a good credit reputation with suppliers, it is important to have an accounting system that ensures prompt payment of invoices.
- A well-run accounting system provides management with information about cash: cash required to pay suppliers, short-term loans needed to cover temporary cash shortages, and cash available for short-term investments.
- Separate accounts for recording purchases, freight charges, and purchases returns and allowances make it easy to analyze the elements in the cost of purchases.

Thinking Critically

As a manager, what internal controls would you put in your accounting system?

For firms that do not have freight charges, the amount of net purchases is calculated as follows.

Purchases	$28,125
Less Purchases Returns and Allowances	4,250
Net Purchases	$23,875

In Chapter 13 you will see how the complete income statement for a merchandising business is prepared. You will learn about the Cost of Goods Sold section and how the net delivered cost of purchases is used in calculating the results of operations.

7 Objective

Demonstrate a knowledge of the procedures for effective internal control of purchases.

Internal Control of Purchases

Because of the large amount of money spent to buy goods, most businesses develop careful procedures for the control of purchases and payments. Some firms have a *voucher system,* a special system used to achieve internal control. Whether the voucher system is used or not, a business should be sure that its control process includes sufficient safeguards. The objectives of the controls are to

- create written proof that purchases and payments are authorized;
- ensure that different people are involved in the process of buying goods, receiving goods, and making payments.

Separating duties among employees provides a system of checks and balances. In a small business with just a few employees, it might be difficult or impossible to separate duties. However, the business should design as effective a set of control procedures as the company's resources will allow. Effective systems have the following controls in place.

1. All purchases should be made only after proper authorization has been given in writing.
2. Goods should be carefully checked when they are received. They should then be compared with the purchase order and with the invoice received from the supplier.
3. The purchase order, receiving report, and invoice should be checked to confirm that the information on the documents is in agreement.
4. The computations on the invoice should be checked for accuracy.
5. Authorization for payment should be made by someone other than the person who ordered the goods, and this authorization should be given only after all the verifications have been made.
6. Another person should write the check for payment.
7. Prenumbered forms should be used for purchase requisitions, purchase orders, and checks. Periodically the numbers of the documents issued should be verified to make sure that all forms can be accounted for.

About Accounting

Employee Fraud

According to the U.S. Chamber of Commerce, businesses lose $20 to $40 billion each year to employee fraud. The best defense against fraud is to use good internal controls: Have multiple employees in contact with suppliers and screen employees and vendors to reduce fraud opportunities.

Lands' End, Inc. reported a 2.7 percent decrease in the cost of purchases in fiscal 2000. The company believes this decrease is the result of more efficient negotiations with its suppliers. Effective internal controls verify that the agreed price is accurately reflected on the invoice received from the supplier.

Section 2 Self Review

Questions

1. A firm has a debit balance of $55,160 in its **Purchases** account and a credit balance of $2,520 in its **Purchases Returns and Allowances** account. Calculate net purchases for the period.
2. A firm receives an invoice that reflects the price of goods as $1,120 and the freight charge as $84. How is this transaction recorded?
3. What is the purpose of the schedule of accounts payable?

Exercises

4. The net delivered cost of purchases for the period appears on the
   a. balance sheet.
   b. income statement.
   c. schedule of accounts payable.
   d. statement of owner's equity.
5. In the accounts payable ledger, a supplier's account has a beginning balance of $2,400. A transaction of $800 is posted from the purchases journal. What is the balance of the supplier's account?
   a. $1,600 debit
   b. $1,600 credit
   c. $3,200 debit
   d. $3,200 credit

Analysis

6. In the general ledger, the **Accounts Payable** account has a balance of $12,500. The schedule of accounts payable lists accounts totaling $17,500. What could cause this error?

(Answers to Section 2 Self Review are on page 289.)

CHAPTER 8 Review and Applications

Review

Chapter Summary

In this chapter, you have learned about the accounting journals and ledgers required for the efficient processing of purchases for a business. Businesses with strong internal controls establish and follow procedures for approving requests for new merchandise, choosing suppliers, placing orders with suppliers, checking goods after they arrive, identifying invoices, and approving payments.

Learning Objectives

1 Record purchases of merchandise on credit in a three-column purchases journal.

Purchases and payments on account must be entered in the firm's accounting records promptly and accurately. Most merchandising businesses normally purchase goods on credit. The most efficient system for recording purchases on credit is the use of a special purchases journal. With this type of journal, only one line is needed to enter all the data.

The purchases journal is used only to record the credit purchase of goods for resale. General business expenses are not recorded in the purchases journal.

2 Post from the three-column purchases journal to the general ledger accounts.

The use of the three-column purchases journal simplifies the posting process because nothing is posted to the general ledger until the month's end. Then, summary postings are made to the **Purchases, Freight In,** and **Accounts Payable** accounts.

3 Post purchases on credit from the purchases journal to the accounts payable subsidiary ledger.

An accounts payable subsidiary ledger helps a firm keep track of the amounts it owes to creditors. Postings are made to this ledger on a daily basis.

- Each credit purchase is posted from the purchases journal to the accounts payable subsidiary ledger.
- Each payment on account is posted from the cash payments journal to the accounts payable subsidiary ledger.

4 Record purchases returns and allowances in the general journal and post them to the accounts payable subsidiary ledger.

Returns and allowances on purchases of goods are credited to an account called **Purchases Returns and Allowances.** These transactions may be recorded in the general journal or in a special purchases returns and allowances journal. Each return or allowance on a credit purchase is posted to the accounts payable subsidiary ledger.

5 Prepare a schedule of accounts payable.

At the month's end, a schedule of accounts payable is prepared. The schedule lists the balances owed to the firm's creditors and proves the accuracy of the subsidiary ledger. The total of the schedule of accounts payable is compared with the balance of the **Accounts Payable** account in the general ledger, which acts as a control account. The two amounts should be equal.

6 Compute the net delivered cost of purchases.

The net delivered cost of purchases is computed by adding the cost of purchases and freight in, then subtracting any purchases returns and allowances. Net delivered cost of purchases is reported in the Cost of Goods Sold section of the income statement.

7 Demonstrate a knowledge of the procedures for effective internal control of purchases.

Purchases and payments should be properly authorized and processed with appropriate documentation to provide a system of checks and balances. A division of responsibilities within the purchases process ensures strong internal controls.

8 Define the accounting terms new to this chapter.

CHAPTER 8 GLOSSARY

Accounts payable ledger (p. 262) A subsidiary ledger that contains a separate account for each creditor

Cash discount (p. 259) A discount offered by suppliers for payment received within a specified period of time

Cost of goods sold (p. 256) The actual cost to the business of the merchandise sold to customers

Freight In account (p. 256) An account showing transportation charges for items purchased

Purchase allowance (p. 263) A price reduction from the amount originally billed

Purchase invoice (p. 254) A bill received for goods purchased

Purchase order (p. 254) An order to the supplier of goods specifying items needed, quantity, price, and credit terms

Purchase requisition (p. 254) A list sent to the purchasing department showing the items to be ordered

Purchase return (p. 263) Return of unsatisfactory goods

Purchases account (p. 256) An account used to record cost of goods bought for resale during a period

Purchases discount (p. 259) A cash discount offered to the customer for payment within a specified period

Purchases journal (p. 256) A special journal used to record the purchase of goods on credit

Receiving report (p. 254) A form showing quantity and condition of goods received

Sales discount (p. 259) A cash discount offered by the supplier for payment within a specified period

Sales invoice (p. 254) A supplier's billing document

Schedule of accounts payable (p. 265) A list of all balances owed to creditors

Transportation In account (p. 256) See Freight In account

Comprehensive Self Review

1. What is the difference between a receiving report and an invoice?
2. What is the purpose of a purchase requisition? A purchase order?
3. What is the purpose of the **Freight In** account?
4. What is a cash discount and why is it offered?
5. What type of account is **Purchases Returns and Allowances?**

(Answers to Comprehensive Self Review are on page 289.)

Discussion Questions

1. How is the net delivered cost of purchases computed?
2. Why is it useful for a business to have an accounts payable ledger?
3. What type of accounts are kept in the accounts payable ledger?
4. What is the relationship of the **Accounts Payable** account in the general ledger to the accounts payable subsidiary ledger?
5. What is a schedule of accounts payable? Why is it prepared?
6. What is a purchase return?
7. What is a purchase allowance?
8. What is the purpose of a credit memorandum?
9. What major safeguards should be built into a system of internal control for purchases of goods?
10. Why are the invoice date and terms recorded in the purchases journal?
11. A business has purchased some new equipment for use in its operations, not for resale to customers. The terms of the invoice are n/30. Should this transaction be entered in the purchases journal? If not, where should it be recorded?
12. What do the following credit terms mean?
    - **a.** n/30
    - **b.** 2/10, n/30
    - **c.** n/10 EOM
    - **d.** n/20
    - **e.** 1/10, n/20
    - **f.** 3/5, n/30
    - **g.** n/15 EOM
13. Why is the use of a **Purchases Returns and Allowances** account preferred to crediting these transactions to **Purchases?**
14. On what financial statement do the accounts related to purchases of merchandise appear? In which section of this statement are they reported?
15. What is the normal balance of the **Purchases** account?
16. What is the difference between a purchase invoice and a sales invoice?
17. What journals can be used to enter various merchandise purchase transactions?

Applications

EXERCISES

Identifying journals used to record purchases and related transactions.

◄ **Exercise 8-1**
Objective 1

The following transactions took place at Mountain Hike and Bike Shop. Indicate the general ledger account numbers that would be debited and credited to record each transaction.

GENERAL LEDGER ACCOUNTS

101 Cash
205 Accounts Payable
501 Purchases
502 Freight In
503 Purchases Returns and Allowances

TRANSACTIONS

1. Purchased merchandise for $1,000; the terms are 2/10, n/30.
2. Returned damaged merchandise to a supplier and received a credit memorandum for $200.
3. Issued a check for $400 to a supplier as a payment on account.
4. Purchased merchandise for $1,200 plus a freight charge of $130; the supplier's invoice is payable in 30 days.
5. Received an allowance for merchandise that was damaged but can be sold at a reduced price; the supplier's credit memorandum is for $300.
6. Purchased merchandise for $2,100 in cash.

Identifying the journals used to record purchases and related transactions.

◄ **Exercise 8-2**
Objective 1

The accounting system of Discount Rack includes the following journals. Indicate which journal is used to record each transaction.

JOURNALS

Cash receipts journal
Cash payments journal
Purchases journal
Sales journal
General journal

TRANSACTIONS

1. Purchased merchandise for $1,500; the terms are 2/10, n/30.
2. Returned damaged merchandise to a supplier and received a credit memorandum for $700.
3. Issued a check for $1,800 to a supplier as a payment on account.
4. Purchased merchandise for $1,000 plus a freight charge of $70; the supplier's invoice is payable in 30 days.
5. Received an allowance for merchandise that was damaged but can be sold at a reduced price; the supplier's credit memorandum is for $360.
6. Purchased merchandise for $1,750 in cash.

Exercise 8-3 ► Objective 1

Recording credit purchases.

The following transactions took place at Metroplex Auto Parts and Detailing Center during the first week of July. Indicate how these transactions would be entered in a purchases journal like the one shown in this chapter.

DATE		TRANSACTIONS
July	1	Purchased batteries for $3,900 plus a freight charge of $64 from Car Parts Corporation; received Invoice 2168, dated June 27, which has terms of n/30.
	3	Purchased mufflers for $1,560 plus a freight charge of $40 from Sharpe Company; received Invoice 144, dated June 30, which has terms of 1/10, n/60.
	5	Purchased car radios for $4,900 plus freight of $50 from Sounds From Above, Inc.; received Invoice 1056, dated July 1, which has terms of 2/10, n/30.
	10	Purchased truck tires for $3,900 from Big Wheel Tire Company; received Invoice 2011, dated July 8, which has terms of 2/10, n/30.

Exercise 8-4 ► Objective 4

Recording a purchase return.

On February 9, 20--, City Appliance Center, a retail store, received Credit Memorandum 442 for $1,960 from Broken Bow Corporation. The credit memorandum covered a return of damaged trash compactors originally purchased on Invoice 1041 dated January 3. Prepare the general journal entry that City Appliance Center would make for this transaction.

Exercise 8-5 ► Objective 4

Recording a purchase allowance.

On March 15, 20--, The Ides of March Company was given an allowance of $500 by City Appliance Center, which issued Credit Memorandum 333. The allowance was for scratches on stoves that were originally purchased on Invoice 686 dated February 20. Prepare the general journal entry that The Ides of March Company would make for this transaction.

Exercise 8-6 ► Objective 4

Determining the cost of purchases.

On June 30 the general ledger of Fashion World, a clothing store, showed a balance of $35,360 in the **Purchases** account, a balance of $1,156 in the **Freight In** account, and a balance of $3,620 in the **Purchases Returns and Allowances** account. What was the delivered cost of the purchases made during June? What was the net delivered cost of these purchases?

Exercise 8-7 ► Objectives 1, 4

Errors in recording purchase transactions.

The following errors were made in recording transactions in posting from the purchases journal. How will these errors be detected?

a. A credit of $1,000 to Zant Furniture Company account in the accounts payable ledger was posted as $100.

b. The Accounts Payable column total of the purchases journal was understated by $100.

c. An invoice of $840 for merchandise from Davis Company was recorded as having been received from Darrin Company, another supplier.

d. A $500 payment to Darrin Company was debited to Davis Company.

Determining the cost of purchases.

◄ **Exercise 8-8**
Objective 4

Complete the following schedule by supplying the missing information.

Net Delivered Cost of Purchases	Case A	Case B
Purchases	(a)	83,600
Freight In	3,000	(c)
Delivered Cost of Purchases	93,600	(d)
Less Purchases Returns and Allowances	(b)	3,600
Net Delivered Cost of Purchases	88,640	93,100

Problems

Selected problems can be completed using:
Peachtree **QuickBooks** **Spreadsheets**

PROBLEM SET A

Journalizing credit purchases and purchases returns and allowances and posting to the general ledger.

◄ **Problem 8-1A**
Objectives 1, 2, 3

Picture Perfect Photo Mart is a retail store that sells cameras and photography supplies. The firm's credit purchases and purchases returns and allowances transactions for June 20-- appear below and on page 276, along with the general ledger accounts used to record these transactions. The balance shown in **Accounts Payable** is for the beginning of June.

INSTRUCTIONS

1. Open the general ledger accounts and enter the balance of **Accounts Payable** for June 1, 20--.
2. Record the transactions in a three-column purchases journal and in a general journal. Use 13 as the page number for the purchases journal and 37 as the page number for the general journal.
3. Post entries from the general journal to the general ledger accounts.
4. Total and rule the purchases journal as of June 30.
5. Post the column total from the purchases journal to the proper general ledger accounts.
6. Compute the net purchases of the firm for the month of June.

GENERAL LEDGER ACCOUNTS

205 Accounts Payable, $6,952 Cr.
501 Purchases
502 Freight In
503 Purchases Returns and Allowances

DATE		TRANSACTIONS
June	1	Purchased instant cameras for $3,990 plus a freight charge of $90 from Jarvis Company, Invoice 1442, dated May 26; the terms are 60 days net.
	8	Purchased film for $695 from Photographic Products, Invoice 2101, dated June 3, net payable in 45 days.
	12	Purchased lenses for $453 from The Optical Mart, Invoice 3872, dated June 9; the terms are 1/10, n/60.
		Continued

DATE	(8-1A cont.) TRANSACTIONS
June 18	Received Credit Memorandum 112 for $450 from Jarvis Company for defective cameras that were returned; they were originally purchased on Invoice 1442, dated May 26.
20	Purchased color film for $2,100 plus freight of $50 from Photographic Products, Invoice 2151, dated June 15, net payable in 45 days.
23	Purchased camera cases for $970 from Dallas Case Company, Invoice 8310, dated June 18, net due and payable in 45 days.
28	Purchased disk cameras for $4,940 plus freight of $60 from Penn Corporation, Invoice 2750, dated June 24; the terms are 2/10, n/30.
30	Received Credit Memorandum 1120 for $120 from Dallas Case Company; the amount is an allowance for damaged but usable goods purchased on Invoice 8310, dated June 18.

(**Note:** Save your working papers for use in Problem 8-2A.)

Analyze: What total purchases were posted to the **Purchases** general ledger account for June?

Problem 8-2A ►
Objectives 4, 6

Posting to the accounts payable ledger and preparing a schedule of accounts payable.

This problem is a continuation of Problem 8-1A.

INSTRUCTIONS

1. Set up an accounts payable subsidiary ledger for Picture Perfect Photo Mart. Open an account for each of the creditors listed below and enter the balances as of June 1, 20--.
2. Post the individual entries from the purchases journal and the general journal prepared in Problem 8-1A.
3. Prepare a schedule of accounts payable for June 30.
4. Check the total of the schedule of accounts payable against the balance of the **Accounts Payable** account in the general ledger. The two amounts should be equal.

Creditors

Name	Terms	Balance
Dallas Case Company	n/45	$ 600
Jarvis Company	n/60	
The Optical Mart	1/10, n/60	1,112
Penn Corporation	2/10, n/30	
Photographic Products	n/45	5,240

Analyze: What amount is owed to The Optical Mart on June 30?

Problem 8-3A ►
Objectives 1, 2, 3, 4, 5, 6

Journalizing credit purchases and purchases returns and allowances, computing the net delivered cost of goods, posting to the general ledger, posting to the accounts payable ledger, and preparing a schedule of accounts payable.

The Garden Center is a retail store that sells garden equipment, furniture, and supplies. Its credit purchases and purchases returns and allowances for July are listed below. The general ledger accounts used to record these transactions are also provided. The balance shown is for the beginning of July 20--.

INSTRUCTIONS

Part I

1. Open the general ledger accounts and enter the balance of **Accounts Payable** for July 1.
2. Record the transactions in a three-column purchases journal and in a general journal. Use 7 as the page number for the purchases journal and 19 as the page number for the general journal.
3. Post the entries from the general journal to the proper general ledger accounts.
4. Total, prove, and rule the purchases journal as of July 31.
5. Post the column totals from the purchases journal to the proper general ledger accounts.
6. Compute the net delivered cost of the firm's purchases for the month of July.

GENERAL LEDGER ACCOUNTS

205 Accounts Payable, $17,940 Cr.
501 Purchases
502 Freight In
503 Purchases Returns and Allowances

DATE		TRANSACTIONS
July	1	Purchased lawn mowers for $9,400 plus a freight charge of $260 from Bronze Corporation, Invoice 1077, dated June 26, net due and payable in 60 days.
	5	Purchased outdoor chairs and tables for $8,740 plus a freight charge of $276 from Bailey Garden Furniture Company, Invoice 936, dated July 2, net due and payable in 45 days.
	9	Purchased grass seed for $1,900 from Parks and Gardens Lawn Products, Invoice 4681, dated July 5; the terms are 30 days net.
	16	Received Credit Memorandum 110 for $400 from Bailey Garden Furniture Company; the amount is an allowance for scratches on some of the chairs and tables originally purchased on Invoice 936, dated July 2.
	19	Purchased fertilizer for $2,400 plus a freight charge of $128 from Parks and Garden Lawn Products, Invoice 5139, dated July 15; the terms are 30 days net.
	28	Received Credit Memorandum 322 for $600 from Bush Rubber Company for damaged hoses that were returned; the goods were purchased on Invoice 5817, dated June 17.
	31	Purchased lawn sprinkler systems for $11,400 plus a freight charge of $320 from Woods Industrial Products, Invoice 5889, dated July 26; the terms are 2/10, n/30.

INSTRUCTIONS

Part II

1. Set up an accounts payable subsidiary ledger for The Garden Center. Open an account for each of the creditors listed below and enter the balances as of July 1.
2. Post the individual entries from the purchases journal and the general journal prepared in Part I.
3. Prepare a schedule of accounts payable for July 31, 20--.
4. Check the total of the schedule of accounts payable against the balance of the **Accounts Payable** account in the general ledger. The two amounts should be equal.

Creditors

Name	Terms	Balance
Bailey Garden Furniture Company	n/45	$5,560
Bronze Corporation	n/60	9,060
Bush Rubber Company	1/15, n/60	
Parks and Garden Lawn Products	n/30	3,320
Woods Industrial Products	2/10, n/30	

Analyze: What total freight charges were posted to the general ledger for the month of July?

Problem 8-4A ►
Objectives 1, 2, 3, 4, 5, 6

Journalizing credit purchases and purchases returns and allowances, posting to the general ledger, posting to the accounts payable ledger, and preparing a schedule of accounts payable.

Essential Office Products Center is a retail business that sells office equipment, furniture, and supplies. Its credit purchases and purchases returns and allowances for September are shown on page 279. The general ledger accounts and the creditors' accounts in the accounts payable subsidiary ledger used to record these transactions are also provided. All balances shown are for the beginning of September.

INSTRUCTIONS

1. Open the general ledger accounts and enter the balance of **Accounts Payable** for September 1, 20--.
2. Open the creditors' accounts in the accounts payable ledger and enter the balances for September 1.
3. Record the transactions in a three-column purchases journal and in a general journal. Use 5 as the page number for the purchases journal and 14 as the page number for the general journal.
4. Post to the accounts payable ledger daily.
5. Post the entries from the general journal to the proper general ledger accounts at the end of the month.
6. Total and rule the purchases journal as of September 30.
7. Post the column totals from the purchases journal to the proper general ledger accounts.
8. Prepare a schedule of accounts payable and compare the balance of the **Accounts Payable** control account with the schedule of accounts payable.

GENERAL LEDGER ACCOUNTS

205 Accounts Payable, $14,128 Cr.
501 Purchases
502 Freight In
503 Purchases Returns and Allowances

Creditors

Name	Terms	Balance
American Office Machines, Inc.	n/60	$5,480
Badge Paper Company	1/10, n/30	1,060
Brint Corporation	n/30	
City Office Furniture Company	n/30	4,788
Depot Furniture, Inc.	2/10, n/30	2,800

DATE		TRANSACTIONS
Sept.	3	Purchased desks for $3,960 plus a freight charge of $106 from City Office Furniture Company, Invoice 1342, dated August 29; the terms are 30 days net.
	7	Purchased computers for $5,650 from American Office Machines, Inc., Invoice 1792, dated September 2, net due and payable in 60 days.
	10	Received Credit Memorandum 561 for $300 from City Office Furniture Company; the amount is an allowance for damaged but usable desks purchased on Invoice 1342, dated August 29.
	16	Purchased file cabinets for $1,278 plus a freight charge of $62 from Brint Corporation, Invoice 6680, dated September 11; the terms are 30 days net.
	20	Purchased electronic desk calculators for $500 from American Office Machines, Inc., Invoice 6556, dated September 15, net due and payable in 60 days.
	23	Purchased bond paper and copy machine paper for $3,750 plus a freight charge of $50 from Badge Paper Company, Invoice 9864, dated September 18; the terms are 1/10, n/30.
	28	Received Credit Memorandum 296 for $440 from American Office Machines, Inc., for defective calculators that were returned; the calculators were originally purchased on Invoice 6556, dated September 15.
	30	Purchased office chairs for $1,920 plus a freight charge of $80 from Depot Furniture, Inc., Invoice 966, dated September 25, the terms are 2/10, n/30.

Analyze: What total amount was recorded for purchases returns and allowances in the month of September? What percentage of total purchases does this represent?

PROBLEM SET B

Problem 8-1B ►
Objectives 1, 2, 3

Journalizing credit purchases and purchases returns and allowances and posting to the general ledger.

Colorado Ski Shop is a retail store that sells ski equipment and clothing. The firm's credit purchases and purchases returns and allowances during May 20-- follow, along with the general ledger accounts used to record these transactions. The balance shown in **Accounts Payable** is for the beginning of May.

INSTRUCTIONS

1. Open the general ledger accounts and enter the balance of **Accounts Payable** for May 1, 20--.
2. Record the transactions in a three-column purchases journal and in a general journal. Use 14 as the page number for the purchases journal and 37 as the page number for the general journal.
3. Post the entries from the general journal to the proper general ledger accounts.
4. Total and rule the purchases journal as of May 30.
5. Post the column total from the purchases journal to the proper general ledger accounts.
6. Compute the net purchases of the firm for the month of May.

GENERAL LEDGER ACCOUNTS

205 Accounts Payable, $10,804 Cr.
501 Purchases
502 Freight In
503 Purchases Returns and Allowances

DATE	TRANSACTIONS
May 1	Purchased ski boots for $3,300 plus a freight charge of $110 from Denver Shop for Skiers, Invoice 7265, dated April 28; the terms are 45 days net.
8	Purchased skis for $5,550 from Andover Industries, Invoice 1649, dated May 2; the terms are net payable in 30 days.
9	Received Credit Memorandum 551 for $800 from Denver Shop for Skiers for damaged ski boots that were returned; the boots were originally purchased on Invoice 7265, dated April 28.
12	Purchased ski jackets for $2,500 from Chilly Winter Fashions, Inc., Invoice 869, dated May 11, net due and payable in 60 days.
16	Purchased ski poles for $1,580 from Andover Industries, Invoice 1766, dated May 15; the terms are n/30.
22	Purchased ski pants for $1,120 from Chilton Clothing Company, Invoice 1940, dated May 16; the terms are 1/10, n/60.
	Continued

DATE	(8-1B cont.) TRANSACTIONS
May 28	Received Credit Memorandum 83 for $210 from Andover Industries for defective ski poles that were returned; the items were originally purchased on Invoice 1766, dated May 15.
31	Purchased sweaters for $1,650 plus a freight charge of $50 from Knit Ski Goods, Invoice 5483, dated May 27; the terms are 2/10, n/30.

(**Note:** Save your working papers for use in Problem 8-2B.)

Analyze: What total accounts payable were posted from the purchases journal to the general ledger for the month?

◄ Problem 8-2B
Objectives 4, 6

Posting to the accounts payable ledger and preparing a schedule of accounts payable.

This problem is a continuation of Problem 8-1B.

INSTRUCTIONS

1. Set up an accounts payable subsidiary ledger for Colorado Ski Shop. Open an account for each of the creditors listed and enter the balances as of May 1, 20--.
2. Post the individual entries from the purchases journal and the general journal prepared in Problem 8-1B.
3. Prepare a schedule of accounts payable for May 31.
4. Check the total of the schedule of accounts payable against the balance of the **Accounts Payable** account in the general ledger. The two amounts should be equal.

Creditors

Name	Terms	Balance
Andover Industries	n/30	$ 850
Chilly Winter Fashions, Inc.	n/60	4,360
Chilton Clothing Company	1/10, n/60	2,500
Denver Shop for Skiers	n/45	3,094
Knit Ski Goods	2/10, n/30	

Analyze: What amount did Colorado Ski Shop owe to its supplier, Denver Shop for Skiers, on May 31?

◄ Problem 8-3B
Objectives 1, 2, 3, 4, 5, 6

Journalizing credit purchases and purchases returns and allowances, computing the net delivered cost of goods, posting to the general ledger, posting to the accounts payable ledger, and preparing a schedule of accounts payable.

The Flower and Garden Nursery is a retail store that sells garden equipment, furniture, and supplies. Its credit purchases and purchases returns and allowances for December are shown on page 282. The general ledger accounts used to record these transactions are also provided. The balance shown is for the beginning of December 20--.

INSTRUCTIONS

Part I

1. Open the general ledger accounts and enter the balance of **Accounts Payable** for December 1.
2. Record the transactions in a three-column purchases journal and in a general journal. Use 7 as the page number for the purchases journal and 19 as the page number for the general journal.
3. Post the entries from the general journal to the proper general ledger accounts.
4. Total, prove, and rule the purchases journal as of December 31.
5. Post the column totals from the purchases journal to the proper general ledger accounts.
6. Compute the net delivered cost of the firm's purchases for the month of December.

GENERAL LEDGER ACCOUNTS

205 Accounts Payable, $6,745 Cr.
501 Purchases
502 Freight In
503 Purchases Returns and Allowances

DATE	TRANSACTIONS
Dec. 1	Purchased lawn mowers for $2,890 plus a freight charge of $78 from River Corporation, Invoice 1021, dated November 26, net due and payable in 45 days.
5	Purchased outdoor chairs and tables for $2,850 plus a freight charge of $50 from Garden Furniture Shop, Invoice 363, dated December 2; the terms are 1/15, n/60.
9	Purchased grass seed for $574 from Springtime Lawn Center, Invoice 2711, dated December 4; the terms are 30 days net.
16	Received Credit Memorandum 101 for $200 from Garden Furniture Shop; the amount is an allowance for scratches on some of the chairs and tables originally purchased on Invoice 363, dated December 2.
19	Purchased fertilizer for $800 plus a freight charge of $78 from Springtime Lawn Center, Invoice 3157, dated December 15; the terms are 30 days net.
21	Purchased garden hoses for $380 plus a freight charge of $38 from City Rubber Company, Invoice 1785, dated December 17; the terms are n/60.
28	Received Credit Memorandum 209 for $75 from City Rubber Company for damaged hoses that were returned; the goods were purchased on Invoice 1785, dated December 17.
31	Purchased lawn sprinkler systems for $1,850 plus a freight charge of $40 from Carlton Industries, Invoice 1988, dated December 26; the terms are 2/10, n/30.

INSTRUCTIONS

Part II

1. Set up an accounts payable subsidiary ledger for The Flower and Garden Nursery. Open an account for each of the following creditors and enter the balances as of December 1.
2. Post the individual entries from the purchases journal and the general journal prepared in Part I.
3. Prepare a schedule of accounts payable for December 31.
4. Check the total of the schedule of accounts payable against the balance of the **Accounts Payable** account in the general ledger. The two amounts should be equal.

CREDITORS

Name	Terms	Balance
Carlton Industries	2/10, n/30	$1,075
City Rubber Company	n/60	1,925
Garden Furniture Shop	1/15, n/60	
River Corporation	n/45	2,421
Springtime Lawn Center	n/30	1,324

Analyze: By what amount did **Accounts Payable** increase during the month of December?

◄ **Problem 8-4B**
Objectives 1, 2, 3, 4, 5, 6

Journalizing credit purchases and purchases returns and allowances, posting to the general ledger, posting to the accounts payable ledger, and preparing a schedule of accounts payable.

Rochelle's Cards and Stuff is a retail card, novelty, and business supply store. Its credit purchases and purchases returns and allowances for February 20-- appear on page 284. The general ledger accounts and the creditors' accounts in the accounts payable subsidiary ledger used to record these transactions are also provided. The balance shown is for the beginning of February.

INSTRUCTIONS

1. Open the general ledger accounts and enter the balance of **Accounts Payable** for February.
2. Open the creditors' accounts in the accounts payable ledger and enter the balances for February 1, 20--.
3. Record each transaction in the appropriate journal, purchases or general. Use page 3 in the purchases journal and page 11 in the general journal.
4. Post entries to the accounts payable ledger daily.
5. Post entries in the general journal to the proper general ledger accounts at the end of the month.
6. Total and rule the purchases journal as of February 28.
7. Post the totals to the appropriate general ledger accounts.
8. Calculate the net delivered cost of purchases.
9. Prepare a schedule of accounts payable and compare the balance of the **Accounts Payable** control account with the schedule of accounts payable.

GENERAL LEDGER ACCOUNTS

203 Accounts Payable, $7,600 credit balance
501 Purchases
502 Freight In
503 Purchases Returns and Allowances

Creditors		
Name	Terms	Balance
Cards & Gifts for Holidays	2/10, n/30	$2,000
Forms for Business, Inc.	n/30	4,000
Office Supplies, Packing & Mailing, Inc.	2/10, n/30	1,600
Unique Business Cards	1/10, n/45	

DATE		TRANSACTIONS
Feb.	5	Purchased copy paper from Office Supplies, Packing & Mailing, Inc., for $1,000 plus $50 shipping charges on Invoice 502, dated February 2.
	8	Purchased assorted holiday cards from Cards & Gifts for Holidays on Invoice 8028, $950, dated February 5.
	12	Purchased five boxes of novelty items from Cards & Gifts for Holidays for a total cost of $600, Invoice 9032, dated February 8.
	13	Purchased tray of cards from Unique Business Cards on Invoice 1320 for $550, dated February 9.
	19	Purchased supply of forms from Forms for Business, Inc., for $990 plus shipping charges of $30 on Invoice 1920, dated February 16.
	20	One box of cards purchased on February 8 from Cards & Gifts for Holidays was water damaged. Received Credit Memorandum 1002 for $100.
	21	Toner supplies are purchased from Unique Business Cards for $1,800 plus shipping charges of $100, Invoice 1420, dated February 19.
	27	Received Credit Memorandum 1022 for $120 from Cards & Gifts for Holidays as an allowance for damaged novelty items purchased on February 12.

Analyze: What total amount did Rochelle's Cards and Stuff pay in freight charges during the month of February? What percentage of delivered cost of purchases does this represent?

CHAPTER 8 CHALLENGE PROBLEM

Merchandising: Sales and Purchases

Casual Fashions is a retail clothing store. Sales of merchandise and purchases of goods on account for January 20--, the first month of operations, appear on pages 285–286.

INSTRUCTIONS

1. Record the purchases of goods on account on page 5 of a three-column purchases journal.
2. Record the sales of merchandise on account on page 1 of a sales journal.
3. Post the entries from the purchases journal and the sales journal to the individual accounts in the accounts payable and accounts receivable subsidiary ledgers.
4. Total, prove, and rule the journals as of January 31.
5. Post the column totals from the special journals to the proper general ledger accounts.
6. Prepare a schedule of accounts payable for January 31.
7. Prepare a schedule of accounts receivable for January 31.

		PURCHASES OF GOODS ON ACCOUNT
Jan.	3	Purchased dresses for $2,500 plus a freight charge of $50 from Fashion World, Invoice 101, dated December 26; the terms are net 30 days.
	5	Purchased handbags for $1,740 plus a freight charge of $40 from Modern Handbags, Invoice 322, dated December 28; the terms are 2/10, n/30.
	7	Purchased blouses for $1,950 plus a freight charge of $30 from Trendsetters, Inc., Invoice 655, dated January 3; the terms are 2/10, n/30.
	9	Purchased casual pants for $1,180 from The Trousers Company, Invoice 109, dated January 5; terms are n/30.
	12	Purchased business suits for $2,700 plus a freight charge of $50 from Suits for Executives, Invoice 104, dated January 9; the terms are 2/10, n/30.
	18	Purchased shoes for $1,560 plus freight of $40 from Larry's Shoes, Invoice 111, dated January 14; the terms are n/60.
	25	Purchased hosiery for $700 from Socks Warehouse, Invoice 1211, dated January 20; the terms are 2/10, n/30.
	29	Purchased scarves and gloves for $800 from The Trousers Company, Invoice 809, dated January 26; the terms are n/30.
	31	Purchased party dresses for $2,500 plus a freight charge of $50 from Carolyn's Wholesale Shop, Invoice 1033, dated January 27; the terms are 2/10, n/30.

	SALES OF MERCHANDISE ON ACCOUNT
Jan. 4	Sold two dresses to Selena Ramirez; issued Sales Slip 101 for $400 plus $24 sales tax.
5	Sold a handbag to Ruby Darbandi; issued Sales Slip 102 for $200 plus $12 sales tax.
6	Sold four blouses to Gloria Hughes; issued Sales Slip 103 for $200 plus $12 sales tax.
10	Sold casual pants and a blouse to Brenda Davis; issued Sales Slip 104 for $500 plus $30 sales tax.
14	Sold a business suit to Linda Washington; issued Sales Slip 105 for $400 plus $24 sales tax.
17	Sold hosiery, shoes, and gloves to Lisa Mariani; issued Sales Slip 106 for $600 plus $36 sales tax.
21	Sold dresses and scarves to Rosa Maria Vasquez; issued Sales Slip 107 for $1,000 plus $60 sales tax.
24	Sold a business suit to Emily Adams; issued Sales Slip 108 for $200 plus $12 sales tax.
25	Sold shoes to Natasha Wells; issued Sales Slip 109 for $150 plus $9 sales tax.
29	Sold a casual pants set to Melissa Anderson; issued Sales Slip 110 for $200 plus $12 sales tax.
31	Sold a dress and handbag to Denise Cooper; issued Sales Slip 111 for $300 plus $18 sales tax.

Analyze: What is the net delivered cost of purchases for the month of January?

CHAPTER 8 CRITICAL THINKING PROBLEM

Internal Control

Kim Coda, owner of The Linen Shop, was preparing checks for payment of the current month's purchase invoices when she realized that there were two invoices from Romantic Towel Company, each for the purchase of 100 red, heart-imprinted bath towels. Coda thinks that Romantic Towel Company must have billed The Linen Shop twice for the same shipment because she knows the shop would not have needed two orders for 100 red bath towels within a month.

1. How can Coda determine whether Romantic Towel Company billed The Linen Shop in error or whether The Linen Shop placed two identical orders for red, heart-imprinted bath towels?
2. If two orders were placed, how can Coda prevent duplicate purchases from happening in the future?

Business Connections

MANAGERIAL FOCUS **Cash Management** ◄ Connection 1

1. Why should management be concerned about the timely payment of invoices?
2. Why is it important for a firm to maintain a satisfactory credit rating?
3. Suppose you are the new controller of a small but growing company and you find that the firm has a policy of paying cash for all purchases of goods even though it could obtain credit. The president of the company does not like the idea of having debts, but the vice president thinks this is a poor business policy that will hurt the firm in the future. The president has asked your opinion. Would you agree with the president or the vice president? Why?
4. Why should management be concerned about the internal control of purchases?
5. How can good internal control of purchases protect a firm from fraud and errors and from excessive investment in merchandise?
6. In what ways would excessive investment in merchandise harm a business?

Ethical DILEMMA **Favor for a Friend** Assume that you are a sales clerk in a retail clothing store. One of your friends regularly shops at this store and has asked you to ring some items at a price substantially below their marked price. Would you do this for your friend? ◄ Connection 2

Street WISE: Questions from the Real World **Accounts Payable and Cost of Merchandise** Refer to the *1999 Annual Report* for The Home Depot, Inc. in Appendix B. ◄ Connection 3

1. Locate the consolidated balance sheets. What is the reported amount of accounts payable at January 30, 2000? Has this balance increased or decreased since the prior fiscal year-end? By what amount?
2. Review Management's Discussion and Analysis of Results of Operations and Financial Condition for The Home Depot, Inc. What factors contributed to the lower cost of merchandise for the operating period?

FINANCIAL STATEMENT ANALYSIS **Income Statement** The following financial statement excerpt is taken from the *2000 Annual Report* for Lands' End, Inc. ◄ Connection 4

LANDS' END DIRECT MERCHANTS

Consolidated Statements of Operations

(In thousands, except per share data)	*For the period ended January 28, 2000*	*January 29, 1999*
Net Sales	*$ 1,319,823*	*$ 1,371,375*
Cost of Sales	*727,271*	*754,661*
Gross Profit	*$ 592,552*	*$ 616,714*

1. The Cost of Sales amount on Lands' End, Inc. consolidated statements of operations represents the net cost of the goods that were sold for the period. For fiscal 2000, what percentage of net sales was the cost of sales? For fiscal 1999?
2. What factors might affect a merchandising company's cost of sales from one period to another?

Analyze Online: On the Lands' End, Inc. Web site **(www.landsend.com),** locate the investor information section.

3. Review the consolidated statements of operations found in the current year's annual report.
4. What amount is reported for cost of sales?
5. What amount is reported for net sales?

Connection 5 ► *Extending the Thought* **Timing** A purchase order expresses an authorized intent to buy a particular item at a specific price from a supplier. Some companies record a debit to **Purchases** and a credit to **Accounts Payable** at the time the purchase order is issued. Other companies wait until the invoice for the merchandise arrives and then record the purchase. Which method do you think is better? Why?

Connection 6 ► **Business Communication** **Memo** You own a retail gourmet cooking supply store. As the owner of the business, you have noticed that your manager, bookkeeper, and sales clerk all place orders with suppliers, sometimes resulting in duplicate orders and confusion in processing invoices. You need to strengthen your internal controls in regard to the purchase of goods for resale. Prepare a memo to your staff that outlines proper procedures for placement of merchandise orders, receipt of goods, and payment of invoices.

Connection 7 ► **TeamWork** **System Design** Form teams of three to four individuals. Create an idea for a merchandising business needed in your community. Then, design an automated purchasing system that will support strong internal controls over order placement and invoice payment for this business. The system should use current technologies that will free managers or store clerks from the necessity of calling suppliers when merchandise is needed. In a presentation to the class, describe the automated system that you have designed. Use a visual flowchart to demonstrate the flow of purchasing tasks including who will complete each task, how merchandise orders should be placed, what merchandise is needed, when orders are placed, and how invoices are processed.

inter NET CONNECTION **AIPB** The Web site address of the American Institute of Professional Bookkeepers (AIPB) is **www.aipb.com.** List two of the goals of the Certified Bookkeeper Program. What are the eligibility requirements to become a certified bookkeeper? List some of the benefits of becoming a certified bookkeeper.

◄ **Connection 8**

Answers to Self Reviews

Answers to Section 1 Self Review

1. Merchandise purchased on credit for resale.
2. It saves time and effort, and it strengthens the audit trail.
3. Locating suitable suppliers, obtaining price quotations and credit terms, and placing orders.
4. **c.** Purchase requisition
5. **b.** Purchase order
6. The business will receive a 2 percent discount if the invoice is paid within 10 days. If the invoice is not paid within 10 days, the total amount is due within 30 days.

Answers to Section 2 Self Review

1. $52,640
2. Purchases 1,120.00
   Freight In 84.00
   Accounts Payable 1,204.00

Purchases	1,120.00	
Freight In	84.00	
Accounts Payable		1,204.00

3. It lists all of the creditors to whom money is owed.
4. **b.** income statement.
5. **d.** $3,200 credit
6. A payment was made and recorded in the general ledger account, but was not recorded in the creditor's subsidiary ledger account.

Answers to Comprehensive Self Review

1. The receiving report shows the quantity of goods received and the condition of the goods. The invoice shows quantities and prices; it is the document from which checks are prepared in payment of purchases.
2. The purchase requisition is used by a sales department to notify the purchasing department of the items wanted. The purchase order is prepared by the purchasing department to order the necessary goods at an appropriate price from the selected supplier.
3. To accumulate freight charges paid for purchases.
4. A price reduction offered to encourage quick payment of invoices by customers.
5. A contra cost of goods sold account.

CHAPTER 9

Learning Objectives

1. Record cash receipts in a cash receipts journal.
2. Account for cash short or over.
3. Post from the cash receipts journal to subsidiary and general ledgers.
4. Record cash payments in a cash payments journal.
5. Post from the cash payments journal to subsidiary and general ledgers.
6. Demonstrate a knowledge of procedures for a petty cash fund.
7. Demonstrate a knowledge of internal control routines for cash.
8. Write a check, endorse checks, prepare a bank deposit slip, and maintain a checkbook balance.
9. Reconcile the monthly bank statement.
10. Record any adjusting entries required from the bank reconciliation.
11. Define the accounting terms new to this chapter.

Cash Receipts, Cash Payments, and Banking Procedures

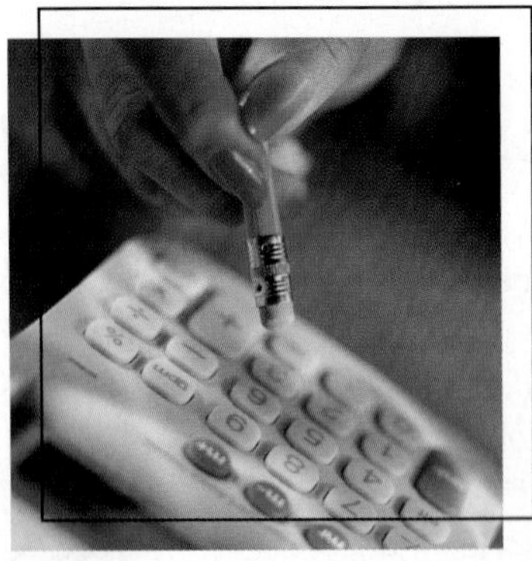

H&R BLOCK

www.hrblock.com

In 1955 the founders of H&R Block made a decision to shift the focus of services away from bookkeeping to tax return preparation. A small ad purchased in *The Kansas City Star* newspaper pictured a man behind an eight ball and a simple headline, "Taxes, $5." The office was flooded with new customers and the strategy proved successful—business tripled over the previous year's volume.

Today, in more than 9,000 U.S. tax offices, the company handles approximately one in every seven regular returns and nearly one-half of all electronic returns filed with the Internal Revenue Service. Receipts for services, products, and royalties totaled $2.5 billion in 2000. Payments for expenses, which included items such as employee compensation, office rent, supplies, and postage, totaled $2.1 billion.

Thinking Critically

What types of daily receipts and payments do you think occur in a single H&R Block office location?

For more information on H&R Block, go to: collegeaccounting.glencoe.com.

New Terms

Bank reconciliation statement
Blank endorsement
Bonding
Canceled check
Cash
Cash payments journal
Cash receipts journal
Cash register proof
Cash Short or Over account
Check
Credit memorandum
Debit memorandum
Deposit in transit
Deposit slip
Dishonored (NSF) check
Drawee
Drawer
Endorsement
Full endorsement
Negotiable
Outstanding checks
Payee
Petty cash analysis sheet
Petty cash fund
Petty cash voucher
Postdated check
Promissory note
Restrictive endorsement
Service charge
Statement of account

Section 1

Cash Receipts

Section Objectives

1. **Record cash receipts in a cash receipts journal.**

   WHY IT'S IMPORTANT
   The cash receipts journal is an efficient option for recording incoming cash.

2. **Account for cash short or over.**

   WHY IT'S IMPORTANT
   Discrepancies in cash are a possible indication that cash is mismanaged.

3. **Post from the cash receipts journal to subsidiary and general ledgers.**

   WHY IT'S IMPORTANT
   The subsidiary and general ledgers must hold accurate, up-to-date information about cash transactions.

Terms to Learn

cash
cash receipts journal
cash register proof
Cash Short or Over account
petty cash fund
promissory note
statement of account

Cash is the business asset that is most easily lost, mishandled, or even stolen. A well-managed business has careful procedures for controlling cash and recording cash transactions.

Cash Transactions

In accounting, the term **cash** is used for currency, coins, checks, money orders, and funds on deposit in a bank. Most cash transactions involve checks.

Cash Receipts

The type of cash receipts depends on the nature of the business. Supermarkets receive checks as well as currency and coins. Department stores receive checks in the mail from charge account customers. Cash received by wholesalers is usually in the form of checks.

Cash Payments

For safety and convenience, most businesses make payments by check. Sometimes a limited number of transactions are paid with currency and coins. The **petty cash fund** is used to handle payments involving small amounts of money, such as postage stamps, delivery charges, and minor purchases of office supplies. Some businesses maintain a fund to provide cash for business-related travel and entertainment expenses.

The Cash Receipts Journal

To improve the recordkeeping of cash receipts, many businesses use a special **cash receipts journal**. The cash receipts journal simplifies the recording of transactions and eliminates repetition in posting.

Recording Transactions in the Cash Receipts Journal

1 Objective
Record cash receipts in a cash receipts journal.

The format of the cash receipts journal varies according to the needs of each business. Figure 9-1 on page 293 shows the cash receipts journal for The Trend Center. The Trend Center has two major sources of cash receipts: checks from credit customers who are making payments on account, and currency and coins from cash sales.

The cash receipts journal has separate columns for the accounts frequently used when recording cash receipts. There are columns for

- debits to **Cash,**
- credits to **Accounts Receivable** for payments received on account,
- credits to **Sales** and **Sales Tax Payable** for cash sales.

At the end of the month, the totals of these columns are posted to the general ledger.

CASH RECEIPTS JOURNAL PAGE 1

DATE		DESCRIPTION	POST. REF.	ACCOUNTS RECEIVABLE CREDIT	SALES TAX PAYABLE CREDIT	SALES CREDIT	OTHER ACCOUNTS CREDIT			CASH DEBIT
							ACCOUNT NAME	POST. REF.	AMOUNT	
20--										
Jan.	7	John Allen		428 00						428 00
	8	Cash Sales			212 80	3 040 00				3 252 80
	11	Clyde Davis		267 50						267 50
	12	Investment					S. Harris, Capital		10 000 00	10 000 00
	13	Blake Howard		535 00						535 00
	15	Cash Sales			275 10	3 930 00	Cash Short/Over		9 00	4 196 10
	16	Kim Johnson		107 00						107 00
	17	Cash Refund					Supplies		50 00	50 00
	22	Ed Ramirez		200 00						200 00
	22	Cash Sales			295 40	4 220 00				4 515 40
	29	Cash Sales			49 00	700 00	Cash Short/Over		7 00	756 00
	31	Linda Sanchez		107 00						107 00
	31	Newton Wu		260 00						260 00
	31	Cash Sales			231 70	3 310 00				3 541 70
	31	Collection of					Notes Receivable		400 00	
		note/Jeff Wells					Interest Income		18 00	418 00

▲ **FIGURE 9-1**
Cash Receipts Journal

Notice the Other Accounts Credit section, which is for entries that do not fit into one of the special columns. Entries in the Other Accounts Credit section are individually posted to the general ledger.

Cash Sales and Sales Taxes. The Trend Center uses a cash register to record cash sales and to store currency and coins. As each transaction is entered, the cash register prints a receipt for the customer. It also records the sale and the sales tax on an audit tape locked inside the machine. At the end of the day, when the machine is cleared, the cash register prints the transaction totals on the audit tape. The manager of the store removes the audit tape, and a cash register proof is prepared. The **cash register proof** is a verification that the amount in the cash register agrees with the amount shown on the audit tape. The cash register proof is used to record cash sales and sales tax in the cash receipts journal. The currency and coins are deposited in the firm's bank.

Refer to Figure 9-1, the cash receipts journal for The Trend Center. To keep it simple, it shows weekly, rather than daily, cash sales entries. Look at the January 8 entry. The steps to record the January 8 sales follow.

1. Enter the sales tax collected, $212.80, in the Sales Tax Payable Credit column.
2. Enter the sales, $3,040.00, in the Sales Credit column.
3. Enter the cash received, $3,252.80, in the Cash Debit column.
4. Confirm that total credits equal total debits ($212.80 + $3,040.00 = $3,252.80).

About Accounting

Automated Teller Machines
The banking industry paved the way for the Internet's self-service applications (such as ordering products online) with ATMs.

❷ Objective
Account for cash short or over.

Cash Short or Over. Occasionally errors occur when making change. When errors happen, the cash in the cash register is either more than or less than the cash listed on the audit tape. When cash in the register is more than the audit tape, cash is *over*. When cash in the register is less than the

Important!

Cash Short or Over

Expect errors when employees make change, but investigate large and frequent errors. They may indicate dishonesty or incompetence.

audit tape, cash is *short.* Cash tends to be short more often than over because customers are more likely to notice and complain if they receive too little change.

Record short or over amounts in the **Cash Short or Over account**. If the account has a credit balance, there is an overage, which is treated as revenue. If the account has a debit balance, there is a shortage, which is treated as an expense.

Figure 9-1 shows how cash overages and shortages appear in the cash receipts journal. Look at the January 29 entry. Cash sales were $700. Sales tax collected was $49. The cash drawer was over $7. Overages are recorded as credits. Notice that the account name and the overage are entered in the Other Accounts Credit section.

Now look at the January 15 entry. This time the cash register was short. Shortages are recorded as debits. Debits are not the normal balance of the Other Accounts Credit column, so the debit entry is circled.

Businesses that have frequent entries for cash shortages and overages add a Cash Short or Over column to the cash receipts journal.

Cash Received on Account. The Trend Center makes sales on account and bills customers once a month. It sends a **statement of account** that shows the transactions during the month and the balance owed. Customers are asked to pay within 30 days of receiving the statement. Checks from credit customers are entered in the cash receipts journal, and then the checks are deposited in the bank.

Figure 9-1 shows how cash received on account is recorded. Look at the January 7 entry for John Allen. The check amount is entered in the Accounts Receivable Credit and the Cash Debit columns.

Cash Discounts on Sales. The Trend Center, like most retail businesses, does not offer cash discounts. However, many wholesale businesses offer cash discounts to customers who pay within a certain time period. For example, a wholesaler may offer a 1 percent discount if the customer pays within 10 days. To the wholesaler this is a *sales discount.* Sales discounts are recorded when the payment is received. Sales discounts are recorded in a contra revenue account, **Sales Discounts.** Businesses with many sales discounts add a Sales Discounts Debit column to the cash receipts journal.

Additional Investment by the Owner. Figure 9-1 shows that on January 12, the owner Stacee Harris invested an additional $10,000 in The Trend Center. She intends to use the money to expand the product line. The account name and amount are entered in the Other Accounts Credit section. The debit is entered in the Cash Debit column.

Receipt of a Cash Refund. Sometimes a business receives a cash refund for supplies, equipment, or other assets that are returned to the supplier. Figure 9-1 shows that on January 17, The Trend Center received a $50 cash refund for supplies that were returned to the seller. The account name and amount are entered in the Other Accounts Credit section. The debit is entered in the Cash Debit column.

Collection of a Promissory Note and Interest. A **promissory note** is a written promise to pay a specified amount of money on a certain date. Most notes require that interest is paid at a specified rate. Businesses use promissory notes to extend credit for some sales transactions.

Sometimes promissory notes are used to replace an accounts receivable balance when the account is overdue. For example, on July 31 The Trend Center accepted a six-month promissory note from Jeff Wells, who owed $400 on account (see Figure 9-2). Wells had asked for more time to pay his balance. The Trend Center agreed to grant more time if Wells signed a promissory note with 9 percent annual interest. The note provides more legal protection than an account receivable. The interest is compensation for the delay in receiving payment.

$ *400.00* *July 31, 20--*

Six Months AFTER DATE *I* PROMISE TO PAY

TO THE ORDER OF *The Trend Center*

Four Hundred and no/100 DOLLARS

PAYABLE AT *First Security National Bank*

VALUE RECEIVED *with interest at 9%*

NO. *30* DUE *January 31, 20--* *Jeff Wells*

◄ **FIGURE 9-2**
A Promissory Note

On the date of the transaction, July 31, The Trend Center recorded a general journal entry to increase notes receivable and to decrease accounts receivable for $400. The asset account, **Notes Receivable,** was debited and **Accounts Receivable** was credited.

GENERAL JOURNAL PAGE *16*

	DATE		DESCRIPTION	POST. REF.	DEBIT	CREDIT	
1	20--						1
2	July	31	Notes Receivable	109	400 00		2
3			Accounts Receivable/Jeff Wells	111 / ✓		400 00	3
4			Received a 6-month, 9% note from				4
5			Jeff Wells to replace open account				5

On January 31, the due date of the note, The Trend Center received a check for $418 from Wells. This sum covered the amount of the note ($400) and the interest owed for the six-month period ($18). Figure 9-1 shows the entry in the cash receipts journal. The account names, **Notes Receivable** and **Interest Income,** and the amounts are entered on two lines in the Other Accounts Credit section. The debit is in the Cash Debit column.

Posting from the Cash Receipts Journal

❸ Objective

Post from the cash receipts journal to subsidiary and general ledgers.

During the month the amounts recorded in the Accounts Receivable Credit column are posted to individual accounts in the accounts receivable subsidiary ledger. Similarly, the amounts that appear in the Other Accounts Credit column are posted individually to the general ledger accounts during the month. The "CR1" posting references in the **Cash Short or Over** general ledger account on page 296 show that the entries appear on the first page of the cash receipts journal.

ACCOUNT *Cash Short or Over* ACCOUNT NO. *617*

DATE		DESCRIPTION	POST. REF.	DEBIT	CREDIT	BALANCE DEBIT	BALANCE CREDIT
20--							
Jan.	*15*		*CR1*	*9 00*		*9 00*	
	29		*CR1*		*7 00*	*2 00*	

Posting the Column Totals. At the end of the month, the cash receipts journal is totaled and the equality of debits and credits is proved.

PROOF OF CASH RECEIPTS JOURNAL

	Debits
Cash Debit column	$28,634.50

	Credits
Accounts Receivable Credit column	$ 1,904.50
Sales Tax Payable Credit column	1,064.00
Sales Credit column	15,200.00
Other Accounts Credit column	10,466.00
Total Credits	$28,634.50

Figure 9-3 shows The Trend Center's cash receipts journal after all posting is completed.

FIGURE 9-3 ▼
Posted Cash Receipts Journal

CASH RECEIPTS JOURNAL PAGE *1*

DATE		DESCRIPTION	POST. REF.	ACCOUNTS RECEIVABLE CREDIT	SALES TAX PAYABLE CREDIT	SALES CREDIT	OTHER ACCOUNTS CREDIT: ACCOUNT NAME	POST. REF.	AMOUNT	CASH DEBIT
20--										
Jan.	*7*	*John Allen*	✓	*428 00*						*428 00*
	8	*Cash Sales*			*212 80*	*3 040 00*				*3 252 80*
	11	*Clyde Davis*	✓	*267 50*						*267 50*
	12	*Investment*					*S. Harris, Capital*	*301*	*10 000 00*	*10 000 00*
	13	*Blake Howard*	✓	*535 00*						*535 00*
	15	*Cash Sales*			*275 10*	*3 930 00*	*Cash Short/Over*	*617*	*9 00*	*4 196 10*
	16	*Kim Johnson*	✓	*107 00*						*107 00*
	17	*Cash Refund*					*Supplies*	*129*	*50 00*	*50 00*
	22	*Ed Ramirez*	✓	*200 00*						*200 00*
	22	*Cash Sales*			*295 40*	*4 220 00*				*4 515 40*
	29	*Cash Sales*			*49 00*	*700 00*	*Cash Short/Over*	*617*	*7 00*	*756 00*
	31	*Linda Sanchez*	✓	*107 00*						*107 00*
	31	*Newton Wu*	✓	*260 00*						*260 00*
	31	*Cash Sales*			*231 70*	*3 310 00*				*3 541 70*
	31	*Collection of*					*Notes Receivable*	*109*	*400 00*	
		note/Jeff Wells					*Interest Income*	*491*	*18 00*	*418 00*
	31	*Totals*		*1 904 50*	*1 064 00*	*15 200 00*			*10 466 00*	*28 634 50*
				(111)	*(231)*	*(401)*			*(X)*	*(101)*

When the cash receipts journal has been proved, rule the columns and post the totals to the general ledger. Figure 9-4 on page 297 shows how to post from the cash receipts journal to the general ledger accounts.

FIGURE 9-4 ▼
Posting from the Cash Receipts Journal

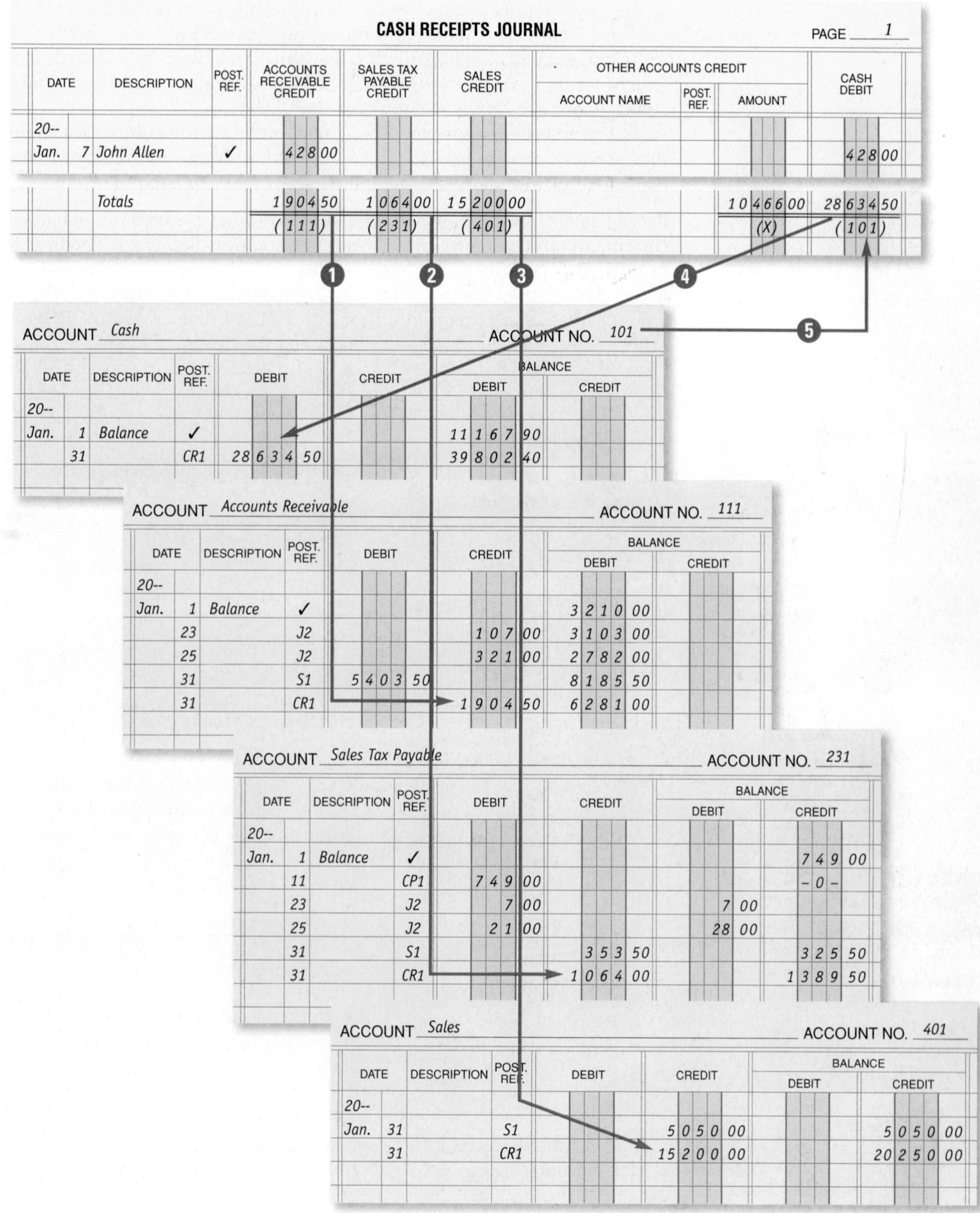

CASH RECEIPTS JOURNAL PAGE 1

DATE		DESCRIPTION	POST. REF.	ACCOUNTS RECEIVABLE CREDIT	SALES TAX PAYABLE CREDIT	SALES CREDIT	OTHER ACCOUNTS CREDIT ACCOUNT NAME	POST. REF.	AMOUNT	CASH DEBIT
20--										
Jan.	7	John Allen	✓	428 00						428 00
		Totals		1 904 50	1 064 00	15 200 00			10 466 00	28 634 50
				(111)	(231)	(401)			(X)	(101)

ACCOUNT Cash ACCOUNT NO. 101

DATE		DESCRIPTION	POST. REF.	DEBIT	CREDIT	BALANCE DEBIT	BALANCE CREDIT
20--							
Jan.	1	Balance	✓			11 167 90	
	31		CR1	28 634 50		39 802 40	

ACCOUNT Accounts Receivable ACCOUNT NO. 111

DATE		DESCRIPTION	POST. REF.	DEBIT	CREDIT	BALANCE DEBIT	BALANCE CREDIT
20--							
Jan.	1	Balance	✓			3 210 00	
	23		J2		107 00	3 103 00	
	25		J2		321 00	2 782 00	
	31		S1	5 403 50		8 185 50	
	31		CR1		1 904 50	6 281 00	

ACCOUNT Sales Tax Payable ACCOUNT NO. 231

DATE		DESCRIPTION	POST. REF.	DEBIT	CREDIT	BALANCE DEBIT	BALANCE CREDIT
20--							
Jan.	1	Balance	✓				749 00
	11		CP1	749 00			-0-
	23		J2	7 00		7 00	
	25		J2	21 00		28 00	
	31		S1		353 50		325 50
	31		CR1		1 064 00		1 389 50

ACCOUNT Sales ACCOUNT NO. 401

DATE		DESCRIPTION	POST. REF.	DEBIT	CREDIT	BALANCE DEBIT	BALANCE CREDIT
20--							
Jan.	31		S1		5 050 00		5 050 00
	31		CR1		15 200 00		20 250 00

To post a column total to a general ledger account, enter "CR1" in the Posting Reference column to show that the entry is from the first page of the cash receipts journal. Enter the column total in the general ledger account Debit or Credit column. Figure 9-4 shows the entries to **Accounts Receivable** (1), **Sales Tax Payable** (2), **Sales** (3), and **Cash** (4). Compute the new balance for each account and enter it in the Balance Debit or Balance Credit column.

Enter the general ledger account numbers under the column totals on the cash receipts journal. The (X) in the Other Accounts Credit Amount column indicates that the individual amounts were posted, not the total.

Posting to the Accounts Receivable Ledger. To keep customer balances current, accountants post entries from the Accounts Receivable Credit column to the customers' accounts in the accounts receivable subsidiary ledger daily. For example, on January 7, $428 was posted to John Allen's account in the subsidiary ledger. The "CR1" in the Posting Reference column indicates that the transaction appears on page 1 of the cash receipts journal. The check mark (✓) in the Posting Reference column in the cash receipts journal (Figure 9-4 on page 297) shows that the amount was posted to John Allen's account in the accounts receivable subsidiary ledger.

NAME *John Allen*

ADDRESS *1313 Broken Arrow Road, Dallas, Texas 75267-6205*

DATE		DESCRIPTION	POST. REF.	DEBIT	CREDIT	BALANCE
20--						
Jan.	1	Balance	✓			428 00
	3	Sales Slip 1101	S1	214 00		642 00
	7		CR1		428 00	214 00
	31	Sales Slip 1110	S1	267 50		481 50

Advantages of the Cash Receipts Journal

The cash receipts journal

- saves time and effort when recording and posting cash receipts,
- allows for the division of work among the accounting staff,
- strengthens the audit trail by recording all cash receipts transactions in one place.

Self Review

Questions

1. What is a promissory note? In what situation would a business accept a promissory note?
2. How and when are the amounts in the Accounts Receivable Credit column posted?
3. What is a cash shortage? A cash overage? How are they recorded?

Exercises

4. Which items are considered cash?
   a. Currency
   b. Funds on deposit in the bank
   c. Money orders
   d. All of the above
5. Collection of a note receivable is recorded in the
   a. accounts receivable journal.
   b. cash receipts journal.
   c. general journal.
   d. promissory note journal.

Analysis

6. You notice that the **Cash Short or Over** account has 15 entries during the month. The ending balance is a $5 shortage for the month. Is this a problem? Why or why not?

(Answers to Section 1 Self Review are on page 348.)

Section 2

Cash Payments

A good system of internal control requires that payments be made by check. In a good internal control system one employee approves payments, another employee prepares the checks, and another employee records the transactions.

The Cash Payments Journal

Unless a business has just a few cash payments each month, the process of recording these transactions in the general journal is time consuming. The **cash payments journal** is a special journal used to record transactions involving the payment of cash.

Recording Transactions in the Cash Payments Journal

Refer to Figure 9-5 on page 300 for The Trend Center's cash payments journal. Notice that there are separate columns for the accounts frequently used when recording cash payments—**Cash, Accounts Payable,** and **Purchases Discounts.** At the end of the month, the totals of these columns are posted to the general ledger.

The Other Accounts Debit section is for entries that do not fit into one of the special columns. Entries in the Other Accounts Debit section are individually posted to the general ledger.

Payments for Expenses. Businesses write checks for a variety of expenses each month. In January The Trend Center issued checks for rent, electricity, telephone service, advertising, and salaries. Refer to the January 3 entry for rent expense in Figure 9-5. Notice that the account name and amount are entered in the Other Accounts Debit section. The credit is in the Cash Credit column.

In 1999 JC Penney Company, Inc. spent $1.05 billion for newspaper, catalog, television, and radio advertising. Payment of these expenses is recorded in the cash payments journal.

Payments on Account. Merchandising businesses usually make numerous payments on account for goods that were purchased on credit. If there is no cash discount, the entry in the cash payments journal is a debit to **Accounts Payable** and a credit to **Cash.** For an example of a payment without a discount, refer to the January 27 entry for Clothes Rack Depot in Figure 9-5.

Purchases Discounts is a contra cost of goods sold account that appears in the Cost of Goods Sold section of the income statement. Purchases discounts are subtracted from purchases to obtain net purchases.

For an example of a payment with a discount, refer to the January 13 entry for Sebrina's Clothing Store in Figure 9-5. The Trend Center takes a

Section Objectives

4 **Record cash payments in a cash payments journal.**

Why It's Important
The cash payments journal is an efficient option for recording payments by check.

5 **Post from the cash payments journal to subsidiary and general ledgers.**

Why It's Important
The subsidiary and general ledgers must hold accurate, up-to-date information about cash transactions.

6 **Demonstrate a knowledge of procedures for a petty cash fund.**

Why It's Important
Businesses use the petty cash fund to pay for small operating expenditures.

7 **Demonstrate a knowledge of internal control routines for cash.**

Why It's Important
Internal controls safeguard business assets.

Terms to Learn

bonding
cash payments journal
petty cash analysis sheet
petty cash voucher

4 Objective

Record cash payments in a cash payments journal.

CASH PAYMENTS JOURNAL

PAGE 1

DATE		CK. NO.	DESCRIPTION	POST. REF.	ACCOUNTS PAYABLE DEBIT	OTHER ACCOUNTS DEBIT: ACCOUNT NAME	POST. REF.	AMOUNT	PURCHASES DISCOUNT CREDIT	CASH CREDIT
20--										
Jan.	3	111	January rent			Rent Expense		1 400 00		1 400 00
	10	112	Store fixtures			Store Equipment		1 200 00		1 200 00
	11	113	Tax remittance			Sales Tax Payable		749 00		749 00
	11	114	Fashion World		1 000 00					1 000 00
	13	115	Sebrina's Clothing Store		3 250 00				65 00	3 185 00
	14	116	Store supplies			Supplies		750 00		750 00
	15	117	Withdrawal			Stacee Harris, Drawing		2 400 00		2 400 00
	17	118	Electric bill			Utilities Expense		300 00		300 00
	17	119	The Style Shop		4 300 00					4 300 00
	21	120	Telephone bill			Telephone Expense		250 00		250 00
	25	121	Newspaper ad			Advertising Expense		420 00		420 00
	27	122	Clothes Rack Depot		1 200 00					1 200 00
	30	123	Sebrina's Clothing Store		400 00					400 00
	31	124	Fashion World		2 560 00				51 20	2 508 80
	31	125	January payroll			Salaries Expense		4 200 00		4 200 00
	31	126	Purchase of goods			Purchases		2 400 00		2 400 00
	31	127	Freight charge			Freight In		150 00		150 00
	31	128	Cash refund			Sales Returns & Allow.		80 00		
						Sales Tax Payable		5 60		85 60
	31	129	Note paid to Dallas			Notes Payable		3 000 00		
			Equipment Company			Interest Expense		150 00		3 150 00
	31	130	Establish petty cash fund			Petty Cash Fund		200 00		200 00

▲ **FIGURE 9-5**
Cash Payments Journal

2 percent discount for paying within the discount period ($3,250 × 0.02 = $65). When there is a cash discount, three elements must be recorded.

- Debit **Accounts Payable** for the invoice amount, $3,250.
- Credit **Purchases Discounts** for the amount of the discount, $65.
- Credit **Cash** for the amount of cash paid, $3,185.

Discount Terms

The terms 2/10, n/30 mean that if payment is made within 10 days, the customer can take a 2 percent discount. Otherwise, payment in full is due in 30 days.

Kroger Corporation reported accounts payable of $2.87 billion at January 29, 2000.

Cash Purchases of Equipment and Supplies. Businesses use cash to purchase equipment, supplies, and other assets. These transactions are recorded in the cash payments journal. In January The Trend Center issued checks for store fixtures and store supplies. Refer to the entries on January 10 and 14 in Figure 9-5. Notice that the account names and amounts appear in the Other Accounts Debit section. The credits are recorded in the Cash Credit column.

Payment of Taxes. Retail businesses collect sales tax from their customers. Periodically the sales tax is remitted to the taxing authority. Refer to the entry on January 11 in Figure 9-5. The Trend Center issued a check for $749 to pay the December sales tax. Notice that the account name and amount appear in the Other Accounts Debit section. The credit is in the Cash Credit column.

Cash Purchases of Merchandise. Most merchandising businesses buy their goods on credit. Occasionally purchases are made for cash. These purchases are recorded in the cash payments journal. Refer to the January 31 entry for the purchase of goods in Figure 9-5.

Payment of Freight Charges. Freight charges on purchases of goods are handled in two ways. In some cases, the seller pays the freight charge and then includes it on the invoice. This method was covered in Chapter 8. The other method is for the buyer to pay the transportation company when the goods arrive. The buyer issues a check for the freight charge and records it in the cash payments journal. Refer to the entry on January 31 in Figure 9-5. The account name and amount appear in the Other Accounts Debit section. The credit is in the Cash Credit column.

Currency

If an American business buys a product from a French company and promises to pay in 90 days, does the business pay in euros or dollars? The accountant reads the terms of the invoice before making payment. If the invoice is in euros, the accountant uses the exchange rate to calculate the amount of the payment.

Payment of a Cash Refund. When a customer purchases goods for cash and later returns them or receives an allowance, the customer is usually given a cash refund. Refer to the January 31 entry in Figure 9-5. The Trend Center issued a check for $85.60 to a customer who returned a defective item. When there is a cash refund, three elements are recorded.

- Debit **Sales Returns and Allowances** for the amount of the purchase, $80.00.
- Debit **Sales Tax Payable** for the sales tax, $5.60.
- Credit **Cash** for the amount of cash paid, $85.60.

Notice that the debits in the Other Accounts Debit section appear on two lines because two general ledger accounts are debited.

Payment of a Promissory Note and Interest. A promissory note can be issued to settle an overdue account or to obtain goods, equipment, or other property. For example, on August 2 The Trend Center issued a six-month promissory note for $3,000 to purchase store fixtures from Dallas Equipment Company. The note had an interest rate of 10 percent. The Trend Center recorded this transaction in the general journal by debiting **Store Equipment** and crediting **Notes Payable,** a liability account.

GENERAL JOURNAL PAGE 16

	DATE		DESCRIPTION	POST. REF.	DEBIT	CREDIT	
1	20--						1
2	Aug.	2	Store Equipment	131	3 000 00		2
3			Notes Payable	201		3 000 00	3
4			Issued a 6-month, 10% note to Dallas				4
5			Equipment Company for purchase of				5
6			new store fixtures				6
7							7

On January 31 The Trend Center issued a check for $3,150 in payment of the note, $3,000, and the interest, $150. This transaction was recorded in the cash payments journal in Figure 9-5.

- Debit **Notes Payable,** $3,000.
- Debit **Interest Expense,** $150.
- Credit **Cash,** $3,150.

Notice that the debits in the Other Accounts Debit section appear on two lines.

5 Objective

Post from the cash payments journal to subsidiary and general ledgers.

Posting from the Cash Payments Journal

During the month the amounts recorded in the Accounts Payable Debit column are posted to individual accounts in the accounts payable subsidiary ledger. The amounts in the Other Accounts Debit column are also posted individually to the general ledger accounts during the month. For example, the January 3 entry in the cash payments journal was posted to the **Rent Expense** account. The "CP1" indicates that the entry is recorded on page 1 of the cash payments journal.

ACCOUNT *Rent Expense* ACCOUNT NO. *634*

DATE		DESCRIPTION	POST. REF.	DEBIT	CREDIT	BALANCE DEBIT	BALANCE CREDIT
20--							
Jan.	*3*		*CP1*	*1 400 00*		*1 400 00*	

Posting the Column Totals. At the end of the month, the cash payments journal is totaled and proved. The total debits must equal total credits.

PROOF OF CASH PAYMENTS JOURNAL

	Debits
Accounts Payable Debit column	$12,710.00
Other Accounts Debit column	17,654.60
Total Debits	$30,364.60

	Credits
Purchases Discount Credit column	$ 116.20
Cash Credit column	30,248.40
Total Credits	$30,364.60

Figure 9-6 on page 303 shows the January cash payments journal after posting for The Trend Center. Notice that the account numbers appear in the Posting Reference column of the Other Accounts Debit section to show that the amounts were posted.

When the cash payments journal has been proved, rule the columns and post the totals to the general ledger. Figure 9-7 on page 304 shows how to post from the cash payments journal to the general ledger accounts.

To post a column total to a general ledger account, enter "CP1" in the Posting Reference column to show that the entry is from page 1 of the cash payments journal.

Enter the column total in the general ledger account Debit or Credit column. Figure 9-7 shows the entries to **Accounts Payable** (1), **Purchases Discounts** (2), and **Cash** (3). Compute the new balance and enter it in the Balance Debit or Balance Credit column.

Enter the general ledger account numbers under the column totals on the cash payments journal. The (X) in the Other Accounts Debit column indicates that the individual accounts were posted, not the total.

Posting to the Accounts Payable Ledger. To keep balances current, accountants post entries from the Accounts Payable Debit column of the cash payments journal to the vendor accounts in the accounts payable subsidiary ledger daily. For example, on January 13, $3,250 was posted to Sebrina's Clothing Store account in the subsidiary ledger. The "CP1" in

anything with payments (cash going out)

CASH PAYMENTS JOURNAL PAGE 1

DATE		CK. NO.	DESCRIPTION	POST. REF.	ACCOUNTS PAYABLE DEBIT	OTHER ACCOUNTS DEBIT: ACCOUNT NAME	POST. REF.	AMOUNT	PURCHASES DISCOUNT CREDIT	CASH CREDIT
20--										
Jan.	3	111	January rent			Rent Expense	634	1 400 00		1 400 00
	10	112	Store fixtures			Store Equipment	131	1 200 00		1 200 00
	11	113	Tax remittance			Sales Tax Payable	231	749 00		749 00
	11	114	Fashion World	✓	1 000 00					1 000 00
	13	115	Sebrina's Clothing Store	✓	3 250 00				65 00	3 185 00
	14	116	Store supplies			Supplies	129	750 00		750 00
	15	117	Withdrawal			Stacee Harris, Drawing	302	2 400 00		2 400 00
	17	118	Electric bill			Utilities Expense	643	300 00		300 00
	17	119	The Style Shop	✓	4 300 00					4 300 00
	21	120	Telephone bill			Telephone Expense	649	250 00		250 00
	25	121	Newspaper ad			Advertising Expense	614	420 00		420 00
	27	122	Clothes Rack Depot	✓	1 200 00					1 200 00
	30	123	Sebrina's Clothing Store	✓	400 00					400 00
	31	124	Fashion World	✓	2 560 00				51 20	2 508 80
	31	125	January payroll			Salaries Expense	637	4 200 00		4 200 00
	31	126	Purchase of goods			Purchases	501	2 400 00		2 400 00
	31	127	Freight charge			Freight In	502	150 00		150 00
	31	128	Cash refund			Sales Returns & Allow.	451	80 00		
						Sales Tax Payable	231	5 60		85 60
	31	129	Note paid to Dallas			Notes Payable	201	3 000 00		
			Equipment Company			Interest Expense	691	150 00		3 150 00
	31	130	Establish petty cash fund			Petty Cash Fund	105	200 00		200 00
	31		Totals		12 710 00			17 654 60	116 20	30 248 40
					(205)			(X)	(504)	(101)

▲ **FIGURE 9-6**
Posted Cash Payments Journal

the Posting Reference column indicates that the entry is recorded on page 1 of the cash payments journal. The check mark (✓) in the Posting Reference column of the cash payments journal (Figure 9-7 on page 304) shows that the amount was posted to the supplier's account in the accounts payable subsidiary ledger.

NAME *Sebrina's Clothing Store* TERMS *2/10, n/30*
ADDRESS *5671 Preston Road, Dallas, Texas 75267-6205*

DATE		DESCRIPTION	POST. REF.	DEBIT	CREDIT	BALANCE
20--						
Jan.	1	Balance	✓			1 100 00
	3	Invoice 8434, 12/29/--	P1		3 250 00	4 350 00
	13		CP1	3 250 00		1 100 00
	30		CP1	400 00		700 00

Advantages of the Cash Payments Journal

The cash payments journal

- saves time and effort when recording and posting cash payments,
- allows for a division of labor among the accounting staff,
- improves the audit trail because all cash payments are recorded in one place and listed by check number.

FIGURE 9-7 ▼
Posting from the Cash Payments Journal

CASH PAYMENTS JOURNAL PAGE 1

DATE		CK. NO.	DESCRIPTION	POST. REF.	ACCOUNTS PAYABLE DEBIT	OTHER ACCOUNTS DEBIT			PURCHASES DISCOUNT CREDIT	CASH CREDIT
						ACCOUNT NAME	POST. REF.	AMOUNT		
20--										
Jan.	3	111	January rent			Rent Expense	634	1 400 00		1 400 00
	10	112	Store fixtures			Store Equipment	131	1 200 00		1 200 00
	11	113	Tax remittance			Sales Tax Payable	231	749 00		749 00
	11	114	Fashion World	✓	1 000 00					1 000 00
	13	115	Sebrina's Clothing Store	✓	3 250 00				65 00	3 185 00
	31		Totals		12 710 00			17 654 60	116 20	30 248 40
					(205)			(X)	(504)	(101)

ACCOUNT *Cash* ACCOUNT NO. *101*

DATE		DESCRIPTION	POST. REF.	DEBIT	CREDIT	BALANCE DEBIT	BALANCE CREDIT
20--							
Jan.	1	Balance	✓			11 167 90	
	31		CR1	28 634 50		39 802 40	
	31		CP1		30 248 40	9 554 00	

ACCOUNT *Accounts Payable* ACCOUNT NO. *205*

DATE		DESCRIPTION	POST. REF.	DEBIT	CREDIT	BALANCE DEBIT	BALANCE CREDIT
20--							
Jan.	1	Balance	✓				5 400 00
	18		J1	500 00			4 900 00
	31		P1		18 750 00		23 650 00
	31		CP1	12 710 00			10 940 00

ACCOUNT *Purchases Discounts* ACCOUNT NO. *504*

DATE		DESCRIPTION	POST. REF.	DEBIT	CREDIT	BALANCE DEBIT	BALANCE CREDIT
20--							
Jan.	31		CP1		116 20		116 20

6 Objective

Demonstrate a knowledge of procedures for a petty cash fund.

The Petty Cash Fund

In a well-managed business, most bills are paid by check. However, there are times when small expenditures are made with currency and coins. Most businesses use a petty cash fund to pay for small expenditures. Suppose that in the next two hours the office manager needs a $3 folder for a customer. It is not practical to obtain an approval and write a check for $3 in the time available. Instead, the office manager takes $3 from the petty cash fund to purchase the folder.

Establishing the Fund

The amount of the petty cash fund depends on the needs of the business. Usually the office manager, cashier, or assistant is in charge of the petty cash fund. The Trend Center's cashier is responsible for petty cash. To set up the petty cash fund, The Trend Center wrote a $200 check to the cashier. She cashed the check and put the currency in a locked cash box.

The establishment of the petty cash fund should be recorded in the cash payments journal. Debit **Petty Cash Fund** in the Other Accounts Debit section of the journal, and enter the credit in the Cash Credit column.

Important!

Petty Cash
Only one person controls the petty cash fund. That person keeps receipts for all expenditures.

Making Payments from the Fund

Petty cash fund payments are limited to small amounts. A **petty cash voucher** is used to record the payments made from the petty cash fund. The petty cash voucher shows the voucher number, amount, purpose of the expenditure, and account to debit. The person receiving the funds signs the voucher, and the person who controls the petty cash fund initials the voucher. Figure 9-8 shows a petty cash voucher for $17.50 for office supplies.

◄ **FIGURE 9-8**
Petty Cash Voucher

PETTY CASH VOUCHER 1
NOTE: This form must be computer processed or filled out in black ink.

DESCRIPTION OF EXPENDITURE	ACCOUNTS TO BE CHARGED	AMOUNT	
Office supplies	Supplies 129	17	50
	Total	17	50

RECEIVED THE SUM OF Seventeen -- DOLLARS AND 50/100 CENTS
SIGNED *A.C. Albot* DATE *2/3/--* APPROVED BY *D.W.* DATE *2/3/--*
Delta Office Supply Co.

The Petty Cash Analysis Sheet

Most businesses use a **petty cash analysis sheet** to record transactions involving petty cash. The Receipts column shows cash put in the fund, and the Payments column shows the cash paid out. There are special columns for accounts that are used frequently, such as **Supplies, Freight In,** and **Miscellaneous Expense.** There is an Other Accounts Debit column for entries that do not fit in a special column. Figure 9-9 on page 306 shows the petty cash analysis sheet for The Trend Center for February.

Replenishing the Fund. The total vouchers plus the cash on hand should always equal the amount of the fund—$200 for The Trend Center. Replenish the petty cash fund at the end of each month or sooner if the fund is low. Refer to Figures 9-9 and 9-10 on page 306 as you learn how to replenish the petty cash fund.

1. Total the columns on the petty cash analysis sheet.
2. Prove the petty cash fund by adding cash on hand and total payments. This should equal the petty fund balance ($33 + $167 = $200).
3. Write a check to restore the petty cash fund to its original balance.
4. Record the check in the cash payments journal. Refer to the petty cash analysis sheet for the accounts and amounts to debit. Notice that the debits appear on four lines of the Other Accounts Debit section. The credit appears in the Cash Credit column.

FIGURE 9-9 ▼
Petty Cash Analysis Sheet

PETTY CASH ANALYSIS PAGE 1

DATE		VOU. NO.	DESCRIPTION	RECEIPTS	PAYMENTS	SUPPLIES DEBIT	DELIVERY EXPENSE DEBIT	MISC. EXPENSE DEBIT	OTHER ACCOUNTS DEBIT	
									ACCOUNT NAME	AMOUNT
20--										
Feb.	1		Establish fund	200 00						
	4	1	Office supplies		17 50	17 50				
	6	2	Delivery service		25 00		25 00			
	11	3	Withdrawal		30 00				S. Harris, Drawing	30 00
	15	4	Postage stamps		33 00			33 00		
	20	5	Delivery service		18 50		18 50			
	26	6	Window washing		28 00			28 00		
	28	7	Store supplies		15 00	15 00				
	28		Totals	200 00	167 00	32 50	43 50	61 00		30 00
	28		Balance on hand		33 00					
				200 00	200 00					
	28		Balance on hand	33 00						
	28		Replenish fund	167 00						
	28		Carried forward	200 00						

CASH PAYMENTS JOURNAL PAGE 1

DATE		CK. NO.	DESCRIPTION	POST. REF.	ACCOUNTS PAYABLE DEBIT	OTHER ACCOUNTS DEBIT			PURCHASES DISCOUNT CREDIT	CASH CREDIT
						ACCOUNT NAME	POST. REF.	AMOUNT		
20--										
Feb.	28	191	Replenish petty cash fund			Supplies	129	32 50		
						S. Harris, Drawing	302	30 00		
						Delivery Expense	658	43 50		
						Miscellaneous Expense	693	61 00		167 00

FIGURE 9-10 ▲
Reimbursing the Petty Cash Fund

Internal Control of the Petty Cash Fund

Whenever there is valuable property or cash to protect, appropriate safeguards must be established. Petty cash is no exception. The following internal control procedures apply to petty cash.

1. Use the petty cash fund only for small payments that cannot conveniently be made by check.
2. Limit the amount set aside for petty cash to the approximate amount needed to cover one month's payments from the fund.
3. Write petty cash fund checks to the person in charge of the fund, not to the order of "Cash."
4. Assign one person to control the petty cash fund. This person has sole control of the money and is the only one authorized to make payments from the fund.
5. Keep petty cash in a safe, a locked cash box, or a locked drawer.
6. Obtain a petty cash voucher for each payment. The voucher should be signed by the person who receives the money and should show the payment details. This provides an audit trail for the fund.

Internal Control over Cash

7 Objective

Demonstrate a knowledge of internal control routines for cash.

In a well-managed business, there are internal control procedures for handling and recording cash receipts and cash payments. The internal control over cash should be tailored to the needs of the business. Accountants play a vital role in designing, establishing, and monitoring the cash control system. In developing internal control procedures for cash, certain basic principles must be followed.

Control of Cash Receipts

As noted already, cash is the asset that is most easily stolen, lost, or mishandled. Yet cash is essential to carrying on business operations. It is important to protect all cash receipts to make sure that funds are available to pay expenses and take care of other business obligations. The following are essential cash receipt controls.

1. Have only designated employees receive and handle cash whether it consists of checks and money orders, or currency and coins. These employees should be carefully chosen for reliability and accuracy and should be carefully trained. In some businesses employees who handle cash are bonded. **Bonding** is the process by which employees are investigated by an insurance company. Employees who pass the background check can be bonded; that is, the employer can purchase insurance on the employees. If the bonded employees steal or mishandle cash, the business is insured against the loss.
2. Keep cash receipts in a cash register, a locked cash drawer, or a safe while they are on the premises.
3. Make a record of all cash receipts as the funds come into the business. For currency and coins, this record is the audit tape in a cash register or duplicate copies of numbered sales slips. The use of a cash register provides an especially effective means of control because the machine automatically produces a tape showing the amounts entered. This tape is locked inside the cash register until it is removed by a supervisor.
4. Before a bank deposit is made, check the funds to be deposited against the record made when the cash was received. The employee who checks the deposit is someone other than the one who receives or records the cash.
5. Deposit cash receipts in the bank promptly—every day or several times a day. Deposit the funds intact—do not make payments directly from the cash receipts. The person who makes the bank deposit is someone other than the one who receives and records the funds.
6. Enter cash receipts transactions in the accounting records promptly. The person who records cash receipts is not the one who receives or deposits the funds.
7. Have the monthly bank statement sent to and reconciled by someone other than the employees who handle, record, and deposit the funds.

One of the advantages of efficient procedures for handling and recording cash receipts is that the funds reach the bank sooner. Cash receipts are not kept on the premises for more than a short time, which means that the funds are safer and are readily available for paying bills owed by the firm.

Control of Cash Payments

It is important to control cash payments so that the payments are made only for authorized business purposes. The following are essential cash payment controls.

1. Make all payments by check except for payments from special-purpose cash funds such as a petty cash fund or a travel and entertainment fund.
2. Issue checks only with an approved bill, invoice, or other document that describes the reason for the payment.
3. Have only designated personnel, who are experienced and reliable, approve bills and invoices.
4. Have checks prepared and recorded in the checkbook or check register by someone other than the person who approves the payments.
5. Have still another person sign and mail the checks to creditors.
6. Use prenumbered check forms. Periodically the numbers of the checks that were issued and the numbers of the blank check forms remaining should be verified to make sure that all check numbers are accounted for.
7. During the bank reconciliation process, compare the canceled checks to the checkbook or check register. The person who does the bank reconciliation should be someone other than the person who prepares or records the checks.
8. Enter promptly in the accounting records all cash payment transactions. The person who records cash payments should not be the one who approves payments or the one who writes the checks.

Small businesses usually cannot achieve the division of responsibility recommended for cash receipts and cash payments. However, no matter what size the firm, efforts should be made to set up effective control procedures for cash.

Section 2 Self Review

Questions

1. Why does a business use a petty cash fund?
2. What cash payments journal entry records a cash withdrawal by the owner of a sole proprietorship?
3. How and when are amounts in the Other Accounts Debit column of the cash payments journal posted?

Exercises

4. Cash purchases of merchandise are recorded in the
   a. cash payments journal.
   b. general journal.
   c. merchandise journal.
   d. purchases journal.
5. To take the discount, what is the payment date for an invoice dated January 20 with terms 3/15, n/30?
   a. February 3
   b. February 4
   c. February 5
   d. February 6

Analysis

6. Your employer keeps a $50 petty cash fund. She asked you to replenish the fund. She is missing a receipt for $6.60, which she says she spent on postage. How should you handle this?

(Answers to Section 2 Self Review are on page 348.)

Section 3

Banking Procedures

Businesses with good internal control systems safeguard cash. Many businesses make a daily bank deposit, and some make two or three deposits a day. Keeping excess cash is a dangerous practice. Also, frequent bank deposits provide a steady flow of funds for the payment of expenses.

Writing Checks

A **check** is a written order signed by an authorized person, the **drawer**, instructing a bank, the **drawee**, to pay a specific sum of money to a designated person or business, the **payee**. The checks in Figure 9-11 on page 310 are **negotiable**, which means that ownership of the checks can be transferred to another person or business.

Before writing the check, complete the check stub. In Figure 9-11, the check stub for Check 111 shows

- Balance brought forward: $11,167.90
- Check amount: $1,400
- Balance: $9,767.90
- Date: January 3, 20--
- Payee: Turner Real Estate Associates
- Purpose: January rent

Once the stub has been completed, fill in the check. Carefully enter the date, the payee, and the amount in figures and words. Draw a line to fill any empty space after the payee's name and after the amount in words. To be valid, checks need an authorized signature. For The Trend Center only Stacee Harris, the owner, is authorized to sign checks.

Figure 9-11 shows the check stub for Check 112, a cash purchase from The Merchandising Equipment Center for $1,200. After Check 112, the account balance is $8,567.90 ($9,767.90 − $1,200.00).

Endorsing Checks

Each check needs an endorsement to be deposited. The **endorsement** is a written authorization that transfers ownership of a check. After the payee transfers ownership to the bank by an endorsement, the bank has a legal right to collect payment from the drawer, the person or business that issued the check. If the check cannot be collected, the payee guarantees payment to all subsequent holders.

Several forms of endorsement are shown in Figure 9-12 on page 310. Endorsements are placed on the back of the check, on the left, near the perforated edge where the check was separated from the stub.

A **blank endorsement** is the signature of the payee that transfers ownership of the check without specifying to whom or for what purpose. Checks with a blank endorsement can be further endorsed by anyone who has the check, even if the check is lost or stolen.

Section Objectives

8 Write a check, endorse checks, prepare a bank deposit slip, and maintain a checkbook balance.

WHY IT'S IMPORTANT
Banking tasks are basic practices in every business.

9 Reconcile the monthly bank statement.

WHY IT'S IMPORTANT
Reconciliation of the bank statement provides a good control of cash.

10 Record any adjusting entries required from the bank reconciliation.

WHY IT'S IMPORTANT
Certain items are not recorded in the accounting records during the month.

Terms to Learn

bank reconciliation statement
blank endorsement
canceled check
check
credit memorandum
debit memorandum
deposit in transit
deposit slip
dishonored (NSF) check
drawee
drawer
endorsement
full endorsement
negotiable
outstanding checks
payee
postdated check
restrictive endorsement
service charge

No. 111	BAL BRO'T FOR'D	11,167	90
January 3 20 --			
Turner Real Estate Assoc. TO ORDER OF			
January rent FOR			
	TOTAL	11,167	90
	AMOUNT THIS CHECK	1,400	00
	BALANCE	9,767	90

The Trend Center No. 111
1010 Red Bird Lane 11-8640/1210
Dallas, TX 75268-7783

DATE January 3 20 --

PAY TO THE ORDER OF Turner Real Estate Associates $ 1,400.00

One thousand four hundred 00/100 DOLLARS

FIRST SECURITY NATIONAL BANK
Dallas, TX 75267-6205

MEMO Rent for January Stacee Harris

⑆1210⑈8640⑆ ⑈19⑈0767889⑈

No. 112	BAL BRO'T FOR'D	9,767	90
January 10 20 --			
The Merch. Equip. Ctr. TO ORDER OF			
store fixtures FOR			
	TOTAL	9,767	90
	AMOUNT THIS CHECK	1,200	00
	BALANCE	8,567	90

The Trend Center No. 112
1010 Red Bird Lane 11-8640/1210
Dallas, TX 75268-7783

DATE January 10 20 --

PAY TO THE ORDER OF The Merchandising Equipment Center $ 1,200.00

One thousand two hundred 00/100 DOLLARS

FIRST SECURITY NATIONAL BANK
Dallas, TX 75267-6205

MEMO store fixtures Stacee Harris

⑆1210⑈8640⑆ ⑈19⑈0767889⑈

▲ **FIGURE 9-11**
Checks and Check Stubs

A **full endorsement** is a signature transferring a check to a specific person, business, or bank. Only the person, business, or bank named in the full endorsement can transfer it to someone else.

The safest endorsement is the **restrictive endorsement**. A restrictive endorsement is a signature that transfers the check to a specific party for a specific purpose, usually for deposit to a bank account. Most businesses restrictively endorse the checks they receive using a rubber stamp.

FIGURE 9-12 ►
Types of Check Endorsement

Full Endorsement

PAY TO THE ORDER OF
FIRST SECURITY NATIONAL BANK
THE TREND CENTER
19-07-67889

Blank Endorsement

Stacee Harris
19-07-67889

Restrictive Endorsement

PAY TO THE ORDER OF
FIRST SECURITY NATIONAL BANK
FOR DEPOSIT ONLY
THE TREND CENTER
19-07-67889

8 Objective

Write a check, endorse checks, prepare a bank deposit slip, and maintain a checkbook balance.

Preparing the Deposit Slip

Businesses prepare a **deposit slip** to record each deposit of cash or checks to a bank account. Usually the bank provides deposit slips preprinted with the account name and number. Figure 9-13 on page 311 shows the deposit slip for the January 8 deposit for The Trend Center.

CHECKING ACCOUNT DEPOSIT		CURRENCY	DOLLARS	CENTS
			1350	00
DATE *January 8, 20--*		COIN	109	90
	ENTER ADDITIONAL CHECKS ON OTHER SIDE	1 11-8182	240	80
		2 11-8182	230	00
		3 11-5216	171	20
		4 11-5216	280	00
THE TREND CENTER		5 11-7450	460	50
1010 Red Bird Lane		6 11-7450	410	40
Dallas, TX 75268-7783		7		
		8		
		9		
		10		
FIRST SECURITY NATIONAL BANK		11		
Dallas, TX 75267-6205		12		
		TOTAL FROM OTHER SIDE OR ATTACHED LIST		
Checks and other items are received for deposit subject to the terms and conditions of this bank's collection agreement.		**TOTAL**	3,252.80	
⑆1210⑉8640⑆ ⑈19⑈07 67889⑈				

FIGURE 9-13
Deposit Slip

Notice the printed numbers on the lower edge of the deposit slip. These are the same numbers on the bottom of the checks, Figure 9-11. The numbers are printed using a special *magnetic ink character recognition (MICR)* type that can be "read" by machine. Deposit slips and checks encoded with MICR are rapidly and efficiently processed by machine.

- The 12 indicates that the bank is in the 12th Federal Reserve District.
- The 10 is the routing number used in processing the document.
- The 8640 identifies First Security National Bank.
- The 19 07 67889 is The Trend Center account number.

The deposit slip for The Trend Center shows the date, January 8. *Currency* is the paper money, $1,350.00. *Coin* is the amount in coins, $109.90. The checks and money orders are individually listed. Some banks ask that the *American Bankers Association (ABA) transit number* for each check be entered on the deposit slip. The transit number appears on the top part of the fraction that appears in the upper right corner of the check. In Figure 9-11, the transit number is 11-8640.

Handling Postdated Checks

Occasionally a business will receive a postdated check. A **postdated check** is dated some time in the future. If the business receives a postdated check, it should not deposit it before the date on the check. Otherwise, the check could be refused by the drawer's bank. Postdated checks are written by drawers who do not have sufficient funds to cover the check. The drawer expects to have adequate funds in the bank by the date on the check. Issuing or accepting postdated checks is not a proper business practice.

Reconciling the Bank Statement

9 Objective
Reconcile the monthly bank statement.

Once a month the bank sends a statement of the deposits received and the checks paid for each account. Figure 9-14 on page 313 shows the bank statement for The Trend Center. It shows a day-to-day listing of all transactions during the month. A code, explained at the bottom,

Computers in Accounting

Banking on Computer Technologies

The banking industry has long been a major user of computer technologies to process and maintain accurate records for internal operations and customer accounts. As early as 1950, the banking industry adopted magnetic ink character recognition (MICR) type to be printed along the bottom edge of checks and deposit slips. Using MICR readers, banks process millions of checks and deposit slips annually. MICR readers are also used in retail stores where checks are accepted.

Bank computer systems use real-time processing. Every banking transaction is recorded immediately in the bank's accounting records, and customer account balances are instantly updated.

Banking consumers today rely heavily on automated teller machines (ATMs). The banking industry has invested billions of dollars to maintain and upgrade teller machines to offer the services that their customers demand. Newer ATMs allow customers to cash checks, purchase stamps, and withdraw money in bills and coins.

Online banking is a service now offered by most financial institutions. Password-protected Web sites offer customers an easy-to-use interface where many banking transactions are completed. Consumers now pay bills, transfer funds, purchase IRAs, download bank statements, and review their account activity using home or office computers. Some consumers have abandoned the bricks-and-mortar bank altogether. Again, the banking industry has responded quickly with investment in Internet technologies and security software applications necessary to serve the needs of customers.

Thinking Critically

As a banking customer, what concerns do you have about online banking? What benefits and disadvantages can you identify?

Internet Application

Locate the Web site for your banking institution. What online banking services are offered? What costs are associated with these services?

identifies transactions that do not involve checks or deposits. For example, *SC* indicates a service charge. The last column of the bank statement shows the account balance at the beginning of the period, after each day's transactions, and at the end of the period.

Often the bank encloses canceled checks with the bank statement. **Canceled checks** are checks paid by the bank during the month. The bank stamps the word *PAID* across the face of each check. Canceled checks are proof of payment. They are filed after the bank reconciliation is complete.

Usually there is a difference between the ending balance shown on the bank statement and the balance shown in the checkbook. A bank reconciliation determines why the difference exists and brings the records into agreement.

Changes in the Checking Account Balance

A **credit memorandum** explains any addition, other than a deposit, to the checking account. For example, when a note receivable is due, the bank may collect the note from the maker and place the proceeds in the checking account. The amount collected appears on the bank statement, and the credit memorandum showing the details of the transaction is enclosed with the bank statement.

FIGURE 9-14
Bank Statement

FIRST SECURITY NATIONAL BANK

THE TREND CENTER
1010 Red Bird Lane
Dallas, TX 75268-7783

Account Number: 19-07-67889

Period Ending January, 31, 20--

CHECKS		DEPOSITS	DATE	BALANCE
Beginning Balance			December 31	11,167.90
1,400.00-		428.00+	January 7	10,195.90
1,200.00-		3,252.80+	January 8	12,248.70
749.00-		267.50+	January 11	11,767.20
1,000.00-		10,000.00+	January 12	20,767.20
3,185.00-		535.00+	January 13	18,117.20
750.00-		4,196.10+	January 15	21,563.30
2,400.00-		107.00+	January 16	19,270.30
250.00-	300.00-	50.00+	January 17	18,770.30
420.00-	4,300.00-	200.00+	January 22	14,250.30
800.00-	1,200.00-	4,515.40+	January 22	16,765.70
250.00- DM		756.00+	January 29	17,271.70
20.00- SC		107.00+	January 31	17,358.70
400.00-		260.00+	January 31	17,218.70
		418.00+	January 31	17,636.70

LAST AMOUNT IN THIS COLUMN IS YOUR BALANCE

Codes:

CC	Certified Check	EC	Error Correction
CM	Credit Memorandum	OD	Overdrawn
DM	Debit Memorandum	SC	Service Charge

PLEASE EXAMINE THIS STATEMENT UPON RECEIPT AND REPORT ANY ERRORS WITHIN TEN DAYS.

A **debit memorandum** explains any deduction, other than a check, to the checking account. Service charges and dishonored checks appear as debit memorandums.

Bank **service charges** are fees charged by banks to cover the costs of maintaining accounts and providing services, such as the use of the night deposit box and the collection of promissory notes. The debit memorandum shows the type and amount of each service charge.

Figure 9-15 on page 314 shows a debit memorandum for a $250 dishonored check. A **dishonored check** is one that is returned to the depositor unpaid. Normally, checks are dishonored because there are insufficient funds in the drawer's account to cover the check. The bank usually stamps the letters *NSF* for *Not Sufficient Funds* on the check. The business records a journal entry to create an account receivable from the drawer for the amount of the dishonored check.

When a check is dishonored, the business contacts the drawer to arrange for collection. The drawer can ask the business to redeposit the check because the funds are now in the account. If so, the business records the check deposit again. Sometimes, the business requests a cash payment.

FIGURE 9-15 ►
Debit Memorandum

DEBIT: **THE TREND CENTER**
1010 Red Bird Lane
Dallas, TX 75268-7783

FIRST SECURITY NATIONAL BANK

19-07-67889

DATE: *January 31, 20--*

NSF Check - Bridgette Wilson	*250 00*

APPROVED: *DCP*

The Bank Reconciliation Process: An Illustration

When the bank statement is received, it is reconciled with the financial records of the business. On February 5 The Trend Center received the bank statement shown in Figure 9-14. The ending cash balance according to the bank is $17,636.70. On January 31 the **Cash** account, called the *book balance of cash,* is $9,554.00. The same amount appears on the check stub at the end of January.

Sometimes the difference between the bank balance and the book balance is due to errors. The bank might make an arithmetic error, give credit to the wrong depositor, or charge a check against the wrong account. Many banks require that errors in the bank statement be reported within a short period of time, usually 10 days. The errors made by businesses include not recording a check or deposit, or recording a check or deposit for the wrong amount.

Other than errors, there are four reasons why the book balance of cash may not agree with the balance on the bank statement.

1. **Outstanding checks** are checks that are recorded in the cash payments journal but have not been paid by the bank.
2. **Deposit in transit** is a deposit that is recorded in the cash receipts journal but that reaches the bank too late to be shown on the monthly bank statement.
3. Service charges and other deductions are not recorded in the business records.
4. Deposits, such as the collection of promissory notes, are not recorded in the business records.

Figure 9-16 on page 315 shows a **bank reconciliation statement** that accounts for the differences between the balance on the bank statement and the book balance of cash. The bank reconciliation statement format is:

First Section	
	Bank statement balance
+	deposits in transit
−	outstanding checks
+ or −	bank errors
	Adjusted bank balance

Second Section	
	Book balance
+	deposits not recorded
−	deductions
+ or −	errors in the books
	Adjusted book balance

When the bank reconciliation statement is complete, the adjusted bank balance must equal the adjusted book balance.

FIGURE 9-16
Bank Reconciliation Statement

The Trend Center Bank Reconciliation Statement January 31, 20--		
Bank statement balance		17 6 3 6 70
Additions:		
Deposits of January 31 in transit	3 5 4 1 70	
Check incorrectly charged to account	8 0 0 00	4 3 4 1 70
		21 9 7 8 40
Deductions for outstanding checks:		
Check 124 of January 31	2 5 0 8 80	
Check 125 of January 31	4 2 0 0 00	
Check 126 of January 31	2 4 0 0 00	
Check 127 of January 31	1 5 0 00	
Check 128 of January 31	8 5 60	
Check 129 of January 31	3 1 5 0 00	
Check 130 of January 31	2 0 0 00	
Total outstanding checks		12 6 9 4 40
Adjusted bank balance		9 2 8 4 00
Book balance		9 5 5 4 00
Deductions:		
NSF Check	2 5 0 00	
Bank service charge	2 0 00	2 7 0 00
Adjusted book balance		9 2 8 4 00

Use the following steps to prepare the bank reconciliation statement:

First Section

1. Enter the balance on the bank statement, $17,636.70.
2. Compare the deposits in the checkbook with the deposits on the bank statement. The Trend Center had one deposit in transit. On January 31 receipts of $3,541.70 were placed in the bank's night deposit box. The bank recorded the deposit on February 1. The deposit will appear on the February bank statement.
3. List the outstanding checks.
   - Put the canceled checks in numeric order.
   - Compare the canceled checks to the check stubs, verifying the check numbers and amounts.
   - Examine the endorsements to make sure that they agree with the names of the payees.
   - List the checks that have not cleared the bank.
   - The Trend Center has seven outstanding checks totaling $12,694.40.
4. While reviewing the canceled checks for The Trend Center, Stacee Harris found an $800 check issued by Trudie's Dress Barn. The $800 was deducted from The Trend Center's account; it should have been deducted from the account for Trudie's Dress Barn. This is a bank error. Stacee Harris contacted the bank about the error. The correction will appear on the next bank statement. The bank error amount is added to the bank statement balance on the bank reconciliation statement.
5. The adjusted bank balance is $9,284.

Cash

- It is important to safeguard cash against loss and theft.
- Management and the accountant need to work together
  - to make sure that there are effective controls for cash receipts and cash payments,
  - to monitor the internal control system to make sure that it functions properly,
  - to develop procedures that ensure the quick and efficient recording of cash transactions.
- To make decisions, management needs up-to-date information about the cash position so that it can anticipate cash shortages and arrange loans or arrange for the temporary investment of excess funds.
- Management and the accountant need to establish controls over the banking activities—depositing funds, issuing checks, recording checking account transactions, and reconciling the monthly bank statement.

Thinking Critically

How would you determine how much cash to keep in the business checking account, as opposed to in a short-term investment?

Adjusted Book Balance

Make journal entries to record additions and deductions that appear on the bank statement but that have not been recorded in the general ledger.

Second Section

1. Enter the balance in books from the **Cash** account, $9,554.
2. Record any deposits made by the bank that have not been recorded in the accounting records. The Trend Center did not have any.
3. Record deductions made by the bank. There are two items:
   - the NSF check for $250,
   - the bank service charge for $20.
4. Record any errors in the accounting records that were discovered during the reconciliation process. The Trend Center did not have any errors in January.
5. The adjusted book balance is $9,284.

Notice that the adjusted bank balance and the adjusted book balance agree.

⑩ Objective

Record any adjusting entries required from the bank reconciliation.

Adjusting the Financial Records

Items in the second section of the bank reconciliation statement include additions and deductions made by the bank that do not appear in the accounting records. Businesses prepare journal entries to record these items in the books.

For The Trend Center, two entries must be made. The first entry is for the NSF check from Bridgette Wilson, a credit customer. The second entry is for the bank service charge. The effect of the two items is a decrease in the **Cash** account balance.

Business Transaction

The January bank reconciliation statement (Figure 9-16 on page 315) shows an NSF check of $250 and a bank service charge of $20.

Analysis

The asset account, **Accounts Receivable,** is increased by $250 for the returned check. The expense account, **Bank Fees Expense,** is increased by $20 for the service charge. The asset account, **Cash,** is decreased by $270 ($250 + $20).

Debit-Credit Rules

DEBIT Increases to assets are debits. Debit **Accounts Receivable** for $250. Increases to expenses are debits. Debit **Bank Fees Expense** for $20.

CREDIT Decreases to assets are credits. Credit **Cash** for $270.

T-Account Presentation

Accounts Receivable +	Accounts Receivable −	Bank Fees Expense +	Bank Fees Expense −	Cash +	Cash −
250		20			270

General Journal Entry

GENERAL JOURNAL PAGE 16

	DATE		DESCRIPTION	POST. REF.	DEBIT	CREDIT	
29	Jan.	31	Accounts Receivable/ Bridgette Wilson		250 00		29
30			Bank Fees Expense		20 00		30
31			Cash			270 00	31
32			To record NSF check and service charge				32

The Bottom Line

Adjusting Entries

Income Statement

Expenses	↑ 20
Net Income	↓ 20

Balance Sheet

Assets	↓ 20
Equity	↓ 20

After these entries are posted, the **Cash** account appears as follows.

ACCOUNT Cash ACCOUNT NO. 101

DATE		DESCRIPTION	POST. REF.	DEBIT	CREDIT	BALANCE DEBIT	BALANCE CREDIT
20--							
Jan.	1	Balance	✓			11 167 90	
	31		CR1	28 634 50		39 802 40	
	31		CP1		30 248 40	9 554 00	
	31		J16		270 00	9 284 00	

Notice that $9,284 is the adjusted bank balance, the adjusted book balance, and the general ledger **Cash** balance. A notation is made on the latest check stub to deduct the amounts ($250 and $20). The notation includes the reasons for the deductions.

Sometimes the bank reconciliation reveals an error in the firm's financial records. For example, the February bank reconciliation for The Trend Center found that Check 151 was written for $355. The amount on the bank statement is $355. However, the check was recorded in the accounting records as $345. The business made a $10 error when recording the check. The Trend Center prepared the following journal entry to correct the error. The $10 is also deducted on the check stub.

GENERAL JOURNAL — PAGE 17

	DATE		DESCRIPTION	POST. REF.	DEBIT	CREDIT	
1	20--						1
2	Feb.	28	Advertising Expense	614	10 00		2
3			Cash	101		10 00	3
4			To correct error for Check 151 of				4
5			Feb. 21				5

Internal Control of Banking Activities

Well-run businesses put the following internal controls in place.

1. Limit access to the checkbook to designated employees. When the checkbook is not in use, keep it in a locked drawer or cabinet.
2. Use prenumbered check forms. Periodically, verify and account for all checks. Examine checks before signing them. Match each check to an approved invoice or other payment authorization.
3. Separate duties.
   - The person who writes the check should not sign or mail the check.
   - The person who performs the bank reconciliation should not handle or deposit cash receipts or write, record, sign, or mail checks.
4. File all deposit receipts, canceled checks, voided checks, and bank statements for future reference. These documents provide a strong audit trail for the checking account.

Section 3 Self Review

Questions

1. What is a postdated check? When should postdated checks be deposited?
2. Which bank reconciliation items require journal entries?
3. Why does a payee endorse a check before depositing it?

Exercises

4. On the bank reconciliation statement, you would not find a list of
   a. canceled checks.
   b. deposits in transit.
   c. outstanding checks.
   d. NSF checks.
5. Which of the following does not require an adjustment to the financial records?
   a. NSF check
   b. Bank service charge
   c. Check that was incorrectly recorded at $65, but was written and paid by the bank as $56
   d. Deposits in transit

Analysis

6. James is one of several accounting clerks at Avery Beverage Company. His job duties include recording invoices as they are received, filing the invoices, and writing the checks for accounts payable. He is a fast and efficient clerk and usually has some time available each day to help other clerks. It has been suggested that reconciling the bank statement should be added to his job duties. Do you agree or disagree? Why or why not?

(Answers to Section 3 Self Review are on page 348.)

CHAPTER 9 Review and Applications

Review

Chapter Summary

In this chapter, you have learned the basic principles of accounting for cash payments and cash receipts.

Learning Objectives

1. **Record cash receipts in a cash receipts journal.**
   Use of special journals leads to an efficient recording process for cash transactions. The cash receipts journal has separate columns for the accounts used most often for cash receipt transactions.

2. **Account for cash short or over.**
   Errors can occur when making change. Cash register discrepancies should be recorded using the expense account **Cash Short or Over.**

3. **Post from the cash receipts journal to subsidiary and general ledgers.**
   Individual accounts receivable amounts are posted to the subsidiary ledger daily. Figures in the Other Accounts Credit column are posted individually to the general ledger during the month. All other postings are done on a summary basis at month-end.

4. **Record cash payments in a cash payments journal.**
   The cash payments journal has separate columns for the accounts used most often, eliminating the need to record the same account names repeatedly.

5. **Post from the cash payments journal to subsidiary and general ledgers.**
   Individual accounts payable amounts are posted daily to the accounts payable subsidiary ledger. Amounts listed in the Other Accounts Debit column are posted individually to the general ledger during the month. All other postings are completed on a summary basis at the end of the month.

6. **Demonstrate a knowledge of procedures for a petty cash fund.**
   Although most payments are made by check, small payments are often made through a petty cash fund. A petty cash voucher is prepared for each payment and signed by the person receiving the money. The person in charge of the fund records expenditures on a petty cash analysis sheet. The fund is replenished with a check for the sum spent. An entry is made in the cash payments journal to debit the accounts involved.

7. **Demonstrate a knowledge of internal control routines for cash.**
   All businesses need a system of internal controls to protect cash from theft and mishandling and to ensure accurate records of cash transactions. A checking account is essential to store cash safely and to make cash payments efficiently. For maximum control over outgoing cash, all payments should be made by check except those from carefully controlled special-purpose cash funds such as a petty cash fund.

8. **Write a check, endorse checks, prepare a bank deposit slip, and maintain a checkbook balance.**
   Check writing requires careful attention to details. If a standard checkbook is used, the stub should be completed before the check so that it will not be forgotten. The stub gives the data needed to journalize the payment.

9. **Reconcile the monthly bank statement.**
   A bank statement should be immediately reconciled with the cash balance in the firm's financial records. Usually, differences are due to deposits in transit, outstanding checks, and bank service charges, but many factors can cause lack of agreement between the bank balance and the book balance.

10. **Record any adjusting entries required from the bank reconciliation.**
    Some differences between the bank balance and the book balance may require that the firm's records be adjusted after the bank statement is reconciled. Journal entries are recorded and then posted to correct the **Cash** account balance and the checkbook balance.

11. **Define the accounting terms new to this chapter.**

CHAPTER 9 GLOSSARY

Bank reconciliation statement (p. 314) A statement that accounts for all differences between the balance on the bank statement and the book balance of cash

Blank endorsement (p. 309) A signature of the payee written on the back of the check that transfers ownership of the check without specifying to whom or for what purpose

Bonding (p. 307) The process by which employees are investigated by an insurance company that will insure the business against losses through employee theft or mishandling of funds

Canceled check (p. 312) A check paid by the bank on which it was drawn

Cash (p. 292) In accounting, currency, coins, checks, money orders, and funds on deposit in a bank

Cash payments journal (p. 299) A special journal used to record transactions involving the payment of cash

Cash receipts journal (p. 292) A special journal used to record and post transactions involving the receipt of cash

Cash register proof (p. 293) A verification that the amount of currency and coins in a cash register agrees with the amount shown on the cash register audit tape

Cash Short or Over account (p. 294) An account used to record any discrepancies between the amount of currency and coins in the cash register and the amount shown on the audit tape

Check (p. 309) A written order signed by an authorized person instructing a bank to pay a specific sum of money to a designated person or business

Credit memorandum (p. 312) A form that explains any addition, other than a deposit, to a checking account

Debit memorandum (p. 313) A form that explains any deduction, other than a check, from a checking account

Deposit in transit (p. 314) A deposit that is recorded in the cash receipts journal but that reaches the bank too late to be shown on the monthly bank statement

Deposit slip (p. 310) A form prepared to record the deposit of cash or checks to a bank account

Dishonored check (p. 313) A check returned to the depositor unpaid because of insufficient funds in the drawer's account; also called an NSF check

Drawee (p. 309) The bank on which a check is written

Drawer (p. 309) The person or firm issuing a check

Endorsement (p. 309) A written authorization that transfers ownership of a check

Full endorsement (p. 310) A signature transferring a check to a specific person, firm, or bank

Negotiable (p. 309) A financial instrument whose ownership can be transferred to another person or business

Outstanding checks (p. 314) Checks that have been recorded in the cash payments journal but have not yet been paid by the bank

Payee (p. 309) The person or firm to whom a check is payable

Petty cash analysis sheet (p. 305) A form used to record transactions involving petty cash

Petty cash fund (p. 292) A special-purpose fund used to handle payments involving small amounts of money

Petty cash voucher (p. 305) A form used to record the payments made from a petty cash fund

Postdated check (p. 311) A check dated some time in the future

Promissory note (p. 294) A written promise to pay a specified amount of money on a specific date

Restrictive endorsement (p. 310) A signature that transfers a check to a specific party for a stated purpose

Service charge (p. 313) A fee charged by a bank to cover the costs of maintaining accounts and providing services

Statement of account (p. 294) A form sent to a firm's customers showing transactions during the month and the balance owed

Comprehensive Self Review

1. What does the term *cash* mean in business?
2. What are the advantages of using special journals for cash receipts and cash payments?
3. Describe a full endorsement.
4. What is a petty cash voucher?
5. When is the petty cash fund replenished?

(Answers to Comprehensive Self Review are on page 348.)

Discussion Questions

1. Why are MICR numbers printed on deposit slips and checks?
2. What is a check?
3. What type of information is entered on a check stub? Why should a check stub be prepared before the check is written?
4. What information is shown on the bank statement?
5. Why is a bank reconciliation prepared?
6. What is the book balance of cash?
7. Give some reasons why the bank balance and the book balance of cash might differ.
8. Why are journal entries sometimes needed after the bank reconciliation statement is prepared?
9. What procedures are used to achieve internal control over banking activities?

10. Explain the meaning of the following terms.
    - **a.** Canceled check
    - **b.** Outstanding check
    - **c.** Deposit in transit
    - **d.** Debit memorandum
    - **e.** Credit memorandum
    - **f.** Dishonored check
    - **g.** Blank endorsement
    - **h.** Deposit slip
    - **i.** Drawee
    - **j.** Restrictive endorsement
    - **k.** Payee
    - **l.** Drawer
    - **m.** Service charge
11. Describe the major controls for cash receipts.
12. Explain what *bonding* means. How does bonding relate to safeguarding cash?
13. Describe the major controls for cash payments.
14. What is a promissory note? What entry is made to record the collection of a promissory note and interest? Which journal is used?
15. Why do some wholesale businesses offer cash discounts to their customers?
16. How does a wholesale business record a check received on account from a customer when a cash discount is involved? Which journal is used?
17. How does a firm record a payment on account to a creditor when a cash discount is involved? Which journal is used?
18. What type of account is **Purchases Discounts?** How is this account presented on the income statement?
19. When are petty cash expenditures entered in a firm's accounting records?
20. Describe the major controls for petty cash.
21. How are cash shortages and overages recorded?
22. Which type of endorsement is most appropriate for a business to use?

Applications

EXERCISES

Recording cash receipts.

◄ **Exercise 9-1**
Objective 1

The following transactions took place at Comfort Zone Shoe Store during the first week of September 20--. Indicate how these transactions would be entered in a cash receipts journal.

DATE		TRANSACTIONS
Sept.	1	Had cash sales of $2,800 plus sales tax of $112; there was a cash overage of $4.
	2	Collected $360 on account from Brenda Joy, a credit customer.
	3	Had cash sales of $2,500 plus sales tax of $100.
	4	Angela Sadler, the owner, made an additional cash investment of $14,000.
	5	Had cash sales of $3,200 plus sales tax of $128; there was a cash shortage of $10.

Recording cash payments.

◄ **Exercise 9-2**
Objective 4

The following transactions took place at Comfort Zone Shoe Store during the first week of September 20--. Indicate how these transactions would be entered in a cash payments journal.

DATE		TRANSACTIONS
Sept.	1	Issued Check 5038 for $1,200 to pay the monthly rent.
	1	Issued Check 5039 for $2,440 to Amos Company, a creditor, on account.
	2	Issued Check 5040 for $5,120 to purchase new equipment.
	2	Issued Check 5041 for $992 to remit sales tax to the state sales tax authority.
	3	Issued Check 5042 for $1,372 to Nathan Company, a creditor, on account for invoice of $1,400 less cash discount of $28.
	4	Issued Check 5043 for $1,180 to purchase merchandise.
	5	Issued Check 5044 for $1,500 as a cash withdrawal for personal use by Angela Sadler, the owner.

Recording the establishment of a petty cash fund.

◄ **Exercise 9-3**
Objective 6

On January 2 Davis Insurance Company issued Check 7921 for $150 to establish a petty cash fund. Indicate how this transaction would be recorded in a cash payments journal.

Recording the replenishment of a petty cash fund.

◄ **Exercise 9-4**
Objective 6

On January 31 Fox Inc. issued Check 4431 to replenish its petty cash fund. An analysis of payments from the fund showed these totals: **Supplies,** $84; **Delivery Expense,** $72; and **Miscellaneous Expense,** $60. Indicate how this transaction would be recorded in a cash payments journal.

Exercise 9-5 ► Objective 9

Analyzing bank reconciliation items.

At Marshall Security Company the following items were found to cause a difference between the bank statement and the firm's records. Indicate whether each item will affect the bank balance or the book balance when the bank reconciliation statement is prepared. Also indicate which items will require an accounting entry after the bank reconciliation is completed.

1. A deposit in transit.
2. A debit memorandum for a dishonored check.
3. A credit memorandum for a promissory note that the bank collected for Marshall.
4. An error found in Marshall's records, which involves the amount of a check. The firm's checkbook and cash payments journal indicate $404 as the amount, but the canceled check itself and the listing on the bank statement show that $440 was the actual sum.
5. An outstanding check.
6. A bank service charge.
7. A check issued by another firm that was charged to Marshall's account by mistake.

Exercise 9-6 ► Objectives 9, 10

Determining an adjusted bank balance.

Gagliardi Corporation received a bank statement showing a balance of $29,840 as of October 31, 20--. The firm's records showed a book balance of $28,724 on October 31. The difference between the two balances was caused by the following items. Prepare the adjusted bank balance section and the adjusted book balance section of the bank reconciliation statement. Also prepare the necessary journal entry.

1. A debit memorandum for an NSF check from Jim Night for $600.
2. Three outstanding checks: Check 7107 for $258, Check 7125 for $130 and Check 7147 for $3,066.
3. A bank service charge of $24.
4. A deposit in transit of $1,714.

Exercise 9-7 ► Objective 9

Preparing a bank reconciliation statement.

Wilner Building Supply Company received a bank statement showing a balance of $135,810 as of March 31, 20--. The firm's records showed a book balance of $138,774 on March 31. The difference between the two balances was caused by the following items. Prepare a bank reconciliation statement for the firm as of March 31 and the necessary journal entries from the statement.

1. A debit memorandum for $42, which covers the bank's collection fee for the note.
2. A deposit in transit of $7,440.
3. A check for $534 issued by another firm that was mistakenly charged to Wilner's account.
4. A debit memorandum for an NSF check of $11,550 issued by Ames Construction Company, a credit customer.
5. Outstanding checks: Check 8237 for $4,260; Check 8244 for $342.
6. A credit memorandum for a $12,000 noninterest-bearing note receivable that the bank collected for the firm.

Problems

Selected problems can be completed using:
Peachtree QuickBooks Spreadsheets

PROBLEM SET A

Journalizing cash receipts and posting to the general ledger.

◄ **Problem 9-1A**
Objectives 1, 2, 3

Movies To Go is a retail store that rents movies and sells blank and prerecorded videocassettes. The firm's cash receipts for February are listed below and on page 326. The general ledger accounts used to record these transactions appear below.

INSTRUCTIONS

1. Open the general ledger accounts and enter the balances as of February 1, 20--.
2. Record the transactions in a cash receipts journal. Use 3 as the page number.
3. Post the individual entries from the Other Accounts Credit section of the cash receipts journal to the proper general ledger accounts.
4. Total, prove, and rule the cash receipts journal as of February 28, 20--.
5. Post the column totals from the cash receipts journal to the proper general ledger accounts.

GENERAL LEDGER ACCOUNTS

101 Cash	$ 9,920 Dr.	401 Sales
109 Notes Receivable	700 Dr.	620 Cash Short or Over
111 Accounts Receivable	2,050 Dr.	691 Interest Income
129 Supplies	1,220 Dr.	
231 Sales Tax Payable	590 Cr.	
301 Durwood McGrew, Capital	68,000 Cr.	

DATE		TRANSACTIONS
Feb.	3	Received $250 from Kirk Walker, a credit customer, on account.
	5	Received a cash refund of $60 for damaged supplies.
	7	Had cash sales of $4,280 plus sales tax of $214 during the first week of February; there was a cash shortage of $10.
	9	Durwood McGrew, the owner, invested an additional $10,000 cash in the business.
	12	Received $190 from Kim Reno, a credit customer, in payment of her account.
	14	Had cash sales of $3,520 plus sales tax of $176 during the second week of February; there was an overage of $4.
	16	Received $420 from Kelly Rock, a credit customer, to apply toward her account.
	19	Received a check from Michael Lane to pay his $700 promissory note plus interest of $14.
	21	Had cash sales of $3,240 plus sales tax of $162 during the third week of February.
		Continued

DATE	(9-1A cont.) TRANSACTIONS
Feb. 25	Jason Bolima, a credit customer, sent a check for $290 to pay the balance he owes.
28	Had cash sales of $3,960 plus sales tax of $198 during the fourth week of February; there was a cash shortage of $6.

Analyze: What total accounts receivable were collected in February?

Problem 9-2A ►
Objectives 4, 5, 6

Journalizing cash payments, recording petty cash, and posting to the general ledger.

The cash payments of Crown Jewelry Store, a retail business, for June are listed below and on page 327. The general ledger accounts used to record these transactions appear below.

INSTRUCTIONS

1. Open the general ledger accounts and enter the balances as of June 1.
2. Record all payments by check in a cash payments journal; use 8 as the page number.
3. Record all payments from the petty cash fund on a petty cash analysis sheet; use 8 as the sheet number.
4. Post the individual entries from the Other Accounts Debit section of the cash payments journal to the proper general ledger accounts.
5. Total, prove, and rule the petty cash analysis sheet as of June 30. Record the replenishment of the fund and the final balance on the sheet.
6. Total, prove, and rule the cash payments journal as of June 30.
7. Post the column totals from the cash payments journal to the proper general ledger accounts.

GENERAL LEDGER ACCOUNTS

101	Cash	$48,960 Dr.
105	Petty Cash Fund	
129	Supplies	2,120 Dr.
201	Notes Payable	2,800 Cr.
205	Accounts Payable	17,840 Cr.
231	Sales Tax Payable	3,920 Cr.
302	Lenny Jefferson, Drawing	
451	Sales Returns and Allowances	
504	Purchases Discounts	
611	Delivery Expense	
620	Rent Expense	
623	Salaries Expense	
626	Telephone Expense	
634	Interest Expense	
635	Miscellaneous Expense	

DATE	TRANSACTIONS
June 1	Issued Check 1241 for $2,400 to pay the monthly rent.
2	Issued Check 1242 for $3,920 to remit the state sales tax.
3	Issued Check 1243 for $2,300 to Digital Watch Company, a creditor, in payment of Invoice 8086, dated May 5.

Continued

DATE		(9-2A cont.) TRANSACTIONS
June	4	Issued Check 1244 for $400 to establish a petty cash fund. (After journalizing this transaction, be sure to enter it on the first line of the petty cash analysis sheet.)
	5	Paid $60 from the petty cash fund for office supplies, Petty Cash Voucher 1.
	7	Issued Check 1245 for $2,884 to Evergreen Corporation in payment of a $2,800 promissory note and interest of $84.
	8	Paid $40 from the petty cash fund for postage stamps, Petty Cash Voucher 2.
	10	Issued Check 1246 for $520 to a customer as a cash refund for a defective watch that was returned; the original sale was made for cash.
	12	Issued Check 1247 for $312 to pay the telephone bill.
	14	Issued Check 1248 for $4,900 to Rudy Importers, a creditor, in payment of Invoice 2986, dated May 6 ($5,000), less a cash discount ($100).
	15	Paid $37 from the petty cash fund for delivery service, Petty Cash Voucher 3.
	17	Issued Check 1249 for $700 to purchase store supplies.
	20	Issued Check 1250 for $2,744 to Flashy Chains, Inc., a creditor, in payment of Invoice 3115, dated June 12 ($2,800), less a cash discount ($56).
	22	Paid $48 from the petty cash fund for a personal withdrawal by Lenny Jefferson, the owner, Petty Cash Voucher 4.
	25	Paid $60 from the petty cash fund to have the store windows washed and repaired, Petty Cash Voucher 5.
	27	Issued Check 1251 for $3,560 to Emerald Creations, a creditor, in payment of Invoice 566, dated May 30.
	30	Paid $47 from the petty cash fund for delivery service, Petty Cash Voucher 6.
	30	Issued Check 1252 for $7,000 to pay the monthly salaries.
	30	Issued Check 1253 for $6,000 to Lenny Jefferson, the owner, as a withdrawal for personal use.
	30	Issued Check 1254 for $292 to replenish the petty cash fund. (Foot the columns of the petty cash analysis sheet in order to determine the accounts that should be debited and the amounts involved.)

Analyze: What total payments were made from the petty cash fund for the month?

Journalizing sales and cash receipts and posting to the general ledger.

◄ **Problem 9-3A**
Objectives 1, 2, 3

Sounds Unlimited is a wholesale business that sells musical instruments. Transactions involving sales and cash receipts for the firm during April 20-- follow, along with the general ledger accounts used to record these transactions.

INSTRUCTIONS

1. Open the general ledger accounts and enter the balances as of April 1, 20--.
2. Record the transactions in a sales journal, a cash receipts journal, and a general journal. Use 6 as the page number for each of the special journals and 16 as the page number for the general journal.
3. Post the entries from the general journal to the general ledger.
4. Total, prove, and rule the special journals as of April 30, 20--.
5. Post the column totals from the special journals to the proper general ledger accounts.
6. Prepare the heading and the Revenue section of the firm's income statement for the month ended April 30.

GENERAL LEDGER ACCOUNTS

101	Cash	$ 8,200 Dr.
109	Notes Receivable	
111	Accounts Receivable	10,500 Dr.
401	Sales	
451	Sales Returns and Allowances	
452	Sales Discounts	

DATE		TRANSACTIONS
April	1	Sold merchandise for $3,700 to Alto Music Center; issued Invoice 1239 with terms of 2/10, n/30.
	3	Received a check for $1,430.80 from Band Shop in payment of Invoice 1237 of March 24 ($1,460), less a cash discount ($29.20).
	5	Sold merchandise for $1,270 in cash to a new customer who has not yet established credit.
	8	Sold merchandise for $4,840 to The Music Store; issued Invoice 1240 with terms of 2/10, n/30.
	10	Alto Music Center sent a check for $3,626 in payment of Invoice 1239 of April 1 ($3,700), less a cash discount ($74).
	15	Accepted a return of damaged merchandise from The Music Store; issued Credit Memorandum 108 for $700; the original sale was made on Invoice 1240 of April 8.
	19	Sold merchandise for $10,340 to Emporium Music Center; issued Invoice 1241 with terms of 2/10, n/30.
	23	Collected $2,960 from Golden Oldies Shop for Invoice 1232 of March 25.
	26	Accepted a two-month promissory note for $5,200 from Webster's Country Music Store in settlement of its overdue account; the note has an interest rate of 12 percent.
	28	Received a check for $10,133.20 from Emporium Music Center in payment of Invoice 1241, dated April 19 ($10,340), less a cash discount ($206.80).
	30	Sold merchandise for $8,990 to Jam Sounds, Inc.; issued Invoice 1242 with terms of 2/10, n/30.

Analyze: What total sales on account were made in the month of April prior to any returns or allowances?

Journalizing purchases, cash payments, and purchases discounts; posting to the general ledger.

◄ **Problem 9-4A**
Objectives 4, 5

The Joggers Outlet Center is a retail store. Transactions involving purchases and cash payments for the firm during June 20-- are listed below and on page 330. The general ledger accounts used to record these transactions appear below.

INSTRUCTIONS

1. Open the general ledger accounts and enter the balances as of June 1, 20--.
2. Record the transactions in a purchases journal, a cash payments journal, and a general journal. Use 7 as the page number for each of the special journals and 18 as the page number for the general journal.
3. Post the entries from the general journal and from the Other Accounts Debit section of the cash payments journal to the proper general ledger accounts.
4. Total, prove, and rule the special journals as of June 30.
5. Post the column totals from the special journals to the general ledger.
6. Show how the firm's net cost of purchases would be reported on its income statement for the month ended June 30.

GENERAL LEDGER ACCOUNTS

101 Cash	$19,660 Dr.	503 Purchases Ret. and Allow.
131 Equipment	28,000 Dr.	504 Purchases Discounts
201 Notes Payable		611 Rent Expense
205 Accounts Payable	2,440 Cr.	614 Salaries Expense
501 Purchases		617 Telephone Expense

DATE		TRANSACTIONS
June	1	Issued Check 1580 for $1,450 to pay the monthly rent.
	3	Purchased merchandise for $2,200 from Variety Shoe Shop, Invoice 476, dated May 30; the terms are 2/10, n/30.
	5	Purchased new store equipment for $3,000 from Wilson Company, Invoice 6790 dated June 4, net payable in 30 days.
	7	Issued Check 1581 for $1,380 to Hikers and Bikers Clothing Company, a creditor, in payment of Invoice 4233 of May 9.
	8	Issued Check 1582 for $2,156 to Variety Shoe Shop, a creditor, in payment of Invoice 476 dated May 30 ($2,200), less a cash discount ($44).
	12	Purchased merchandise for $1,700 from Mundy's Coat Shop, Invoice 2992, dated June 9, net due and payable in 30 days.
	15	Issued Check 1583 for $190 to pay the monthly telephone bill.

Continued

DATE		(9-4A cont.) TRANSACTIONS
June	18	Received Credit Memorandum 423 for $530 from Mundy's Coat Shop for defective goods that were returned; the original purchase was made on Invoice 2992 dated June 9.
	21	Purchased new store equipment for $8,000 from Smith Company; issued a three-month promissory note with interest at 11 percent.
	23	Purchased merchandise for $4,500 from Racing Products, Invoice 7219, dated June 20; terms of 2/10, n/30.
	25	Issued Check 1584 for $1,060 to Mundy's Coat Shop, a creditor, in payment of Invoice 1674 dated May 28.
	28	Issued Check 1585 for $4,410 to Racing Products, a creditor, in payment of Invoice 7219 of June 20 ($4,500), less a cash discount ($90).
	30	Purchased merchandise for $1,820 from Running Shoes Store, Invoice 1347, dated June 26; the terms are 1/10, n/30.
	30	Issued Check 1586 for $3,600 to pay the monthly salaries of the employees.

Analyze: What total liabilities does the company have at month-end?

Problem 9-5A ►
Objectives 9, 10

Preparing a bank reconciliation statement and journalizing entries to adjust the cash balance.

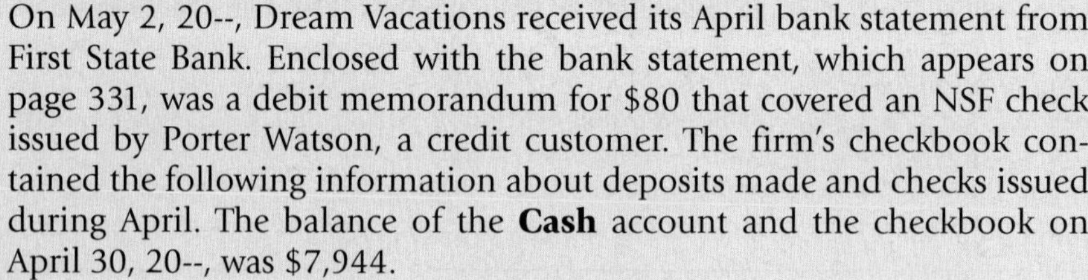
On May 2, 20--, Dream Vacations received its April bank statement from First State Bank. Enclosed with the bank statement, which appears on page 331, was a debit memorandum for $80 that covered an NSF check issued by Porter Watson, a credit customer. The firm's checkbook contained the following information about deposits made and checks issued during April. The balance of the **Cash** account and the checkbook on April 30, 20--, was $7,944.

DATE		TRANSACTIONS	
April	1	Balance	$12,178
	1	Check 1144	200
	3	Check 1145	600
	5	Deposit	700
	5	Check 1146	550
	10	Check 1147	4,000
	17	Check 1148	100
	19	Deposit	300
	22	Check 1149	18
	23	Deposit	300
	26	Check 1150	400
	28	Check 1151	36
	30	Check 1152	30
	30	Deposit	400

FIRST STATE BANK

Dream Vacations 895 Martin Luther King Drive Atlanta, GA 30305	Account Number: 56-7874-09 Period Ending April 30, 20--

CHECKS		DEPOSITS	DATE	BALANCE
			Beginning Balance	
			March 31	12,178.00
200.00-		700.00+	April 6	12,678.00
550.00-	600.00-		April 10	11,528.00
4,000.00-			April 13	7,528.00
3.30- SC			April 14	7,524.70
		300.00+	April 20	7,824.70
100.00-			April 22	7,724.70
		300.00+	April 25	8,024.70
18.00-			April 26	8,006.70
400.00-	80.00- DM		April 29	7,526.70

INSTRUCTIONS

1. Prepare a bank reconciliation statement for the firm as of April 30, 20--.
2. Record general journal entries for any items on the bank reconciliation statement that must be journalized. Date the entries May 2, 20--.

Analyze: What checks remain outstanding after the bank statement has been reconciled?

◄ Problem 9-6A
Objectives 9, 10

Preparing a bank reconciliation statement and journalizing entries to adjust the cash balance.

On August 31, 20--, the balance in the checkbook and the **Cash** account of the Jefferson Inn was $23,098. The balance shown on the bank statement on the same date was $23,564.10.

Notes

a. The firm's records indicate that a $1,759.20 deposit dated August 30 and a $953.60 deposit dated August 31 do not appear on the bank statement.

b. A service charge of $9 and a debit memorandum of $160 covering an NSF check have not yet been entered in the firm's records. (The check was issued by Don Grant, a credit customer.)

c. The following checks were issued but have not yet been paid by the bank.

Check 684, $221.00
Check 685, $23.20
Check 688, $476.40
Check 708, $1,152.60
Check 711, $154.70
Check 713, $290.00

d. A credit memorandum shows that the bank collected a $1,000 note receivable and interest of $30 for the firm. These amounts have not yet been entered in the firm's records.

INSTRUCTIONS

1. Prepare a bank reconciliation statement for the firm as of August 31.
2. Record general journal entries for items on the bank reconciliation statement that must be journalized. Date the entries September 4, 20--.

Analyze: What effect did the journal entries recorded as a result of the bank reconciliation have on the fundamental accounting equation?

Problem 9-7A ►
Objectives 9, 10

Correcting errors revealed by a bank reconciliation.

During the bank reconciliation process at Teel Company on May 2, 20--, the following two errors were discovered in the firm's records.

a. The checkbook and the cash payments journal indicated that Check 4021 dated April 10 was issued for $700 to make a cash purchase of supplies. However, examination of the canceled check and the listing on the bank statement showed that the actual amount of the check was $70.

b. The checkbook and the cash payments journal indicated that Check 4712 dated April 18 was issued for $332 to pay a utility bill. However, examination of the canceled check and the listing on the bank statement showed that the actual amount of the check was $372.

INSTRUCTIONS

1. Prepare the adjusted book balance section of the firm's bank reconciliation statement. The book balance as of April 30 was $17,126. The errors listed above are the only two items that affect the book balance.
2. Prepare general journal entries to correct the errors. Date the entries May 2, 20--. Check 4021 was debited to **Supplies** on April 10, and Check 4712 was debited to **Utilities Expense** on April 18.

Analyze: If the errors described had not been corrected, would net income for the period be overstated or understated? By what amount?

PROBLEM SET B

Problem 9-1B ►
Objectives 1, 2, 3

Journalizing cash receipts and posting to the general ledger.

The Reading Den is a retail store that sells books, cards, business supplies, and novelties. The firm's cash receipts during June 20-- are shown on page 333. The general ledger accounts used to record these transactions appear below.

INSTRUCTIONS

1. Open the general ledger accounts and enter the balances as of June 1.
2. Record the transactions in a cash receipts journal. (Use page 12.)
3. Post the individual entries from the Other Accounts Credit section of the cash receipts journal to the proper general ledger accounts.
4. Total, prove, and rule the cash receipts journal as of June 30.
5. From the cash receipts journal, post the totals to the general ledger.

GENERAL LEDGER ACCOUNTS

102 Cash	$ 600	231 Sales Tax Payable	$ 200
111 Accounts Receivable	4,200	302 James Walker, Capital	3,800
115 Notes Receivable	1,400	401 Sales	
129 Office Supplies	500	791 Interest Income	

DATE		TRANSACTIONS
June	3	Received $200 from Night Hawk Copy Center, a credit customer.
	4	Received a check for $1,500 from Juan Gonzo to pay his note receivable; the total included $100 of interest.
	5	Received a $180 refund for damaged supplies purchased from Cards-R-Us.
	7	Recorded cash sales of $1,400 plus sales tax payable of $84.
	10	Received $700 from Vicky Neal, a credit customer.
	13	James Walker, the owner, contributed additional capital of $5,000 to the business.
	14	Recorded cash sales of $800 plus sales tax of $48.
	18	Received $580 from David Jackson, a credit customer.
	19	Received $600 from Jane Todd, a credit customer.
	21	Recorded cash sales of $1,300 plus sales tax of $78.
	27	Received $400 from Richard Sneed, a credit customer.

Analyze: What are total assets for The Reading Den at June 30, 20--?

Journalizing cash payments and recording petty cash; posting to the general ledger.

◄ **Problem 9-2B**
Objectives 4, 5, 6

The cash payments of International Gift Shop, a retail business, for September are listed below and on pages 334–335. The general ledger accounts used to record these transactions appear below and on page 334.

INSTRUCTIONS

1. Open the general ledger accounts and enter the balances as of September 1, 20--.
2. Record all payments by check in a cash payments journal. Use 10 as the page number.
3. Record all payments from the petty cash fund on a petty cash analysis sheet with special columns for **Delivery Expense** and **Miscellaneous Expense.** Use 10 as the sheet number.
4. Post the individual entries from the Other Accounts Debit section of the cash payments journal to the proper general ledger accounts.
5. Total, prove, and rule the petty cash analysis sheet as of September 30, then record the replenishment of the fund and the final balance on the sheet.
6. Total, prove, and rule the cash payments journal as of September 30.
7. Post the column totals from the cash payments journal to the proper general ledger accounts.

GENERAL LEDGER ACCOUNTS

101	Cash	$10,765	Dr.
105	Petty Cash Fund		
141	Equipment	21,500	Dr.
201	Notes Payable	840	Cr.
205	Accounts Payable	3,985	Cr.
231	Sales Tax Payable	672	Cr.

GENERAL LEDGER ACCOUNTS (cont.)

302 Peter Chen, Drawing
451 Sales Ret. and Allow.
504 Purchases Discounts
511 Delivery Expense
620 Rent Expense
623 Salaries Expense
626 Telephone Expense
631 Interest Expense
634 Miscellaneous Expense

DATE		TRANSACTIONS
Sept.	1	Issued Check 394 for $672 to remit sales tax to the state tax commission.
	2	Issued Check 395 for $850 to pay the monthly rent.
	4	Issued Check 396 for $75 to establish a petty cash fund. (After journalizing this transaction, be sure to enter it on the first line of the petty cash analysis sheet.)
	5	Issued Check 397 for $1,176 to Crystal Glassware, a creditor, in payment of Invoice 9367, dated August 28 ($1,200), less a cash discount ($24).
	6	Paid $10.50 from the petty cash fund for delivery service, Petty Cash Voucher 1.
	9	Purchased store equipment for $500; issued Check 398.
	11	Paid $8 from the petty cash fund for office supplies, Petty Cash Voucher 2 (charge to **Miscellaneous Expense**).
	13	Issued Check 399 for $485 to Scott Company, a creditor, in payment of Invoice 2579, dated August 15.
	14	Issued Check 400 for $57 to a customer as a cash refund for a defective watch that was returned; the original sale was made for cash.
	16	Paid $15 from the petty cash fund for a personal withdrawal by Peter Chen, the owner, Petty Cash Voucher 3.
	18	Issued Check 401 for $92 to pay the monthly telephone bill.
	21	Issued Check 402 for $735 to European Imports, a creditor, in payment of Invoice 2218, dated September 13 ($750), less a cash discount ($15).
	23	Paid $12 from the petty cash fund for postage stamps, Petty Cash Voucher 4.
	24	Issued Check 403 for $854 to Simpson Corporation in payment of an $840 promissory note and interest of $14.
	26	Issued Check 404 for $620 to Pacific Ceramics, a creditor, in payment of Invoice 1035, dated August 29.
	27	Paid $9 from the petty cash fund for delivery service, Petty Cash Voucher 5.
	28	Issued Check 405 for $1,200 to Peter Chen, the owner, as a withdrawal for personal use.
		Continued

DATE	(9-2B cont.) TRANSACTIONS
Sept. 30	Issued Check 406 for $1,900 to pay the monthly salaries of the employees.
30	Issued Check 407 for $68 to replenish the petty cash fund. (Foot the columns of the petty cash analysis sheet in order to determine the accounts that should be debited and the amounts involved.)

Analyze: What was the amount of total debits to general ledger liability accounts during the month of September?

Journalizing sales and cash receipts and posting to the general ledger.

◄ **Problem 9-3B**
Objectives 1, 2, 3

Thomas Construction Company is a wholesale business. The transactions involving sales and cash receipts for the firm during August 20-- are listed below and on page 336. The general ledger accounts used to record these transactions are listed below.

INSTRUCTIONS

1. Open the general ledger accounts and enter the balances as of August 1, 20--.
2. Record the transactions in a sales journal, a cash receipts journal, and a general journal. Use 9 as the page number for each of the special journals and 25 as the page number for the general journal.
3. Post the entries from the general journal to the proper general ledger accounts.
4. Total, prove, and rule the special journals as of August 31, 20--.
5. Post the column totals from the special journals to the proper general ledger accounts.
6. Prepare the heading and the Revenue section of the firm's income statement for the month ended August 31, 20--.

GENERAL LEDGER ACCOUNTS

101 Cash	$12,680 Dr.	401 Sales	
109 Notes Receivable		451 Sales Returns and Allowances	
111 Accounts Receivable	20,200 Dr.	452 Sales Discounts	

DATE	TRANSACTIONS
Aug. 1	Received a check for $5,390 from Builders Supply Company in payment of Invoice 7782 dated July 21 ($5,500), less a cash discount ($110).
2	Sold merchandise for $14,960 to Wilson Builders; issued Invoice 7928 with terms of 2/10, n/30.
4	Accepted a three-month promissory note for $9,000 from Henderson Homes to settle its overdue account; the note has an interest rate of 11 percent.
7	Sold merchandise for $18,690 to Colonial Construction Company; issued Invoice 7929 with terms of 2/10, n/30.
11	Collected $14,660.80 from Wilson Builders for Invoice 7928 dated August 2 ($14,960), less a cash discount ($299.20).

Continued

DATE	(9-3B cont.) TRANSACTIONS
Aug. 14	Sold merchandise for $3,500 in cash to a new customer who has not yet established credit.
16	Colonial Construction Company sent a check for $18,316.20 in payment of Invoice 7929 dated August 7 ($18,690), less a cash discount ($373.80).
22	Sold merchandise for $6,260 to Modern Homes; issued Invoice 7930 with terms of 2/10, n/30.
24	Received a check for $5,000 from Harrison Homes Center to pay Invoice 7778, dated July 23.
26	Accepted a return of damaged merchandise from Modern Homes; issued Credit Memorandum 311 for $420; the original sale was made on Invoice 7930, dated August 22.
31	Sold merchandise for $12,740 to Warren County Builders; issued Invoice 7931 with terms of 2/10, n/30.

Analyze: What total sales on account were made in August? Include sales returns and allowances in your computation.

Problem 9-4B ►
Objectives 4, 5

Journalizing purchases, cash payments, and purchase discounts; posting to the general ledger.

Best Value Center is a retail store that sells a variety of household appliances. Transactions involving purchases and cash payments for the firm during December 20-- are listed on page 337. The general ledger accounts used to record these transactions appear below.

INSTRUCTIONS

1. Open the general ledger accounts and enter the balances in these accounts as of December 1, 20--.
2. Record the transactions in a purchases journal, a cash payments journal, and a general journal. Use 11 as the page number for each of the special journals and 32 as the page number for the general journal.
3. Post the entries from the general journal and from the Other Accounts Debit section of the cash payments journal to the proper accounts in the general ledger.
4. Total, prove, and rule the special journals as of December 31, 20--.
5. Post the column totals from the special journals to the general ledger accounts.
6. Show how the firm's cost of purchases would be reported on its income statement for the month ended December 31, 20--.

GENERAL LEDGER ACCOUNTS

101 Cash	$45,700 Dr.
131 Equipment	62,000 Dr.
201 Notes Payable	
205 Accounts Payable	3,800 Cr.
501 Purchases	
503 Purchases Returns and Allowances	
504 Purchases Discounts	
611 Rent Expense	
614 Salaries Expense	
617 Telephone Expense	

DATE		TRANSACTIONS
Dec.	1	Purchased merchandise for $6,400 from Axis Products for Homes, Invoice 5965, dated November 28; the terms are 2/10, n/30.
	2	Issued Check 1506 for $2,800 to pay the monthly rent.
	4	Purchased new store equipment for $13,000 from Blaine Company; issued a two-month promissory note with interest at 10 percent.
	6	Issued Check 1507 for $6,272 to Axis Products for Homes, a creditor, in payment of Invoice 5965, dated November 28 ($6,400), less a cash discount ($128).
	10	Purchased merchandise for $8,900 from the Parr Corporation, Invoice 9115, dated December 7; terms of 2/10, n/30.
	13	Issued Check 1508 for $240 to pay the monthly telephone bill.
	15	Issued Check 1509 for $8,722 to Parr Corporation, a creditor, in payment of Invoice 9115, dated December 7 ($8,900), less a cash discount ($178).
	18	Purchased merchandise for $11,800 from Appliance Center, Invoice 8372, dated December 16; terms of 3/10, n/30.
	20	Purchased new store equipment for $4,000 from Security Systems Inc., Invoice 635, dated December 17, net payable in 45 days.
	21	Issued Check 1510 for $3,800 to Hogan Lighting and Appliances, a creditor, in payment of Invoice 1378, dated November 23.
	22	Purchased merchandise for $5,300 from Davis Corporation, Invoice 6131, dated December 19, net due in 30 days.
	24	Issued Check 1511 for $11,446 to Appliance Center, a creditor, in payment of Invoice 8372, dated December 16 ($11,800), less a cash discount ($354).
	28	Received Credit Memorandum 128 for $900 from Security Systems Inc. for damaged goods that were returned; the original purchase was made on Invoice 635, dated December 17.
	31	Issued Check 1512 for $5,400 to pay the monthly salaries of the employees.

Analyze: List the dates for transactions in December that would be categorized as expenses of the business.

◄ **Problem 9-5B**
Objectives 9, 10

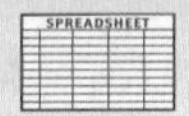

Preparing a bank reconciliation statement and journalizing entries to adjust the cash balance.

On October 5, 20--, Sam Yao, Attorney at Law, received his September bank statement from First Security National Bank. Enclosed with the bank statement, which appears on page 338, was a debit memorandum for $112 that covered an NSF check issued by Julia Anderson, a credit customer. The firm's checkbook contained the following information about deposits made and checks issued during September. The balance of the **Cash** account and the checkbook on September 30 was $16,622.

DATE		TRANSACTIONS	
Sept.	1	Balance	$13,000
	1	Check 124	200
	3	Check 125	20
	3	Deposit	1,000
	6	Check 126	450
	10	Deposit	820
	11	Check 127	400
	15	Check 128	150
	21	Check 129	120
	22	Deposit	1,460
	25	Check 130	8
	25	Check 131	40
	27	Check 132	70
	28	Deposit	1,800

FIRST SECURITY NATIONAL BANK

Sam Yao, Attorney-at-Law
2222 Sam Houston Lane
Columbus, OH 44106

Account Number: 11-4568-03

Period Ending September 30, 20--

CHECKS		DEPOSITS	DATE	BALANCE
Beginning Balance			August 31	13,000.00
		1,000.00+	September 3	14,000.00
200.00-			September 6	13,800.00
400.00-	20.00-	820.00+	September 11	14,200.00
450.00-			September 15	13,750.00
120.00-			September 19	13,630.00
		1,460.00+	September 23	15,090.00
40.00-	8.00-		September 25	15,042.00
7.50- SC	112.00- DM		September 28	14,922.50

INSTRUCTIONS

1. Prepare a bank reconciliation statement for the firm as of September 30, 20--.
2. Record general journal entries for any items on the bank reconciliation statement that must be journalized. Date the entries October 5, 20--.

Analyze: How many checks were paid (cleared the bank) according to the September 30 bank statement?

Preparing a bank reconciliation statement and journalizing entries to adjust the cash balance.

◄ **Problem 9-6B**
Objectives 9, 10

On June 30, 20--, the balance in Wilson Builder's checkbook and **Cash** account was $12,837.18. The balance shown on the bank statement on the same date was $15,084.06.

Notes

a. The following checks were issued but have not yet been paid by the bank: Check 335 for $297.90, Check 337 for $195, and Check 339 for $850.80.

b. A credit memorandum shows that the bank has collected a $3,000 note receivable and interest of $60 for the firm. These amounts have not yet been entered in the firm's records.

c. The firm's records indicate that a deposit of $1,888.14 made on June 30 does not appear on the bank statement.

d. A service charge of $28.68 and a debit memorandum of $240 covering an NSF check have not yet been entered in the firm's records. (The check was issued by Alan Hutchins, a credit customer.)

INSTRUCTIONS

1. Prepare a bank reconciliation statement for the firm as of June 30, 20--.

2. Record general journal entries for any items on the bank reconciliation statement that must be journalized. Date the entries July 3, 20--.

Analyze: After all journal entries have been recorded and posted, what is the balance in the **Cash** account?

Correcting errors revealed by a bank reconciliation.

◄ **Problem 9-7B**
Objectives 9, 10

During the bank reconciliation process at ABC Liquidators Corporation on March 3, 20--, the following errors were discovered in the firm's records.

a. The checkbook and the cash payments journal indicated that Check 1285 dated February 7 was issued for $158 to pay for hauling expenses. However, examination of the canceled check and the listing on the bank statement showed that the actual amount of the check was $154.

b. The checkbook and the cash payments journal indicated that Check 1292 dated February 23 was issued for $202 to pay a telephone bill. However, examination of the canceled check and the listing on the bank statement showed that the actual amount of the check was $220.

INSTRUCTIONS

1. Prepare the adjusted book balance section of the firm's bank reconciliation statement. The book balance as of February 28, 20--, was $38,902. The errors listed are the only two items that affect the book balance.

2. Prepare general journal entries to correct the errors. Date the entries March 3, 20--. Check 1285 was debited to **Hauling Expense** on February 7, and Check 1292 was debited to **Telephone Expense** on February 23.

Analyze: What net change to the **Cash** account occurred as a result of the correcting journal entries?

CHAPTER 9 CHALLENGE PROBLEM

Special Journals

During September 20-- Jo's Specialty Shop, a retail store, had the transactions listed on pages 342–343. The general ledger accounts used to record these transactions are provided on page 341.

INSTRUCTIONS

1. Open the general ledger accounts and enter the balances as of September 1, 20--.
2. Record the transactions in a sales journal, a cash receipts journal, a purchases journal, a cash payments journal, and a general journal. Use page 11 as the page number for each of the special journals and page 31 as the page number for the general journal.
3. Post the entries from the general journal to the proper general ledger accounts.
4. Post the entries from the Other Accounts Credit section of the cash receipts journal to the proper general ledger accounts.
5. Post the entries from the Other Accounts Debit section of the cash payments journal to the proper general ledger accounts.
6. Total, prove, and rule the special journals as of September 30.
7. Post the column totals from the special journals to the proper general ledger accounts.
8. Set up an accounts receivable ledger for Jo's Specialty Shop. Open an account for each of the customers listed below, and enter the balances as of September 1. All of these customers have terms of n/30.

Credit Customers

Name	Balance 9/01/--
Marty Cooper	
Theresa Den	$ 630.00
Kevin Kaylor	865.20
Lacie Lawson	
George Polk	525.00
Michael Turner	
Ralph Wall	1,050.00

9. Post the individual entries from the sales journal, cash receipts journal, and the general journal to the accounts receivable subsidiary ledger.
10. Prepare a schedule of accounts receivable for September 30, 20--.
11. Check the total of the schedule of accounts receivable against the balance of the **Accounts Receivable** account in the general ledger. The two amounts should be the same.

Creditors		
Name	Balance 9/01/--	Terms
Baker Mills		n/45
McDavid Corporation	$11,000	1/10, n/30
Northern Craft Products		2/10, n/30
Reed Company		n/30
Robertson Mills		2/10, n/30
Sadie's Floor Coverings	3,880	n/30
Wilson Products	4,240	n/30

12. Set up an accounts payable subsidiary ledger for Jo's Specialty Shop. Open an account for each of the creditors listed above, and enter the balances as of September 1, 20--.
13. Post the individual entries from the purchases journal, the cash payments journal, and the general journal to the accounts payable subsidiary ledger.
14. Prepare a schedule of accounts payable for September 1, 20--.
15. Check the total of the schedule of accounts payable against the balance of the **Accounts Payable** account in the general ledger. The two amounts should be the same.

GENERAL LEDGER ACCOUNTS

101	Cash	$37,890.00 Dr.
109	Notes Receivable	
111	Accounts Receivable	3,070.20 Dr.
121	Supplies	1,420.00 Dr.
201	Notes Payable	
205	Accounts Payable	19,120.00 Cr.
231	Sales Tax Payable	
301	Eric Flores, Capital	91,200.00 Cr.
401	Sales	
451	Sales Returns and Allowances	
501	Purchases	
502	Freight In	
503	Purchases Returns and Allowances	
504	Purchases Discounts	
611	Cash Short or Over	
614	Rent Expense	
617	Salaries Expense	
619	Utilities Expense	

DATE	TRANSACTIONS
Sept. 1	Received a check for $525.00 from George Polk to pay his account.
1	Issued Check 1372 for $3,880 to Sadie's Floor Coverings, a creditor, in payment of Invoice 5236 dated August 3.
2	Issued Check 1373 for $2,400 to pay the monthly rent.
3	Sold a table on credit for $1,330 plus sales tax of $66.50 to Lacie Lawson, Sales Slip 1972.
5	Eric Flores, the owner, invested an additional $14,000 cash in the business in order to expand operations.
6	Had cash sales of $3,560 plus sales tax of $178 during the period September 1–6; there was a cash shortage of $10.
6	Purchased carpeting for $8,900 from Robertson Mills, Invoice 728, dated September 3; terms of 2/10, n/30.
6	Issued Check 1374 for $122 to City Trucking Company to pay the freight charge on goods received from Robertson Mills.
8	Purchased store supplies for $740 from Reed Company, Invoice 0442, dated September 6, net amount due in 30 days.
8	Sold chairs on credit for $1,860 plus sales tax of $93.00 to Michael Turner, Sales Slip 1973.
11	Accepted a two-month promissory note for $1,050 from Ralph Wall to settle his overdue account; the note has an interest rate of 10 percent.
11	Issued Check 1375 for $8,722 to Robertson Mills, a creditor, in payment of Invoice 728 dated September 3 ($8,900) less a cash discount ($178).
13	Had cash sales of $3,920 plus sales tax of $196 during the period September 8–13.
14	Purchased carpeting for $7,400 plus a freight charge of $84 from Wilson Products, Invoice 3594, dated September 11, net due and payable in 30 days.
15	Collected $630 on account from Theresa Den.
17	Gave a two-month promissory note for $11,000 to McDavid Corporation, a creditor, to settle an overdue balance; the note bears interest at 12 percent.
19	Sold a lamp on credit to Marty Cooper for $480 plus sales tax of $24, Sales Slip 1974.
20	Had cash sales of $3,300 plus sales tax of $165 during the period September 15–20; there was a cash shortage of $4.50.
21	Purchased area rugs for $5,600 from Northern Craft Products, Invoice 776, dated September 18; the terms are 2/10, n/30.
	Continued

DATE	(cont.) TRANSACTIONS
Sept. 22	Issued Check 1376 for $360 to pay the monthly utility bill.
23	Granted an allowance to Marty Cooper for scratches on the lamp that she bought on Sales Slip 1974 of September 19; issued Credit Memorandum 651 for $42, which includes a price reduction of $40 and sales tax of $2.
24	Received Credit Memorandum 14 for $600 from Northern Craft Products for a damaged rug that was returned; the original purchase was made on Invoice 776 dated September 18.
24	Kevin Kaylor sent a check for $865.20 to pay the balance he owes.
25	Issued Check 1377 for $3,300 to make a cash purchase of merchandise.
26	Issued Check 1378 for $4,900 to Northern Craft Products, a creditor, in payment of Invoice 776 of September 18 ($5,600), less a return ($600) and a cash discount ($100).
27	Purchased hooked rugs for $8,200 plus a freight charge of $112 from Baker Mills, Invoice 1368, dated September 23, net payable in 45 days.
27	Had cash sales of $4,310 plus sales tax of $215.50 during the period September 22–27.
28	Issued Check 1379 for $4,240 to Wilson Products, a creditor, in payment of Invoice 1184 dated August 30.
29	Sold a cabinet on credit to Theresa Den for $1,180 plus sales tax of $59, Sales Slip 1975.
30	Had cash sales of $1,440 plus sales tax of $72 for September 29–30; there was a cash overage of $2.20.
30	Issued Check 1380 for $5,200 to pay the monthly salaries of the employees.

Analyze: What were the total cash payments for September?

CHAPTER 9 CRITICAL THINKING PROBLEM

Cash Controls

James Wilson is the owner of a successful small construction company. He spends most of his time out of the office supervising work at various construction sites, leaving the operation of the office to the company's cashier/bookkeeper, Roberta Smith. Roberta makes bank deposits, pays the company's bills, maintains the accounting records, and prepares monthly bank reconciliations.

Recently a friend told James that while he was at a party he overheard Roberta bragging that she paid for her new dress with money from the company's cash receipts. She said her boss would never know because he never checks the cash records.

James admits that he does not check on Roberta 's work. He now wants to know if Roberta is stealing from him. He asks you to examine the company's cash records to determine whether Roberta has stolen cash from the business and, if so, how much.

Your examination of the company's cash records reveals the following information.

1. Roberta prepared the following August 31, 20--, bank reconciliation.

Balance in books, August 31, 20--		$37,572
Additions:		
Outstanding checks		
Check 2778	$1,584	
Check 2792	3,638	
Check 2814	768	5,390
		$42,962
Deductions:		
Deposit in transit, August 28, 20--	$9,764	
Bank service charge	20	9,784
Balance on bank statement, July 31, 20--		$33,178

2. An examination of the general ledger shows the **Cash** account with a balance of $37,572 on August 31, 20--.
3. The August 31 bank statement shows a balance of $33,178.
4. The August 28 deposit of $9,764 does not appear on the August 31 bank statement.
5. A comparison of canceled checks returned with the August 31 bank statement with the cash payments journal reveals the following checks as outstanding:

Check 2419	$ 526
Check 2508	2,436
Check 2724	972
Check 2778	1,584
Check 2792	3,638
Check 2814	768

Prepare a bank statement using the format presented in this chapter for the month of August. Assume there were no bank or bookkeeping errors in August. Did Roberta take cash from the company? If so, how much and how did she try to conceal the theft? What changes would you recommend to James to provide better internal control over cash?

Business Connections

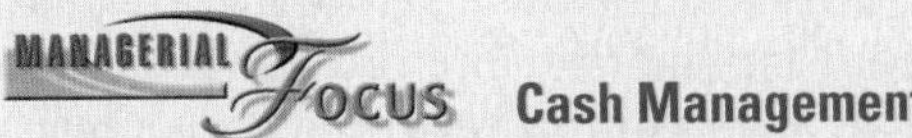

Cash Management

◄ Connection 1

1. The new accountant for Asheville Hardware Center, a large retail store, found the following weaknesses in the firm's cash-handling procedures. How would you explain to management why each of these procedures should be changed?
   a. No cash register proof is prepared at the end of each day. The amount of money in the register is considered the amount of cash sales for the day.
   b. Small payments are sometimes made from the currency and coins in the cash register. (The store has no petty cash fund.)
   c. During busy periods for the firm, cash receipts are sometimes kept on the premises for several days before a bank deposit is made.
   d. When funds are removed from the cash register at the end of each day, they are placed in an unlocked office cabinet until they are deposited.
   e. The person who makes the bank deposits also records them in the checkbook, journalizes cash receipts, and reconciles the bank statement.
2. Why should management be concerned about having accurate information about the firm's cash position available at all times?
3. Many banks now offer a variety of computer services to clients. Why is it not advisable for a firm to pay its bank to complete the reconciliation procedure at the end of each month?
4. Assume that you are the newly hired controller at Norton Company and that you have observed the following banking procedures in use at the firm. Would you change any of these procedures? Why or why not?
   a. A blank endorsement is made on all checks to be deposited.
   b. The checkbook is kept on the top of a desk so that it will be handy.
   c. The same person prepares bank deposits, issues checks, and reconciles the bank statement.
   d. The reconciliation process usually takes place two or three weeks after the bank statement is received.
   e. The bank statement and the canceled checks are thrown away after the reconciliation process is completed.
   f. As a shortcut in the reconciliation process, there is no attempt to compare the endorsements on the back of the canceled checks with the names of the payees shown on the face of these checks.
5. Why should management be concerned about achieving effective internal control over cash receipts and cash payments?
6. How does management benefit when cash transactions are recorded quickly and efficiently?
7. Why do some companies require that all employees who handle cash be bonded?
8. Why is it a good practice for a business to make all payments by check except for minor payments from a petty cash fund?

Connection 2 ► **Ethical DILEMMA** **Out of Balance** Assume that you are a sales clerk in a retail clothing store. The owner of the business frequently takes cash out of your cash register without explanation and provides you with an IOU slip so that you can reconcile the cash intake with the cash register tape. When you questioned the owner about the use of the funds, he replied, "It's my store, I can take whatever I want."

What do you think of the owner's actions? Is he being ethical?

Connection 3 ► *Street WISE:* Questions from the Real World **Cash** Refer to the *1999 Annual Report* of The Home Depot, Inc. in Appendix B.

1. Review the consolidated balance sheet. Store operations provide the company with a significant source of cash. What amount is reported for "Cash and Cash Equivalents" for January 30, 2000? For January 31, 1999? By what percentage has this figure increased?
2. Locate the report named "Selected Consolidated Statements of Earnings Data." How many sales transactions were reported for 1999? What is the average sale per transaction? If 40 percent of these sales were comprised of cash transactions (as opposed to credit transactions), what total cash receipts would have been recorded in 1999?

Connection 4 ► Armstrong **FINANCIAL STATEMENT ANALYSIS** **Balance Sheet** Armstrong Holdings, Inc. is a global leader in the design, innovation, and manufacture of floors and ceilings. In 1999 Armstrong's net sales totaled more than $3.4 billion. The following excerpt was taken from the company's *1999 Annual Report.*

Consolidated Balance Sheets

	As of December 31	
Millions except for numbers of shares and per-share data	*1999*	*1998*
ASSETS		
Current Assets:		
*Cash and cash equivalents**	*$ 35.6*	*$ 38.2*
Accounts and notes receivable	*436.0*	*440.4*
Total current assets	*$1,029.9*	*$1,121.1*

** Cash and Cash Equivalents: Short-term investments that have maturities of three months or less when purchased are considered to be cash equivalents.*

Analyze:

1. What percentage of total current assets is made up of cash and cash equivalents for fiscal 1999?
2. Cash receipt and cash payment transactions affect the total value of a company's assets. By what amount did the category "Cash and cash equivalents" change from 1998 to 1999?
3. If accountants at Armstrong failed to record cash receipts of $125,000 on the final day of fiscal 1999, what impact would this error have on the balance sheet category "Cash and cash equivalents"?

Analyze Online: Find the *Corporate Information* link on the Web site for Armstrong Holdings, Inc. **(www.armstrong.com).** Review the most recent annual report.

4. What amount is reported for the balance sheet line item "Cash and cash equivalents"?
5. Does this amount represent an increase or decrease from the amount reported in fiscal 1999? By what amount has this figure changed?

Extending the Thought **E-commerce** A small gift shop has just launched a new Web site where customers can purchase products. The Web site's e-commerce software systems automatically generate daily sales reports and forward the reports to the gift shop's accountant. The gift shop uses an online e-cash processing company, which deposits cash receipts to the gift shop's bank account automatically. What strategies should the gift shop implement to ensure proper accounting for cash receipts generated from online sales?

◄ **Connection 5**

Business Communication **Agenda** You have just been hired as the chief financial officer for a software development company. In an effort to familiarize yourself with the processes of the accounting office, you have requested a meeting with the accounting manager to discuss the company's internal control procedures. To prepare for the meeting, create a list of questions and topics that you would like to discuss. Your list should include questions that will help you verify that the department is enforcing the appropriate controls over cash payments and cash receipts.

◄ **Connection 6**

TeamWork **Petty Cash** Your photo supply store has established a petty cash fund of $200. Form two teams to enact five petty cash transactions.

1. Team 1 should create five receipts that will represent payments from the petty cash fund. Present each receipt individually to Team 2 to receive cash from the fund.
2. Team 2 will act as the manager of the petty cash fund and should prepare the appropriate vouchers as payments are made.
3. After all five payments are made, Team 2 should prepare a petty cash analysis sheet so that the petty cash fund can be replenished to its original balance.

◄ **Connection 7**

interNET CONNECTION **"The Fed"** The Federal Reserve System is the central bank of the United States. Go to the Web site at **www.federalreserve.gov.** From the *Board of Governors* site, access the related Web site for the *National Information Center of Banking.* Name the three largest banks and the total assets of each bank. From the *Board of Governors* site, access the site for *Federal Reserve Banks.* In which of the 12 Federal Reserve Districts do you live?

◄ **Connection 8**

Answers to Self Reviews

Answers to Section 1 Self Review

1. A written promise to pay a specified amount of money on a specified date. To grant credit in certain sales transactions or to replace open-account credit when a customer has an overdue balance.
2. Amounts from the Accounts Receivable Credit column are posted as credits to the individual customers' accounts in the accounts receivable subsidiary ledger daily. The total of the Accounts Receivable Credit column is posted as a credit to the **Accounts Receivable** control account in the general ledger at the end of the accounting period.
3. A cash shortage occurs when cash in the register is less than the audit tape; an overage occurs when cash is more than the audit tape. Debit shortages and credit overages in the **Cash Short or Over** account.
4. **d.** all of the above
5. **b.** cash receipts journal
6. The frequency of cash discrepancies indicates that a problem exists in the handling of the cash.

Answers to Section 2 Self Review

1. To make small expenditures that require currency and coins.
2. Record the name of the owner's drawing account and the amount in the Other Accounts Debit section of the cash payments journal, and record the amount in the Cash Credit column.
3. Amounts in the Other Accounts Debit section are posted individually to the general ledger accounts daily. The total of the Other Accounts Debit column is not posted because the individual amounts were previously posted to the general ledger.
4. **a.** cash payments journal
5. **b.** February 4
6. You should explain to your employer that she must keep all receipts regardless of the amount. Ask your employer to complete a voucher for that amount, then record the entry in the proper account.

Answers to Section 3 Self Review

1. A check that is dated in the future. It should not be deposited before its date because the drawer of the check may not have sufficient funds in the bank to cover the check at the current time.
2. Items in the second section of the bank reconciliation statement require entries in the firm's financial records to correct the **Cash** account balance and make it equal to the checkbook balance. These may include bank fees, debit memorandums, NSF checks, and interest income.
3. Endorsement is the legal process by which the payee transfers ownership of the check to the bank.
4. **a.** canceled checks
5. **d.** Deposits in transit
6. Disagree. Good internal control requires separation of duties.

Answers to Comprehensive Self Review

1. Checks, money orders, and funds on deposit in a bank as well as currency and coins.
2. They eliminate repetition in postings; the initial recording of transactions is faster.
3. A full endorsement contains the name of the payee plus the name of the firm or bank to whom the check is payable.
4. A record of when a payment is made from petty cash, the amount and purpose of the expenditure, and the account to be charged.
5. Petty cash can be replenished at any time if the fund runs low, but it should be replenished at the end of each month so that all expenses for the month are recorded.

PART 3

Payroll Records and Procedures

SAS e-Intelligence

Executives at SAS Institute Inc., a leading provider of business intelligence software and services, believe that happy employees are productive ones. The software leader's award-winning culture earned a No. 2 ranking in *Fortune* magazine's "100 Best Companies to Work For in America" in 2000.

Thinking Critically

What types of benefits, philosophies, or company policies contribute to a happy workforce?

CHAPTER 10

Learning Objectives

1. Explain the major federal laws relating to employee earnings and withholding.
2. Compute gross earnings of employees.
3. Determine employee deductions for social security tax.
4. Determine employee deductions for Medicare tax.
5. Determine employee deductions for income tax.
6. Enter gross earnings, deductions, and net pay in the payroll register.
7. Journalize payroll transactions in the general journal.
8. Maintain an earnings record for each employee.
9. Define the accounting terms new to this chapter.

Payroll Computations, Records, and Payment

New Terms

- Commission basis
- Compensation record
- Employee
- Employee's Withholding Allowance Certificate (Form W-4)
- Exempt employees
- Federal unemployment taxes
- Hourly rate basis
- Independent contractor
- Individual earnings record
- Medicare tax
- Payroll register
- Piece-rate basis
- Salary basis
- Social Security Act
- Social security (FICA) tax
- State unemployment taxes
- Tax-exempt wages
- Time and a half
- Wage-bracket table method
- Workers' compensation insurance

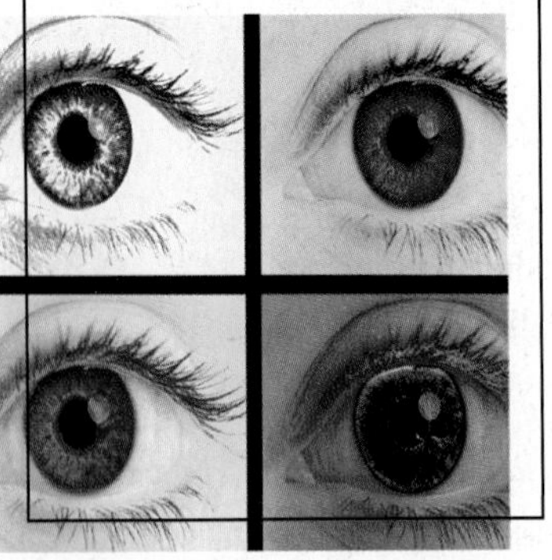

Adobe

www.adobe.com

"Hire the best and treat them well." Adobe Systems Incorporated is committed to providing rewarding work experiences for its employees. The company was recognized by *Inter@ctive Week* magazine as one of the "Top 10 Companies to Work For"[1] and placed number 30 in *Fortune* magazine's "100 Best Companies to Work for in America".[2]

Adobe Systems Incorporated distributes paychecks for a workforce of 2,800 employees worldwide. Salaried and hourly wages are computed. Calculations for federal, state, and social security taxes are made and employee payroll records must be updated after each payroll period.

[1] Adobe Press Release, April 12, 2000

[2] Adobe Press Release, December 20, 2000

Thinking Critically

What types of benefits would be important to you if you worked for a company like Adobe Systems Incorporated?

For more information on Adobe Systems Incorporated, go to: collegeaccounting.glencoe.com.

Section 1

Section Objective

1 Explain the major federal laws relating to employee earnings and withholding.

WHY IT'S IMPORTANT
Tax and labor laws protect the rights of both the employee and the employer. Income tax withholding laws ensure continued funding of certain federal and state programs.

Terms to Learn

employee
federal unemployment taxes
independent contractor
Medicare tax
Social Security Act
social security (FICA) tax
state unemployment taxes
time and a half
workers' compensation insurance

Payroll Laws and Taxes

A large component of the activity of any business is concerned with payroll work. Payroll accounting is so important that it requires special consideration.

Who Is an Employee?

Payroll accounting relates only to earnings of those individuals classified as employees. An **employee** is hired by and works under the control and direction of the employer. Usually the employer provides the tools or equipment used by the employee, sets the employee's working hours, and determines how the employee completes the job. Examples of employees are the company president, the bookkeeper, the sales clerk, and the warehouse worker.

In contrast to an employee, an **independent contractor** is paid by the company to carry out a specific task or job, but is not under the direct supervision or control of the company. The independent contractor is told what needs to be done, but the means of doing the job is left to the independent contractor. Examples of independent contractors are the accountant who performs the independent audit, the outside attorney who renders legal advice, and the consultant who installs a new accounting system.

This text addresses issues related to employees but not to independent contractors. When dealing with independent contractors, businesses do not have to follow federal labor laws regulating minimum rates of pay and maximum hours of employment. The business is not required to withhold or match payroll taxes on amounts paid to independent contractors.

1 Objective

Explain the major federal laws relating to employee earnings and withholding.

Federal Employee Earnings and Withholding Laws

Since the 1930s many federal and state laws have affected the relationship between employers and employees. Some of these laws deal with working conditions, including hours and earnings. Others relate to income tax withholding. Some concern taxes that are levied against the employer to provide specific employee benefits.

The Fair Labor Standards Act

The *Fair Labor Standards Act* of 1938, often referred to as the Wage and Hour Law, applies only to firms engaged directly or indirectly in interstate commerce. It sets a minimum hourly rate of pay and maximum hours of work per week to be performed at the regular rate of pay. When this book was printed, the minimum hourly rate of pay was $5.15, and the maximum number of hours at the regular pay rate was 40 hours per week. When an employee works more than 40 hours in a week, the employee earns at least one and one-half times the regular hourly rate of pay. This overtime rate is called **time and a half**. Even if the federal law does not apply to them, many employers pay time and a half for overtime because of union contracts or simply as good business practice.

Social Security Tax

The *Federal Insurance Contributions Act (FICA)* is commonly referred to as the **Social Security Act**. The act, first passed in the 1930s, has been amended frequently. The Social Security Act provides the following benefits:

- Retirement benefits, or pension, when a worker reaches age 62.
- Benefits for the dependents of the retired worker.
- Benefits for the worker and the worker's dependents when the worker is disabled.

These retirement and disability benefits are paid by the **social security tax**, sometimes called the **FICA tax**. Both the employer and the employee pay an equal amount of social security tax. The employer is required to withhold social security tax from the employee's pay. Periodically the employer sends the social security tax withheld to the federal government.

The rate of the social security tax and the calendar year earnings base to which it applies are frequently changed by Congress. In recent years, the social security tax rate has remained constant at 6.2 percent. The earnings base to which the tax applies has increased yearly. In 2000 the social security tax rate was 6.2 percent of the first $76,200 of salary or wages paid to each employee. In examples and problems, this text uses a social security tax rate of 6.2 percent of the first $76,200 of salary or wages.

Medicare Tax

The Medicare tax is closely related to the social security tax. Prior to 1992 it was a part of the social security tax. The **Medicare tax** is a tax levied equally on employees and employers to provide medical care for the employee and the employee's spouse after each has reached age 65.

In recent years, the Medicare tax rate has remained constant at 1.45 percent. The Medicare tax applies to all salaries and wages paid during the year. The employer is required to withhold the Medicare tax from the employee's pay and periodically send it to the federal government.

Note that the social security tax has an earnings base limit. The Medicare tax does not have an earnings base limit. The Medicare tax applies to *all* earnings paid during the year.

Important!

Wage Base Limit

The social security tax has a wage base limit. There is no wage base limit for the Medicare tax. All salaries and wages are subject to the Medicare tax.

Federal Income Tax

Employers are required to withhold from employees' earnings an estimated amount of income tax that will be payable by the employee on the earnings. The amount depends on several factors. Later in this chapter you will learn how to determine the amount to withhold from an employee's paycheck.

State and Local Taxes

Most states, and many local governments, require employers to withhold income taxes from employees' earnings to prepay the employees' state and local income taxes. These rules are generally almost identical to those governing federal income tax withholding, but they require separate general ledger accounts in the firm's accounting system.

Employer's Payroll Taxes and Insurance Costs

Remember that employers withhold social security and Medicare taxes from employees' earnings. In addition, employers pay social security and Medicare taxes on their employees' earnings. Employers are also required to pay federal and state taxes for unemployment benefits and to carry workers' compensation insurance.

Social Security Tax

The employer's share of the social security tax is 6.2 percent up to the earnings base. (In this text, the social security tax is 6.2 percent of the first $76,200 of earnings.) Periodically the employer pays to the federal government the social security tax withheld plus the employer's share of the social security tax.

	FICA
Employee (withheld)	6.2%
Employer (match)	6.2
Total	12.4%

Medicare Tax

The employer's share of Medicare tax is 1.45 percent of earnings. Periodically the employer pays to the federal government the Medicare tax withheld plus the employer's share of the Medicare tax.

The total social security and Medicare taxes the employer remits to the federal government are shown below.

	Medicare
Employee (withheld)	1.45%
Employer (match)	1.45
Total	2.90%

Federal Unemployment Tax

The *Federal Unemployment Tax Act* (*FUTA*) provides benefits for employees who become unemployed. Taxes levied by the federal government against employers to benefit unemployed workers are called **federal unemployment taxes (FUTA)**. Employers pay the entire amount of these taxes. In this text we assume that the taxable earnings base is $7,000. That is, the tax applies to the first $7,000 of each employee's earnings for the year. The FUTA tax rate is 6.2 percent.

Accounting On The Job

Human Services

Industry Overview

The human services field provides essential services to those who are not fully equipped to help themselves. Social disabilities, economic disadvantage, employment difficulties, food and housing hardships, and alcohol and drug dependencies are issues addressed by professionals in this field.

Career Opportunities

- Child Support Payment Specialist
- Social Worker
- Senior Accounting Supervisor—Human Services
- Income Maintenance Program Advisor
- Social Services Grant Administrator
- Budget Analyst—U.S. Administration on Aging

Preparing for a Human Services Career

- Demonstrate an understanding of and sensitivity to individual, ethnic, and cultural differences among individuals and families.
- Complete governmental accounting courses to prepare for administration of human service department budgets and funds.
- Develop proficiencies in electronic spreadsheets and database applications to manage client files, administer benefits, and track human services programs.
- Obtain certification or an associate's degree in social work or human services for middle management or entry-level positions.
- Secure a bachelor's degree for supervisory or managerial positions with an emphasis in human services management, social work, behavioral science, math, science, child development, world languages, computer science, or consumer science.
- Apply to participate in a Presidential Management Internship Program with the U.S. Department of Health and Human Services.

Thinking Critically

Social worker planners and policymakers develop programs to address issues such as homelessness, poverty, and violence. What skills or proficiencies do you think might be beneficial to these professionals as they identify specific problems, create plans of action, and suggest solutions?

Internet Application

Locate the Web site for the U.S. Department of Health and Human Services. Describe the purpose of this human services agency. What is the department's budget for the current year? How many individuals does this agency employ?

State Unemployment Tax

The federal and state unemployment programs work together to provide benefits for employees who become unemployed. Employers pay all of the **state unemployment taxes (SUTA)**. Usually the earnings base for the federal and state unemployment taxes are the same, the first $7,000 of each employee's earnings for the year. For many states the SUTA tax rate is 5.4 percent.

The federal tax rate (6.2 percent) can be reduced by the rate charged by the state (5.4 percent in this example), so the FUTA rate can be as low as 0.8 percent (6.2% − 5.4%).

SUTA tax		5.4%
FUTA tax rate	6.2%	
Less SUTA tax	(5.4)	
Net FUTA tax		0.8
Total federal and state unemployment tax		6.2%

Workers' Compensation Insurance

Workers' compensation insurance protects employees against losses from job-related injuries or illnesses, or compensates their families if death occurs in the course of the employment. Workers' compensation requirements are defined by each state. Most states mandate workers' compensation insurance.

Employee Records Required by Law

Some companies outsource payroll duties to professional payroll companies. ADP, Inc., is the world's largest provider of payroll services and employee information systems.

Federal laws require that certain payroll records be maintained. For each employee the employer must keep a record of

- the employee's name, address, social security number, and date of birth;
- hours worked each day and week, and wages paid at the regular and overtime rates (certain exceptions exist for employees who earn salaries);
- cumulative wages paid throughout the year;
- amount of income tax, social security tax, and Medicare tax withheld for each pay period;
- proof that the employee is a United States citizen or has a valid work permit.

Section 1 Self Review

Questions

1. What is "time and a half"?
2. How are social security benefits financed?
3. How are unemployment insurance benefits financed?

Exercises

4. The earnings base limit for Medicare
   a. is the same as the earnings base limit for social security.
   b. is lower than the earnings base limit for social security.
   c. is higher than the earnings base limit for social security.
   d. does not exist.
5. The purpose of FUTA is to provide benefits for
   a. employees who become unemployed.
   b. employees who become injured while on the job.
   c. retired workers.
   d. disabled employees.

Analysis

6. Julie Kerns was hired by Jacob's Architects to create three oil paintings for the president's office. Is Kerns an employee? Why or why not?

(Answers to Section 1 Self Review are on page 387.)

Section 2

Calculating Earnings and Taxes

On Line Furnishings is a sole proprietorship owned and managed by Roberta Rosario. On Line Furnishings imports furniture and novelty items to sell over the Internet. It has five employees. The three shipping clerks and the shipping supervisor are paid on an hourly basis. The office clerk is paid a weekly salary. Payday is each Monday; it covers the wages and salaries earned the previous week. The employees are subject to withholding of social security, Medicare, and federal income taxes. The business pays social security and Medicare taxes, and federal and state unemployment insurance taxes. The business is required by state law to carry workers' compensation insurance. Since it is involved in interstate commerce, On Line Furnishings is subject to the Fair Labor Standards Act.

From time to time, Roberta Rosario, the owner, makes cash withdrawals to cover her personal expenses. The withdrawals of the owner of a sole proprietorship are not treated as salaries or wages.

Computing Total Earnings of Employees

The first step in preparing payroll is to compute the gross wages or salary for each employee. There are several ways to compute earnings.

- **Hourly rate basis** workers earn a stated rate per hour. Gross pay depends on the number of hours worked.
- **Salary basis** workers earn an agreed-upon amount for each week, month, or other period.
- **Commission basis** workers, usually salespeople, earn a percentage of net sales.
- **Piece-rate basis** manufacturing workers are paid based on the number of units produced.

Wal-Mart Stores, Inc., has approximately 889,000 employees in its U.S. operations, which include Wal-Mart Discount Stores, SAM's Clubs, the distribution centers, and the home office. The company reports that 65 percent of Wal-Mart managers, who are compensated on a salary basis, first entered the company as hourly rate basis employees.

Determining Pay for Hourly Employees

Two pieces of data are needed to compute gross pay for hourly rate basis employees: the number of hours worked during the payroll period, and the rate of pay.

Section Objectives

2 Compute gross earnings of employees.

WHY IT'S IMPORTANT
Payroll is a large part of business activity.

3 Determine employee deductions for social security tax.

WHY IT'S IMPORTANT
Employers are legally responsible for collecting and remitting this tax.

4 Determine employee deductions for Medicare tax.

WHY IT'S IMPORTANT
Employers have legal responsibility.

5 Determine employee deductions for income tax.

WHY IT'S IMPORTANT
Employers are legally responsible.

6 Enter gross earnings, deductions, and net pay in the payroll register.

WHY IT'S IMPORTANT
The payroll register provides information needed to prepare paychecks.

Terms to Learn

commission basis
Employee's Withholding Allowance Certificate (Form W-4)
exempt employees
hourly rate basis
payroll register
piece-rate basis
salary basis
tax-exempt wages
wage-bracket table method

❷ Objective

Compute gross earnings of employees.

Owner Withdrawals
Withdrawals by the owner of a sole proprietorship are debited to a temporary owner's equity account (in this case, **Roberta Rosario, Drawing**). Withdrawals are not treated as salary or wages.

International INSIGHTS

Salaries

More than three million Americans live and work overseas. One of the reasons may be the salary. Americans working abroad can earn up to 300 percent more than the same job pays in the United States.

Hours Worked

At On Line Furnishings, the shipping supervisor keeps a weekly time sheet. Each day she enters the hours worked by each shipping clerk. At the end of the week, the office clerk uses the time sheet to compute the total hours worked and to prepare the payroll.

Many businesses use time clocks for hourly employees. Each employee has a time card and inserts it in the time clock to record the times of arrival and departure. The payroll clerk collects the cards at the end of the week, determines the hours worked by each employee, and multiplies the number of hours by the pay rate to compute the *gross pay.* Some time cards are machine readable. A computer determines the hours worked and makes the earnings calculations.

Gross Pay

Cindy Taylor, Edward Gallegos, and Bill Turner are shipping clerks at On Line Furnishings. They are hourly employees. Their gross pay for the week ended January 6 is determined as follows:

- Taylor worked 40 hours. She earns \$9 an hour. Her gross pay is \$360 (40 hours × \$9).
- Turner worked 40 hours. He earns \$7.50 an hour. His gross pay is \$300 (40 × \$7.50).
- Gallegos earns \$8 per hour. He worked 45 hours. He is paid 40 hours at regular pay and 5 hours at time and a half. There are two ways to compute Gallegos' gross pay:

1. The Wage and Hour Law method identifies the *overtime premium,* the amount the firm could have saved if all the hours were paid at the regular rate. The overtime premium rate is \$4, one-half of the regular rate (\$8 × 1/2 = \$4).

Total hours × regular rate:	
45 hours × \$8	\$360.00
Overtime premium:	
5 hours × \$4	20.00
Gross pay	\$380.00

2. The second method identifies how much the employee earned by working overtime.

Regular earnings:	
40 hours × \$8	\$320.00
Overtime earnings:	
5 hours × \$12 (\$8 × 1 1/2)	60.00
Gross pay	\$380.00

Cecilia Lin is the shipping supervisor at On Line Furnishings. She is an hourly employee. She earns \$13 an hour, and she worked 40 hours. Her gross pay is \$520 (40 × \$13).

Withholdings for Hourly Employees Required by Law

Recall that three deductions from employees' gross pay are required by federal law. They are FICA (social security) tax, Medicare tax, and federal income tax withholding.

❸ Objective

Determine employee deductions for social security tax.

Social Security Tax. The social security tax is levied on both the employer and the employee. This text calculates social security tax using a 6.2 percent tax rate on the first $76,200 of wages paid during the calendar year. **Tax-exempt wages** are earnings in excess of the base amount set by the Social Security Act ($76,200). Tax-exempt wages are not subject to FICA withholding.

If an employee works for more than one employer during the year, the FICA tax is deducted and matched by each employer. When the employee files a federal income tax return, any excess FICA tax withheld from the employee's earnings is refunded by the government or applied to payment of the employee's federal income taxes.

To determine the amount of social security tax to withhold from an employee's pay, multiply the taxable wages by the social security tax rate. Round the result to the nearest cent.

The following shows the social security tax deductions for On Line Furnishings' hourly employees.

Employee	Gross Pay	Tax Rate	Tax
Cindy Taylor	$360.00	6.2%	$22.32
Edward Gallegos	380.00	6.2	23.56
Bill Turner	300.00	6.2	18.60
Cecilia Lin	520.00	6.2	32.24
Total social security tax			$96.72

❹ Objective

Determine employee deductions for Medicare tax.

Medicare Tax. The Medicare tax is levied on both the employee and the employer. To compute the Medicare tax to withhold from the employee's paycheck, multiply the wages by the Medicare tax rate, 1.45 percent. The following shows the Medicare tax deduction for hourly employees.

Employee	Gross Pay	Tax Rate	Tax
Cindy Taylor	$360.00	1.45%	$ 5.22
Edward Gallegos	380.00	1.45	5.51
Bill Turner	300.00	1.45	4.35
Cecilia Lin	520.00	1.45	7.54
Total Medicare tax			$22.62

❺ Objective

Determine employee deductions for income tax.

Federal Income Tax. A substantial portion of the federal government's revenue comes from the income tax on individuals. Employers are required to withhold federal income tax from employees' pay. Periodically the employer pays the federal income tax withheld to the federal government. After the end of the year, the employee files an income tax return. If the amount of federal income tax withheld does not cover the amount of income tax due, the employee pays the balance. If too much federal income tax has been withheld, the employee receives a refund.

According to tax collection statistics reported by the IRS for 1997, employers withheld more than $580 billion from the paychecks of their employees for income taxes.

Pay-As-You-Go
Employee income tax withholding is designed to place employees on a pay-as-you-go basis in paying their federal income tax.

Withholding Allowances. The amount of federal income tax to withhold from an employee's earnings depends on the

- earnings during the pay period,
- length of the pay period,
- marital status,
- number of withholding allowances.

Determining the number of withholding allowances for some taxpayers is complex. In the simplest circumstances, a taxpayer claims a withholding allowance for

- the taxpayer,
- a spouse who does not also claim an allowance,
- each dependent for whom the taxpayer provides more than half the support during the year.

As the number of withholding allowances increases, the amount of federal income tax withheld decreases. The goal is to claim the number of withholding allowances so that the federal income tax withheld is about the same as the employee's tax liability.

Important!

Get It in Writing
Employers need a signed Form W-4 in order to change the employee's federal income tax withholding.

To claim withholding allowances, employees complete **Employee's Withholding Allowance Certificate, Form W-4**. The employee gives the completed Form W-4 to the employer. If the number of exemption allowances decreases, the employee must file a new Form W-4 within 10 days. If the number of exemption allowances increases, the employee may, but is not required to, file another Form W-4. If an employee does not file a Form W-4, the employer withholds federal income tax based on zero withholding allowances.

Figure 10-1 shows Form W-4 for Cindy Taylor. Notice that on Line 5, Taylor claims one withholding allowance.

FIGURE 10-1 ▼
Form W-4 (Partial)

Cut here and give the certificate to your employer. Keep the top portion for your records.

Form **W-4** Department of the Treasury Internal Revenue Service	**Employee's Withholding Allowance Certificate** ► **For Privacy Act and Paperwork Reduction Act Notice, see page 2.**	OMB No. 1545-0010 **20--**

1 Type or print your first name and middle initial	Last Name	2 Your social security number
Cindy M.	Taylor	123 XX XXXX

Home address (number and street or rural route) 6480 Oak Tree Drive	3 ☐ Single ☑ Married ☐ Married, but withhold at higher Single rate **Note:** *If married, but legally separated, or spouse is a nonresident alien, check the Single box.*
City or town, state, and ZIP code Denton, TX 76209-6789	4 **If your last name differs from that on your social security card, check here. You must call 1-800-772-1213 for a new card.** ► ☐

5 Total number of allowances you are claiming (from line **H** above **or** from the applicable worksheet on page 2) . . .	5	1
6 Additional amount, if any, you want deducted from each paycheck	6	$
7 I claim exemption from withholding for 20--, and I certify that I meet **both** of the following conditions for exemption: • Last year I had a right to a refund of **all** Federal income tax withheld because I had **no** tax liability **and** • This year I expect a refund of **all** Federal income tax withheld because I expect to have **no** tax liability. If you meet both conditions, write "Exempt" here . . . . ►	7	

Under penalty of perjury, I certify that I am entitled to the number of withholding allowances claimed on this certificate, or I am entitled to claim exempt status.

Employee's signature (Form is not valid unless you sign it.) ► *Cindy Taylor* **Date** ► *December 1,* 20 *--*

8 Employer's name and address (Employer: Complete lines 8 and 10 only if sending to IRS.)	9 Office code (optional)	10 Employer identification number

Cat. No. 10220Q

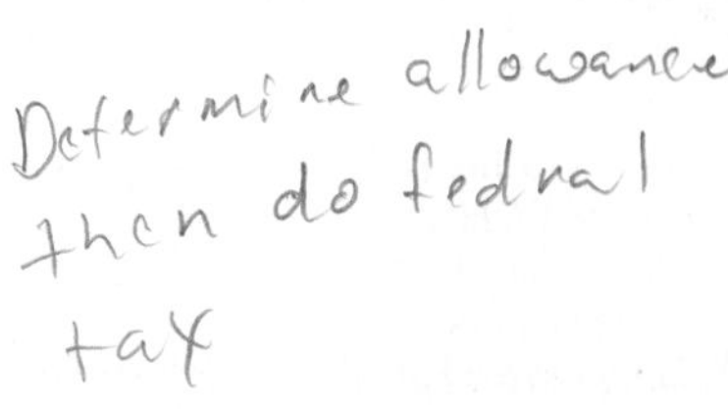

Computing Federal Income Tax Withholding. Although there are several ways to compute the federal income tax to withhold from an employee's earnings, the **wage-bracket table method** is almost universally used. The wage-bracket tables are in *Publication 15, Circular E.* This publication contains withholding tables for weekly, biweekly, semimonthly, monthly, and daily or miscellaneous payroll periods for single and married persons. Figure 10-2 on pages 362–363 shows partial tables for single and married persons who are paid weekly.

Use the following steps to determine the amount to withhold:

1. Choose the table for the pay period and the employee's marital status.
2. Find the row in the table that matches the wages earned. Find the column that matches the number of withholding allowances claimed on Form W-4. The income tax to withhold is the intersection of the row and the column.

As an example, let's determine the amount to withhold from Cecilia Lin's gross pay. Lin is married, claims two withholding allowances, and earned $520 for the week.

1. Go to the table for married persons paid weekly, Figure 10-2b.
2. Find the line covering wages between $520 and $530. Find the column for two withholding allowances. The tax to withhold is $44; this is where the row and the column intersect.

Using the wage-bracket tables, can you find the federal income tax amounts to withhold for Taylor, Gallegos, and Turner?

Employee	Gross Pay	Marital Status	Withholding Allowances	Income Tax Withholding
Cindy Taylor	$360.00	Married	1	$ 28.00
Edward Gallegos	380.00	Single	1	42.00
Bill Turner	300.00	Single	3	14.00
Cecilia Lin	520.00	Married	2	44.00
				$128.00

Other Deductions Required by Law. Most states and some local governments require employers to withhold state and local income taxes from earnings. In some states employers are also required to withhold unemployment tax or disability tax. The procedures are similar to those for federal income tax withholding. Apply the tax rate to the earnings, or use withholding tables.

Withholdings Not Required by Law

There are many payroll deductions not required by law but made by agreement between the employee and the employer. Some examples are

- group life insurance,
- group medical insurance,
- company retirement plans,
- bank or credit union savings plans or loan repayments,
- United States saving bonds purchase plans,
- stocks and other investment purchase plans,
- employer loan repayments,
- union dues.

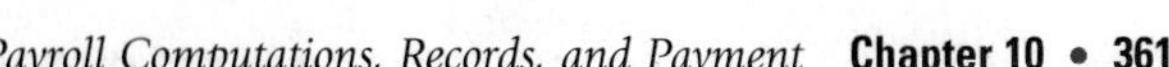

FIGURE 10-2a ►
Federal Withholding Tax Tables (Partial)
Single Persons—Weekly Payroll Period

SINGLE Persons—WEEKLY Payroll Period (For Wages Paid in 20--)

If the wages are –		And the number of withholding allowances claimed is –										
At least	But less than	0	1	2	3	4	5	6	7	8	9	10
		The amount of income tax to be withheld is –										
$0	$55	0	0	0	0	0	0	0	0	0	0	0
55	60	1	0	0	0	0	0	0	0	0	0	0
60	65	2	0	0	0	0	0	0	0	0	0	0
65	70	2	0	0	0	0	0	0	0	0	0	0
70	75	3	0	0	0	0	0	0	0	0	0	0
75	80	4	0	0	0	0	0	0	0	0	0	0
80	85	5	0	0	0	0	0	0	0	0	0	0
85	90	5	0	0	0	0	0	0	0	0	0	0
90	95	6	0	0	0	0	0	0	0	0	0	0
95	100	7	0	0	0	0	0	0	0	0	0	0
100	105	8	0	0	0	0	0	0	0	0	0	0
105	110	8	0	0	0	0	0	0	0	0	0	0
110	115	9	1	0	0	0	0	0	0	0	0	0
115	120	10	2	0	0	0	0	0	0	0	0	0
120	125	11	3	0	0	0	0	0	0	0	0	0
125	130	11	3	0	0	0	0	0	0	0	0	0
130	135	12	4	0	0	0	0	0	0	0	0	0
135	140	13	5	0	0	0	0	0	0	0	0	0
140	145	14	6	0	0	0	0	0	0	0	0	0
145	150	14	6	0	0	0	0	0	0	0	0	0
150	155	15	7	0	0	0	0	0	0	0	0	0
155	160	16	8	0	0	0	0	0	0	0	0	0
160	165	17	9	1	0	0	0	0	0	0	0	0
165	170	17	9	1	0	0	0	0	0	0	0	0
170	175	18	10	2	0	0	0	0	0	0	0	0
175	180	19	11	3	0	0	0	0	0	0	0	0
180	185	20	12	4	0	0	0	0	0	0	0	0
185	190	20	12	4	0	0	0	0	0	0	0	0
190	195	21	13	5	0	0	0	0	0	0	0	0
195	200	22	14	6	0	0	0	0	0	0	0	0
200	210	23	15	7	0	0	0	0	0	0	0	0
210	220	25	17	8	0	0	0	0	0	0	0	0
220	230	26	18	10	2	0	0	0	0	0	0	0
230	240	28	20	11	3	0	0	0	0	0	0	0
240	250	29	21	13	5	0	0	0	0	0	0	0
250	260	31	23	14	6	0	0	0	0	0	0	0
260	270	32	24	16	8	0	0	0	0	0	0	0
270	280	34	26	17	9	1	0	0	0	0	0	0
280	290	35	27	19	11	3	0	0	0	0	0	0
290	300	37	29	20	12	4	0	0	0	0	0	0
300	310	38	30	22	14	6	0	0	0	0	0	0
310	320	40	32	23	15	7	0	0	0	0	0	0
320	330	41	33	25	17	9	1	0	0	0	0	0
330	340	43	35	26	18	10	2	0	0	0	0	0
340	350	44	36	28	20	12	4	0	0	0	0	0
350	360	46	38	29	21	13	5	0	0	0	0	0
360	370	47	39	31	23	15	7	0	0	0	0	0
370	380	49	41	32	24	16	8	0	0	0	0	0
380	390	50	42	34	26	18	10	2	0	0	0	0
390	400	52	44	35	27	19	11	3	0	0	0	0
400	410	53	45	37	29	21	13	5	0	0	0	0
410	420	55	47	38	30	22	14	6	0	0	0	0
420	430	56	48	40	32	24	16	8	0	0	0	0
430	440	58	50	41	33	25	17	9	1	0	0	0
440	450	59	51	43	35	27	19	11	3	0	0	0
450	460	61	53	44	36	28	20	12	4	0	0	0
460	470	62	54	46	38	30	22	14	6	0	0	0
470	480	64	56	47	39	31	23	15	7	0	0	0
480	490	65	57	49	41	33	25	17	9	0	0	0
490	500	67	59	50	42	34	26	18	10	2	0	0
500	510	68	60	52	44	36	28	20	12	3	0	0
510	520	70	62	53	45	37	29	21	13	5	0	0
520	530	71	63	55	47	39	31	23	15	6	0	0
530	540	73	65	56	48	40	32	24	16	8	0	0
540	550	75	66	58	50	42	34	26	18	9	1	0
550	560	78	68	59	51	43	35	27	19	11	3	0
560	570	81	69	61	53	45	37	28	21	12	4	0
570	580	84	71	62	54	46	38	30	22	14	6	0
580	590	87	72	64	56	48	40	32	24	16	7	0
590	600	89	74	65	57	49	41	33	25	17	9	1

FIGURE 10-2b Federal Withholding Tax Tables (Partial) Married Persons—Weekly Payroll Period

MARRIED Persons—WEEKLY Payroll Period (For Wages Paid in 20--)

If the wages are –		And the number of withholding allowances claimed is –										
At least	But less than	0	1	2	3	4	5	6	7	8	9	10
		The amount of income tax to be withheld is –										
$0	$125	0	0	0	0	0	0	0	0	0	0	0
125	130	1	0	0	0	0	0	0	0	0	0	0
130	135	1	0	0	0	0	0	0	0	0	0	0
135	140	2	0	0	0	0	0	0	0	0	0	0
140	145	3	0	0	0	0	0	0	0	0	0	0
145	150	4	0	0	0	0	0	0	0	0	0	0
150	155	4	0	0	0	0	0	0	0	0	0	0
155	160	5	0	0	0	0	0	0	0	0	0	0
160	165	6	0	0	0	0	0	0	0	0	0	0
165	170	7	0	0	0	0	0	0	0	0	0	0
170	175	7	0	0	0	0	0	0	0	0	0	0
175	180	8	0	0	0	0	0	0	0	0	0	0
180	185	9	1	0	0	0	0	0	0	0	0	0
185	190	10	1	0	0	0	0	0	0	0	0	0
190	195	10	2	0	0	0	0	0	0	0	0	0
195	200	11	3	0	0	0	0	0	0	0	0	0
200	210	12	4	0	0	0	0	0	0	0	0	0
210	220	14	6	0	0	0	0	0	0	0	0	0
220	230	15	7	0	0	0	0	0	0	0	0	0
230	240	17	9	0	0	0	0	0	0	0	0	0
240	250	18	10	2	0	0	0	0	0	0	0	0
250	260	20	12	3	0	0	0	0	0	0	0	0
260	270	21	13	5	0	0	0	0	0	0	0	0
270	280	23	15	6	0	0	0	0	0	0	0	0
280	290	24	16	8	0	0	0	0	0	0	0	0
290	300	26	18	9	1	0	0	0	0	0	0	0
300	310	27	19	11	3	0	0	0	0	0	0	0
310	320	29	21	12	4	0	0	0	0	0	0	0
320	330	30	23	14	6	0	0	0	0	0	0	0
330	340	32	24	15	7	0	0	0	0	0	0	0
340	350	33	25	17	9	1	0	0	0	0	0	0
350	360	35	27	18	10	2	0	0	0	0	0	0
360	370	36	28	20	12	4	0	0	0	0	0	0
370	380	38	30	21	13	5	0	0	0	0	0	0
380	390	39	31	23	15	7	0	0	0	0	0	0
390	400	41	33	24	16	8	0	0	0	0	0	0
400	410	42	34	26	18	10	2	0	0	0	0	0
410	420	44	36	27	19	11	3	0	0	0	0	0
420	430	45	37	29	21	13	5	0	0	0	0	0
430	440	47	39	30	22	14	6	0	0	0	0	0
440	450	48	40	32	24	16	8	0	0	0	0	0
450	460	50	42	33	25	17	9	1	0	0	0	0
460	470	51	43	35	27	19	11	3	0	0	0	0
470	480	53	45	36	28	20	12	4	0	0	0	0
480	490	54	46	38	30	22	14	6	0	0	0	0
490	500	56	48	39	31	23	15	7	0	0	0	0
500	510	57	49	41	33	25	17	9	1	0	0	0
510	520	59	51	42	34	26	18	10	2	0	0	0
520	530	60	52	44	36	28	20	12	4	0	0	0
530	540	62	54	45	37	29	21	13	5	0	0	0
540	550	63	55	47	39	31	23	15	7	0	0	0
550	560	65	57	48	40	32	24	16	8	0	0	0
560	570	66	58	50	42	34	26	18	10	2	0	0
570	580	68	60	51	43	35	27	19	11	3	0	0
580	590	69	61	53	45	37	29	21	13	5	0	0
590	600	71	63	54	46	38	30	22	14	6	0	0
600	610	72	64	56	48	40	32	24	16	8	0	0
610	620	74	66	57	49	41	33	25	17	9	1	0
620	630	75	67	59	51	43	35	27	19	11	2	0
630	640	77	69	60	52	44	36	28	20	12	4	0
640	650	78	70	62	54	46	38	30	22	14	5	0
650	660	80	72	63	55	47	39	31	23	15	7	0
660	670	81	73	65	57	49	41	33	25	17	8	0
670	680	83	75	66	58	50	42	34	26	18	10	2
680	690	84	76	68	60	52	44	36	28	20	11	3
690	700	86	78	69	61	53	45	37	29	21	13	5
700	710	87	79	71	63	55	47	39	31	23	14	6
710	720	89	81	72	64	56	48	40	32	24	16	8
720	730	90	82	74	66	58	50	42	34	26	17	9
730	740	92	84	75	67	59	51	43	35	27	19	11

These and other payroll deductions increase the payroll recordkeeping work but do not involve any new principles or procedures. They are handled in the same way as the deductions for social security, Medicare, and federal income taxes.

On Line Furnishings pays all medical insurance premiums for each employee. If the employee chooses to have medical coverage for a spouse or dependent, On Line Furnishings deducts $20 per week for coverage for the spouse and each dependent. Turner and Lin each have $20 per week deducted to obtain the medical coverage.

Determining Pay for Salaried Employees

A salaried employee earns a specific sum of money for each payroll period. The office clerk at On Line Furnishings earns a weekly salary.

Hours Worked

Salaried workers who do not hold supervisory jobs are covered by the provisions of the Wage and Hour Law that deal with maximum hours and overtime premium pay. Employers keep time records for all nonsupervisory salaried workers to make sure that their hourly earnings meet the legal requirements.

Salaried employees who hold supervisory or managerial positions are called **exempt employees**. They are not subject to the maximum hour and overtime premium pay provisions of the Wage and Hour Law.

Gross Earnings

Selena Anderson is the office clerk at On Line Furnishings. During the first week of January, she worked 40 hours, her regular schedule. There are no overtime earnings because she did not work more than 40 hours during the week. Her salary of $400 is her gross pay for the week.

Withholdings for Salaried Employees Required by Law

The procedures for withholding taxes for salaried employees is the same as withholding for hourly rate employees. Apply the tax rate to the earnings, or use withholding tables.

FIGURE 10-3 ▼
Payroll Register

PAYROLL REGISTER **WEEK BEGINNING** *January 1, 20--*

NAME	NO. OF ALLOW.	MARITAL STATUS	CUMULATIVE EARNINGS	NO. OF HRS.	RATE/ SALARY	EARNINGS REGULAR	EARNINGS OVERTIME	EARNINGS GROSS AMOUNT	CUMULATIVE EARNINGS
Taylor, Cindy	*1*	*M*		*40*	*9.00*	*360 00*		*360 00*	*360 00*
Gallegos, Edward	*1*	*S*		*45*	*8.00*	*320 00*	*60 00*	*380 00*	*380 00*
Turner, Bill	*3*	*S*		*40*	*7.50*	*300 00*		*300 00*	*300 00*
Lin, Cecilia	*2*	*M*		*40*	*13.00*	*520 00*		*520 00*	*520 00*
Anderson, Selena	*1*	*S*		*40*	*400.00*	*400 00*		*400 00*	*400 00*
						1 900 00	*60 00*	*1 960 00*	*1 960 00*
(A)	*(B)*		*(C)*	*(D)*	*(E)*	*(F)*	*(G)*	*(H)*	*(I)*

Recording Payroll Information for Employees

6 Objective

Enter gross earnings, deductions, and net pay in the payroll register.

A payroll register is prepared for each pay period. The **payroll register** shows all the payroll information for the pay period.

The Payroll Register

Figure 10-3 on pages 364–365 shows the payroll register for On Line Furnishings for the week ended January 6. Note that all employees were paid for eight hours on January 1, a holiday. To learn how to complete the payroll register, refer to Figure 10-3 and follow these steps.

1. *Columns A, B, and E.* Enter the employee's name (Column A), number of withholding allowances and marital status (Column B), and rate of pay (Column E). In a computerized payroll system, this information is entered once and is automatically retrieved each time payroll is prepared.
2. *Column C.* The Cumulative Earnings column (Column C) shows the total earnings for the calendar year before the current pay period. This figure is needed to determine whether the employee has exceeded the earnings limit for the FICA and FUTA taxes. Since this is the first payroll period of the year, there are no cumulative earnings prior to the current pay period.
3. *Column D.* In Column D enter the total number of hours worked in the current period. This data comes from the weekly time sheet.
4. *Columns F, G, and H.* Using the hours worked and the pay rate, calculate regular pay (Column F), the overtime earnings (Column G), and gross pay (Column H).
5. *Column I.* Calculate the cumulative earnings after this pay period (Column I) by adding the beginning cumulative earnings (Column C) and the current period's gross pay (Column H).
6. *Columns J, K, and L.* The Taxable Wages columns show the earnings subject to taxes for social security (Column J), Medicare (Column K), and FUTA (Column L). Only the earnings at or under the earnings limit are included in these columns.

AND ENDING January 6, 20-- **PAID** January 8, 20--

TAXABLE WAGES			DEDUCTIONS						DISTRIBUTION	
SOCIAL SECURITY	MEDICARE	FUTA	SOCIAL SECURITY	MEDICARE	INCOME TAX	HEALTH INSURANCE	NET AMOUNT	CHECK NO.	OFFICE SALARIES	SHIPPING WAGES
360 00	360 00	360 00	22 32	5 22	28 00		304 46	1725		360 00
380 00	380 00	380 00	23 56	5 51	42 00		308 93	1726		380 00
300 00	300 00	300 00	18 60	4 35	14 00	20 00	243 05	1727		300 00
520 00	520 00	520 00	32 24	7 54	44 00	20 00	416 22	1728		520 00
400 00	400 00	400 00	24 80	5 80	45 00		324 40	1729	400 00	
1 960 00	1 960 00	1 960 00	121 52	28 42	173 00	40 00	1 597 06		400 00	1 560 00
(J)	(K)	(L)	(M)	(N)	(O)	(P)	(Q)	(R)	(S)	(T)

7. *Columns M, N, O, and P.* The Deductions columns show the withholding for social security tax (Column M), Medicare tax (Column N), federal income tax (Column O), and medical insurance (Column P).
8. *Column Q.* Subtract the deductions (Columns M, N, O, and P) from the gross earnings (Column H). Enter the results in the Net Amount column (Column Q). This is the amount paid to each employee.
9. *Column R.* Enter the check number in Column R.
10. *Columns S and T.* The payroll register's last two columns classify employee earnings as office salaries (Column S) or shipping wages (Column T).

When the payroll data for all employees has been entered in the payroll register, total the columns. Check the balances of the following columns:

- Total regular earnings plus total overtime earnings must equal the gross amount (Columns F + G = Column H).
- The total gross amount less total deductions must equal the total net amount.

Gross amount		$1,960.00
Less deductions:		
Social security tax	$121.52	
Medicare tax	28.42	
Income tax	173.00	
Health insurance	40.00	
Total deductions		362.94
Net amount		$1,597.06

- The office salaries and the shipping wages must equal gross earnings (Columns S + T = Column H).

The payroll register supplies all the information to make the journal entry to record the payroll. Journalizing the payroll is discussed in Section 3.

Section 2 Self Review

Questions

1. What three payroll deductions does federal law require?
2. List four payroll deductions that are not required by law but can be made by agreement between the employee and the employer.
3. What factors determine the amount of federal income tax to be withheld from an employee's earnings?

Exercises

4. Casey Klein worked 46 hours during the week ending October 19. His regular rate is $8 per hour. Calculate his gross earnings for the week.
   a. $320
   b. $392
   c. $368
   d. $344
5. Which of the following affects the amount of Medicare tax to be withheld from an hourly rate employee's pay?
   a. medical insurance premium
   b. marital status
   c. withholding allowances claimed on Form W-4
   d. hours worked

Analysis

6. Maria Sanchez left a voice mail asking you to withhold an additional $20 of federal income tax from her wages each pay period, starting May 1. When should you begin withholding the extra amount?

(Answers to Section 2 Self Review are on page 387.)

Section 3

Recording Payroll Information

Section Objectives

7. **Journalize payroll transactions in the general journal.**

   WHY IT'S IMPORTANT
   Payroll cost is an operating expense.

8. **Maintain an earnings record for each employee.**

   WHY IT'S IMPORTANT
   Federal law requires that employers maintain records.

Terms to Learn

compensation record
individual earnings record

In this section you will learn how to prepare paychecks and journalize and post payroll transactions by following the January payroll activity for On Line Furnishings.

Recording Payroll

Recording payroll involves two separate entries: one to record the payroll expense and another to pay the employees. The general journal entry to record the payroll expense is based on the payroll register. The gross pay is debited to **Shipping Wages Expense** for the shipping clerks and supervisor and to **Office Salaries Expense** for the office clerk. Each type of deduction is credited to a separate liability account **(Social Security Tax Payable, Medicare Tax Payable, Employee Income Tax Payable, Health Insurance Premiums Payable).** Net pay is credited to the liability account, **Salaries and Wages Payable.**

7 Objective
Journalize payroll transactions in the general journal.

Refer to Figure 10-3 on pages 364–365 to see how the data on the payroll register is used to prepare the January 8 payroll journal entry for On Line Furnishings. Following is an analysis of the entry.

Business Transaction

The information in the payroll register (Figure 10-3) is used to record the payroll expense.

Analysis

The expense account, **Office Salaries Expense,** is increased by $400.00. The expense account, **Shipping Wages Expense,** is increased by $1,560.00. The liability account for each deduction is increased: **Social Security Tax Payable,** $121.52; **Medicare Tax Payable,** $28.42; **Employee Income Tax Payable,** $173.00; **Health Insurance Premiums Payable,** $40.00. The liability account, **Salaries and Wages Payable,** is increased by the net amount of the payroll, $1,597.06.

Debit-Credit Rules

DEBIT Increases in expenses are recorded as debits. Debit **Office Salaries Expense** for $400.00. Debit **Shipping Wages Expense** for $1,560.00.

CREDIT Increases in liability accounts are recorded as credits. Credit **Social Security Tax Payable** for $121.52. Credit **Medicare Tax Payable** for $28.42. Credit **Employee Income Tax Payable** for $173.00. Credit **Health Insurance Premiums Payable** for $40.00. Credit **Salaries and Wages Payable** for $1,597.06

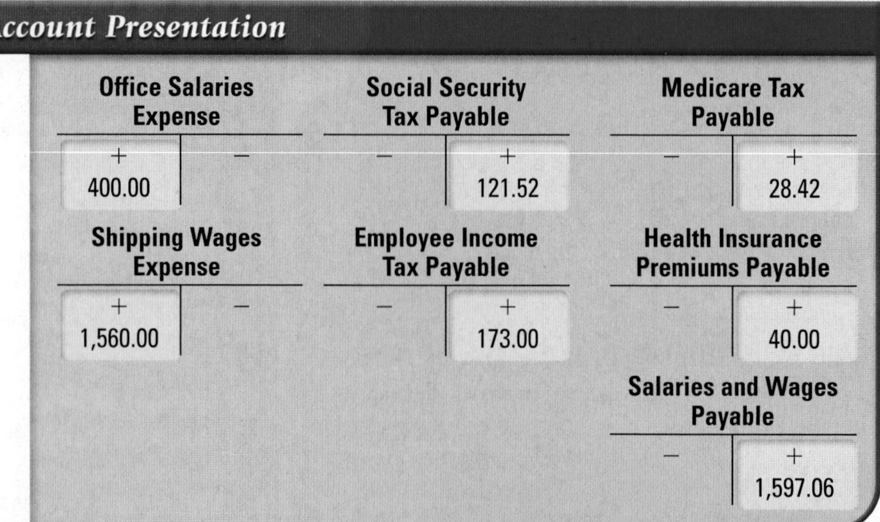

General Journal Entry

GENERAL JOURNAL PAGE 1

	DATE		DESCRIPTION	POST. REF.	DEBIT	CREDIT	
1	20--						1
2	Jan.	8	Office Salaries Expense		400 00		2
3			Shipping Wages Expense		1 560 00		3
4			Social Security Tax Payable			121 52	4
5			Medicare Tax Payable			28 42	5
6			Employee Income Tax Payable			173 00	6
7			Health Insurance Premiums Payable			40 00	7
8			Salaries and Wages Payable			1 597 06	8
9			Payroll for week ending Jan. 6				9

The Bottom Line

Record Payroll

Income Statement

Expenses	↑ 1,960
Net Income	↓ 1,960

Balance Sheet

Liabilities	↑ 1,960
Equity	↓ 1,960

Southwest Airlines Co. recorded salaries, wages, and benefits of more than $1.4 billion for the year ended December 31, 1999.

Paying Employees

Most businesses pay their employees by check or by direct deposit. By using these methods, the business avoids the inconvenience and risk involved in dealing with currency.

Paying by Check

Important!

Payroll Liabilities
Deductions from employee paychecks are liabilities for the employer.

Paychecks may be written on the firm's regular checking account or on a payroll bank account. The check stub shows information about the employee's gross earnings, deductions, and net pay. Employees detach the stubs and keep them as a record of their payroll data. The check number is entered in the Check Number column of the payroll register (Figure 10-3, Column R). The canceled check provides a record of the payment, and the employee's endorsement serves as a receipt. Following is an analysis of the transaction to pay On Line Furnishings' employees.

Business Transaction

On January 8 On Line Furnishings wrote five checks for payroll, Check numbers 1725–1729.

Analysis

The liability account, **Salaries and Wages Payable,** is decreased by $1,597.06. The asset account, **Cash,** is decreased by $1,597.06.

Debit-Credit Rules

DEBIT Decreases to liability accounts are recorded as debits. Debit **Salaries and Wages Payable** for $1,597.06.

CREDIT Decreases to assets are credits. Credit **Cash** for $1,597.06.

T-Account Presentation

Salaries and Wages Payable	
−	+
1,597.06	

Cash	
+	−
	1,597.06

General Journal Entry

GENERAL JOURNAL PAGE *1*

DATE		DESCRIPTION	POST. REF.	DEBIT	CREDIT
Jan.	*8*	*Salaries and Wages Payable*		*1 5 9 7 06*	
		Cash			*1 5 9 7 06*
		To record payment of salaries and wages			
		for week ended Jan. 6			

The Bottom Line

Issue Paychecks

Income Statement

No effect on net income

Balance Sheet

Assets	↓1,597.06
Liabilities	↓1,597.06

No effect on equity

Checks Written on Regular Checking Account. The above entry is shown in general journal form for illustration purposes only. When paychecks are written on the regular checking account, the entries are recorded in the cash payments journal. Figure 10-4 on page 370 shows the January 8 entries to pay employees. Notice that there is a separate Salaries and Wages Payable Debit column.

Checks Written on a Separate Payroll Account. Many businesses write payroll checks from a separate payroll bank account. This is a two-step process.

1. A check is drawn on the regular bank account for the total amount of net pay and deposited in the payroll bank account.
2. Individual payroll checks are issued from the payroll bank account.

Using a separate payroll account simplifies the bank reconciliation of the regular checking account and makes it easier to identify outstanding payroll checks.

Important!

Separate Payroll Account
Using a separate payroll account facilitates the bank reconciliation and provides better internal control.

FIGURE 10-4 ►
Cash Payments Journal

CASH PAYMENTS JOURNAL PAGE 1

DATE		CK. NO.	DESCRIPTION	POST. REF.	ACCOUNTS PAYABLE DEBIT	SALARIES AND WAGES PAYABLE DEBIT	PURCHASES DISCOUNT CREDIT	CASH CREDIT
Jan.	2	1711	Discount Furniture Company		1 200 00		24 00	1 176 00
	8	1725	Cindy Taylor			304 46		304 46
	8	1726	Edward Gallegos			308 93		308 93
	8	1727	Bill Turner			243 05		243 05
	8	1728	Cecilia Lin			416 22		416 22
	8	1729	Selena Anderson			324 40		324 40
	31		Totals		XX X X X XX	6 388 24	XX X X X XX	XX X X X XX

Paying by Direct Deposit

A popular method of paying employees is the direct deposit method. The bank electronically transfers net pay from the employer's account to the personal account of the employee. On payday the employee receives a statement showing gross earnings, deductions, and net pay.

8 Objective

Maintain an earnings record for each employee.

Individual Earnings Records

An **individual earnings record**, also called a **compensation record**, is created for each employee. This record contains the employee's name, address, social security number, date of birth, number of withholding allowances claimed, rate of pay, and any other information needed to compute earnings and complete tax reports.

The payroll register provides the details that are entered on the employee's individual earnings record for each pay period. Figure 10-5 on page 371 shows the earnings record for Cindy Taylor.

Laws and Controls

- It is management's responsibility to ensure that the payroll procedures and records comply with federal, state, and local laws.
- For most businesses, wages and salaries are a large part of operating expenses. Payroll records help management to keep track of and control expenses.
- Management should investigate large or frequent overtime expenditures.
- To prevent errors and fraud, management periodically should have the payroll records audited and payroll procedures evaluated.
- Two common payroll frauds are the overstatement of hours worked and the issuance of checks to nonexistent employees.

Thinking Critically

What controls would you put in place to prevent payroll fraud?

			EARNINGS RECORD FOR 20--		
NAME	Cindy Taylor	RATE	$9 per hour	SOCIAL SECURITY NO.	123-XX-XXXX
ADDRESS	6480 Oak Tree Drive, Denton, TX 76209-6789			DATE OF BIRTH	November 23, 1979
WITHHOLDING ALLOWANCES	1			MARITAL STATUS	M

PAYROLL NO.	DATE WK. END.	DATE PAID	HOURS RG	HOURS OT	EARNINGS REGULAR	EARNINGS OVERTIME	EARNINGS TOTAL	EARNINGS CUMULATIVE	DEDUCTIONS SOCIAL SECURITY	DEDUCTIONS MEDICARE	DEDUCTIONS INCOME TAX	DEDUCTIONS OTHER	NET PAY
1	1/06	1/08	40		360 00		360 00	360 00	22 32	5 22	28 00		304 46
2	1/13	1/15	40		360 00		360 00	720 00	22 32	5 22	28 00		304 46
3	1/20	1/22	40		360 00		360 00	1080 00	22 32	5 22	28 00		304 46
4	1/27	1/29	40		360 00		360 00	1440 00	22 32	5 22	28 00		304 46
	January				1440 00		1440 00	1440 00	89 28	20 88	112 00		1217 84

▲ **FIGURE 10-5**
An Individual Earnings Record

The earnings record shows the payroll period, the date paid, the regular and overtime hours, the regular and overtime earnings, the deductions, and the net pay. The cumulative earnings on the earnings record agrees with Column I of the payroll register (Figure 10-3). The earnings records are totaled monthly and at the end of each calendar quarter. This provides information needed to make tax payments and file tax returns.

Completing January Payrolls

Figure 10-6 on pages 371–372 shows the entire cycle of computing, paying, journalizing, and posting payroll data. In order to complete the

▼ **FIGURE 10-6** Journalizing and Posting Payroll Data

AND ENDING January 6, 20-- PAID January 8, 20--

TAXABLE WAGES SOCIAL SECURITY	TAXABLE WAGES MEDICARE	TAXABLE WAGES FUTA	DEDUCTIONS SOCIAL SECURITY	DEDUCTIONS MEDICARE	DEDUCTIONS INCOME TAX	DEDUCTIONS HEALTH INSURANCE	NET AMOUNT	CHECK NO.	DISTRIBUTION OFFICE SALARIES	DISTRIBUTION SHIPPING WAGES
360 00	360 00	360 00	22 32	5 22	28 00		304 46	1725		360 00
380 00	380 00	380 00	23 56	5 51	42 00		308 93	1726		380 00
300 00	300 00	300 00	18 60	4 35	14 00	20 00	243 05	1727		300 00
520 00	520 00	520 00	32 24	7 54	44 00	20 00	416 22	1728		520 00
400 00	400 00	400 00	24 80	5 80	45 00		324 40	1729	400 00	
1 960 00	1 960 00	1 960 00	121 52	28 42	173 00	40 00	1 597 06		400 00	1 560 00
(J)	(K)	(L)	(M)	(N)	(O)	(P)	(Q)	(R)	(S)	(T)

1	20--						1
2	Jan.	8	Office Salaries Expense	641	400 00		2
3			Shipping Wages Expense	642	1 560 00		3
4			Social Security Tax Payable	221		121 52	4
5			Medicare Tax Payable	222		28 42	5
6			Employee Income Tax Payable	223		173 00	6
7			Health Insurance Premiums Payable	224		40 00	7
8			Salaries and Wages Payable	229		1 597 06	8
9			Payroll for week ending Jan. 6				9

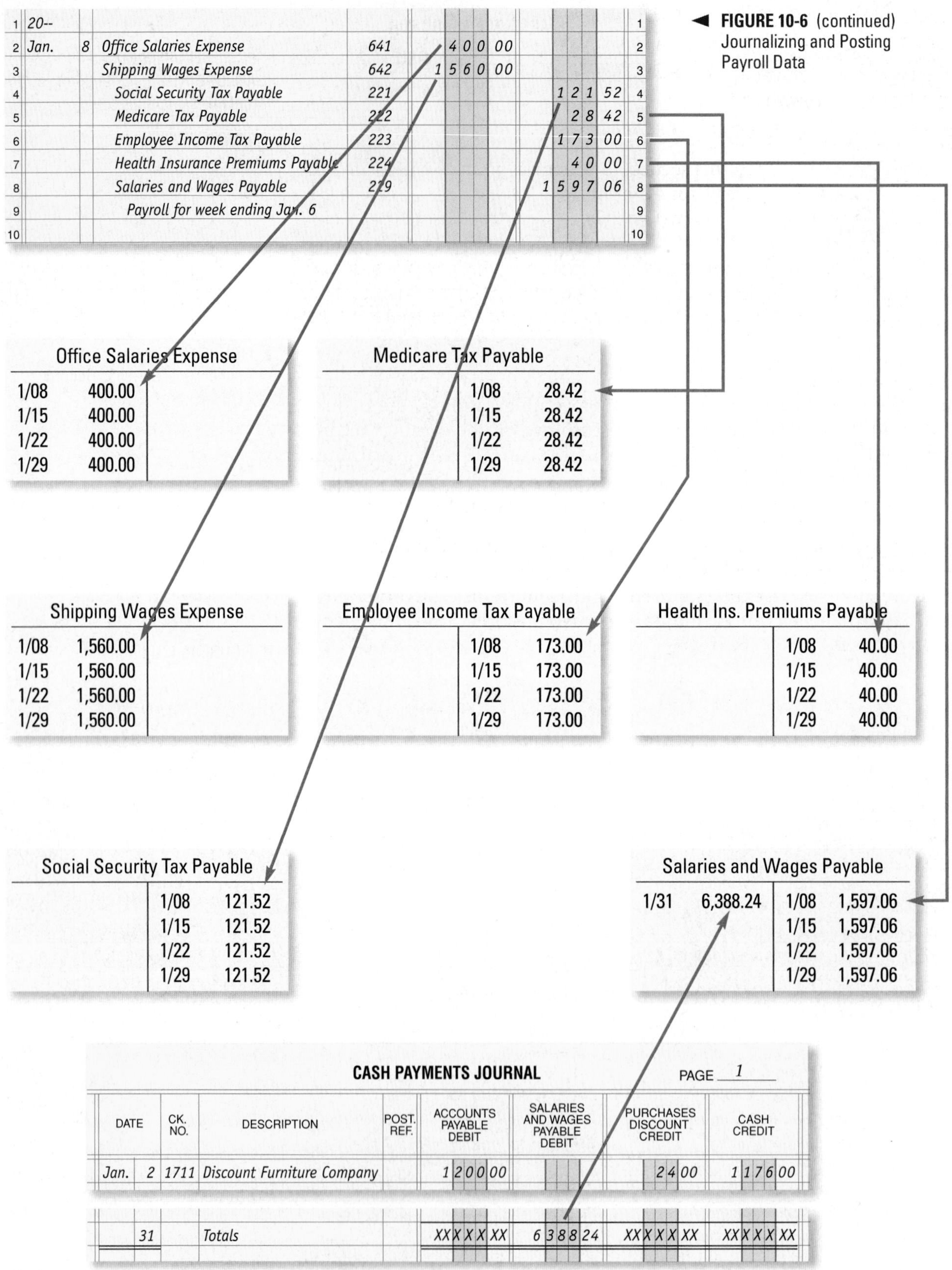

1	20--						1
2	Jan.	8	Office Salaries Expense	641	400 00		2
3			Shipping Wages Expense	642	1 560 00		3
4			Social Security Tax Payable	221		121 52	4
5			Medicare Tax Payable	222		28 42	5
6			Employee Income Tax Payable	223		173 00	6
7			Health Insurance Premiums Payable	224		40 00	7
8			Salaries and Wages Payable	229		1 597 06	8
9			Payroll for week ending Jan. 6				9
10							10

Office Salaries Expense

1/08	400.00		
1/15	400.00		
1/22	400.00		
1/29	400.00		

Medicare Tax Payable

		1/08	28.42
		1/15	28.42
		1/22	28.42
		1/29	28.42

Shipping Wages Expense

1/08	1,560.00		
1/15	1,560.00		
1/22	1,560.00		
1/29	1,560.00		

Employee Income Tax Payable

		1/08	173.00
		1/15	173.00
		1/22	173.00
		1/29	173.00

Health Ins. Premiums Payable

		1/08	40.00
		1/15	40.00
		1/22	40.00
		1/29	40.00

Social Security Tax Payable

		1/08	121.52
		1/15	121.52
		1/22	121.52
		1/29	121.52

Salaries and Wages Payable

1/31	6,388.24	1/08	1,597.06
		1/15	1,597.06
		1/22	1,597.06
		1/29	1,597.06

CASH PAYMENTS JOURNAL PAGE 1

DATE		CK. NO.	DESCRIPTION	POST. REF.	ACCOUNTS PAYABLE DEBIT	SALARIES AND WAGES PAYABLE DEBIT	PURCHASES DISCOUNT CREDIT	CASH CREDIT
Jan.	2	1711	Discount Furniture Company		1 200 00		24 00	1 176 00
	31		Totals		XX X X X XX	6 388 24	XX X X X XX	XX X X X XX

FIGURE 10-6 (continued) Journalizing and Posting Payroll Data

January payroll for On Line Furnishings, assume that all employees worked the same number of hours each week of the month as they did the first week. Thus they had the same earnings, deductions, and net pay each week.

Entry to Record Payroll

As illustrated earlier in this section, one general journal entry is made to record the weekly payroll for all employees of On Line Furnishings. This general journal entry records the payroll expense and liability, but not the payments to employees. Since we are assuming an identical payroll for each week of the month, each of the four weekly payrolls requires general journal entries identical to the one shown in Figure 10-6. Notice how the payroll register column totals are recorded in the general journal.

Entry to Record Payment of Payroll

The weekly entries in the cash payments journal to record payments to employees are the same as the January 8 entries in Figure 10-4 on page 370. At the end of January, the columns in the cash payments journal are totaled, including the Salaries and Wages Payable Debit column.

Postings to Ledger Accounts

The entries to record the weekly payroll expense and liability amounts are posted from the general journal to the accounts in the general ledger. The total of the Salaries and Wages Payable Debit column in the cash payments journal is posted to the **Salaries and Wages Payable** general ledger account.

About Accounting

Tax Returns
Research conducted by the Tax Foundation found that Americans spend 5.4 billion hours each year completing their tax returns.

Section 3 Self Review

Questions

1. What accounts are debited and credited when individual payroll checks are written on the regular checking account?
2. What is the purpose of a payroll bank account?
3. What appears on an individual earnings record?

Exercises

4. Payroll deductions are recorded in a separate
   a. asset account.
   b. expense account.
   c. liability account.
   d. revenue account.
5. Details related to all employees' gross earnings, deductions, and net pay for a period are found in the
   a. payroll register.
   b. individual earnings record.
   c. general journal.
   d. cash payments journal.

Analysis

6. This general journal entry was made to record the payroll liability.

Account	Debit	Credit
Ofc. Salaries Exp.	*300.00*	
Shipping Wages Exp.	*1,292.00*	
Health Ins. Prem. Exp.	*20.00*	
Soc. Sec. Taxes Exp.		*103.48*
Medicare Taxes Pay.		*23.88*
Employee Income Tax Payable		*133.00*
Cash		*1,311.64*

What corrections should be made to this journal entry?

(Answers to Section 3 Self Review are on page 387.)

CHAPTER 10 Review and Applications

Review

Chapter Summary

The main goal of payroll work is to compute the gross wages or salaries earned by each employee, the amounts to be deducted for various taxes and other purposes, and the net amount payable.

Learning Objectives

1 Explain the major federal laws relating to employee earnings and withholding.

Several federal laws affect payroll.

- The federal Wage and Hour Law limits to 40 the number of hours per week an employee can work at the regular rate of pay. For more than 40 hours of work a week, an employer involved in interstate commerce must pay one and one-half times the regular rate.
- Federal laws require that the employer withhold at least three taxes from the employee's pay: the employee's share of social security tax, the employee's share of Medicare tax, and federal income tax. Instructions for computing these taxes are provided by the government.
- If they are required, state and city income taxes can also be deducted. Some states require the employer to withhold contributions to an unemployment fund from the employee's paycheck.
- Voluntary deductions can also be made.

2 Compute gross earnings of employees.

To compute gross earnings for an employee, it is necessary to know whether the employee is paid using an hourly rate basis, a salary basis, a commission basis, or a piece-rate basis.

3 Determine employee deductions for social security tax.

The social security tax is levied in an equal amount on both the employer and the employee. The tax is a percentage of the employee's gross wages during a calendar year up to a wage base limit.

4 Determine employee deductions for Medicare tax.

The Medicare tax is levied in an equal amount on both the employer and the employee. There is no wage base limit for Medicare taxes.

5 Determine employee deductions for income tax.

Income taxes are deducted from an employee's paycheck by the employer and then are paid to the government periodically. Although several methods can be used to compute the amount of federal income tax to be withheld from employee earnings, the wage-bracket table method is most often used. The wage-bracket tables are in *Publication 15, Circular E, Employer's Tax Guide.* Withholding tables for various pay periods for single and married persons are contained in *Circular E.*

6 Enter gross earnings, deductions, and net pay in the payroll register.

Daily records of the hours worked by each nonsupervisory employee are kept. Using these hourly time sheets, the payroll clerk computes the employees' earnings, deductions, and net pay for each payroll period and records the data in a payroll register.

7 Journalize payroll transactions in the general journal.

The payroll register is used to prepare a general journal entry to record payroll expense and liability amounts. A separate journal entry is made to record payments to employees.

8 Maintain an earnings record for each employee.

At the beginning of each year, the employer sets up an individual earnings record for each employee. The amounts in the payroll register are posted to the individual earnings records throughout the year so that the firm has detailed payroll information for each employee. At the end of the year, employers provide reports that show gross earnings and total deductions to each employee.

9 Define the accounting terms new to this chapter.

CHAPTER 10 GLOSSARY

Commission basis (p. 357) A method of paying employees according to a percentage of net sales

Compensation record (p. 370) See Individual earnings record

Employee (p. 352) A person who is hired by and works under the control and direction of the employer

Employee's Withholding Allowance Certificate, Form W-4 (p. 360) A form used to claim exemption (withholding) allowances

Exempt employees (p. 364) Salaried employees who hold supervisory or managerial positions who are not subject to the maximum hour and overtime pay provisions of the Wage and Hour Law

Federal unemployment taxes (FUTA) (p. 354) Taxes levied by the federal government against employers to benefit unemployed workers

Hourly rate basis (p. 357) A method of paying employees according to a stated rate per hour

Independent contractor (p. 352) One who is paid by a company to carry out a specific task or job but is not under the direct supervision or control of the company

Individual earnings record (p. 370) An employee record that contains information needed to compute earnings and complete tax reports

Medicare tax (p. 353) A tax levied on employees and employers to provide medical care for the employee and the employee's spouse after each has reached age 65

Payroll register (p. 365) A record of payroll information for each employee for the pay period

Piece-rate basis (p. 357) A method of paying employees according to the number of units produced

Salary basis (p. 357) A method of paying employees according to an agreed-upon amount for each week or month

Social Security Act (p. 353) A federal act providing certain benefits for employees and their families; officially the Federal Insurance Contributions Act

Social security (FICA) tax (p. 353) A tax imposed by the Federal Insurance Contributions Act and collected on employee earnings to provide retirement and disability benefits

State unemployment taxes (SUTA) (p. 355) Taxes levied by a state government against employers to benefit unemployed workers

Tax-exempt wages (p. 359) Earnings in excess of the base amount set by the Social Security Act

Time and a half (p. 353) Rate of pay for an employee's work in excess of 40 hours a week

Wage-bracket table method (p. 361) A simple method to determine the amount of federal income tax to be withheld using a table provided by the government

Workers' compensation insurance (p. 356) Insurance that protects employees against losses from job-related injuries or illnesses, or compensates their families if death occurs in the course of the employment

Comprehensive Self Review

1. What is the purpose of workers' compensation insurance?
2. How is the amount of social security tax to be withheld from an employee's earnings determined?
3. What is the purpose of the payroll register?
4. From an accounting and internal control viewpoint, would it be preferable to pay employees by check or cash? Explain.
5. How does an independent contractor differ from an employee?

(Answers to Comprehensive Self Review are on page 387.)

Discussion Questions

1. How does the salary basis differ from the hourly rate basis of paying employees?
2. What publication of the Internal Revenue Service provides information about the current federal income tax rates and the procedures that employers should use to withhold federal income tax from an employee's earnings?
3. What is the simplest method for finding the amount of federal income tax to be deducted from an employee's gross pay?
4. What are the four bases for determining employee gross earnings?
5. How does the direct deposit method of paying employees operate?
6. What is the purpose of the social security tax?
7. What is the purpose of the Medicare tax?
8. How are earnings determined when employees are paid on the hourly rate basis?
9. Does the employer bear any part of the SUTA tax? Explain.
10. How are the federal and state unemployment taxes related?
11. What is an exempt employee?
12. Give two examples of common payroll fraud.
13. What aspects of employment are regulated by the Fair Labor Standards Act? What is another commonly used name for this act?
14. How does the Fair Labor Standards Act affect the wages paid by many firms? What types of firms are regulated by the act?
15. What factors affect how much federal income tax must be withheld from an employee's earnings?

Applications

EXERCISES

Computing gross earnings.

◄ **Exercise 10-1**
Objective 2

The hourly rates of four employees of High Water Company follow, along with the hours that these employees worked during one week. Determine the gross earnings of each employee.

Employee No.	Hourly Rate	Hours Worked
1	$8.20	38
2	8.25	40
3	6.90	40
4	9.15	35

Computing regular earnings, overtime earnings, and gross pay.

◄ **Exercise 10-2**
Objective 2

During one week four production employees of Costal Manufacturing Company worked the hours shown below. All these employees receive overtime pay at one and one-half times their regular hourly rate for any hours worked beyond 40 in a week. Determine the regular earnings, overtime earnings, and gross earnings for each employee.

Employee No.	Hourly Rate	Hours Worked
1	$8.75	44
2	8.50	48
3	9.00	33
4	9.25	45

Determining social security withholding.

◄ **Exercise 10-3**
Objective 3

The monthly salaries for December and the year-to-date earnings of the employees of Seattle Broadcasting Company as of November 30 follow.

Employee No.	December Salary	Year-to-Date Earnings through November 30
1	$9,000	$85,800
2	5,000	71,500
3	8,800	80,860
4	4,000	57,200

Determine the amount of social security tax to be withheld from each employee's gross pay for December. Assume a 6.2 percent social security tax rate and an earnings base of $76,200 for the calendar year.

Determining deduction for Medicare tax.

◄ **Exercise 10-4**
Objective 4

Using the earnings data given in Exercise 10-3, determine the amount of Medicare tax to be withheld from each employee's gross pay for December. Assume a 1.45 percent Medicare tax rate and that all salaries and wages are subject to the tax.

Exercise 10-5 ►
Objective 5

Determining federal income tax withholding.

Data about the marital status, withholding allowances, and weekly salaries of the four office workers at Taylor Publishing Company follow. Use the tax tables in Figure 10-2 on pages 362–363 to find the amount of federal income tax to be deducted from each employee's gross pay.

Employee No.	Marital Status	Withholding Allowances	Weekly Salary
1	S	1	$550
2	M	3	675
3	S	2	480
4	M	1	420

Exercise 10-6 ►
Objective 7

Recording payroll transactions in the general journal.

Jackson Corporation has two office employees. A summary of their earnings and the related taxes withheld from their pay for the week ending June 6, 20--, follows.

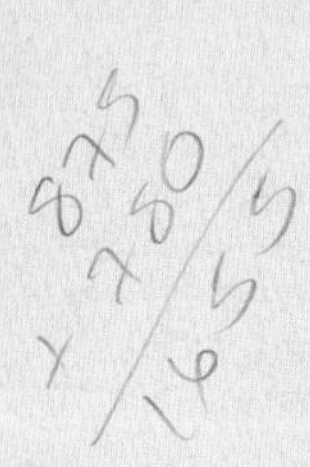

	Scott Barkley	Jill Wrenn
Gross earnings	$780.00	$875.00
Social security deduction	(48.36)	(54.25)
Medicare deduction	(11.31)	(12.69)
Income tax withholding	(83.00)	(96.00)
Net pay for week	$637.33	$712.06

1. Give the general journal entry to record the company's payroll for the week. Use the account names given in this chapter.
2. Give the general journal entry to summarize the checks to pay the weekly payroll.

Exercise 10-7 ►
Objective 7

Journalizing payroll transactions.

On June 30, 20--, the payroll register of Food Products Wholesale Company showed the following totals for the month: gross earnings, $19,200; social security tax, $1,190; Medicare tax, $278; income tax, $1,520; and net amount due, $16,212. Of the total earnings, $15,200 was for sales salaries and $4,000 was for office salaries. Prepare a general journal entry to record the monthly payroll of the firm on June 30, 20--.

Problems

Selected problems can be completed using:
Peachtree **QuickBooks** **Spreadsheets**

PROBLEM SET A

Problem 10-1A ►
Objectives 2, 3, 4, 5, 6, 7

  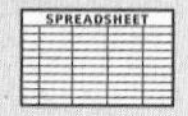

Computing gross earnings, determining deductions, preparing payroll register, journalizing payroll transactions.

Movie Time Theaters has four employees and pays them on an hourly basis. During the week beginning June 1 and ending June 7, 20--, these employees worked the hours shown below. Information about hourly rates, marital status, withholding allowances, and cumulative earnings prior to the current pay period also appears below.

Employee	Hours Worked	Hourly Rate	Marital Status	Withholding Allowances	Cumulative Earnings
Gary Smith	45	$9.25	M	4	$ 9,620
Ben Lewis	43	9.75	S	1	10,140
Shawn Jones	37	8.90	S	2	9,256
Debbie Watson	47	9.00	M	1	9,360

INSTRUCTIONS

1. Enter the basic payroll information for each employee in a payroll register. Record the employee's name, number of withholding allowances, marital status, total and overtime hours, and hourly rate. Consider any hours worked more than 40 in the week as overtime hours.
2. Compute the regular, overtime, and gross earnings for each employee. Enter the figures in the payroll register.
3. Compute the amount of social security tax to be withheld from each employee's earnings. Assume a 6.2 percent social security rate on the first $76,200 earned by the employee during the year. Enter the figures in the payroll register.
4. Compute the amount of Medicare tax to be withheld from each employee's earnings. Assume a 1.45 percent Medicare tax rate on all salaries and wages earned by the employee during the year. Enter the figures in the payroll register.
5. Determine the amount of federal income tax to be withheld from each employee's total earnings. Use the tax tables in Figure 10-2 on pages 362–363. Enter the figures in the payroll register.
6. Compute the net pay of each employee and enter the figures in the payroll register.
7. Total and prove the payroll register. Watson is an office worker. All other employees work in the theater.
8. Prepare a general journal entry to record the payroll for the week ended June 7, 20--.
9. Record the general journal entry to summarize payment of the payroll on June 10, 20--.

Analyze: What are Gary Smith's cumulative earnings on June 7?

◄ Problem 10-2A
Objectives 2, 3, 4, 5, 6, 7

Computing gross earnings, determining deductions, preparing payroll register, journalizing payroll transactions.

Tom Phillips operates Same Day Delivery Service. He has four employees who are paid on an hourly basis. During the work week beginning December 12 and ending December 18, 20--, his employees worked the following number of hours. Information about their hourly rates, marital status, and withholding allowances also follows, along with their cumulative earnings for the year prior to the December 12–18 payroll period.

Employee	Hours Worked	Hourly Rate	Marital Status	Withholding Allowances	Cumulative Earnings
Jason Knight	44	$ 9.85	M	3	$19,700
Aaron Fuller	39	26.50	S	1	55,120
Jon Perot	46	22.75	M	2	47,320
Kelly Aikman	43	10.50	S	0	21,840

INSTRUCTIONS

1. Enter the basic payroll information for each employee in a payroll register. Record the employee's name, number of withholding allowances, marital status, total and overtime hours, and hourly rate. Consider any hours worked more than 40 in the week as overtime hours.
2. Compute the regular, overtime, and gross earnings for each employee. Enter the figures in the payroll register.
3. Compute the amount of social security tax to be withheld from each employee's gross earnings. Assume a 6.2 percent social security rate on the first $76,200 earned by the employee during the year. Enter the figures in the payroll register.
4. Compute the amount of Medicare tax to be withheld from each employee's gross earnings. Assume a 1.45 percent Medicare tax rate on all salaries and wages earned by the employee during the year. Enter the figures in the payroll register.
5. Determine the amount of federal income tax to be withheld from each employee's total earnings. Fuller's withholding is $197, and Perot's is $142. Use the tax tables in Figure 10-2 on pages 362–363 to determine the withholding for Knight and Aikman. Enter the figures in the payroll register.
6. Compute the net amount due each employee and enter the figures in the payroll register.
7. Total and prove the payroll register. Knight and Aikman are office workers. Fuller and Perot are delivery workers.
8. Prepare a general journal entry to record the payroll for the week ended December 18, 20--.
9. Give the entry in general journal form on December 20, 20--, to summarize payment of wages for the week.

Analyze: What percentage of total taxable wages was delivery wages?

PROBLEM SET B

Problem 10-1B ►
Objectives 2, 3, 4, 5, 6, 7

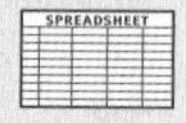

Computing earnings, determining deductions and net amount due, preparing payroll register, journalizing payroll transactions.

The four employees of Swan's Ice Cream Parlor are paid on an hourly basis. During the week March 6–12, 20--, these employees worked the following number of hours. Information about their hourly rates, marital status, withholding allowances, and cumulative earnings prior to the current pay period also follows.

Employee	Hours Worked	Hourly Rate	Marital Status	Withholding Allowances	Cumulative Earnings
Corey Hunter	45	$8.75	M	4	$2,800.00
Peter Black	26	7.50	M	1	2,400.00
Latoya Snow	43	7.75	S	0	2,480.00
Haven England	13	7.25	S	2	0.00

INSTRUCTIONS

1. Enter the basic payroll information for each employee in a payroll register. Record the employee's name, number of withholding allowances, marital status, total number of hours worked, overtime hours, and hourly rate. Consider any hours worked beyond 40 in the week as overtime hours.
2. Compute the regular earnings, overtime earnings, and gross earnings for each employee. Enter the figures in the payroll register.
3. Compute the amount of social security tax to be withheld from each employee's gross earnings. Assume a 6.2 percent social security tax rate on the first $76,200 earned by each employee during the year. Enter the figures in the payroll register.
4. Compute the amount of Medicare tax to be withheld from each employee's gross earnings. Assume a 1.45 percent Medicare tax rate on all earnings for each employee during the year. Enter the figure on the payroll register.
5. Determine the amount of federal income tax to be withheld from each employee's gross earnings. Use the tax tables in Figure 10-2 on pages 362–363. Enter the amounts in the payroll register.
6. Compute the net amount due each employee and enter the figures in the payroll register.
7. Complete the payroll register. All employees are classified as store employees.
8. Prepare a general journal entry to record the payroll for the week ended March 12, 20--.
9. Record the general journal entry to summarize the payment on March 14, 20-- of the net amount due employees.

Analyze: What is the difference between the amount credited to the **Cash** account on March 14 for the payroll week ended March 12 and the amount debited to **Store Wages Expenses** for the same payroll period? What causes the difference between these two figures?

◄ **Problem 10-2B**
Objectives 2, 3, 4, 5, 6, 7

Computing earnings, determining deductions and net amount due, preparing payroll register, journalizing payroll transactions.

David Flores operates Flores Consulting Service. He has four employees and pays them on an hourly basis. During the week November 6–12, 20--, his employees worked the following number of hours. Information about their hourly rates, marital status, withholding allowances, and cumulative earnings for the year prior to the current pay period also follows.

Employee	Hours Worked	Hourly Rate	Marital Status	Withholding Allowances	Cumulative Earnings
Barbara Cain	43	$ 8.50	M	2	$15,640
Casey Bryant	36	8.25	S	1	15,180
Linda Hogan	45	28.00	M	3	51,520
Leona Stewart	41	33.00	S	1	77,500

INSTRUCTIONS

1. Enter the basic payroll information for each employee in a payroll register. Record the employee's name, number of withholding allowances, marital status, total hours, overtime hours, and hourly rate. Consider any hours worked beyond 40 in the week as overtime hours.
2. Compute the regular earnings, overtime earnings, and gross earnings for each employee. Enter the figures in the payroll register.
3. Compute the amount of social security tax to be withheld from each employee's gross earnings. Assume a 6.2 percent social security rate on the first $76,200 earned by the employee during the year. Enter the figures in the payroll register.
4. Compute the amount of Medicare tax to be withheld from each employee's gross earnings. Assume a 1.45 percent Medicare tax rate on all earnings paid during the year. Enter the figures in the payroll register.
5. Determine the amount of federal income tax to be withheld from each employee's earnings. Federal income tax to be withheld from Hogan's pay is $189 and from Stewart's pay is $296. Use the tax tables in Figure 10-2 on pages 362–363 to determine the withholding for Cain and Bryant. Enter the figures in the payroll register.
6. Compute the net amount due each employee and enter the figures in the payroll register.
7. Complete the payroll register. Cain and Bryant are office workers. Earnings for Hogan and Stewart are charged to consulting wages.
8. Prepare a general journal entry to record the payroll for the week ended November 12, 20--. Use the account names given in this chapter.
9. Give the general journal entry to summarize payment of amounts due employees on November 15, 20--.

Analyze: What total deductions were taken from employee paychecks for the pay period ended November 12?

CHAPTER 10 CHALLENGE PROBLEM

Payroll Accounting

Bueno Company pays salaries and wages on the last day of each month. Payments made on November 30, 20--, for amounts incurred during November are shown below. Cumulative amounts paid prior to November 30 to the persons named are also shown.

a. Jason Jackson, president, gross monthly salary $14,000; gross earnings paid prior to November 30, $140,000.

b. Laura Peters, vice president, gross monthly salary $11,000; gross earnings paid prior to November 30, $55,000.

c. Martha Spiller, independent accountant who audits the company's accounts and performs certain consulting services, $13,000; gross amount paid prior to November 30, $5,000.

d. Pat Hammon, treasurer, gross monthly salary $5,000; gross earnings paid prior to November 30, $50,000.

e. Payment to Anderson Security Services for Neal Black, a security guard who is on duty on Saturdays and Sundays, $900; amount paid to Anderson Security prior to November 30, $10,500.

INSTRUCTIONS

1. Using the tax rates and earnings bases given in this chapter, prepare a schedule showing this information:

   a. Each employee's cumulative earnings prior to November 30, 20--.

   b. Each employee's gross earnings for November.

   c. The amounts to be withheld for each payroll tax from each employee's earnings (employee income tax withholdings for Jackson are $3,700; for Peters, $3,200; and for Hammon, $875).

   d. The net amount due each employee.

   e. The total gross earnings, the total of each payroll tax deduction, and the total net amount payable to employees.

2. Record the general journal entry for the company's payroll on November 30, 20--.

3. Record the general journal entry for payments to employees on November 30, 20--.

Analyze: What is the balance of the **Salaries Payable** account after all payroll entries have been posted for the month?

CHAPTER 10 CRITICAL THINKING PROBLEM

Payroll Internal Controls

Several years ago, Hector Martinez opened the Fajita Grill, a restaurant specializing in homemade Mexican food. The restaurant was so successful that Martinez was able to expand, and his company now operates seven restaurants in the local area.

Martinez tells you that when he first started, he handled all aspects of the business himself. Now that there are seven Fajita Grills, he depends on the managers of each restaurant to make decisions and oversee day-to-day operations. Hector oversees operations at the company's headquarters, which is located at the first Fajita Grill.

Each manager interviews and hires new employees for a restaurant. The new employee is required to complete a Form W-4, which is sent by the manager to the headquarters office. Each restaurant has a time clock, and employees are required to clock in as they arrive or depart. Blank time cards are kept in a box under the time clock. At the beginning of each week, employees complete the top of the card they will use during the week. The manager collects the cards at the end of the week and sends them to headquarters.

Hector hired his cousin Rosa Maria to prepare the payroll instead of assigning this task to the accounting staff. Since she is a relative, Hector trusts her and has confidence that confidential payroll information will not be divulged to other employees.

When Rosa Maria receives a Form W-4 for a new employee, she sets up an individual earnings record for the employee. Each week, using the time cards sent by each restaurant's manager, she computes the gross pay, deductions, and net pay for all employees. She then posts details to the employees' earnings records and prepares and signs the payroll checks. The checks are sent to the managers, who distribute them to the employees.

As long as Rosa Maria receives a time card for an employee, she prepares a paycheck. If she fails to get a time card for an employee, she checks with the manager to see if the employee was terminated or has quit. At the end of the month, Rosa Maria reconciles the payroll bank account. She also prepares quarterly and annual payroll tax returns.

1. Identify any weaknesses in Fajita Grill's payroll system.
2. Identify one way a manager could defraud Fajita Grill under the present payroll system.
3. What internal control procedures would you recommend to Hector to protect against the fraud you identified above?

Business Connections

MANAGERIAL FOCUS **Cash Management** ◄ Connection 1

1. Why should managers check the amount spent for overtime?
2. The new controller for Ellis Company, a manufacturing firm, has suggested to management that the business change from paying the factory employees in cash to paying them by check. What reasons would you offer to support this suggestion?
3. Why should management make sure that a firm has an adequate set of payroll records?
4. How can detailed payroll records help managers to control expenses?

Ethical DILEMMA **Clocking Out** You are employed by a firm that uses a time clock for employees to punch in when they arrive at work and punch out at quitting time. One employee asks you to punch out for him on a day that he plans to leave work two hours early. What will you do? ◄ Connection 2

Street WISE: Questions from the Real World **Human Resources** Refer to the *1999 Annual Report* of The Home Depot in Appendix B. ◄ Connection 3

1. Locate the letter written by the president and chief executive officer to the stockholders, customers, and associates. Describe the goals and company vision in regard to the employees of The Home Depot. Based on your knowledge of The Home Depot stores and the financial information presented in Appendix B, what types of positions do you think the company hires? Describe whether you think each job position listed is paid on hourly rate, commission, or salary basis.
2. Locate the financial discussion titled "Fiscal year ended January 30, 2000 compared to January 31, 1999." Describe the financial data regarding payroll expenses. What factors contributed to increases in payroll expenses?

FINANCIAL STATEMENT ANALYSIS **Income Statement** Southwest Airlines Co. reported the following data on its consolidated statement of income for the years ended December 31, 1999, 1998, and 1997. ◄ Connection 4

SOUTHWEST

Southwest Airlines Co.
Consolidated Statement of Income

(in thousands except per share amounts)	Years Ended December 31		
	1999	***1998***	***1997***
Operating expenses:			
Salaries, wages, and benefits	*1,455,237*	*1,285,942*	*1,136,542*
Total operating expenses	*3,954,011*	*3,480,369*	*3,292,582*

Analyze:

1. The amounts reported for the line item "Salaries, wages, and benefits" include expenses for company retirement plans and profit-sharing plans. If Southwest Airlines Co. spent approximately $1,263,237,000 on wages and salaries alone, compute the employer's Medicare tax expense for 1999. Use a rate of 1.45 percent.
2. What percentage of total operating expenses was spent on salaries, wages, and benefits in 1999?
3. By what amount did salaries, wages, and benefits increase from 1997 to 1999?

Analyze Online: Go to the company Web site for Southwest Airlines Co. **(www.southwest.com).** Locate the company fact sheet within the *About SWA* section of the site.

4. How many employees does Southwest Airlines Co. employ?
5. How many resumes were submitted to the company for consideration in the current year?

Connection 5 ► *Extending the Thought* **Exempt Employees** Salaried exempt employees generally work for a predetermined annual rate regardless of the actual number of hours they work. In many cases, supervisors and managers work considerably more than 40 hours per week. What do you think of this practice from the employee's perspective? From the employer's perspective?

Connection 6 ► Business Communication **Pie Chart** Employees should understand how take-home, or net, pay is computed. As the payroll manager, you have been asked to make a presentation to the employees of Broad Street Bakery on how their gross earnings are allocated to taxes and net pay. You decide that a visual representation of the allocation would be most effective. Create a pie chart for the following information.

Employee: Carol Blakley		Federal income tax:	$ 35.00
Gross earnings:	$312.00	State income tax:	6.71
Social security tax:	20.79	Medical insurance:	4.10
Medicare tax:	4.86	Net pay:	240.54

Connection 7 ► TeamWork **Career Research** ADP, Inc., provides payroll services to clients worldwide. The company processes paychecks for 29 million workers each payday. As a team, research career opportunities found on the ADP Web site **(www.adp.com).** Identify one job title of interest to each member of your team and prepare a report comparing the jobs.

Connection 8 ► interNET CONNECTION **U.S. Department of Labor** The federal government makes a great deal of information available related to wages and earnings. Visit the Department of Labor Web site at **www.dol.gov.** What is the current minimum wage? Give three examples of employees who are exempt from both minimum wage and overtime pay requirements. When both the federal and state laws apply, which standard of laws must be observed?

Answers to Self Reviews

Answers to Section 1 Self Review

1. The federal requirement that covered employees be paid at a rate equal to one and one-half times their normal hourly rate for each hour worked in excess of 40 hours per week.
2. By a tax levied equally on both employers and employees. The tax amount is based on the earnings.
3. By state and federal taxes levied on the employer.
4. **d.** does not exist.
5. **a.** employees who become unemployed.
6. She is not an employee. She is an independent contractor because she has been hired to complete a specific job and is not under the control of the employer.

Answers to Section 2 Self Review

1. Social security tax, Medicare tax, and federal income tax
2. Health insurance premiums, life insurance premiums, union dues, retirement plans
3. Amount of earnings, period covered by the payment, employee's marital status, and the number of withholding allowances
4. **b.** $392
5. **d.** hours worked
6. When you receive a signed Form W-4 for the change in withholding.

Answers to Section 3 Self Review

1. Debit **Salaries and Wages Payable** and credit **Cash.**
2. Using a separate payroll account simplifies the bank reconciliation procedure and makes it easier to identify outstanding payroll checks.
3. Employee's name, address, social security number, date of birth, number of withholding allowances claimed, rate of pay, and any other information needed to compute earnings and complete tax reports.
4. **c.** liability account.
5. **a.** payroll register.
6. **Health Insurance Premiums Expense** Dr. 20.00 should be **Health Insurance Premiums Payable** Cr. 20.00; **Social Security Taxes Expense** Cr. 103.48 should be **Social Security Tax Payable** Cr. 103.48; **Cash** Cr. 1,311.64 should be **Salaries and Wages Payable** Cr. 1,311.64

Answers to Comprehensive Self Review

1. To compensate workers for losses suffered from job-related injuries or to compensate their families if the employee's death occurs in the course of employment.
2. Social security taxes are determined by multiplying the amount of taxable earnings by the social security tax rate.
3. To record in one place all information about an employee's earnings and withholdings for the period.
4. By check because there is far less possibility of mistake, lost money, or fraud. The check serves as a receipt and permanent record of the transaction.
5. An employee is one who is hired by the employer and who is under the control and direction of the employer. An independent contractor is paid by the company to carry out a specific task or job and is not under the direct supervision and control of the employer.

CHAPTER 11

Learning Objectives

1. Explain how and when payroll taxes are paid to the government.
2. Compute and record the employer's social security and Medicare taxes.
3. Record deposit of social security, Medicare, and employee income taxes.
4. Prepare an Employer's Quarterly Federal Tax Return, Form 941.
5. Prepare Wage and Tax Statement (Form W-2) and Annual Transmittal of Wage and Tax Statements (Form W-3).
6. Compute and record liability for federal and state unemployment taxes and record payment of the taxes.
7. Prepare an Employer's Federal Unemployment Tax Return, Form 940 or 940-EZ.
8. Compute and record workers' compensation insurance premiums.
9. Define the accounting terms new to this chapter.

Payroll Taxes, Deposits, and Reports

LANDS' END
DIRECT MERCHANTS

www.landsend.com

In 1963 the first Lands' End store opened in the old tannery district of Chicago. It started with catalog sales of sailing equipment, duffel bags, and clothing suitable for sailing. Now the company operates 16 outlet stores in the United States and two outlet stores in the United Kingdom and Japan. Lands' End is also on the Internet.

In 1999 the company employed approximately 7,200 individuals. During the peak holiday season (September to December), the employee count increases to 9,700. Keeping accurate payroll records for a workforce of this size requires an effective payroll system and a knowledgeable accounting staff.

Thinking Critically

Lands' End hires a large number of seasonal employees. What challenges does this present to the payroll accounting department?

For more information on Lands' End, go to: collegeaccounting.glencoe.com.

New Terms

Employer's Annual Federal Unemployment Tax Return, Form 940 or Form 940-EZ

Employer's Quarterly Federal Tax Return, Form 941

Experience rating system

Merit rating system

Transmittal of Wage and Tax Statements, Form W-3

Unemployment insurance program

Wage and Tax Statement, Form W-2

Withholding statement

Section 1

Section Objectives

1. **Explain how and when payroll taxes are paid to the government.**
   WHY IT'S IMPORTANT
   Employers are required by law to deposit payroll taxes.
2. **Compute and record the employer's social security and Medicare taxes.**
   WHY IT'S IMPORTANT
   Accounting records should reflect all liabilities.
3. **Record deposit of social security, Medicare, and employee income taxes.**
   WHY IT'S IMPORTANT
   Payments decrease the payroll tax liability.
4. **Prepare an Employer's Quarterly Federal Tax Return, Form 941.**
   WHY IT'S IMPORTANT
   Completing a federal tax return is part of the employer's legal obligation.
5. **Prepare Wage and Tax Statement (Form W-2) and Annual Transmittal of Wage and Tax Statements (Form W-3).**
   WHY IT'S IMPORTANT
   Employers are legally required to provide end-of-year payroll information.

Terms to Learn

Employer's Quarterly Federal Tax Return, Form 941
Transmittal of Wage and Tax Statements, Form W-3
Wage and Tax Statement, Form W-2
withholding statement

Social Security, Medicare, and Employee Income Tax

In Chapter 10 you learned that the law requires employers to act as collection agents for certain taxes due from employees. In this chapter you will learn how to compute the employer's taxes, make tax payments, and file the required tax returns and reports.

Payment of Payroll Taxes

The payroll register provides information about wages subject to payroll taxes. Figure 11-1 on page 391 shows a portion of the payroll register for On Line Furnishings for the week ending January 6.

Employers make tax deposits for federal income tax withheld from employee earnings, the employees' share of social security and Medicare taxes withheld from earnings, and the employer's share of social security and Medicare taxes. The deposits are made in a Federal Reserve Bank or other authorized financial institution. Businesses usually make payroll tax deposits at their own bank. There are two ways to deposit payroll taxes: by electronic deposit or with a tax deposit coupon.

The *Electronic Federal Tax Payment System (EFTPS)* is a system for electronically depositing employment taxes using a telephone or a computer. Any employer can use EFTPS. An employer *must* use EFTPS if the annual federal tax deposits are more than $200,000. Employers who are required to make electronic deposits and do not do so can be subject to a 10 percent penalty.

Employers who are not required to use EFTPS may deposit payroll taxes using a *Federal Tax Deposit Coupon, Form 8109*. The employer's name, tax identification number, and address are preprinted on Form 8109. The employer enters the deposit amount on the form and makes the payment with a check, money order, or cash.

In some cases an employer may use Form 8109-B. *Form 8109-B* is a coupon that is *not* preprinted. Form 8109-B may be used if a new employer has been assigned an identification number but has not yet received a supply of Forms 8109, or an employer has not received a resupply of Forms 8109. Figure 11-2 on page 391 shows the completed Form 8109-B for On Line Furnishings.

The frequency of deposits depends on the amount of tax liability. The amount currently owed is compared to the tax liability threshold. For simplicity this textbook uses $1,000 as the tax liability threshold.

The deposit schedules are not related to how often employees are paid. The deposit schedules are based on the amount currently owed and the amount reported in the lookback period. The *lookback period* is a four-quarter period ending on June 30 of the preceding year.

AND ENDING *January 6, 20--* **PAID** *January 8, 20--*

TAXABLE WAGES			DEDUCTIONS				DISTRIBUTION			
SOCIAL SECURITY	MEDICARE	FUTA	SOCIAL SECURITY	MEDICARE	INCOME TAX	HEALTH INSURANCE	NET AMOUNT	CHECK NO.	OFFICE SALARIES	SHIPPING WAGES
360 00	360 00	360 00	22 32	5 22	28 00		304 46	1725		360 00
380 00	380 00	380 00	23 56	5 51	42 00		308 93	1726		380 00
300 00	300 00	300 00	18 60	4 35	14 00	20 00	243 05	1727		300 00
520 00	520 00	520 00	32 24	7 54	44 00	20 00	416 22	1728		520 00
400 00	400 00	400 00	24 80	5 80	45 00		324 40	1729	400 00	
1 960 00	1 960 00	1 960 00	121 52	28 42	173 00	40 00	1 597 06		400 00	1 560 00

▲ **FIGURE 11-1**
Portion of a Payroll Register

1. If the amount owed is less than $1,000, payment is due quarterly with the payroll tax return (Form 941).

   Example. An employer's tax liability is as follows:

January	$290
February	320
March	310
	$920

   Since at no time during the quarter is the accumulated tax liability $1,000 or more, no deposit is required during the quarter. The employer may pay the amount with the payroll tax returns.

2. If the amount owed is $1,000 or more, the schedule is determined from the total taxes reported on Form 941 during the lookback period.
   a. If the amount reported in the lookback period was $50,000 or less, the employer is subject to the *Monthly Deposit Schedule Rule.* Monthly payments are due on the 15th day of the following month. For example, the January payment is due by February 15.
   b. If the amount reported in the lookback period was more than $50,000, the employer is subject to the *Semiweekly Deposit Schedule Rule.* "Semiweekly" refers to the fact that deposits are due on either Wednesdays or Fridays, depending on the employer's payday.

1 Objective

Explain how and when payroll taxes are paid to the government.

▼ **FIGURE 11-2**
Federal Tax Deposit Coupon, Form 8109-B

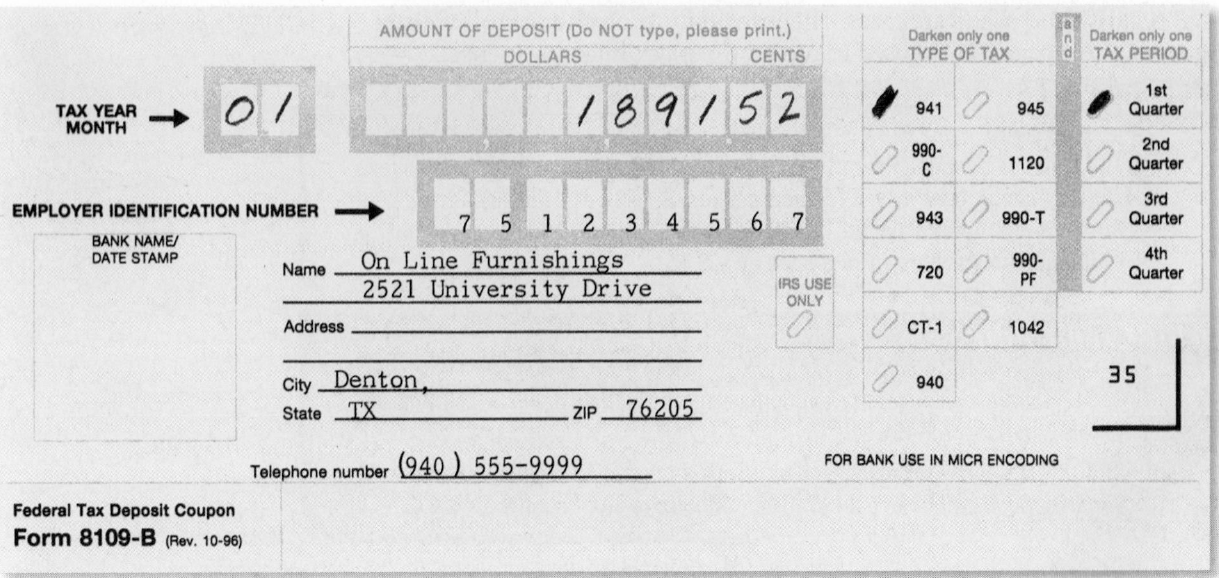

AMOUNT OF DEPOSIT (Do NOT type, please print.)
DOLLARS | CENTS
1891 | 52

TAX YEAR MONTH → 01

EMPLOYER IDENTIFICATION NUMBER → 75-1234567

BANK NAME/ DATE STAMP

Name On Line Furnishings
2521 University Drive
Address
City Denton,
State TX ZIP 76205

Telephone number (940) 555-9999

IRS USE ONLY

Darken only one TYPE OF TAX: 941 (darkened), 945, 990-C, 1120, 943, 990-T, 720, 990-PF, CT-1, 1042, 940

Darken only one TAX PERIOD: 1st Quarter (darkened), 2nd Quarter, 3rd Quarter, 4th Quarter

35

FOR BANK USE IN MICR ENCODING

Federal Tax Deposit Coupon
Form 8109-B (Rev. 10-96)

- If payday is a Wednesday, Thursday, or Friday, the deposit is due on the following Wednesday.
- If payday is a Saturday, Sunday, Monday, or Tuesday, the deposit is due on the following Friday.

c. For new employers with no lookback period, if the amount owed is $1,000 or more, payments are due under the Monthly Deposit Schedule Rule.

3. If the total accumulated tax liability reaches $100,000 or more on any day, a deposit is due on the next banking day. This applies even if the employer is on a monthly or a semiweekly deposit schedule.

2 Objective

Compute and record the employer's social security and Medicare taxes.

Employer's Social Security and Medicare Tax Expenses

Remember that both employers and employees pay social security and Medicare taxes. Figure 11-1 shows the *employee's* share of these payroll taxes. The *employer* pays the same amount of payroll taxes. At the assumed rate of 6.2 percent for social security and 1.45 percent for Medicare tax, the employer's tax liability is $299.88.

Tax Liability

The employer's tax liability is the amount owed for

- employee withholdings (income tax, social security tax, Medicare tax);
- employer's share of social security and Medicare taxes.

	Employee (Withheld)		Employer (Matched)
Social security	$121.52		$121.52
Medicare	28.42		28.42
	$149.94		$149.94
Total		$299.88	

In Chapter 10 you learned how to record employee payroll deductions. The entry to record the employer's share of social security and Medicare taxes is made at the end of each payroll period. The debit is to the **Payroll Taxes Expense** account. The credits are to the same liability accounts used to record the employee's share of payroll taxes.

Business Transaction

On January 8 On Line Furnishings recorded the employer's share of social security and Medicare taxes. The information on the payroll register (Figure 11-1 on page 391) is used to record the payroll taxes expense.

Analysis

The expense account, **Payroll Taxes Expense,** is increased by the employer's share of social security and Medicare taxes, $149.94. The liability account, **Social Security Tax Payable,** is increased by $121.52. The liability account, **Medicare Tax Payable,** is increased by $28.42.

Debit-Credit Rules

DEBIT Increases to expense accounts are recorded as debits. Debit **Payroll Taxes Expense** for $149.94.

CREDIT Increases to liability accounts are recorded as credits. Credit **Social Security Tax Payable** for $121.52. Credit **Medicare Tax Payable** for $28.42.

T-Account Presentation

General Journal Entry

GENERAL JOURNAL PAGE 1

	DATE		DESCRIPTION	POST. REF.	DEBIT	CREDIT	
1	20--						1
2	Jan.	8	Payroll Taxes Expense		149 94		2
3			Social Security Tax Payable			121 52	3
4			Medicare Tax Payable			28 42	4
5			To record social security and				5
6			Medicare taxes for Jan. 8 payroll				6

The Bottom Line

Employer's Payroll Taxes

Income Statement	
Expenses	↑ 149.94
Net Income	↓ 149.94
Balance Sheet	
Liabilities	↑ 149.94
Equity	↓ 149.94

According to the American Payroll Association, the Social Security Administration provides benefits to approximately 44 million men, women, and children. It is essential that earnings are correctly reported so that future benefits can be calculated accurately.

Recording the Payment of Taxes Withheld

3 Objective

Record deposit of social security, Medicare, and employee income taxes.

At the end of January, the accounting records for On Line Furnishings contained the following information.

	Employee (Withheld)	Employer (Matched)	Total
Social security	$ 486.08	$486.08	$ 972.16
Medicare	113.68	113.68	227.36
Federal income tax	692.00	–	692.00
Total	$1,291.76	$599.76	$1,891.52

On Line Furnishings is on a monthly payment schedule. The amount reported in the lookback period is less than $50,000. The current payroll tax liability is more than $1,000. (Recall that this textbook uses $1,000 as the tax liability threshold.) A tax payment is due on the 15th day of the following month, February 15.

Figure 11-2 on page 391 shows the Federal Tax Deposit Coupon for On Line Furnishings. Notice that the type of tax (Form 941) and the tax period (first quarter) are indicated on the form. The coupon is accompanied by a check from On Line Furnishings for $1,891.52 written to First State Bank, an authorized financial institution.

The entry to record the tax deposit is shown on page 394. The entry is shown in general journal form for illustration purposes only. (On Line Furnishings actually uses a cash payments journal.)

	DATE		DESCRIPTION	POST. REF.	DEBIT	CREDIT	
			GENERAL JOURNAL			PAGE 2	
1	20--						1
22	Feb.	15	*Social Security Tax Payable*		972 16		22
23			*Medicare Tax Payable*		227 36		23
24			*Employee Income Tax Payable*		692 00		24
25			*Cash*			1 891 52	25
26			*Deposit of payroll taxes withholding*				26
27			*at First State Bank*				27

February Payroll Records

There were four weekly payroll periods in February. Each hourly employee worked the same number of hours each week and had the same gross pay and deductions as in January. The office clerk earned her regular salary and had the same deductions as in January. At the end of the month

- the individual earnings records were updated;
- Form 8109, Federal Tax Deposit Coupon, was prepared, and the taxes were deposited before March 15;
- the tax deposit was recorded in the cash payments journal.

March Payroll Records

There were five weekly payroll periods in March. Assume that the payroll period ended on March 31, and the payday was on March 31. Also assume that the earnings and deductions of the employees were the same for each week as in January and February. At the end of the month the individual earnings records were updated, the taxes were deposited, and the tax deposit was recorded in the cash payments journal.

Quarterly Summary of Earnings Records

At the end of each quarter, the individual earnings records are totaled. This involves adding the columns in the Earnings, Deductions, and Net Pay sections. Figure 11-3 on page 395 shows the earnings record, posted and summarized, for Cindy Taylor for the first quarter.

Table 11-1 below shows the quarterly totals for each employee of On Line Furnishings. This information is taken from the individual earnings records. Through the end of the first quarter, no employee has exceeded the social security earnings limit ($76,200) or the FUTA/SUTA limit ($7,000).

TABLE 11-1 ▼ Summary of Earnings

Summary of Earnings, Quarter Ended March 31, 20--

	Taxable Earnings				Deductions		
Employee	Total Earnings	Social Security	Medicare	SUTA & FUTA	Social Security	Medicare Tax	Income Tax
Cindy Taylor	4,680	4,680	4,680	4,680	290.16	67.86	364.00
Edward Gallegos	4,940	4,940	4,940	4,940	306.28	71.63	546.00
Bill Turner	3,900	3,900	3,900	3,900	241.80	56.55	182.00
Cecilia Lin	6,760	6,760	6,760	6,760	419.12	98.02	572.00
Selena Anderson	5,200	5,200	5,200	5,200	322.40	75.40	585.00
Totals	25,480	25,480	25,480	25,480	1,579.76	369.46	2,249.00

EARNINGS RECORD FOR 20--

NAME Cindy Taylor **RATE** $9 per hour **SOCIAL SECURITY NO.** 123-XX-XXXX
ADDRESS 6480 Oak Tree Drive, Denton, TX 76209-6789 **DATE OF BIRTH** November 23, 1979
WITHHOLDING ALLOWANCES 1 **MARITAL STATUS** M

PAYROLL NO.	DATE		HOURS		EARNINGS				DEDUCTIONS				NET PAY
	WK. END.	PAID	RG	OT	REGULAR	OVERTIME	TOTAL	CUMULATIVE	SOCIAL SECURITY	MEDICARE	INCOME TAX	OTHER	
1	1/06	1/08	40		360 00		360 00	360 00	22 32	5 22	28 00		304 46
2	1/13	1/15	40		360 00		360 00	720 00	22 32	5 22	28 00		304 46
3	1/20	1/22	40		360 00		360 00	1080 00	22 32	5 22	28 00		304 46
4	1/27	1/29	40		360 00		360 00	1440 00	22 32	5 22	28 00		304 46
	January				1440 00		1440 00	1440 00	89 28	20 88	112 00		1217 84
1	2/03	2/05	40		360 00		360 00	360 00	22 32	5 22	28 00		304 46
2	2/10	2/12	40		360 00		360 00	720 00	22 32	5 22	28 00		304 46
3	2/17	2/19	40		360 00		360 00	1080 00	22 32	5 22	28 00		304 46
4	2/24	2/25	40		360 00		360 00	1440 00	22 32	5 22	28 00		304 46
	February				1440 00		1440 00	1440 00	89 28	20 88	112 00		1217 84
1	3/03	3/05	40		360 00		360 00	360 00	22 32	5 22	28 00		304 46
2	3/10	3/12	40		360 00		360 00	720 00	22 32	5 22	28 00		304 46
3	3/17	3/19	40		360 00		360 00	1080 00	22 32	5 22	28 00		304 46
4	3/24	3/26	40		360 00		360 00	1440 00	22 32	5 22	28 00		304 46
5	3/31	3/31	40		360 00		360 00	1800 00	22 32	5 22	28 00		304 46
	March				1800 00		1800 00	1800 00	111 60	26 10	140 00		1522 30
	First Quarter				4680 00		4680 00	4680 00	290 16	67 86	364 00		3957 98

▲ **FIGURE 11-3**
Individual Earnings Record

Employer's Quarterly Federal Tax Return

4 Objective

Prepare an Employer's Quarterly Federal Tax Return, Form 941.

Each quarter an employer files an **Employer's Quarterly Federal Tax Return, Form 941** with the Internal Revenue Service. Form 941 must be filed by all employers subject to federal income tax withholding, social security tax, or Medicare tax, with certain exceptions as specified in *Publication 15, Circular E.* This tax return provides information about employee earnings, the tax liability for each month in the quarter, and the deposits made.

The Social Security Administration administers the Old Age and Survivors, Disability Insurance, and Supplemental Security Income Programs. These programs are funded by the social security taxes collected from employees and matched by employers. In 1999 more than $462 billion of social security taxes were collected by the Social Security Administration.

Quarters

A quarter is a three-month period. There are four quarters in a year:

- 1st quarter: January, February, March
- 2nd quarter: April, May, June
- 3rd quarter: July, August, September
- 4th quarter: October, November, December

When to File Form 941. The due date for Form 941 is the last day of the month following the end of each calendar quarter. If the taxes for the quarter were deposited when due, the due date is extended by 10 days.

Completing Form 941. Figure 11-4 on page 397 shows Form 941 for On Line Furnishings. Form 941 is prepared using the data on the quarterly summary of earnings records, Table 11-1. Let's examine Form 941.

- Use the preprinted form if it is available. Otherwise, enter the employer's name, address, and identification number at the top of Form 941. Enter the date the quarter ended.
- *Line 1* is completed for the first quarter only. Enter the number of employees in the pay period that includes March 12.
- *Line 2* shows total wages and tips subject to withholding. For On Line Furnishings, the total subject to withholding is $25,480.
- *Line 3* shows the total employee income tax withheld during the quarter, $2,249.
- *Line 4* shows adjustments of income tax withheld in prior quarters of the year. This line would be used to show corrections of errors made in previous withholdings.
- *Line 5* shows the adjusted income tax withheld. Since there were no adjustments on Line 4, the amount on Line 5 is the same as on Line 3, $2,249.
- *Line 6a* shows the total amount of wages that are subject to social security taxes, $25,480. The amount is multiplied by the combined social security tax rate, 12.4 percent.

Social security tax:	
Employee's share	6.2%
Employer's share	6.2
Total	12.4%

Working Abroad

The IRS has tax treaties with more than 50 countries including Canada, Germany, and France. These tax treaties spell out exactly how income taxes are handled for U.S. citizens working abroad.

- *Line 6b* shows the amount of social security taxes, $3,159.52.
- *Line 6c* is for reporting social security tips. It is blank for On Line Furnishings.
- *Line 7a* shows the amount of wages and tips that are subject to Medicare taxes, $25,480. The amount is multiplied by the combined Medicare tax rate, 2.9 percent.

Medicare tax:	
Employee's share	1.45%
Employer's share	1.45
Total	2.90%

Tax Calculations

Social security and Medicare taxes are calculated by multiplying the taxable wages by the tax rate.

- *Line 7b* shows the amount of Medicare taxes, $738.92.
- *Line 8* shows the total social security and Medicare taxes, $3,898.44 ($3,159.52 + $738.92).
- *Line 9* is blank. There were no adjustments.
- *Line 10* shows the adjusted social security and Medicare taxes, $3,898.44. It is the same as Line 8 because there were no adjustments on Line 9.
- *Line 11* shows the total tax liability for employee income tax withheld plus social security and Medicare taxes, $6,147.44 ($2,249.00 + $3,898.44).

  Don't be surprised if there is a small difference between the tax withheld that is computed on Form 941 and the tax withheld that is computed on the sum of the payroll registers. Any small difference that is due to rounding is settled on Form 941.

Form **941** (Rev. October 2000) Department of the Treasury Internal Revenue Service

Employer's Quarterly Federal Tax Return

▶ **See separate instructions for information on completing this return.**

Please type or print.

Enter state code for state in which deposits were made **only** if different from state in address to the right ▶ (see page 2 of instructions).

OMB No. 1545-0029

Name (as distinguished from trade name): *Roberta Rosario*	Date quarter ended: *March 31, 20--*	T
Trade name, if any: *On Line Furnishings*	Employer identification number: *75-1234567*	FF
Address (number and street): *2521 University Drive*	City, state, and ZIP code: *Denton, TX 76205*	FD
		FP
		I
		T

If address is different from prior return, check here ▶ ☐ — IRS Use

1 1 1 1 1 1 1 1 1 1 2 3 3 3 3 3 3 3 3 4 4 4 5 5 5

6 7 8 8 8 8 8 8 8 8 9 9 9 9 9 10 10 10 10 10 10 10 10 10 10

If you do not have to file returns in the future, check here ▶ ☐ and enter date final wages paid ▶

If you are a seasonal employer, see **Seasonal employers** on page 1 of the instructions and check here ▶ ☐

1	Number of employees in the pay period that includes March 12th ▶ 5		
2	Total wages and tips, plus other compensation	2	25,480 00
3	Total income tax withheld from wages, tips, and sick pay	3	2,249 00
4	Adjustment of withheld income tax for preceding quarters of calendar year	4	
5	Adjusted total of income tax withheld (line 3 as adjusted by line 4—see instructions)	5	2,249 00
6	Taxable social security wages — 6a 25,480 00 × 12.4% (.124) =	6b	3,159 52
	Taxable social security tips — 6c × 12.4% (.124) =	6d	
7	Taxable Medicare wages and tips — 7a 25,480 00 × 2.9% (.029) =	7b	738 92
8	Total social security and Medicare taxes (add lines 6b, 6d, and 7b). Check here if wages are not subject to social security and/or Medicare tax ▶ ☐	8	3,898 44
9	Adjustment of social security and Medicare taxes (see instructions for required explanation) Sick Pay $ ____ ± Fractions of Cents $ ____ ± Other $ ____ =	9	
10	Adjusted total of social security and Medicare taxes (line 8 as adjusted by line 9—see instructions)	10	3,898 44
11	**Total taxes** (add lines 5 and 10)	11	6,147 44
12	Advance earned income credit (EIC) payments made to employees	12	
13	Net taxes (subtract line 12 from line 11). **If $1,000 or more, this must equal line 17, column (d) below (or line D of Schedule B (Form 941))**	13	6,147 44
14	Total deposits for quarter, including overpayment applied from a prior quarter	14	6,147 44
15	**Balance due** (subtract line 14 from line 13). See instructions	15	0 00
16	**Overpayment.** If line 14 is more than line 13, enter excess here ▶ $ ____ and check if to be: ☐ Applied to next return **or** ☐ Refunded.		

All filers: If line 13 is less than $1,000, you need not complete line 17 or Schedule B (Form 941).

Semiweekly schedule depositors: Complete Schedule B (Form 941) and check here ▶ ☐

Monthly schedule depositors: Complete line 17, columns (a) through (d), and check here ▶ ☒

17 Monthly Summary of Federal Tax Liability. Do not complete if you were a semiweekly schedule depositor

(a) First month liability	**(b)** Second month liability	**(c)** Third month liability	**(d)** Total liability for quarter
1,891.52	1,891.52	2,364.40	6,147.44

Sign Here Under penalties of perjury, I declare that I have examined this return, including accompanying schedules and statements, and to the best of my knowledge and belief, it is true, correct, and complete.

Signature ▶ *Roberta Rosario* Print Your Name and Title ▶ *Roberta Rosario, Owner* Date ▶ *April 30, 20--*

For Privacy Act and Paperwork Reduction Act Notice, see back of Payment Voucher. Cat. No. 17001Z Form **941** (Rev. 10-2000)

▲ **FIGURE 11-4** Employer's Quarterly Federal Tax Return, Form 941

- *Line 12* is blank. There were no advance earned income credit payments.
- *Line 13* shows total net taxes for the quarter, $6,147.44.
- *Line 14* shows total deposits for the quarter, $6,147.44. On Line Furnishings deposited all the taxes during the quarter.
- *Line 15* and *Line 16* are blank. There is no balance due and no overpayment.

Read Line 13 carefully. The taxes for On Line Furnishings were more than $1,000, so Line 17 is completed. This section shows the taxes for each month during the quarter. Line 17(d) and Line 13 must be equal.

If the employer did not make sufficient deposits, a check for the balance due is mailed to the Internal Revenue Service with Form 941. An employer may instead make a deposit at an authorized financial institution.

If the employer did not deduct enough taxes from an employee's earnings, the business pays the difference. The deficiency is debited to **Payroll Taxes Expense.**

5 Objective

Prepare Wage and Tax Statement (Form W-2) and Annual Transmittal of Wage and Tax Statements (Form W-3).

Wage and Tax Statement, Form W-2

Employers provide a **Wage and Tax Statement, Form W-2**, to each employee by January 31 of the following year. Form W-2 is sometimes called a **withholding statement**. Form W-2 contains information about the employee's earnings and tax withholdings for the year. The information for Form W-2 comes from the employee's earnings record.

Employees who stop working for the business during the year may ask that a Form W-2 be issued early. The Form W-2 must be issued within 30 days after the request or after the final wage payment, whichever is later.

Figure 11-5 on page 399 shows Form W-2 for Cindy Taylor. This is the standard form provided by the Internal Revenue Service (IRS). Some employers use a "substitute" Form W-2 that is approved by the IRS. The substitute form permits the employer to list total deductions and to reconcile the gross earnings, the deductions, and the net pay. If the firm issues 250 or more Forms W-2, the returns must be filed electronically or on magnetic media (tape or disk).

Important!

Form W-2

The employer must provide each employee with a Wage and Tax Statement, Form W-2, by January 31 of the following year.

At least four copies of each of Form W-2 are prepared:

1. One copy for the employer to send to the Social Security Administration, which shares the information with the IRS.
2. One copy for the employee to attach to the federal income tax return.
3. One copy for the employee's records.
4. One copy for the employer's records.

If there is a state income tax, two more copies of Form W-2 are prepared:

5. One copy for the employer to send to the state tax department.
6. One copy for the employee to attach to the state income tax return.

Additional copies are prepared if there is a city or county income tax.

FedEx Corporation prepared and distributed 106,300 Forms W-2 to its employees for 1998.

| Federal | State | Records | Employee

a Control number		Void ☐	**For Official Use Only ▶** **OMB No. 1545-0008**	
b Employer identification number 75-1234567			**1** Wages, tips, other compensation 18,720.00	**2** Federal income tax withheld 1,456.00
c Employer's name, address, and ZIP code On Line Furnishings 2521 University Drive Denton, TX 76205			**3** Social security wages 18,720.00	**4** Social security tax withheld 1,160.64
			5 Medicare wages and tips 18,720.00	**6** Medicare tax withheld 271.44
			7 Social security tips	**8** Allocated tips
d Employee's social security number 123-XX-XXXX			**9** Advance EIC payment	**10** Dependent care benefits
e Employee's name (first, middle initial, last) Cindy Taylor			**11** Nonqualified plans	**12** Benefits included in box 1
6480 Oak Tree Drive Denton, TX 76209–6789			**13** See instrs. for box 13	**14** Other
f Employee's address and ZIP code			**15** Statutory employee ☐ Deceased ☐ Pension plan ☐ Legal rep. ☐ Deferred compensation ☐	

16 State	Employer's state I.D. no.	**17** State wages, tips, etc.	**18** State income tax	**19** Locality name	**20** Local wages, tips, etc.	**21** Local income tax
TX	12-98765	18,720.00				

Form **W-2** **Wage and Tax Statement** **20--**

Department of the Treasury—Internal Revenue Service

For Privacy Act and Paperwork Reduction Act Notice, see separate instructions.

Copy A For Social Security Administration—Send this entire page with Form W-3 to the Social Security Administration; photocopies are **not** acceptable.

Cat. No. 10134D

▲ **FIGURE 11-5**
Wage and Tax Statement, Form W-2

Annual Transmittal of Wage and Tax Statements, Form W-3

The **Transmittal of Wage and Tax Statements, Form W-3**, is submitted with Forms W-2 to the Social Security Administration. Form W-3 reports the total social security wages; total Medicare wages; total social security tax withheld; total Medicare tax withheld; total wages, tips, and other compensation; total federal income tax withheld; and other information.

A copy of Form W-2 for each employee is attached to Form W-3. Form W-3 is due by the last day of February following the end of the calendar year. The Social Security Administration shares the tax information on Forms W-2 with the Internal Revenue Service. Figure 11-6 on page 400 shows the completed Form W-3 for On Line Furnishings.

The amounts on Form W-3 must equal the sums of the amounts on the attached Forms W-2. For example, the amount entered in Box 1 of Form W-3 must equal the sum of the amounts entered in Box 1 of all the Forms W-2.

About Accounting

IRS Electronic Filing

More than 19 million taxpayers have filed their tax returns electronically. Returns that are filed electronically are more accurate than paper returns. Electronic filing means refunds in half the time, especially if the taxpayer chooses direct deposit of the refund.

for the Employer

FIGURE 11-6 ► Transmittal of Wage and Tax Statements, Form W-3

a Control number	33333	For Official Use Only ► OMB No. 1545-0008	
b Kind of Payer ► 941 [X] Military [ ] 943 [ ] CT-1 [ ] Hshld. emp. [ ] Medicare govt. emp. [ ]		1 Wages, tips, other compensation 101,920.00	2 Federal income tax withheld 8,996.00
		3 Social security wages 101,920.00	4 Social security tax withheld 6,319.04
c Total number of Forms W-2 5	d Establishment number	5 Medicare wages and tips 101,920.00	6 Medicare tax withheld 1,477.84
e Employer identification number 75-1234567		7 Social security tips	8 Allocated tips
f Employer's name Roberta Rosario		9 Advance EIC payments	10 Dependent care benefits
On Line Furnishings 2521 University Drive Denton, TX 76205		11 Nonqualified plans	12 Deferred compensation
		13	
g Employer's address and ZIP code		14	
h Other EIN used this year		15 Income tax withheld by third-party payer	
i Employer's state I.D. no. 12-98765			
Contact person Roberta Rosario	Telephone number (940) 555-9999	Fax number (940) 555-8018	E-mail address

Under penalties of perjury, I declare that I have examined this return and accompanying documents, and, to the best of my knowledge and belief, they are true, correct, and complete.

Signature ► Roberta Rosario Title ► Owner Date ► February 10, 20--

Form **W-3 Transmittal of Wage and Tax Statements 20--** Department of the Treasury Internal Revenue Service

The amounts on Form W-3 also must equal the sums of the amounts reported on the Forms 941 during the year. For example, the social security wages reported on the Form W-3 must equal the sum of the social security wages reported on the four Forms 941.

The filing of Form W-3 marks the end of the routine procedures needed to account for payrolls and for payroll tax withholdings.

Section 1 Self Review

Questions

1. Where does a business deposit federal payroll taxes?
2. What is the purpose of Form 941?
3. What is the purpose of Form W-2?

Exercises

4. Employers usually record social security taxes in the accounting records at the end of
   a. each payroll period.
   b. each month.
   c. each quarter.
   d the year.
5. Which tax is shared equally by the employee and employer?
   a. Federal income tax
   b. State income tax
   c. Social security tax
   d. Federal unemployment tax

Analysis

6. Your business currently owes $2,550 in payroll taxes. During the lookback period, your business paid $10,000 in payroll taxes. How often does your business need to make payroll tax deposits?

(Answers to Section 1 Self Review are on page 426.)

Section 2

Unemployment Tax and Workers' Compensation

In Section 1 we discussed taxes that are withheld from employees' earnings and in some cases matched by the employer. In this section we will discuss payroll related expenses that are paid solely by the employer.

Unemployment Compensation Insurance Taxes

The unemployment compensation tax program, often called the **unemployment insurance program**, provides unemployment compensation through a tax levied on employers.

Coordination of Federal and State Unemployment Rates

The unemployment insurance program is a federal program that encourages states to provide unemployment insurance for employees working in the state. The federal government allows a credit—or reduction—in the federal unemployment tax for amounts charged by the state for unemployment taxes.

This text assumes that the federal unemployment tax rate is 6.2 percent less a state unemployment tax credit of 5.4 percent; thus the federal tax rate is reduced to 0.8 percent (6.2% − 5.4%). The earnings limits for the federal and the state unemployment tax are usually the same, $7,000.

A few states levy an unemployment tax on the employee. The tax is withheld from employee pay and remitted by the employer to the state.

For businesses that provide steady employment, the state unemployment tax rate may be lowered based on an **experience rating system**, or a **merit rating system**. Under the experience rating system, the state tax rate may be reduced to less than 1 percent for businesses that provide steady employment. In contrast, some states levy penalty rates as high as 10 percent for employers with poor records of providing steady employment.

The reduction of state unemployment taxes because of favorable experience ratings does not affect the credit allowable against the federal tax. An employer may take a credit against the federal unemployment tax as though it were paid at the normal state rate even though the employer actually pays the state a lower rate.

Because of its experience rating, On Line Furnishings pays state unemployment tax of 4.0 percent, which is less than the standard rate of 5.4 percent. Note that the business may take the credit for the full amount of the state rate (5.4%) against the federal rate, even though the business actually pays a state rate of 4.0%.

Section Objectives

6 **Compute and record liability for federal and state unemployment taxes and record payment of the taxes.**

WHY IT'S IMPORTANT
Businesses need to record all payroll tax liabilities.

7 **Prepare an Employer's Federal Unemployment Tax Return, Form 940 or 940-EZ.**

WHY IT'S IMPORTANT
The unemployment insurance programs provide support to individuals during temporary periods of unemployment.

8 **Compute and record workers' compensation insurance premiums.**

WHY IT'S IMPORTANT
Businesses need insurance to cover workplace injury claims.

Terms to Learn

Employer's Annual Federal Unemployment Tax Return, Form 940 or Form 940-EZ
experience rating system
merit rating system
unemployment insurance program

6 Objective

Compute and record liability for federal and state unemployment taxes and record payment of the taxes.

Computing and Recording Unemployment Taxes

On Line Furnishings records its state and federal unemployment tax expense at the end of each payroll period. The unemployment taxes for the payroll period ending January 6 are as follows.

Federal unemployment tax	($1,960 × 0.008)	=	$15.68
State unemployment tax	($1,960 × 0.040)	=	78.40
Total unemployment taxes		=	$94.08

The entry to record the employer's unemployment payroll taxes follows.

GENERAL JOURNAL PAGE *1*

	DATE		DESCRIPTION	POST. REF.	DEBIT	CREDIT	
8	*Jan.*	*8*	*Payroll Taxes Expense*		*94 08*		8
9			*Federal Unemployment Tax Payable*			*15 68*	9
10			*State Unemployment Tax Payable*			*78 40*	10
11			*Unemployment taxes on*				11
12			*weekly payroll*				12

Reporting and Paying State Unemployment Taxes

In most states the due date for the unemployment tax return is the last day of the month following the end of the quarter. Generally the tax is paid with the return.

Employer's Quarterly Report. Figure 11-7 on page 403 shows the Employer's Quarterly Report for the State of Texas filed by On Line Furnishings in April for the first quarter. The report for Texas is similar to the tax forms of other states. The top of the form contains information about the company.

- *Block 4* at the top of the form shows the tax rate assigned by the state based on the experience rating. The tax rate for On Line Furnishings is 4.0 percent.
- *Block 10* (3 boxes) shows the number of employees in the state on the 12th day of each month of the quarter.
- *Line 13* shows the total wages paid during the quarter to employees in the state, $25,480.
- *Line 14* shows the total *taxable* wages paid during the quarter, $25,480. Note that the limit on taxable wages is $7,000. Table 11-1 on page 394 shows that at the end of the first quarter, no employee earned more than $7,000. All wages and salaries are taxable for state unemployment. Actually, the base in Texas was changed to $9,000 for 1989 and later years. We use a base of $7,000 for the sake of simplicity and because the increase to $9,000 was intended to be "temporary."
- *Line 15* shows the total tax for the quarter. Taxable wages are multiplied by the tax rate ($25,480 × 0.04 = $1,019.20).
- *Lines 16a* and *b* are a breakdown of the amount on Line 15. In Texas, part of the 4 percent tax is set aside for job training and other incentive programs. Box 4a contains the tax rate for the unemployment tax (3.9%). Box 4b contains the tax rate for training incentives or *Smart Jobs Assessment* (0.1%).

Unemployment State

TEXAS WORKFORCE COMMISSION
AUSTIN, TEXAS 78714-9037
(512)-463-2222

11111

EMPLOYER'S QUARTERLY REPORT

1. ACCOUNT NUMBER	2. COUNTY CODE	3. TAX AREA	4. TAX RATE	5. SIC CODE	6. FEDERAL I.D. NUMBER	7. QTR. YR.
12-98765	121	2	4.0 %	59	75-1234567	1st/20--

8. EMPLOYER NAME AND ADDRESS (SEE ITEM 25 FOR CHANGES TO NAME, ADDRESS, ETC.)

Roberta Rosario, DBA
On Line Furnishings
2521 University Drive
Denton, TX 76205

9. TELEPHONE NUMBER: (940) 555-9999

4a. UI TAX RATE	4b. SMART JOBS ASSESSMENT
3.9 %	.1 %

ALIGNMENT

9A. QUARTER ENDING

9B. PENALTIES WILL BE ASSESSED IF REPORT IS NOT POSTMARKED BY

1st Month	2nd Month	3rd Month
5	5	5

10. Enter in the boxes above the number of employees both full-time and part-time, in pay periods that include 12th day of the calendar month. (ENTER NUMERALS ONLY)

11. SHOW THE COUNTY CODE (see list on the back of this form) in which you had the greatest number of employees: 121

12. IF you have employees in more than one county in TEXAS, how many are outside the county shown in Item 11?

		DOLLARS	CENTS
13. Total (Gross) Wages Paid During this Quarter to Texas Employees		25,480	00
14. Taxable Wages paid this quarter to each employee up to $7000, the annual maximum amount. **(If none, enter "0")**		25,480	00
15. Tax Due (Multiply Taxable Wages By Tax Rate, Item 4 Above)		1,019	20
16a. UI TAX	993.72		
b. Smart Jobs Assessment	25.48		
17. Interest, If Tax is Past Due			
18. Penalty, If Report Is Past Due			
19. Balance Due From Prior Periods (Subtract Credit Or Add Debit)			
20. Total Due - Make Remittance Payable To TEXAS WORKFORCE COMMISSION		1,019	20

You must FILE this return even though you had no payroll this quarter. If you had no payroll show '0' in item 13 and sign the declaration (Item 26) on this form.

14a. Mark box with an "X" if reporting wages to another state during the year for employees listed in Item 22.

FOR TWC USE ONLY

	MONTH	DAY	YEAR
POSTMARK DATE C3			
POSTMARK DATE S			
EX DATE C3			
EX DATE S			

Est

DOLLARS	CENTS	INITIALS

AMOUNT RECEIVED

	21. SOCIAL SECURITY NUMBER	22. EMPLOYEE NAME (1ST INIT, 2ND INIT, LAST NAME)	23. TOTAL WAGES PAID THIS QUARTER
1	587-XX-XXXX	S. Anderson	5,200.00
2	427-XX-XXXX	E. Gallegos	4,940.00
3	687-XX-XXXX	C. Lin	6,760.00
4	123-XX-XXXX	C. Taylor	4,680.00
5	587-XX-XXXX	B. Turner	3,900.00
6			
7			
8			
9			
10			
		24. PAGE TOTAL	25,480.00

26. I DECLARE that the information herein is true and correct to the best of my knowledge and belief.

SIGNATURE Roberta Rosario

TITLE Owner DATE 4/29/20--

PREPARERS NAME Roberta Rosario

PREPARERS PHONE NUMBER (940) 555-9999

For assistance in completing form call,

MAIL REPORT AND REMITTANCE TO:
CASHIER
TEXAS WORKFORCE COMMISSION
P.O. BOX 149037
AUSTIN, TEXAS 78714-9037

DO NOT STAPLE REPORT
(Write Account No. On Check)

FORM C - 3 (6/99)
SCANC3

25. MAKE CHANGES TO EMPLOYER INFORMATION USING C-3 **INSTRUCTION SHEET.** CHANGES NOTED ON THIS FORM MAY NOT BE CAPTURED DURING PROCESSING.

▲ **FIGURE 11-7** Employer's Quarterly Report Form for State Unemployment Taxes

- *Lines 17* and *18* are blank. There are no penalties or interest because no taxes or reports are past due.
- *Line 19* is blank. There is no balance due from prior periods.
- *Line 20* shows the tax due.

On Line Furnishings submits the report and issues a check payable to the state tax authority for the amount shown on Line 20. The entry is recorded in the cash payments journal. The transaction is shown here in general journal form for purposes of illustration.

1	20--						1
2	Apr.	29	State Unemployment Tax Payable		1 019 20		2
3			Cash			1 019 20	3
4			Paid SUTA taxes for quarter				4
5			ending March 31				5
6							6

Earnings in Excess of Base Amount. State unemployment tax is paid on the first $7,000 of annual earnings for each employee. Earnings over $7,000 are not subject to state unemployment tax.

For example, suppose Cindy Taylor earns $360 every week of the year. Table 11-1 on page 394 shows that she earned $4,680 at the end of the first quarter. In the four weeks of April, she earned $1,440 ($360 × 4). She earned $360 in the first week and in the second week of May. So far, all of Taylor's earnings are subject to state unemployment tax.

	Earnings	Cumulative Earnings
First quarter	$4,680	$4,680
April	1,440	6,120
May, week 1	360	6,480
May, week 2	360	6,840

In the third week of May, Taylor earned $360, but only $160 of it is subject to state unemployment tax ($7,000 earnings limit − $6,840 cumulative earnings = $160). For the rest of the calendar year, Taylor's earnings are not subject to state unemployment tax.

Reporting and Paying Federal Unemployment Taxes

The rules for reporting and depositing federal unemployment taxes differ from those used for social security and Medicare taxes.

Depositing Federal Unemployment Taxes. There are two ways to make federal unemployment tax deposits: with electronic deposits using EFTPS or with a Federal Tax Deposit Coupon, Form 8109, at an authorized financial institution. Deposits are made quarterly and are due on the last day of the month following the end of the quarter.

The federal unemployment tax is calculated at the end of each quarter. It is computed by multiplying the first $7,000 of each employee's wages by 0.008. A deposit is required when more than $100 of federal unemployment tax is owed. If $100 or less is owed, no deposit is due.

For example, suppose that a business calculates its federal unemployment tax to be $80 at the end of the first quarter. Since it is not more than $100, no deposit is due. At the end of the second quarter, it calculates its federal unemployment taxes on second quarter wages to be $65. The total undeposited unemployment tax now is more than $100, so a deposit is required.

First quarter undeposited tax	$ 80
Second quarter undeposited tax	65
Total deposit due	$145

In the case of On Line Furnishings, the company owed $203.84 in federal unemployment tax at the end of March. Since this is more than $100, a deposit of $203.84 is due by April 30.

Month	Taxable Earnings Paid	Rate	Tax Due	Deposit Due Date
January	$ 7,840	0.008	$ 62.72	April 30
February	7,840	0.008	62.72	April 30
March	9,800	0.008	78.40	April 30
Total	$25,480		$203.84	

On April 30 On Line Furnishings records the payment of federal unemployment tax in the cash payments journal. The transaction is shown here in general journal form for illustration purposes.

8	Apr.	30	Federal Unemployment Tax Payable	203 84		8
9			Cash		203 84	9
10			Deposit FUTA due			10
11						11

7 Objective

Prepare an Employer's Federal Unemployment Tax Return, Form 940 or 940-EZ.

Reporting Federal Unemployment Tax, Form 940 or 940-EZ. Tax returns are not due quarterly for the federal unemployment tax. The employer submits an annual return. The **Employer's Annual Federal Unemployment Tax Return, Form 940 or 940-EZ**, is a preprinted government form used to report unemployment taxes for the calendar year. It is due by January 31 of the following year. The due date is extended to February 10 if all tax deposits were made on time. Instead of using Form 940, businesses can use Form 940-EZ if

- they paid unemployment tax to only one state,
- they paid all federal unemployment taxes by January 31 of the following year,
- all wages that were taxable for federal unemployment were also taxable for state unemployment.

On Line Furnishings prepares Form 940-EZ. The information needed to complete Form 940-EZ comes from the annual summary of individual earnings records and from the state unemployment tax returns filed during the year.

Figure 11-8 on page 406 shows Form 940-EZ prepared for On Line Furnishings. Refer to it as you learn how to complete Form 940-EZ.

- *Line A* shows the total state unemployment tax paid. All five employees of On Line Furnishings reached the earnings limit during the year. Wages subject to state unemployment tax are $35,000 ($7,000 × 5 employees). The state rate is 4 percent. On Line Furnishings paid state unemployment tax of $1,400 ($35,000 × 0.04).

Due at end of the year

Form **940-EZ**

Department of the Treasury
Internal Revenue Service (99)

Employer's Annual Federal Unemployment (FUTA) Tax Return

See separate Instructions for Form 940-EZ for information on completing this form.

OMB No. 1545-1110

20--

T	
FF	
FD	
FP	
I	
T	

Name (as distinguished from trade name): *Roberta Rosario*

Calendar year 20--

Trade name, if any: *On Line Furnishings*

Address and ZIP code: *2521 University Drive, Denton, TX 76205*

Employer identification number: *75:1234567*

Answer the questions under **Who May Use Form 940-EZ** *on page 2. If you cannot use Form 940-EZ, you must use Form 940.*

A Enter the amount of contributions paid to your state unemployment fund. (See separate instructions.) . . . ▶ $ 1,400 00

B (1) Enter the name of the state where you have to pay contributions . . . . ▶ TX

(2) Enter your state reporting number as shown on your state unemployment tax return ▶ 12-98765

If you will not have to file returns in the future, check here (see **Who Must File** in separate instructions), **and complete and sign the return.** ▶ ☐

If this is an Amended Return, check here . . . . ▶ ☐

Part I Taxable Wages and FUTA Tax

1	Total payments (including payments shown on lines 2 and 3) during the calendar year for services of employees			1	101,920 00
2	Exempt payments. (Explain all exempt payments, attaching additional sheets if necessary.) ▶	2			
3	Payments of more than $7,000 for services. Enter only amounts over the first $7,000 paid to each employee. Do not include any exempt payments from line 2. (See separate instructions.) The $7,000 amount is the Federal wage base. Your state wage base may be different. **Do not use your state wage limitation**	3	66,920 00		
4	Total exempt payments (add lines 2 and 3)			4	66,920 00
5	**Total taxable wages** (subtract line 4 from line 1) . . . . ▶			5	35,000 00
6	**FUTA tax.** Multiply the wages on line 5 by .008 and enter here. **(If the result is over $100, also complete Part II.)**			6	280 00
7	Total FUTA tax deposited for the year, including any overpayment applied from a prior year			7	280 00
8	**Balance due** (subtract line 7 from line 6). Pay to the **"United States Treasury"** . . . . ▶ If you owe more than $100, see **Depositing FUTA tax** in separate instructions.			8	0 00
9	**Overpayment** (subtract line 6 from line 7). Check if it is to be: ☐ **Applied to next return or** ☐ **Refunded** ▶			9	

Part II Record of Quarterly Federal Unemployment Tax Liability (Do not include state liability.) Complete only if line 6 is over $100.

Quarter	First (Jan. 1 – Mar. 31)	Second (Apr. 1 – June 30)	Third (July 1 – Sept. 30)	Fourth (Oct. 1 – Dec. 31)	Total for year
Liability for quarter	203.84	76.16	-0-	-0-	280.00

Under penalties of perjury, I declare that I have examined this return, including accompanying schedules and statements, and, to the best of my knowledge and belief, it is true, correct, and complete, and that no part of any payment made to a state unemployment fund claimed as a credit was, or is to be, deducted from the payments to employees.

Signature ▶ *Roberta Rosario* Title (Owner, etc.) ▶ *Owner* Date ▶ *January 31, 20--*

For Privacy Act and Paperwork Reduction Act Notice, see separate instructions. Cat. No. 10983G Form **940-EZ** (20--)

DETACH HERE

Form **940-EZ(V)**

Department of the Treasury
Internal Revenue Service

Form 940-EZ Payment Voucher

Use this voucher only when making a payment with your return.

OMB No. 1545-1110

20--

Complete boxes 1, 2, 3, and 4. Do not send cash, and do not staple your payment to this voucher. Make your check or money order payable to the **"United States Treasury."** Be sure to enter your employer identification number, "Form 940-EZ," and "20--" on your payment.

1 Enter the first four letters of your last name (business name if partnership or corporation).	2 Enter your employer identification number.	3 Enter the amount of your payment. $.
Instructions for Box 1 —Individuals (sole proprietors, trusts, and estates)—Enter the first four letters of your last name. —Corporations and partnerships—Enter the first four characters of your business name (omit "The" if followed by more than one word).	4 Enter your business name (individual name for sole proprietors) Enter your address Enter your city, state, and ZIP code	

▲ **FIGURE 11-8** Employer's Annual Federal Unemployment Tax Return, Form 940-EZ

PART I: Taxable Wages and FUTA Tax

- *Line 1* shows the total compensation paid to employees, $101,920.
- *Line 2* is blank because there were no exempt payments for On Line Furnishings.
- *Line 3* shows the compensation that exceeds the $7,000 earnings limit, $66,920 ($101,920 − $35,000).
- *Line 4* shows the wages not subject to federal unemployment tax, $66,920.
- *Line 5* shows the taxable wages for the year, $35,000. This amount must agree with the total taxable FUTA wages shown on the individual employee earnings records for the year.
- *Line 6* shows the FUTA tax, $280 ($35,000 × 0.008).
- *Line 7* shows the FUTA tax deposited during the year, $280.
- *Line 8* shows the balance due. On Line Furnishings deposited $280, so there is no balance due.
- *Line 9* is blank because there is no overpayment.

PART II: Record of Quarterly Federal Unemployment Tax Liability shows the FUTA tax due for each quarter. The total for the year must equal Line 6.

Computers in Accounting

Payroll Applications

Southwest Airlines processes more than 29,000 paychecks every pay period. It would be impossible to manually prepare this many checks every two weeks. Instead, companies with large numbers of employees use computerized payroll systems to process payroll. Computerized payroll applications can access current tax laws and tax forms using Internet connections.

Setting up a computerized payroll system begins by creating a master file for the employer. The employer's name, address, and federal employer identification number are entered. A master file is then prepared for each employee.

At the end of each pay period, the accountant enters the hours worked for hourly employees and any bonuses or commissions. The software calculates gross earnings, tax deductions, voluntary deductions, and net pay for all employees. A payroll proof report is printed and reviewed by the accountant. Once the payroll proof report is approved, the system automatically updates the earnings records for each employee. Paycheck forms are inserted into the printer, and paychecks are printed.

If the payroll module is integrated with a general ledger system, the payroll entries are posted to the general ledger accounts. Sophisticated payroll applications send reminders to the accountant when payroll tax deposits are due.

At the end of each calendar quarter and year, the payroll system generates summary reports to use in preparing Forms 940 and 941, as well as state unemployment returns. At year-end, Forms W-2 are generated using the payroll application.

Thinking Critically

When an accountant reviews the payroll proof report, what types of information do you think the accountant checks?

Internet Application

Go to the Web site for the American Payroll Association. What resources does the site offer on selecting a payroll system?

8 Objective

Compute and record workers' compensation insurance premiums.

Workers' Compensation Insurance

Workers' compensation provides benefits for employees who are injured on the job. The insurance premium, which is paid by the employer, depends on the risk involved with the work performed. It is important to classify earnings according to the type of work the employees perform and to summarize labor costs according to the insurance premium classifications.

There are two ways to handle workers' compensation insurance. The method a business uses depends on the number of its employees.

Estimated Annual Premium in Advance. Employers who have few employees pay an estimated premium in advance. At the end of the year, the employer calculates the actual premium. If the actual premium is more than the estimated premium paid, the employer pays the balance due. If the actual premium is less than the estimated premium paid, the employer receives a refund.

On Line Furnishings has two work classifications: office work and shipping work. The workers' compensation premium rates are

Office workers	$0.40 per $100 of labor costs
Shipping workers	1.20 per $100 of labor costs

The insurance premium rates recognize that injuries are more likely to occur to shipping workers than to office workers. Based on employee earnings for the previous year, On Line Furnishings paid an estimated premium of $1,000 for the new year. The payment was made on January 15.

1	*20--*						1
14	*Jan.*	*15*	*Workers' Compensation Insurance Expense*		*1 000 00*		14
15			*Cash*			*1 000 00*	15
16			*Estimated workers' compensation*				16
17			*insurance for 20--*				17
18							18

At the end of the year, the actual premium was computed, $1,056.64. The actual premium was computed by applying the proper rates to the payroll data for the year:

- The office wages were $20,800.
  ($20,800 ÷ $100) × $0.40 =
  208 × $0.40 = $ 83.20
- The shipping wages were $81,120.
  ($81,120 ÷ $100) × $1.20 =
  811.2 × $1.20 = $ 973.44

Total premium for year = $1,056.64

Classification	Payroll	Rate	Premium
Office work	$20,800	$0.40 per $100	$ 83.20
Shipping work	81,120	1.20 per $100	973.44
Total premium for year			$1,056.64
Less estimated premium paid			1,000.00
Balance of premium due			$ 56.64

Payroll Taxes

- Management must ensure that payroll taxes are computed properly and paid on time.
- In order to avoid penalties, it is essential that a business prepares its payroll tax returns accurately and files the returns and required forms promptly.
- The payroll system should ensure that payroll reports are prepared in an efficient manner.
- Managers need to be familiar with all payroll taxes and how they impact operating expenses.
- Managers must be knowledgeable about unemployment tax regulations in their state because favorable experience ratings can reduce unemployment tax expense.
- Management is responsible for developing effective internal control procedures over payroll operations and ensuring that they are followed.

Thinking Critically

What accounting records are used to prepare Form 941?

On December 31 the balance due to the insurance company is recorded as a liability by an adjusting entry. On Line Furnishings owes $56.64 ($1,056.64 – $1,000.00) for the workers' compensation insurance.

1	*20--*						1
2	*Dec.*	*31*	*Workers' Compensation Insurance Expense*		*56 64*		2
3			*Workers' Compensation Insurance Payable*			*56 64*	3
4							4

Suppose that on January 15 On Line Furnishings had paid an estimated premium of $1,200 instead of $1,000. The actual premium at the end of the year was $1,056.64. On Line Furnishings would be due a refund from the insurance company for the amount overpaid, $143.36 ($1,200.00 – $1,056.64).

1	*20--*						1
2	*Dec.*	*31*	*Workers' Compensation Refund Receivable*		*143 36*		2
3			*Workers' Compensation Insurance Expense*			*143 36*	3
4							4

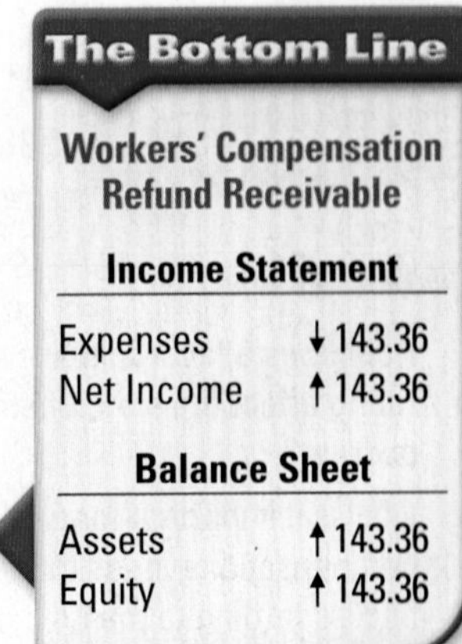

Deposit and Monthly Premium Payments. Employers with many employees use a different method to handle workers' compensation insurance. At the beginning of the year, they make large deposits, often 25 percent of the estimated annual premium. From January through November, they pay the actual premium due based on an audit of the month's wages. The premium for the last month is deducted from the deposit. Any balance is refunded or applied toward the following year's deposit.

Internal Control over Payroll Operations

Now that we have examined the basic accounting procedures used for payrolls and payroll taxes, let's look at some internal control procedures that are recommended to protect payroll operations.

1. Assign only highly responsible, well-trained employees to work in payroll operations.
2. Keep payroll records in locked files. Train payroll employees to maintain confidentiality about pay rates and other information in the payroll records.
3. Add new employees to the payroll system and make all changes in employee pay rates only with proper written authorization from management.
4. Make changes to an employee's withholding allowances based only on a Form W-4 properly completed and signed by the employee.
5. Make voluntary deductions from employee earnings based only on a signed authorization from the employee.
6. Have the payroll checks examined by someone other than the person who prepares them. Compare each check to the entry for the employee in the payroll register.
7. Have payroll checks distributed to the employees by someone other than the person who prepares them.
8. Have the monthly payroll bank account statement received and reconciled by someone other than the person who prepares the payroll checks.
9. Use prenumbered forms for the payroll checks. Periodically the numbers of the checks issued and the numbers of the unused checks should be verified to make sure that all checks can be accounted for.
10. Maintain files of all authorization forms for adding new employees, changing pay rates, and making voluntary deductions. Also retain all Forms W-4.

Section 2 Self Review

Questions

1. How does a favorable experience rating affect the state unemployment tax rate?
2. Why is it important for workers' compensation wages to be classified according to the type of work performed?
3. Who pays the federal unemployment tax? The state unemployment tax?

Exercises

4. State unemployment taxes are filed
   - **a.** monthly.
   - **b.** quarterly.
   - **c.** yearly.
   - **d.** at the end of each pay period.
5. The federal unemployment taxes are reported on
   - **a.** Form 941.
   - **b.** Form 8109.
   - **c.** Form W-3.
   - **d.** Form 940.

Analysis

6. At the end of the year, the business has a balance due for workers' compensation insurance. If no adjusting entry is made, will the amount of net income reported be correct? If not, how will it be wrong?

(Answers to Section 2 Self Review are on page 426.)

CHAPTER 11

Review and Applications

Review

Chapter Summary

Employers must pay social security, SUTA, FUTA, and Medicare taxes. They must also collect federal and state taxes from their employees and then remit those taxes to the appropriate taxing authorities. In this chapter, you have learned how to compute the employer's taxes and how to file the required tax returns and reports.

Learning Objectives

1 Explain how and when payroll taxes are paid to the government.
Employers act as collection agents for social security, Medicare, and federal income taxes withheld from employee earnings. Employers must remit these sums, with their own share of social security and Medicare taxes, to the government. The taxes must be deposited in an authorized depository, usually a commercial bank. The methods and schedules for deposits vary according to the sums involved.

2 Compute and record the employer's social security and Medicare taxes.
Employers should multiply the social security and Medicare tax rates by taxable wages to compute the employer's portion of taxes due.

3 Record deposit of social security, Medicare, and employee income taxes.
As taxes are paid to the government, the accounting records should be updated to reflect the payment, thereby reducing tax liability accounts.

4 Prepare an Employer's Quarterly Federal Tax Return, Form 941.
The Form 941 reports wages paid, federal income tax withheld, and applicable social security and Medicare taxes.

5 Prepare Wage and Tax Statement (Form W-2) and Annual Transmittal of Wage and Tax Statements (Form W-3).
By the end of January each employee must be given a Wage and Tax Statement, Form W-2, showing the previous year's earnings and withholdings for social security, Medicare, and employee income tax. The employer files a Transmittal of Wage and Tax Statements, Form W-3, with copies of employees' Forms W-2. Form W-3 is due by the last day of February following the end of the calendar year.

6 Compute and record liability for federal and state unemployment taxes and record payment of the taxes.
Unemployment insurance taxes are paid by the employer to both state and federal governments. State unemployment tax returns differ from state to state but usually require a list of employees, their social security numbers, and taxable wages paid. The rate of state unemployment tax depends on the employer's experience rating. The net federal unemployment tax rate can be as low as 0.8 percent.

7 Prepare an Employer's Federal Unemployment Tax Return, Form 940 or 940-EZ.
An Employer's Annual Federal Unemployment Tax Return, Form 940 or 940-EZ, must be filed in January for the preceding calendar year. The form shows the total wages paid, the amount of wages subject to unemployment tax, and the federal unemployment tax owed for the year. A credit is allowed against gross federal tax for unemployment tax charged under state plans, up to 5.4 percent of wages subject to the federal tax.

8 Compute and record workers' compensation insurance premiums.
By state law, employers might be required to carry workers' compensation insurance. For companies with a few employees, an estimated premium is paid at the start of the year. A final settlement is made with the insurance company on the basis of an audit of the payroll after the end of the year. Premiums vary according to the type of work performed by each employee. Other premium payment plans can be used for larger employers.

9 Define the accounting terms new to this chapter.

CHAPTER 11 GLOSSARY

Employer's Annual Federal Unemployment Tax Return, Form 940 (p. 405) Preprinted government form used by the employer to report unemployment taxes for the calendar year

Employer's Annual Federal Unemployment Tax Return, Form 940-EZ (p. 405) See Employer's Annual Federal Unemployment Tax Return, Form 940

Employer's Quarterly Federal Tax Return, Form 941 (p. 395) Preprinted government form used by the employer to report payroll tax information relating to social security, Medicare, and employee income tax withholding to the Internal Revenue Service

Experience rating system (p. 401) A system that rewards an employer for maintaining steady employment conditions by reducing the firm's state unemployment tax rate

Merit rating system (p. 401) See Experience rating system

Transmittal of Wage and Tax Statements, Form W-3 (p. 399) Preprinted government form submitted with Forms W-2 to the Social Security Administration

Unemployment insurance program (p. 401) A program that provides unemployment compensation through a tax levied on employers

Wage and Tax Statement, Form W-2 (p. 398) Preprinted government form that contains information about an employee's earnings and tax withholdings for the year

Withholding statement (p. 398) See Wage and Tax Statement, Form W-2

Comprehensive Self Review

1. Which of the following factors determine the frequency of deposits of social security, Medicare, and income tax withholdings?
   - **a.** Experience rating.
   - **b.** Amount of taxes reported in the lookback period.
   - **c.** Company's net income.
   - **d.** Amount of taxes currently owed.
   - **e.** How often employees are paid.
2. Under the monthly deposit schedule rule, when must deposits for employee income tax and other withheld taxes be made?
3. Is the ceiling on earnings subject to unemployment taxes larger than or smaller than the ceiling on earnings subject to the social security tax?
4. How do the FUTA and SUTA taxes relate to each other?
5. What is Form W-3?

(Answers to Comprehensive Self Review are on page 426.)

Discussion Questions

1. Why was the unemployment insurance system established?
2. What is the purpose of allowing a credit against the FUTA for state unemployment taxes?
3. What is the purpose of Form 940? How often is it filed?
4. A state charges a basic SUTA tax rate of 5.4 percent. Because of an excellent experience rating, an employer in the state has to pay only 1.0 percent of the taxable payroll as state tax. What is the percentage to be used in computing the credit against the federal unemployment tax?
5. Is the employer required to deposit the federal unemployment tax during the year? Explain.
6. What is Form 941? How often is the form filed?
7. Who pays for workers' compensation insurance?
8. When is the premium for workers' compensation insurance usually paid?
9. How can an employer keep informed about changes in the rates and bases for the social security, Medicare, and FUTA taxes?
10. What government form is prepared to accompany deposits of federal taxes?
11. What happens if the employer fails to deduct enough federal income tax or FICA tax from employee earnings?
12. When must Form W-2 be issued? To whom is it sent?
13. What is the purpose of Form W-3? When must it be issued? To whom is it sent?
14. What is the lookback period?
15. What are the four taxes levied on employers?
16. What is a business tax identification number?
17. When is the use of Form 8109-B permitted?
18. What is EFTPS? When is EFTPS required?
19. What does "semiweekly" refer to in the Semiweekly Deposit Schedule Rule?
20. What does "monthly" refer to in the Monthly Deposit Schedule Rule?
21. Which of the following are withheld from employees' earnings?
    - **a.** FUTA
    - **b.** income tax
    - **c.** Medicare
    - **d.** social security
    - **e.** SUTA
    - **f.** workers' compensation

Applications

EXERCISES

Exercise 11-1 ► Objective 1

Depositing payroll taxes.

The amounts of federal income tax withheld and social security and Medicare taxes (both employee and employer shares) shown below were owed by different businesses on the specified dates. In each case decide whether the firm is required to deposit the sum in an authorized financial institution. If a deposit is necessary, give the date by which it should be made. The employers are monthly depositors.

1. Total taxes of $4,375 owed on February 28, 20--.
2. Total taxes of $600 owed on March 31, 20--.
3. Total taxes of $825 owed on April 30, 20--.
4. Total taxes of $275 owed on July 31, 20--.

Exercise 11-2 ► Objective 3

Recording deposit of social security, Medicare, and income taxes.

After Elite Corporation paid its employees on July 15, 20--, and recorded the corporation's share of payroll taxes for the payroll paid that date, the firm's general ledger showed a balance of $10,080 in the **Social Security Tax Payable** account, a balance of $2,322 in the **Medicare Tax Payable** account, and a balance of $9,180 in the **Employee Income Tax Payable** account. On July 16 the business issued a check to deposit the taxes owed in the Northstar National Bank. Record this transaction in general journal form.

Exercise 11-3 ► Objectives 2, 6

Computing employer's payroll taxes.

At the end of the weekly payroll period on June 30, 20--, the payroll register of Tanaka Professional Consultants Company showed employee earnings of $65,400. Determine the firm's payroll taxes for the period. Use a social security rate of 6.2 percent, Medicare rate of 1.45 percent, FUTA rate of 0.8 percent, and SUTA rate of 5.4 percent. Consider all earnings subject to social security tax and Medicare tax and $33,000 subject to FUTA and SUTA taxes.

Exercise 11-4 ► Objective 6

Depositing federal unemployment tax.

On March 31, 20--, the **Federal Unemployment Tax Payable** account in the general ledger of The Boston Trading Company showed a balance of $576. This represents the FUTA tax owed for the first quarter of the year. On April 30, 20--, the firm issued a check to deposit the amount owed in the Provident National Bank. Record this transaction in general journal form.

Exercise 11-5 ► Objective 6

Computing SUTA tax.

On April 29, 20--, Thompson Furniture Company prepared its state unemployment tax return for the first quarter of the year. The firm had taxable wages of $90,600. Because of a favorable experience rating, Thompson pays SUTA tax at a rate of 1.6 percent. How much SUTA tax did the firm owe for the quarter?

Exercise 11-6 ► Objective 6

Paying SUTA tax.

On June 30, 20--, the **State Unemployment Tax Payable** account in the general ledger of Gulf Shore Sea Food Company showed a balance of

$1,368. This represents the SUTA tax owed for the second quarter of the year. On July 31, 20--, the business issued a check to the state unemployment insurance fund for the amount due. Record this payment in general journal form.

◄ **Exercise 11-7**
Objective 6

Computing FUTA tax.

On January 31 Simply Beautiful Salon prepared its Employer's Annual Federal Unemployment Tax Return, Form 940. During the previous year, the business paid total wages of $374,400 to its eight employees. Of this amount, $112,000 was subject to FUTA tax. Using a rate of 0.8 percent, determine the FUTA tax owed and the balance due on January 31, 20--, when Form 940 was filed. A deposit of $748.80 was made during the year.

◄ **Exercise 11-8**
Objective 8

Computing workers' compensation insurance premiums.

Electronic Computer Services Company estimates that its office employees will earn $160,000 next year and its factory employees will earn $840,000. The firm pays the following rates for workers' compensation insurance: $0.30 per $100 of wages for the office employees and $6.00 per $100 of wages for the factory employees. Determine the estimated premium for each group of employees and the total estimated premium for next year.

Problems

Selected problems can be completed using:
Peachtree QuickBooks Spreadsheets

PROBLEM SET A

◄ **Problem 11-1A**
Objectives 2, 6

Computing and recording employer's payroll tax expense.

The payroll register of Goree Lawn Equipment Company showed total employee earnings of $2,400 for the payroll period ended June 14, 20--.

INSTRUCTIONS

1. Compute the employer's payroll taxes for the period. Use rates of 6.2 percent for the employer's share of the social security tax, 1.45 percent for Medicare tax, 0.8 percent for FUTA tax, and 5.4 percent for SUTA tax. All earnings are taxable.
2. Prepare a general journal entry to record the employer's payroll taxes for the period.

Analyze: Which of the above taxes are paid by the employee and matched by the employer?

◄ **Problem 11-2A**
Objectives 2, 3, 4, 6

Computing employer's social security tax, Medicare tax, and unemployment taxes and recording payment of taxes; preparing employer's quarterly federal tax return.

A payroll summary for Nelson Sullivan, who owns and operates Sullivan Broadcasting Company, for the quarter ending June 30, 20--, appears on page 416. The firm prepared the required tax deposit forms and issued checks as follows.

a. Federal Tax Deposit Coupon, Form 8109, check for April taxes, paid on May 15.
b. Federal Tax Deposit Coupon, Form 8109, check for May taxes, paid on June 17.

Date Wages Paid		Total Earnings	Social Security Tax Deducted	Medicare Tax Deducted	Income Tax Withheld
April	8	$ 2,120.00	$ 131.44	$ 30.74	$ 210.00
	15	2,200.00	136.40	31.90	216.00
	22	2,120.00	131.44	30.74	210.00
	29	2,160.00	133.92	31.32	214.00
		$ 8,600.00	$ 533.20	$124.70	$ 850.00
May	5	$ 2,080.00	$ 128.96	$ 30.16	206.00
	12	2,120.00	131.44	30.74	210.00
	19	2,120.00	131.44	30.74	210.00
	26	2,160.00	133.92	31.32	214.00
		$ 8,480.00	$ 525.76	$122.96	$ 840.00
June	2	$ 2,200.00	$ 136.40	$ 31.90	$ 216.00
	9	2,120.00	131.44	30.74	210.00
	16	2,160.00	133.92	31.32	214.00
	23	2,120.00	131.44	30.74	210.00
	30	2,080.00	128.96	30.16	206.00
		$10,680.00	$ 662.16	$154.86	$1,056.00
Total		$27,760.00	$1,721.12	$402.52	$2,746.00

INSTRUCTIONS

1. Using the tax rates given below, and assuming that all earnings are taxable, make the general journal entry on April 8, 20--, to record the employer's payroll tax expense on the payroll ending that date.

Social security	6.2 percent
Medicare	1.45
FUTA	0.8
SUTA	5.4

2. Give the entries in general journal form to record deposit of the employee income tax withheld and the social security and Medicare taxes (employee and employer shares) on May 15 for April taxes and on June 17 for May taxes.
3. On July 15, the firm issued a check to deposit the federal income tax withheld and the FICA tax (both employee and employer shares) for the third month (June). In general journal form, record issuance of the check.
4. Complete Form 941 in accordance with the discussions in this chapter. Use a 12.4 percent social security rate and a 2.9 percent Medicare rate in computations. Use the following address for the company: 3465 Merit Drive, Dallas, TX 75201. Use 75-3333333 as the employer identification number. Date the return July 31, 20--.

Analyze: Based on the entries you have recorded, what is the balance of the **Employee Income Tax Payable** account at July 15?

Problem 11-3A ►
Objectives 6, 7

Computing and recording unemployment taxes; completing Form 940.

Certain transactions and procedures relating to federal and state unemployment taxes follow for The Fashion Center, a retail store owned by

Debra Jones. The firm's address is 1112 Misty Mountain Drive, Denton, TX 76209. The employer's federal and state identification numbers are 75-4444444 and 12-44444, respectively. Carry out the procedures as instructed in each of the following steps.

INSTRUCTIONS

1. Compute the state unemployment insurance tax owed on the employees' wages for the quarter ended March 31, 2004. This information will be shown on the employer's quarterly report to the state agency that collects SUTA tax. The employer has recorded the tax on each payroll date. Although the state charges a 5.4 percent unemployment tax rate, The Fashion Center's rate is only 1.7 percent because of its experience rating. The employee earnings for the first quarter are shown below. All earnings are subject to SUTA tax.

Name of Employee	Total Earnings
Gus Salvage	$ 4,020
Marvel Turner	3,720
Sadie Judge	4,030
Paul Torres	4,000
Nelsy Li	3,800
Nita Williams	4,200
Steven Holmes	4,450
Total	$28,220

2. On April 30, 2004, the firm issued a check to the state employment commission for the amount computed above. In general journal form, record the issuance of the check.
3. Complete Form 940-EZ, the Employer's Annual Federal Unemployment Tax Return, on January 15, 2005. Assume that all wages have been paid and that all quarterly payments have been submitted to the state as required. The payroll information appears below. The required federal tax deposit forms and checks were submitted as follows: a deposit of $225.76 on April 21, a deposit of $211.92 on July 22, and a deposit of $72.00 on October 21. Date the unemployment tax return January 28, 2005. A check for the balance due will be sent with Form 940-EZ.

Quarter Ended	Total Wages Paid	Wages Paid in Excess of $7,000	State Unemployment Tax Paid
Mar. 31	$ 28,220.00	–0–	$ 479.74
June 30	29,520.00	$ 3,030.00	450.33
Sept. 30	29,720.00	20,720.00	153.00
Dec. 31	30,820.00	27,700.00	53.04
Totals	$118,280.00	$51,450.00	$1,136.11

4. In general journal form, record the issuance of a check on January 28, 2005, for the balance of FUTA tax due.

Analyze: What total debits were made to liability accounts for the entries you have recorded?

Problem 11-4A ► Objective 8

Computing and recording workers' compensation insurance premiums.

The following information relates to Mason Manufacturing Company's workers' compensation insurance premiums for 2004. On January 15, 2004, the company estimated its premium for workers' compensation insurance for the year on the basis of that data.

Work Classification	Amount of Estimated Wages	Insurance Rates
Office work	$ 66,000	$0.30/$100
Shop work	300,000	$4.00/$100

INSTRUCTIONS

1. Compute the estimated premiums.
2. Record in general journal form payment of the estimated premium on January 15, 2004.
3. On January 4, 2005, an audit of the firm's payroll records showed that it had actually paid wages of $76,000 to its office employees and wages of $302,000 to its shop employees. Compute the actual premium for the year and the balance due the insurance company or the credit due the firm.
4. Give the general journal entry to adjust the **Workers' Compensation Insurance Expense** account as of the end of 2004. Date the entry December 31, 2004.

Analyze: If all wages were attributable to shop employees, what premium estimate would have been calculated and recorded on January 15, 2004?

PROBLEM SET B

Problem 11-1B ► Objectives 2, 6

Computing and recording employer's payroll tax expense.

The payroll register of Kline Automotive Repair Shop showed total employee earnings of $2,160 for the week ended April 8, 20--.

INSTRUCTIONS

  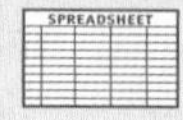

1. Compute the employer's payroll taxes for the period. The tax rates are as follows:

Social security	6.2 percent
Medicare	1.45
FUTA	0.8
SUTA	2.2

2. Prepare a general journal entry to record the employer's payroll taxes for the period.

Analyze: If the FUTA tax rate had been 1.2 percent, what total employer payroll taxes would have been recorded?

◄ Problem 11-2B
Objectives 2, 3, 4, 6

QB

Computing employer's social security tax, Medicare tax, and unemployment taxes and recording payment of taxes; preparing employer's federal tax return.

A payroll summary for Jenny Schwartz, who owns and operates The Dress Shop, for the quarter ending September 30, 20--, appears below. The business prepared the tax deposit forms and issued checks as follows during the quarter.

a. Federal Tax Deposit Coupon, Form 8109, check for July taxes, paid on August 15.

b. Federal Tax Deposit Coupon, Form 8109, check for August taxes, paid on September 15.

Date Wages Paid		Total Earnings	Social Security Tax Withheld	Medicare Tax Withheld	Income Tax Withheld
July	7	$ 1,800.00	$ 111.60	$ 26.10	$ 175.00
	14	1,800.00	111.60	26.10	175.00
	21	2,100.00	130.20	30.45	205.00
	28	1,800.00	111.60	26.10	175.00
		$ 7,500.00	$ 465.00	$108.75	$ 730.00
Aug.	4	$ 2,100.00	$ 130.20	$ 30.45	205.00
	11	2,700.00	167.40	39.15	265.00
	18	2,700.00	167.40	39.15	265.00
	25	2,400.00	148.80	34.80	235.00
		$ 9,900.00	$ 613.80	$143.55	$ 970.00
Sept.	3	$ 1,800.00	$ 111.60	$ 26.10	$ 175.00
	10	2,100.00	130.20	30.45	205.00
	17	2,100.00	130.20	30.45	205.00
	24	2,100.00	130.20	30.45	205.00
	31	1,800.00	111.60	26.10	175.00
		$ 9,900.00	$ 613.80	$143.55	$ 965.00
Total		$27,300.00	$1,692.60	$395.85	$2,665.00

INSTRUCTIONS

1. Prepare the general journal entry on July 7, 20--, to record the employer's payroll tax expense on the payroll ending that date. All earnings are subject to the following taxes:

Social security	6.2 percent
Medicare	1.45
FUTA	0.8
SUTA	2.2

2. Make the entries in general journal form to record deposit of the employee income tax withheld and the social security and Medicare taxes (both employees' withholding and employer's matching portion) on August 15 for July taxes and on September 15 for the August taxes.
3. On October 15 the firm issued a check to deposit the federal income tax withheld and the social security and Medicare taxes for September (both employees' withholding and employer's matching portion). Record the issuance of this check in your general journal.

4. Complete Form 941 in accordance with the discussions in this chapter and the instructions on the form itself. Use the tax rates of 12.4 percent for social security and 2.9 percent for Medicare in computations. Use the following company information: The Dress Shop, 2001 University Drive, Waco, TX 76706. Use the following employer identification number, 75-89023920. Date the return October 31, 20--.

Analyze: What total taxes were deposited with the IRS for the quarter ended September 30, 20--?

Problem 11-3B ►
Objectives 6, 7

Computing and recording unemployment taxes; completing Form 940.

Certain transactions and procedures relating to federal and state unemployment taxes are given below for The Saddle Shop, a retail store owned by Guy Gagliardi. The firm's address is 4560 LBJ Freeway, Dallas, TX 75201. The employer's federal and state identification numbers are 75-7777777 and 12-12345, respectively. Carry out the procedures as instructed in each step.

INSTRUCTIONS

1. Compute the state unemployment insurance tax owed for the quarter ended March 31, 2004. This information will be shown on the employer's quarterly report to the state agency that collects SUTA tax. The employer has recorded the tax expense and liability on each payroll date. Although the state charges a 5.4 percent unemployment tax rate, The Saddle Shop has received a favorable experience rating and therefore pays only a 2.3 percent state tax rate. The employee earnings for the first quarter are given below. All earnings are subject to SUTA tax.

Name of Employee	Total Earnings
Susan Benson	$ 3,275
Emma Johnson	3,500
John Alexander	3,100
Selena Ramos	3,250
Patricia Reed	2,975
Melvin Miller	2,980
Total	$19,080

2. On April 30, 2004, the firm issued a check for the amount computed above. Record the transaction in general journal form.
3. Complete Form 940-EZ, the Employer's Annual Federal Unemployment Tax Return. Assume that all wages have been paid and that all quarterly payments have been submitted to the state as required. The FUTA deposits made during the year were $152.64 on April 12, $159.80 on July 14, and $74.40 on October 12. Date the unemployment tax return January 22, 2005. A check for the balance due will be sent with Form 940. The payroll information is given in the following table.

Quarter Ended	Total Wages Paid	Wages Paid in Excess of $7,000	State Unemployment Tax Paid
Mar. 31	$19,080.00	–0–	$ 438.84
June 30	19,975.00	–0–	459.43
Sept. 30	17,245.00	$ 8,200.00	208.04
Dec. 31	20,400.00	19,700.00	16.10
Totals	$76,700.00	$27,900.00	$1,122.41

4. On January 25, 2005, the firm issued a check for the amount shown on line 8, Part I, of Form 940-EZ. In general journal form, record issuance of the check.

Analyze: What is the balance of the **Federal Unemployment Tax Payable** account on January 26, 2005?

Computing and recording premiums on workers' compensation insurance.

◄ **Problem 11-4B**
Objective 8

The following information is for Taylor's Office Supply workers' compensation insurance premiums. On January 15, 2004, the company estimated its premium for workers' compensation insurance for the year on the basis of the following data.

Work Classification	Amount of Estimated Wages	Insurance Rates
Office work	$ 76,000	$0.40/$100
Factory work	370,000	$8.00/$100

INSTRUCTIONS

1. Use the information to compute the estimated premium for the year.
2. A check was issued to pay the estimated premium on January 15, 2004. Record the transaction in general journal form.
3. On January 17, 2005, an audit of the firm's payroll records showed that it had actually paid wages of $72,800 to its office employees and wages of $357,000 to its factory employees. Compute the actual premium for the year and the balance due the insurance company or the credit due the firm.
4. Give the general journal entry to adjust the **Workers' Compensation Insurance Expense** account. Date the entry December 31, 2004.

Analyze: What is the balance of the **Workers' Compensation Insurance Expense** account at December 31, 2004, after all journal entries have been posted?

CHAPTER 11 CHALLENGE PROBLEM

Determining Employee Status

In each of the following independent situations, decide whether the business organization should treat the person being paid as an employee and should withhold social security, Medicare, and employee income taxes from the payment made.

1. Munich Corporation carries on very little business activity. It merely holds land and certain assets. The board of directors has concluded that they need no employees. They have decided instead to pay Harry White, one of the shareholders, a consulting fee of $12,000 per year to serve as president, secretary, and treasurer and to manage all the affairs of the company. White spends an average of one hour per week on the corporation's business affairs. However, his fee is fixed regardless of how few or how many hours he works.
2. Patrick Hicks owns and operates a crafts shop, using the sole proprietorship form of business. Each week a check for $1,000 is written on the crafts shop's bank account as a salary payment to Hicks.
3. Clare Parks is a public stenographer, or court reporter. She has an office at the Trenton Court Reporting Center but pays no rent. The manager of the center receives requests from attorneys for public stenographers to take depositions at legal hearings. The manager then chooses a stenographer who best meets the needs of the client and contacts the stenographer chosen. The stenographer has the right to refuse to take on the job, and the stenographer controls his or her working hours and days. Clients make payments to the center, which deducts a 25 percent fee for providing facilities and rendering services to support the stenographer. The balance is paid to the stenographer. During the current month, the center collected fees of $20,000 for Clare, deducted $5,000 for the center's fee, and remitted the proper amount to Clare.
4. David, a registered nurse, has retired from full-time work. However, because of his experience and special skills, on each Monday, Wednesday, and Thursday afternoon he assists Dr. Nancy Heart, a dermatologist. David is paid an hourly fee by Dr. Heart. During the current week, his hourly fees totaled $800.
5. After working several years as an editor for a magazine publisher, Leola quit her job to stay at home with her two small children. Later the publisher asked her to work in her home performing editorial work as needed. Leola is paid an hourly fee for the work she performs. In some cases she goes to the publishing company's offices to pick up or return a manuscript, and in other cases the firm sends a manuscript to her or she returns one by mail. During the current month Leola's hourly earnings totaled $1,800.

Analyze: What characteristics do the persons you identified as "employees" have in common?

CHAPTER 11 CRITICAL THINKING PROBLEM

Comparing Employees and Independent Contractors

The *City Record Chronicle* is a local newspaper that is published Monday through Friday. It sells 90,000 copies daily. The paper is currently in a profit squeeze, and the publisher, Amanda Lewis, is looking for ways to reduce expenses.

A review of current distribution procedures reveals that the *City Record Chronicle* employs 100 truck drivers to drop off bundles of newspapers to 1,200 teenagers who deliver papers to individual homes. The drivers are paid an hourly wage while the teenagers receive 3 cents for each paper they deliver.

Lewis is considering an alternative method of distributing the papers, which she says has worked in other cities the size of Denton (where the *City Record Chronicle* is published). Under the new system, the newspaper would retain 25 truck drivers to transport papers to four distribution centers around the city. The distribution centers are operated by independent contractors who would be responsible for making their own arrangements to deliver papers to subscribers' homes. The 25 drivers retained by the *City Record Chronicle* would receive the same hourly rate as they currently earn, and the independent contractors would receive 15 cents for each paper delivered.

1. What payroll information does Lewis need in order to make a decision about adopting the alternative distribution method?
2. Assume the following information:
   a. The average driver earns $44,000 per year.
   b. Average federal income tax withholding is 17 percent.
   c. The social security tax is 6.2 percent of the first $76,200 of earnings.
   d. The Medicare tax is 1.45 percent of all earnings.
   e. The state unemployment tax is 4 percent, and the federal unemployment tax is 0.8 percent of the first $7,000 of earnings.
   f. Workers' compensation insurance is 90 cents per $100 of wages.
   g. The paper pays $290 per month for health insurance for each driver and contributes $220 per month to each driver's pension plan.
   h. The paper has liability insurance coverage for all teenage carriers that costs $120,000 per year.

   Prepare a schedule showing the costs of distributing the newspapers under the current system and the proposed new system. Based on your analysis, which system would you recommend to Lewis?
3. What other factors, monetary and nonmonetary, might influence your decision?

Business Connections

Connection 1 ►

Payroll

1. Davis Company recently discovered that a payroll clerk had issued checks to nonexistent employees for several years and cashed the checks himself. The firm does not have any internal control procedures for its payroll operations. What specific controls might have led to the discovery of this fraud more quickly or discouraged the payroll clerk from even attempting the fraud?
2. Johnson Company has 20 employees. Some employees work in the office, others in the warehouse, and still others in the retail store. In the company's records, all employees are simply referred to as "general employees." Explain to management why this is not an acceptable practice.
3. Why should management be concerned about the accuracy and promptness of payroll tax deposits and payroll tax returns?
4. What is the significance to management of the experience rating system used to determine the employer's tax under the state unemployment insurance laws?

Connection 2 ►

Ethical DILEMMA **Personal Expenses** You work in the payroll department of State University where you attend college. You use the copy machine, fax, and telephone to make personal copies, fax letters to family and friends, and call family and friends out of town. State University prohibits personal use of these items and requires employees to sign a statement at the end of each month certifying that all copies, calls, and faxes were made for business use. You sign the statement each month. Are your actions ethical? Why or why not?

Connection 3 ►

Payroll and Promotions Refer to The Home Depot, Inc. *1999 Annual Report* in Appendix B.

1. Locate the consolidated balance sheets. When The Home Depot, Inc. records payroll tax liabilities, which category reflected on the balance sheet most likely contains these obligations?
2. The Home Depot, Inc. employed 201,400 associates at the close of fiscal 1999. According to the company's employment strategies, store managers are rarely recruited externally. Most store managers are promoted from within the organization. Discuss why you think The Home Depot, Inc. employs this strategy. What advantages and disadvantages do you think the company experiences as a result of this procedure?

Connection 4 ►

H&R BLOCK

Income Statement The following excerpt was taken from H&R Block, Inc.'s consolidated statements of earnings for the year ended April 30, 2000.

H&R Block			
Consolidated Statements of Earnings			
(Amounts in thousands, except per share amounts)			
	Year Ended April 30		
	2000	**1999**	**1998**
Expenses:			
Employee compensation and benefits	963,536	610,866	483,951
Occupancy and equipment	253,171	182,701	157,995
Interest	153,500	69,338	38,899
Depreciation and amortization	147,218	74,605	54,972
Marketing and advertising	140,683	90,056	71,594
Supplies, freight and postage	64,599	57,157	51,705
Bad debt	51,719	71,662	53,736
Other	273,902	133,206	85,612
Total Operating Expenses	2,048,328	1,289,591	998,464

Analyze:

1. What percentage of total operating expenses was spent on employee compensation and benefits in the year ended April 30, 2000?
2. Assume that FICA (social security) wages for the first quarter of 2000 were $251,694,000. What deposit did H&R Block send to the federal government for FICA taxes for the quarter? (Assume FICA rate of 6.2%.)
3. By what percentage did employee compensation and benefits increase from the years ended April 30, 1998 to 1999; and 1999 to 2000?

Analyze Online: Find the H&R Block Web site **(www.hrblock.com).** Locate *Investor Relations* within the *About* section of the Web site. Find the most recent annual report.

4. What percentage of total operating expenses was spent on employee compensation and benefits?
5. Which expense line had the highest percentage increase in the last two years?

Extending the Thought **Unemployment Insurance** Businesses must pay unemployment insurance taxes required by federal and state agencies. The program provides benefits to unemployed workers. Your business has never fired or laid off an employee, yet you are required to pay the minimum tax rate on gross salaries. Do you agree or disagree with this system? Why?

◄ **Connection 5**

Business Communication **Memo—Payroll Forms** You have opened a new office supply store and plan to hire 10 employees to help with sales, inventory maintenance, and advertising. You would like your payroll clerk to set up his office to prepare for the year's payroll duties. Write a memo to your payroll clerk requesting that he gather all the necessary employee forms, payroll tax return forms, and accounting forms that will be needed for payroll. Include a detailed list of the items that should be gathered.

◄ **Connection 6**

Connection 7 ► **TeamWork** **Taxation** Taxation can be based on a progressive, regressive, or proportional basis. As a team, research the definitions of each type of taxation. Create index cards for each type of taxation with arguments that support or refute the taxation basis. Use these cards for a class discussion on the topic.

Connection 8 ► **interNET CONNECTION** **IRS** The Internal Revenue Service (IRS) processes approximately 205 million tax returns a year while assisting 99 million taxpayers by telephone and 6.3 million taxpayers at walk-in offices throughout the country. Go to its Web site at **www.irs.gov.** What is an ITIN? Can you receive an ITIN if you have a social security number? What is Revenue Procedure 96-13?

Answers to Self Reviews

Answers to Section 1 Self Review

1. Federal Reserve Bank or a commercial bank that is designated as a federal depository.
2. Form 941 shows income taxes withheld, social security and Medicare taxes due for the quarter, and tax deposits. The form is due on the last day of the month following the end of the quarter.
3. Form W-2 provides information to enable the employees to complete their federal income tax return. Copies are given to the employee and to the federal government (and to other governmental units that levy an income tax).
4. **a.** each payroll period.
5. **c.** Social security tax
6. Monthly

Answers to Section 2 Self Review

1. It reduces the rate of SUTA tax that must actually be paid.
2. The amount of the premium depends on the type of work the employee performs.
3. The employer pays FUTA. Usually the employer pays SUTA, although a few states also levy SUTA on employees.
4. **b.** quarterly.
5. **d.** Form 940.
6. Expenses will be understated. Net income will be overstated.

Answers to Comprehensive Self Review

1. **b.** Amount of taxes reported in the lookback period.
   d. Amount of taxes currently owed.
2. By the 15th day of the following month.
3. Smaller
4. A credit, with limits, is allowed against the federal tax for unemployment tax charged by the state.
5. Form W-3 is sent to the Social Security Administration. It reports the total social security wages; total Medicare wages; total social security and Medicare taxes withheld; total wages, tips, and other compensation; total federal income tax withheld; and other information.

PART 4

Summarizing and Reporting Financial Information

Johnson & Johnson In January 2001 Johnson & Johnson announced worldwide pharmaceutical segment sales of $12 billion in 2000, an 11.8 percent increase over 1999 sales. The company recorded and summarized millions of transactions to arrive at the sales figure for 2000.

Thinking Critically

What importance do you think financial measurements hold for a company like Johnson & Johnson? What implications do these milestones carry in the investment community and within the organization?

CHAPTER 12

Learning Objectives

1. Determine the adjustment for merchandise inventory, and enter the adjustment on the worksheet.
2. Compute adjustments for accrued and prepaid expense items, and enter the adjustments on the worksheet.
3. Compute adjustments for accrued and deferred income items, and enter the adjustments on the worksheet.
4. Complete a ten-column worksheet.
5. Define the accounting terms new to this chapter.

Accruals, Deferrals, and the Worksheet

AMERICAN EAGLE OUTFITTERS

www.ae.com

Clothing from American Eagle Outfitters, Inc. is hip, fun, and youthful. The company designs, markets, and sells its own brand of casual classics including AE khakis, jeans, accessories, footwear, and T-shirts. The company targets men and women between the ages of 16 and 34. The prices are affordable, and the styles hit the mark. Apparently U.S. consumers like the mix. Sales have increased at an average annual rate of 37 percent since 1996. AE styles have been seen on television shows such as *Dawson's Creek,* in major Hollywood films, and in national newspapers and magazines, resulting in exposure to more than 1.5 billion viewers in 1999.

Thinking Critically

American Eagle Outfitters, Inc.'s plans for 2000 included opening 90 new stores and remodeling more than 40 existing stores. What types of adjustments do you think the accountants at American Eagle Outfitters, Inc. recorded as a result of this expansion activity?

For more information on American Eagle Outfitters, Inc., go to: collegeaccounting.glencoe.com.

New Terms

Accrual basis
Accrued expenses
Accrued income
Deferred expenses
Deferred income
Inventory sheet
Net income line
Prepaid expenses
Property, plant, and equipment
Unearned income
Updated account balances

Section 1

Section Objectives

1. **Determine the adjustment for merchandise inventory, and enter the adjustment on the worksheet.**

   WHY IT'S IMPORTANT
   The change in merchandise inventory affects the financial statements.

2. **Compute adjustments for accrued and prepaid expense items, and enter the adjustments on the worksheet.**

   WHY IT'S IMPORTANT
   Each expense item needs to be assigned to the accounting period in which it helped to earn revenue.

3. **Compute adjustments for accrued and deferred income items, and enter the adjustments on the worksheet.**

   WHY IT'S IMPORTANT
   The accrual basis of accounting states that income is recognized in the period it is earned.

Terms to Learn

accrual basis
accrued expenses
accrued income
deferred expenses
deferred income
inventory sheet
prepaid expenses
property, plant, and equipment
unearned income

Calculating and Recording Adjustments

In Chapter 5 you learned how to make adjustments so that all revenue and expenses that apply to a fiscal period appear on the income statement for that period. In this chapter you will learn more about adjustments and how they affect Modern Casuals, a retail merchandising business.

The Accrual Basis of Accounting

Financial statements usually are prepared using the **accrual basis** of accounting because it most nearly attains the goal of matching expenses and revenue in an accounting period.

- *Revenue is recognized when earned, not necessarily when the cash is received.* Revenue is recognized when the sale is complete. A sale is complete when title to the goods passes to the customer or when the service is provided. For sales on account, revenue is recognized when the sale occurs even though the cash is not collected immediately.
- *Expenses are recognized when incurred or used, not necessarily when cash is paid.* Each expense is assigned to the accounting period in which it helped to earn revenue for the business, even if cash is not paid at that time. This is often referred to as *matching revenues and expenses.*

Sometimes cash changes hands before the revenue or expense is recognized. For example, insurance premiums are normally paid in advance, and the coverage extends over several accounting periods. In other cases cash changes hands after the revenue or expense has been recognized. For example, employees might work during December but be paid in January of the following year. Because of these timing differences, adjustments are made to ensure that revenue and expenses are recognized in the appropriate period.

Using the Worksheet to Record Adjustments

The worksheet is used to assemble data about adjustments and to organize the information for the financial statements. Figure 12-1 on pages 432–433 shows the first two sections of the worksheet for Modern Casuals. Let's review how to prepare the worksheet.

- Enter the trial balance in the Trial Balance section. Total the columns. Be sure that total debits equal total credits.
- Enter the adjustments in the Adjustments section. Use the same letter to identify the debit part and the credit part of each adjustment. Total the columns. Be sure that total debits equal total credits.

- For each account, combine the amounts in the Trial Balance section and the Adjustments section. Enter the results in the Adjusted Trial Balance section, total the columns, and make sure that total debits equal total credits.
- Extend account balances to the Income Statement and Balance Sheet sections and complete the worksheet.

Recognize

The word "recognize" means to record in the accounting records.

Adjustment for Merchandise Inventory

1 Objective

Determine the adjustment for merchandise inventory, and enter the adjustment on the worksheet.

Merchandise inventory consists of the goods that a business has on hand for sale to customers. An asset account for merchandise inventory is maintained in the general ledger. During the accounting period, all purchases of merchandise are debited to the **Purchases** account. All sales of merchandise are credited to the revenue account **Sales.**

Notice that no entries are made directly to the **Merchandise Inventory** account during the accounting period. Consequently, when the trial balance is prepared at the end of the period, the **Merchandise Inventory** account still shows the *beginning* inventory for the period. At the end of each period a business determines the *ending* balance of the **Merchandise Inventory** account. The first step in determining the ending inventory is to count the number of units of each type of item on hand. As the merchandise is counted, the quantity on hand is entered on an inventory sheet. The **inventory sheet** lists the quantity of each type of goods a firm has in stock. For each item the quantity is multiplied by the unit cost to find the totals per item. The totals for all items are added to compute the total cost of merchandise inventory.

The trial balance for Modern Casuals shows **Merchandise Inventory** of $51,500. Based on a count taken on December 31, merchandise inventory at the end of the year actually totaled $46,000. Modern Casuals needs to adjust the **Merchandise Inventory** account to reflect the balance at the end of the year.

Income Summary

The **Income Summary** account is a temporary owner's equity account used in the closing process.

The adjustment is made in two steps, using the accounts **Merchandise Inventory** and **Income Summary.**

1. The beginning inventory ($51,500) is taken off the books by transferring the account balance to the **Income Summary** account. This entry is labeled **(a)** on the worksheet in Figure 12-1 and is illustrated in T-account form below.

Merchandise Inventory			
Bal.	51,500	Adj.	51,500 (a)

Income Summary			
Adj.	51,500 (a)		

2. The ending inventory ($46,000) is placed on the books by debiting **Merchandise Inventory** and crediting **Income Summary.** This entry is labeled **(b)** on the worksheet in Figure 12-1.

Merchandise Inventory			
Bal.	51,500	Adj.	51,500 (a)
Adj.	46,000 (b)		

Income Summary			
Adj.	51,500 (a)	Adj.	46,000 (b)

Modern Casuals
Worksheet
Year Ended December 31, 2004

	ACCOUNT NAME	TRIAL BALANCE		ADJUSTMENTS	
		DEBIT	CREDIT	DEBIT	CREDIT
1	*Cash*	*21,136.00*			
2	*Petty Cash Fund*	*100.00*			
3	*Notes Receivable*	*1,200.00*			
4	*Accounts Receivable*	*32,000.00*			
5	*Allowance for Doubtful Accounts*		*100.00*		*(c) 750.00*
6	*Interest Receivable*			*(m) 24.00*	
7	*Merchandise Inventory*	*51,500.00*		*(b) 46,000.00*	*(a) 51,500.00*
8	*Prepaid Insurance*	*7,200.00*			*(k) 3,600.00*
9	*Prepaid Interest*	*225.00*			*(l) 150.00*
10	*Supplies*	*6,300.00*			*(j) 4,975.00*
11	*Store Equipment*	*20,000.00*			
12	*Accumulated Depreciation—Store Equipment*				*(d) 2,250.00*
13	*Office Equipment*	*7,000.00*			
14	*Accumulated Depreciation—Office Equipment*				*(e) 1,200.00*
15	*Notes Payable—Trade*		*2,000.00*		
16	*Notes Payable—Bank*		*9,000.00*		
17	*Accounts Payable*		*24,129.00*		
18	*Interest Payable*				*(i) 20.00*
19	*Social Security Tax Payable*		*1,084.00*		*(g) 93.00*
20	*Medicare Tax Payable*		*250.00*		*(g) 21.75*
21	*Employee Income Taxes Payable*		*990.00*		
22	*Federal Unemployment Tax Payable*				*(h) 12.00*
23	*State Unemployment Tax Payable*				*(h) 81.00*
24	*Salaries Payable*				*(f) 1,500.00*
25	*Sales Tax Payable*		*7,200.00*	*(n) 144.00*	
26	*Sonia Sanchez, Capital*		*61,221.00*		
27	*Sonia Sanchez, Drawing*	*27,600.00*			
28	*Income Summary*			*(a) 51,500.00*	*(b) 46,000.00*
29	*Sales*		*559,650.00*		
30	*Sales Returns and Allowances*	*13,000.00*			
31	*Interest Income*		*136.00*		*(m) 24.00*
32	*Miscellaneous Income*		*366.00*		*(n) 144.00*
33	*Purchases*	*320,500.00*			
34	*Freight In*	*8,800.00*			
35	*Purchases Returns and Allowances*		*3,050.00*		
36	*Purchase Discounts*		*3,130.00*		
37	*Salaries Expense—Sales*	*78,490.00*		*(f) 1,500.00*	
38	*Advertising Expense*	*7,425.00*			
39	*Cash Short or Over*	*125.00*			
40	*Supplies Expense*			*(j) 4,975.00*	

▲ **FIGURE 12-1**
10-Column Worksheet—Partial

	ACCOUNT NAME	TRIAL BALANCE DEBIT	TRIAL BALANCE CREDIT	ADJUSTMENTS DEBIT	ADJUSTMENTS CREDIT
41	*Depreciation Expense—Store Equipment*			(d) 2 250 00	
42	*Rent Expense*	27 600 00			
43	*Salaries Expense—Office*	26 500 00			
44	*Insurance Expense*			(k) 3 600 00	
45	*Payroll Taxes Expense*	7 205 00		(g) 114 75	
46				(h) 93 00	
47	*Telephone Expense*	1 875 00			
48	*Uncollectible Accounts Expense*			(c) 750 00	
49	*Utilities Expense*	5 925 00			
50	*Depreciation Expense—Office Equipment*			(e) 1 200 00	
51	*Interest Expense*	600 00		(i) 20 00	
52				(l) 150 00	
53	*Totals*	672 306 00	672 306 00	112 320 75	112 320 75
54					

▲ **FIGURE 12-1 (continued)**
10-Column Worksheet—Partial

The effect of this adjustment is to remove the beginning merchandise inventory balance and replace it with the ending merchandise inventory balance. Merchandise inventory is adjusted in two steps on the worksheet because both the beginning and the ending inventory figures appear on the income statement, which is prepared directly from the worksheet.

2 Objective

Compute adjustments for accrued and prepaid expense items, and enter the adjustments on the worksheet.

Adjustment for Loss from Uncollectible Accounts

Credit sales are made with the expectation that the customers will pay the amount due later. Sometimes the account receivable is never collected. Losses from uncollectible accounts are classified as operating expenses.

Under accrual accounting, the expense for uncollectible accounts is recorded in the same period as the related sale. The expense is estimated because the actual amount of uncollectible accounts is not known until later periods. To match the expense for uncollectible accounts with the sales revenue for the same period, the estimated expense is debited to an account named **Uncollectible Accounts Expense.**

Several methods exist for estimating the expense for uncollectible accounts. Modern Casuals uses the *percentage of net credit sales* method. The rate used is based on the company's past experience with uncollectible accounts and management's assessment of current business conditions. Modern Casuals estimates that three-fourths of 1 percent (0.75 percent) of net credit sales will be uncollectible. Net credit sales for the year were $100,000. The estimated expense for uncollectible accounts is $750 ($100,000 × 0.0075).

The entry to record the expense for uncollectible accounts includes a credit to a contra asset account, **Allowance for Doubtful Accounts.** This account appears on the balance sheet as follows.

Accounts Receivable	$32,000
Allowance for Doubtful Accounts	(750)
Net Accounts Receivable	$31,250

Adjustment **(c)** appears on the worksheet in Figure 12-1 for the expense for uncollectible accounts.

The Bottom Line

Uncollectible Accounts Expense

Income Statement	
Expenses	↑ 750
Net income	↓ 750
Balance Sheet	
Assets	↓ 750
Equity	↓ 750

Uncollectible Accounts Expense			
Adj.	750		

Allowance for Doubtful Accounts			
		Bal.	100
		Adj.	750

(c)

When a specific account becomes uncollectible, it is written off.

- The entry is a debit to **Allowance for Doubtful Accounts** and a credit to **Accounts Receivable.**
- The customer's account in the accounts receivable subsidiary ledger is also reduced.

Uncollectible Accounts Expense is not affected by the write-off of individual accounts identified as uncollectible. It is used only when the end-of-period adjustment is recorded.

Notice that net income is decreased at the end of the period when the adjustment for *estimated* expense for uncollectible accounts is made. When a specific customer account is written off, net income is *not* affected. The write-off of a specific account affects only the balance sheet accounts **Accounts Receivable** (asset) and **Allowance for Doubtful Accounts** (contra asset).

The balance of **Allowance for Doubtful Accounts** is reduced throughout the year as customer accounts are written off. Notice that **Allowance for Doubtful Accounts** already has a credit balance of $100 in the Trial Balance section of the worksheet. When the estimate of uncollectible accounts expense is based on sales, any remaining balance from previous periods is not considered when recording the adjustment.

Adjustments for Depreciation

Most businesses have long-term assets that are used in the operation of the business. These are often referred to as **property, plant, and equipment**. Property, plant, and equipment includes buildings, trucks, automobiles, machinery, furniture, fixtures, office equipment, and land.

Property, plant, and equipment costs are not charged to expense accounts when purchased. Instead, the cost of a long-term asset is allocated over the asset's expected useful life by depreciation. This process involves the gradual transfer of acquisition cost to expense. There is one exception. Land is not depreciated.

There are many ways to calculate depreciation. Modern Casuals uses the straight-line method, so an equal amount of depreciation is taken in each year of the asset's useful life. The formula for straight-line depreciation is

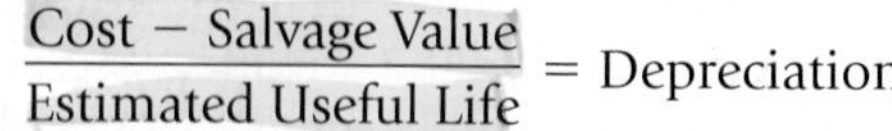

$$\frac{\text{Cost} - \text{Salvage Value}}{\text{Estimated Useful Life}} = \text{Depreciation}$$

Salvage value is an estimate of the amount that could be obtained from the sale or disposition of an asset at the end of its useful life. Cost minus salvage value is called the *depreciable base*.

Important!

Depreciation

To calculate monthly straight-line depreciation, divide the depreciable base by the number of months in the useful life.

Depreciation of Store Equipment. The trial balance shows that Modern Casuals has $20,000 of store equipment. What is the amount of annual depreciation expense using the straight-line method?

Cost of store equipment	$20,000
Salvage value	(2,000)
Depreciable base	$18,000
Expected useful life	8 years

$$\frac{\$20{,}000 - \$2{,}000}{8 \text{ years}} = \$2{,}250 \text{ Per year}$$

The annual depreciation expense is $2,250. Adjustment **(d)** appears on the worksheet in Figure 12-1 for the depreciation expense for store equipment.

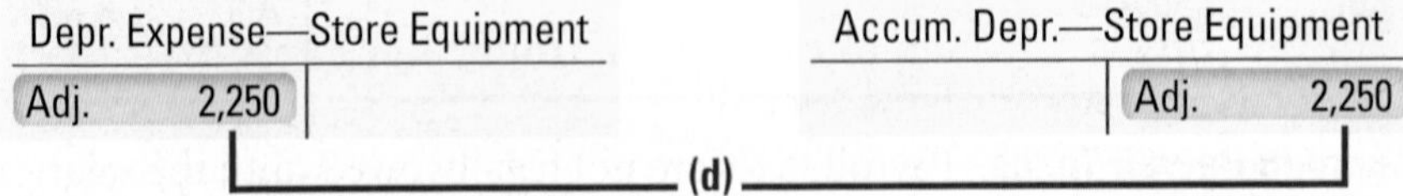

Depreciation of Office Equipment. Modern Casuals reports $7,000 of office equipment on the trial balance. What is the amount of annual depreciation expense using the straight-line method?

Cost of office equipment	$7,000
Salvage value	(1,000)
Depreciable base	$6,000
Expected useful life	5 years

$$\frac{\$7{,}000 - \$1{,}000}{5 \text{ Years}} = \$1{,}200 \text{ Per year}$$

Annual depreciation expense is $1,200. Adjustment **(e)** appears on the worksheet in Figure 12-1 for depreciation expense for office equipment.

Depr. Expense—Office Equipment	
Adj. 1,200	

Accum. Depr.—Office Equipment	
	Adj. 1,200

(e)

Adjustments for Accrued Expenses

Many expense items are paid for, recorded, and used in the same accounting period. However, some expense items are paid for and recorded in one period but used in a later period. Other expense items are used in one period and paid for in a later period. In these situations adjustments are made so that the financial statements show all expenses in the appropriate period.

Accrued expenses are expenses that relate to (are used in) the current period but have not yet been paid and do not yet appear in the accounting records. Modern Casuals makes adjustments for three types of accrued expenses:

- accrued salaries
- accrued payroll taxes
- accrued interest on notes payable

Because accrued expenses involve amounts that must be paid in the future, the adjustment for each item is a debit to an expense account and a credit to a liability account.

Electronic Payments

Congress ordered the U.S. Treasury Department to begin electronic payments for all checks except taxpayer refunds by January 2, 1999. The initiative saves taxpayers an estimated $100 million per year.

Accrued Salaries. At Modern Casuals all full-time sales and office employees are paid semimonthly—on the 15th and the last day of the month. The trial balance in Figure 12-1 shows the correct salaries expense for the full-time employees for the year. From December 28 to January 3, the firm hired several part-time sales clerks for the year-end sale. Through December 31, 2004, these employees earned $1,500. The part-time salaries expense has not yet been recorded because the employees will not be paid until January 3, 2005. An adjustment is made to record the amount owed, but not yet paid, as of the end of December.

Adjustment **(f)** appears on the worksheet in Figure 12-1 for accrued salaries.

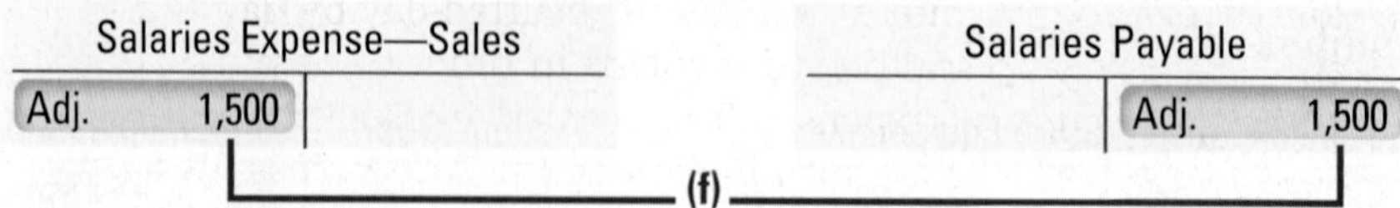

Accrued Payroll Taxes. Payroll taxes are not legally owed until the salaries are paid. Businesses that want to match revenue and expenses in the appropriate period make adjustments to accrue the employer's payroll taxes even though the taxes are technically not yet due. Modern Casuals makes adjustments for accrued employer's payroll taxes.

Important!

Matching

Adjustments for accrued expenses match the expense to the period in which the expense was used.

The payroll taxes related to the full-time employees of Modern Casuals have been recorded and appear on the trial balance. However, the payroll taxes for the part-time sales clerks have not been recorded. None of the part-time clerks have reached the social security wage base limit. The entire $1,500 of accrued salaries is subject to the employer's share of social security and Medicare taxes. The accrued employer's payroll taxes are

Social security tax	$1,500	×	0.0620	=	$ 93.00
Medicare tax	1,500	×	0.0145	=	21.75
Total accrued payroll taxes					$114.75

Adjustment **(g)** appears on the worksheet in Figure 12-1 for accrued payroll taxes.

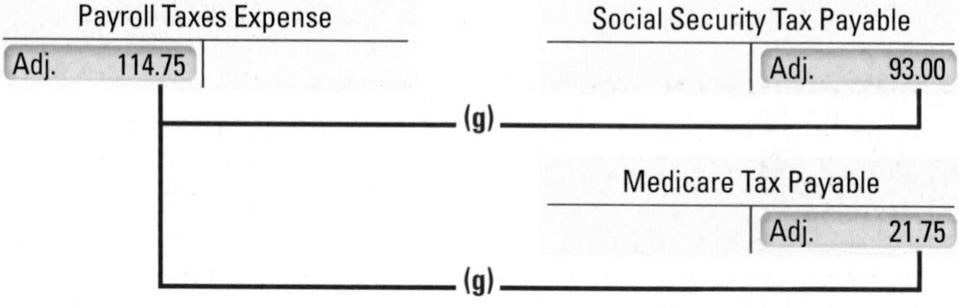

The entire $1,500 of accrued salaries is also subject to unemployment taxes. The unemployment tax rates for Modern Casuals are 0.8 percent for federal and 5.4 percent for state.

Federal unemployment tax	$1,500	×	0.008	=	$12.00
State unemployment tax	1,500	×	0.054	=	81.00
Total accrued taxes					$93.00

Adjustment **(h)** appears on the worksheet in Figure 12-1 for accrued unemployment taxes.

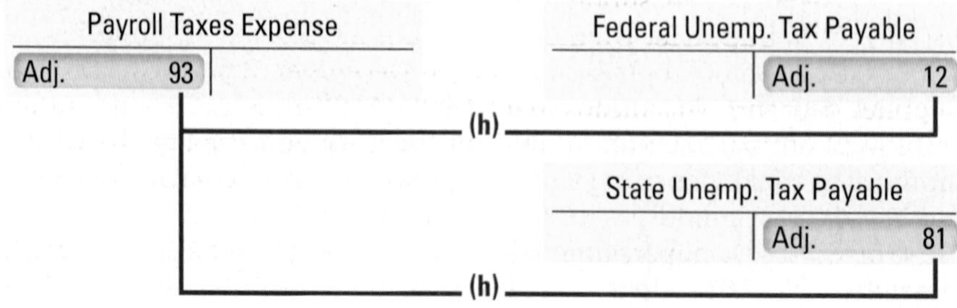

Accrued Interest on Notes Payable. On December 1, 2004, Modern Casuals issued a two-month note for $2,000, with annual interest of 12 percent. The note was recorded in the **Notes Payable—Trade** account. Modern Casuals will pay the interest when the note matures on February 1, 2005. However, the interest expense is incurred day by day and should be allocated to each fiscal period involved in order to obtain a complete and accurate picture of expenses. The accrued interest amount is determined by using the interest formula *Principal × Rate × Time.*

Principal	×	Rate	×	Time
$2,000	×	0.12	×	1/12 = $20

The fraction 1/12 represents one month, which is 1/12 of a year.

Adjustment **(i)** appears on the worksheet in Figure 12-1 for the accrued interest expense.

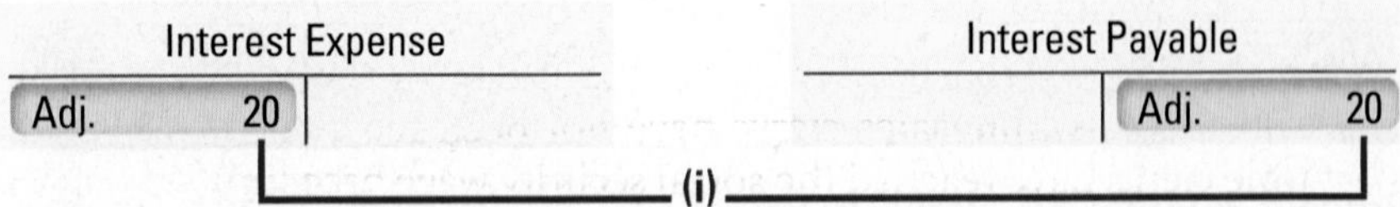

Other Accrued Expenses. Many businesses pay property taxes to state and local governments. They accrue these taxes at the end of the accounting period. Adjustments might also be necessary for commissions, professional services, and many other accrued expenses.

Adjustments for Prepaid Expenses

Prepaid expenses, or **deferred expenses**, are expenses that are paid for and recorded before they are used. Often a portion of a prepaid item remains unused at the end of the period; it is applicable to future periods. When paid for, these items are recorded as assets. At the end of the period, an adjustment is made to recognize as an expense the portion used during the period. Modern Casuals makes adjustments for three types of prepaid expenses:

- prepaid supplies
- prepaid insurance
- prepaid interest on notes payable

Avery Dennison Corporation reported prepaid expenses of $23.7 million at January 1, 2000. Adjustments are made to these accounts to allocate expenses to the appropriate period.

Supplies Used. When supplies are purchased, they are debited to the asset account **Supplies.** On the trial balance in Figure 12-1, **Supplies** has a balance of $6,300. A physical count on December 31 showed $1,325 of supplies on hand. This means that $4,975 ($6,300 − $1,325) of supplies were used during the year. An adjustment is made to charge the cost of supplies used to the current year's operations and to reflect the value of the supplies on hand.

Adjustment **(j)** appears on the worksheet in Figure 12-1 for supplies expense.

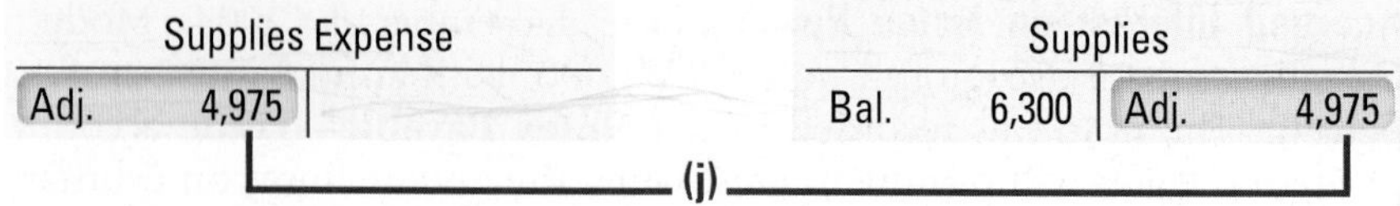

Expired Insurance. On January 1, 2004, Modern Casuals wrote a check for \$7,200 for a two-year insurance policy. The asset account **Prepaid Insurance** was debited for \$7,200. On December 31, 2004, one year of insurance had expired. An adjustment for \$3,600 (\$7,200 × 1/2) was made to charge the cost of the expired insurance to operations and to decrease **Prepaid Insurance** to reflect the prepaid insurance premium that remains.

Adjustment **(k)** appears on the worksheet in Figure 12-1 for the insurance.

Insurance Expense				Prepaid Insurance			
Adj.	3,600			Bal.	7,200	Adj.	3,600

(k)

Prepaid Interest on Notes Payable. On November 1, 2004, Modern Casuals borrowed \$9,000 from its bank and signed a three-month note at an annual interest rate of 10 percent. The bank deducted the entire amount of interest in advance. The interest for three months is \$225.

Principal	×	**Rate**	×	**Time**		
\$9,000	×	0.10	×	3/12	=	\$225

Modern Casuals received \$8,775 (\$9,000 − \$225). The transaction was recorded as a debit to **Cash** for \$8,775, a debit to **Prepaid Interest** for \$225, and a credit to **Notes Payable—Bank** for \$9,000.

On December 31 two months of prepaid interest (\$225 × 2/3 = \$150) had been incurred and needed to be recorded as an expense. The adjustment consists of a debit to **Interest Expense** and a credit to **Prepaid Interest.**

Adjustment **(l)** appears on the worksheet in Figure 12-1 for the interest expense.

Interest Expense				Prepaid Interest			
Adj.	150			Bal.	225	Adj.	150

(l)

Other Prepaid Expenses. Other common prepaid expenses are prepaid rent, prepaid advertising, and prepaid taxes. When paid, the amounts are debited to the asset accounts **Prepaid Rent, Prepaid Advertising,** and **Prepaid Taxes.** At the end of each period, an adjustment is made to transfer the portion used from the asset account to an expense account. For example, the adjustment for expired rent would be a debit to **Rent Expense** and a credit to **Prepaid Rent.**

Alternative Method. Some businesses use a different method for prepaid expenses. At the time cash is paid, they debit an expense account (not an asset account). At the end of each period, they make an adjustment to transfer the portion that is not used from the expense account to an asset account.

Suppose that Modern Casuals used this alternative method when it purchased the two-year insurance policy. On January 1, 2004, the transaction would have been recorded as a debit to **Insurance Expense** for \$7,200 and

Accounting On The Job

Business & Administration

Industry Overview

Business and administration services extend into every sector of the economy. The coordination and support of business operations is required in organizations ranging from insurance firms to government offices, steel manufacturers to retail stores.

Career Opportunities

- Account Executive
- Cost Accountant
- Payroll Supervisor
- Human Resources Manager
- Facility Manager
- Contract Administrator
- Chief Financial Officer

Preparing for a Career in Business & Administration

- Develop solid communication and analytical skills. Be flexible, decisive, and capable of coordinating many activities at once. Develop strategies to cope with deadlines.
- Attain certification specific to your area of interest. For example, the Certified Administrative Manager (CAM) is offered by the Institute of Certified Professional Managers.
- Complete a bachelor's degree with a major in accounting, finance, management, management information systems, marketing, or production and operations management.
- Become proficient in database, spreadsheet, and word processing applications.
- Complete a degree in engineering, architecture, business administration, or facility management for a career as a facility manager.
- Become familiar with basic office equipment such as fax machines, telephone systems, and personal computers.
- Gain a solid understanding of standard business forms such as purchase orders, invoices, contracts, and packing slips.
- Be prepared to interpret and analyze financial statements to effectively contribute to business discussions and decisions.

Thinking Critically

Describe 10 business tasks or responsibilities involved in the operation of Southwest Airlines Co. or a similar company.

Internet Application

The Internet contains a wealth of information provided to help individuals as they launch new businesses. Using an Internet search engine, list five resources that offer entrepreneurs guidance on their new endeavors. Describe the information or resources offered at each Web site.

a credit to **Cash** for $7,200. On December 31, 2004, after the insurance coverage for one year had expired, coverage for one year remained. The adjustment would be recorded as a debit to **Prepaid Insurance** for $3,600 ($7,200 × 1/2) and a credit to **Insurance Expense** for $3,600.

Identical amounts appear on the financial statements at the end of each fiscal period no matter which method is used to handle prepaid expenses.

Adjustments for Accrued Income

3 Objective

Compute adjustments for accrued and deferred income items, and enter the adjustments on the worksheet.

Accrued income is income that has been earned but not yet received and recorded. On December 31, 2004, Modern Casuals had two types of accrued income: accrued interest on notes receivable and accrued commission on sales tax.

Accrued Interest on Notes Receivable. Interest-bearing notes receivable are recorded at face value and are carried in the accounting records at this value until they are collected. The interest income is recorded when it is received, which is normally when the note matures. However, interest income is earned day by day. At the end of the period, an adjustment is made to recognize interest income earned but not yet received or recorded.

On November 1, 2004, Modern Casuals accepted from a customer a four-month, 12 percent note for $1,200. The note and interest are due on March 1, 2005. As of December 31, 2004, two months (November and December) of interest income was earned but not received. The amount of earned interest income is $24.

Principal	×	**Rate**	×	**Time**		
$1,200	×	0.12	×	2/12	=	$24

Adjustment **(m)** appears on the worksheet in Figure 12-1 for the interest income. To record the interest income of $24 earned, but not yet received, an adjustment debiting the asset account **Interest Receivable** and crediting a revenue account called **Interest Income** is made.

Interest Receivable			
Adj.	24		

Interest Income			
		Bal.	136
		Adj.	24

(m)

Accrued Commission on Sales Tax. Modern Casuals collects sales tax on retail sales. It sends the tax to the state agency on a quarterly basis. The state sales tax law allows firms that file the quarterly tax returns and pay the tax promptly to keep 2 percent of the tax. On December 31, 2004, Modern Casuals owed $7,200 of sales tax. In January the tax will be paid less the permitted commission of $144 ($7,200 × 0.02). The commission represents income earned and is recorded in the **Miscellaneous Income** account.

Adjustment **(n)** appears on the worksheet in Figure 12-1. The adjustment decreases the sales tax liability.

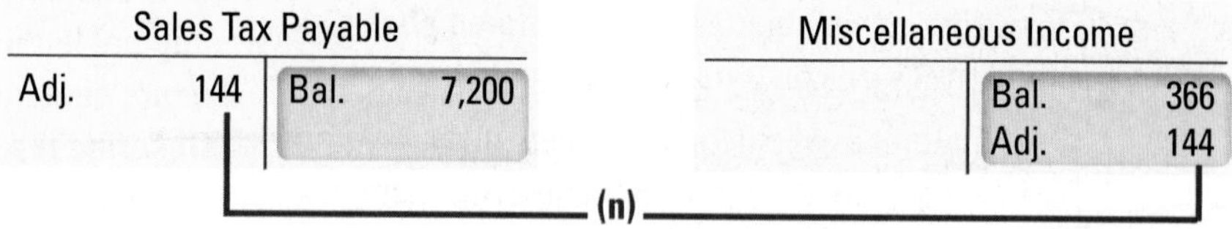

Adjustments for Unearned Income

Unearned income, or **deferred income**, exists when income is received before it is earned. Under the accrual basis of accounting, only income that has been earned appears on the income statement. Modern Casuals has no unearned income. The following is an example of unearned income for another business.

Unearned Subscription Income for a Publisher. Magazine publishers receive cash in advance for subscriptions. When the publisher receives the cash, it is unearned income and is a liability. It is a liability because the publisher has an obligation to provide magazines during the subscription period. As the magazines are sent to the subscribers, income is earned and the liability decreases.

Hitech Publishing Corporation publishes *Computer Trends and Techniques*. When subscriptions are received, **Cash** is debited and **Unearned Subscription Income,** a liability account, is credited. At the end of the year, **Unearned Subscription Income** had a balance of $450,000. During the year $184,000 of magazines were delivered; income was earned in the amount of $184,000. The adjustment to recognize income is a debit to **Unearned Subscription Income** for $184,000 and a credit to **Subscription Income** for $184,000.

After the adjustment the **Unearned Subscription Income** account has a balance of $266,000, which represents subscriptions for future periods.

Unearned Subscription Income	
	12/31 Bal. 450,000
12/31 Adj. 184,000	
	12/31 Bal. 266,000

Other Unearned Income Items. Other types of unearned income include management fees, rental income, legal fees, architectural fees, construction fees, and advertising income. The cash received in advance is recorded as unearned income. As the income is earned, the amount is transferred from the liability account to a revenue account.

Alternative Method. Some businesses use a different method to handle unearned income. At the time the cash is received, a credit is made to a revenue account (not a liability account). At the end of each period, the adjustment transfers the portion that is not earned to a liability account. For example, suppose Hitech Publishing Corporation uses this method. When cash for subscriptions is received, it is credited to **Subscription Income.** At the end of the period, an adjustment is made to transfer the unearned income to a liability account. The entry is a debit to **Subscription Income** and a credit to **Unearned Subscription Income.**

Identical amounts appear on the financial statements at the end of each fiscal period no matter which method is used to handle unearned income.

Section 1 Self Review

Questions

1. Under the accrual basis of accounting, when is revenue recognized?
2. Under the accrual basis of accounting, when are the costs of merchandise inventory normally recorded?
3. Under the accrual basis of accounting, when are operating expenses recognized?

Exercises

4. Under the accrual basis of accounting, it is appropriate to recognize revenue from a credit sale
   a. on the date of the sale.
   b. on the date that the account is collected in full.
   c. each time a customer payment is received.
   d. on the date the monthly statement is sent to the customer.
5. Accrued income is income that has been
   a. received but not earned.
   b. earned but not received.
   c. earned and received.
   d. expected to be received within the next accounting period.

Analysis

6. A company makes an end-of-period adjustment for uncollectible accounts expense. Does net accounts receivable change when a specific customer's account is later identified as being uncollectible and is written off? Why or why not?

(Answers to Section 1 Self Review are on page 469.)

Section 2

Section Objective

4 Complete a ten-column worksheet.

WHY IT'S IMPORTANT
Using the worksheet is a convenient way to gather the information needed for the financial statements.

Terms to Learn

net income line
updated account balances

Completing the Worksheet

After all adjustments have been entered on the worksheet, total the Adjustments Debit and Credit columns and verify that debits and credits are equal. The next step in the process is to prepare the Adjusted Trial Balance section.

Preparing the Adjusted Trial Balance Section

4 Objective
Complete a ten-column worksheet.

Figure 12-2 on pages 444–447 shows the completed worksheet for Modern Casuals. The Adjusted Trial Balance section of the worksheet is completed as follows.

1. Combine the amount in the Trial Balance section and the Adjustments section for each account.
2. Enter the results in the Adjusted Trial Balance section. The accounts that do not have adjustments are simply extended from the Trial Balance section to the Adjusted Trial Balance section. For example, the balance of the **Cash** account is recorded in the Debit column of the Adjusted Trial Balance section without change.
3. The accounts that are affected by adjustments are recomputed. Follow these rules to combine amounts on the worksheet.

Trial Balance Section	Adjustments Section	Action
Debit	Debit	Add
Debit	Credit	Subtract
Credit	Credit	Add
Credit	Debit	Subtract

- If the account has a debit balance in the Trial Balance section and a debit entry in the Adjustments section, add the two amounts. Look at the **Salaries Expense—Sales** account. It has a $78,490 debit balance in the Trial Balance section and a $1,500 debit entry in the Adjustments section. The new balance is $79,990 ($78,490 + $1,500). It is entered in the Debit column of the Adjusted Trial Balance section.
- If the account has a debit balance in the Trial Balance section and a credit entry in the Adjustments section, subtract the credit amount. Look at the **Supplies** account. It has a $6,300 debit balance in the Trial Balance section and a $4,975 credit entry in the Adjustments section. The new balance is $1,325 ($6,300 − $4,975). It is entered in the Debit column of the Adjusted Trial Balance section.
- If the account has a credit balance in the Trial Balance section and a credit entry in the Adjustments section, add the two amounts. Look at **Allowance for Doubtful Accounts.** It has a $100 credit balance

in the Trial Balance section and a $750 credit entry in the Adjustments section. The new balance is $850 ($100 + $750). It is entered in the Credit column of the Adjusted Trial Balance section.

- If the account has a credit balance in the Trial Balance section and a debit entry in the Adjustments section, subtract the debit amount. Look at the **Sales Tax Payable** account. It has a $7,200 Credit balance in the Trial Balance section and a $144 debit entry in the Adjustments section. The new balance is $7,056 ($7,200 − $144). It is entered in the Credit column of the Adjusted Trial Balance section.

The Adjusted Trial Balance section now contains the **updated account balances**.

Look at the **Income Summary** account. Recall that the debit entry removed the *beginning* balance from **Merchandise Inventory** and the credit entry added the *ending* balance to **Merchandise Inventory.** (See pages 444–447.) Notice that the debit and credit amounts in **Income Summary** are not combined in the Adjusted Trial Balance section.

Once all the updated account balances have been entered in the Adjusted Trial Balance section, total and rule the columns. Confirm that total debits equal total credits.

Two Sets of Books

A Russian company called Inotec sells computers, supports innovations in international accounting, and distributes software made by other companies. Inotec distributes Microsoft's Solution Provider software. The software allows companies to comply with separate accounting requirements, such as U.S. generally accepted accounting principles and the accounting standards of other countries.

Preparing the Balance Sheet and Income Statement Sections

To complete the Income Statement and Balance Sheet sections of the worksheet, identify the accounts that appear on the balance sheet. On Figure 12-2 the accounts from **Cash** through **Sonia Sanchez, Drawing** appear on the balance sheet. For each account enter the amount in the appropriate Debit or Credit column of the Balance Sheet section of the worksheet.

For accounts that appear on the income statement, **Sales** through **Interest Expense,** enter the amounts in the appropriate Debit or Credit column of the Income Statement section. The **Income Summary** debit and credit amounts are also entered in the Income Statement section of the worksheet. Notice that the debit and credit amounts in **Income Summary** are not combined in the Income Statement section.

Calculating Net Income or Net Loss

Once all account balances have been entered in the financial statement sections of the worksheet, the net income or net loss for the period is determined.

1. Total the Debit and Credit columns in the Income Statement section. For Modern Casuals, the debits total $564,197.75 and the credits total $612,500.00. Since the credits exceed the debits, the difference represents net income of $48,302.25.
2. To balance the Debit and the Credit columns in the Income Statement section, enter $48,302.25 in the Debit column of the Income Statement section. Total each column again and record the final total of each column ($612,500.00) on the worksheet.
3. Total the columns in the Balance Sheet section. Total debits are $160,060.00 and total credits are $111,757.75. The difference must equal the net income for the year, $48,302.25.

Modern Casuals
Worksheet
Year Ended December 31, 2004

	ACCOUNT NAME	TRIAL BALANCE DEBIT	TRIAL BALANCE CREDIT	ADJUSTMENTS DEBIT	ADJUSTMENTS CREDIT
1	*Cash*	21,136.00			
2	*Petty Cash Fund*	100.00			
3	*Notes Receivable*	1,200.00			
4	*Accounts Receivable*	32,000.00			
5	*Allowance for Doubtful Accounts*		100.00		(c) 750.00
6	*Interest Receivable*			(m) 24.00	
7	*Merchandise Inventory*	51,500.00		(b) 46,000.00	(a) 51,500.00
8	*Prepaid Insurance*	7,200.00			(k) 3,600.00
9	*Prepaid Interest*	225.00			(l) 150.00
10	*Supplies*	6,300.00			(j) 4,975.00
11	*Store Equipment*	20,000.00			
12	*Accumulated Depreciation—Store Equipment*				(d) 2,250.00
13	*Office Equipment*	7,000.00			
14	*Accumulated Depreciation—Office Equipment*				(e) 1,200.00
15	*Notes Payable—Trade*		2,000.00		
16	*Notes Payable—Bank*		9,000.00		
17	*Accounts Payable*		24,129.00		
18	*Interest Payable*				(i) 20.00
19	*Social Security Tax Payable*		1,084.00		(g) 93.00
20	*Medicare Tax Payable*		250.00		(g) 21.75
21	*Employee Income Taxes Payable*		990.00		
22	*Federal Unemployment Tax Payable*				(h) 12.00
23	*State Unemployment Tax Payable*				(h) 81.00
24	*Salaries Payable*				(f) 1,500.00
25	*Sales Tax Payable*		7,200.00	(n) 144.00	
26	*Sonia Sanchez, Capital*		61,221.00		
27	*Sonia Sanchez, Drawing*	27,600.00			
28	*Income Summary*			(a) 51,500.00	(b) 46,000.00
29	*Sales*		559,650.00		
30	*Sales Returns and Allowances*	13,000.00			
31	*Interest Income*		136.00		(m) 24.00
32	*Miscellaneous Income*		366.00		(n) 144.00
33	*Purchases*	320,500.00			
34	*Freight In*	8,800.00			
35	*Purchases Returns and Allowances*		3,050.00		
36	*Purchase Discounts*		3,130.00		
37	*Salaries Expense—Sales*	78,490.00		(f) 1,500.00	
38	*Advertising Expense*	7,425.00			
39	*Cash Short or Over*	125.00			
40	*Supplies Expense*			(j) 4,975.00	

▲ **FIGURE 12-2** 10-Column Worksheet—Complete

ADJUSTED TRIAL BALANCE		INCOME STATEMENT		BALANCE SHEET		
DEBIT	CREDIT	DEBIT	CREDIT	DEBIT	CREDIT	
21136 00				21136 00		1
100 00				100 00		2
1200 00				1200 00		3
32000 00				32000 00		4
	850 00				850 00	5
24 00				24 00		6
46000 00				46000 00		7
3600 00				3600 00		8
75 00				75 00		9
1325 00				1325 00		10
20000 00				20000 00		11
	2250 00				2250 00	12
7000 00				7000 00		13
	1200 00				1200 00	14
	2000 00				2000 00	15
	9000 00				9000 00	16
	24129 00				24129 00	17
	20 00				20 00	18
	1177 00				1177 00	19
	271 75				271 75	20
	990 00				990 00	21
	12 00				12 00	22
	81 00				81 00	23
	1500 00				1500 00	24
	7056 00				7056 00	25
	61221 00				61221 00	26
27600 00				27600 00		27
51500 00	46000 00	51500 00	46000 00			28
	559650 00		559650 00			29
13000 00		13000 00				30
	160 00		160 00			31
	510 00		510 00			32
320500 00		320500 00				33
8800 00		8800 00				34
	3050 00		3050 00			35
	3130 00		3130 00			36
79990 00		79990 00				37
7425 00		7425 00				38
125 00		125 00				39
4975 00		4975 00				40

▲ **FIGURE 12-2 (continued)** 10-Column Worksheet—Complete

	ACCOUNT NAME	TRIAL BALANCE DEBIT	TRIAL BALANCE CREDIT	ADJUSTMENTS DEBIT	ADJUSTMENTS CREDIT
41	*Depreciation Expense—Store Equipment*			(d) 2,250.00	
42	*Rent Expense*	27,600.00			
43	*Salaries Expense—Office*	26,500.00			
44	*Insurance Expense*			(k) 3,600.00	
45	*Payroll Taxes Expense*	7,205.00		(g) 114.75	
46				(h) 93.00	
47	*Telephone Expense*	1,875.00			
48	*Uncollectible Accounts Expense*			(c) 750.00	
49	*Utilities Expense*	5,925.00			
50	*Depreciation Expense—Office Equipment*			(e) 1,200.00	
51	*Interest Expense*	600.00		(i) 20.00	
52				(l) 150.00	
53	*Totals*	672,306.00	672,306.00	112,320.75	112,320.75
54	*Net Income*				
55					
56					

▲ **FIGURE 12-2 (continued)** 10-Column Worksheet—Complete

Effect of Adjustments on Financial Statements

- If managers are to know the true revenue, expenses, and net income or net loss for a period, the matching process is necessary.
- If accounts are not adjusted, the financial statements will be incomplete, misleading, and of little help in evaluating operations.
- Managers need to be familiar with the procedures and underlying assumptions used by the accountant to make adjustments because adjustments increase or decrease net income.
- Managers need information about uncollectible accounts expense in order to review the firm's credit policy. If losses are too high, management might tighten the requirements for obtaining credit. If losses are very low, management might investigate whether easing credit requirements would increase net income.
- The worksheet is a useful device for gathering data about adjustments and for preparing the financial statements.
- Managers are keenly interested in receiving timely financial statements, especially the income statement, which shows the results of operations.
- Managers are also interested in the prompt preparation of the balance sheet because it shows the financial position of the business at the end of the period.

Thinking Critically

What are some possible consequences of not making adjusting entries?

ADJUSTED TRIAL BALANCE		INCOME STATEMENT		BALANCE SHEET	
DEBIT	CREDIT	DEBIT	CREDIT	DEBIT	CREDIT
2,250.00		2,250.00			
27,600.00		27,600.00			
26,500.00		26,500.00			
3,600.00		3,600.00			
7,412.75		7,412.75			
1,875.00		1,875.00			
750.00		750.00			
5,925.00		5,925.00			
1,200.00		1,200.00			
770.00		770.00			
724,257.75	724,257.75	564,197.75	612,500.00	160,060.00	111,757.75
		48,302.25			48,302.25
		612,500.00	612,500.00	160,060.00	160,060.00

▲ **FIGURE 12-2 (continued)**
10-Column Worksheet—Complete

4. Enter $48,302.25 in the Credit column of the Balance Sheet section. Total each column again and record the final total in each column ($160,060.00).
5. Rule the Debit and Credit columns in all sections to show that the worksheet is complete.

Notice that the net income is recorded in two places on the **net income line** of the worksheet. It is recorded in the Credit column of the Balance Sheet section because net income *increases* owner's equity. It is recorded in the Debit column of the Income Statement section to balance the two columns in that section.

Section 2 Self Review

Questions

1. What is merchandise inventory?
2. How is the amount of ending merchandise inventory determined?
3. How many entries are made to adjust **Merchandise Inventory** on the worksheet? What are the entries?

Exercises

4. **Allowance for Doubtful Accounts** is reported in the
   a. Assets section of the balance sheet.
   b. Operating Expenses section of the income statement.
   c. Liabilities section of the balance sheet.
   d. Owner's Equity section of the balance sheet.
5. The amount of net income appears on the worksheet in the
   a. Income Statement Debit column only.
   b. Income Statement Debit and the Balance Sheet Credit columns.
   c. Income Statement Credit and the Balance Sheet Debit Columns.
   d. Balance Sheet Credit column only.

Analysis

6. If the accountant does not adjust **Merchandise Inventory,** how is the balance sheet affected?

(Answers to Section 2 Self Review are on page 469.)

CHAPTER 12 Review and Applications

Review

Chapter Summary

Accrual basis accounting requires that all revenue and expenses for a fiscal period to be matched and reported on the income statement to determine net income or net loss for the period. In this chapter, you have learned the techniques used to adjust accounts so that they accurately reflect the operations of the period.

Learning Objectives

1 Determine the adjustment for merchandise inventory, and enter the adjustment on the worksheet.
Merchandise inventory consists of goods that a business has on hand for sale to customers. When the trial balance is prepared at the end of the period, the **Merchandise Inventory** account still reflects the beginning inventory. Before the financial statements can be prepared, **Merchandise Inventory** must be updated to reflect the ending inventory for the period. The actual quantity of the goods on hand at the end of the period must be counted. Then the adjustment is completed in two steps:

1. Remove the beginning inventory balance from the **Merchandise Inventory** account. Debit **Income Summary;** credit **Merchandise Inventory.**
2. Add the ending inventory to the **Merchandise Inventory** account. Debit **Merchandise Inventory;** credit **Income Summary.**

2 Compute adjustments for accrued and prepaid expense items, and enter the adjustments on the worksheet.
Expense accounts are adjusted at the end of the period so that they correctly reflect the current period. Examples of adjustments include provision for uncollectible accounts and depreciation. Other typical adjustments of expense accounts involve accrued expenses and prepaid expenses.

- Accrued expenses are expense items that have been incurred or used but not yet paid or recorded. They include salaries, payroll taxes, interest on notes payable, and property taxes.
- Prepaid expenses are expense items that a business pays for and records before it actually uses the items. Rent, insurance, and advertising paid in advance are examples.

3 Compute adjustments for accrued and deferred income items, and enter the adjustments on the worksheet.
Revenue accounts are adjusted at the end of the period so that they correctly reflect the current period.

- Adjustments can affect either accrued income or deferred income.
- Accrued income is income that has been earned but not yet received and recorded.
- Deferred, or unearned, income is income that has not yet been earned but has been received.

4 Complete a ten-column worksheet.
When all adjustments have been entered on the worksheet, the worksheet is completed so that the financial statements can be prepared easily.

1. Figures in the Trial Balance section are combined with the adjustments to obtain an adjusted trial balance.
2. Each item in the Adjusted Trial Balance section is extended to the Income Statement and Balance Sheet sections of the worksheet.
3. The Income Statement columns are totaled and the net income or net loss is determined and entered in the net income line.
4. The amount of net income or net loss is entered in the net income line in the Balance Sheet section. After net income or net loss is added, the total debits must equal the total credits in the Balance Sheet section columns.

5 Define the accounting terms new to this chapter.

CHAPTER 12 GLOSSARY

Accrual basis (p. 430) A system of accounting by which all revenues and expenses are matched and reported on financial statements for the applicable period, regardless of when the cash related to the transaction is received or paid

Accrued expenses (p. 435) Expense items that relate to the current period but have not yet been paid and do not yet appear in the accounting records

Accrued income (p. 439) Income that has been earned but not yet received and recorded

Deferred expenses (p. 437) See Prepaid expenses

Deferred income (p. 440) See Unearned income

Inventory sheet (p. 431) A form used to list the volume and type of goods a firm has in stock

Net income line (p. 447) The worksheet line immediately following the column totals on which net income (or net loss) is recorded in two places: the Income Statement section and the Balance Sheet section

Prepaid expenses (p. 437) Expenses that are paid for and recorded before they are used, such as rent or insurance

Property, plant, and equipment (p. 434) Long-term assets that are used in the operation of a business and that are subject to depreciation (except for land, which is not depreciated)

Unearned income (p. 440) Income received before it is earned

Updated account balances (p. 443) The amounts entered in the Adjusted Trial Balance section of the worksheet

Comprehensive Self Review

1. What is the purpose of the accrual basis of accounting?
2. Why must the accounts be examined carefully at the end of a fiscal period before financial statements are prepared?
3. What types of accounts appear in the Income Statement section of the worksheet?
4. What types of accounts appear in the Balance Sheet section of the worksheet?
5. What are accrued expenses?

(Answers to Comprehensive Self Review are on page 469.)

Discussion Questions

1. What are the advantages of preparing a worksheet?
2. Should the estimated expense for uncollectible accounts be recorded at the time each of these accounts actually becomes worthless or before the losses from individual accounts actually occur?
3. What adjustment is made to record the estimated expense for uncollectible accounts?
4. Why is depreciation recorded?
5. What types of assets are subject to depreciation? Give three examples of such assets.
6. Explain the meaning of the following terms that relate to depreciation.
   - **a.** Salvage value
   - **b.** Depreciable base
   - **c.** Useful life
   - **d.** Straight-line method
7. What adjustment is made for depreciation on office equipment?
8. What is an accrued expense? Give three examples of items that often become accrued expenses.
9. What adjustment is made to record accrued salaries?
10. What is a prepaid expense? Give three examples of prepaid expense items.
11. How is the cost of an insurance policy recorded when the policy is purchased?
12. What adjustment is made to record expired insurance?
13. What is the alternative method of handling prepaid expenses?
14. What is accrued income? Give an example of an item that might produce accrued income.
15. What adjustment is made for accrued interest on a note receivable?
16. What is unearned income? Give two examples of items that would be classified as unearned income.
17. How is unearned income recorded when it is received?
18. What adjustment is made to record income earned during a period?
19. What is the alternative method of handling unearned income?
20. How does the worksheet help the accountant to prepare financial statements more efficiently?
21. **Unearned Fees Income** is classified as which type of account?

Applications

EXERCISES

Determining the adjustments for inventory.

◄ Exercise 12-1
Objective 1

The beginning inventory of a merchandising business was $126,000, and the ending inventory is $112,000. What entries are needed at the end of the fiscal period to adjust **Merchandise Inventory?**

Determining the adjustments for inventory.

◄ Exercise 12-2
Objective 1

The Income Statement section of the worksheet of Bryan Company for the year ended December 31, 20--, has $144,000 recorded in the Debit column and $168,000 in the Credit column on the line for the **Income Summary** account. What were the beginning and ending balances for **Merchandise Inventory?**

Computing adjustments for accrued and prepaid expense items.

◄ Exercise 12-3
Objective 2

For each of the following independent situations, indicate the adjusting entry that must be made on the December 31, 20--, worksheet. Omit descriptions.

a. During the year 20--, Janus Company had net credit sales of $850,000. Past experience shows that 0.9 percent of the firm's net credit sales result in uncollectible accounts.

b. Equipment purchased by Quick Burger Center for $26,000 on January 2, 20--, has an estimated useful life of five years and an estimated salvage value of $3,500. What adjustment for depreciation should be recorded on the firm's worksheet for the year ended December 31, 20--?

c. On December 31, 20--, Lawson Metal Company owed wages of $5,200 to its factory employees, who are paid weekly.

d. On December 31, 20--, Lawson Metal Company owed the employer's social security (6.2%) and Medicare (1.45%) taxes on the entire $5,200 of accrued wages for its factory employees.

e. On December 31, 20--, Lawson Metal Company owed federal (0.8%) and state (5.4%) unemployment taxes on the entire $5,200 of accrued wages for its factory employees.

Computing adjustments for accrued and prepaid expense items.

◄ Exercise 12-4
Objective 2

For each of the following independent situations, indicate the adjusting entry that must be made on the December 31, 20--, worksheet. Omit descriptions.

a. On December 31, 20--, the **Notes Payable** account at Mercado Manufacturing Company had a balance of $9,000. This balance represented a three-month, 12 percent note issued on November 1.

b. On January 2, 20--, Valdez Word Processing Service purchased floppy disks, paper, and other supplies for $4,800 in cash. On December 31, 20--, an inventory of supplies showed that items costing $1,140 were on hand. The **Supplies** account has a balance of $4,800.

c. On August 1, 20--, Homegrown Company paid a premium of $9,720 in cash for a one-year insurance policy. On December 31, 20--, an examination of the insurance records showed that coverage for a period of five months had expired.

d. On April 1, 20--, Capside Restaurant signed a one-year advertising contract with a local radio station and issued a check for $11,520 to pay the total amount owed. On December 31, 20--, the **Prepaid Advertising** account has a balance of $11,520.

Exercise 12-5 ►
Objective 2

Recording adjustments for accrued and prepaid expense items.

On December 1, 20--, Clear Camera Center borrowed $20,000 from its bank in order to expand its operations. The firm issued a four-month, 12 percent note for $20,000 to the bank and received $19,200 in cash because the bank deducted the interest for the entire period in advance. In general journal form, show the entry that would be made to record this transaction and the adjustment for prepaid interest that should be recorded on the firm's worksheet for the year ended December 31, 20--. Omit descriptions.

Exercise 12-6 ►
Objective 2

Recording adjustments for accrued and prepaid expense items.

On December 31, 20--, the **Notes Payable** account at McNear's Antique Shop had a balance of $40,000. This amount represented funds borrowed on a four-month, 12 percent note from the firm's bank on December 1. Record the journal entry for interest expense on this note that should be recorded on the firm's worksheet for the year ended December 31, 20--. Omit descriptions.

Exercise 12-7 ►
Objective 3

Recording adjustments for accrued and deferred income items.

For each of the following independent situations, indicate the adjusting entry that must be made on the December 31, 20--, worksheet. Omit descriptions.

a. On December 31, 20--, the **Notes Receivable** account at Denton Company had a balance of $9,600, which represented a six-month, 10 percent note received from a customer on August 1.

b. On December 31, 20--, the **Sales Tax Payable** account at Lane Shoe Store had a balance of $1,290. This balance represented the sales tax owed for the fourth quarter. The firm is scheduled to send the amount to the state sales tax agency on January 15. At that time the firm will deduct a commission of 2 percent of the tax due, as allowed by state law.

c. During the week ended January 7, 20--, Jordan Magazines Company received $24,000 from customers for subscriptions to its magazine *Modern Business*. On December 31, 20--, an analysis of the **Unearned Subscription Revenue** account showed that $12,000 of the subscriptions were earned in 20--.

d. On September 1, 20--, Eaton Realty Company rented a commercial building to a new tenant and received $30,000 in advance to cover the rent for six months.

Exercise 12-8 ►
Objective 4

Completing a ten-column worksheet.

Indicate whether each of the following accounts would appear in the Income Statement Debit or Credit column or the Balance Sheet Debit or Credit column of the worksheet.

ACCOUNTS

Purchases	Jerome Newton, Capital
Purchases Returns and Allowances	Income Summary
Purchases Discounts	Accumulated Depreciation—Equipment
Unearned Rent	Sales Discounts
Subscription Revenue	

Problems

Selected problems can be completed using:
Peachtree **QuickBooks** **Spreadsheets**

PROBLEM SET A

◄ **Problem 12-1A**
Objectives 2, 3

Recording adjustments for accrued and prepaid expense items and unearned income.

On July 1, 20--, David Watson established his own accounting practice. Selected transactions for the first few days of July follow.

INSTRUCTIONS

1. Record the transactions on page 1 of the general journal. Omit descriptions. Assume that the firm initially records prepaid expenses as assets and unearned income as a liability.
2. Record the adjusting journal entries that must be made on July 31, 20--, on page 2 of the general journal. Omit descriptions.

DATE		TRANSACTIONS
July	1	Signed a lease for an office and issued Check 101 for $12,000 to pay the rent in advance for six months.
	1	Borrowed money from First National Bank by issuing a four-month, 12 percent note for $18,000; received $17,280 because the bank deducted the interest in advance.
	1	Signed an agreement with Young Company to provide accounting and tax services for one year at $4,000 per month; received the entire fee of $48,000 in advance.
	1	Purchased office equipment for $15,600 from Office Supplies; issued a two-month, 12 percent note in payment. The equipment is estimated to have a useful life of six years and a $1,200 salvage value. The equipment will be depreciated using the straight-line method.
	1	Purchased a one-year insurance policy and issued Check 102 for $1,920 to pay the entire premium.
	3	Purchased office furniture for $16,800 from Office Warehouse; issued Check 103 for $8,400 and agreed to pay the balance in 60 days. The equipment has an estimated useful life of five years and a $1,200 salvage value. The office furniture will be depreciated using the straight-line method.
	5	Purchased office supplies for $2,160 with Check 104. Assume $800 of supplies are on hand July 31, 20--.

Analyze: What balance should be reflected in **Unearned Accounting Fees** at July 31, 20--?

Problem 12-2A ► Objectives 2, 3

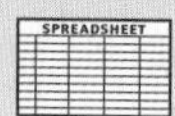

Recording adjustments for accrued and prepaid expense items and earned income.

On July 31, 20--, after one month of operation, the general ledger of Hillary Rao, Consultant, contained the accounts and balances given below.

INSTRUCTIONS

1. Prepare a partial worksheet with the following sections: Trial Balance, Adjustments, and Adjusted Trial Balance. Use the data about the firm's accounts and balances to complete the Trial Balance section.
2. Enter the adjustments described below in the Adjustments section. Identify each adjustment with the appropriate letter.
3. Complete the Adjusted Trial Balance section.

ACCOUNTS AND BALANCES

Cash	$22,200	Dr.
Accounts Receivable	1,300	Dr.
Supplies	860	Dr.
Prepaid Rent	9,000	Dr.
Prepaid Insurance	1,680	Dr.
Prepaid Interest	400	Dr.
Furniture	11,800	Dr.
Accumulated Depreciation—Furniture		
Equipment	6,400	Dr.
Accumulated Depreciation—Equipment		
Notes Payable	18,400	Cr.
Accounts Payable	4,000	Cr.
Interest Payable		
Unearned Consulting Fees	3,600	Cr.
Hillary Rao, Capital	25,220	Cr.
Hillary Rao, Drawing	2,000	Dr.
Consulting Fees	8,000	Cr.
Salaries Expense	3,200	Dr.
Utilities Expense	220	Dr.
Telephone Expense	160	Dr.
Supplies Expense		
Rent Expense		
Insurance Expense		
Depreciation Expense—Furniture		
Depreciation Expense—Equipment		
Interest Expense		

ADJUSTMENTS

a. On July 31 an inventory of the supplies showed that items costing $760 were on hand.

b. On July 1 the firm paid $9,000 in advance for six months of rent.

c. On July 1 the firm purchased a one-year insurance policy for $1,680.

d. On July 1 the firm paid $400 interest in advance on a four-month note that it issued to the bank.

e. On July 1 the firm purchased office furniture for $11,800. The furniture is expected to have a useful life of five years and a salvage value of $1,000.

f. On July 1 the firm purchased office equipment for $6,400. The equipment is expected to have a useful life of five years and a salvage value of $1,600.

g. On July 1 the firm issued a two-month, 12 percent note for $6,400.

h. On July 1 the firm received a consulting fee of $3,600 in advance for a one-year period.

Analyze: By what total amount were the expense accounts of the business adjusted?

Recording adjustments and completing the worksheet.

◄ **Problem 12-3A**
Objectives 1, 2, 3, 4

The Garden House is a retail store that sells plants, soil, and decorative pots. On December 31, 2005, the firm's general ledger contained the accounts and balances that appear below and on page 456.

INSTRUCTIONS

1. Prepare the Trial Balance section of a ten-column worksheet. The worksheet covers the year ended December 31, 2005.
2. Enter the adjustments below in the Adjustments section of the worksheet. Identify each adjustment with the appropriate letter.
3. Complete the worksheet.

ACCOUNTS AND BALANCES

Account	Balance	
Cash	$ 4,700	Dr.
Accounts Receivable	3,100	Dr.
Allowance for Doubtful Accounts	52	Cr.
Merchandise Inventory	11,800	Dr.
Supplies	1,200	Dr.
Prepaid Advertising	960	Dr.
Store Equipment	7,000	Dr.
Accumulated Depreciation—Store Equipment	1,300	Cr.
Office Equipment	1,600	Dr.
Accumulated Depreciation—Office Equipment	280	Cr.
Accounts Payable	1,750	Cr.
Social Security Tax Payable	430	Cr.
Medicare Tax Payable	98	Cr.
Federal Unemployment Tax Payable		
State Unemployment Tax Payable		
Salaries Payable		
Tony Rowe, Capital	25,712	Cr.
Tony Rowe, Drawing	20,000	Dr.
Sales	89,768	Cr.
Sales Returns and Allowances	1,100	Dr.
Purchases	46,400	Dr.
Purchases Returns and Allowances	430	Cr.
Rent Expense	6,000	Dr.
Telephone Expense	590	Dr.
Salaries Expense	14,100	Dr.
Payroll Taxes Expense	1,270	Dr.
Income Summary		
Supplies Expense		

ACCOUNTS AND BALANCES (cont.)

Advertising Expense
Depreciation Expense—Store Equipment
Depreciation Expense—Office Equipment
Uncollectible Accounts Expense

ADJUSTMENTS

a.–b. Merchandise inventory on December 31, 2005, is $13,000.

c. During 2005 the firm had net credit sales of $35,000; the firm estimates that 0.6 percent of these sales will result in uncollectible accounts.

d. On December 31, 2005, an inventory of the supplies showed that items costing $350 were on hand.

e. On October 1, 2005, the firm signed a six-month advertising contract for $960 with a local newspaper and paid the full amount in advance.

f. On January 2, 2004, the firm purchased store equipment for $7,000. At that time, the equipment was estimated to have a useful life of five years and a salvage value of $500.

g. On January 2, 2004, the firm purchased office equipment for $1,600. At that time the equipment was estimated to have a useful life of five years and a salvage value of $200.

h. On December 31, 2005, the firm owed salaries of $1,500 that will not be paid until 2006.

i. On December 31, 2005, the firm owed the employer's social security tax (assume 6.2 percent) and Medicare tax (assume 1.45 percent) on the entire $1,500 of accrued wages.

j. On December 31, 2005, the firm owed federal unemployment tax (assume 0.8 percent) and state unemployment tax (assume 5.4 percent) on the entire $1,500 of accrued wages.

Analyze: By what total amount were the net assets of the business affected by adjustments?

Problem 12-4A ►
Objectives 1, 2, 3, 4

Recording adjustments and completing the worksheet.

Fitness Foods Company is a distributor of nutritious snack foods such as granola bars. On December 31, 2005, the firm's general ledger contained the accounts and balances that follow.

INSTRUCTIONS

1. Prepare the Trial Balance section of a ten-column worksheet. The worksheet covers the year ended December 31, 2005.
2. Enter the adjustments in the Adjustments section of the worksheet. Identify each adjustment with the appropriate letter.
3. Complete the worksheet.

Note: This problem will be required to complete Problem 13-3A in Chapter 13.

ACCOUNTS AND BALANCES

Account	Balance	
Cash	$30,600	Dr.
Accounts Receivable	35,200	Dr.
Allowance for Doubtful Accounts	420	Cr.
Merchandise Inventory	86,000	Dr.

ACCOUNTS AND BALANCES (cont.)

Account	Balance	
Supplies	$ 10,400	Dr.
Prepaid Insurance	5,400	Dr.
Office Equipment	7,800	Dr.
Accum. Depreciation—Office Equipment	2,800	Cr.
Warehouse Equipment	28,000	Dr.
Accum. Depreciation—Warehouse Equipment	9,600	Cr.
Notes Payable—Bank	30,000	Cr.
Accounts Payable	12,200	Cr.
Interest Payable		
Social Security Tax Payable	1,680	Cr.
Medicare Tax Payable	388	Cr.
Federal Unemployment Tax Payable		
State Unemployment Tax Payable		
Salaries Payable		
Warren Jones, Capital	110,534	Cr.
Warren Jones, Drawing	56,000	Dr.
Sales	653,778	Cr.
Sales Returns and Allowances	10,000	Dr.
Purchases	350,000	Dr.
Purchases Returns and Allowances	9,200	Cr.
Income Summary		
Rent Expense	36,000	Dr.
Telephone Expense	2,200	Dr.
Salaries Expense	160,000	Dr.
Payroll Taxes Expense	13,000	Dr.
Supplies Expense		
Insurance Expense		
Depreciation Expense—Office Equip.		
Depreciation Expense—Warehouse Equip.		
Uncollectible Accounts Expense		
Interest Expense		

ADJUSTMENTS

a.–b. Merchandise inventory on December 31, 2005, is $84,000.

c. During 2005 the firm had net credit sales of $560,000; past experience indicates that 0.5 percent of these sales should result in uncollectible accounts.

d. On December 31, 2005, an inventory of supplies showed that items costing $1,200 were on hand.

e. On May 1, 2005, the firm purchased a one-year insurance policy for $5,400.

f. On January 2, 2003, the firm purchased office equipment for $7,800. At that time the equipment was estimated to have a useful life of five years and a salvage value of $800.

g. On January 2, 2003, the firm purchased warehouse equipment for $28,000. At that time the equipment was estimated to have a useful life of five years and a salvage value of $4,000.

h. On November 1, 2005, the firm issued a four-month, 11 percent note for $30,000.

i. On December 31, 2005, the firm owed salaries of $5,000 that will not be paid until 2006.

j. On December 31, 2005, the firm owed the employer's social security tax (assume 6.2 percent) and Medicare tax (assume 1.45 percent) on the entire $5,000 of accrued wages.

k. On December 31, 2005, the firm owed the federal unemployment tax (assume 0.8 percent) and the state unemployment tax (assume 5.4 percent) on the entire $5,000 of accrued wages.

Analyze: When the financial statements for Fitness Foods Company are prepared, what net income will be reported for the period ended December 31, 2005?

PROBLEM SET B

Problem 12-1B ►
Objectives 2, 3

Recording adjustments for accrued and prepaid expense items and unearned income.

On June 1, 20--, Jane Sadler established her own advertising firm. Selected transactions for the first few days of June follow.

INSTRUCTIONS

1. Record the transactions on page 1 of the general journal. Omit descriptions. Assume that the firm initially records prepaid expenses as assets and unearned income as a liability.
2. Record the adjusting journal entries that must be made on June 30, 20--, on page 2 of the general journal. Omit descriptions.

DATE		TRANSACTIONS
June	1	Signed a lease for an office and issued Check 101 for $14,400 to pay the rent in advance for six months.
	1	Borrowed money from National Trust Bank by issuing a three-month, 10 percent note for $16,000; received $15,600 because the bank deducted interest in advance.
	1	Signed an agreement with Universe of Fashion Clothing Store to provide advertising consulting for one year at $5,000 per month; received the entire fee of $60,000 in advance.
	1	Purchased office equipment for $21,600 from The Furniture Store; issued a three-month, 12 percent note in payment. The equipment is estimated to have a useful life of five years and a $1,200 salvage value and will be depreciated using the straight-line method.
	1	Purchased a one-year insurance policy and issued Check 102 for $2,160 to pay the entire premium.
	3	Purchased office furniture for $19,200 from Office Furniture Mart; issued Check 103 for $9,600 and agreed to pay the balance in 60 days. The equipment is estimated to have a useful life of five years and a $1,200 salvage value and will be depreciated using the straight-line method.
	5	Purchased office supplies for $2,800 with Check 104; assume $1,200 of supplies are on hand June 30, 20--.

Analyze: At the end of the year, what total rent expense should have been recorded?

Recording adjustments for accrued and prepaid expense items and unearned income.

◄ **Problem 12-2B**
Objectives 2, 3

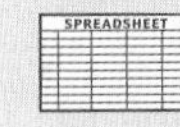

On September 30, 20--, after one month of operation, the general ledger of Professional Skills Company contained the accounts and balances shown below.

INSTRUCTIONS

1. Prepare a partial worksheet with the following sections: Trial Balance, Adjustments, and Adjusted Trial Balance. Use the data about the firm's accounts and balances to complete the Trial Balance section.
2. Enter the adjustments described below in the Adjustments section. Identify each adjustment with the appropriate letter.
3. Complete the Adjusted Trial Balance section.

ACCOUNTS AND BALANCES

Account	Balance
Cash	$27,000 Dr.
Supplies	740 Dr.
Prepaid Rent	4,200 Dr.
Prepaid Advertising	2,400 Dr.
Prepaid Interest	450 Dr.
Furniture	5,600 Dr.
Accumulated Depreciation—Furniture	
Equipment	9,000 Dr.
Accumulated Depreciation—Equipment	
Notes Payable	20,600 Cr.
Accounts Payable	4,000 Cr.
Interest Payable	
Unearned Course Fees	22,000 Cr.
Durwood Becknell, Capital	6,730 Cr.
Durwood Becknell, Drawing	2,000 Dr.
Course Fees	
Salaries Expense	1,600 Dr.
Telephone Expense	120 Dr.
Entertainment Expense	220 Dr.
Supplies Expense	
Rent Expense	
Advertising Expense	
Depreciation Expense—Furniture	
Depreciation Expense—Equipment	
Interest Expense	

ADJUSTMENTS

a. On September 30 an inventory of the supplies showed that items costing $640 were on hand.

b. On September 1 the firm paid $4,200 in advance for six months of rent.

c. On September 1 the firm signed a six-month advertising contract for $2,400 and paid the full amount in advance.

d. On September 1 the firm paid $450 interest in advance on a three-month note that it issued to the bank.

e. On September 1 the firm purchased office furniture for $5,600. The furniture is expected to have a useful life of five years and a salvage value of $800.

f. On September 3 the firm purchased equipment for $9,000. The equipment is expected to have a useful life of five years and a salvage value of $1,200.

g. On September 1 the firm issued a two-month, 9 percent note for $5,600.

h. During September the firm received $22,000 fees in advance. An analysis of the firm's records shows that $7,000 applies to services provided in September and the rest pertains to future months.

Analyze: What was the net dollar effect of the adjustments to the accounting records of the business?

Problem 12-3B ►
Objectives 1, 2, 3, 4

Recording adjustments and completing the worksheet.

Eastwood Toys is a retail store that sells toys, games, and bicycles. On December 31, 2005, the firm's general ledger contained the following accounts and balances.

INSTRUCTIONS

1. Prepare the Trial Balance section of a ten-column worksheet. The worksheet covers the year ended December 31, 2005.
2. Enter the adjustments below in the Adjustments section of the worksheet. Identify each adjustment with the appropriate letter.
3. Complete the worksheet.

ACCOUNTS AND BALANCES

Account	Balance	
Cash	$ 27,600	Dr.
Accounts Receivable	21,200	Dr.
Allowance for Doubtful Accounts	320	Cr.
Merchandise Inventory	138,000	Dr.
Supplies	11,600	Dr.
Prepaid Advertising	5,280	Dr.
Store Equipment	32,800	Dr.
Accumulated Depreciation—Store Equipment	5,760	Cr.
Office Equipment	8,400	Dr.
Accumulated Depreciation—Office Equipment	1,440	Cr.
Accounts Payable	8,600	Cr.
Social Security Tax Payable	5,920	Cr.
Medicare Tax Payable	1,368	Cr.
Federal Unemployment Tax Payable		
State Unemployment Tax Payable		
Salaries Payable		
Ross Moss, Capital	113,520	Cr.
Ross Moss, Drawing	100,000	Dr.
Sales	1,042,392	Cr.
Sales Returns and Allowances	17,200	Dr.
Purchases	507,600	Dr.
Purchases Returns and Allowances	5,040	Cr.
Rent Expense	120,000	Dr.
Telephone Expense	4,280	Dr.

ACCOUNTS AND BALANCES (cont.)

Salaries Expense	$ 169,200	Dr.
Payroll Taxes Expense	15,200	Dr.
Income Summary		
Supplies Expense		
Advertising Expense	6,000	Dr.
Depreciation Expense—Store Equipment		
Depreciation Expense—Office Equipment		
Uncollectible Accounts Expense		

ADJUSTMENTS

a.–b. Merchandise inventory on December 31, 2005, is $144,000.

c. During 2005 the firm had net credit sales of $440,000. The firm estimates that 0.7 percent of these sales will result in uncollectible accounts.

d. On December 31, 2005, an inventory of the supplies showed that items costing $2,800 were on hand.

e. On September 1, 2005, the firm signed a six-month advertising contract for $5,280 with a local newspaper and paid the full amount in advance.

f. On January 2, 2004, the firm purchased store equipment for $32,800. At that time the equipment was estimated to have a useful life of five years and a salvage value of $4,000.

g. On January 2, 2004, the firm purchased office equipment for $8,400. At that time the equipment was estimated to have a useful life of five years and a salvage value of $1,200.

h. On December 31, 2005, the firm owed salaries of $6,000 that will not be paid until 2006.

i. On December 31, 2005, the firm owed the employer's social security tax (assume 6.2 percent) and Medicare tax (assume 1.45 percent) on the entire $6,000 of accrued wages.

j. On December 31, 2005, the firm owed federal unemployment tax (assume 0.8 percent) and state unemployment tax (assume 5.4 percent) on the entire $6,000 of accrued wages.

Analyze: If the adjustment for advertising had not been recorded, what would the reported net income have been?

Recording adjustments and completing the worksheet.

◄ **Problem 12-4B**
Objectives 1, 2, 3, 4

Village Novelties is a retail seller of cards, novelty items, and business products. On December 31, 2005, the firm's general ledger contained the following accounts and balances.

INSTRUCTIONS

1. Prepare the Trial Balance section of a ten-column worksheet. The worksheet covers the year ended December 31, 2005.
2. Enter the adjustments in the Adjustments section of the worksheet. Identify each adjustment with the appropriate letter.
3. Complete the worksheet.

Note: This problem will be required to complete Problem 13-3B in Chapter 13.

ACCOUNTS AND BALANCES

Account	Balance	
Cash	$ 1,180	Dr.
Accounts Receivable	2,200	Dr.
Allowance for Doubtful Accounts	600	Cr.
Merchandise Inventory	17,600	Dr.
Supplies	600	Dr.
Prepaid Insurance	2,400	Dr.
Store Equipment	6,000	Dr.
Accumulated Depreciation—Store Equip.		
Store Fixtures	15,000	Dr.
Accumulated Depreciation—Store Fixtures		
Notes Payable	4,000	Cr.
Accounts Payable	600	Cr.
Interest Payable		
Social Security Tax Payable		
Medicare Tax Payable		
Federal Unemployment Tax Payable		
State Unemployment Tax Payable		
Salaries Payable		
Jordi Riker, Capital	39,780	Cr.
Jordi Riker, Drawing	8,000	Dr.
Sales	235,600	Cr.
Sales Returns and Allowances	6,000	Dr.
Purchases	160,000	Dr.
Purchases Returns and Allowances	2,000	Cr.
Income Summary		
Rent Expense	18,000	Dr.
Telephone Expense	2,400	Dr.
Salaries Expense	40,000	Dr.
Payroll Tax Expense	3,200	Dr.
Supplies Expense		
Insurance Expense		
Depreciation Expense—Store Equipment		
Depreciation Expense—Store Fixtures		
Uncollectible Accounts Expense		
Interest Expense		

ADJUSTMENTS

a.–b. Merchandise inventory on hand on December 31, 2005, is $16,000.

c. During 2005 the firm had net credit sales of $160,000. Past experience indicates that 0.8 percent of these sales should result in uncollectible accounts.

d. On December 31, 2005, an inventory of supplies showed that items costing $200 were on hand.

e. On July 1, 2005, the firm purchased a one-year insurance policy for $2,400.

f. On January 2, 2003, the firm purchased store equipment for $6,000. The equipment was estimated to have a five-year useful life and a salvage value of $1,000.

g. On January 4, 2003, the firm purchased store fixtures for $15,000. At the time of the purchase, the fixtures were assumed to have a useful life of seven years and a salvage value of $1,000.

h. On October 1, 2005, the firm issued a six-month, $4,000 note payable at 9 percent interest with a local bank.

i. At year-end (December 31, 2005), the firm owed salaries of $1,200 that will not be paid until January 2006.

j. On December 31, 2005, the firm owed the employer's social security tax (assume 6.2 percent) and Medicare tax (assume 1.45 percent) on the entire $1,200 of accrued wages.

k. On December 31, 2005, the firm owed federal unemployment tax (assume 1.0 percent) and state unemployment tax (assume 5.0 percent) on the entire $1,200 of accrued wages.

Analyze: After all adjustments have been recorded, what is the total value of the company's assets?

CHAPTER 12 CHALLENGE PROBLEM

Completing the Worksheet

The unadjusted trial balance of Quick Stop Discount Store on December 31, 20--, the end of its accounting period, appears on page 464.

INSTRUCTIONS

1. Copy the unadjusted trial balance onto a worksheet and complete the worksheet using the following information.
   - **a.–b.** Ending merchandise inventory, $99,360.
   - **c.** Uncollectible accounts expense, $1,000.
   - **d.** Store supplies on hand December 31, 20--, $550.
   - **e.** Office supplies on hand December 31, 20--, $380.
   - **f.** Depreciation on store equipment, $11,000.
   - **g.** Depreciation on office equipment, $3,000.
   - **h.** Accrued sales salaries, $4,000, and accrued office salaries, $1,000.
   - **i.** Social security tax on accrued salaries, $326; Medicare tax on accrued salaries, $76.
   - **j.** Federal unemployment tax on accrued salaries, $56; state unemployment tax on accrued salaries, $270.
2. Journalize the adjusting entries on page 30 of the general journal. Omit descriptions.
3. Journalize the closing entries on page 32 of the general journal. Omit descriptions.
4. Compute the following:
   - **a.** net sales
   - **b.** net delivered cost of purchases
   - **c.** cost of goods sold
   - **d.** net income or net loss
   - **e.** balance of **Don Black, Capital** on December 31, 20--.

Analyze: What change(s) to **Don Black, Capital** will be reported on the statement of owner's equity?

QUICK STOP DISCOUNT STORE
Trial Balance
December 31, 20--

Account	Balance	
Cash	$ 12,950	Dr
Accounts Receivable	50,000	Dr.
Allowance for Doubtful Accounts	2,000	Cr.
Merchandise Inventory	106,630	Dr.
Store Supplies	3,840	Dr.
Office Supplies	2,950	Dr.
Store Equipment	113,590	Dr.
Accumulated Depreciation—Store Equipment	12,620	Cr.
Office Equipment	27,320	Dr.
Accumulated Depreciation—Office Equipment	4,770	Cr.
Accounts Payable	4,390	Cr.
Salaries Payable		
Social Security Tax Payable		
Medicare Tax Payable		
Federal Unemployment Tax Payable		
State Unemployment Tax Payable		
Don Black, Capital	168,000	Cr.
Don Black, Drawing	30,000	Dr.
Income Summary		
Sales	862,230	Cr.
Sales Returns and Allowances	7,580	Dr.
Purchases	505,430	Dr.
Purchases Returns and Allowances	4,240	Cr.
Purchases Discounts	10,770	Cr.
Freight In	7,000	Dr.
Salaries Expense—Sales	75,950	Dr.
Rent Expense	36,000	Dr.
Advertising Expense	12,300	Dr.
Store Supplies Expense		
Depreciation Expense—Store Equipment		
Salaries Expense—Office	77,480	Dr.
Payroll Taxes Expense		
Uncollectible Accounts Expense		
Office Supplies Expense		
Depreciation Expense—Office Equipment		

CHAPTER 12 CRITICAL THINKING PROBLEM

Net Profit

When Reuben Van Gogh's father became seriously ill and had to go to the hospital, Reuben stepped in to run the family business, Van Gogh's Cab Company. Under his father's direction, the cab company was a successful operation and provided ample money to meet the family's needs, including Reuben's college tuition.

Reuben was majoring in psychology in college and knew little about business or accounting, but he was eager to do a good job of running the business in his father's absence. Since all the service performed by the cab company was for cash, Reuben figured that he would do all right as long as the **Cash** account increased. Thus he was delighted to watch the cash balance increase from $31,642 at the beginning of the first month to $70,850 at the end of the second month—an increase of $39,208. Reuben assumed that the company had made $39,208 during the two months he was in charge. He did not understand why the income statement prepared by the company's bookkeeper did not show that amount as income but instead reported a lower amount as net income.

Knowing that you are taking an accounting class, Reuben brings the income statement, shown below, to you and asks if you can explain the difference.

VAN GOGH'S CAB COMPANY Income Statement For the Past Two Months		
Operating Revenue		
Fares Income		$192,934
Operating Expenses		
Salaries Expense	$120,000	
Gasoline and Oil Expense	26,000	
Repairs Expense	5,570	
Supplies Expense	2,268	
Insurance Expense	3,166	
Depreciation Expense	17,000	
Total Operating Expense		174,004
Net Income		$ 18,930

In addition, Reuben permits you to examine the accounting records, which show that **Salaries Payable** were $2,680 at the beginning of the first month but had increased to $3,240 at the end of the second month. Most of the **Insurance Expense** account reflects monthly insurance payments covering only one month. However, the **Prepaid Insurance** account had decreased $450 during the two months, and all supplies had been purchased before Reuben took over. The balances of the company's other asset and liability accounts showed no changes.

1. Explain the cause of the difference between the increase in the **Cash** account balance and the net income for the two months.
2. Prepare a schedule that accounts for this difference.

Business Connections

Connection 1 ►

Adjustments

1. Assume that you are the newly hired controller for Timmons Company, a wholesale firm that sells most of its goods on credit. You have found that the business does not make an adjustment for estimated uncollectible accounts at the end of each year. Instead, the expense for uncollectible accounts is recorded during the year as individual accounts are identified as bad debts. Would you recommend that the firm continue its present accounting treatment of uncollectible accounts? Why or why not?
2. On July 1, 20--, Secrist Company rented a portion of its warehouse to another business for a one-year period and received the full amount of $4,200 in advance. At the end of Secrist's fiscal year on December 31, 20--, the firm's income statement showed $2,100 as rental income. The other $2,100 appeared in the liabilities section of the firm's balance sheet as unearned rental income. The owner, Omer Secrist, felt that the entire sum should have been reported on the income statement as income because all the cash was received in 20--. How would you explain to Omer why the accountant's treatment of the $4,200 was correct?
3. Some firms initially record the cost of an insurance policy as an expense and then make an adjustment at the end of the fiscal year to transfer the unexpired amount to an asset account. Does this method produce financial results different from the method used by Modern Casuals? Explain.
4. Why is it important for management to understand the accounting methods used to report data on the firm's financial statements?

Connection 2 ►

Ethical DILEMMA **Out of Balance** As the accountant of a company, you were overwhelmed with work at the end of March and could not begin the process of closing the accounts and preparing the quarterly financial statements until almost mid-April. You are under pressure to have the financial statements ready for a meeting of the company's management on April 14.

To your distress, you discovered that the March 31 trial balance does not balance. The debits exceed the credits by $4,800. After spending several hours trying to find the reason for the error, you have concluded that the $4,800 is not a critical error. You are considering simply adding $4,800 to the **Sales** account in order to bring the accounts into balance and to enable you to complete the statements on time. You believe that if you do this, you will have time to find the reason for the trial balance error after the meeting of the management. At that time you can correct the $4,800 adjustment.

Will you "force" the accounts to balance? Discuss your decision from an ethical perspective.

Street WISE:
Questions from the Real World **Balance Sheet Accounts** Refer to the *1999 Annual Report* for The Home Depot, Inc. found in Appendix B.

◄ **Connection 3**

1. Review the balance sheet. Based only on the asset account categories shown, list two types of adjusting entries you think are required each fiscal period. Which accounts are affected?
2. Based on the account categories found in the Liabilities section, describe two types of adjusting entries that may be recorded by The Home Depot, Inc. in an effort to match revenues with expenses.

FINANCIAL STATEMENT ANALYSIS **Balance Sheet** The following financial data was reported in the DuPont *1999 Annual Report.*

◄ **Connection 4**

DUPONT

Consolidated Balance Sheet
As of December 31

(Dollars in millions, except per share)	***1999***	***1998***
Assets		
Current Assets		
Cash and Cash Equivalents	*$ 1,466*	*$ 1,059*
Marketable Securities	*116*	*10*
Accounts and Notes Receivable	*5,318*	*4,201*
Inventories	*5,057*	*3,129*
Prepaid Expenses	*202*	*192*
Deferred Income Taxes	*494*	*645*
Total Current Assets	*12,653*	*9,236*
Property, Plant and Equipment	*35,416*	*34,728*
Less: Accumulated Depreciation	*20,545*	*20,597*
Net Property, Plant and Equipment	*14,871*	*14,131*

Analyze:

1. Based on the information presented above, which categories do you think might require adjustments at the end of an operating period?
2. List the potential adjusting entries that would be necessary. Do not worry about the dollar amounts.
3. By what percentage did DuPont's inventories increase from 1998 to 1999?

Analyze Online: Log on to the DuPont Web site **(www.dupont.com).** Review the current annual report and answer the following questions.

4. What method is used to depreciate property, plant, and equipment at DuPont?
5. What is the company's policy for revenue recognition?

Connection 5 ► *Extending the Thought* **Catalog Sales** JC Penney Company, Inc., records sales for in-store purchases, catalog, and Internet transactions. For catalog orders, sales are not recorded in the accounting records until customers pick up the merchandise they have ordered. Other retailers record catalog or Internet sales at the point that an order is placed and credit card information has been submitted. Do you agree or disagree with the method that JC Penney, Inc., uses to record catalog sales? Prepare a statement supporting your opinion.

Connection 6 ► **Business Communication** **Memo** You are the owner of a raw furniture company that sells products via two channels of distribution: the Internet and catalogs. Your accounting clerk has prepared a ten-column worksheet for the month ended September 30, 20--. As you review the worksheet, you notice the following errors.

1. The balances of the **Depreciation Expense** account and the **Insurance Expense** account were carried over into the Balance Sheet Debit columns in error.
2. There were no adjustments recorded for **Merchandise Inventory.**

Prepare a memo to the accounting clerk outlining the errors you have noticed. Explain the impact of the errors on the financial statements. Be sure to explain the importance of the adjustment to the **Merchandise Inventory** account.

Connection 7 ► **TeamWork** **Gift Certificates** Have you ever purchased a gift card or gift certificate from a retail business? How do these companies recognize gift certificate revenue? As a team, research the revenue recognition practices for retail businesses of your choice. Publicly traded companies often provide financial statements online where you find a discussion of revenue recognition with the notes that accompany the statements. Write a report on your findings.

Connection 8 ► **interNET CONNECTION** **E-commerce** The United States has developed a framework for dealing with electronic commerce. Go to **www.ecommerce.gov** to see the *United States Electronic Commerce Policy*. What are two other sites that you can link to from this site? Click on *International Sites.* What does the acronym APEC mean? What does the abbreviation EU stand for?

Answers to Self Reviews

Answers to Section 1 Self Review

1. When a sale of goods is completed or when the service is provided, regardless of when payment is received.
2. When the purchases are made, regardless of when payment is received.
3. They are normally recognized for the period in which they help to earn revenue.
4. **a.** on the date of the sale.
5. **b.** earned but not received.
6. Net accounts receivable does not change because the entry is a debit to **Allowance For Doubtful Accounts** (contra asset) and a credit to **Accounts Receivable** (asset).

Answers to Section 2 Self Review

1. The stock of goods that a business has on hand for sale to customers.
2. **a.** The quantity of each type of goods in stock is listed on the inventory sheet.
   b. The quantity is multiplied by the unit cost to find the total cost of the item.
   c. The totals for all the different items on hand are added to find the cost of the entire inventory.
3. Two entries are made.
   - The beginning inventory is taken off the books by transferring the beginning inventory balance to the **Income Summary** account. This is accomplished by debiting the **Income Summary** account and crediting the **Merchandise Inventory** account.
   - The ending inventory is placed on the books by debiting the **Merchandise Inventory** account and crediting the **Income Summary** account.
4. **a.** Assets section of the balance sheet.
5. **b.** Income Statement Debit and the Balance Sheet Credit columns.
6. The assets would be overstated if inventory is less than the account balance or understated if inventory is more than the account balance.

Answers to Comprehensive Self Review

1. To match revenues and expenses of specific fiscal periods.
2. To see if each account contains amounts of revenue or expense that should be allocated to other periods.
3. The revenue, expense, and cost of goods sold accounts. **Purchases** is an example of a cost of goods sold account. The figures for the beginning and ending inventory accounts also appear in the Income Statement section in the **Income Summary** account.
4. Assets, liabilities, and owner's equity (including drawing) accounts.
5. Expenses that relate to the current period but have not yet been paid.

CHAPTER 13

Learning Objectives

1. Prepare a classified income statement from the worksheet.
2. Prepare a statement of owner's equity from the worksheet.
3. Prepare a classified balance sheet from the worksheet.
4. Journalize and post the adjusting entries.
5. Journalize and post the closing entries.
6. Prepare a postclosing trial balance.
7. Journalize and post reversing entries.
8. Define the accounting terms new to this chapter.

Financial Statements and Closing Procedures

www.safeway.com

Safeway Inc. is one of the largest food and drug retailers in North America, operating 1,754 stores in the United States and western Canada. For many consumers, a trip to the grocery story is synonymous with a trip to Safeway. Even pop culture has embraced the Safeway name. Marge Simpson shops at Safeway for pacifiers and Fred Flintstone tried to sell Wilma's gravelberry pies to the "Safestone" Market.

As Safeway stores spread across the United States from 1926 to the present, a network of supporting distribution, manufacturing, and food processing facilities emerged. Safeway owns and operates 41 milk, ice cream, soft drink bottling, bread-baking plants, and other food processing facilities.

Thinking Critically

If you owned stock in Safeway Inc., what types of financial information would be most important to you?

For more information on Safeway Inc., go to: collegeaccounting.glencoe.com.

New Terms

- **Classified financial statement**
- **Current assets**
- **Current liabilities**
- **Current ratio**
- **Gross profit**
- **Gross profit percentage**
- **Inventory turnover**
- **Liquidity**
- **Long-term liabilities**
- **Multiple-step income statement**
- **Plant and equipment**
- **Reversing entries**
- **Single-step income statement**

Section 1

Section Objectives

1. **Prepare a classified income statement from the worksheet.**

   WHY IT'S IMPORTANT
   To help decision-makers, financial information needs to be presented in a meaningful and easy-to-use way.

2. **Prepare a statement of owner's equity from the worksheet.**

   WHY IT'S IMPORTANT
   The statement of owner's equity reports changes to and balances of the owner's equity account.

3. **Prepare a classified balance sheet from the worksheet.**

   WHY IT'S IMPORTANT
   Grouping accounts helps financial statement users to identify total assets, equity, and financial obligations of the business.

Terms to Learn

classified financial statement
current assets
current liabilities
gross profit
liquidity
long-term liabilities
multiple-step income statement
plant and equipment
single-step income statement

1 Objective

Prepare a classified income statement from the worksheet.

Preparing the Financial Statements

The information needed to prepare the financial statements is on the worksheet in the Income Statement and Balance Sheet sections. At the end of the period, Modern Casuals prepares three financial statements: income statement, statement of owner's equity, and balance sheet. The income statement and the balance sheet are arranged in a classified format. On **classified financial statements**, revenues, expenses, assets, and liabilities are divided into groups of similar accounts and a subtotal is given for each group. This makes the financial statements more useful to the readers.

> The annual report of The Coca-Cola Company includes Consolidated Balance Sheets, Consolidated Statements of Income, and Consolidated Statements of Share-Owners' Equity. The annual report also contains a statement of Selected Financial Data that reports 11 consecutive years of summarized financial information.

The Classified Income Statement

A classified income statement is sometimes called a **multiple-step income statement** because several subtotals are computed before net income is calculated. The simpler income statement you learned about in previous chapters is called a **single-step income statement**. It lists all revenues in one section and all expenses in another section. Only one computation is necessary to determine the net income (Total Revenue − Total Expenses = Net Income).

Figure 13-1 on page 474 shows the classified income statement for Modern Casuals. Refer to it as you learn how to prepare a multiple-step income statement.

Operating Revenue

The first section of the classified income statement contains the revenue from operations. This is the revenue earned from normal business activities. Other income is presented separately near the bottom of the statement. For Modern Casuals all operating revenue comes from sales of merchandise.

Because Modern Casuals is a retail firm, it does not offer sales discounts to its customers. If it did, the sales discounts would be deducted from total sales in order to compute net sales. The net sales amount is computed as follows.

Sales
(Sales Returns and Allowances)
(Sales Discounts)
Net Sales

The parentheses indicate that the amount is subtracted. Net sales for Modern Casuals is $546,650.

Cost of Goods Sold

The Cost of Goods Sold section contains information about the cost of the merchandise that was sold during the period. Three elements are needed to compute the cost of goods sold: beginning inventory, net delivered cost of purchases, and ending inventory. The format is

Purchases
\+ Freight In
(Purchases Returns and Allowances)
(Purchases Discounts)
Net Delivered Cost of Purchases

Beginning Merchandise Inventory
\+ Net Delivered Cost of Purchases
Total Merchandise Available for Sale
(Ending Merchandise Inventory)
Cost of Goods Sold

For Modern Casuals the net delivered cost of purchases is $323,120 and the cost of goods sold is $328,620. **Merchandise Inventory** is the one account that appears on both the income statement and the balance sheet. Beginning and ending merchandise inventory balances appear on the income statement. Ending merchandise inventory also appears on the balance sheet in the Assets section.

Gross Profit on Sales

The **gross profit** on sales is the difference between the net sales and the cost of goods sold. For Modern Casuals net sales is the revenue earned from selling clothes. Cost of goods sold is what Modern Casuals paid for the clothes that were sold during the fiscal period. Gross profit is what is left to cover operating expenses and provide a profit. The format is

Net Sales
(Cost of Goods Sold)
Gross Profit on Sales

For Modern Casuals gross profit on sales is $218,030.

Operating Expenses

Operating expenses are expenses that arise from normal business activities. Modern Casuals separates operating expenses into two categories: *Selling Expenses* and *General and Administrative Expenses.* The selling expenses relate directly to the sale and delivery of goods. The general and administrative expenses are necessary for business operations but are not directly connected with the sales function. Rent, utilities, and salaries for office employees are examples of general and administrative expenses.

Modern Casuals
Income Statement
Year Ended December 31, 2004

Operating Revenue				
Sales				559,650.00
Less Sales Returns and Allowances				13,000.00
Net Sales				546,650.00
Cost of Goods Sold				
Merchandise Inventory, Jan. 1, 2004			51,500.00	
Purchases		320,500.00		
Freight In		8,800.00		
Delivered Cost of Purchases		329,300.00		
Less Purchases Returns and Allowances	3,050.00			
Purchases Discounts	3,130.00	6,180.00		
Net Delivered Cost of Purchases			323,120.00	
Total Merchandise Available for Sale			374,620.00	
Less Merchandise Inventory, Dec. 31, 2004			46,000.00	
Cost of Goods Sold				328,620.00
Gross Profit on Sales				218,030.00
Operating Expenses				
Selling Expenses				
Salaries Expense—Sales		79,990.00		
Advertising Expense		7,425.00		
Cash Short or Over		125.00		
Supplies Expense		4,975.00		
Depreciation Expense—Store Equipment		2,250.00		
Total Selling Expenses			94,765.00	
General and Administrative Expenses				
Rent Expense		27,600.00		
Salaries Expense—Office		26,500.00		
Insurance Expense		3,600.00		
Payroll Taxes Expense		7,412.75		
Telephone Expense		1,875.00		
Uncollectible Accounts Expense		750.00		
Utilities Expense		5,925.00		
Depreciation Expense—Office Equipment		1,200.00		
Total General and Administrative Expenses			74,862.75	
Total Operating Expenses				169,627.75
Net Income from Operations				48,402.25
Other Income				
Interest Income		160.00		
Miscellaneous Income		510.00		
Total Other Income			670.00	
Other Expenses				
Interest Expense			770.00	
Net Nonoperating Expense				100.00
Net Income for Year				48,302.25

Classified Income Statement

Net Income or Net Loss from Operations

Keeping operating and nonoperating income separate helps financial statement users learn about the operating efficiency of the firm. The format for determining net income (or net loss) from operations is

Gross Profit on Sales
(Total Operating Expenses)
Net Income (or Net Loss) from Operations

For Modern Casuals net income from operations is $48,402.25.

Other Income and Other Expenses

Income that is earned from sources other than normal business activities appears in the Other Income section. For Modern Casuals other income includes interest on notes receivable and one miscellaneous income item.

Expenses that are not directly connected with business operations appear in the Other Expenses section. The only other expense for Modern Casuals is interest expense.

Net Income or Net Loss

Net income is all the revenue minus all the expenses. For Modern Casuals net income is $48,302.25. If there is a net loss, it appears in parentheses. Net income or net loss is used to prepare the statement of owner's equity.

The Statement of Owner's Equity

2 Objective

Prepare a statement of owner's equity from the worksheet.

The statement of owner's equity reports the changes that occurred in the owner's financial interest during the period. Figure 13-2 shows the statement of owner's equity for Modern Casuals. The ending capital balance for Sonia Sanchez, $81,923.25, is used to prepare the balance sheet.

◄ **FIGURE 13-2**
Statement of Owner's Equity

Modern Casuals Statement of Owner's Equity Year Ended December 31, 2004		
Sonia Sanchez, Capital, January 1, 2004		61 221 00
Net Income for Year	48 302 25	
Less Withdrawals for the Year	27 600 00	
Increase in Capital		20 702 25
Sonia Sanchez, Capital, December 31, 2004		81 923 25

The Classified Balance Sheet

3 Objective

Prepare a classified balance sheet from the worksheet.

The classified balance sheet divides the various assets and liabilities into groups. Figure 13-3 on page 476 shows the balance sheet for Modern Casuals. Refer to it as you learn how to prepare a classified balance sheet.

Current Assets

Current assets consist of cash, items that will normally be converted into cash within one year, and items that will be used up within one year.

Current assets are usually listed in order of liquidity. **Liquidity** is the ease with which an item can be converted into cash. Current assets are vital to the survival of a business because they provide the funds needed to pay bills and meet expenses. The current assets for Modern Casuals total $104,610.

FIGURE 13-3 ► Classified Balance Sheet

Modern Casuals
Balance Sheet
December 31, 2004

Assets			
Current Assets			
Cash			21,136.00
Petty Cash Fund			100.00
Notes Receivable			1,200.00
Accounts Receivable		32,000.00	
Less Allowance for Doubtful Accounts		850.00	31,150.00
Interest Receivable			24.00
Merchandise Inventory			46,000.00
Prepaid Expenses			
Supplies		1,325.00	
Prepaid Insurance		3,600.00	
Prepaid Interest		75.00	5,000.00
Total Current Assets			104,610.00
Plant and Equipment			
Store Equipment	20,000.00		
Less Accumulated Depreciation	2,250.00	17,750.00	
Office Equipment	7,000.00		
Less Accumulated Depreciation	1,200.00	5,800.00	
Total Plant and Equipment			23,550.00
Total Assets			128,160.00
Liabilities and Owner's Equity			
Current Liabilities			
Notes Payable—Trade			2,000.00
Notes Payable—Bank			9,000.00
Accounts Payable			24,129.00
Interest Payable			20.00
Social Security Tax Payable			1,177.00
Medicare Tax Payable			271.75
Employee Income Tax Payable			990.00
Federal Unemployment Tax Payable			12.00
State Unemployment Tax Payable			81.00
Salaries Payable			1,500.00
Sales Tax Payable			7,056.00
Total Current Liabilities			46,236.75
Owner's Equity			
Sonia Sanchez, Capital			81,923.25
Total Liabilities and Owner's Equity			128,160.00

Plant and Equipment

Noncurrent assets are called *long-term assets.* An important category of long-term assets is plant and equipment. **Plant and equipment** consists of property that will be used in the business for longer than one year. For many businesses plant and equipment represents a sizable investment. The balance sheet shows three amounts for each category of plant and equipment:

Asset
(Accumulated depreciation)
Book value

For Modern Casuals total plant and equipment is $23,550.

Book Value

Book value is the portion of the original cost that has not been depreciated. Often book value bears no relation to the market value of the asset.

Current Liabilities

Current liabilities are the debts that must be paid within one year. They are usually listed in order of priority of payment. Management must ensure that funds are available to pay current liabilities when they become due in order to maintain the firm's good credit reputation. For Modern Casuals total current liabilities are $46,236.75.

Long-Term Liabilities

Long-term liabilities are debts of the business that are due more than one year in the future. Although repayment of long-term liabilities might not be due for several years, management must make sure that periodic interest is paid promptly. Long-term liabilities include mortgages, notes payable, and loans payable. Modern Casuals had no long-term liabilities on December 31, 2004.

Owner's Equity

Modern Casuals prepares a separate statement of owner's equity that reports all information about changes that occurred in the owner's financial interest during the period. The ending balance from that statement is transferred to the Owner's Equity section of the balance sheet.

International **INSIGHTS**

Paying Bills

According to a payment survey conducted by Dun & Bradstreet, businesses in Germany are more likely to pay their bills on time; only 20 percent of invoices were paid more than 15 days after their due date. In contrast, the European average was 35 percent.

Section 1 Self Review

Questions

1. What are classified financial statements?
2. What is the purpose of the income statement?
3. What is gross profit on sales?

Exercises

4. Which of the following is not a current asset?
   a. Equipment
   b. Prepaid Insurance
   c. Merchandise Inventory
   d. Accounts Receivable
5. Purchases are shown in the
   a. Current Assets section of the balance sheet.
   b. Plant and Equipment section of the balance sheet.
   c. Cost of Goods Sold section of the income statement.
   d. Operating Expenses section of the income statement.

Analysis

6. Assume that a business listed the **Freight In** account in the Operating Expense section of the income statement. What is the effect on net purchases? On total operating expenses? On net income from operations?

(Answers to Section 1 Self Review are on page 514.)

Section 2

Section Objectives

4 Journalize and post the adjusting entries.

Why It's Important
Adjusting entries match revenue and expenses to the proper periods.

5 Journalize and post the closing entries.

Why It's Important
The temporary accounts are closed in order to prepare for the next accounting period.

6 Prepare a postclosing trial balance.

Why It's Important
The general ledger must remain in balance.

7 Journalize and post reversing entries.

Why It's Important
Reversing entries are made so that transactions can be recorded in the usual way in the next accounting period.

Terms to Learn

current ratio
gross profit percentage
inventory turnover
reversing entries

Completing the Accounting Cycle

The complete accounting cycle was presented in Chapter 6 (pages 176–177). In this section we will complete the accounting cycle for Modern Casuals.

Journalizing and Posting the Adjusting Entries

All adjustments are shown on the worksheet. After the financial statements have been prepared, the adjustments are made a permanent part of the accounting records. They are recorded in the general journal as adjusting journal entries and are posted to the general ledger.

Journalizing the Adjusting Entries

Figure 13-4 on pages 479–481 shows the adjusting journal entries for Modern Casuals. Each adjusting entry shows how the adjustment was calculated. Supervisors and auditors need to understand, without additional explanation, why the adjustment was made.

Let's review the types of adjusting entries made by Modern Casuals:

Type of Adjustment	Worksheet Reference	Purpose
Inventory	(a–b)	Removes beginning inventory and adds ending inventory to the accounting records.
Expense	(c–e)	Matches expense to revenue for the period; the credit is to a contra asset account.
Accrued Expense	(f–i)	Matches expense to revenue for the period; the credit is to a liability account.
Prepaid Expense	(j–l)	Matches expense to revenue for the period; the credit is to an asset account.
Accrued Income	(m–n)	Recognizes income earned in the period. The debit is to an asset account **(Interest Receivable)** or a liability account **(Sales Tax Payable).**

4 Objective

Journalize and post the adjusting entries.

Posting the Adjusting Entries

After the adjustments have been recorded in the general journal, they are promptly posted to the general ledger. The word *Adjusting* is entered in the Description column of the general ledger account. This distinguishes it from entries for transactions that occurred during that period. After the adjusting entries have been posted, the general ledger account balances match the amounts shown in the Adjusted Trial Balance section of the worksheet in Figure 12-2.

GENERAL JOURNAL

PAGE 25

DATE		DESCRIPTION	POST. REF.	DEBIT	CREDIT
		Adjusting Entries			
2004		*(Adjustment a)*			
Dec.	*31*	*Income Summary*	*399*	*51,500.00*	
		Merchandise Inventory	*121*		*51,500.00*
		To transfer beginning inventory			
		to Income Summary			
		(Adjustment b)			
	31	*Merchandise Inventory*	*121*	*46,000.00*	
		Income Summary	*399*		*46,000.00*
		To record ending inventory			
		(Adjustment c)			
	31	*Uncollectible Accounts Expense*	*685*	*750.00*	
		Allowance For Doubtful Accounts	*112*		*750.00*
		To record estimated loss			
		from uncollectible accounts			
		based on 0.75% of net			
		credit sales of $100,000			
		(Adjustment d)			
	31	*Depreciation Expense—Store Equip.*	*620*	*2,250.00*	
		Accum. Depreciation—Store Equip.	*132*		*2,250.00*
		To record depreciation			
		for 2004 as shown by			
		schedule on file			
		(Adjustment e)			
	31	*Depreciation Expense—Office Equip.*	*689*	*1,200.00*	
		Accum. Depreciation—Office Equip.	*142*		*1,200.00*
		To record depreciation			
		for 2004 as shown by			
		schedule on file			
		(Adjustment f)			
	31	*Salaries Expense—Sales*	*602*	*1,500.00*	
		Salaries Payable	*229*		*1,500.00*
		To record accrued salaries			
		of part-time sales clerks			
		for Dec. 28–31			

▲ **FIGURE 13-4** Adjusting Entries in the General Journal

GENERAL JOURNAL

PAGE 26

DATE		DESCRIPTION	POST. REF.	DEBIT	CREDIT
		Adjusting Entries			
2004		*(Adjustment g)*			
Dec.	*31*	*Payroll Taxes Expense*	*665*	*114 75*	
		Social Security Tax Payable	*221*		*93 00*
		Medicare Tax Payable	*223*		*21 75*
		To record accrued payroll			
		taxes on accrued salaries			
		for Dec. 28–31			
		(Adjustment h)			
	31	*Payroll Taxes Expense*	*665*	*93 00*	
		Fed. Unemployment Tax Payable	*225*		*12 00*
		State Unemployment Tax Payable	*227*		*81 00*
		To record accrued payroll			
		taxes on accrued salaries			
		for Dec. 28–31			
		(Adjustment i)			
	31	*Interest Expense*	*695*	*20 00*	
		Interest Payable	*216*		*20 00*
		To record interest on a			
		2-month, $2,000, 12%			
		note payable dated			
		Dec. 1, 2004			
		(Adjustment j)			
	31	*Supplies Expense*	*615*	*4975 00*	
		Supplies	*129*		*4975 00*
		To record supplies used			
		(Adjustment k)			
	31	*Insurance Expense*	*660*	*3600 00*	
		Prepaid Insurance	*126*		*3600 00*
		To record expired			
		insurance on 2-year			
		policy purchased for			
		$7,200 on Jan. 1, 2004			

▲ **FIGURE 13-4 (continued)** Adjusting Entries in the General Journal

GENERAL JOURNAL PAGE 27

DATE		DESCRIPTION		POST. REF.	DEBIT	CREDIT
2004		(Adjustment l)				
Dec.	31	Interest Expense		695	150 00	
		Prepaid Interest		127		150 00
		To record transfer of 2/3				
		of prepaid interest of				
		$225 for a 3-month,				
		10% note payable issued				
		to bank on Nov. 1, 2004				
		(Adjustment m)				
	31	Interest Receivable		116	24 00	
		Interest Income		491		24 00
		To record accrued interest				
		earned on a 4-month,				
		12% note receivable				
		dated Nov. 1, 2004				
		($1,200 x 0.12 x 2/12)				
		(Adjustment n)				
	31	Sales Tax Payable		231	144 00	
		Miscellaneous Income		493		144 00
		To record accrued				
		commission earned on				
		sales tax owed for fourth				
		quarter of 2004:				
		Sales Tax Payable	$7,200			
		Commission rate	x 0.02			
		Commission due	$ 144			

▲ **FIGURE 13-4 (continued)** Adjusting Entries in the General Journal

Journalizing and Posting the Closing Entries

At the end of the period, the temporary accounts are closed. The temporary accounts are the revenue, cost of goods sold, expense, and drawing accounts.

Journalizing the Closing Entries

5 Objective

Journalize and post the closing entries.

The Income Statement section of the worksheet in Figure 12-2 on pages 444–447 provides the data needed to prepare closing entries. There are four steps in the closing process.

1. Close revenue accounts and cost of goods sold accounts with credit balances to **Income Summary.**

2. Close expense accounts and cost of goods sold accounts with debit balances to **Income Summary.**
3. Close **Income Summary,** which now reflects the net income or loss for the period, to owner's capital.
4. Close the drawing account to owner's capital.

Step 1: Closing the Revenue Accounts and the Cost of Goods Sold Accounts with Credit Balances. The first entry closes the revenue accounts and other temporary income statement accounts with credit balances. Look at the Income Statement section of the worksheet in Figure 12-2. There are five items listed in the Credit column, not including **Income Summary.** Debit each account, *except* **Income Summary,** for its balance. Credit **Income Summary** for the total, $566,500.

GENERAL JOURNAL PAGE *28*

	DATE		DESCRIPTION	POST. REF.	DEBIT	CREDIT	
1	*2004*		*Closing Entries*				1
2	*Dec.*	*31*	*Sales*	*401*	*559 650 00*		2
3			*Interest Income*	*491*	*1 600 00*		3
4			*Miscellaneous Income*	*493*	*5 100 00*		4
5			*Purchases Returns and Allowances*	*503*	*3 050 00*		5
6			*Purchases Discounts*	*504*	*3 130 00*		6
7			*Income Summary*			*566 500 00*	7

Step 2: Closing the Expense Accounts and the Cost of Goods Sold Accounts with Debit Balances. The Debit column of the Income Statement section of the worksheet in Figure 12-2 shows the expense accounts and the cost of goods sold accounts with debit balances. Credit each account, *except* **Income Summary,** for its balance. Debit **Income Summary** for the total, $512,697.75.

GENERAL JOURNAL PAGE *28*

	DATE		DESCRIPTION	POST. REF.	DEBIT	CREDIT	
9	*Dec.*	*31*	*Income Summary*	*399*	*512 697 75*		9
10			*Sales Returns and Allowances*	*451*		*13 000 00*	10
11			*Purchases*	*501*		*320 500 00*	11
12			*Freight In*	*502*		*8 800 00*	12
13			*Salaries Expense—Sales*	*602*		*79 990 00*	13
14			*Advertising Expense*	*605*		*7 425 00*	14
15			*Cash Short or Over*	*610*		*125 00*	15
16			*Supplies Expense*	*615*		*4 975 00*	16
17			*Depreciation Expense—Store Equip.*	*620*		*2 250 00*	17
18			*Rent Expense*	*640*		*27 600 00*	18
19			*Salaries Expense—Office*	*645*		*26 500 00*	19
20			*Insurance Expense*	*660*		*3 600 00*	20
21			*Payroll Taxes Expense*	*665*		*7 412 75*	21
22			*Telephone Expense*	*680*		*1 875 00*	22
23			*Uncollectible Accounts Expense*	*685*		*750 00*	23
24			*Utilities Expense*	*687*		*5 925 00*	24
25			*Depreciation Expense—Office Equip.*	*689*		*1 200 00*	25
26			*Interest Expense*	*695*		*770 00*	26

Step 3: Closing the Income Summary Account. After the first two closing entries have been posted, the balance of the **Income Summary** account is net income or net loss for the period. The third closing entry transfers the **Income Summary** balance to the owner's capital account. **Income Summary** after the second closing entry has a balance of $48,302.25.

	Income Summary			
Adjusting Entries (a–b)	12/31	51,500.00	12/31	46,000.00
Closing Entries	12/31	512,697.75	12/31	566,500.00
		564,197.75		612,500.00
			Bal.	48,302.25

For Modern Casuals the third closing entry is as follows. This closes the **Income Summary** account, which remains closed until it is used in the end-of-period process for the next year.

GENERAL JOURNAL — PAGE 28

	DATE		DESCRIPTION	POST. REF.	DEBIT	CREDIT	
28	Dec.	31	Income Summary	399	48 302 25		28
29			Sonia Sanchez, Capital	301		48 302 25	29

Step 4: Closing the Drawing Account. This entry closes the drawing account and updates the capital account so that its balance agrees with the ending capital reported on the statement of owner's equity and on the balance sheet.

GENERAL JOURNAL — PAGE 28

	DATE		DESCRIPTION	POST. REF.	DEBIT	CREDIT	
31	Dec.	31	Sonia Sanchez, Capital	301	27 600 00		31
32			Sonia Sanchez, Drawing	302		27 600 00	32

Posting the Closing Entries

The closing entries are posted from the general journal to the general ledger. This process brings the temporary account balances to zero. The word *Closing* is entered in the Description column. After the closing entry is posted, the account balance is zero.

Preparing a Postclosing Trial Balance

6 Objective

Prepare a postclosing trial balance.

After the closing entries have been posted, prepare a postclosing trial balance to confirm that the general ledger is in balance. Only the accounts that have balances—the asset, liability and owner's capital accounts—appear on the postclosing trial balance. The postclosing trial balance matches the amounts reported on the balance sheet. To verify this, compare the postclosing trial balance, Figure 13-5 on page 484, with the balance sheet, Figure 13-3 on page 476.

If the postclosing trial balance shows that the general ledger is out of balance, find and correct the error or errors immediately. Any necessary correcting entries must be journalized and posted so that the general ledger is in balance before any transactions can be recorded for the new period.

FIGURE 13-5 ►
Postclosing Trial Balance

Modern Casuals Postclosing Trial Balance December 31, 2004		
ACCOUNT NAME	DEBIT	CREDIT
Cash	21 136 00	
Petty Cash Fund	100 00	
Notes Receivable	1 200 00	
Accounts Receivable	32 000 00	
Allowance for Doubtful Accounts		850 00
Interest Receivable	24 00	
Merchandise Inventory	46 000 00	
Supplies	1 325 00	
Prepaid Insurance	3 600 00	
Prepaid Interest	75 00	
Store Equipment	20 000 00	
Accumulated Depreciation—Store Equipment		2 250 00
Office Equipment	7 000 00	
Accumulated Depreciation—Office Equipment		1 200 00
Notes Payable—Trade		2 000 00
Notes Payable—Bank		9 000 00
Accounts Payable		24 129 00
Interest Payable		20 00
Social Security Tax Payable		1 177 00
Medicare Tax Payable		271 75
Employee Income Taxes Payable		990 00
Federal Unemployment Tax Payable		12 00
State Unemployment Tax Payable		81 00
Salaries Payable		1 500 00
Sales Tax Payable		7 056 00
Sonia Sanchez, Capital		81 923 25
Totals	132 460 00	132 460 00

Interpreting the Financial Statements

Interested parties analyze the financial statements to evaluate the results of operations and to make decisions. Interpreting financial statements requires an understanding of the business and the environment in which it operates as well as the nature and limitations of accounting information. Ratios and other measurements are used to analyze and interpret financial statements. Three such measurements are used by Modern Casuals.

The **gross profit percentage** reveals the amount of gross profit from each sales dollar. The gross profit percentage is calculated by dividing gross profit by net sales. For Modern Casuals, for every dollar of net sales, gross profit was almost 40 cents.

Important!

Current Ratio

Banks and other lenders look closely at the current ratio of each loan applicant.

$$\frac{\text{Gross profit}}{\text{Net sales}} = \frac{\$218{,}030}{\$546{,}650} = 0.399 = 39.9\%$$

The **current ratio** is a relationship between current assets and current liabilities that provides a measure of a firm's ability to pay its current debts. Modern Casuals has $2.26 in current assets for every dollar of current liabilities. The current ratio is calculated in the following manner.

$$\frac{\text{Current assets}}{\text{Current liabilities}} = \frac{\$104{,}610.00}{\$\ 46{,}236.75} = 2.26 \text{ to } 1$$

Caterpillar Inc. reported current assets of $11.7 billion and current liabilities of $8.2 billion on December 31, 1999. The current ratio shows that the business has $1.43 of current assets for every dollar of current liabilities.

Inventory turnover shows the number of times inventory is replaced during the accounting period. Inventory turnover is calculated in the following manner.

$$\text{Inventory turnover} = \frac{\text{Cost of goods sold}}{\text{Average inventory}}$$

$$\text{Average inventory} = \frac{\text{Beginning inventory} + \text{Ending inventory}}{2}$$

$$\text{Average inventory} = \frac{\$51{,}500 + \$46{,}000}{2} = \$48{,}750$$

$$\text{Inventory turnover} = \frac{\$328{,}620}{\$\ 48{,}750} = 6.74 \text{ times}$$

For Modern Casuals the average inventory for the year was $48,750. The inventory turnover was 6.74; that is, inventory was replaced about seven times during the year.

Journalizing and Posting Reversing Entries

7 Objective

Journalize and post reversing entries.

Some adjustments made at the end of one period can cause problems in the next period. **Reversing entries** are made to reverse the effect of certain adjustments. This helps prevent errors in recording payments or cash receipts in the new accounting period.

Let's use adjustment **(f)** as an illustration of how reversing entries are helpful. On December 31 Modern Casuals owed $1,500 of salaries to its part-time sales clerks. The salaries will be paid in January. To recognize the salaries expense in December, adjustment **(f)** was made to debit **Salaries Expense—Sales** for $1,500 and credit **Salaries Payable** for $1,500. The adjustment was recorded and posted in the accounting records.

Accrual Basis

Revenues are recognized when earned, and expenses are recognized when incurred or used, regardless of when cash is received or paid.

By payday on January 3, the part-time sales clerks have earned $2,000:

$1,500 earned in December
$ 500 earned in January

The entry to record the January 3 payment of the salaries is a debit to **Salaries Expense—Sales** for $500, a debit to **Salaries Payable** for $1,500, and a credit to **Cash** for $2,000. This entry recognizes the salary expense for January and reduces the **Salaries Payable** account to zero.

Salaries Expense—Sales

Date	Debit	Date	Credit
1/3	500		

Cash

Date	Debit	Date	Credit
12/31	21,136	1/3	2,000
Bal.	19,136		

Salaries Payable

Date	Debit	Date	Credit
1/3	1,500	12/31	1,500
		Bal.	0

To record this transaction, the accountant had to review the adjustment in the end-of-period records and divide the amount paid between the expense and liability accounts. This review is time consuming, can cause errors, and is sometimes forgotten.

Reversing entries provide a way to guard against oversights, eliminate the review of accounting records, and simplify the entry made in the new period. As an example of a reversing entry, we will analyze the same transaction (January 3 payroll of $2,000) if reversing entries are made.

First, record the adjustment on December 31. Then record the reversing entry on January 1. Note that the reversing entry is the exact opposite (the reverse) of the adjustment. After the reversing entry is posted, the **Salaries Payable** account shows a zero balance and the **Salaries Expense—Sales** account has a credit balance. This is unusual because the normal balance of an expense account is a debit.

Computers in Accounting

Tools for Success: Decision Support Systems

Executives and managers use financial statements to make decisions about the future. Transportation of goods might be moved from trucking vendors to air vendors. Staff reductions or increases might be in order. These managerial decisions are made while keeping in mind the goals of the company.

Computerized decision support systems help managers make the best possible decisions. *Decision support system (DSS)* is a term used to describe computer software designed to assemble, arrange, and analyze data in order to find the most profitable plan of action. For example, an automobile manufacturing company might use the software to determine the most cost-efficient manufacturing method. In this case the decision support system would extract information from the manufacturing, engineering, accounting information, and production planning systems. The various costs associated with different techniques for body formation, engineering models, and assembly processes would be assembled and combined in potential groupings.

Then the DSS would make projections based on "what-if" scenarios, calculating outcome on profits or operational costs. For example, would costs decrease if manufacturing of glass components were completed by an outside firm? Would profits increase if steel fabrication contained different composite materials? A DSS can provide executives a vision of the integrated relationships between manufacturing processes and the bottom line.

A computerized decision support system, however, cannot integrate the human elements into decisions. For example, a DSS might reveal a change in the production process that positively affects the bottom line, but doesn't reveal its impact on employees. How will the change affect job satisfaction or stress levels? Is retraining required? A business that uses DSS in combination with human element considerations will have the information to make decisions that positively impact not only the bottom line, but also the entire organization.

Thinking Critically

Companies select among a variety of transportation methods when moving goods from suppliers to warehouses or to retail locations. Describe how you think a decision support system could be used to evaluate the various shipping methods.

Internet Application

Using a search engine on the Internet, find a decision support system used in the farming, aviation, robotics, or natural or biological resources management industry. Write a one-page report on the decision support system. Describe the goal of the software, the types of data needed, and the benefits provided.

GENERAL JOURNAL PAGE 25

	DATE		DESCRIPTION	POST. REF.	DEBIT	CREDIT	
1	2004		Adjusting Entries				1
35			(Adjustment f)				35
36	Dec.	31	Salaries Expense—Sales	602	1 5 0 0 00		36
37			Salaries Payable	229		1 5 0 0 00	37

GENERAL JOURNAL PAGE 29

	DATE		DESCRIPTION	POST. REF.	DEBIT	CREDIT	
1	2005		Reversing Entries				1
2	Jan.	1	Salaries Payable	229	1 5 0 0 00		2
3			Salaries Expense—Sales	602		1 5 0 0 00	3

ACCOUNT Salaries Payable ACCOUNT NO. 229

DATE		DESCRIPTION	POST. REF.	DEBIT	CREDIT	BALANCE DEBIT	BALANCE CREDIT
2004							
Dec.	31	Adjusting	J25		1 5 0 0 00		1 5 0 0 00
2005							
Jan.	1	Reversing	J29	1 5 0 0 00			—0—

ACCOUNT Salaries Expense—Sales ACCOUNT NO. 602

DATE		DESCRIPTION	POST. REF.	DEBIT	CREDIT	BALANCE DEBIT	BALANCE CREDIT
2004							
Dec.	31	Balance				78 4 9 0 00	
	31	Adjusting	J25	1 5 0 0 00		79 9 9 0 00	
	31	Closing	J28		79 9 9 0 00	—0—	
2005							
Jan.	1	Reversing	J29		1 5 0 0 00		1 5 0 0 00

On January 3 the payment of $2,000 of salaries is recorded in the normal manner. Notice that this entry reduces cash and increases the expense account for the entire $2,000. It does not allocate the $2,000 between the expense and liability accounts.

GENERAL JOURNAL PAGE 30

	DATE		DESCRIPTION	POST. REF.	DEBIT	CREDIT	
1	2005						1
2	Jan.	3	Salaries Expense—Sales	602	2 0 0 0 00		2
3			Cash	101		2 0 0 0 00	3

After this entry is posted, the expenses are properly divided between the two periods: $1,500 in December and $500 in January. The **Salaries Payable** account has a zero balance. The accountant did not have to review the previous records or allocate the payment between two accounts.

ACCOUNT *Salaries Expense—Sales* ACCOUNT NO. *602*

DATE		DESCRIPTION	POST. REF.	DEBIT	CREDIT	BALANCE DEBIT	BALANCE CREDIT
2004							
Dec.	*31*	*Balance*				*78490 00*	
	31	*Adjusting*	*J25*	*1500 00*		*79990 00*	
	31	*Closing*	*J28*		*79990 00*	*—0—*	
2005							
Jan.	*1*	*Reversing*	*J29*		*1500 00*		*1500 00*
	3		*J30*	*2000 00*		*500 00*	

Identifying Items for Reversal

Not all adjustments need to be reversed. Normally, reversing entries are made for accrued items that involve future payments or receipts of cash. Reversing entries are not made for uncollectible accounts, depreciation, and prepaid expenses—if they are initially recorded as assets. However, when prepaid expenses are initially recorded as expenses (the alternative method), the end-of-period adjustment needs to be reversed.

Modern Casuals makes reversing entries for:

- accrued salaries—adjustment **(f),**
- accrued payroll taxes—adjustments **(g)** and **(h),**
- interest payable—adjustment **(i),**
- interest receivable—adjustment **(m).**

Journalizing Reversing Entries

We just analyzed the reversing entry for accrued salaries, adjustment **(f).** The next two reversing entries are for accrued payroll taxes. Making these reversing entries means that the accountant does not have to review the year-end adjustments before recording the payment of payroll taxes in the next year.

GENERAL JOURNAL PAGE *29*

DATE		DESCRIPTION	POST. REF.	DEBIT	CREDIT
Jan.	*1*	*Social Security Tax Payable*	*221*	*93 00*	
		Medicare Tax Payable	*223*	*21 75*	
		Payroll Taxes Expense	*665*		*114 75*
		To reverse adjusting entry			
		(g) made Dec. 31, 2004			
	1	*Federal Unemployment Tax Payable*	*225*	*12 00*	
		State Unemployment Tax Payable	*227*	*81 00*	
		Payroll Taxes Expense	*665*		*93 00*
		To reverse adjusting entry			
		(h) made Dec. 31, 2004			

The next reversing entry is for accrued interest expense. The reversing entry that follows prevents recording difficulties when the note is paid on February 1.

	DATE		DESCRIPTION	POST. REF.	DEBIT	CREDIT	
18	Jan.	1	Interest Payable	216	20 00		18
19			Interest Expense	695		20 00	19
20			To reverse adjusting entry				20
21			(i) made Dec. 31, 2004				21
22							22

GENERAL JOURNAL — PAGE 29

In addition to adjustments for accrued expenses, Modern Casuals made two adjustments for accrued income items. The next reversing entry is for accrued interest income on the note receivable. Modern Casuals will receive cash for the note and the interest on March 1. The reversing entry eliminates any difficulties in recording the interest income when the note is paid on March 1.

GENERAL JOURNAL — PAGE 29

	DATE		DESCRIPTION	POST. REF.	DEBIT	CREDIT	
23	Jan.	1	Interest Income	491	24 00		23
24			Interest Receivable	116		24 00	24
25			To reverse adjusting entry				25
26			(m) made Dec. 31, 2004				26
27							27

After the reversing entry has been posted, the **Interest Receivable** account has a zero balance and the **Interest Income** account has a debit balance of $24. This is unusual because the normal balance of **Interest Income** is a credit.

On March 1 Modern Casuals received a check for $1,248 in payment of the note ($1,200) and the interest ($48). The transaction is recorded in the normal manner as a debit to **Cash** for $1,248, a credit to **Notes Receivable** for $1,200, and a credit to **Interest Income** for $48.

Refer to the **Interest Income** general ledger account on page 490. After this entry has been posted, note that interest income is properly divided between the two periods, $24 in the previous year and $24 in the current year. The balance of **Interest Receivable** is zero. The accountant does not have to review the year-end adjustments before recording the receipt of the principal and interest relating to the note receivable.

ACCOUNT Interest Receivable — ACCOUNT NO. 116

DATE		DESCRIPTION	POST. REF.	DEBIT	CREDIT	BALANCE DEBIT	BALANCE CREDIT
2004							
Dec.	31	Adjusting	J27	24 00		24 00	
2005							
Jan.	1	Reversing	J29		24 00	–0–	

ACCOUNT *Interest Income* ACCOUNT NO. *491*

DATE		DESCRIPTION	POST. REF.	DEBIT	CREDIT	BALANCE DEBIT	BALANCE CREDIT
2004							
Dec.	*31*	*Balance*					*136 00*
	31	*Adjusting*	*J27*		*24 00*		*160 00*
	31	*Closing*	*J28*	*160 00*			*–0–*
2005							
Jan.	*1*	*Reversing*	*J29*	*24 00*		*24 00*	
Mar.	*1*		*CR3*		*48 00*		*24 00*

Notice that the adjustment for sales tax commission, adjustment **(n)**, is not reversed. Since no cash will be received in the new year when the sales tax return is filed, there is no need to reverse the adjustment.

Review of the Accounting Cycle

In Chapters 7, 8, and 9, The Trend Center was used to introduce accounting procedures, records, and statements for merchandising businesses. In Chapters 12 and 13, Modern Casuals was used to illustrate the end-of-period activities for merchandising businesses. Underlying the various procedures described were the steps in the accounting cycle. Let's review the accounting cycle.

Professional Conduct
In September 1998 the Securities and Exchange Commission (SEC) defined improper professional conduct by accountants. The new rule allows the SEC to censure, suspend, or bar accountants who violate it. The American Institute of Certified Public Accountants (AICPA) supported the rule.

1. ***Analyze transactions.*** Transaction data comes into an accounting system from a variety of source documents—sales slips, purchase invoices, credit memorandums, check stubs, and so on. Each document is analyzed to determine the accounts and amounts affected.
2. ***Journalize the data about transactions.*** Each transaction is recorded in either a special journal or the general journal.
3. ***Post the data about transactions.*** Each transaction is transferred from the journal to the ledger accounts. Merchandising businesses typically maintain several subsidiary ledgers in addition to the general ledger.
4. ***Prepare a worksheet.*** At the end of each period, a worksheet is prepared. The Trial Balance section of the worksheet is used to prove the equality of the debits and credits in the general ledger. Adjustments are entered in the Adjustments section so that the financial statements will be prepared using the accrual basis of accounting. The Adjusted Trial Balance section is used to prove the equality of the debit and credits of the updated account balances. The Income Statement and Balance Sheet sections are used to arrange data in an orderly manner.
5. ***Prepare financial statements.*** A formal set of financial statements is prepared to report information to interested parties.
6. ***Journalize and post adjusting entries.*** Adjusting entries are journalized and posted in the accounting records. This creates a permanent record of the changes shown on the worksheet.
7. ***Journalize and post closing entries.*** Closing entries are journalized and posted in order to transfer the results of operations to owner's equity and to prepare the temporary accounts for the next period. The closing entries reduce the temporary account balances to zero.

8. ***Prepare a postclosing trial balance.*** The postclosing trial balance confirms that the general ledger is still in balance and that the temporary accounts have zero balances.
9. ***Interpret the financial information.*** The accountant, owners, managers, and other interested parties interpret the information shown on the financial statements and other less formal financial reports that might be prepared. This information is used to evaluate the results of operations and the financial position of the business and to make decisions.

In addition to the nine steps listed here, some firms record reversing entries. Reversing entries simplify the recording of cash payments for accrued expenses and cash receipts for accrued income.

Figure 13-6 on page 492 shows the flow of data through an accounting system that uses special journals and subsidiary ledgers. The system is composed of subsystems that perform specialized functions.

The accounts receivable area records transactions involving sales and cash receipts and maintains the individual accounts for credit customers. This area also handles billing for credit customers.

The accounts payable area records transactions involving purchases and cash payments and maintains the individual accounts for creditors.

Financial Statements

- Managers carefully study the financial statements to evaluate the operating efficiency and financial strength of the business.
- A common analysis technique is to compare the data on current statements with the data from previous statements. This can reveal developing trends.
- In large businesses, financial statements are compared with the published financial reports of other companies in the same industry.
- In order to evaluate information on classified financial statements, managers need to understand the nature and significance of the groupings.
- Management ensures that closing entries are promptly made so that transactions for the new period can be recorded. Any significant delay means that valuable information, such as the firm's cash position, will not be available or up to date.
- The efficiency and effectiveness of the adjusting and closing procedures can have a positive effect on the annual independent audit. For example, detailed descriptions in the general journal make it easy for the auditor to understand the adjusting entries.

Thinking Critically

How can managers use the financial statements to learn about a company's operating efficiency?

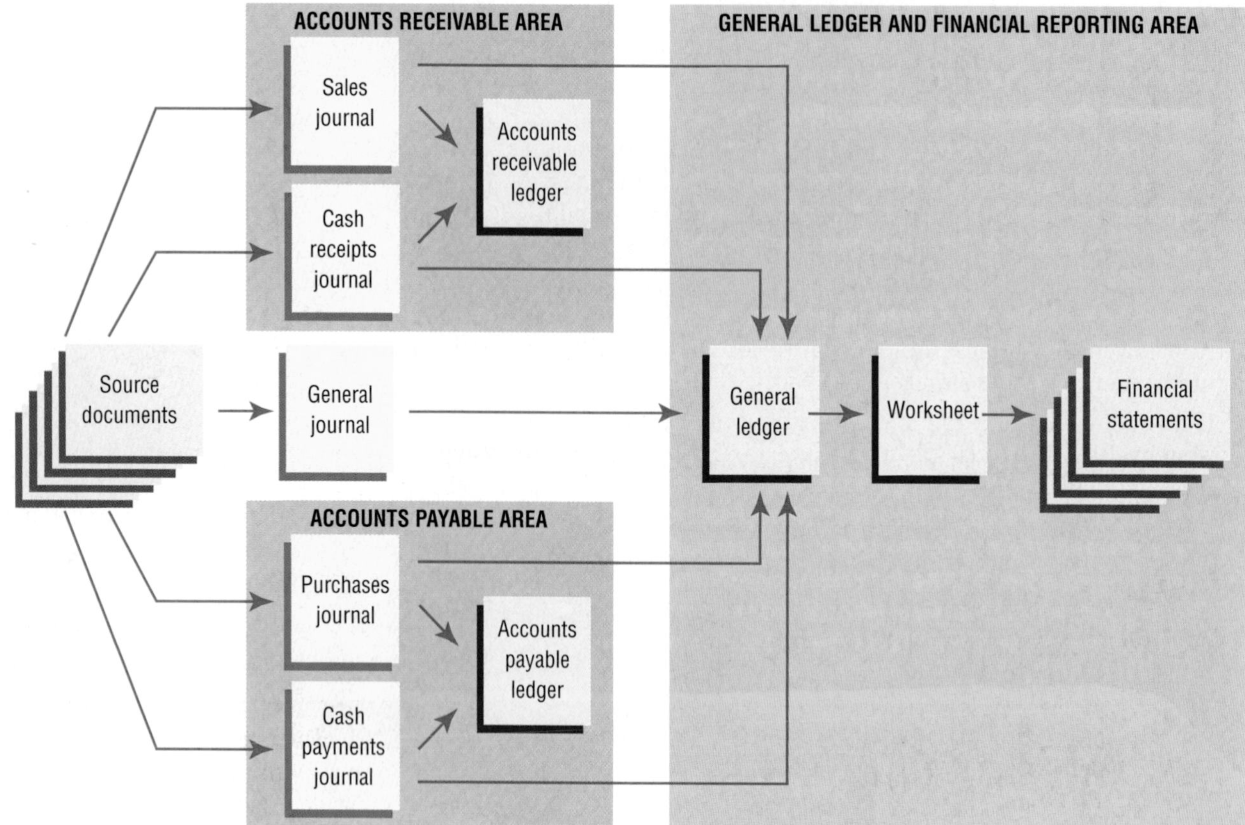

FIGURE 13-6 ▲
Flow of Financial Data through an Accounting System

The general ledger and financial reporting area records transactions in the general journal, maintains the general ledger accounts, performs the end-of-period procedures, and prepares financial statements. This area is the focal point for the accounting system because all transactions eventually flow into the general ledger. In turn, the general ledger provides the data that appears on the financial statements.

Section 2 Self Review

Questions

1. Since adjustments already appear on the worksheet, why is it necessary to journalize and post them?
2. Why do adjusting entries need detailed explanations in the general journal?
3. What do the four steps in the closing process accomplish?

Exercises

4. A reversing entry is made for an end-of-period adjustment that recorded
   a. depreciation.
   b. an accrued expense that involves future cash payments.
   c. a transfer of an amount from a prepaid asset account to an expense account.
   d. the change in merchandise inventory.
5. The current ratio is
   a. current liabilities divided by current assets.
   b. total assets divided by total current liabilities.
   c. total assets divided by total liabilities.
   d. current assets divided by current liabilities.

Analysis

6. At the end of the previous accounting period, an adjusting entry to record accrued employer payroll taxes was made. Reversing entries were not made for the current accounting period. What effect will this have on the current financial statements?

(Answers to Section 2 Self Review are on page 514.)

CHAPTER 13 Review and Applications

Review

Chapter Summary

In this chapter, you have learned how to prepare classified financial statements from the worksheet and how to close the accounting records for the period.

Learning Objectives

1. **Prepare a classified income statement from the worksheet.**
   - A classified income statement for a merchandising business usually includes these sections: Operating Revenue, Cost of Goods Sold, Gross Profit on Sales, Operating Expenses, and Net Income.
   - To make the income statement even more useful, operating expenses may be broken down into categories, such as selling expenses and general and administrative expenses.

2. **Prepare a statement of owner's equity from the worksheet.**
   A statement of owner's equity is prepared to provide detailed information about the changes in the owner's financial interest during the period. The ending owner's capital balance is used to prepare the balance sheet.

3. **Prepare a classified balance sheet from the worksheet.**
   - Assets are usually presented in two groups—current assets, and plant and equipment. Current assets consist of cash, items to be converted into cash within one year, and items to be used up within one year. Plant and equipment consists of property that will be used for a long time in the operations of the business.
   - Liabilities are also divided into two groups—current liabilities and long-term liabilities. Current liabilities will normally be paid within one year. Long-term liabilities are due in more than one year.

4. **Journalize and post the adjusting entries.**
   When the year-end worksheet and financial statements have been completed, adjusting entries are recorded in the general journal and posted to the general ledger. The data comes from the worksheet Adjustments section.

5. **Journalize and post the closing entries.**
   After the adjusting entries have been journalized and posted, the closing entries should be recorded in the records of the business. The data in the Income Statement section of the worksheet can be used to journalize the closing entries.

6. **Prepare a postclosing trial balance.**
   To confirm that the general ledger is still in balance after the adjusting and closing entries have been posted, a postclosing trial balance is prepared.

7. **Journalize and post reversing entries.**
   At the start of each new period, many firms follow the practice of reversing certain adjustments that were made in the previous period.
   - This is done to avoid recording problems with transactions that will occur in the new period.
   - Usually, only adjusting entries for accrued expenses and accrued income need be considered for reversing. Of these, usually only accrued expense and income items involving future payments and receipts of cash can cause difficulties later and should therefore be reversed.
   - The use of reversing entries is optional. Reversing entries save time, promote efficiency, and help to achieve a proper matching of revenue and expenses in each period.
   - With reversing entries, there is no need to examine each transaction to see whether a portion applies to the past period and then divide the amount of the transaction between the two periods.

8. **Define the accounting terms new to this chapter.**

CHAPTER 13 GLOSSARY

Classified financial statement (p. 472) A format by which revenues and expenses on the income statement, and assets and liabilities on the balance sheet, are divided into groups of similar accounts and a subtotal is given for each group

Current assets (p. 475) Assets consisting of cash, items that normally will be converted into cash within one year, or items that will be used up within one year

Current liabilities (p. 477) Debts that must be paid within one year

Current ratio (p. 484) A relationship between current assets and current liabilities that provides a measure of a firm's ability to pay its current debts (current ratio = current assets ÷ current liabilities)

Gross profit (p. 473) The difference between net sales and the cost of goods sold (gross profit = net sales − cost of goods sold)

Gross profit percentage (p. 484) The amount of gross profit from each dollar of sales (gross profit percentage = gross profit ÷ net sales)

Inventory turnover (p. 485) The number of times inventory is purchased and sold during the accounting period (inventory turnover = cost of good sold ÷ average inventory)

Liquidity (p. 476) The ease with which an item can be converted into cash

Long-term liabilities (p. 477) Debts of a business that are due more than one year in the future

Multiple-step income statement (p. 472) A type of income statement on which several subtotals are computed before the net income is calculated

Plant and equipment (p. 477) Property that will be used in the business for longer than one year

Reversing entries (p. 485) Journal entries made to reverse the effect of certain adjusting entries involving accrued income or accrued expenses to avoid problems in recording future payments or receipts of cash in a new accounting period

Single-step income statement (p. 472) A type of income statement where only one computation is needed to determine the net income (total revenue − total expenses = net income)

Comprehensive Self Review

1. Explain the difference between a single-step income statement and a multiple-step income statement.
2. How is net income from operations determined?
3. Why would a factory machine not be considered a current asset?
4. After closing entries are posted, which of the following types of accounts will have zero balances?
   a. asset accounts
   b. revenue accounts
   c. owner's drawing account
   d. liability accounts

e. Income Summary account
f. expense accounts
g. owner's capital account
h. cost of goods sold accounts

5. Describe the entry that would be made to close the **Income Summary** account in each of the following cases. The owner of the firm is Harold Hicks.
   a. There is a net income of $62,000.
   b. There is a net loss of $28,000.

(Answers to Comprehensive Self Review are on page 514.)

Discussion Questions

1. What is the difference between operating revenue and other revenues or income?
2. What are operating expenses?
3. Which section of the income statement contains information about the purchases made during the period and the beginning and ending merchandise inventory?
4. What is the purpose of the balance sheet?
5. What are current assets? Give four examples of items that would be considered current assets.
6. What is plant and equipment? Give two examples of items that would be considered plant and equipment.
7. How do current liabilities and long-term liabilities differ?
8. What information is provided by the statement of owner's equity?
9. What is the purpose of the postclosing trial balance?
10. What types of accounts appear on the postclosing trial balance?
11. Why are reversing entries helpful?
12. What types of adjustments are reversed?
13. On December 31 Chan Company made an adjusting entry debiting **Interest Receivable** and crediting **Interest Income** for $30 of accrued interest. What reversing entry would be recorded for this item as of January 1?
14. Various adjustments made at Smith Company are listed below. Which ones should normally be reversed?
    a. An adjustment for the estimated loss from uncollectible accounts
    b. An adjustment for depreciation on equipment
    c. An adjustment for accrued salaries expense
    d. An adjustment for accrued payroll taxes expense
    e. An adjustment for accrued interest expense
    f. An adjustment for supplies used
    g. An adjustment for expired insurance
    h. An adjustment for accrued interest income
15. Name the steps of the accounting cycle.

Applications

EXERCISES

Exercise 13-1 ► Objective 1

Classifying income statement items.

The following accounts appear on the worksheet of Huntsville Variety Store. Indicate the section of the classified income statement in which each account will be reported.

SECTIONS OF CLASSIFIED INCOME STATEMENT

- **a.** Operating Revenue
- **b.** Cost of Goods Sold
- **c.** Operating Expenses
- **d.** Other Income
- **e.** Other Expenses

ACCOUNTS

1. Purchases
2. Salaries Expense—Sales
3. Sales
4. Interest Expense
5. Merchandise Inventory
6. Interest Income
7. Freight In
8. Sales Returns and Allowances
9. Utilities Expense
10. Purchases Discounts

Exercise 13-2 ► Objective 3

Classifying balance sheet items.

The following accounts appear on the worksheet of Huntsville Record Store. Indicate the section of the classified balance sheet in which each account will be reported.

SECTIONS OF CLASSIFIED BALANCE SHEET

- **a.** Current Assets
- **b.** Plant and Equipment
- **c.** Current Liabilities
- **d.** Long-Term Liabilities
- **e.** Owner's Equity

ACCOUNTS

1. Sales Tax Payable
2. Cash
3. Mike Valdez, Capital
4. Building
5. Accounts Payable
6. Store Supplies
7. Mortgage Payable

8. Prepaid Insurance
9. Delivery Van
10. Accounts Receivable

Preparing a classified income statement.

◄ **Exercise 13-3**
Objective 1

The worksheet of Village Auto Supply contains the following revenue, cost, and expense accounts. Prepare a classified income statement for this firm for the year ended December 31, 20--. The merchandise inventory amounted to $54,000 on January 1, 20--, and $50,400 on December 31, 20--. The expense accounts numbered 611 through 617 represent selling expenses, and those numbered 631 through 646 represent general and administrative expenses.

ACCOUNTS

401	Sales	$247,000	Cr.
451	Sales Returns and Allowances	5,200	Dr.
491	Miscellaneous Income	220	Cr.
501	Purchases	102,000	Dr.
502	Freight In	1,800	Dr.
503	Purchases Returns and Allowances	3,000	Cr.
504	Purchases Discounts	1,600	Cr.
611	Salaries Expense—Sales	44,000	Dr.
614	Store Supplies Expense	2,200	Dr.
617	Depreciation Expense—Store Equipment	1,600	Dr.
631	Rent Expense	12,000	Dr.
634	Utilities Expense	2,800	Dr.
637	Salaries Expense—Office	20,000	Dr.
640	Payroll Taxes Expense	5,000	Dr.
643	Depreciation Expense—Office Equipment	400	Dr.
646	Uncollectible Accounts Expense	640	Dr.
691	Interest Expense	520	Dr.

Preparing a statement of owner's equity.

◄ **Exercise 13-4**
Objective 2

The worksheet of Village Auto Supply contains the following owner's equity accounts. Use this data and the net income determined in Exercise 13-3 to prepare a statement of owner's equity for the year ended December 31, 20--. No additional investments were made during the period.

ACCOUNTS

301	Sue Davis, Capital	$60,120	Cr.
302	Sue Davis, Drawing	42,000	Dr.

Preparing a classified balance sheet.

◄ **Exercise 13-5**
Objective 3

The worksheet of Village Auto Supply contains the following asset and liability accounts. The balance of the **Notes Payable** account consists of notes that are due within a year. Prepare a balance sheet dated December 31, 20--. Obtain the ending capital for the period from the statement of owner's equity completed in Exercise 13-4.

ACCOUNTS

101	Cash	$10,800	Dr.
107	Change Fund	400	Dr.
111	Accounts Receivable	5,400	Dr.
112	Allowance for Doubtful Accounts	760	Cr.

ACCOUNTS (cont.)

121	Merchandise Inventory	$50,400 Dr.
131	Store Supplies	2,000 Dr.
133	Prepaid Interest	80 Dr.
141	Store Equipment	10,200 Dr.
142	Accum. Depreciation—Store Equipment	1,600 Cr.
151	Office Equipment	3,200 Dr.
152	Accum. Depreciation—Office Equipment	400 Cr.
201	Notes Payable	5,400 Cr.
203	Accounts Payable	3,600 Cr.
216	Interest Payable	60 Cr.
231	Sales Tax Payable	2,480 Cr.

Exercise 13-6 ► Objective 5

Recording closing entries.

On December 31, 20--, the Income Statement section of the worksheet for Lozozo Company contained the following information. Give the entries that should be made in the general journal to close the revenue, cost of goods sold, expense, and other temporary accounts.

INCOME STATEMENT SECTION

	Debit	Credit
Income Summary	$ 38,000	$ 40,000
Sales		245,000
Sales Returns and Allowances	3,100	
Sales Discounts	2,300	
Interest Income		100
Purchases	125,000	
Freight In	1,700	
Purchases Returns and Allowances		1,900
Purchases Discounts		2,200
Rent Expense	8,400	
Utilities Expense	2,100	
Telephone Expense	1,300	
Salaries Expense	65,000	
Payroll Taxes Expense	5,150	
Supplies Expense	1,600	
Depreciation Expense	2,400	
Interest Expense	350	
Totals	$256,400	$289,200

Assume further that the owner of the firm is Lexi Lozozo and that the **Lexi Lozozo, Drawing** account had a balance of $26,000 on December 31, 20--.

Exercise 13-7 ► Objective 7

Journalizing reversing entries.

Examine the following adjusting entries and determine which ones should be reversed. Show the reversing entries that should be recorded in the general journal as of January 1, 2005. Include appropriate descriptions.

2004	(Adjustment a)		
Dec. 31	Uncollectible Accounts Expense	3,600.00	
	Allowance for Doubtful Accounts		3 ,600.00
	To record estimated loss from uncollectible accounts based on 0.5% of net credit sales, $720,000		

		Debit	Credit
	(Adjustment b)		
Dec. 31	Supplies Expense	4,640.00	
	Supplies		4,640.00
	To record supplies used during the year		
	(Adjustment c)		
31	Insurance Expense	1,800.00	
	Prepaid Insurance		1,800.00
	To record expired insurance on 1-year $5,400 policy purchased on Sept. 1		
	(Adjustment d)		
31	Depreciation. Exp.—Store Equipment	15,400.00	
	Accum. Depreciation—Store Equip.		15,400.00
	To record depreciation		
	(Adjustment e)		
31	Salaries Expense—Office	2,360.00	
	Salaries Payable		2,360.00
	To record accrued salaries for Dec. 29–31		
	(Adjustment f)		
31	Payroll Tax Expense	180.54	
	Social Security Tax Payable		146.32
	Medicare Tax Payable		34.22
	To record accrued payroll taxes on accrued salaries: social security, 6.2% × 2,360 = $146.32; Medicare, 1.45% × 2,360 = $34.22		
	(Adjustment g)		
31	Interest Expense	660.00	
	Interest Payable		660.00
	To record accrued interest on a 4-month, 11% trade note payable dated Oct. 1: $24,000 × 0.11 × 3/12 = $660		
	(Adjustment h)		
31	Interest Receivable	100.00	
	Interest Income		100.00
	To record interest earned on 6-month, 10% note receivable dated Nov. 1: $6,000 ×0.10 × 2/12 = $100		

Preparing a postclosing trial balance.

◄ **Exercise 13-8**
Objective 6

The Adjusted Trial Balance section of the worksheet for Lucas Implement Company follows. The owner made no additional investments during the year. Prepare a postclosing trial balance for the firm on December 31, 20--.

ACCOUNTS	Debit	Credit
Cash	$ 20,400	
Accounts Receivable	40,800	
Allowance for Doubtful Accounts		$ 120
Merchandise Inventory	189,000	
Supplies	7,140	

ACCOUNTS (cont.)	Debit	Credit
Prepaid Insurance	$ 3,060	
Equipment	51,000	
Accumulated Depreciation—Equipment		$ 16,800
Notes Payable		10,500
Accounts Payable		8,700
Social Security Tax Payable		1,392
Medicare Tax Payable		324
Don Lucas, Capital		233,430
Don Lucas, Drawing	84,000	
Income Summary	180,000	189,000
Sales		768,000
Sales Returns and Allowances	14,400	
Purchases	477,000	
Freight In	5,400	
Purchases Returns and Allowances		10,500
Purchases Discounts		6,900
Rent Expense	21,600	
Telephone Expense	3,246	
Salaries Expense	124,140	
Payroll Taxes Expense	11,100	
Supplies Expense	3,600	
Insurance Expense	660	
Depreciation Expense—Equipment	9,000	
Uncollectible Accounts Expense	120	
Totals	$1,245,666	$1,245,666

Problems

Selected problems can be completed using:
Peachtree QuickBooks Spreadsheets

PROBLEM SET A

Problem 13-1A ►
Objectives 1, 2, 3

Preparing classified financial statements.

Mayfair Company distributes electronic components to small manufacturers. The adjusted trial balance data given below is from the firm's worksheet for the year ended December 31, 20--.

INSTRUCTIONS

1. Prepare a classified income statement for the year ended December 31, 20--. The expense accounts represent warehouse expenses, selling expenses, and general and administrative expenses.
2. Prepare a statement of owner's equity for the year ended December 31, 20--. No additional investments were made during the period.
3. Prepare a classified balance sheet as of December 31, 20--. The mortgage and the loans extend for more than a year.

ACCOUNTS	Debit	Credit
Cash	$27,100	
Petty Cash Fund	400	
Notes Receivable	10,800	
Accounts Receivable	54,500	
Allowance for Doubtful Accounts		$5,000

ACCOUNTS (cont.)	Debit	Credit
Merchandise Inventory	$ 224,000	
Warehouse Supplies	2,760	
Office Supplies	1,320	
Prepaid Insurance	7,200	
Land	36,000	
Building	168,000	
Accumulated Depreciation—Building		$ 48,000
Warehouse Equipment	32,000	
Accumulated Depreciation—Warehouse Equipment		14,400
Delivery Equipment	46,000	
Accumulated Depreciation—Delivery Equipment		17,600
Office Equipment	20,000	
Accumulated Depreciation—Office Equipment		9,000
Notes Payable		19,200
Accounts Payable		42,000
Interest Payable		480
Mortgage Payable		56,000
Loans Payable		12,000
Jeff London, Capital (Jan. 1)		397,640
Jeff London, Drawing	126,000	
Income Summary	234,000	224,000
Sales		1,673,600
Sales Returns and Allowances	17,200	
Interest Income		1,480
Purchases	770,400	
Freight In	12,800	
Purchases Returns and Allowances		7,440
Purchases Discounts		10,160
Warehouse Wages Expense	189,600	
Warehouse Supplies Expense	6,100	
Depreciation Expense—Warehouse Equipment	4,800	
Salaries Expense—Sales	259,200	
Travel and Entertainment Expense	20,500	
Delivery Wages Expense	84,000	
Depreciation Expense—Delivery Equipment	8,800	
Salaries Expense—Office	69,600	
Office Supplies Expense	3,000	
Insurance Expense	5,200	
Utilities Expense	9,600	
Telephone Expense	5,520	
Payroll Taxes Expense	54,000	
Property Taxes Expense	4,600	
Uncollectible Accounts Expense	4,800	
Depreciation Expense—Building	8,000	
Depreciation Expense—Office Equipment	3,000	
Interest Expense	7,200	
Totals	$2,538,000	$2,538,000

Analyze: What is the current ratio for this business?

Problem 13-2A
Objectives 1, 2, 3

QB

Preparing classified financial statements.

Superior Auto Products distributes automobile parts to service stations and repair shops. The adjusted trial balance data that follows is from the firm's worksheet for the year ended December 31, 20--.

INSTRUCTIONS

1. Prepare a classified income statement for the year ended December 31, 20--. The expense accounts represent warehouse expenses, selling expenses, and general and administrative expenses.
2. Prepare a statement of owner's equity for the year ended December 31, 20--. No additional investments were made during the period.
3. Prepare a classified balance sheet as of December 31, 20--. The mortgage and the long-term notes extend for more than one year.

ACCOUNTS	Debit	Credit
Cash	$ 86,000	
Petty Cash Fund	400	
Notes Receivable	10,000	
Accounts Receivable	101,200	
Allowance for Doubtful Accounts		$ 2,800
Interest Receivable	200	
Merchandise Inventory	124,000	
Warehouse Supplies	2,300	
Office Supplies	600	
Prepaid Insurance	3,640	
Land	15,000	
Building	92,000	
Accumulated Depreciation—Building		14,400
Warehouse Equipment	18,800	
Accumulated Depreciation—Warehouse Equipment		9,600
Office Equipment	8,400	
Accumulated Depreciation—Office Equipment		3,040
Notes Payable—Short-Term		14,000
Accounts Payable		59,000
Interest Payable		300
Notes Payable—Long-Term		10,000
Mortgage Payable		20,000
Luis Garcia, Capital (Jan. 1)		327,020
Luis Garcia, Drawing	64,000	
Income Summary	130,400	124,000
Sales		990,200
Sales Returns and Allowances	7,400	
Interest Income		480
Purchases	438,000	
Freight In	8,800	
Purchases Returns and Allowances		11,560
Purchases Discounts		8,240
Warehouse Wages Expense	107,200	
Warehouse Supplies Expense	4,800	
Depreciation Expense—Warehouse Equipment	2,400	
Salaries Expense—Sales	150,200	
Travel Expense	23,000	
Delivery Expense	36,400	
Salaries Expense—Office	84,000	
Office Supplies Expense	1,120	
Insurance Expense	8,800	
Utilities Expense	6,000	
Telephone Expense	3,180	
Payroll Taxes Expense	30,600	

ACCOUNTS (cont.)	Debit	Credit
Building Repairs Expense	$ 2,700	
Property Taxes Expense	12,400	
Uncollectible Accounts Expense	2,580	
Depreciation Expense—Building	3,600	
Depreciation Expense—Office Equipment	1,520	
Interest Expense	3,000	
Totals	$1,594,640	$1,594,640

Analyze: What percentage of total operating expenses is attributable to warehouse expenses?

◄ **Problem 13-3A**
Objectives 4, 5, 7

Journalizing adjusting, closing, and reversing entries.

Obtain all data that is necessary from the worksheet prepared for Fitness Foods Company in Problem 12-4A. Then follow the instructions to complete this problem.

INSTRUCTIONS

1. Record adjusting entries in the general journal as of December 31, 2005. Use 25 as the first journal page number. Include descriptions for the entries.
2. Record closing entries in the general journal as of December 31, 2005. Include descriptions.
3. Record reversing entries in the general journal as of January 1, 2006. Include descriptions.

Analyze: Assuming that the firm did not record a reversing entry for salaries payable, what entry is required when salaries of $5,000 are paid in January?

◄ **Problem 13-4A**
Objectives 4, 7

Journalizing adjusting and reversing entries.

The data below concerns adjustments to be made at Lakers Company.

INSTRUCTIONS

1. Record the adjusting entries in the general journal as of December 31, 2004. Use 25 as the first journal page number. Include descriptions.
2. Record reversing entries in the general journal as of January 1, 2005. Include descriptions.

ADJUSTMENTS

a. On September 1, 2004, the firm signed a lease for a warehouse and paid rent of $16,800 in advance for a six-month period.

b. On December 31, 2004, an inventory of supplies showed that items costing $1,840 were on hand. The balance of the **Supplies** account was $11,120.

c. A depreciation schedule for the firm's equipment shows that a total of $7,800 should be charged off as depreciation for 2004.

d. On December 31, 2004, the firm owed salaries of $4,400 that will not be paid until January 2005.

e. On December 31, 2004, the firm owed the employer's social security (6.2 percent) and Medicare (1.45 percent) taxes on all accrued salaries.

f. On November 1, 2004, the firm received a four-month, 10 percent note for $5,400 from a customer with an overdue balance.

Analyze: After the adjusting entries have been posted, what is the balance of the **Prepaid Rent** account on January 1?

PROBLEM SET B

Problem 13-1B ► Objectives 1, 2, 3

Preparing classified financial statements.

The Net Store is a retail store that sells computers and computer supplies. The adjusted trial balance data given below is from the firm's worksheet for the year ended December 31, 20--.

INSTRUCTIONS

1. Prepare a classified income statement for the year ended December 31, 20--. The expense accounts represent warehouse expenses, selling expenses, and general and administrative expenses.
2. Prepare a statement of owner's equity for the year ended December 31, 20--. No additional investments were made during the period.
3. Prepare a classified balance sheet as of December 31, 20--. The mortgage and the loans extend for more than one year.

ACCOUNTS	Debit	Credit
Cash	$ 8,924	
Petty Cash Fund	100	
Notes Receivable	3,200	
Accounts Receivable	16,326	
Allowance for Doubtful Accounts		$ 2,250
Merchandise Inventory	36,000	
Warehouse Supplies	750	
Office Supplies	730	
Prepaid Insurance	2,200	
Land	7,000	
Building	48,000	
Accum. Depr.—Building		12,000
Warehouse Equipment	9,000	
Accumulated Depreciation—Warehouse Equipment		2,600
Delivery Equipment	14,000	
Accumulated Depreciation—Delivery Equipment		3,600
Office Equipment	6,000	
Accumulated Depreciation—Office Equipment		2,500
Notes Payable		5,000
Accounts Payable		12,800
Interest Payable		240
Mortgage Payable		16,000
Loans Payable		4,000
Carol Hall, Capital (Jan. 1)		60,490
Carol Hall, Drawing	24,000	
Income Summary	34,000	36,000
Sales		430,500
Sales Returns and Allowances	3,150	
Interest Income		420
Purchases	185,550	
Freight In	2,200	
Purchases Returns and Allowances		1,920
Purchases Discounts		2,350
Warehouse Wages Expense	39,400	
Warehouse Supplies Expense	1,790	
Depreciation Expense—Warehouse Equipment	1,400	

ACCOUNTS (cont.)	Debit	Credit
Salaries Expense—Sales	$ 70,200	
Travel and Entertainment Expense	6,300	
Delivery Wages Expense	24,000	
Depreciation Expense—Delivery Equipment	2,400	
Salaries Expense—Office	15,900	
Office Supplies Expense	950	
Insurance Expense	1,500	
Utilities Expense	2,800	
Telephone Expense	1,380	
Payroll Taxes Expense	15,100	
Property Taxes Expense	1,750	
Uncollectible Accounts Expense	1,050	
Depreciation Expense—Building	3,000	
Depreciation Expense—Office Equipment	1,020	
Interest Expense	1,600	
Totals	$592,670	$592,670

Analyze: What is the gross profit percentage for the period ended December 31, 20--?

◄ **Problem 13-2B**
Objectives 1, 2, 3

Preparing classified financial statements.

Motor Center is a retail firm that sells motorcycles, parts, and accessories. The adjusted trial balance data given below is from the firm's worksheet for the year ended December 31, 20--.

INSTRUCTIONS

1. Prepare a classified income statement for the year ended December 31, 20--. The expense accounts represent warehouse expenses, selling expenses, and general and administrative expenses.
2. Prepare a statement of owner's equity for the year ended December 31, 20--. No additional investments were made during the period.
3. Prepare a classified balance sheet as of December 31, 20--. The mortgage and the long-term notes extend for more than one year.

ACCOUNTS	Debit	Credit
Cash	$ 13,200	
Petty Cash Fund	200	
Notes Receivable	6,000	
Accounts Receivable	55,000	
Allowance for Doubtful Accounts		$ 5,000
Interest Receivable	200	
Merchandise Inventory	85,000	
Warehouse Supplies	3,700	
Office Supplies	1,800	
Prepaid Insurance	7,200	
Land	18,000	
Building	54,000	
Accumulated Depreciation—Building		8,400
Warehouse Equipment	24,000	
Accumulated Depreciation—Warehouse Equipment		4,000
Office Equipment	12,800	
Accumulated Depreciation—Office Equipment		1,800
Notes Payable—Short-Term		8,000
Accounts Payable		32,500

ACCOUNTS (cont.)	Debit	Credit
Interest Payable		$ 600
Notes Payable—Long-Term		6,000
Mortgage Payable		32,000
Ruby Mitchell, Capital (Jan. 1)		200,170
Ruby Mitchell, Drawing	$ 56,000	
Income Summary	89,000	85,000
Sales		602,902
Sales Returns and Allowances	9,400	
Interest Income		720
Purchases	225,000	
Freight In	9,600	
Purchases Returns and Allowances		6,200
Purchases Discounts		4,340
Warehouse Wages Expense	63,500	
Warehouse Supplies Expense	4,300	
Depreciation Expense—Warehouse Equipment	2,400	
Salaries Expense—Sales	79,100	
Travel Expense	21,000	
Delivery Expense	35,400	
Salaries Expense—Office	46,000	
Office Supplies Expense	1,360	
Insurance Expense	9,120	
Utilities Expense	6,912	
Telephone Expense	3,740	
Payroll Taxes Expense	28,800	
Building Repairs Expense	3,100	
Property Taxes Expense	11,700	
Uncollectible Accounts Expense	2,620	
Depreciation Expense—Building	3,200	
Depreciation Expense—Office Equipment	1,680	
Interest Expense	3,600	
Totals	$997,632	$997,632

Analyze: What is the inventory turnover for Motor Center?

Problem 13-3B ►
Objectives 4, 5, 7

Journalizing adjusting, closing, and reversing entries.

Obtain all data that is necessary from the worksheet prepared for Village Novelties in Problem 12-4B. Then follow the instructions to complete this problem.

INSTRUCTIONS

1. Record adjusting entries in the general journal as of December 31, 2005. Use 29 as the first journal page number. Include descriptions for the entries.
2. Record closing entries in the general journal as of December 31, 2005. Include descriptions.
3. Record reversing entries in the general journal as of January 1, 2006. Include descriptions.

Analyze: Assuming that the company did not record a reversing entry for salaries payable, what entry is required when salaries of $1,200 are paid in January?

Journalizing adjusting and reversing entries.

◄ **Problem 13-4B**
Objectives 4, 7

The data below concerns adjustments to be made at Najar Company.

INSTRUCTIONS

1. Record the adjusting entries in the general journal as of December 31, 2005. Use 25 as the first journal page number. Include descriptions.
2. Record reversing entries in the general journal as of January 1, 2006. Include descriptions.

ADJUSTMENTS

a. On August 1, 2005, the firm signed a one-year advertising contract with a trade magazine and paid the entire amount, $6,000, in advance. **Prepaid Advertising** has a balance of $6,000.

b. On December 31, 2005, an inventory of supplies showed that items costing $1,500 were on hand. The balance of the **Supplies** account was $6,980.

c. A depreciation schedule for the firm's equipment shows that a total of $5,260 should be charged off as depreciation for 2005.

d. On December 31, 2005, the firm owed salaries of $3,200 that will not be paid until January 2006.

e. On December 31, 2005, the firm owed the employer's social security (6.2 percent) and Medicare (1.45 percent) taxes on all accrued salaries.

f. On October 1, 2005, the firm received a six-month, 12 percent note for $4,400 from a customer with an overdue balance.

Analyze: Assuming that the company did not make a reversing entry for salaries payable, what entry would be required to record the payment of salaries of $3,500 in January?

CHAPTER 13 CHALLENGE PROBLEM

Year-End Processing

Software Center is a retail firm that sells computer programs for home and business use. On December 31, 2005, its general ledger contained the accounts and balances shown below.

ACCOUNTS	BALANCES
Cash	$ 13,600 Dr.
Accounts Receivable	27,200 Dr.
Allowance for Doubtful Accounts	80 Cr.
Merchandise Inventory	62,000 Dr.
Supplies	4,760 Dr.
Prepaid Insurance	2,040 Dr.
Equipment	34,000 Dr.
Accumulated Depreciation—Equipment	11,200 Cr.
Notes Payable	7,000 Cr.
Accounts Payable	5,800 Cr.
Social Security Tax Payable	560 Cr.
Medicare Tax Payable	130 Cr.
Matt Alexi, Capital	92,246 Cr.
Matt Alexi, Drawing	50,000 Dr.
Sales	512,348 Cr.
Sales Returns and Allowances	9,600 Dr.
Purchases	318,000 Dr.
Freight In	3,600 Dr.
Purchases Returns and Allowances	7,000 Cr.
Purchases Discounts	4,600 Cr.
Rent Expense	14,400 Dr.
Telephone Expense	2,164 Dr.
Salaries Expense	92,000 Dr.
Payroll Taxes Expense	7,400 Dr.
Interest Expense	200 Dr.

The following accounts had zero balances:

Interest Payable
Salaries Payable
Income Summary
Supplies Expense
Insurance Expense
Depreciation Expense—Equipment
Uncollectible Accounts Expense

The data needed for the adjustments on December 31 are as follows:

a.–b. Ending merchandise inventory, $68,000.

c. Uncollectible accounts, 0.6 percent of net credit sales of $230,000.

d. Supplies on hand December 31, $1,100.

e. Expired insurance, $1,190.

f. **Depreciation Expense—Equipment,** $5,600.

g. Accrued interest expense on notes payable, $280.

h. Accrued salaries, $1,600.

i. **Social Security Tax Payable** (6.2 percent) and **Medicare Tax Payable** (1.45 percent) of accrued salaries.

INSTRUCTIONS

1. Prepare a worksheet for the year ended December 31, 2005.
2. Prepare a classified income statement. The firm does not divide its operating expenses into selling and administrative expenses.
3. Prepare a statement of owner's equity. No additional investments were made during the period.
4. Prepare a classified balance sheet. All notes payable are due within one year.
5. Journalize the adjusting entries.
6. Journalize the closing entries.
7. Journalize the reversing entries.

Analyze: By what percentage did the owner's capital account change in the period from January 1, 2005, to December 31, 2005?

CHAPTER 13 CRITICAL THINKING PROBLEM

Classified Balance Sheet

Tommie Jones is the owner of Clothing Galore, a store specializing in women's and children's sweaters. During the past year, in response to increased demand, Tommie doubled her selling space by expanding into the vacant store next to Clothing Galore. This expansion has been expensive because of the need to increase inventory and to purchase new store fixtures and equipment. Tommie notes that the company's cash position has gone down, and she is worried about paying for the expansion. Tommie shows you balance sheet data for the current year and last year and asks your opinion on the company's ability to pay for the recent expansion.

	December 31, 2004		December 31, 2005	
Assets				
Cash	100,000		20,000	
Accounts Receivable	30,000		61,000	
Inventory	70,000		156,000	
Prepaid Expenses	4,000		6,000	
Store Fixtures and Equipment	120,000		260,000	
Total Assets		324,000		503,000
Liabilities and Owner's Equity				
Liabilities				
Notes Payable (due in 5 years)	60,000		160,000	
Accounts Payable	88,000		114,000	
Salaries Payable	12,000		13,000	
Total Liabilities		160,000		287,000
Owner's Equity				
Tommie Jones, Capital		164,000		216,000
Total Liabilities and Owner's Equity		324,000		503,000

INSTRUCTIONS

1. Prepare classified balance sheets for Clothing Galore for the years 2004 and 2005.
2. Based on the information that is presented in the classified balance sheets, what is your opinion of Clothing Galore's ability to pay its current bills in a timely manner?
3. What is the advantage of a classified balance sheet over a balance sheet that is not classified?

Business Connections

MANAGERIAL FOCUS **Understanding Financial Statements** ◄ **Connection 1**

1. Why should management be concerned about the efficiency of the end-of-period procedures?
2. Spector Company had an increase in sales and net income during its last fiscal year, but cash decreased and the firm was having difficulty paying its bills by the end of the year. What factors might cause a shortage of cash even though a firm is profitable?
3. For the last three years, the balance sheet of Desai Hardware Center, a large retail store, has shown a substantial increase in merchandise inventory. Why might management be concerned about this development?
4. Why is it important to compare the financial statements of the current year with those of prior years?
5. Should a manager be concerned if the balance sheet shows a large increase in current liabilities and a large decrease in current assets? Explain your answer.
6. The latest income statement prepared at Wilkes Company shows that net sales increased by 10 percent over the previous year and selling expenses increased by 25 percent. Do you think that management should investigate the reasons for the increase in selling expenses? Why or why not?
7. Why is it useful for management to compare a firm's financial statements with financial information from other companies in the same industry?

Ethical DILEMMA **Current or Long-Term?** The owner of the health and beauty aids store where you are employed has received a bank loan of $50,000 that requires her to maintain a current ratio of at least 1.3 to 1. On December 31 the business also owes $135,000 on a mortgage on the company's land and building. Of the $135,000, $15,000 falls due within the next 12 months. The current assets on December 31 are $125,000, and other current liabilities are $94,000. Sue, the owner, suggests that you include the entire $135,000 mortgage balance as long-term so that the bank loan covenant will be met ($125,000/$94,000 = 1.33 to 1). What will you do in response to this suggestion? ◄ **Connection 2**

Street ***WISE:*** Questions from the Real World **Financial Performance** Refer to The Home Depot, Inc. *1999 Annual Report* in Appendix B. ◄ **Connection 3**

1. Locate the consolidated statements of earnings. What gross profit was reported for the year ended January 30, 2000? For January 31,1999? If the company had targeted a 25 percent increase in gross profit between fiscal 1998 and fiscal 1999, was the goal achieved?
2. Using the financial statements, calculate the following measurements of financial performance and condition for The Home Depot, Inc. as of January 30, 2000.

a. Gross profit percentage

b. Current ratio

Connection 4 ► **FINANCIAL $TATEMENT ANALYSIS** **Balance Sheet** The following excerpts were taken from the Mattel, Inc. *1999 Annual Report.*

Consolidated Balance Sheets

(in thousands)	December 31 *1999*	*1998*
Assets		
Current Assets		
Cash and short-term investments	*$ 275,024*	*$ 469,213*
Accounts receivable, less allowances of $229.2 million at December 31, 1999, and $125.1 million at December 31, 1998	*1,270,005*	*1,150,051*
Inventories	*544,296*	*644,270*
Prepaid expenses and other current assets	*330,702*	*371,772*
Total current assets	*2,420,027*	*2,635,306*
Liabilities and Stockholders' Equity		
Current Liabilities		
Short-term borrowings	*$ 369,549*	*$ 199,006*
Current portion of long-term liabilities	*3,173*	*33,666*
Accounts payable	*360,609*	*362,467*
Accrued liabilities	*825,874*	*748,837*
Income taxes payable	*258,319*	*299,058*
Total current liabilities	*1,817,524*	*1,643,034*

Analyze:

1. What is the current ratio for 1999? For 1998?
2. Has the ratio improved from 1998 to 1999? Why or why not?
3. The company reported net sales of $5,514,950,000 and gross profit of $2,601,040,000 for the period ended December 31, 1999. What is the gross profit percentage for this period?

Analyze Online: On the Mattel, Inc. Web site **(www.mattel.com),** find the investor relations section. Locate the consolidated statements of operations and the consolidated balance sheets within the most recent annual report. Answer the following questions.

4. What is the current ratio?
5. What is the gross profit percentage?
6. Compare these calculations with your calculations for 1999. Based on these two measurements, do you think the company is in a better financial position than it was in 1999? Why or why not?

Extending the Thought **Annual Report** Once the year-end financial statements have been prepared, companies often publish an annual report, containing both financial and nonfinancial information about the company's operation over the past fiscal year.

◄ **Connection 5**

In addition to the financial statements for the period, the report frequently includes

- a letter to its shareholders,
- management's discussion and analysis of the company's performance,
- notes that accompany the financial statements.

Although there is no comprehensive list of items that should be disclosed in an annual report, the accountants of the business must use their best professional judgement when deciding what information to include. What types of information do you think should be included in a company's annual report? Why?

Business Communication **Memo** You have been placed in charge of the closing process for Magnolia Tree Services for the period ending December 31. Time is short, and you must delegate the closing tasks to three accountants in your department: Brenda Calhoun, Sean Miele, and Cassandra Wilson. Write an e-mail to your co-workers, assigning each of them specific tasks to complete by the end of the week. In the e-mail, list the required closing tasks and identify which employee is responsible for each task. Make sure that your co-workers understand the order of the tasks that they are to perform.

◄ **Connection 6**

TeamWork **Interpreting Financial Statements** Locate the Web site for a major corporation such as Sara Lee Corporation or McDonald's Corporation. Then do the following:

◄ **Connection 7**

- Locate the most recent annual report found in the company's investor relations section of the site.
- Review the balance sheet and statement of earnings for the corporation.
- Compute the gross profit percentage and the current ratio for the current year and the previous year.
- Write a report about the trends you discover based on these computations.

interNET CONNECTION **Credit Counseling** The National Foundation for Credit Counseling is a national nonprofit agency that provides counseling for credit problems. Go to the organization's Web site at **www.nfcc.org.** How often do they recommend checking your credit report? Under what circumstances are you able to obtain a free report?

◄ **Connection 8**

Answers to Self Reviews

Answers to Section 1 Self Review

1. Statements on which the revenues, expenses, assets, and liabilities are divided into groups of similar accounts with a subtotal given for each group.
2. To show the results of operations for a specific period of time.
3. The difference between the net sales and the cost of goods sold.
4. **a.** Equipment
5. **c.** Cost of Goods Sold section of the income statement.
6. Net delivered cost of purchases are understated. Operating expenses are overstated. The net income from operations is unchanged.

Answers to Section 2 Self Review

1. To complete the financial records for the accounting period.
2. To show how the adjustments were determined.
3. **a.** Debit the revenue accounts and other temporary accounts with credit balances. Credit **Income Summary** for the total.
   b. Debit the **Income Summary** account for the total of the balances of the expense accounts and other temporary accounts with debit balances. Credit each account balance listed.
   c. Transfer the balance of the **Income Summary** account to the owner's capital account.
   d. Transfer the balance of the owner's drawing account to the owner's capital account.
4. **a.** depreciation.
5. **d.** current assets divided by current liabilities.
6. If the accountant correctly allocates the payment between the payroll taxes expense account and the liability account, there will be no effect on financial statements in the current period.
   If the accountant records the entire payment in the payroll taxes expense account, payroll taxes expense will be overstated for the period, net income will be understated, and payroll tax liabilities will be overstated.

Answers to Comprehensive Self Review

1. Single-step: all revenues are listed in one section and all expenses in another section. Multiple step: various sections in which subtotals and totals are computed before the net income is presented.
2. Deduct the total of the operating expenses from the gross profit on sales.
3. Long-term asset, classified as plant and equipment.
4. **b.** revenue accounts
   c. owner's drawing account
   e. Income Summary account
   f. expense accounts
   h. cost of goods sold accounts
5. **a.** Debit **Income Summary** and credit **Harold Hicks, Capital** for $62,000.
   b. Debit **Harold Hicks, Capital** and credit **Income Summary** for $28,000.

MINI-PRACTICE SET 2

Merchandising Business Accounting Cycle

Best for Less

Best for Less is a retail merchandising business that sells brand-name clothing at discount prices. The firm is owned and managed by Peg Rezak, who started the business on May 1, 2004. This project will give you an opportunity to put your knowledge of accounting into practice as you handle the accounting work of Best for Less during the month of October 2004.

INTRODUCTION

Best for Less has a monthly accounting period. The firm's chart of accounts is shown on page 516. The journals used to record transactions are the sales journal, purchases journal, cash receipts journal, cash payments journal, and general journal. Postings are made from the journals to the accounts receivable ledger, accounts payable ledger, and general ledger. The employees are paid at the end of the month. A computerized payroll service prepares all payroll records and checks.

INSTRUCTIONS

1. Open the general ledger accounts and enter the balances for October 1, 2004. Obtain the necessary figures from the postclosing trial balance prepared on September 30, 2004, which is shown on page 520. (If you are using the *Study Guide & Working Papers,* you will find that the general ledger accounts are already open.)
2. Open the subsidiary ledger accounts and enter the balances for October 1, 2004. Obtain the necessary figures from the schedule of accounts payable and schedule of accounts receivable prepared on September 30, 2004, which appear on page 520. (If you are using the *Study Guide & Working Papers,* you will find that the subsidiary ledger accounts are already open.)
3. Analyze the transactions for October and record each transaction in the proper journal. (Use 10 as the number for the first page of each special journal and 16 as the number for the first page of the general journal.)
4. Post the individual entries that involve customer and creditor accounts from the journals to the subsidiary ledgers on a daily basis. Post the individual entries that appear in the general journal and in the Other Accounts sections of the cash receipts and cash payments journals to the general ledger on a daily basis.
5. Total, prove, and rule the special journals as of October 31, 2004.
6. Post the column totals from the special journals to the general ledger accounts.

Best for Less
Chart of Accounts

Assets	Revenue
101 Cash	401 Sales
111 Accounts Receivable	402 Sales Returns and Allowances
112 Allowance for Doubtful Accounts	**Cost of Goods Sold**
121 Merchandise Inventory	501 Purchases
131 Supplies	502 Freight In
133 Prepaid Insurance	503 Purchases Returns and Allowances
135 Prepaid Advertising	504 Purchases Discounts
141 Equipment	**Expenses**
142 Accumulated Depreciation—Equipment	611 Advertising Expense
Liabilities	614 Depreciation Expense—Equipment
203 Accounts Payable	617 Insurance Expense
221 Social Security Tax Payable	620 Uncollectible Accounts Expense
222 Medicare Tax Payable	623 Payroll Processing Expense
223 Federal Income Tax Withholding Payable	626 Payroll Taxes Expense
225 Federal Unemployment Tax Payable	629 Rent Expense
227 State Unemployment Tax Payable	632 Salaries Expense
229 Salaries Payable	635 Supplies Expense
231 Sales Tax Payable	638 Telephone Expense
Owner's Equity	644 Utilities Expense
301 Peg Rezak, Capital	
302 Peg Rezak, Drawing	
399 Income Summary	

7. Check the accuracy of the subsidiary ledgers by preparing a schedule of accounts receivable and a schedule of accounts payable as of October 31, 2004. Compare the totals with the balances of the **Accounts Receivable** account and the **Accounts Payable** account in the general ledger.
8. Check the accuracy of the general ledger by preparing a trial balance in the first two columns of a 10-column worksheet. Make sure that the total debits and the total credits are equal.
9. Complete the Adjustments section of the worksheet. Use the following data. Identify each adjustment with the appropriate letter.
   a. During October the firm had net credit sales of $9,240. From experience with similar businesses, the previous accountant had estimated that 0.8 percent of the firm's net credit sales would result in uncollectible accounts. Record an adjustment for the expected loss from uncollectible accounts for the month of October.

- **b.** On October 31 an inventory of the supplies showed that items costing $2,840 were on hand. Record an adjustment for the supplies used in October.
- **c.** On September 30, 2004, the firm purchased a one-year insurance policy for $8,100. Record an adjustment for the expired insurance for October.
- **d.** On October 1 the firm signed a four-month advertising contract for $2,800 with a local radio station and paid the full amount in advance. Record an adjustment for the expired advertising for October.
- **e.** On May 1, 2004, the firm purchased equipment for $83,000. The equipment was estimated to have a useful life of five years and a salvage value of $8,600. Record an adjustment for depreciation on the equipment for October.
- **f.–g.** Based on a physical count, ending merchandise inventory was determined to be $80,200.

10. Complete the Adjusted Trial Balance section of the worksheet.

11. Determine the net income or net loss for October and complete the worksheet.

12. Prepare a classified income statement for the month ended October 31, 2004. (The firm does not divide its operating expenses into selling and administrative expenses.)

13. Prepare a statement of owner's equity for the month ended October 31, 2004.

14. Prepare a classified balance sheet as of October 31, 2004.

15. Journalize and post the adjusting entries using general journal page 17.

16. Prepare and post the closing entries using general journal page 18.

17. Prepare a postclosing trial balance.

DATE		TRANSACTIONS
Oct.	1	Issued Check 601 for $3,200 to pay the monthly rent.
	1	Signed a four-month radio advertising contract for $2,800; issued Check 602 to pay the full amount in advance.
	2	Received $470 from Carol Damus, a credit customer, in payment of her account.
	2	Issued Check 603 for $17,820 to remit the sales tax owed for July through September to the state sales tax agency.
	2	Issued Check 604 for $6,701.24 to Able Fashions, a creditor, in payment of Invoice 9387 ($6,838.00), less a cash discount ($136.76).
	3	Sold merchandise on credit for $2,480 plus sales tax of $124 to Vince Ramos, Sales Slip 241.
		Continued

DATE		(cont.) TRANSACTIONS
Oct.	4	Issued Check 605 for $1,000 to purchase supplies.
	4	Issued Check 606 for $8,547.56 to Young Togs, a creditor, in payment of Invoice 5671 ($8,722.00), less a cash discount ($174.44).
	5	Collected $1,220 on account from Sharon Scott, a credit customer.
	5	Accepted a return of merchandise from Vince Ramos. The merchandise was originally sold on Sales Slip 241, dated October 3; issued Credit Memorandum 18 for $630, which includes sales tax of $30.
	5	Issued Check 607 for $1,470 to Classic Styles Inc., a creditor, in payment of Invoice 3292 ($1,500), less a cash discount ($30).
	6	Had cash sales of $17,200 plus sales tax of $860 during October 1–6.
	8	Keith Larson, a credit customer, sent a check for $832 to pay the balance he owes.
	8	Issued Check 608 for $1,884 to deposit social security tax ($702), Medicare tax ($162), and federal income tax withholding ($1,020) from the September payroll.
	9	Sold merchandise on credit for $1,840 plus sales tax of $92 to Diane Nichols, Sales Slip 242.
	10	Issued Check 609 for $2,000 to pay for a newspaper advertisement that appeared in October.
	11	Purchased merchandise for $4,820 from Able Fashions, Invoice 9422, dated October 8; the terms are 2/10, n/30.
	12	Issued Check 610 for $300 to pay freight charges to the trucking company that delivered merchandise from Able Fashions on September 27 and October 11.
	13	Had cash sales of $11,520 plus sales tax of $576 during October 8–13.
	15	Sold merchandise on credit for $1,940 plus sales tax of $97 to Keith Larson, Sales Slip 243.
	16	Made a purchase of discontinued merchandise; paid for it immediately with Check 611 for $4,600.
	16	Received $486 on account from Vince Ramos, a credit customer.
	16	Issued Check 612 for $4,723.60 to Able Fashions, a creditor, in payment of Invoice 9422 ($4,820.00), less a cash discount ($96.40).

Continued

DATE	(cont.) TRANSACTIONS
Oct. 18	Issued Check 613 for $6,000 to Peg Rezak as a withdrawal for personal use.
20	Had cash sales of $12,800 plus sales tax of $640 during October 15–20.
22	Issued Check 614 for $760 to pay the monthly electric bill.
24	Sold merchandise on credit for $820 plus sales tax of $41 to Carol Damus, Sales Slip 244.
25	Purchased merchandise for $3,120 from Classic Styles Inc., Invoice 3418, dated October 23; the terms are 2/10, n/30.
26	Issued Check 615 for $480 to pay the monthly telephone bill.
27	Had cash sales of $12,240 plus sales tax of $612 during October 22–27.
29	Received Credit Memorandum 175 for $430 from Classic Styles Inc. for defective goods that were returned. The original purchase was made on Invoice 3418, dated October 23.
29	Sold merchandise on credit for $2,760 plus sales tax of $138 to Sharon Scott, Sales Slip 245.
29	Recorded the October payroll. The records prepared by the payroll service show the following totals: earnings, $10,800; social security, $702; Medicare, $162; income tax, $1,020; and net pay, $8,916.
29	Recorded the employer's payroll taxes, which were calculated by the payroll service: social security, $702; Medicare, $162; federal unemployment tax, $118; and state unemployment tax, $584.
30	Purchased merchandise for $2,300 from Young Togs, Invoice 5821, dated October 26; the terms are 1/10, n/30.
31	Issued Check 616 for $8,916 to pay the October payroll.
31	Issued Check 617 for $200 to pay the fee owed to the payroll service for processing the October payroll.
31	Had cash sales of $1,440 plus sales tax of $72 for October 29–31.

Analyze: Compare the end-of-period accounting procedures of Best for Less to the end-of-period procedures for Carter Consulting Services in Chapters 2–6. How do the procedures for a merchandising business differ from the procedures for a service business? How are they similar?

Best for Less
Postclosing Trial Balance
September 30, 2004

ACCOUNT NAME	DEBIT	CREDIT
Cash	60 700 00	
Accounts Receivable	5 188 00	
Allowance for Doubtful Accounts		234 00
Merchandise Inventory	87 400 00	
Supplies	4 400 00	
Prepaid Insurance	8 100 00	
Equipment	83 000 00	
Accumulated Depreciation—Equipment		6 060 00
Accounts Payable		17 060 00
Social Security Tax Payable		702 00
Medicare Tax Payable		162 00
Federal Income Tax Withholding Payable		1 020 00
Federal Unemployment Tax Payable		512 00
State Unemployment Tax Payable		1 268 00
Sales Tax Payable		17 820 00
Peg Rezak, Capital		203 950 00
Totals	248 788 00	248 788 00

Best for Less
Schedule of Accounts Payable
September 30, 2004

Able Fashions	6 838 00
Classic Styles Inc.	1 500 00
Young Togs	8 722 00
Total	17 060 00

Best for Less
Schedule of Accounts Receivable
September 30, 2004

Jan Adams	820 00
Carol Damus	470 00
Keith Larson	832 00
Diane Nichols	224 00
Michael O'Mara	1 136 00
Vince Ramos	486 00
Sharon Scott	1 220 00
Total	5 188 00

APPENDIX A

Combined Journal

Most small businesses have just a few employees and can devote only a limited amount of time to the preparation of accounting records. To serve the needs of these businesses, accountants have developed certain types of record systems that have special time-saving and labor-saving features but still produce all the necessary financial information for management. One example of such a system is the combined journal discussed in this appendix.

Small firms play an important role in our economy today. In fact, almost one-half of the businesses in the United States are classified as small firms. Despite their limited size, these businesses need good accounting systems that can produce accurate and timely information.

Systems Involving the Combined Journal

The **combined journal**, also called the *combination journal*, provides the cornerstone for a simple yet effective accounting system in many small firms. As its name indicates, this journal combines features of the general journal and the special journals in a single record.

If a small business has enough transactions to make the general journal difficult to use but too few transactions to make it worthwhile to set up special journals, the combined journal offers a solution. It has many of the advantages of special journals but provides the simplicity of a single journal. Like the special journals, the combined journal contains separate money columns for the accounts used most often to record a firm's transactions. This speeds up the initial entry of transactions and permits summary postings at the end of the month. Most transactions can be recorded on a single line, and the need to write account names is minimized.

Other Accounts columns allow the recording of transactions that do not fit into any of the special columns. These columns are also used for entries that would normally appear in the general journal, such as adjusting and closing entries.

Some small firms just use a combined journal and a general ledger in their accounting systems. Others need one or more subsidiary ledgers in addition to the general ledger.

Designing a Combined Journal

To function effectively, a combined journal must be designed to meet the specific needs of a firm. For a new business, the accountant first studies the proposed operations and develops an appropriate chart of accounts. Then the accountant decides which accounts are likely to be used often enough in recording daily transactions to justify special columns in the combined journal.

COMBINED JOURNAL

	DATE		CK. NO.	DESCRIPTION	POST. REF.	CASH		ACCOUNTS RECEIVABLE	
						DEBIT	CREDIT	DEBIT	CREDIT
1	2005								
2	Jan.	3	842	Rent for month			900 00		
3		5		David Levine	✓			60 00	
4		6		United Chemicals Inc.	✓				
5		7		Cash sales		1150 00			
6		7	843	Payroll			520 00		
7		10		Marion Brown	✓	45 00			45 00
8		12		Pacific Products Corp.	✓				
9		13		Thomas Nolan	✓	70 00			70 00
10		14		Cash sales		1385 00			
11		14	844	Payroll			520 00		
12		17		Joyce Miller	✓			55 00	
13		18		Alvarez Company	✓				
14		19	845	Telephone service			82 00		
15		20		Carl Janowski	✓	64 00			64 00
16		20		Dorothy Russell	✓			33 00	
17		21		Cash sales		1270 00			
18		21	846	Payroll	✓		520 00		
19		24		Ace Plastic Bags	✓				
20		25		Roger DeKoven	✓			56 00	
21		26	847	Bell Corporation			230 00		
22		28		Cash sales		1100 00			
23		28	848	Payroll			520 00		
24		30		Note issued for purchase					
25				of cleaning equipment					
26		31		Leslie Stewart	✓			41 00	
27		31		Totals		5084 00	3292 00	245 00	179 00
28						(101)	(101)	(111)	(111)

▲ **FIGURE A-1** Combined Journal

Consider the combined journal shown above which belongs to the B & H Laundry and Dry Cleaning Services, a small business that provides laundry and dry cleaning services. In designing this journal before the firm opened, the accountant established a Cash section with Debit and Credit columns because it was known that the business would constantly be receiving cash from customers and paying out cash for expenses and other obligations. Debit and Credit columns were also set up in Accounts Receivable and Accounts Payable sections because the firm planned to offer credit to qualified customers and would make credit purchases of supplies and other items.

After further analysis it was realized that the business would have numerous entries for the sale of services, the payment of employee salaries, and the purchase of supplies. Therefore, columns were established for recording credits to **Sales,** debits to **Salaries Expense,** and debits to **Supplies.** Finally, a column was set up for an Other Accounts section to take care of transactions that cannot be entered in the special columns.

PAGE 1

ACCOUNTS PAYABLE DEBIT	ACCOUNTS PAYABLE CREDIT	SALES CREDIT	SUPPLIES EXPENSE DEBIT	SALARIES EXPENSE DEBIT	OTHER ACCOUNTS: ACCOUNT NAME	POST REF.	DEBIT	CREDIT	
									1
					Rent expense	*511*	*900 00*		2
		60 00							3
	210 00		*210 00*						4
		1150 00							5
				520 00					6
									7
	90 00		*90 00*						8
									9
		1385 00							10
				520 00					11
		55 00							12
	600 00				*Equipment*	*131*	*600 00*		13
					Telephone exp.	*514*	*82 00*		14
									15
		33 00							16
		1270 00							17
				520 00					18
	145 00		*145 00*						19
		56 00							20
230 00									21
		1100 00							22
				520 00					23
									24
					Equipment	*131*	*1500 00*		25
		41 00			*Notes Payable*	*201*		*1500 00*	26
230 00	*1045 00*	*5150 00*	*445 00*	*2080 00*			*3082 00*	*1500 00*	27
(202)	*(202)*	*(401)*	*(121)*	*(517)*			*(X)*	*(X)*	28

Recording Transactions in the Combined Journal

The combined journal shown in Figure A-1 contains the January 2005 transactions of B & H Laundry and Dry Cleaning Services. Notice that most of these transactions require only a single line and involve the use of just the special columns. The entries for major types of transactions are explained in the following paragraphs.

Payment of Expenses. During January, B & H Laundry and Dry Cleaning Services issued checks to pay three kinds of expenses: rent, telephone service, and employee salaries. Notice how the payment of the monthly rent on January 3 was recorded in the combined journal. Since there is no special column for rent expense, the debit part of this entry appears in the Other Accounts section. The offsetting credit appears in the Cash Credit column. The payment of the monthly telephone bill on January 19 was recorded in a similar manner. However, when employee salaries were paid on January 7, 14, 21, and 28, both parts of the entries could be made in special columns. Because the firm has a weekly payroll period, a separate column in the combined journal was set up for debits to Salaries Expense.

Sales on Credit. On January 5, 17, 20, 25, and 31, B & H Laundry and Dry Cleaning Services sold services on credit. The necessary entries were made in two special columns of the combined journal—the Accounts Receivable Debit column and the Sales Credit column.

Cash Sales. Entries for the firm's weekly cash sales were recorded on January 7, 14, 21, and 28. Again, special columns were used—the Cash Debit column and the Sales Credit column.

Cash Received on Account. When B & H Laundry and Dry Cleaning Services collected cash on account from credit customers on January 10, 13, and 20, the transactions were entered in the Cash Debit column and the Accounts Receivable Credit column.

Purchases of Supplies on Credit. Because the firm's combined journal includes a Supplies Debit column and an Accounts Payable Credit column, all purchases of supplies on credit can be recorded in special columns. Refer to the entries made on January 6, 12, and 24.

Purchases of Equipment on Credit. On January 18, B & H Laundry and Dry Cleaning Services bought some store equipment on credit. Since there is no special column for equipment, the debit part of the entry was made in the Other Accounts section. The offsetting credit appears in the Accounts Payable Credit column.

Payments on Account. Any payments made on account to creditors are recorded in two special columns—Accounts Payable Debit and Cash Credit, as shown in the entry of January 26.

Issuance of a Promissory Note. On January 30 the business purchased new cleaning equipment and issued a promissory note to the seller. Notice that both the debit to Equipment and the credit to Notes Payable had to be recorded in the Other Accounts section.

Posting from the Combined Journal

One of the advantages of the combined journal is that it simplifies the posting process. All amounts in the special columns can be posted to the general ledger on a summary basis at the end of the month. Only the figures that appear in the Other Accounts section require individual postings to the general ledger during the month. Of course, if the firm has subsidiary ledgers, individual postings must also be made to these ledgers.

Daily Postings. The procedures followed at B & H Laundry and Dry Cleaning Services will illustrate the techniques used to post from the combined journal. Each day any entries appearing in the Other Accounts section are posted to the proper accounts in the general ledger. For example, refer to the combined journal shown on pages A-2 and A-3. The five amounts listed in the Other Accounts Debit and Credit columns were posted individually during the month. The account numbers recorded in the Posting Reference column of the Other Accounts section show that the postings have been made.

Because B & H Laundry and Dry Cleaning Services has subsidiary ledgers for accounts receivable and accounts payable, individual postings were also made on a daily basis to these ledgers. As each amount was posted, a check mark was placed in the Posting Reference column of the combined journal.

End-of-Month Postings. At the end of the month, the combined journal is totaled, proved, and ruled. Then the totals of the special columns are posted to the general ledger. Proving the combined journal involves a comparison of the column totals to make sure that the debits and credits are equal. The following procedure is used:

Proof of Combined Journal

	Debits
Cash Debit Column	$ 5,084
Accounts Receivable Debit Column	245
Accounts Payable Debit Column	230
Supplies Expense Debit Column	445
Salaries Expense Debit Column	2,080
Other Accounts Debit Column	3,082
	$11,166

	Credits
Cash Credit Column	$ 3,292
Accounts Receivable Credit Column	179
Accounts Payable Credit Column	1,045
Sales Credit Column	5,150
Other Accounts Credit Column	1,500
	$11,166

After the combined journal is proved, all column totals except those in the Other Accounts section are posted to the appropriate general ledger accounts. As each total is posted, the account number is entered beneath the column in the journal. Notice that an X is used to indicate that the column totals in the Other Accounts section are not posted, since the individual amounts were posted on a daily basis.

Typical Uses of the Combined Journal

The combined journal is used most often in small professional offices and small service businesses. It is less suitable for merchandising businesses but is sometimes used in firms of this type if they are very small and have only a limited number of transactions.

Professional Offices. The combined journal can be ideal to record the transactions that occur in a professional office, such as the office of a doctor, lawyer, accountant, or architect. However, special journals are more efficient if transactions become very numerous or are too varied.

Service Businesses. The use of the combined journal to record the transactions of B & H Laundry and Dry Cleaning Services has already been illustrated. The combined journal may be advantageous for a small service business, provided that the volume of transactions does not become excessive and the nature of the transactions does not become too complex.

Merchandising Businesses. The combined journal can be used by a merchandising business, but only if the firm is quite small and has a limited number and variety of transactions involving few accounts. However, even for a small merchandising business, the use of special journals might prove more advantageous.

Disadvantages of the Combined Journal

If the variety of transactions is so great that many different accounts are required, the combined journal will not work well. Either the business will have to set up so many columns that the journal will become unwieldy, or it will be necessary to record so many transactions in the Other Accounts columns that little efficiency will result. As a general rule, if the transactions of a business are numerous enough to merit the use of special journals, any attempt to substitute the combined journal is a mistake. Remember that each special journal can be designed for maximum efficiency in recording transactions.

Excerpts from The Home Depot, Inc. 1999 Annual Report

To Our Stockholders, Customers and Associates:

On the heels of fiscal 1998's record performance, many of our investors wondered, "What will The Home Depot do for an encore?" The encore we performed during fiscal 1999 is worthy of a "Bravo!" response. We are extremely proud of our accomplishments during fiscal 1999, particularly because they demonstrate the ongoing commitment of 201,000 associates who understand that superior customer service is the key to success for them, the Company and our investors.

We entered fiscal 1999 with confidence and a list of goals, which fit into three main categories:

1. To continue a pattern of strong and consistent sales and earnings growth.
2. To increase our ability to be a total solutions provider to do-it-yourself and professional home improvement customers.
3. To lead the marketplace to a better world.

We achieved all of our goals, exceeding most of them. As a result, we further strengthened our competitive position in the home improvement industry and solidly positioned the Company for long-term success.

Strong and Consistent Growth

Net earnings grew 44% during fiscal 1999, a key area where we exceeded our goal.

One hundred sixty-nine new stores and a 10% increase in sales at existing stores contributed to a 27% total sales gain for the year. A healthy economic environment helped, but the strength in sales was due mainly to new products and services, sharper product assortments and customer service enhancements.

We reduced product costs through efforts such as product line reviews, and imports and logistics efficiencies. These improvements gave us the financial flexibility to make further customer service-related investments in our stores, as well as invest in long-term growth initiatives, even as we recorded our 14th consecutive year of record earnings and our strongest year-over-year earnings gain since 1992.

We are firmly positioned to continue this pattern of consistent growth. New stores are planned to open at a steady rate of 21–22%. When combined with many new initiatives to enhance customer service, sales and productivity in our existing stores, we

During fiscal 1999, The Home Depot was recognized for its industry and stock market leadership by being added to the Dow Jones Industrial Average.

are confident in our ability to continue the consistent sales and earnings growth our stockholders have come to expect.

Providing Total Solutions

We reached further into our industry to find new ways to serve customers.

Our commitment to new and existing customers has expanded inside and outside the walls of Home Depot stores. As the North American home-ownership base has grown and become more diverse, so have our customers' needs. Plain vanilla is not enough – our customers want what they want, when they want it and where they want it.

In response, we added new products and services to our stores during the year. For example, we introduced a broad assortment of major appliances at nearly 150 Home Depot stores. Appliances are a natural extension of the products and services we currently offer. They also provide us with another opportunity to extend the trusting relationship we have with our customers. We expect to offer appliances in all remaining U.S. Home Depot stores during fiscal 2000.

We expanded our line of proprietary brands to include highly recognized names, such as General Electric® and Thomasville®. During fiscal 1999, we completed the introduction of GE SmartWater™ water heaters into all our stores. We also reached agreements to begin selling a new line of kitchen cabinets under the Thomasville name beginning in fiscal 2000. These new product lines are excellent examples of our merchants' creativity in developing proprietary brands that provide our customers with more choices of quality products at value prices – available only at The Home Depot.

Nearly 50,000 customers sharpened their do-it-yourself skills at Home Depot University℠, a four-week customer education program that premiered in all our stores during fiscal 1999. In addition, we added tool rental centers to 104 stores during the year, bringing the total to 150. We also further refined our test of new services for professional customers in three markets, and we added this package of services to ten additional markets.

Behind the scenes, we worked to enhance the customer service experience in our stores. We implemented new systems, tested new store formats and tweaked our staffing models, all with the mission to make our stores easier to shop and our associates more accessible to customers. We firmly believe that there is always room for improvement.

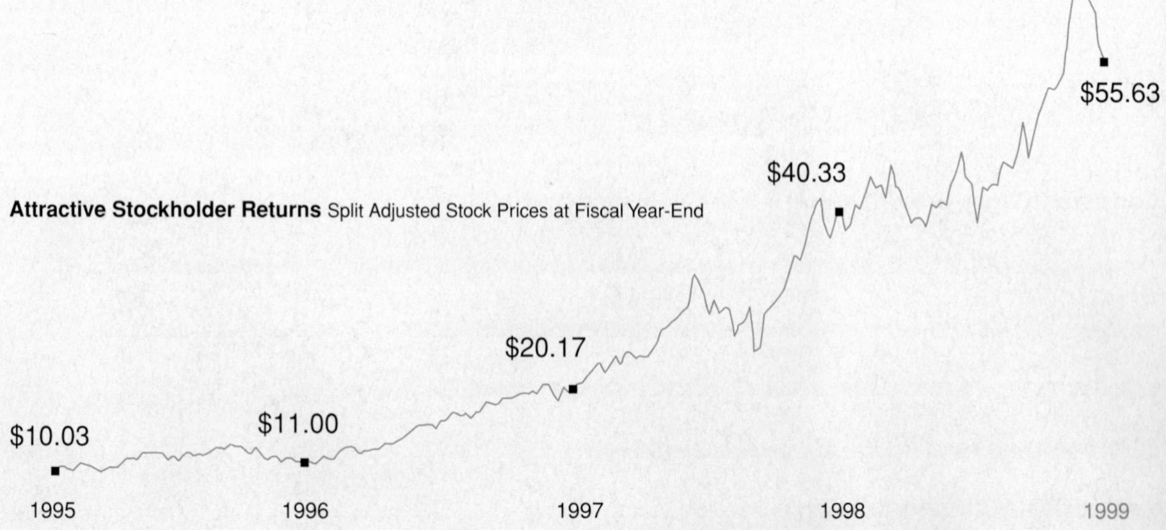

Developing Our Capabilities

We're smart enough to know what we don't know. If we don't have the expertise or experience we need, we get it. During fiscal 1999, we acquired two companies for the purpose of developing our capabilities in two important segments of the home improvement business. Georgia Lighting, purchased in June 1999, is known throughout the lighting industry for its expertise in lighting design, sourcing, merchandising and training programs. Home Depot and EXPO Design Center stores are benefiting today from this acquisition in all four areas.

In January 2000, we acquired Apex Supply Company, a wholesale distributor of plumbing, HVAC and related products. Going forward, we plan to leverage Apex's expertise and resources to better serve the needs of professional plumbers shopping in Home Depot stores.

Exploring E-Commerce

As the world watched the developments of electronic commerce, we were busy laying the foundation for our own e-commerce efforts. We view the Internet not as an *alternate* channel but as an *additional* channel to provide flexibility and convenience to our customers. Therefore, our e-commerce strategy starts with our stores.

Beginning in fiscal 2000, Home Depot customers in our initial launch markets will be able to purchase electronically all of the products available in their local Home Depot store. If they want the products delivered, we'll deliver them. If they want the to pick them up at the store, we'll have the order ready for them. With nearly 1,000 Home Depot stores spread across North America, we will have the inventory and delivery systems instantly in place to serve e-commerce customers. During this period of dot-com mania, we firmly believe that, in the long run, the most successful online retailers will be those who know how to extend to the Internet the power of their brands, the leverage of their bricks-and-mortar assets and the value of their customer service.

Launching New Ventures

Outside the walls of Home Depot, we made great progress with EXPO Design Center. We opened seven EXPO Design Center stores during fiscal 1999, and each store opening was more successful than the one before it. More customers doing remodeling and decorating projects are attracted by EXPO's ability to complete design work, product

Consistent Store Growth Number of Stores at Fiscal Year-End

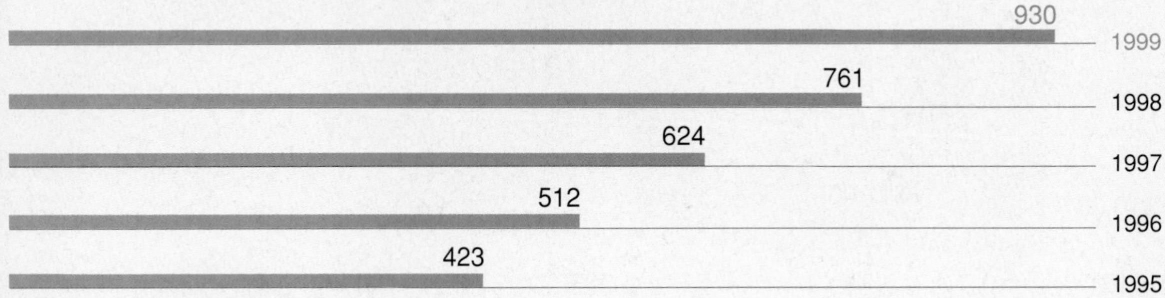

selection and installation coordination – all under one roof. Like Home Depot 20 years ago, EXPO is poised to revolutionize this segment of the home improvement market.

We also learned more about serving the hardware convenience customer. During fiscal 1999, we opened two Villager's Hardware test stores in New Jersey. Designed primarily to serve smaller project or home enhancement customers, Villager's Hardware complements Home Depot stores with its product mix differences and a different type of shopping experience. We plan to open two more test stores in fiscal 2000. Villager's Hardware is a good example of our willingness to test new ideas and prove their success before rolling them out. By doing this, our customers and our stockholders win.

Expanding Globally

Global expansion will become a more important part of our growth plans during the next decade. Like the Internet, trends in global retailing are accelerating, as retailers consolidate, capitalize on the power of their brands throughout the world and create the scale to achieve greater operating efficiencies. The opportunities we see to serve homeowners around the world, combined with our experiences to-date in Canada, Chile and Puerto Rico, make us excited about our long-term prospects for successful expansion outside North America. Our primary focus continues to be on growing our presence in Latin America. However, we are also exploring other opportunities around the world for further international growth.

These and many other initiatives support our goal of providing total solutions to our customers. Coupled with this goal is our objective that every initiative maintain or enhance our current return on invested capital. Given this high hurdle, for every initiative we undertake, many others have been discarded. Even so, there are still many opportunities for us to continue to widen our leadership position in the industry.

Leading the Marketplace to a Better World

Every day, we have the ability to touch millions of lives.

During fiscal 1999, we completed 797 million customer transactions. With each transaction, we had the opportunity to touch the lives of our customers by providing them with a wide assortment of low-priced home improvement products. In many cases, we also gave our do-it-yourself customers the knowledge and confidence to complete their own projects.

Career Opportunities Number of Associates at Fiscal Year-End

Year	Number of Associates
1999	201,400
1998	156,700
1997	124,400
1996	98,100
1995	80,800

At the end of fiscal 1999, we employed over 201,000 associates. We have the opportunity to touch each of their lives by building a better workplace in which every associate understands the culture and values upon which this Company was built. We have a responsibility to build an inclusive and diverse organization of the very best people, and foster an environment that supports diversity, providing the opportunity for everyone to excel.

During fiscal 1999, The Home Depot gave $15 million to support disaster relief and the building of affordable housing, to aid youth at risk and to protect the environment. We touched thousands of lives through our financial support and thousands more through our volunteer efforts.

Our actions today in protecting the environment will touch millions of lives for many years to come. Last year, we told you about our commitment to leadership in addressing sustainable forestry and certification issues. This year, we put the stake in the ground by pledging to stop selling any wood products from endangered regions by the end of 2002. Further, we will give preference to vendors that supply us with products made from certified wood. We will use the power of our purchasing dollars to promote products that do the most to preserve environmentally sensitive areas and make the most efficient use of wood.

The key to our success in this area is in the partnerships we develop with environmental groups and suppliers. I am happy to report that many environmental organizations have publicly voiced their support of our efforts, and our vendors are quickly climbing on the bandwagon. As The Home Depot expands its global presence, sustaining the environment will become an even more important issue for the Company and our vendor partners.

During fiscal 1999, The Home Depot celebrated its 20th year of business. We have achieved so much in just 20 years of history. But even more opportunity exists for us in the next 20 years. The encore performance in fiscal 1999 was outstanding – but the curtain remains wide open.

Arthur M. Blank
President & Chief Executive Officer
February 25, 2000

Management's Discussion and Analysis of Results of Operations and Financial Condition

The Home Depot, Inc. and Subsidiaries

The data below reflect selected sales data, the percentage relationship between sales and major categories in the Consolidated Statements of Earnings and the percentage change in the dollar amounts of each of the items.

Selected Consolidated Statements of Earnings Data

	Fiscal Year[1]			Percentage Increase (Decrease) in Dollar Amounts	
	1999	1998	1997	1999 vs. 1998	1998 vs. 1997
Net Sales	100.0%	100.0%	100.0%	27.2%	25.1%
Gross Profit	29.7	28.5	28.1	32.6	26.9
Operating Expenses:					
Selling and Store Operating[2]	17.8	17.7	17.8	27.9	24.1
Pre-Opening	0.3	0.3	0.3	28. 4	35.4
General and Administrative	1.7	1.7	1.7	30.3	24.7
Non-Recurring Charge	–	–	0.4	NM[3]	NM[3]
Total Operating Expenses	19.8	19.7	20.2	28.1	21.7
Operating Income	9.9	8.8	7.9	42.6	40.3
Interest Income (Expense):					
Interest and Investment Income	0.1	0.1	0.2	23.3	(31.8)
Interest Expense	(0.1)	(0.1)	(0.2)	(24.3)	(11.9)
Interest, net	–	–	–	(228.6)	(450.0)
Earnings Before Income Taxes	9.9	8.8	7.9	43.3	39.8
Income Taxes	3.9	3.5	3.1	42.7	40.9
Net Earnings	6.0%	5.3%	4.8%	43.7%	39.1%
Selected Sales Data[4]					
Number of Transactions (000s)	797,229	665,125	550,226	19.9%	20.9%
Average Sale per Transaction	$ 47.87	$ 45.05	$ 43.63	6.3	3.3
Weighted Average Weekly Sales per Operating Store	$876,000	$844,000	$829,000	3.8	1.8
Weighted Average Sales per Square Foot	$ 422.53	$ 409.79	$ 405.56	3.1	1.0

(1) Fiscal years 1999, 1998 and 1997 refer to the fiscal years ended January 30, 2000; January 31, 1999; and February 1, 1998, respectively.
(2) Minority interest has been reclassified to selling and store operating expenses.
(3) Not meaningful.
(4) Excludes wholly-owned subsidiaries: Apex Supply Company, Georgia Lighting, Maintenance Warehouse, and National Blinds and Wallpaper.

Forward-Looking Statements

Certain written and oral statements made by The Home Depot, Inc. and subsidiaries (the "Company") or with the approval of an authorized executive officer of the Company may constitute "forward-looking statements" as defined under the Private Securities Litigation Reform Act of 1995. Words or phrases such as "should result," "are expected to," "we anticipate," "we estimate," "we project" or similar expressions are intended to identify forward-looking statements. These statements are subject to certain risks and uncertainties that could cause actual results to differ materially from the Company's historical experience and its present expectations or projections. These risks and uncertainties include, but are not limited to, unanticipated weather conditions; stability of costs and availability of sourcing channels; the ability to attract, train and retain highly-qualified associates; conditions affecting the availability, acquisition, development and ownership of real estate; general economic conditions; the impact of competition; and regulatory and litigation matters. Caution should be taken not to place undue reliance on any such forward-looking statements, since such statements speak only as of the date of the making of such statements. Additional information concerning these risks and uncertainties is contained in the Company's filings with the Securities and Exchange Commission, including the Company's Annual Report on Form 10-K.

Results of Operations

For an understanding of the significant factors that influenced the Company's performance during the past three fiscal years, the following discussion should be read in conjunction with the consolidated financial statements and the notes to consolidated financial statements presented in this annual report.

Fiscal year ended January 30, 2000 compared to January 31, 1999

Net sales for fiscal 1999 increased 27.2% to $38.4 billion from $30.2 billion in fiscal 1998. This increase was attributable to, among other things, full year sales from the 138 new stores opened during fiscal 1998, a 10% comparable store-for-store sales increase, and 169 new store openings and 6 store relocations during fiscal 1999.

Gross profit as a percent of sales was 29.7% for fiscal 1999 compared to 28.5% for fiscal 1998. The rate increase was primarily attributable to a lower cost of merchandise resulting from product line reviews and increased sales of imported products, other merchandising initiatives begun in prior years and continued during fiscal 1999, and sales mix shifts to higher gross margin product categories and assortments. In addition, inventory and refund systems improvements and more effective training resulted in better inventory shrink results and lower product markdowns.

Operating expenses as a percent of sales were 19.8% for fiscal 1999 compared to 19.7% for fiscal 1998. Selling and store operating expenses as a percent of sales increased to 17.8% in fiscal 1999 from 17.7% in fiscal 1998. The increase was primarily attributable to higher store selling payroll expenses resulting from market wage pressures and an increase in employee longevity, as well as to the Company's continued investment in new customer service initiatives. In addition, medical costs increased due to higher family enrollment in the Company's medical plans, increased claims and higher prescription drug costs. The Company's strong financial performance during fiscal 1999 also resulted in higher bonus expenses as a percent of sales. Credit card discounts increased as a result of higher penetrations of credit card sales and increases in non-private label discount rates. Partially offsetting these increases were lower net advertising expenses resulting from higher cooperative advertising participation by vendors and economies realized from the increased use of national advertising.

Pre-opening expenses as a percent of sales were 0.3% for both fiscal 1999 and 1998. The Company opened 169 new stores and relocated 6 stores in fiscal 1999, compared to 138 new stores and 4 store relocations in fiscal 1998. Pre-opening expenses averaged $643,000 per store in fiscal 1999 compared to $618,000 per store in fiscal 1998. The higher average expense was primarily due to the opening of more EXPO Design Center stores and expansion into certain new Home Depot markets, which involved longer pre-opening periods and higher training, travel and relocation costs.

General and administrative expenses as a percent of sales were 1.7% for both fiscal 1999 and 1998. Incremental expenses related to long-term growth and business planning initiatives, including Internet development, international operations and the opening of four new divisional offices, were offset by efficiencies realized from increased sales.

Interest and investment income as a percent of sales was 0.1% for both fiscal 1999 and 1998. Interest expense as a percent of sales was 0.1% for both comparable periods.

The Company's combined federal and state effective income tax rate decreased to 39.0% for fiscal 1999 from 39.2% for fiscal 1998. The decrease was attributable to higher tax credits in fiscal 1999 compared to fiscal 1998.

Net earnings as a percent of sales were 6.0% for fiscal 1999 compared to 5.3% for fiscal 1998, reflecting a higher gross profit rate partially offset by higher operating expenses as a percent of sales as described above. Diluted earnings per share were $1.00 for fiscal 1999 compared to $0.71 for fiscal 1998.

Consolidated Statements of Earnings

The Home Depot, Inc. and Subsidiaries

amounts in millions, except per share data

	Fiscal Year Ended		
	January 30, 2000	January 31, 1999	February 1, 1998
Net Sales	$ 38,434	$ 30,219	$ 24,156
Cost of Merchandise Sold	27,023	21,614	17,375
Gross Profit	11,411	8,605	6,781
Operating Expenses:			
Selling and Store Operating	6,832	5,341	4,303
Pre-Opening	113	88	65
General and Administrative	671	515	413
Non-Recurring Charge (note 8)	–	–	104
Total Operating Expenses	7,616	5,944	4,885
Operating Income	3,795	2,661	1,896
Interest Income (Expense):			
Interest and Investment Income	37	30	44
Interest Expense (note 2)	(28)	(37)	(42)
Interest, net	9	(7)	2
Earnings Before Income Taxes	3,804	2,654	1,898
Income Taxes (note 3)	1,484	1,040	738
Net Earnings	$ 2,320	$ 1,614	$ 1,160
Basic Earnings Per Share (note 7)	$ 1.03	$ 0.73	$ 0.53
Weighted Average Number of Common Shares Outstanding	2,244	2,206	2,188
Diluted Earnings Per Share (note 7)	$ 1.00	$ 0.71	$ 0.52
Weighted Average Number of Common Shares Outstanding Assuming Dilution	2,342	2,320	2,287

See accompanying notes to consolidated financial statements.

Consolidated Balance Sheets

The Home Depot, Inc. and Subsidiaries

amounts in millions, except per share data

	January 30, 2000	January 31, 1999
Assets		
Current Assets:		
Cash and Cash Equivalents	$ 168	$ 62
Short-Term Investments, including current maturities of long-term investments	2	–
Receivables, net	587	469
Merchandise Inventories	5,489	4,293
Other Current Assets	144	109
Total Current Assets	6,390	4,933
Property and Equipment, at cost:		
Land	3,248	2,739
Buildings	4,834	3,757
Furniture, Fixtures and Equipment	2,279	1,761
Leasehold Improvements	493	419
Construction in Progress	791	540
Capital Leases (notes 2 and 5)	245	206
	11,890	9,422
Less Accumulated Depreciation and Amortization	1,663	1,262
Net Property and Equipment	10,227	8,160
Long-Term Investments	15	15
Notes Receivable	48	26
Cost in Excess of the Fair Value of Net Assets Acquired, net of accumulated amortization of $33 at January 30, 2000 and $24 at January 31, 1999	311	268
Other	90	63
	$ 17,081	$ 13,465
Liabilities and Stockholders' Equity		
Current Liabilities:		
Accounts Payable	$ 1,993	$ 1,586
Accrued Salaries and Related Expenses	541	395
Sales Taxes Payable	269	176
Other Accrued Expenses	763	586
Income Taxes Payable	61	100
Current Installments of Long-Term Debt (notes 2 and 5)	29	14
Total Current Liabilities	3,656	2,857
Long-Term Debt, excluding current installments (notes 2 and 5)	750	1,566
Other Long-Term Liabilities	237	208
Deferred Income Taxes (note 3)	87	85
Minority Interest	10	9
Stockholders' Equity (notes 2, 4 and 6)		
Common Stock, par value $0.05. Authorized: 5,000,000,000 shares; issued and outstanding – 2,304,317,000 shares at January 30, 2000 and 2,213,178,000 shares at January 31, 1999	115	111
Paid-In Capital	4,319	2,817
Retained Earnings	7,941	5,876
Accumulated Other Comprehensive Income	(27)	(61)
	12,348	8,743
Less Shares Purchased for Compensation Plans (notes 4 and 6)	7	3
Total Stockholders' Equity	12,341	8,740
Commitments and Contingencies (notes 5 and 9)		
	$ 17,081	$ 13,465

See accompanying notes to consolidated financial statements.

Consolidated Statements of Stockholders' Equity and Comprehensive Income

The Home Depot, Inc. and Subsidiaries

amounts in millions, except per share data

	Common Stock		Paid-In Capital	Retained Earnings	Accumulated Other Comprehensive Income	Other	Total Stockholders' Equity	Comprehensive Income[1]
	Shares	Amount						
Balance, February 2, 1997	2,163	$ 108	$ 2,439	$ 3,407	$ 2	$ (1)	$ 5,955	
Shares Sold Under Employee Stock Purchase and Option Plans, net of retirements (note 4)	12	1	123	–	–	–	124	
Tax Effect of Sale of Option Shares by Employees	–	–	26	–	–	–	26	
Net Earnings	–	–	–	1,160	–	–	1,160	$1,160
Translation Adjustments	–	–	–	–	(30)	–	(30)	(30)
Immaterial Pooling of Interests	21	1	1	2	–	–	4	
Shares Purchased for Compensation Plans (notes 4 and 6)	–	–	–	–	–	(2)	(2)	
Cash Dividends ($0.063 per share)	–	–	–	(139)	–	–	(139)	
Comprehensive Income for Fiscal 1997								$ 1,130
Balance, February 1, 1998	2,196	$ 110	$ 2,589	$ 4,430	$ (28)	$ (3)	$ 7,098	
Shares Sold Under Employee Stock Purchase and Option Plans, net of retirements (note 4)	17	1	165	–	–	–	166	
Tax Effect of Sale of Option Shares by Employees	–	–	63	–	–	–	63	
Net Earnings	–	–	–	1,614	–	–	1,614	1,614
Translation Adjustments	–	–	–	–	(33)	–	(33)	(33)
Cash Dividends ($0.077 per share)	–	–	–	(168)	–	–	(168)	
Comprehensive Income for Fiscal 1998								$ 1,581
Balance, January 31, 1999	2,213	$ 111	$ 2,817	$ 5,876	$ (61)	$ (3)	$ 8,740	
Shares Sold Under Employee Stock Purchase and Option Plans, net of retirements (note 4)	19	1	273	–	–	–	274	
Tax Effect of Sale of Option Shares by Employees	–	–	132	–	–	–	132	
Conversion of 3 1/4% Convertible Subordinated Notes, net (note 2)	72	3	1,097	–	–	–	1,100	
Net Earnings	–	–	–	2,320	–	–	2,320	2,320
Translation Adjustments	–	–	–	–	34	–	34	34
Shares Purchased for Compensation Plans (notes 4 and 6)	–	–	–	–	–	(4)	(4)	
Cash Dividends ($0.113 per share)	–	–	–	(255)	–	–	(255)	
Comprehensive Income for Fiscal 1999								$ 2,354
Balance, January 30, 2000	2,304	$ 115	$ 4,319	$ 7,941	$ (27)	$ (7)	$ 12,341	

[1] Components of comprehensive income are reported net of related taxes.

See accompanying notes to consolidated financial statements.

APPENDIX B

Consolidated Statements of Cash Flows

The Home Depot, Inc. and Subsidiaries

amounts in millions

	Fiscal Year Ended		
	January 30, 2000	January 31, 1999	February 1, 1998
Cash Provided from Operations:			
Net Earnings	$ 2,320	$ 1,614	$ 1,160
Reconciliation of Net Earnings to Net Cash Provided by Operations:			
Depreciation and Amortization	463	373	283
(Increase) Decrease in Receivables, net	(85)	85	(166)
Increase in Merchandise Inventories	(1,142)	(698)	(885)
Increase in Accounts Payable and Accrued Expenses	820	423	577
Increase in Income Taxes Payable	93	59	83
Other	(23)	61	(23)
Net Cash Provided by Operations	2,446	1,917	1,029
Cash Flows from Investing Activities:			
Capital Expenditures, net of $37, $41 and $44 of non-cash capital expenditures in fiscal 1999, 1998 and 1997, respectively	(2,581)	(2,053)	(1,420)
Purchase of Remaining Interest in The Home Depot Canada	–	(261)	–
Payments for Businesses Acquired, net	(101)	(6)	(61)
Proceeds from Sales of Property and Equipment	87	45	85
Purchases of Investments	(32)	(2)	(194)
Proceeds from Maturities of Investments	30	4	599
Advances Secured by Real Estate, net	(25)	2	20
Net Cash Used in Investing Activities	(2,622)	(2,271)	(971)
Cash Flows from Financing Activities:			
(Repayments) Issuance of Commercial Paper Obligations, net	(246)	246	–
Proceeds from Long-Term Borrowings, net	522	–	15
Repayments of Long-Term Debt	(14)	(8)	(40)
Proceeds from Sale of Common Stock, net	267	167	122
Cash Dividends Paid to Stockholders	(255)	(168)	(139)
Minority Interest Contributions to Partnership	7	11	10
Net Cash Provided by (Used in) Financing Activities	281	248	(32)
Effect of Exchange Rate Changes on Cash and Cash Equivalents	1	(4)	–
Increase (Decrease) in Cash and Cash Equivalents	106	(110)	26
Cash and Cash Equivalents at Beginning of Year	62	172	146
Cash and Cash Equivalents at End of Year	$ 168	$ 62	$ 172
Supplemental Disclosure of Cash Payments Made for:			
Interest, net of interest capitalized	$ 26	$ 36	$ 42
Income Taxes	$ 1,396	$ 940	$ 685

See accompanying notes to consolidated financial statements.

> Note 1

Summary of Significant Accounting Policies

The Company operates Home Depot stores, which are full-service, warehouse-style stores averaging approximately 108,000 square feet in size. The stores stock approximately 40,000 to 50,000 different kinds of building materials, home improvement supplies and lawn and garden products that are sold primarily to do-it-yourselfers, but also to home improvement contractors, tradespeople and building maintenance professionals. In addition, the Company operates EXPO Design Center stores, which offer products and services primarily related to design and renovation projects, and is currently testing two Villager's Hardware stores, a convenience hardware concept that offers products and services for home enhancement and smaller project needs. At the end of fiscal 1999, the Company was operating 930 stores, including 854 Home Depot stores, 15 EXPO Design Center stores and 2 Villager's Hardware stores in the United States; 53 Home Depot stores in Canada; 4 Home Depot stores in Chile; and 2 Home Depot stores in Puerto Rico. Included in the Company's Consolidated Balance Sheets at January 30, 2000 were $707 million of net assets of the Canada, Chile and Argentina operations.

Fiscal Year

The Company's fiscal year is a 52- or 53-week period ending on the Sunday nearest to January 31. Fiscal years 1999, 1998 and 1997, which ended January 30, 2000, January 31, 1999 and February 1, 1998, respectively, consisted of 52 weeks.

Basis of Presentation

The consolidated financial statements include the accounts of the Company, its wholly-owned subsidiaries, and its majority-owned partnership. All significant intercompany transactions have been eliminated in consolidation.

Stockholders' equity, share and per share amounts for all periods presented have been adjusted for a three-for-two stock split effected in the form of a stock dividend on December 30, 1999, a two-for-one stock split effected in the form of a stock dividend on July 2, 1998, and a three-for-two stock split effected in the form of a stock dividend on July 3, 1997.

Cash Equivalents

The Company considers all highly liquid investments purchased with a maturity of three months or less to be cash equivalents. The Company's cash and cash equivalents are carried at fair market value and consist primarily of commercial paper, money market funds, U.S. government agency securities and tax-exempt notes and bonds.

Merchandise Inventories

Inventories are stated at the lower of cost (first-in, first-out) or market, as determined by the retail inventory method.

Investments

The Company's investments, consisting primarily of high-grade debt securities, are recorded at fair value and are classified as available-for-sale.

Income Taxes

The Company provides for federal, state and foreign income taxes currently payable, as well as for those deferred because of timing differences between reporting income and expenses for financial statement purposes versus tax purposes. Federal, state and foreign incentive tax credits are recorded as a reduction of income taxes. Deferred tax assets and liabilities are recognized for the future tax consequences attributable to differences between the financial statement carrying amounts of existing assets and liabilities and their respective tax bases. Deferred tax assets and liabilities are measured using enacted tax rates expected to apply to taxable income in the years in which those temporary differences are expected to be recovered or settled. The effect of a change in tax rates is recognized as income or expense in the period that includes the enactment date.

The Company and its eligible subsidiaries file a consolidated U.S. federal income tax return. Non-U.S. subsidiaries, which are consolidated for financial reporting, are not eligible to be included in consolidated U.S. federal income tax returns, and separate provisions for income taxes have been determined for these entities. The Company intends to reinvest the unremitted earnings of its non-U.S. subsidiaries and postpone their remittance. Accordingly, no provision for U.S. income taxes for non-U.S. subsidiaries was required for any year presented.

Depreciation and Amortization

The Company's buildings, furniture, fixtures and equipment are depreciated using the straight-line method over the estimated useful lives of the assets. Improvements to leased premises are amortized using the straight-line method over the life of the lease or the useful life of the improvement, whichever is shorter. The Company's property and equipment is depreciated using the following estimated useful lives:

	Life
Buildings	10–45 years
Furniture, fixtures and equipment	5–20 years
Leasehold improvements	5–30 years
Computer software	3–5 years

Advertising

Television and radio advertising production costs are amortized over the fiscal year in which the advertisements first appear. All media placement costs are expensed in the month the advertisement appears. Included in Current Assets in the Company's Consolidated Balance Sheets were $24.4 million and $22.6 million at the end of fiscal 1999 and 1998, respectively, relating to prepayments of production costs for print and broadcast advertising.

Cost in Excess of the Fair Value of Net Assets Acquired

Goodwill, which represents the excess of purchase price over fair value of net assets acquired, is amortized on a straight-line basis over 40 years. The Company assesses the recoverability of this intangible asset by determining whether the amortization of the goodwill balance over its remaining useful life can be recovered through undiscounted future operating cash flows of the acquired operation. The amount of goodwill impairment, if any, is measured based on projected discounted future operating cash flows using a discount rate reflecting the Company's average cost of funds.

Store Pre-Opening Costs

Non-capital expenditures associated with opening new stores are expensed as incurred.

Impairment of Long-Lived Assets

The Company reviews long-lived assets for impairment when circumstances indicate the carrying amount of an asset may not be recoverable. An impairment is recognized to the extent the sum of undiscounted estimated future cash flows expected to result from the use of the asset is less than the carrying value. Accordingly, when the Company commits to relocate or close a store, the estimated unrecoverable costs are charged to selling and store operating expense. Such costs include the estimated loss on the sale of land and buildings, the book value of abandoned fixtures, equipment and leasehold improvements, and a provision for the present value of future lease obligations, less estimated sub-lease income.

Stock Compensation

Statement of Financial Accounting Standards No. 123 ("SFAS 123"), "Accounting for Stock-Based Compensation," encourages the use of a fair-value-based method of accounting. As allowed by SFAS 123, the Company has elected to account for its stock-based compensation plans under the intrinsic value-based method of accounting prescribed by Accounting Principles Board Opinion No. 25 ("APB No. 25"), "Accounting for Stock Issued to Employees." Under APB No. 25, compensation expense would be recorded on the date of grant if the current market price of the underlying stock exceeded the exercise price. The Company has adopted the disclosure requirements of SFAS 123.

Comprehensive Income

Comprehensive income includes net earnings adjusted for certain revenues, expenses, gains and losses that are excluded from net earnings under generally accepted accounting principles. Examples include foreign currency translation adjustments and unrealized gains and losses on investments.

Foreign Currency Translation

The assets and liabilities denominated in a foreign currency are translated into U.S. dollars at the current rate of exchange on the last day of the reporting period, revenues and expenses are translated at the average monthly exchange rates, and all other equity transactions are translated using the actual rate on the day of the transaction.

Use of Estimates

Management of the Company has made a number of estimates and assumptions relating to the reporting of assets and liabilities and the disclosure of contingent assets and liabilities to prepare these financial statements in conformity with generally accepted accounting principles. Actual results could differ from these estimates.

Reclassifications

Certain balances in prior fiscal years have been reclassified to conform with the presentation in the current fiscal year.

> Note 2

Long-Term Debt

The Company's long-term debt at the end of the fiscal 1999 and 1998 consisted of the following (amounts in millions):

	January 30, 2000	January 31, 1999
3 1/4% Convertible Subordinated Notes, due October 1, 2001; converted into shares of common stock of the Company at a conversion price of $15.3611 per share in October 1999	$ –	$ 1,103
6 1/2% Senior Notes, due September 15, 2004; interest payable semi-annually on March 15 and September 15 beginning in 2000	500	–
Commercial Paper; weighted average interest rate of 4.8% at January 31, 1999	–	246
Capital Lease Obligations; payable in varying installments through January 31, 2027 (see note 5)	216	180
Installment Notes Payable; interest imputed at rates between 5.2% and 10.0%; payable in varying installments through 2018	45	27
Unsecured Bank Loan; floating interest rate averaging 6.05% in fiscal 1999 and 5.90% in fiscal 1998; payable in August 2002	15	15
Variable Rate Industrial Revenue Bonds; secured by letters of credit or land; interest rates averaging 2.9% during fiscal 1999 and 3.8% during fiscal 1998; payable in varying installments through 2010	3	9
Total long-term debt	779	1,580
Less current installments	29	14
Long-term debt, excluding current installments	$ 750	$ 1,566

APPENDIX B

> Note 8
Lawsuit Settlements

During fiscal 1997, the Company, without admitting any wrongdoing, entered into a settlement agreement with plaintiffs in the class action lawsuit *Butler et. al. v. Home Depot, Inc.*, in which the plaintiffs had asserted claims of gender discrimination. The Company subsequently reached agreements to settle three other lawsuits seeking class action status, each of which involved claims of gender discrimination.

As a result of these agreements, the Company recorded a pre-tax non-recurring charge of $104 million in fiscal 1997 and, in fiscal 1998, made payments to settle these agreements. The payments made in fiscal 1998 included $65 million to the plaintiff class members and $22.5 million to the plaintiff's attorneys in *Butler*, and approximately $8 million for other related internal costs, including implementation or enhancement of certain human resources programs, as well as the settlement terms of the three other lawsuits. Payments made in fiscal 1999 totaled $3.4 million primarily related to internal costs for human resources staffing and training for store associates. The Company expects to spend the remaining $5 million for additional training programs.

> Note 9
Commitments and Contingencies

At January 30, 2000, the Company was contingently liable for approximately $419 million under outstanding letters of credit issued in connection with purchase commitments.

The Company is involved in litigation arising from the normal course of business. In management's opinion, this litigation is not expected to materially impact the Company's consolidated results of operations or financial condition.

> Note 10
Acquisitions

During the first quarter of fiscal 1998, the Company purchased, for $261 million, the remaining 25% partnership interest held by The Molson Companies in The Home Depot Canada. The excess purchase price over the estimated fair value of net assets of $117 million as of the acquisition date was recorded as goodwill and is being amortized over 40 years. As a result of this transaction, the Company now owns all of The Home Depot's Canadian operations. The Home Depot Canada partnership was formed in 1994 when the Company acquired 75% of Aikenhead's Home Improvement Warehouse for approximately $162 million. The terms of the original partnership agreement provided for a put/call option, which would have resulted in the Company purchasing the remaining 25% of The Home Depot Canada at any time after the sixth anniversary of the original agreement. The companies reached a mutual agreement to complete the purchase transaction at an earlier date.

During fiscal 1999, the Company acquired Apex Supply Company, Inc. and Georgia Lighting, Inc. Both acquisitions were recorded under the purchase method of accounting.

> Note 11
Quarterly Financial Data (unaudited)

The following is a summary of the quarterly results of operations for the fiscal years ended January 30, 2000 and January 31, 1999 (dollars in millions, except per share data):

	Net Sales	Increase In Comparable Store Sales	Gross Profit	Net Earnings	Basic Earnings Per Share	Diluted Earnings Per Share
Fiscal year ended January 30, 2000:						
First quarter	$ 8,952	9%	$ 2,566	$ 489	$ 0.22	$ 0.21
Second quarter	10,431	11%	3,029	679	0.30	0.29
Third quarter	9,877	10%	2,894	573	0.26	0.25
Fourth quarter	9,174	9%	2,922	579	0.25	0.25
Fiscal year	$ 38,434	10%	$ 11,411	$ 2,320	$ 1.03	$ 1.00
Fiscal year ended January 31, 1999:						
First quarter	$ 7,123	7%	$ 1,968	$ 337	$ 0.15	$ 0.15
Second quarter	8,139	7%	2,263	467	0.21	0.21
Third quarter	7,699	7%	2,177	392	0.18	0.17
Fourth quarter	7,258	9%	2,197	418	0.19	0.18
Fiscal year	$ 30,219	7%	$ 8,605	$ 1,614	$ 0.73	$ 0.71

Management's Responsibility for Financial Statements

The financial statements presented in this Annual Report have been prepared with integrity and objectivity and are the responsibility of the management of The Home Depot, Inc. These financial statements have been prepared in conformity with generally accepted accounting principles and properly reflect certain estimates and judgments based upon the best available information.

The Company maintains a system of internal accounting controls, which is supported by an internal audit program and is designed to provide reasonable assurance, at an appropriate cost, that the Company's assets are safeguarded and transactions are properly recorded. This system is continually reviewed and modified in response to changing business conditions and operations and as a result of recommendations by the external and internal auditors. In addition, the Company has distributed to associates its policies for conducting business affairs in a lawful and ethical manner.

The financial statements of the Company have been audited by KPMG LLP, independent auditors. Their accompanying report is based upon an audit conducted in accordance with generally accepted auditing standards, including the related review of internal accounting controls and financial reporting matters.

The Audit Committee of the Board of Directors, consisting solely of outside directors, meets quarterly with the independent auditors, the internal auditors and representatives of management to discuss auditing and financial reporting matters. The Audit Committee, acting on behalf of the stockholders, maintains an ongoing appraisal of the internal accounting controls, the activities of the outside auditors and internal auditors and the financial condition of the Company. Both the Company's independent auditors and the internal auditors have free access to the Audit Committee.

Dennis Carey
Executive Vice President and
Chief Financial Officer

Carol B. Tomé
Senior Vice President,
Finance and Accounting

Independent Auditors' Report

The Board of Directors and Stockholders
The Home Depot, Inc.:

We have audited the accompanying consolidated balance sheets of The Home Depot, Inc. and subsidiaries as of January 30, 2000 and January 31, 1999 and the related consolidated statements of earnings, stockholders' equity and comprehensive income, and cash flows for each of the years in the three-year period ended January 30, 2000. These consolidated financial statements are the responsibility of the Company's management. Our responsibility is to express an opinion on these consolidated financial statements based on our audits.

We conducted our audits in accordance with generally accepted auditing standards. Those standards require that we plan and perform the audit to obtain reasonable assurance about whether the financial statements are free of material misstatement. An audit includes examining, on a test basis, evidence supporting the amounts and disclosures in the financial statements. An audit also includes assessing the accounting principles used and significant estimates made by management, as well as evaluating the overall financial statement presentation. We believe that our audits provide a reasonable basis for our opinion.

In our opinion, the consolidated financial statements referred to above present fairly, in all material respects, the financial position of The Home Depot, Inc. and subsidiaries as of January 30, 2000 and January 31, 1999, and the results of their operations and their cash flows for each of the years in the three-year period ended January 30, 2000 in conformity with generally accepted accounting principles.

KPMG LLP

Atlanta, Georgia
February 25, 2000

Corporate and Stockholder Information

The Home Depot, Inc. and Subsidiaries

Store Support Center

The Home Depot, Inc.
2455 Paces Ferry Road, NW
Atlanta, GA 30339-4024
Telephone: 770-433-8211

The Home Depot Web Site

www.homedepot.com

Transfer Agent and Registrar

Fleet National Bank
c/o EquiServe Limited Partnership
P.O. Box 8040
Boston, MA 02266-8040
Telephone:
1-800-577-0177 (Voice)
1-800-952-9245 (TTY/TDD)
Internet address: www.equiserve.com

Independent Auditors

KPMG LLP
Suite 2000
303 Peachtree Street, NE
Atlanta, GA 30308

Stock Exchange Listing

New York Stock Exchange
Trading Symbol – HD

Annual Meeting

The Annual Meeting of Stockholders will be held at 10:00 a.m., May 31, 2000, at Cobb Galleria Centre, 2 Galleria Parkway, Atlanta, Georgia 30339.

Number of Stockholders

As of April 3, 2000, there were approximately 194,935 stockholders of record. This number excludes individual stockholders holding stock under nominee security position listings.

Dividends per Common Share

	First Quarter	Second Quarter	Third Quarter	Fourth Quarter
Fiscal 1999	$0.020	$0.027	$0.027	$0.040
Fiscal 1998	$0.017	$0.020	$0.020	$0.020

Direct Stock Purchase/Dividend Reinvestment Plan

New investors may make an initial investment and stockholders of record may acquire additional shares of The Home Depot common stock through the Company's direct stock purchase and dividend reinvestment plan. Subject to certain requirements, initial cash investments, quarterly cash dividends and/or additional optional cash purchases may be invested through this plan.

To obtain enrollment materials, including the prospectus, access the Company's Web site, or call 1-800-928-0380. For all other communications regarding these services, contact the Transfer Agent and Registrar.

Financial and Other Company Information

A copy of the Company's Annual Report on Form 10-K for the fiscal year ended January 30, 2000, as filed with the Securities and Exchange Commission, will be mailed upon request to:

The Home Depot, Inc.
Investor Relations
2455 Paces Ferry Road, NW
Atlanta, GA 30339-4024
Telephone: 770-384-4388

In addition, financial reports, recent filings with the Securities and Exchange Commission (including Form 10-K), store locations, news releases and other Company information are available on The Home Depot Web site.

For a copy of the 1999 Home Depot Corporate Social Responsibility Report, which also includes guidelines for applying for philanthropic grants, contact the Community Affairs department at the Store Support Center, or access the Company's Web site.

Quarterly Stock Price Range

	First Quarter	Second Quarter	Third Quarter	Fourth Quarter
Fiscal 1999				
High	$45.29	$46.63	$52.33	$69.75
Low	$35.88	$36.75	$35.75	$49.92
Fiscal 1998				
High	$24.23	$32.67	$30.63	$41.33
Low	$20.42	$22.56	$21.08	$28.75

GLOSSARY

Account balance (p. 64) The difference between the amounts recorded on the two sides of an account

Account form balance sheet (p. 143) A balance sheet that lists assets on the left and liabilities and owner's equity on the right (*see also* Report form balance sheet)

Accounting (p. 4) The process by which financial information about a business is recorded, classified, summarized, interpreted, and communicated to owners, managers, and other interested parties

Accounting cycle (p. 96) A series of steps performed during each accounting period to classify, record, and summarize data for a business and to produce needed financial information

Accounting system (p. 4) A process designed to accumulate, classify, and summarize financial data

Accounts (p. 58) Written records of the assets, liabilities, and owner's equity of a business

Accounts payable (p. 26) Amounts a business must pay in the future

Accounts payable ledger (p. 262) A subsidiary ledger that contains a separate account for each creditor

Accounts receivable (p. 31) Claims for future collection from customers

Accounts receivable ledger (p. 209) A subsidiary ledger that contains credit customer accounts

Accrual basis (p. 430) A system of accounting by which all revenues and expenses are matched and reported on financial statements for the applicable period, regardless of when the cash related to the transaction is received or paid

Accrued expenses (p. 435) Expense items that relate to the current period but have not yet been paid and do not yet appear in the accounting records

Accrued income (p. 439) Income that has been earned but not yet received and recorded

Adjusting entries (p. 131) Journal entries made to update accounts for items that were not recorded during the accounting period

Adjustments (p. 131) See Adjusting entries

Assets (p. 28) Property owned by a business

Audit trail (p. 97) A chain of references that makes it possible to trace information, locate errors, and prevent fraud

Auditing (p. 5) The review of financial statements to assess their fairness and adherence to generally accepted accounting principles

Auditor's report (p. 13) An independent accountant's review of a firm's financial statements

Balance ledger form (p. 105) A ledger account form that shows the balance of the account after each entry is posted

Balance sheet (p. 29) A formal report of a business's financial condition on a certain date; reports the assets, liabilities, and owner's equity of the business

Bank reconciliation statement (p. 314) A statement that accounts for all differences between the balance on the bank statement and the book balance of cash

Blank endorsement (p. 309) A signature of the payee written on the back of the check that transfers ownership of the check without specifying to whom or for what purpose

Bonding (p. 307) The process by which employees are investigated by an insurance company that will insure the business against losses through employee theft or mishandling of funds

Book value (p. 135) That portion of an asset's original cost that has not yet been depreciated

Break even (p. 36) A point at which revenue equals expenses

Business transaction (p. 24) A financial event that changes the resources of a firm

Canceled check (p. 312) A check paid by the bank on which it was drawn

Capital (p. 25) Financial investment in a business; equity

Cash (p. 292) In accounting, currency, coins, checks, money orders, and funds on deposit in a bank

Cash discount (p. 259) A discount offered by suppliers for payment received within a specified period of time

Cash payments journal (p. 299) A special journal used to record transactions involving the payment of cash

Cash receipts journal (p. 292) A special journal used to record and post transactions involving the receipt of cash

Cash register proof (p. 293) A verification that the amount of currency and coins in a cash register agrees with the amount shown on the cash register audit tape

Cash Short or Over account (p. 294) An account used to record any discrepancies between the amount of currency and coins in the cash register and the amount shown on the audit tape

Certified public accountant (CPA) (p. 5) An independent accountant who provides accounting services to the public for a fee

Charge-account sales (p. 221) Sales made through the use of open-account credit or one of various types of credit cards

Chart of accounts (p. 75) A list of the accounts used by a business to record its financial transactions

Check (p. 309) A written order signed by an authorized person instructing a bank to pay a specific sum of money to a designated person or business

Chronological order (p. 96) Organized in the order in which the events occur

Classification (p. 58) A means of identifying each account as an asset, liability, or owner's equity

Classified financial statement (p. 472) A format by which revenues and expenses on the income statement, and assets and liabilities on the balance sheet, are divided into groups of similar accounts and a subtotal is given for each group

Closing entries (p. 164) Journal entries that transfer the results of operations (net income or net loss) to owner's equity and reduce the revenue, expense, and drawing account balances to zero

Combined Journal (p. A-1) A journal that combines features of the general journal and the special journals in a single record

Commission basis (p. 357) A method of paying employees according to a percentage of net sales

Compensation record (p. 370) See Individual earnings record

Compound entry (p. 103) A journal entry with more than one debit or credit

Contra account (p. 135) An account with a normal balance that is opposite that of a related account

Contra asset account (p. 135) An asset account with a credit balance, which is contrary to the normal balance of an asset account

Contra revenue account (p. 211) An account with a debit balance, which is contrary to the normal balance for a revenue account

Control account (p. 216) An account that links a subsidiary ledger and the general ledger since its balance summarizes the balances of the accounts in the subsidiary ledger

Corporation (p. 11) A publicly or privately owned business entity that is separate from its owners and has a legal right to own property and do business in its own name; stockholders are not responsible for the debts or taxes of the business

Correcting entry (p. 110) A journal entry made to correct an erroneous entry

Cost of goods sold (p. 256) The actual cost to the business of the merchandise sold to customers

Credit (p. 72) An entry on the right side of an account

Credit memorandum (p. 210) A note verifying that a customer's account is being reduced by the amount of a sales return or sales allowance plus any sales tax that may have been involved

Credit memorandum (p. 312) A form that explains any addition, other than a deposit, to a checking account

Creditor (p. 9) One to whom money is owed

Current assets (p. 475) Assets consisting of cash, items that normally will be converted into cash within one year, or items that will be used up within one year

Current liabilities (p. 477) Debts that must be paid within one year

Current ratio (p. 484) A relationship between current assets and current liabilities that provides a measure of a firm's ability to pay its current debts (current ratio = current assets ÷ current liabilities)

Debit (p. 72) An entry on the left side of an account

Debit memorandum (p. 313) A form that explains any deduction, other than a check, from a checking account

Deferred expenses (p. 437) See Prepaid expenses

Deferred income (p. 440) See Unearned income

Deposit in transit (p. 314) A deposit that is recorded in the cash receipts journal but that reaches the bank too late to be shown on the monthly bank statement

Deposit slip (p. 310) A form prepared to record the deposit of cash or checks to a bank account

Depreciation (p. 134) Allocation of the cost of a long-term asset to operations during its expected useful life

Discussion memorandum (p. 12) An explanation of a topic under consideration by the Financial Accounting Standards Board

Dishonored check (p. 313) A check returned to the depositor unpaid because of insufficient funds in the drawer's account; also called an NSF check

Double-entry system (p. 72) An accounting system that involves recording the effects of each transaction as debits and credits

Drawee (p. 309) The bank on which a check is written

Drawer (p. 309) The person or firm issuing a check

Drawing account (p. 71) A special type of owner's equity account set up to record the owner's withdrawal of cash from the business

Economic entity (p. 9) A business or organization whose major purpose is to produce a profit for its owners

Employee (p. 352) A person who is hired by and works under the control and direction of the employer

Employee's Withholding Allowance Certificate, Form W-4 (p. 360) A form used to claim exemption (withholding) allowances

Employer's Annual Federal Unemployment Tax Return, Form 940 or 940-EZ (p. 405) Preprinted government form used by the employer to report unemployment taxes for the calendar year

Employer's Quarterly Federal Tax Return, Form 941 (p. 395) Preprinted government form used by the employer to report payroll tax information relating to social security, Medicare, and employee income tax withholding to the Internal Revenue Service

Endorsement (p. 309) A written authorization that transfers ownership of a check

Entity (p. 9) Anything having its own separate identity, such as an individual, a town, a university, or a business

Equity (p. 25) An owner's financial interest in a business

Exempt employees (p. 364) Salaried employees who hold supervisory or managerial positions who are not subject to the maximum hour and overtime pay provisions of the Wage and Hour Law

Expense (p. 31) An outflow of cash, use of other assets, or incurring of a liability

Experience rating system (p. 401) A system that rewards an employer for maintaining steady employment conditions by reducing the firm's state unemployment tax rate

Exposure draft (p. 13) A proposed solution to a problem being considered by the Financial Accounting Standards Board

Fair market value (p. 38) The current worth of an asset or the price the asset would bring if sold on the open market

Federal unemployment taxes (FUTA) (p. 354) Taxes levied by the federal government against employers to benefit unemployed workers

Financial statements (p. 4) Periodic reports of a firm's financial position or operating results

Footing (p. 64) A small pencil figure written at the base of an amount column showing the sum of the entries in the column

Freight In account (p. 256) An account showing transportation charges for items purchased

Full endorsement (p. 310) A signature transferring a check to a specific person, firm, or bank

Fundamental accounting equation (p. 30) The relationship between assets and liabilities plus owner's equity

General journal (p. 96) A financial record for entering all types of business transactions

General ledger (p. 105) A permanent, classified record of all accounts used in a firm's operation; a record of final entry

Generally accepted accounting principles (GAAP) (p. 12) Accounting standards developed and applied by professional accountants

Governmental accounting (p. 6) Accounting work performed for a federal, state, or local governmental unit

Gross profit (p. 473) The difference between net sales and the cost of goods sold

Gross profit percentage (p. 484) The amount of gross profit from each dollar of sales (gross profit percentage = gross profit ÷ net sales)

Hourly rate basis (p. 357) A method of paying employees according to a stated rate per hour

Income statement (p. 35) A formal report of business operations covering a specific period of time; also called a profit and loss statement or a statement of income and expenses

Income Summary account (p. 164) A special owner's equity account that is used only in the closing process to summarize the results of operations

Independent contractor (p. 352) One who is paid by a company to carry out a specific task or job but is not under the direct supervision or control of the company

Individual earnings record (p. 370) An employee record that contains information needed to compute earnings and complete tax reports

International accounting (p. 13) The study of accounting principles used by different countries

Interpret (p. 174) To understand and explain the meaning and importance of something (such as financial statements)

Inventory sheet (p. 431) A form used to list the volume and type of goods a firm has in stock

Inventory turnover (p. 485) The number of times inventory is purchased and sold during the accounting period (inventory turnover = cost of goods sold ÷ average inventory)

Invoice (p. 219) A customer billing for merchandise bought on credit

Journal (p. 96) The record of original entry

Journalizing (p. 96) Recording transactions in a journal

Ledger (p. 105) The record of final entry

Liabilities (p. 28) Debts or obligations of a business

Liquidity (p. 476) The ease with which an item can be converted into cash

List price (p. 218) An established retail price

Long-term liabilities (p. 477) Debts of a business that are due more than one year in the future

Management advisory services (p. 6) Services designed to help clients improve their information systems or their business performance

Managerial accounting (p. 6) Accounting work carried on by an accountant employed by a single business in industry

Manufacturing business (p. 202) A business that sells goods that it has produced

Medicare tax (p. 353) A tax levied on employees and employers to provide medical care for the employee and the employee's spouse after each has reached age 65

Merchandise inventory (p. 202) The stock of goods a merchandising business keeps on hand

Merchandising business (p. 202) A business that sells goods purchased for resale

Merit rating system (p. 401) See Experience rating system

Multiple-step income statement (p. 472) A type of income statement on which several subtotals are computed before the net income is calculated

Negotiable (p. 309) A financial instrument whose ownership can be transferred to another person or business

Net income (p. 36) The result of an excess of revenue over expenses

Net income line (p. 447) The worksheet line immediately following the column totals on which net income (or net loss) is recorded in two places: the Income Statement section and the Balance Sheet section

Net loss (p. 36) The result of an excess of expenses over revenue

Net price (p. 218) The list price less all trade discounts

Net sales (p. 213) The difference between the balance in the **Sales** account and the balance in the **Sales Returns and Allowances** account

Normal balance (p. 65) The increase side of an account

On account (p. 26) An arrangement to allow payment at a later date; also called a charge account or open-account credit

Open-account credit (p. 221) A system that allows the sale of services or goods with the understanding that payment will be made at a later date

Outstanding checks (p. 314) Checks that have been recorded in the cash payments journal but have not yet been paid by the bank

Owner's equity (p. 28) The financial interest of the owner of a business; also called proprietorship or net worth

Partnership (p. 9) A business entity owned by two or more people who are legally responsible for the debts and taxes of the business

Payee (p. 309) The person or firm to whom a check is payable

Payroll register (p. 365) A record of payroll information for each employee for the pay period

Permanent account (p. 76) An account that is kept open from one accounting period to the next

Petty cash analysis sheet (p. 305) A form used to record transactions involving petty cash

Petty cash fund (p. 292) A special-purpose fund used to handle payments involving small amounts of money

Petty cash voucher (p. 305) A form used to record the payments made from a petty cash fund

Piece-rate basis (p. 357) A method of paying employees according to the number of units produced

Plant and equipment (p. 477) Property that will be used in the business for longer than one year

Postclosing trial balance (p. 173) A statement that is prepared to prove the equality of total debits and credits after the closing process is completed

Postdated check (p. 311) A check dated some time in the future

Posting (p. 105) Transferring data from a journal to a ledger

Prepaid expenses (p. 131, 437) Expense items acquired, recorded, and paid for in advance of their use

Promissory note (p. 294) A written promise to pay a specified amount of money on a specific date

Property, plant, and equipment (p. 434) Long-term assets that are used in the operation of a business and that are subject to depreciation (except for land, which is not depreciated)

Public accountants (p. 5) Members of firms that perform accounting services for other companies

Purchase allowance (p. 263) A price reduction from the amount originally billed

Purchase invoice (p. 254) A bill received for goods purchased

Purchase order (p. 254) An order to the supplier of goods specifying items needed, quantity, price, and credit terms

Purchase requisition (p. 254) A list sent to the purchasing department showing the items to be ordered

Purchase return (p. 263) Return of unsatisfactory goods

Purchases account (p. 256) An account used to record cost of goods bought for resale during a period

Purchases discount (p. 259) A cash discount offered to customers buying goods for payment within a specified period

Purchases journal (p. 256) A special journal used to record the purchase of goods on credit

Receiving report (p. 254) A form showing quantity and condition of goods received

Report form balance sheet (p. 143) A balance sheet that lists the asset accounts first, followed by liabilities and owner's equity

Restrictive endorsement (p. 310) A signature that transfers a check to a specific party for a stated purpose

Retail business (p. 202) A business that sells directly to individual consumers

Revenue (p. 30) An inflow of money or other assets that results from the sales of goods or services or from the use of money or property; also called income

Reversing entries (p. 485) Journal entries made to reverse the effect of certain adjusting entries involving accrued income or accrued expenses to avoid problems in recording future payments or receipts of cash in a new accounting period

Salary basis (p. 357) A method of paying employees according to an agreed-upon amount for each week or month

Sales allowance (p. 210) A reduction in the price originally charged to customers for goods or services

Sales discount (p. 259) A cash discount offered by the supplier to customers for payment within a specified period

Sales invoice (p. 254) A supplier's billing document

Sales journal (p. 203) A special journal used to record sales of merchandise on credit

Sales return (p. 210) A firm's acceptance of a return of goods from a customer

Salvage value (p. 134) An estimate of the amount that could be received by selling or disposing of an asset at the end of its useful life

Schedule of accounts payable (p. 265) A list of all balances owed to creditors

Schedule of accounts receivable (p. 216) A listing of all balances of the accounts in the accounts receivable subsidiary ledger

Separate entity assumption (p. 9) The concept of keeping a firm's financial records separate from the owner's personal financial records

Service business (p. 202) A business that sells services

Service charge (p. 313) A fee charged by a bank to cover the costs of maintaining accounts and providing services

Single-step income statement (p. 472) A type of income statement where only one computation is needed to determine the net income (total revenue − total expenses = net income)

Slide (p. 75) An accounting error involving a misplaced decimal point

Social entity (p. 9) A nonprofit organization, such as a city, public school, or public hospital

Social Security Act (p. 353) A federal act providing certain benefits for employees and their families; officially the Federal Insurance Contributions Act

Social security tax (FICA) (p. 353) A tax imposed by the Federal Insurance Contributions Act and collected on employee earnings to provide retirement and disability benefits

Sole proprietorship (p. 9) A business entity owned by one person who is legally responsible for the debts and taxes of the business

Special journal (p. 202) A journal used to record only one type of transaction

State unemployment taxes (SUTA) (p. 355) Taxes levied by a state government against employers to benefit unemployed workers

Statement of account (p. 294) A form sent to a firm's customers showing transactions during the month and the balance owed

Statements of Financial Accounting Standards (p. 12) Accounting principles established by the Financial Accounting Standards Board

Statement of owner's equity (p. 36) A formal report of changes that occurred in the owner's financial interest during a reporting period

Stock (p. 11) Certificates that represent ownership of a corporation

Stockholders (p. 12) The owners of a corporation; also called shareholders

Straight-line depreciation (p. 134) Allocation of an asset's cost in equal amounts to each accounting period of the asset's useful life

Subsidiary ledger (p. 202) A ledger dedicated to accounts of a single type and showing details to support a general ledger account

T account (p. 58) A type of account, resembling a T, used to analyze the effects of a business transaction

Tax accounting (p. 5) A service that involves tax compliance and tax planning

Tax-exempt wages (p. 359) Earnings in excess of the base amount set by the Social Security Act

Temporary account (p. 77) An account whose balance is transferred to another account at the end of an accounting period

Time and a half (p. 353) Rate of pay for an employee's work in excess of 40 hours a week

Trade discount (p. 218) A reduction from list price

Transmittal of Wage and Tax Statements, Form W-3 (p. 399) Preprinted government form submitted with Forms W-2 to the Social Security Administration

Transportation In account (p. 256) See Freight In account

Transposition (p. 75) An accounting error involving misplaced digits in a number

Trial balance (p. 73) A statement to test the accuracy of total debits and credits after transactions have been recorded

Unearned income (p. 440) Income received before it is earned

Unemployment insurance program (p. 401) A program that provides unemployment compensation through a tax levied on employers

Updated account balances (p. 443) The amounts entered in the Adjusted Trial Balance section of the worksheet

Wage and Tax Statement, Form W-2 (p. 398) Preprinted government form that contains information about an employee's earnings and tax withholdings for the year

Wage-bracket table method (p. 361) A simple method to determine the amount of federal income tax to be withheld using a table provided by the government

Wholesale business (p. 218) A business that manufactures or distributes goods to retail businesses or large consumers such as hotels and hospitals

Withdrawals (p. 34) Funds taken from the business by the owner for personal use

Withholding statement (p. 398) See Wage and Tax Statement, Form W-2

Workers' compensation insurance (p. 356) Insurance that protects employees against losses from job-related injuries or illnesses, or compensates their families if death occurs in the course of the employment

Worksheet (p. 130) A form used to gather all data needed at the end of an accounting period to prepare financial statements

INDEX

Note: Page numbers following *def.* refer to pages with definitions. Those following *illus.* refer to pages with illustrations of the topic.

B

C

INDEX

D

E

F

G

K

L

M

N

O

S

Photo Credits

American Eagle Outfitters, Inc. 428–429; Theodore Anderson/The Image Bank 94–95; Mario Bauregard/CORBIS 291(tr); Tim Biber/The Image Bank 23(tr); Peter Dazely/Stone 1; David DeLossy/The Image Bank 57(tr); Ghislain & Marie David DeLossy/The Image Bank 429(tr); Steve Dunwell/The Image Bank 162–163; Jon Feingersh/CORBIS STOCK MARKET 351(tr); Galileo International Inc. 163(tr); Glencoe/McGraw-Hill 199; Guess?, Inc. 56–57; H&R Block, Inc. 290–291; David Hanover/Stone 2–3; Jordan Miller Photography 427; Vicky Kasala/The Image Bank 470–471; Lands' End, Inc. 388–389; John Madere/CORBIS STOCK MARKET 129(tr); James Marshall/CORBIS 200–201; Don Mason/CORBIS STOCK MARKET 350–351; NASA 128–129; Jose L. Pelaez/CORBIS STOCK MARKET 253(tr); Pier 1 Imports 252–253; Mark Richards/PhotoEdit 3(tr); Tim Right/CORBIS 95(tr); Safeway Inc. 471(tr); Mike Eller/Southwest Airlines Co. 22–23; VCG/FPG International 349; Wal-Mart Stores, Inc. 201(tr); Lee White/CORBIS 389(tr).